Post-traumatic Stress Disorder and Psychosis

Post-traumatic Stress Disorder and Psychosis

Editor: Olive Young

MURPHY & MOORE
www.murphy-moorepublishing.com

www.murphy-moorepublishing.com

MURPHY & MOORE

Cataloging-in-Publication Data

Post-traumatic stress disorder and psychosis / edited by Olive Young.
p. cm.
Includes bibliographical references and index.
ISBN 978-1-63987-442-2
1. Post-traumatic stress disorder. 2. Psychosis. 3. Stress (Psychology). 4. Anxiety disorders.
5. Psychology, Pathological. I. Young, Olive.
RC552.P67 P67 2022
616.852 1--dc23

Murphy & Moore Publishing,
1 Rockefeller Plaza,
New York City, NY 10020, USA

ISBN 978-1-63987-442-2 (Hardback)

Contents

Preface

Every book is initially just a concept; it takes months of research and hard work to give it the final shape in which the readers receive it. In its early stages, this book also went through rigorous reviewing. The notable contributions made by experts from across the globe were first molded into patterned chapters and then arranged in a sensibly sequential manner to bring out the best results.

The psychiatric condition wherein a person witnesses or experiences an event which has caused mental trauma, and which leads to disturbing thoughts and feelings related to that event, is termed as post-traumatic stress disorder. The symptoms of PTSD can be broadly categorized into 4 types, namely, intrusion, avoidance, alterations in cognition and alterations in reactivity. Intrusion refers to recurrence of flashbacks and distressing dreams. Avoidance involves trying to avoid the places, people or situations which might remind an individual of the unpleasant memories. Alterations in cognition and mood cause the person to forget aspects of the trauma causing experience as well as distort feelings about themselves. This book contains some path-breaking studies on post-traumatic stress disorder and traumatic psychosis. It discusses the fundamentals as well as modern approaches of research within this field. This book is a collective contribution of a renowned group of international experts.

It has been my immense pleasure to be a part of this project and to contribute my years of learning in such a meaningful form. I would like to take this opportunity to thank all the people who have been associated with the completion of this book at any step.

Editor

1

Exploring the Intersections of Trauma, Structural Adversity, and Psychosis among a Primarily African-American Sample

Cherise Rosen[1†], Nev Jones[2†], Eleanor Longden[3], Kayla A. Chase[4], Mona Shattell[5], Jennifer K. Melbourne[1], Sarah K. Keedy[6] and Rajiv P. Sharma[1,7]*

[1] *Department of Psychiatry, University of Illinois at Chicago, Chicago, IL, USA,* [2] *Felton Institute, San Francisco, CA, USA,* [3] *Greater Manchester West Mental Health NHS Foundation Trust, Psychosis Research Unit, Manchester, UK,* [4] *Department of Psychiatry, University of California San Diego, La Jolla, CA, USA,* [5] *Department of Community, Systems, and Mental Health Nursing, Rush University, Chicago, IL, USA,* [6] *Department of Psychiatry, University of Chicago, Chicago, IL, USA,* [7] *Department of Psychiatry, Jesse Brown Veterans Affairs Medical Center, Chicago, IL, USA*

Edited by:
Kate Hardy,
Stanford University, USA

Reviewed by:
Timo Partonen,
National Institute for Health and Welfare, Finland
Sérgio Saraiva,
Centro Hospitalar Psiquiátrico de Lisboa, Portugal

****Correspondence:***
Cherise Rosen
crosen@psych.uic.edu

†Co-first author.

Traumatic life events (TLEs) have been associated with multiple psychiatric diagnoses, including anxiety disorders, major depression, PTSD, and psychosis. To advance our understanding of the complex interactions between forms of adversity as they manifest across the lifespan, psychosis, and symptom content, we undertook a mixed-methods investigation of TLEs and psychosis. Our research explored the association between cumulative exposures, type of TLE, and proximity to the traumatic event and psychosis; the association between TLEs and clinical symptomology including specific types of delusions and/or hallucinations; and how qualitative data further inform understanding of complex relationships and patterns of past trauma and symptoms as they unfold over time. There were a total of 97 participants in the quantitative study sample, 51 participants with present state psychosis and 46 non-clinical. There were a total of 34 qualitative study participants, all of whom were experiencing psychosis. The quantitative analysis showed that when comparing persons with psychosis to the non-clinical group, there were no group differences in the overall total score of TLEs. However, there was a significant difference in cumulative TLEs that "Happened," demonstrating that as the number of TLEs increased, the likelihood of clinical psychosis also increased. We also found a correlation between lifetime cumulative TLEs that "Happened" and PANSS five-factor analysis: positive, excitement, depression, thought disorder, activation, and paranoia scores. The qualitative analysis further built on these finding by providing rich narratives regarding the timing of trauma-related onset, relationships between trauma and both trauma-related and religious spiritual content, and trauma and hallucinatory modality. Analysis of participant narratives suggests the central role of localized cultural and sociopolitical influences on onset, phenomenology, and coping and contributes to a growing literature calling for strengths-based, client-driven approaches to working with distressing voices and beliefs that centers the exploration of the personal and social meaning of such experiences including links to life narratives. Findings also underscore the clinical importance of trauma assessment and trauma-informed care.

Keywords: psychosis, traumatic life events, delusions, hallucinations, mixed methods

INTRODUCTION

Traumatic life events (TLEs) have been associated with multiple psychiatric diagnoses, including anxiety disorders, major depression, PTSD, and psychosis (1–3). In a recent epidemiological study, the World Mental Health Survey Consortium found that over 70% of respondents in the general population endorsed exposure to at least one TLE, while 30.5% endorsed four or more lifetime exposures to TLEs (4). Recent meta-analyses have found that persons with TLE exposure are three times more likely to experience psychosis than persons with no past trauma (2) and that TLEs significantly increase the risk for subclinical psychosis (5).

In addition to research linking trauma to psychosis, multiple studies have examined the associations between traumatic experiences and specific symptom domains, including auditory hallucinations (voices), paranoia and delusions (6, 7), as well as non-auditory hallucinations (8, 9). Links between trauma and auditory hallucinations (and to a lesser extent other psychotic symptoms) have also been investigated in combat and non-combat-related PTSD (10–12), borderline personality disorder (13), and dissociative identity disorder (14). Several studies have also sought to unpack the relationship between past trauma exposure and the content of delusions and hallucinations, consistently finding strong direct and/or indirect links between dominant content, themes, and past experiences of adversity (15–18). Structural and community adversity, including migration and ethnic density, are also significant risk factors for psychosis (19, 20).

In spite of a large body of research linking TLEs to psychosis and specific symptom domains, mechanisms of action and the interrelationships between multiple social and environmental risk factors are still not well understood (17, 21–23). Childhood adversity, as well as broader lifetime trauma, tends to be correlated with additional environmental factors, including prenatal insults [such as alcohol exposure during gestation (24), poverty/structural adversity[1], and personal substance use (25)]. Muenzenmaier et al. (26), have described "complex trauma reactions" triggered by cumulative social adversities and TLEs leading to a broad range of presenting psychotic or psychotic-like symptoms, including dissociation, flashbacks, hallucinations, and paranoid ideation. Recent debates have centered on the differences and overlap between dissociative phenomena, including hallucinations, and psychotic symptoms as they manifest across traditional diagnostic boundaries [e.g., Ref. (15, 27, 28)].

While a number of studies have investigated the role of migration, far fewer have addressed the relationship between race, non-migration-related racism, trauma, and psychosis (29) and found that dissociation only fully mediated the relationship between trauma and psychotic experiences for African-American (not Hispanic or Asian) young adults; while another investigation found that rates of adversity were substantially higher among ethnic minority participants with psychosis and that adversity partially mediated the relationship between ethnicity and psychosis (30). A recent set of analyses utilizing the National Survey of American Life found that multiple types of adversity increased psychosis risk in African-Americans, including neighborhood difficulties and lack of quality educational options (31). To our knowledge, no previous qualitative studies have explored the intersections between trauma, psychosis, and symptom content among African-Americans in the US, although historical and ethnographic work has drawn attention to significant disparities in diagnosis, treatment, and social responses [e.g., Ref. (32, 33)].

To advance our understanding of the complex interactions between forms of adversity as they manifest across the lifespan, psychosis, and symptom content, we undertook a mixed-methods investigation of TLEs and psychosis. Coding and analysis of a separate qualitative sample followed initial analyses of a quantitative sample. A majority of participants were African-Americans, and the qualitative analyses explicitly focused on the experiences of African-Americans participants. Our research questions were as follows:

(1) Is there an association between cumulative exposure, type of TLE, proximity to the traumatic event, and psychosis?
(2) Is there an association between TLEs and clinical symptomology including specific types of delusions and/or hallucinations and in what ways are trauma and past adversity reflected in the form and content of participant's symptoms?
(3) How does qualitative data further inform our understanding of the complex relationships and patterns of past trauma and adversity and symptoms as they unfold over time?

MATERIALS AND METHODS

This study reports the analyses from a novel mixed-methods investigation into the intercept of TLEs and psychosis. The first set of analyses ($n = 97$) focuses on quantitative data from a sample of individuals with and without psychotic disorders recruited from a large urban university medical center, private referrals, and community treatment facilities from January 2013 through January 2015 in Chicago, IL, USA. Participants were recruited using flyers and direct communication with clinical staff regarding study information from a convenience sample. Participants in the quantitative arm of the study were administered standardized measures that are described in detail in Section "Measures Used to Assess Psychosis and TLEs in the Quantitative Sample."

The second set of analyses ($n = 34$) focuses on a set of individual interviews ($n = 10$) and group interviews ($n = 24$; two focus groups) conducted with individuals reporting experiences of psychosis. The majority of these participants were recruited from a public mental health agency, which serves individuals with serious mental illness and significant, established disability also located in Chicago, Illinois during the same time period. Researchers queried participants about the circumstances surrounding the onset of psychosis; their understanding of the causes and origins of their experiences; and the content, development, and phenomenology of positive symptoms, including the characterological qualities of any voices.

[1]Jones N, Godzikovskaya J, Zhao Z, Vasquez A, Davidson L. Intersecting disadvantage: unpacking sub-optimal outcomes within early intervention in psychosis services. *Early Interv Psychiatry* (under review).

Qualitative interviews and focus groups employed broad, open-ended questions regarding the onset of psychosis or voices; psychosocial context preceding onset; and current symptoms, symptom content, and treatment experiences. Formal diagnostic instruments were intentionally avoided to avoid "clinicalizing" the interviews, and so diagnosis was only recorded through self-report. Background information on past trauma was collected with the demographics. Qualitative data were analyzed using a grounded theory approach (34), which involves focused interview sampling, transcription and summary, coding of data, development of conceptual categories, analytic memoing, and summary of emerging constructs.

Participants

There were a total of 97 participants in the quantitative study sample, of whom 51 reported present state psychosis consisting of 35 (36%) persons diagnosed with schizophrenia and 16 (17%) diagnosed with bipolar disorder with psychotic features, per consensus diagnosis. Consensus diagnosis was determined by reviewing all research data and collateral information by the study personnel that included an Attending Physician, Psychologists, and a Mental Health Nurse Practitioner. Inclusion criteria for the study included participants between the ages of 21 and 60. The clinical sample must have met criteria for schizophrenia or bipolar disorder/psychosis. A group of 46 (47%) non-clinical controls, with no history of DSM-IV-TR Axis 1 diagnosis per the SCID, were also recruited. Exclusion criteria for both groups included current substance dependence, seizure disorders, and neurological conditions. All participants, clinical and non-clinical, were reimbursed equally for their time and transportation. Demographic characteristics for the sample (**Table 1**) and clinical metrics were obtained at the study evaluation.

There were a total of 34 qualitative study participants, all of whom reported either schizophrenia spectrum diagnosis or bipolar disorder with psychotic features. The majority also reported past or comorbid diagnoses of PTSD, dissociative identity disorder, anxiety disorders, and/or major depression. All participants described current hallucinations and/or delusions during interviews and groups. Demographics are listed in **Table 2**. The majority of participants were African-Americans (23/34; 68%). All participants signed consent forms and agreed to be audiotaped for research purposes. Interviews and focus groups lasted from 1.5 to 3 h and were led by an interviewer–facilitator with personal experience of psychosis, which was intentionally disclosed as a part of the interview process.

TABLE 1 | Demographic characteristics of quantitative sample.

Demographic measure	Schizophrenia (n = 35)		Bipolar disorder with psychosis (n = 16)		Non-clinical control (n = 46)		p Value
Sex (male/female)	19/16		7/9		16/30		n.s.
Race							0.02*
African-American	26		13		20		
Caucasian	3		3		11		
Hispanic	4		0		5		
Other	2		0		10		
	Mean	**SD**	**Mean**	**SD**	**Mean**	**SD**	**p Value**
Current age	42	12.31	47	12.19	38	12.27	0.04*

n.s., not significant.
$^*p < 0.05$.

TABLE 2 | Demographic characteristics of qualitative sample.

Demographic measure	Focus groups percent (n)	Individual interviews percent (n)
Sex (male/female)	16/8	4/6
Race		
African-American	18	5
Caucasian	2	3
Hispanic	2	0
Other/mixed	2	2
	Mean	**Mean**
Current age	41.4	49.1

Measures Used to Assess Psychosis and TLEs in the Quantitative Sample

Multiple clinical measures were employed to examine the relationship between TLEs and psychosis. The evaluation of forms of delusions and hallucination was based on the SCID and scored for lifetime exposure as absent (score of "1"), subthreshold ("2"), and threshold or present ("3"). The SCID includes an assessment of forms of delusions (referential, persecutory, grandiose, somatic, religious, guilt, jealous, erotomanic, control, thought insertion, thought withdrawal, and thought broadcasting) and hallucinations (auditory, visual, tactile, gustatory, and olfactory) (35).

The Life Events Checklist consists of 17 items that measure exposure to various TLEs (36). The items consisted of exposure to (1) natural disaster, (2) fire or explosion, (3) transportation accident, (4) serious physical accident, (5) exposure to toxic substance, (6) physical assault, (7) assault with a weapon, (8) sexual assault, (9) other unwanted or uncomfortable sexual experiences, (10) combat or exposure to a war zone, (11) captivity, (12) life-threatening illness or injury, (13) severe human suffering, (14) sudden violent death, (15) sudden unexpected death of someone close, (16) serious injury, and (17) harm or death you caused to someone else or any other very stressful event. For each event, participants were asked to select one or more event by checking all that applied along the following continuum: (a) happened to me, (b) witnessed it, (c) learned about it, (d) not sure, and (e) doesn't apply.

The PANSS was scored along a continuum of severity between one (asymptomatic) to seven (extreme symptom severity). Analysis was conducted *via* data reduction strategies guided by prior empirical studies of symptom domains assessed by the PANSS (37). Scores were calculated for five factors: positive symptoms (delusions, grandiosity, suspiciousness/persecution, and unusual thought content), negative symptoms (blunted affect, emotional withdrawal, poor rapport, passive/apathetic social withdrawal, lack of spontaneity and flow of conversation, and active social avoidance), cognitive disorganization (conceptual disorganization, difficulty in abstract thinking, mannerisms and posturing, disorientation, and poor attention), excitement (excitement, hostility, tension, and poor impulse control), and depression (somatic concern, anxiety, guilt feelings, depression, and preoccupation). Second, PANSS items that have been shown to identify related symptom domains in cluster analyses that assess anergia (blunted affect, emotional withdrawal, motor retardation, and disorientation), thought disturbance (conceptual disorganization, hallucinatory behavior, grandiosity, and unusual thought content), activation (excitement, hostility, tension, poor impulse control), paranoia (suspiciousness/persecution, hostility, and uncooperativeness), and prosocial (active social avoidance, passive social withdrawal, emotional withdrawal, suspiciousness\ persecution, stereotyped thinking, and hallucinations) were also obtained. Items were pooled in this way based on previous factor analytic findings (38, 39). Coefficient alpha, for interrater reliability, was between 0.83 and 0.87.

Data Analyses

Demographic data were analyzed using chi-square tests and analyses of variance (ANOVA). For ANOVAs that yielded significant results (alpha level <0.05), Newman–Keuls *post hoc* tests were used to identify significant pairwise group differences. We conducted a binary logistic regression to examine the probability that cumulative TLEs increased the likelihood of psychosis. An independent sample *t*-test was conducted to compare the association of TLEs and aspects of psychosis. Bivariate spearman correlations were conducted to determine separate associations between TLEs and clinical symptomology with particular attention to forms of delusions and hallucinations between persons with psychosis and the non-clinical group. All quantitative data were analyzed using SPSS software version 24.

For the qualitative component of the project, *a priori* codes were generated following the associations identified as significant and/or unexplained in the quantitative analyses. For example, we explicitly sought to identify and unpack cumulative associations between diverse traumatic events and broader adversity, a topic that the trauma measure utilized in the quantitative study could not address. We also coded the content of participant's symptoms, looking for associations between past adversity, trauma, and the themes of voices and/or unusual beliefs. Transcripts were independently coded at different time points to establish reliability.

RESULTS

Quantitative Analyses

Demographic characteristics of the quantitative sample are presented in **Table 1**. Group comparisons revealed a significant difference in race between diagnostic groups, with a larger proportion of African-American participants in the schizophrenia group relative to both the bipolar/psychosis and non-clinical groups ($\chi^2 = 15.38$, df = 6, $p < 0.02$). In total, just over three quarters (77%) of clinical participants were African-American. We also found a significant difference in age across diagnostic groups, showing that participants with bipolar/psychosis were older than participants with schizophrenia and non-clinical controls ($F_{2,94} = 3.282$, $p < 0.04$). There was no significant sex difference between diagnostic groups or the non-clinical group.

When comparing persons with psychosis (n = 51) to the non-clinical group (n = 46), there were no group differences in the overall total score of TLEs exposure ($t_{95} = 0.43$, $p = 0.67$). However, we did find a significant group difference in the exposure of TLEs that "Happened" to the individual (as opposed to those who "Witnessed" or "Learned" about the event), showing that as lifetime cumulative TLEs exposures that "Happened" to the individual increased, the more likely the individual was to exhibit symptoms of psychosis ($t_{95} = 2.42$, $p = 0.02$). We also examined differences in exposure of TLEs that "Happened" and race and found a significant increase in TLEs that "Happened" in the African-Americans sample ($F_{3,93} = 3.03$, $p = 0.03$) (M = 4.27, SD = 3.19). In addition, we found a significant effect of cumulative TLEs on psychosis (OR = 1.174; $p < 0.02$). Thus, as the number of TLEs increased by one unit, the likelihood of the presence of psychosis also increased.

Spearman's correlations between the number of exposures of TLEs that "Happened" to the individual and clinical symptomology as measured by the PANSS are presented in **Table 3**. We found a positive correlation between lifetime cumulative TLEs that "Happened" to the individual and several, but not all, PANSS symptom domains, showing that as the number of TLE exposures that "Happened" increased, the severity of clinical symptomology increased. There was a positive correlation between the number of TLEs and the following PANSS factor and composite scores: positive ($r = 0.241$, $n = 97$, $p = 0.02$), excitement ($r = 0.302$, $n = 97$, $p = 0.003$), depression ($r = 0.310$, $n = 97$, $p = 0.002$), thought disorder ($r = 0.216$, $n = 97$, $p = 0.03$), activation ($r = 0.266$, $n = 97$, $p = 0.008$), and paranoia ($r = 0.224$, $n = 97$, $p = 0.03$). However, there was no correlation between the number of TLEs and negative, cognitive, anergia, or prosocial symptom domains.

We also examined the correlations between the number of exposures of TLEs that "Happened" to the individual and hallucinations (**Table 4**). With the exception of gustatory hallucination, significant positive correlations were found between TLCs exposure that "Happened" to the individual and all hallucination modalities: auditory hallucinations ($r = 0.196$, $n = 97$, $p = 0.05$), commenting hallucinations ($r = 0.254$, $n = 97$, $p = 0.01$), conversing hallucinations ($r = 0.255$, $n = 97$, $p = 0.012$), visual hallucinations ($r = 0.257$, $n = 97$, $p = 0.011$),; tactile hallucinations

TABLE 3 | Correlations between "Happened" traumatic life events (TLEs) and clinical symptomology.

	Variables	Life Events Checklist (LEC)
1.	LEC	–
2.	PANSS positive	0.241*
3.	PANSS negative	0.113
4.	PANSS cognitive	0.180
5.	PANSS excitement	0.302**
6.	PANSS depression	0.310**
7.	PANSS anergia	0.131
8.	PANSS thought disorder	0.216**
9.	PANSS activation	0.266**
10.	PANSS paranoia	0.224*
11.	PANSS prosocial	0.139

Spearman's correlations between "Happened" TLE and forms of delusions.
*$p < 0.05$.
**$p < 0.01$.

($r = 0.420$, $n = 97$, $p = 0.000$), and olfactory hallucinations ($r = 0.296$, $n = 97$, $p = 0.003$).

Correlations between the number of TLEs that "Happened" to the individual and forms of delusions are reported in **Table 5**. We found positive associations between the number of TLE exposures that "Happened" to the individual and 12 specific forms of delusions, indicating that as the number of TLE exposures that "Happened" increased, the more likely they were to experience specific forms of delusions. However, only associations between the number of TLEs and religious delusions ($r = 0.196$, $n = 97$, $p = 0.05$) and delusions of control ($r = 0.196$, $n = 97$, $p = 0.05$) were statistically significant, with an additional trend in persecutory delusions ($r = 0.191$, $n = 97$, $p = 0.06$). There was no correlation between the number of TLEs that "Happened" and delusions of reference, grandiosity, somatic, guilt, jealous, erotomanic, thought insertion, thought withdrawal, and thought broadcasting.

Given the highly correlated findings between TLEs in both religious delusions and tactile hallucinations, we conducted an independent sample *t*-test to explore associations between specific TLEs involving physical and/or sexual assault, unwanted or uncomfortable sexual experiences, and religious delusions and tactile hallucination. Interestingly, we found a positive relationship between tactile hallucinations and physical assault ($t_{95} = 3.95$, $p = 0.000$), sexual assault ($t_{95} = 4.65$, $p = 0.000$), and unwanted or uncomfortable sexual experiences ($t_{95} = 3.18$, $p = 0.003$). We also found a positive association between religious delusions and unwanted or uncomfortable sexual experiences ($t_{95} = 1.98$, $p = 0.05$).

Qualitative Analyses

Interviews and focus groups were transcribed verbatim, and a modified grounded theory approach was used to identify themes related to the intersections of race, trauma, and psychosis. Transcripts were comprehensively coded and recoded after a 3-month interval to establish reliability (kappa > 0.90). Findings revolve around four major thematic umbrellas: (1) developmental relationships between multiple, intersecting adverse experiences; (2) variations in the timing of onset related to trauma; (3) trauma, spirituality, and religious symptom content; and (4) trauma and hallucinatory modalities.

TABLE 4 | Correlations between "Happened" TLEs and hallucinations.

	Variables	Life Events Checklist (LEC)
1.	LEC	~
2.	Auditory hallucinations	0.196*
3.	Voices commenting	0.254**
4.	Voices conversing	0.255**
5.	Visual hallucinations	0.257**
6.	Tactile hallucinations	0.420***
7.	Gustatory hallucinations	0.125
8.	Olfactory hallucinations	0.296**

Spearman's correlations between "Happened" TLE and hallucinations.
$^{*}p < 0.05$.
$^{**}p < 0.01$.
$^{***}p < 0.001$.

Developmental Relationships between Multiple Adversities

Virtually all participants, and all African-American participants, described some form of trauma and, in the majority of cases, multiple forms of adversity, including structural discrimination and racism that interacted synergistically over the course of childhood, adolescence, and early adulthood. Many participants also reported family members with serious mental illness, poverty, unstable home environments, neglect, verbal and/or physical abuse, and disruption of attachment relationships.

- "The voices that I heard was bad ones for the most part. I came from an abusive background, meaning that my family was abusive physically, emotionally and sexually. I was raped and I just heard all these voices. That's why the doctors thought initially I had schizophrenia."
- "I would get very mad at my mother for being gone. For having passed away. My mother put me in the hospital kind of like my dad. He was in the same hospital, too. He had a mental illness. My father was also in jail. He was put into a hospital in the past too. He was a patient there. He had voices. He often talked to himself and I would wonder why is he talking to himself? Who is he talking to? My dad heard voices. I caught him in that, too, many times talking to himself. Sometimes I would go to church and people were talking like they heard voices. Sometimes I would see my father talking about [voices] and ready to beat me up and he got very angry. He would say, 'Just get out of here. Go on back home.' He would just get really agitated...."
- "Since I was like 12, 13 years old, I used to talk to myself, caught my voices. I didn't know what it was then. I assumed it was me, cuz I heard it very early. I came introverted somewhat cuz there's a lotta violence in the streets. I was more of a homebody. I think, for me being a homebody, that's when the voices got brought up. I just had to entertain myself with the voices and talking."

Narratives of gangs, substance use, and drug trafficking were often woven throughout. One participant described learning (as an older teen) that his mother had been drinking heavily

TABLE 5 | Correlations between "Happened" TLEs and delusions.

	Variables	Life Events Checklist (LEC)
1.	LEC	~
2.	Delusions of reference	0.145
3.	Persecutory delusions	0.191
4.	Grandiose delusions	0.156
5.	Somatic delusions	0.109
6.	Religious delusions	0.196*
7.	Delusions of guilt	−0.023
8.	Jealous delusions	−0.025
9.	Erotomanic delusions	−0.013
10.	Delusions of control	0.196*
11.	Delusions of thought insertion	0.147
12.	Delusions of thought withdrawal	0.092
13.	Delusions of thought broadcasting	0.164

Spearman's correlations between "Happened" TLE and delusions.
$^{*}p < 0.05$.

while pregnant with him, while others described parents with severe addictions throughout their childhoods, as well as parents incarcerated for drug-related offenses. Still others indicated pressure from siblings or peers to start using drugs, as well as more complicated entanglements of money, gangs, and drug use.

- "The kids I hanging with. They got me on drugs. I think it was a negative factor, negative influence on my life, the kids I was with. Other than that, I probably wouldn't be doing drugs. Yeah, definitely drugs is a factor in [my diagnosis]."
- "I was just getting angry, depressed, sad. My parents, I heard my mother say—she was drinking. She was drinking when she [...] was pregnant with me. I heard my father was on my marijuana. Other than them, my mental illness is from both sides of my family, my father and mother's side. They both have mental illness. I'm just sure that I get—I see it in my auntie, too, on my mother's side. I see some mental illness with her and everything. It runs in the family."
- "My mother, she was a heroin addict. I had a problem with her 'cause people wanna take advantage of her. That's where most my problems start. They pissed me off 'bout my mother. I started stickin' up, stealin' to start supplyin' my mother's heroin so she wouldn't have to go out there in the streets. That caused conflict between me and my brother. Me and him got in a fight one time. The second time I shot him in the foot. All that's to say is that I never had no chance at life—childhood or life."

Among African-American men, a strong subtheme was bullying and/or verbal abuse (often from male members of the household or male peers) related to perceptions of effeminate behavior. For example, several participants reported having been bullied due to perceived homosexuality. Several participants reported responding to such accusations by engaging in stereotypically masculine behaviors such as joining a gang or drinking, while others, publicly or in private, embraced gender minority identities, with one engaging in same-sex sex work as a teen.

- "I was bullied, too, in high school and grammar school. I was bullied. People messing with me and everything, beating me up. I got jumped on by some gang bangers. Used to pick on me a lot like I don't know how to defend myself or something. Pick on me and everything. I know how to protect myself, though. I ain't gonna let too many people try to mess me up. My father said that I was gay. He said, 'People think you gonna be gay cuz you don't have many women around. [But] I wasn't gay.... I'm not gay.'"

The above experiences virtually all unfolded in racially segregated neighborhoods and housing projects with high rates of poverty, gang violence, and limited access to quality job and/or secondary education. About half the participants remained in such neighborhoods and explicitly foregrounded the risks of violence in their communities as a major factor in their experiences of ongoing treatment and recovery. Just 2 weeks before, a focus group held at a Chicago South Side drop-in center, for example, participants noted that, only a few blocks away at a public park, over a dozen community members (including children) had been killed or seriously injured in a day-time drive-by shooting.

Timing of Trauma-Related Onset

In discussing the relationship between traumatic events and the onset of psychosis, most participant accounts fell into one of two categories: childhood onset of voices in the midst of acute traumatic experiences (e.g., sexual abuse) and older adolescent or adult onset following a series of adversities (as well as drug or alcohol use) but that was nevertheless temporally disconnected from any *single* traumatic event.

The content and characteristics of voices arising during acute traumatic events in childhood were generally much more likely to mirror real-life abusive figure(s). For instance, voices that began during episodes of severe sexual or physical abuse were typically verbally abusive, telling participants that they "deserved what [they] got," were "whores" or "sluts," would never amount to anything and/or never succeed.

- "There's a lot of voices that I hear. All grown men saying the same thing over and over. I'm no good, I'm worthless. Kill yourself. Just repeatedly over and over and over and over by men."
- "...they keep telling me to kill myself. I'm no good. I'm worthless. To kill myself repeatedly."
- "A lot of negative remarks, they ain't gonna amount to being nothing, they gonna grow up to be nothing, you're a failure, and all that stuff."

One participant with trauma-onset voices described her voices as "glued to your experience through childhood experience." In spite of hearing voices from an early age—typically beginning in early to mid-childhood within this subgroup—most participants reported not receiving a diagnosis of (or treatment for) a psychotic disorder until a much later time point. It was generally ambiguous whether these later diagnoses were exclusively tied to voices, or in fact stemmed from the addition of later onset symptoms and/or functional disability.

For those with later onset and multiple forms of adversity and associated risk taking (substance use, drug trafficking, and participation in street gangs, as described above), connections between psychotic symptoms and particular experiences were less clear—e.g., it was far less common for participants to report voice or symptom contact that amplified or re-played a particular event and associated interpersonal exchanges (such as the messages of an abusive figure). Themes consistent with participants' lives and broad experiences of individual and community adversity and discrimination were nevertheless common, for example, delusions involving gangs or pimps or demonic voices tempting participants to use drugs or engage in illegal activities.

Trauma and Religious–Spiritual Content

The majority of participants described multiple entanglements between religious faith, spiritual beliefs, and their experiences of psychosis and adversity. Examples ranged from distinct voices that reflected demonic forces, or a G-d or Jesus-like messianic figure, ostensible delusions of reference involving messages from G-d or the devil, automatic thoughts related to participants' addictions, and perceived temptations as attributable to the devil while automatic protective thoughts were attributed to G-d; and the involvement of pastors or other religious figures who helped participants make sense of their experiences and distinguish between those that were divine versus demonic in origin.

- "Well, there are voices from above. I label it as G-d. It's a noise, but it's a feeling of 'I must something.' It is like a voice of something talking. Sometimes it's sort of like an amen kind of a noise. Like a church music kind of noise. That kind of noise. There are voices within that."
- "I think they're demons. I think that G-d talks to you and I think that demons talk to you. When I was drinking and using drugs, they was always telling me to kill myself. That I wasn't worthy, that I didn't amount to nothing. When I gave my life to G-d and turned my life over, the devil still tried to come at me. I would hear his voice, but I also read the bible and I believe in the word of G-d. I had to choose G-d's word over what the devil was tellin' me. The bible tells me that the devil is a liar. Whatever he's tellin' me that's negative, he's tellin' me to kill myself, that's not something that G-d would want me to do."
- "When I go to church and all, they teaches me to tell me why the voices are talking like that. [*Interviewer:* Your pastor at church does?] Yeah, tells me not to listen to the voices telling me to hurt yourself."
- "I said that I'll be listening to the preacher preaching, and he's telling me which one is—why you shouldn't listen to the bad side. The bad side try to get you to hurt yourself. He be talking about teaching 'em [voices] how to do good things, too, but he be telling why the bad things be happening, like getting jumped on or getting beat up a lot. They tell you what spirit that is telling you to hurt yourself."

Trauma was often tied to these experiences in both direct and indirect ways. For example, demonic "temptations" (whether communicated through voices or non-auditory messages) often involved risk behaviors deeply interwoven with neighborhood poverty and a lack of supports and access to child and family services such as drug use, drug trafficking, gang involvement, and survival sex. Positive voices, even when not explicitly religious or spiritual in nature, were not infrequently described as forces or entities, which would protect the participant against adversity or violence or to reassure them of their core morality or humanity in spite of "immoral" activities and events they had been exposed to (or previously participated in).

- "One time I go outside at 2:00 a.m. Somethin' tells me that somethin' ain't right. Like you talkin' to me like it's a warning sign. Like you talkin' to me, that's the way—that's how I hear it. Like you talkin' to me. I changed my mind. I'm not gonna catch the bus. I turned around and went upstairs. Where I live there's a park across the street. One of the bus stops is right there. About 2-min long up the steps I heard some shootin'. As I look out the window, I saw a body layin' down and a couple guys runnin'. The very same bus stop I was gonna catch the bus at. That's why I say it's a good voice and a bad voice. The voice that I heard, I feel it was comin' from G-d. If it was an evil voice, I feel that I wouldn't got that notice."

Several participants whose narratives involved accusations and/or internalized concerns about sinful behavior and/or stigmatized gender or sexual identit(ies) described various uses of religious faith or spiritual practice to address their concerns or reassure themselves that they were (in fact) good, ethical people.

- "Jesus [described as a voice earlier in the interview] reassures me...that He loves everyone. Regardless of sexual orientation."
- [Reporting what her voices say]: "I get, 'That's not the right thing to do, Carol [pseudonym].'" *[Pause]* "You can get through this day without thinking about going back and using drugs."

Trauma and Hallucinatory Modality

While participants most frequently described, and spent the most time discussing, ostensible delusions (particularly paranoia) and auditory hallucinations ("voices"), altered perceptual or somatic experiences in other modalities were common. Participants' descriptions generally revolved less around literal "hallucinatory" experiences than they did around more existential alterations of experience and/or "felt presences," which tended to be subtler and harder to describe. In many cases, participants reported that such presences represented ghosts or spirits, generally of deceased loved ones.

- "A smell like, let's see—maybe it tastes like you wanna drink some water cuz I'm dizzy. Almost like a shocking feeling, but the smell it's like maybe more like a taste. Maybe it smells like air, like air." [*Q:* In some way that's different from the air that's already there?] "Right, it's not the same. It's different."
- "I can see my [deceased] aunt and my uncle and you see, I see them. Yeah, I see a lot of people up there when I look up [toward the voices]."
- "I feel like, like it's a lifting, sort of like a lifting feeling, like of something being lifted."
- "For me it's more like a feeling, too. Like something that makes me turn my head. Like something that's there that I—almost like a buzz or a tone or something."

A number of participants connected non-auditory–verbal experiences directly to G-d or spirituality. For example:

- "It's bothersome and there's noise, but then it's like this singing like this noise, and I feel like G-d, you know, G-d makes these noises ['voices']."

In contrast to the previous themes, direct links between these non-verbal experiences and trauma were unclear, and no participant in this sample explicitly described non-auditory experiences as sexual or violent in nature.

DISCUSSION

The urban experience for African-Americans living in segregated neighborhoods and/or housing projects often involves exposure to high rates of poverty, gang violence, and limited access to quality secondary education and job opportunities (40, 41). Increased exposure to TLEs tends to be more frequent in low SES and racial minorities groups (42, 43). In comparison to Caucasians, African-Americans have reported increased exposure to violent assaults (44, 45) including gun-related violence (46, 47). Although racial disparities in access and outcomes are well documented [e.g., Ref.

(48, 49)], relatively little empirical research has focused on the complex relationships between trauma and the subjective experience and phenomenology of psychosis, including symptom content, within specific ethnic/racial/cultural minority communities [for exceptions, see Ref. (33, 50)].

The mixed-methods data reported here replicate existing findings in identifying strong and significant links between cumulative trauma exposure and psychosis that cut across traditional diagnostic boundaries (2, 3, 51, 52). We extend this literature by demonstrating that these findings hold in our predominantly African-American US sample, where the relationship between TLE and psychosis may be particularly relevant due to higher likelihood of TLEs among ethnic minorities. Increased and more nuanced understanding of the role that such environmental factors play in the development of psychotic disorders helps parse the heterogeneous etiology of these illnesses and possibly points toward more personalized treatment conceptualizations.

Beyond demonstrating a general link of greater TLEs and psychosis, we found specific types of psychosis symptoms associated with TLEs, including multiple types of hallucinations, religious delusions, and delusions of control. We further found that tactile hallucinations and religious delusions were significantly correlated with history of unwanted sexual experiences and, for tactile hallucinations, with past physical and sexual assault. We discuss these findings and their implications in the sections that follow.

Our qualitative analyses were designed to further unpack, potentially confirm, and deepen the findings from the quantitative study. The qualitative findings underscore the complex and synergistic relationships between multiple forms of individual trauma (including bullying, harassment, and abuse) as they unfold against a backdrop of racial segregation, poverty, drug trafficking, gang violence, and neighborhood disadvantage. In addition, we report multiple ways in which both individual-level and neighborhood-level themes and dynamics are reflected in the form and content of both voices and unusual beliefs. For example, we found that an array of themes related to participants' childhood experiences and associated attempts to cope with these experiences were reflected in both the content of voices and subject's interpretations of their meaning and significance.

Cumulative Exposure, Type, and Proximity to the Traumatic Event and Psychosis

National comorbidity studies and meta-analysis have reported a potentially causal relationship between cumulative TLEs exposure and psychosis (26, 53, 54). Our data are consistent with other studies that show that the overall lifetime TLE exposure is significantly higher in the African-American population (47, 55, 56). In turn, our finding that cumulative TLE exposures that "Happened" to the individual increased relative to reporting psychotic symptoms is consistent with existing research, highlighting the likelihood of multiple exposures amplifying the risk of psychosis beyond individual stressors alone (5, 25, 57). For example, analysis of the United States National Comorbidity Survey (NCS; $n = 5{,}782$) and the British Psychiatric Morbidity Survey (BPMS; $n = 8{,}580$) found that after adjusting for demographic confounds, substance use, and depression, experiencing two TLEs increased psychosis risk by 3.37 times (NCS) and 4.31 times (BPMS), respectively, compared to 30.16 times (NCS) and 192.97 times (BPMS) for individuals reporting five TLEs (58).

The nature of the relationship between collective trauma and/or socioenvironmental adversity and psychosis indicates that the urban environment may increase the likelihood of exposure to TLE in persons who later develop psychosis (59). Our qualitative findings underscore the synergistic effects of both individual- and neighborhood-level adversity, with both psychological and biological components, including exposure to illicit substances (prenatal and during childhood/adolescence) and chronic background stress. We suggest that future research needs to more explicitly model both biological and (ongoing) psychological mechanisms and associated (adaptive or maladaptive) coping into early adulthood. Participant narratives also suggest that neighborhood adversity, particularly threat of gang-related violence, may be an important maintaining factor for both paranoid beliefs and voices.

TLEs and Participant's Symptoms in Form and Content

Associations between trauma and delusions have been reported in multiple studies (23, 57, 60). A study conducted by Scott et al. (12), examining the association between trauma and delusions found that persons who endorsed any type of delusion were significantly more likely to have been exposed to a traumatic event and that as the exposure to trauma increased, the relative risk of experiencing delusions increased significantly. Exposure to an urban environment has been shown to increase anxiety, negative belief about others, and jumping to conclusions in persons with persecutory delusions when compared to a non-clinical group (61). Interactions amongst discrimination, deprivation, stress, mistrust, social inequality, and lack of social support were proposed as predictors of both affective and non-affective psychosis (62). Likewise, auditory hallucinations across diagnoses have been strongly linked to childhood adversity, particularly sexual abuse (63, 64).

In line with previous research, we also found multiple direct and/or indirect emotional and thematic links between adversity exposure and the content of voices and delusions, including voices that mimicked the sentiments of abusive figures, and paranoia that reflected community contexts characterized by poverty, gang, police activity, and near constant background threat of violence (15, 16, 18). Rather than finding that voices and delusional beliefs predominantly reflected negative trauma-linked content, many of our participants reported positive and/or protective content, including voices perceived to originate from G-d, Jesus, or protective spirits, findings which are consistent with Jones et al. (65). Our finding that several participants reported voices as a source of comfort and support also highlights the need for sensitivity amongst healthcare workers in not treating hallucinations as unilaterally negative experiences, which need to be eradicated.

TLEs, Psychosis, and Spiritual Experiences

In the existing literature, religious beliefs have been reported as a source of strength, comfort, and encouragement in managing psychiatric difficulties related to traumatic events (66, 67). Religion or spirituality may also provide a framework to understand or bring meaning to the individual who experienced a TLE (68, 69). Religious practices such as prayer or meditation, worship, and participation in religious services can engender hope and increased social support among individuals with serious mental illness (70–72). While not universal, religious/spiritual explanations of psychotic experiences, religious themes, and/or content (such as hearing the voices of G-d), and faith-based coping and healing practices (including explicit discussions regarding the navigation of voices with pastors or preachers) were common. For many participants, positive religious or spiritual beliefs, including those entangled directly in their voices and psychotic experiences, were described as offering advice, guidance, moral reassurance, and/or fortification against temptations or demonic intrusions. For at least some clients, these temptations or intrusions (for example, commands such as "take drugs," "shoot him," "have sex," or delusions involving similar themes) were directly associated with past adversity.

Relationship and Patterns of Past Trauma and Symptoms over Time

The causative evidence of the association between trauma and psychosis is the strongest for the manifestation of hallucinations (73). Experiencing trauma has been shown to increase the likelihood of verbal hallucination fivefold (74). The phenomenological associations between trauma and hallucinations have shown that hallucinations with content related to trauma are not only found in psychosis they may actually shape the themes of the hallucinatory experience (16, 73, 75). In a recent systematic literature review of studies investigating voices, the association between trauma and voices has been explored in multiple realms including phenomenology, causal link, neurobiological hypotheses, and treatment interventions (76). Much of the research emphasis has focused on the associations between trauma and verbal hallucinations with much less emphasis between trauma and other types of hallucinations, including tactile or olfactory (77). Our research examined the association of trauma and all forms of hallucinations. Interestingly, the strongest association was found between TLE's that "Happened" and tactile hallucinations, although there was a positive correlation between TLE and most types of hallucinations. Our qualitative data further link the association between a specific traumatic event such as sexual assault and the onset of psychosis and draws attention to a potentially traumatogenic subgroup of patients whose voices began in the midst of acute trauma in childhood but were later diagnosed with a psychotic disorder, and a subgroup who, in spite of significant trauma, did not develop psychosis until early adulthood. This finding further supports the clinical need of evaluating current and past trauma throughout the lifespan as symptoms associated with a TLE may occur during or in close time proximity the event or may not manifest until much later in life (78).

There are limitations of this study in that both quantitative and qualitative datasets reported here are cross-sectional and can only establish correlations and perceived causal connections rather than empirical causality. In addition, our sample was predominantly African-Americans living in a particular, notoriously segregated urban environment; our qualitative analyses are meant to deepen our understanding of the interplay of trauma, psychosis, and spirituality within a particular group and associated sociogeographic context, not to generalize. We also had no mechanism for verifying TLE, although it should be noted that retrospective accounts of adversity amongst psychosis populations have consistently been shown to be reliable and valid and are more likely to underreport than overreport TLEs (79–81).

Finally, our findings echo the extant literature in foregrounding the importance of childhood adversity, neighborhood characteristics, and cumulative adversity with response to both the epidemiology of psychosis and the process of recovery and healing. Experiences described by qualitative participants were far from unilaterally negative, and participants consistently linked the content of symptoms to an array of life events and challenges. Taken together, these findings foreground the importance of trauma assessment and conversations aimed at understanding the role that traumatic experiences have played in clients' lives, in the genesis of their mental health challenges, and in the content of these experiences. From a public health perspective, they add further fuel to calls for both research and preventative interventions aimed at addressing the negative impacts of childhood structural adversity and neighborhood disadvantage.

ETHICS STATEMENT

The quantitative analysis was conducted and approved by University of Illinois at Chicago Institutional Review Board (IRB). The University of Illinois at Chicago Institutional Review Board approved the study, and signed consent was obtained from all participants in accordance with the Declaration of Helsinki before initiation of study procedures. The qualitative analysis by DePaul University's Institutional Review Board where two of the researchers were employed at the time the study was approved and data were collected.

AUTHOR CONTRIBUTIONS

CR, NJ, and RS designed the study. CR and NJ collected the data. CR, NJ, KC, and RS developed the methodology and performed the analysis. CR, NJ, EL, KC, MS, JM, SK, and RS wrote, edited, and approved the final version of the manuscript.

ACKNOWLEDGMENTS

The authors would like to thank all the individuals who participated in this study.

REFERENCES

1. Kendler KS, Karkowski LM, Prescott CA. Causal relationship between stressful life events and the onset of major depression. *Am J Psychiatry* (1999) 156(6):837–41. doi:10.1176/ajp.156.6.837
2. Beards S, Gayer-Anderson C, Borges S, Dewey ME, Fisher HL, Morgan C. Life events and psychosis: a review and meta-analysis. *Schizophr Bull* (2013) 39(4):740–7. doi:10.1093/schbul/sbt065
3. Russo DA, Stochl J, Painter M, Dobler V, Jackson E, Jones PB, et al. Trauma history characteristics associated with mental states at clinical high risk for psychosis. *Psychiatry Res* (2014) 220(1–2):237–44. doi:10.1016/j.psychres.2014.08.028
4. Benjet C, Bromet E, Karam EG, Kessler RC, McLaughlin KA, Ruscio AM, et al. The epidemiology of traumatic event exposure worldwide: results from the world mental health survey consortium. *Psychol Med* (2016) 46(2):327–43. doi:10.1017/S0033291715001981
5. Varese F, Smeets F, Drukker M, Lieverse R, Lataster T, Viechtbauer W, et al. Childhood trauma increases the risk of psychosis: a meta-analysis of patient-control, prospective- and cross-sectional cohort studies. *Schizophr Bull* (2012) 38(4):661–71. doi:10.1093/schbul/sbs050
6. Bentall RP, Wickham S, Shevlin M, Varese F. Do specific early-life adversities lead to specific symptoms of psychosis? A study from the 2007 the adult psychiatric morbidity survey. *Schizophr Bull* (2012) 38(4):734–40. doi:10.1093/schbul/sbs049
7. Bentall RP, de Sousa P, Varese F, Wickham S, Sitko K, Haarmans M, et al. From adversity to psychosis: pathways and mechanisms from specific adversities to specific symptoms. *Soc Psychiatry Psychiatr Epidemiol* (2014) 49(7):1011–22. doi:10.1007/s00127-014-0914-0
8. Longden E, Sampson M, Read J. Childhood adversity and psychosis: generalised or specific effects? *Epidemiol Psychiatr Sci* (2016) 25(4):349–59. doi:10.1017/S204579601500044X
9. Solesvik M, Joa I, Larsen TK, Langeveld J, Johannessen JO, Bjornestad J, et al. Visual hallucinations in first-episode psychosis: association with childhood trauma. *PLoS One* (2016) 11(5):e0153458. doi:10.1371/journal.pone.0153458
10. David D, Kutcher G, Jackson EI, Mellman TA. Psychotic symptoms in PTSD. *New Research Program and Abstracts. American Psychiatric Association Annual Meeting*. (1997).
11. Holmes DS, Tinn LW. The problem of auditory hallucinations in combat PTSD. *Traumatology* (1995) 1(2). doi:10.1177/153476569500100201
12. Scott J, Chant D, Andrews G, Martin G, McGrath J. Association between trauma exposure and delusional experiences in a large community-based sample. *Br J Psychiatry* (2007) 190:339–43. doi:10.1192/bjp.bp.106.026708
13. Kingdon DG, Ashcroft K, Bhandari B, Gleeson S, Warikoo N, Symons M, et al. Schizophrenia and borderline personality disorder: similarities and differences in the experience of auditory hallucinations, paranoia, and childhood trauma. *J Nerv Ment Dis* (2010) 198(6):399–403. doi:10.1097/NMD.0b013e3181e08c27
14. Dorahy MJ, Corry M, Shannon M, Macsherry A, Hamilton G, McRobert G, et al. Complex PTSD, interpersonal trauma and relational consequences: findings from a treatment-receiving northern Irish sample. *J Affect Disord* (2009) 112(1–3):71–80. doi:10.1016/j.jad.2008.04.003
15. Corstens D, Longden E. The origins of voices: links between life history and voice hearing in a survey of 100 cases. *Psychosis* (2013) 5(3):270–85. doi:10.1080/17522439.2013.816337
16. Hardy A, Fowler D, Freeman D, Smith B, Steel C, Evans J, et al. Trauma and hallucinatory experience in psychosis. *J Nerv Ment Dis* (2005) 193(8):501–7. doi:10.1097/01.nmd.0000172480.56308.21
17. Raune D, Bebbington P, Dunn G, Kuipers E. Event attributes and the content of psychotic experiences in first-episode psychosis. *Psychol Med* (2006) 36(2):221–30. doi:10.1017/S003329170500615X
18. Reiff M, Castille DM, Muenzenmaier K, Link B. Childhood abuse and the content of adult psychotic symptoms. *Psychol Trauma* (2012) 4:356–69. doi:10.1037/a0024203
19. Bhavsar V, Boydell J, Murray R, Power P. Identifying aspects of neighbourhood deprivation associated with increased incidence of schizophrenia. *Schizophr Res* (2014) 156(1):115–21. doi:10.1016/j.schres.2014.03.014
20. Morgan C, Charalambides M, Hutchinson G, Murray RM. Migration, ethnicity, and psychosis: toward a sociodevelopmental model. *Schizophr Bull* (2010) 36(4):655–64. doi:10.1093/schbul/sbq051
21. Bebbington P, Wilkins S, Jones P, Foerster A, Murray R, Toone B, et al. Life events and psychosis. Initial results from the Camberwell Collaborative Psychosis Study. *Br J Psychiatry* (1993) 162:72–9. doi:10.1192/bjp.162.1.72
22. Dean K, Murray RM. Environmental risk factors for psychosis. *Dialogues Clin Neurosci* (2005) 7(1):69–80.
23. van Nierop M, Lataster T, Smeets F, Gunther N, van Zelst C, de Graaf R, et al. Psychopathological mechanisms linking childhood traumatic experiences to risk of psychotic symptoms: analysis of a large, representative population-based sample. *Schizophr Bull* (2014) 40(Suppl 2):S123–30. doi:10.1093/schbul/sbt150
24. Bell CC, Chimata R. Prevalence of neurodevelopmental disorders among low-income African Americans at a clinic on Chicago's South Side. *Psychiatr Serv* (2015) 66(5):539–42. doi:10.1176/appi.ps.201400162
25. Morgan C, Reininghaus U, Fearon P, Hutchinson G, Morgan K, Dazzan P, et al. Modelling the interplay between childhood and adult adversity in pathways to psychosis: initial evidence from the AESOP study. *Psychol Med* (2014) 44(2):407–19. doi:10.1017/S0033291713000767
26. Muenzenmaier KH, Seixas AA, Schneeberger AR, Castille DM, Battaglia J, Link BG. Cumulative effects of stressful childhood experiences on delusions and hallucinations. *J Trauma Dissociation* (2015) 16(4):442–62. doi:10.1080/15299732.2015.1018475
27. McCarthy-Jones S, Longden E. Auditory verbal hallucinations in schizophrenia and post-traumatic stress disorder: common phenomenology, common cause, common interventions? *Front Psychol* (2015) 6:1071. doi:10.3389/fpsyg.2015.01071
28. Pilton M, Varese F, Berry K, Bucci S. The relationship between dissociation and voices: a systematic literature review and meta-analysis. *Clin Psychol Rev* (2015) 40:138–55. doi:10.1016/j.cpr.2015.06.004
29. Anglin DM, Polanco-Roman L, Lui F. Ethnic variation in whether dissociation mediates the relation between traumatic life events and attenuated positive psychotic symptoms. *J Trauma Dissociation* (2015) 16(1):68–85. doi:10.1080/15299732.2014.953283
30. Berg AO, Aas M, Larsson S, Nerhus M, Hauff E, Andreassen OA, et al. Childhood trauma mediates the association between ethnic minority status and more severe hallucinations in psychotic disorder. *Psychol Med* (2015) 45(1):133–42. doi:10.1017/S0033291714001135
31. Oh H, Cogburn CD, Anglin D, Lukens E, DeVylder J. Major discriminatory events and risk for psychotic experiences among black Americans. *Am J Orthopsychiatry* (2016) 86(3):277–85. doi:10.1037/ort0000158
32. Metzl JM. *The Protest Psychosis: How Schizophrenia Became a Black Disease*. Boston, MA: Beacon Press (2010).
33. Myers NA, Ziv T. "No one ever even asked me that before": autobiographical power, social defeat, and recovery among African Americans with lived experiences of psychosis. *Med Anthropol Q* (2016) 30(3):395–413. doi:10.1111/maq.12288
34. Strauss A, Corbin J. *Basics of Qualitative Research*. Newbury Park, CA: SAGE (1990). 15 p.
35. First MB, Spitzer RL, Gibbon M, Williams JBW. *Structured Clinical Interview for DSM-IV-TR Axis I Disorders*, Research Version, Patient Edition (SCID-I/P). New York: Biometrics Research, New York State Psychiatric Institute (2002).
36. Gray MJ, Litz BT, Hsu JL, Lombardo TW. Psychometric properties of the life events checklist. *Assessment* (2004) 11(4):330–41. doi:10.1177/1073191104269954
37. Kay SR, Fiszbein A, Opler L. The positive and negative syndrome scale (PANSS) for schizophrenia. *Schizophr Bull* (1987) 13(2):261–76. doi:10.1093/schbul/13.2.261
38. Lindenmayer JP, Bernstein-Hyman R, Grochowski S. Five-factor model of schizophrenia. Initial validation. *J Nerv Ment Dis* (1994) 182(11):631–8. doi:10.1097/00005053-199411000-00006
39. Lehoux C, Gobeil MH, Lefebvre AA, Maziade M, Roy MA. The five-factor structure of the PANSS: a critical review of its consistency across studies. *Clin Schizophr Relat Psychoses* (2009) 3(2):103–10. doi:10.3371/CSRP.3.2.5
40. Orfield G, Lee C. *Why Segregation Matters: Poverty and Educational Inequality (The Civil Rights Project ed.)*. Massachusetts: Harvard University (2005).
41. Wilson WJ. *Being Poor, Black, and American the Impact of Political, Economic, and Cultural Forces*. American Educator (2011).
42. Hatch SL, Dohrenwend BP. Distribution of traumatic and other stressful life events by race/ethnicity, gender, SES and age: a review of the research. *Am J Community Psychol* (2007) 40(3–4):313–32. doi:10.1007/s10464-007-9134-z

43. Marrast L, Himmelstein DU, Woolhandler S. Racial and ethnic disparities in mental health care for children and young adults: a national study. *Int J Health Serv* (2016) 46(4):810–24. doi:10.1177/0020731416662736
44. Breslau N, Davis GC, Andreski P, Peterson E. Traumatic events and post-traumatic stress disorder in an urban population of young adults. *Arch Gen Psychiatry* (1991) 48(3):216–22. doi:10.1001/archpsyc.1991.01810270028003
45. Breslau N, Kessler RC, Chilcoat HD, Schultz LR, Davis GC, Andreski P. Trauma and posttraumatic stress disorder in the community: the 1996 Detroit area survey of trauma. *Arch Gen Psychiatry* (1998) 55(7):626–32. doi:10.1001/archpsyc.55.7.626
46. McCabe KA, Gregory SS. Elderly victimization: an examination beyond the FBI's Index crimes. *Res Aging* (1998) 20:363. doi:10.1177/0164027598203005
47. Turner RJ, Lloyd DA. Stress burden and the lifetime incidence of psychiatric disorder in young adults: racial and ethnic contrasts. *Arch Gen Psychiatry* (2004) 61(5):481–8. doi:10.1001/archpsyc.61.5.481
48. Alegria M, Chatterji P, Wells K, Cao Z, Chen CN, Takeuchi D, et al. Disparity in depression treatment among racial and ethnic minority populations in the United States. *Psychiatr Serv* (2008) 59(11):1264–72. doi:10.1176/appi.ps.59.11.1264
49. Horvitz-Lennon M, Frank RG, Thompson W, Baik SH, Alegria M, Rosenheck RA, et al. Investigation of racial and ethnic disparities in service utilization among homeless adults with severe mental illnesses. *Psychiatr Serv* (2009) 60(8):1032–8. doi:10.1176/appi.ps.60.8.1032
50. Metzl JM, Herzig RM. Medicalisation in the 21st century: introduction. *Lancet* (2007) 369(9562):697–8. doi:10.1016/S0140-6736(07)60317-1
51. Morrison AP, Frame L, Larkin W. Relationships between trauma and psychosis: a review and integration. *Br J Clin Psychol* (2003) 42(Pt 4):331–53. doi:10.1348/014466503322528892
52. van Nierop M, Viechtbauer W, Gunther N, van Zelst C, de Graaf R, Ten Have M, et al. Childhood trauma is associated with a specific admixture of affective, anxiety, and psychosis symptoms cutting across traditional diagnostic boundaries. *Psychol Med* (2015) 45(6):1277–88. doi:10.1017/S0033291714002372
53. Shevlin M, Dorahy MJ, Adamson G. Trauma and psychosis: an analysis of the National Comorbidity Survey. *Am J Psychiatry* (2007) 164(1):166–9. doi:10.1176/ajp.2007.164.1.166
54. Fleming MP, Martin CR. Trauma exposure, schizophrenia symptoms, and the stress vulnerability model. In: Martin CR, Preedy VR, Patel VB, editors. *Comprehensive Guide to Post-Traumatic Stress Disorders*. Switzerland: Springer International Publishing (2016). p. 205–29. doi:10.1007/978-3-319-08359-9_40
55. Biafora FA, Warheit GJ, Vega WA, Gil AG. Stressful life events and changes in substance use among a multiracial/ethnic sample of adolescent boys. *J Community Psychol* (1994) 22:296. doi:10.1002/1520-6629(199410)22:4<296::AID-JCOP2290220403>3.0.CO;2-T
56. Franko DL, Striegel-Moore RH, Brown KM, Barton BA, McMahon RP, Schreiber GB, et al. Expanding our understanding of the relationship between negative life events and depressive symptoms in black and white adolescent girls. *Psychol Med* (2004) 34(7):1319–30. doi:10.1017/S0033291704003186
57. Longden E, Sampson M, Read J. Childhood adversity and psychosis: generalised or specific effects? *Epidemiol Psychiatr Sci* (2016) 25(4):349–59. doi:10.1017/S204579601500044X
58. Shevlin M, Houston JE, Dorahy MJ, Adamson G. Cumulative traumas and psychosis: an analysis of the national comorbidity survey and the British Psychiatric Morbidity Survey. *Schizophr Bull* (2008) 34(1):193–9. doi:10.1093/schbul/sbm069
59. Frissen A, Lieverse R, Drukker M, van Winkel R, Delespaul P; GROUP Investigators. Childhood trauma and childhood urbanicity in relation to psychotic disorder. *Soc Psychiatry Psychiatr Epidemiol* (2015) 50(10):1481–8. doi:10.1007/s00127-015-1049-7
60. Catone G, Pisano S, Broome M, Lindau JF, Pascotto A, Gritti A. Continuity between stressful experiences and delusion content in adolescents with psychotic disorders – a pilot study. *Scand J Child Adolesc Psychiatry Psychol* (2016) 4(1):14–22. doi:10.21307/sjcapp-2016-004
61. Ellett L, Freeman D, Garety PA. The psychological effect of an urban environment on individuals with persecutory delusions: the Camberwell walk study. *Schizophr Res* (2008) 99(1–3):77–84. doi:10.1016/j.schres.2007.10.027
62. Wickham S, Taylor P, Shevlin M, Bentall RP. The impact of social deprivation on paranoia, hallucinations, mania and depression: the role of discrimination social support, stress and trust. *PLoS One* (2014) 9(8):e105140. doi:10.1371/journal.pone.0105140
63. Misiak B, Moustafa AA, Kiejna A, Frydecka D. Childhood traumatic events and types of auditory verbal hallucinations in first-episode schizophrenia patients. *Compr Psychiatry* (2016) 66:17–22. doi:10.1016/j.comppsych.2015.12.003
64. Morgan C, Gayer-Anderson C. Childhood adversities and psychosis: evidence, challenges, implications. *World Psychiatry* (2016) 15(2):93–102. doi:10.1002/wps.20330
65. Jones N, Kelly T, Shattell M. God in the brain: experiencing psychosis in the postsecular United States. *Transcult Psychiatry* (2016) 53(4):488–505. doi:10.1177/1363461516660902
66. Chen YY, Koenig H. Traumatic stress and religion: is there a relationship? A review of empirical findings. *J Relig Health* (2006) 45(3):371–81. doi:10.1007/s10943-006-9040-y
67. Hood RW Jr, Hill PC, Spilka B. *The Psychology of Religion: An Empirical Approach*. New York, NY: Guilford Press (2009).
68. Park CL. *Handbook of the Psychology of Religion and Spirituality*. Guilford Press (2005).
69. Pargament KI, Lomax JW. Understanding and addressing religion among people with mental illness. *World Psychiatry* (2013) 12(1):26–32. doi:10.1002/wps.20005
70. Pargament K. *The Psychology of Religion and Coping: Theory, Research, and Practice*. New York: Guilford Press (1997).
71. Tepper L, Rogers SA, Coleman EM, Malony HN. The prevalence of religious coping among persons with persistent mental illness. *Psychiatr Serv* (2001) 52(5):660–5. doi:10.1176/appi.ps.52.5.660
72. Fallot RD. Spirituality and religion in recovery: some current issues. *Psychiatr Rehabil J* (2007) 30(4):261–70. doi:10.2975/30.4.2007.261.270
73. Read J, Agar K, Argyle N, Aderhold V. Sexual and physical abuse during childhood and adulthood as predictors of hallucinations, delusions and thought disorder. *Psychol Psychother* (2003) 76(Pt 1):1–22. doi:10.1348/14760830260569210
74. Freeman D, Fowler D. Routes to psychotic symptoms: trauma, anxiety and psychosis-like experiences. *Psychiatry Res* (2009) 169(2):107–12. doi:10.1016/j.psychres.2008.07.009
75. Read J, Argyle N. Hallucinations, delusions and thought disorder among adult psychiatric inpatients with a history of child abuse. *Psychiatr Serv* (1999) 50:1467–72. doi:10.1176/ps.50.11.1467
76. Upthegrove R, Broome MR, Caldwell K, Ives J, Oyebode F, Wood SJ. Understanding auditory verbal hallucinations: a systematic review of current evidence. *Acta Psychiatr Scand* (2015) 133:352–67. doi:10.1111/acps.12531
77. Longden E, Read J. Social adversity in the etiology of psychosis: a review of the evidence. *Am J Psychother* (2016) 70(1):5–33.
78. Lu W, Yanos PT, Silverstein SM, Mueser KT, Rosenberg SD, Gottlieb JD, et al. Public mental health clients with severe mental illness and probable posttraumatic stress disorder: trauma exposure and correlates of symptom severity. *J Trauma Stress* (2013) 26(2):266–73. doi:10.1002/jts.21791
79. Darves-Bornoz JM, Lemperiere T, Degiovanni A, Gaillard P. Sexual victimization in women with schizophrenia and bipolar disorder. *Soc Psychiatry Psychiatr Epidemiol* (1995) 30(2):78–84. doi:10.1007/BF00794947
80. Fisher HL, Craig TK, Fearon P, Morgan K, Dazzan P, Lappin J, et al. Reliability and comparability of psychosis patients' retrospective reports of childhood abuse. *Schizophr Bull* (2011) 37(3):546–53. doi:10.1093/schbul/sbp103
81. Goodman LA, Thompson KM, Weinfurt K, Corl S, Acker P, Mueser KT, et al. Reliability of reports of violent victimization and posttraumatic stress disorder among men and women with serious mental illness. *J Trauma Stress* (1999) 12(4):587–99. doi:10.1023/A:1024708916143

2

Childhood Trauma and Minimization/Denial in People with and without a Severe Mental Disorder

*Chelsea Church[1], Ole A. Andreassen[2], Steinar Lorentzen[3], Ingrid Melle[2] and Monica Aas[2]**

[1] School of Psychology, University of Glasgow, Glasgow, United Kingdom, [2] Division of Mental Health and Addiction, NORMENT K.G. Jebsen Centre for Psychosis Research, Oslo University Hospital and Institute of Clinical Medicine, University of Oslo, Oslo, Norway, [3] Institute of Clinical Medicine, University of Oslo, Oslo, Norway

Edited by:
Kim T. Mueser,
Boston University, United States

Reviewed by:
Diane Carol Gooding,
University of Wisconsin-Madison,
United States
Weili Lu,
Rutgers University, The State
University of New Jersey,
United States

***Correspondence:**
Monica Aas
monica.aas@medisin.uio.no

Background: Childhood trauma has garnered extensive research concerning its role in the psychopathology of mental disorders, including psychosis. The Childhood Trauma Questionnaire (CTQ) utilizes a minimization/denial (MD) scale to denote potential under-reporters of trauma, yet MD scores are infrequently reported and validations of the scale are lacking in the literature. Study aim: Elucidate differences in MD between patients with severe mental disorders to healthy individuals, and secondly, investigate if MD influences reports of childhood trauma between the groups.

Methods: We included 621 patients with a DSM-schizophrenia spectrum, bipolar spectrum diagnosis, or major depression disorder with psychotic features and 299 healthy controls as part of the NORMENT study in Oslo, Norway. History of childhood trauma was obtained using the CTQ. Clinical diagnoses were assessed using the Structured Clinical Interview for DSM Disorders.

Results: A significantly greater proportion of healthy controls (42.8%) had a positive MD score compared to patients (26.7%). When controlling for MD, the patient group still exhibited elevated reports of childhood trauma compared to controls (Cohen's $d = 1.27$), concordant with reports of childhood trauma being more frequently reported in a population of severe mental disorders.

Conclusion: Elevated MD in the healthy control group could suggest an enhanced self-serving bias, potentially attenuated in the psychiatric group. Clinicians and researchers would benefit from including the MD component of CTQ when assessing retrospective information on childhood trauma to rule out potential effect of MD.

Keywords: childhood trauma, psychopathology, minimization, schizophrenia, bipolar disorder

INTRODUCTION

A history of childhood trauma is reported at a much greater rate in severe mental disorders compared to healthy individuals (Etain et al., 2008, 2013; Fisher et al., 2010; Mondelli et al., 2010), linked to onset of psychotic experiences (McGrath et al., 2017) and more severe clinical features (Yung et al., 2015). The rate of child maltreatment in the general population has been estimated to 11% for sexual abuse and 24% for physical abuse (United Kingdom, May-Chahal and Cawson, 2005). This compares with numbers closer to 50% in patients with a psychotic illness comprised of both sexual and physical abuse (Read et al., 2005). Most studies, including the above, have used retrospective interviews, such as for example the Childhood Trauma Questionnaire (CTQ) to assess trauma experiences, asking adults about experiences in childhood. Ideally, a history of childhood trauma would be assessed using actual cohort records of childhood neglect and abuse in longitudinal studies. The study by Widom et al. (2005), compared cohort records of childhood neglect and abuse in longitudinal studies vs. self-reported measures of childhood neglect and abuse in retrospective studies showing good validity of the self-reported measures (Widom et al., 2005). Since, it is often not feasible to obtain actual reports of childhood abuse and neglect, the field needs a tool to measure self-report bias when assessing childhood trauma, especially for people with severe mental illness. Not much is known about potential confounders, such as differences in minimization and denial in retrospective reports of childhood trauma. In light of the retrospective nature of the CTQ, a response bias could weaken the validity of the measure. The minimization/denial (MD) scale is designed to detect a response bias that minimizes the extent of childhood trauma experienced. Minimization and denial measured by the MD scale consists of strongly agreeing with the following: "There was nothing I wanted to change in my family"; "I had the perfect childhood"; and "I had the best family in the world" (Bernstein and Fink, 1998). Although minimization has received some recent attention (MacDonald et al., 2015, 2016), research is still sparse regarding the validity of this measure; if differences in minimization are present across populations, or if the amount of "true" abuse/neglect reported depend on level of MD.

Retrospective reports of childhood trauma have been criticized for a tendency to under rather than over report childhood trauma experiences compared to other methods of assessment (health worker notes, sibling interviews, and so on) (Fisher et al., 2011). The MD scale could be used to quantify the potential effect of minimization on childhood trauma data collected retrospectively. The MD scale correlate with the Balanced Inventory of Desirable Responses (BIDRs) (a measure of social desirability) supporting the MD in detecting a social desirability bias (Bernstein and Fink, 1998). Social desirability is a cognitive process of editing relevant information in a socially desirable fashion (Holtgraves, 2004). Social desirability has, in addition to correlating with the MD scale, been linked to higher scores on the trait of self-deception (Holtgraves, 2004). Although the MD scale has been suggested to correlate with editing relevant information in a socially desirable fashion, the scale is rarely reported in the literature in studies of childhood trauma, and validation of the scale is sparse.

The main aim of the study is to investigate potential differences in MD in a large sample of schizophrenia spectrum disorders (SZ), patients with a bipolar spectrum disorder (BD), patients with major depressive disorder with at least one psychotic episode (n = 621) and healthy individuals (n = 299). All patients are part of the broader psychosis continuum disorders (Tesli et al., 2014). Study hypothesis: firstly (based on the study by MacDonald et al., 2015, 2016) we expect differences in MD scores between the patients group and the healthy control group. Based on similar trauma scores within the patient group (Etain et al., 2013; Aas et al., 2017) no differences in MD are expected within the patient group. Secondly, we hypothesized that patients with severe mental disorders will report more childhood trauma experiences than the healthy control group also after correcting for potential differences in MD style.

MATERIALS AND METHODS

Participants

The participants were consecutively recruited from psychiatric units (outpatient and inpatient) in four major hospitals in Oslo as part of the larger NORMENT, Thematically Organized Psychosis (TOP) Research Study. The current study consists of patients recruited any time between 2007 and 2015, and controls recruited any time between 2011 and 2015. A total of 621 participants [with schizophrenia spectrum (n = 368), bipolar spectrum diagnoses (n = 253) or major depressive disorder with psychotic features (n = 24) and healthy individuals (n = 299)] were recruited. Within the schizophrenia spectrum group, the majority had a schizophrenia diagnosis [schizophrenia (n = 195), schizophreniform disorder (n = 27), schizoaffective disorder (n = 51), and psychoses not otherwise specified (NOS) (n = 95)]. Within the bipolar spectrum group the majority had a bipolar 1 diagnosis [bipolar 1 (n = 159), bipolar II (n = 54), and bipolar disorder NOS (n = 16)]. In addition, 24 patients had a diagnosis of major depressive disorder with psychotic features. A history of psychosis in affective patients was based on information retrieved from the SCID interview. The majority of the patients (70%; n = 437) were taking antipsychotic medication at the time of the assessment. In addition, 31% (n = 194) also used antidepressant medication. Furthermore, 27% (n = 169) of the patients were taking mood stabilizers at the time of the assessment. The mean age of the patients was 30.4 ± 10.6 years and 327 (53%) of them were males. Patients with a bipolar disorder with or without psychotic features were included in this study. Among patients with a bipolar I diagnosis, more than two thirds (69%) had at least one psychotic episode, while one third of them (31%) had no psychotic episode. Healthy control group of 299 participants was recruited from the same geographical areas as the patients. The healthy control group was similarly matched in age (mean ± SD: 30.1 ± 7.7) and in gender composition (56% male) as compared to the patient group (age: mean ± SD: 30.4 ± 10.6; 53% males). Both patients and healthy controls were assessed by trained psychiatrists or clinical psychologists. Healthy controls were screened with an interview to capture symptoms of severe mental illness [Primary Care Evaluation of Mental disorders (PRIME-MD); Spitzer et al., 1994]. To help counteract the effects of socio-economic differences between different parts of the city, controls were randomly recruited from the same city areas as patients. The healthy controls were randomly selected from statistical records[1] from the same catchment area as the patients in the Oslo region. The exclusion criteria for all groups were an unstable or uncontrolled medical

[1] www.ssb.no

TABLE 1 | Demographics of the sample divided into presence of minimization.

	No minimization (*N* = 626)		Minimization (*N* = 294)		Statistics	
	N	**%**	***N***	**%**		
Gender (M/F)	337/289	53.8/46.2	158/136	53.7/46.3	$X^2 = 0.001$, df = 1	$P = 0.98$
Diagnosis					$X^2 = 0.73$, df = 2	$P = 0.70$
Schizophrenia	265	58.2	103	62.0		
Bipolar disorder	172	37.8	57.0	34.3		
Major depressive disorder with psychotic features	18	4.0	6	3.6		
Group					$X^2 = 23.99$, df = 1	$P < 0.001$
Patients	455	73.3	166	26.7		
Controls	171	57.2	128	42.8		
Medication						
Antipsychotics *n* (%)	314	50.2	123	41.8	$X^2 = 1.51$, df = 1	$P = 0.21$
Antidepressant *n* (%)	141	22.5	53	18.0	$X^2 = 0.05$, df = 1	$P = 0.82$
Mood stabilizer *n* (%)	117	18.7	52	17.7	$X^2 = 1.93$, df = 1	$P = 0.16$
	Mean	***SD***	**Mean**	***SD***		
Age	30.2	9.7	30.4	9.8	$Z = -0.17$	$P = 0.87$

Skewed data were measures using the Mann–Whitney test.

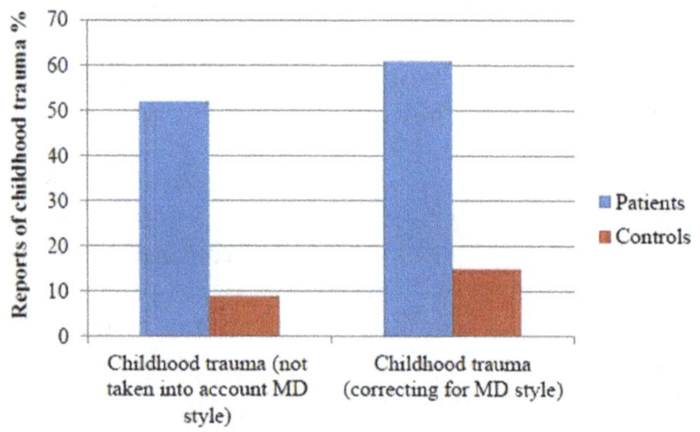

FIGURE 1 | Fifty one % of the patients reported at least one subdomain of childhood trauma, compared to 9% of the controls. When taking into account minimization 61% of the patients reported at least one subdomain of childhood trauma compared to 15% of the healthy controls.

condition that interferes with brain function, and an age outside the range of 18–65 years. The Regional Committee for Medical Research Ethics and the Norwegian Data Inspectorate approved the study. All participants gave their written informed consent.

Clinical Assessment

Trained psychiatrists, physicians and clinical psychologists carried out the clinical assessment, and a diagnosis was based on the research version of the Structured Clinical Interview for DSM-IV Axis I disorders (SCID-I). All patients were assessed on the modules A, B, C, D, and E. In addition, all raters finished a training course in SCID assessment based on the training program at the UCLA (Ventura et al., 1998). The diagnostic reliability was found to be satisfactory (Ringen et al., 2008), with an overall agreement for DSM-IV diagnostic categories of 82% and an overall κ of 0.77 (95% CI: 0.60–0.94).

Childhood Trauma Questionnaire (CTQ)

Traumatic events in childhood were rated using a Norwegian version of the CTQ short version (Bernstein et al., 2003; Aas et al., 2014). This self-report questionnaire with 28 items (Bernstein et al., 2003) yields scores on five subscales of trauma on a Likert scale format, ranging from 1 to 5, ranging from never true, to very often true. The following five subscales were captured: emotional abuse (EA), physical abuse (PA), sexual abuse (SA), physical neglect (PN) and emotional neglect (EN), as well as a trauma total score as described in Bernstein et al. (1994, 2003). The CTQ also includes MD scale to detect underreporting of childhood trauma on the CTQ. Three reverse scored statements are rated on a Likert scale, with high minimization present if the participant would not change anything about their family, their family was the best in the world and they had the 'perfect childhood.' Selecting 'very likely' for any of these statements award one point, allowing a score of 0–3. Bernstein and Fink (1998) stated that any score above 0 indicated minimization. Any scores from 1 to 3 on the CTQ's MD Scale suggests the possible underreporting of maltreatment (false negatives) (Bernstein and Fink, 1998). "No," "low," "intermediate," and "high" minimization and denial corresponds to a MD score of 0–3. A MD score of "yes" correspond to at least one item that measures MD is scored as a 5 ("very often true"). "No" MD corresponds to no item score of 5 ("very often true") on the three items covering MD on the CTQ. The reliability of the MD scale has previously been published in a large multicenter study (MacDonald et al., 2015, 2016), with reliability score of 0.77. In our sample a moderate to good internal consistency of the MD items were observed with a Cronbach's alpha coefficient of 0.75. The validity of the MD scale has been estimated based on a high correlation with The BIDRs (Bernstein and Fink, 1998).

TABLE 2 | Patients reported more childhood trauma than healthy controls also after correcting for MD.

Childhood trauma	*B*	*SE*	Wald	df	Significance	Exp (B)	95% C.I. for Exp (B)	
							Lower	Upper
MD (yes/no)	2.39	0.75	10.27	1	0.001	10.89	2.53	46.93
Patient/control status	3.09	0.74	17.61	1	<0.001	21.98	5.19	93.08
Constant	−4.11	0.71	33.25	1	<0.000	0.02		

**Logistic regression; Childhood trauma (yes/no) is defined as least one subdomain of trauma above cutoff score for moderate to severe trauma; MD style (yes/no) is defined as the following: "MD style yes" = minimizers," score of ≥1 on the MD scale, and "MD style no" = "no minimization" score of 0 on the MD scale. Nagelkerke (r^2) = 0.33.*

Statistical Analyses

Data were analyzed using the Predictive Analytic Software (PASW), Version 21 (formerly SPSS Statistics). The sample was divided into a minimization vs. no minimization group, with minimization operationally defined as a score of 1 or greater on the MD scale. Grading severity of MD (scores rating from 0 to 3) was also included. Differences in categorical variables (gender, diagnosis, and group status) between 'minimizers' and 'non-minimizers' were tested using the chi-square test. As the childhood trauma data were skewed, Mann–Whitney *U*-test was performed to assess CTQ scores in minimizers and non-minimizers with CTQ measured as a continuous variable. For the follow-up analysis, childhood trauma was dichotomized into two groups based on at least one subdomain of childhood trauma reaching levels of moderate to severe reports following the definition by Bernstein et al. (1994, 2003) (see Supplementary Table S1).

Effect sizes were computed using Cohen's *d* (Cohen, 1977). For the effects sizes we compared trauma scores in the patients compared to the control group (Cohen's $d = M_1 - M_2/s_{pooled}$, where $s_{pooled} = \sqrt{[(s_1^2 + s_2^2)/2]}$). According to Rosenthal and Rosnow (1984), effect sizes were considered small for values between 0.20 and 0.50, moderate for values between 0.50 and 0.80, and large for values greater than 0.80. Logistic regression was performed to investigate differences in reports of childhood trauma (reaching above cutoff score for moderate to severe trauma on at least one subdomain) and group status (patients/controls), correcting for MD. Childhood trauma (yes/no) was entered as the dependent variable; MD (yes/no) and group status (patients/controls) as independent variables with a pre-set significance level of 0.05.

RESULTS

Demographics of the Sample According to MD Score

Selected demographics of the minimization (MD) and non-minimization (no MD) groups are presented in **Table 1**. Of the 920 study participants, 32% ($N = 294$) demonstrated a MD score and 68% ($N = 626$) did not. Neither gender ($P = 0.98$), patients group ($P = 0.70$) nor age ($P = 0.87$) had a significant association with MD score (see **Table 1**).

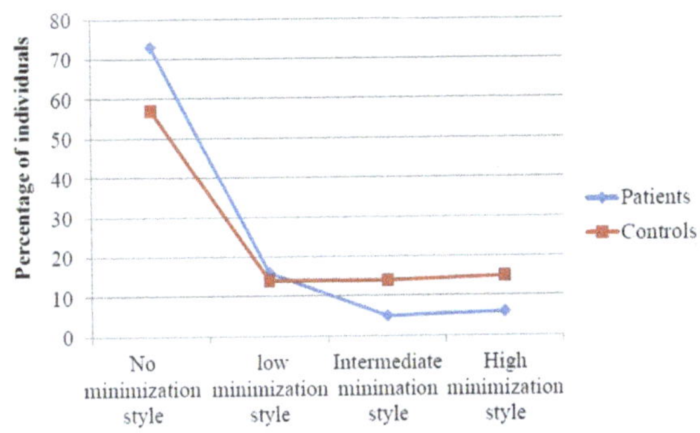

FIGURE 2 | Controls report increased minimization style measured by the minimization/denial (MD) scale compared to patients.

Childhood Trauma and MD Score

42.8% of the controls had a MD score of ≥1 compared to 26.7% of the patients ($X^2 = 23.99$, $P < 0.001$). 51% of the patients reported at least one subdomain of childhood trauma (≥moderate to severe score on CTQ), compared to 9% of the controls ($X^2 = 148.0$, df = 1, $P < 0.001$, Cohen's $d = 1.18$). Excluding participants with MD scores ≥ 1, 61% of patients reported at least one subdomain of childhood trauma (≥ moderate to severe score on CTQ) compared to 15% of the healthy controls ($X^2 = 99.3$, df = 1, $P < 0.001$, Cohen's $d = 1.27$, see **Figure 1**). In the patient group, a MD score of ≥1 was associated with lower CTQ score, compared to the patients with MD < 1 (Mann–Whitney test: $Z = -10.66$, $P < 0.001$). Also in the controls having a MD score of ≥1 was associated with lower CTQ score, compared to controls with MD < 1 (Mann–Whitney test: $Z = -9.29$, $P < 0.001$). Dividing into subdomains of childhood trauma, minimizers (MD score ≥ 1) presented significantly lower CTQ scores across all subtypes of trauma compared to patients and controls with MD < 1 (see Supplementary Figures S1, S2, and Table S2), with the most significant findings for emotional neglect.

A significant difference in childhood trauma (yes/no [defined as at least one subdomain of ≥moderate to severe score on CTQ]) was observed between patients and controls also after controlling for MD [Nagelkerke $r^2 = 0.33$; exp (B) = 0.102, $P < 0.001$, see **Table 2**].

Dividing into no, low, intermediate, and high minimization and denial (MD score of 0–3 respectively), controls had more frequently a score of intermediate or high MD compared to patients ($X^2 = 48.7$, df = 1, $P < 0.00.1$ see **Figure 2**).

DISCUSSION

To our knowledge the current study is one of the first studies to investigate minimization and denial by the MD scale and retrospective reports of childhood trauma amongst healthy individuals and in individuals with a severe mental disorder (SZ, BD, or major depression disorders with at least one psychotic episode). In our study the MD score was elevated in healthy individuals compared to the patient group. A significant negative association was observed between MD and CTQ scores. When we removed participants with MD scores ≥ 1, patients still reported significantly more childhood trauma experiences than the healthy control group (Cohen's $d = 1.27$). No difference in MD was observed within the patient sample (schizophrenia spectrum disorder, patients with a bipolar disorder, or patients with major depressive disorder with at least one psychotic episode). When we examined the impact of MD on CTQ subscale scores, we found the largest effect for patients and controls on the CTQ emotional neglect subscale. Similar findings have been reported in the study by MacDonald et al. (2016). Thus, endorsement of MD seems to be specifically sensitive to emotional neglect. It seems that those with emotional neglect would be less likely to claim that they had a perfect family. As discussed in the paper by MacDonald et al. (2016) reasons for this may include content overlap (for example four of the five items comprising the emotional neglect subscale contain the word "family" as compared to two of the three items comprising the MD score).

Our findings support evidence of a higher prevalence of childhood trauma in patients with severe mental disorders than in the normal population, as consistently reported in the literature (Etain et al., 2008, 2013; Fisher et al., 2010; Mondelli et al., 2010). Similar to the large multicentre study by MacDonald et al. (2016) comprised of healthy individuals and various psychiatric patients, we found that patients had lower minimization than the healthy individuals. This could be due to a larger proportion of individuals without a mental illness to recall life events with a 'rosy view' (Mitchell et al., 1997), a positivity bias recall not demonstrated for example by depressed individuals (Ben-Zeev and Young, 2010). This positivity bias could be a reason for elevated MD amongst healthy individuals in our study, with the reality of traumatic childhood experiences selectively underreported to maintain what Heider coined as the 'individuals positive outlook' (Heider, 1958). This positivity illusion has been repeatedly characterized as a typical cognitive mechanism among healthy individuals in Western cultures (Taylor and Brown, 1994; Greenwald et al., 2002), serving a purpose to preserve mental health. The human desire for esteem and need to view oneself positively form an important function in our psychological self-preservation (Baumeister and Leary, 1995). This may also involve seeing significant others, such as parents, in a more positive light. A meta-analysis of 266 studies support a significantly smaller self-serving attributional bias in psychopathological samples (Cohen's d effect size = 0.48) compared to individuals with no psychopathology (Cohen's $d = 1.28$) (Mezulis et al., 2004). Based on the above, we suggest more studies are needed to investigate if differences in self-serving attribution style influence responses to retrospective questionnaires and interviews across different population groups.

Study Limitations

Childhood trauma was collected using the CTQ, a retrospective measure of childhood trauma experiences with the inherited weakness of its retrospective design. However, retrospective information on childhood trauma is a frequently used measure with high reliability and validity in a psychotic population (Fisher et al., 2011). Reports of childhood trauma has been found stable over time (test–retest reliability) in addition to a large overlap of reports of childhood trauma across different sources [i.e., clinical case notes, questionnaires (convergent validity) (Fisher et al., 2011)]. The validity of the MD measure needs further investigations. We did not have any data on social desirability or attribution style, therefore we can only speculate that differences in minimization between our groups were based on differences in social desirability and attribution style. A further limitation is the failure to assess for the presence of Axis II personality disorders. The high likelihood of unacknowledged Axis II disorders may underestimate the effect of MD. It is well-documented that individuals with a personality disorder, particularly Cluster B (borderline, histrionic, narcissistic, or antisocial) more often report a history of abuse (Molnar et al., 2001). It is likely personality disorder diagnoses were present in the psychiatric population, due to their high comorbidity with Axis I diagnoses Links and Eynan, 2013). The presence of personality disorder diagnoses within the patients' sample may have impacted both CTQ scores and levels of minimization and denial of past-trauma.

CONCLUSION

Higher MD scores were notably observed in the healthy control group which could be based on enhanced self-serving bias, potentially attenuated in the psychiatric group. Clinicians and researchers would benefit from including the MD component of CTQ when assessing retrospective information of childhood trauma to rule out potential effects of MD.

AUTHOR CONTRIBUTIONS

MA, CC, OA, SL, and IM contributed to the study design and writing up process.

ACKNOWLEDGMENTS

We thank the patients who took part in the study and the NORMENT who contributed to the data collection. All authors contributed to the Manuscript.

REFERENCES

Aas, M., Haukvik, U. K., Djurovic, S., Tesli, M., Athanasiu, L., and Melle, I. (2014). Interplay between childhood trauma and BDNF val66met variants on blood BDNF mRNA levels and on hippocampus subfields volumes in schizophrenia spectrum and bipolar disorders. *J. Psychiatr. Res.* 59, 14–21. doi: 10.1016/j.jpsychires.2014.08.011

Aas, M., Kauppi, K., Brandt, C. L., Tesli, M., Kaufmann, T., Steen, N. E., et al. (2017). Childhood trauma is associated with increased brain responses to emotionally negative as compared with positive faces in patients with psychotic disorders. *Psychol. Med.* 47, 1–11. doi: 10.1017/S0033291716002762

Baumeister, R. F., and Leary, M. R. (1995). The need to belong: desire for interpersonal attachments as a fundamental human motivation. *Psychol. Bull.* 117, 497–529. doi: 10.1037/0033-2909.117.3.497

Ben-Zeev, D., and Young, M. A. (2010). Accuracy of hospitalized depressed patients' and healthy controls' retrospective symptom reports: an experience sampling study. *J. Nerv. Ment. Dis.* 198, 280–285. doi: 10.1097/NMD.0b013e3181d6141f

Bernstein, D. P., Fink, L., Handelsman, L., Foote, J., Lovejoy, M., Wenzel, K., et al. (1994). Initial reliability and validity of a new retrospective measure of child abuse and neglect. *Am. J. Psychiatry* 151, 1132–1136. doi: 10.1176/ajp.151.8.1132

Bernstein, D. P., Stein, J. A., Newcomb, M. D., Walker, E., Pogge, D., Ahluvalia, T., et al. (2003). Development and validation of a brief screening version of the Childhood Trauma Questionnaire. *Child Abuse Negl.* 27, 169–190. doi: 10.1016/S0145-2134(02)00541-0

Bernstein, P. B., and Fink, L. (1998). *Childhood Trauma Questionnaire: A Retrospective Self-report Manual.* San Antonio, TX: The Psychological Corporation.

Cohen, J. (1977). *Statistical Power Analysis for the Behavioral Sciences.* New York, NY: Academic Press.

Etain, B., Aas, M., Andreassen, O. A., Lorentzen, S., Dieset, I., Gard, S., et al. (2013). Childhood trauma is associated with severe clinical characteristics of bipolar disorders. *J. Clin. Psychiatry* 74, 991–998. doi: 10.4088/JCP.13m08353

Etain, B., Henry, C., Bellivier, F., Mathieu, F., and Leboyer, M. (2008). Beyond genetics: childhood affective trauma in bipolar disorder. *Bipolar Disord.* 10, 867–876. doi: 10.1111/j.1399-5618.2008.00635.x

Fisher, H. L., Craig, T. K., Fearon, P., Morgan, K., Dazzan, P., Lappin, J., et al. (2011). Reliability and comparability of psychosis patients' retrospective reports of childhood abuse. *Schizophr. Bull.* 37, 546–553. doi: 10.1093/schbul/sbp103

Fisher, H. L., Jones, P. B., Fearon, P., Craig, T. K., Dazzan, P., Morgan, K., et al. (2010). The varying impact of type, timing and frequency of exposure to childhood adversity on its association with adult psychotic disorder. *Psychol. Med.* 40, 1967–1978. doi: 10.1017/S0033291710000231

Greenwald, A. G., Banaji, M. R., Rudman, L. A., Farnham, S. D., Nosek, B. A., and Mellott, D. S. (2002). A unified theory of implicit attitudes, stereotypes, self-esteem, and self-concept. *Psychol. Rev.* 109, 3–25. doi: 10.1037/0033-295X.109.1.3

Heider, F. (1958). *The Psychology of Interpersonal Relations.* Hoboken, NJ: John Wiley & Sons Inc.

Holtgraves, T. (2004). Social desirability and self-reports: testing models of socially desirable responding. *Pers. Soc. Psychol. Bull.* 30, 161–172. doi: 10.1177/0146167203259930

Links, P. S., and Eynan, R. (2013). The relationship between personality disorders and Axis I psychopathology: deconstructing comorbidity. *Annu. Rev. Clin. Psychol.* 9, 529–554. doi: 10.1146/annurev-clinpsy-050212-185624

MacDonald, K., Thomas, M. L., MacDonald, T. M., and Sciolla, A. F. (2015). A perfect childhood? Clinical correlates of minimization and denial on the childhood trauma questionnaire. *J. Interpers. Violence* 30, 988–1009. doi: 10.1177/0886260514539761

MacDonald, K., Thomas, M. L., Sciolla, A. F., Schneider, B., Pappas, K., Bleijenberg, G., et al. (2016). Minimization of childhood maltreatment is common and consequential: results from a large, multinational sample using the childhood trauma questionnaire. *PLoS ONE* 11:e0146058. doi: 10.1371/journal.pone.0146058

May-Chahal, C., and Cawson, P. (2005). Measuring child maltreatment in the United Kingdom: a study of the prevalence of child abuse and neglect. *Child Abuse Negl.* 29, 969–984. doi: 10.1016/j.chiabu.2004.05.009

McGrath, J. J., McLaughlin, K. A., Saha, S., Aguilar-Gaxiola, S., Al- Hamzawi, A., Alonso, J., et al. (2017). The association between childhood adversities and subsequent first onset of psychotic experiences: a cross-national analysis of 23 998 respondents from 17 countries. *Psychol. Med.* 47, 1230–1245. doi: 10.1017/S0033291716003263

Mezulis, A. H., Abramson, L. Y., Hyde, J. S., and Hankin, B. L. (2004). Is there a universal positivity bias in attributions? A meta-analytic review of individual, developmental, and cultural differences in the self-serving attributional bias. *Psychol. Bull.* 130, 711–747. doi: 10.1037/0033-2909.130.5.711

Mitchell, T. R., Thompson, L., Peterson, E., and Cronk, R. (1997). Temporal adjustments in the evaluation of events: the "Rosy View". *J. Exp. Soc. Psychol.* 33, 421–448. doi: 10.1006/jesp.1997.1333

Molnar, B. E., Buka, S. L., and Kessler, R. C. (2001). Child sexual abuse and subsequent psychopathology: results from the National Comorbidity Survey. *Am. J. Public Health* 91, 753–760. doi: 10.2105/AJPH.91.5.753

Mondelli, V., Dazzan, P., Hepgul, N., Di, F. M., Aas, M., D'Albenzio, A., et al. (2010). Abnormal cortisol levels during the day and cortisol awakening response in first-episode psychosis: the role of stress and of antipsychotic treatment. *Schizophr. Res.* 116, 234–242. doi: 10.1016/j.schres.2009.08.013

Read, J., van, O. J., Morrison, A. P., and Ross, C. A. (2005). Childhood trauma, psychosis and schizophrenia: a literature review with theoretical and clinical implications. *Acta Psychiatr. Scand.* 112, 330–350. doi: 10.1111/j.1600-0447.2005.00634.x

Ringen, P. A., Lagerberg, T. V., Birkenaes, A. B., Engn, J., Faerden, A., Jonsdottir, H., et al. (2008). Differences in prevalence and patterns of substance use in schizophrenia and bipolar disorder. *Psychol. Med.* 38, 1241–1249. doi: 10.1017/S003329170700236X

Rosenthal, R., and Rosnow, R. L. (1984). *Essentials of Behavioral Research: Methods and Data Analysis.* New York, NY: McGraw-Hill.

Spitzer, R. L., Williams, J. B., Kroenke, K., Linzer, M., deGruy, F. V. III, Hahn, S. R., et al. (1994). Utility of a new procedure for diagnosing mental disorders in primary care. The PRIME-MD 1000 study. *JAMA* 272, 1749–1756. doi: 10.1001/jama.1994.03520220043029

Taylor, S. E., and Brown, J. D. (1994). Positive illusions and well-being revisited: separating fact from fiction. *Psychol. Bull.* 116, 21–27. doi: 10.1037/0033-2909.116.1.21

Tesli, M., Espeseth, T., Bettella, F., Mattingsdal, M., Aas, M., Melle, I., et al. (2014). Polygenic risk score and the psychosis continuum model. *Acta Psychiatr. Scand.* 130, 311–317. doi: 10.1111/acps.12307

Ventura, J., Liberman, R. P., Green, M. F., Shaner, A., and Mintz, J. (1998). Training and quality assurance with the Structured Clinical Interview for DSM-IV (SCID-I/P). *Psychiatry Res.* 79, 163–173. doi: 10.1016/S0165-1781(98)00038-9

Widom, C. S., Dutton, M. A., Czaja, S. J., and DuMont, K. A. (2005). Development and validation of a new instrument to assess lifetime trauma and victimization history. *J. Trauma Stress* 18, 519–531. doi: 10.1002/jts.20060

Yung, A. R., Cotter, J., Wood, S. J., McGorry, P., Thompson, A. D., Nelson, B., et al. (2015). Childhood maltreatment and transition to psychotic disorder independently predict long-term functioning in young people at ultra-high risk for psychosis. *Psychol. Med.* 45, 3453–3465. doi: 10.1017/S003329171500135X

3

Identifying Four Subgroups of Trauma in Psychosis: Vulnerability, Psychopathology, and Treatment

Lucy H. Stevens[1], Helen M. Spencer[2] and Douglas Turkington[2]*

[1] Tees Esk and Wear Valley NHS Mental Health Foundation Trust, Cleveland, UK, [2] Northumberland, Tyne and Wear NHS Mental Health Foundation Trust, Newcastle upon Tyne, UK

Keywords: schizophrenia, psychosis, trauma, subgroup, PTSD, CBT

Edited by:
Kim T. Mueser, Boston University, USA

Reviewed by:
Craig Steel, University of Reading, UK

****Correspondence:***
Lucy H. Stevens
lucystevens1@nhs.net

INTRODUCTION AND PROPOSAL

Schizophrenia has traditionally been viewed as a unitary diagnostic entity with a single neuropathogenesis (1). However, classification is evolving and schizophrenia is now given less importance in DSM-V (2), with the proposal that schizophrenia spectrum disorders better capture varying manifestations of psychotic symptoms (3). Recent research has pointed to a role for traumatic predisposition in many forms and time points in symptom development. For the first time, four clinical manifestations relating to traumatic vulnerability, trigger, and treatment implications are discussed. Symptoms will be referred to as psychosis, as this has been has been considered an accepted societal term to describe experiences such as hallucinations and delusions (4). However, the focus will remain on symptom presentations seen in schizophrenia spectrum disorders, as the purpose of this piece is to challenge schizophrenia as a unitary diagnostic concept.

SUBGROUP 1: TRAUMATIC PSYCHOSIS

This first clinical manifestation considers the "classical" association between trauma and psychosis, by referring to childhood trauma leading to an overt traumatic and coexisting schematic vulnerability (5, 6). This increases the risk of the emergence of psychotic symptoms in response to later triggers. In addition to the chronicity and multiplicity of the childhood abuse or neglect experienced (7), other factors have been linked with increased risk, such as perceived intent to harm from the victim's perspective (8), the closeness of the relationship between victim and perpetrator (9), and whether the victim is older than 12 or 16 years (9, 10). This indicates why childhood abuse, neglect, and bullying can be particularly harmful. Neurobiological research suggests childhood abuse is more likely to affect brain-derived neurotrophic factor expression, leading to dysregulation of the HPA axis and associated dopamine changes (11, 12) giving a putative marker for this subgroup. A meta-analysis supported the existence of traumatic psychosis by suggesting that if childhood abuse was eradicated, then one-third of adult psychosis would not occur (13).

When these individuals present with psychosis, they are more likely to experience positive symptoms (14). This includes a broad spectrum of hallucinatory experiences often congruent with the trauma history (e.g., somatic, olfactory, gustatory, visual, and auditory hallucinations), and also dissociative phenomena and higher levels of depression, anxiety, guilt, and shame (7, 15–17). From clinical observation, secondary substance misuse to self-manage symptoms and severe weight loss or gain as a somatic defense to help prevent further trauma, can occur. Re-traumatization is almost always present, as the trigger for psychosis is either directly congruent with earlier traumatic experiences, or threatens compensatory schema. For example, delusional formation can be protective of schematic beliefs developed in response to trauma (18), whereby life events threaten compensatory schema and lead to the development of delusional mood followed by delusional perception (19). Resulting psychotic symptoms can either be a direct or metaphorical representation of the earlier trauma (20), such as the relationship between paranoid ideas with prominent hypervigilance and formulation congruent themes of punishment and surveillance. Diagnoses can be unstable (i.e., schizoaffective disorder, schizophrenia, borderline personality disorder, dissociative disorders), given the presence of dissociation and self-harm in this subgroup. Markers of this group can be present prior to trauma disclosure. For example, the occurrence of non-epileptic attacks, which typically abate as disclosure proceeds, is a clinical observation that could be considered a dissociative and conversion phenomenon.

Evidence has suggested this could be a subgroup of people who respond poorly to antipsychotic medication (21) but could be a viable target for various psychological treatment options, including expert cognitive behavioral therapy (CBT), which can lead to stabilization and recovery (22). Techniques include building trust, scaffolding of activities, introducing effective coping strategies as well as grounding and stabilization, psychoeducation around dissociation, and techniques for regulating emotions. Crucially, the development of a maintenance formulation linking past trauma with present triggers and threat (23) is a subsequent stage in therapy, as this link has often not been made by the patient. Highlighting the timeline of events and symptoms and gradually working toward insight into emotional hotspots, particularly guilt and shame, can be longer term therapy targets. This enables reliving or restructuring to proceed, at a pace which can be tolerated by the patient, but it must be considered this may never be processed if too painful.

SUBGROUP 2: NEURODEVELOPMENTAL PSYCHOSIS

The second subgroup is characterized by those who appear to have a chronic and pervasive vulnerability that is genetic and/or organic in nature. For example, research has suggested a link between the C4 gene and excessive neural pruning during adolescence, which has been linked to the development of psychosis (24). This group could be broadened to consider vulnerabilities posed by neurodevelopmental disorders, but this discussion is beyond the scope of this paper. As children, these individuals may be recognized by teachers, as being socially isolated, displaying clumsiness, and suppressing emotional needs. Persistence of these behaviors can lead to alogia/communication difficulties, poor concentration and memory, affective blunting, poor self-care, and reduced motivation, which traditionally could be interpreted as negative symptoms. Given these difficulties, individuals could be at risk of homelessness, or poor quality accommodation, and hence more vulnerable to victimization. As a result, this can increase vulnerability to post-traumatic stress disorder (PTSD), which may occur as a secondary phenomenon of the trajectory of psychosis (25). Unfortunately, substances can be used to self-medicate symptoms of PTSD in this subgroup. Research has reported increased relative risk of substance abuse in those with PTSD (RR = 4.9), even when compared to people who have experienced trauma but do not have PTSD symptoms (RR = 2.0) (26).

It is important to consider Maslow's Hierarchy of Needs (27) before commencing treatment as it is crucial to stabilize basic needs, such as sourcing appropriate accommodation and community care, before attempting to address higher level psychological needs. One opinion is that antipsychotic medication can be efficacious for this group and psychosocial interventions such as family therapy, social skills training, and cognitive remediation may be as effective as CBT. The development of graded activities and approaches such as anxiety management, activity scheduling, and social skills training can allow a gentle cognitive restructuring approach to take place over a period of sessions, with variable length and duration. The presence of PTSD in this subgroup can be difficult to detect, but should be enquired about in all cases.

SUBGROUP 3: PSYCHOTIC PTSD

The third subgroup refers to the symptoms of PTSD developing prior to the onset of psychotic symptoms. This type of psychosis, similar to the traumatic psychosis subgroup, is triggered by trauma, but the symptoms may be a response to an initial trauma of any nature (rather than re-traumatization) and the symptoms of PTSD predate the emergence of the symptoms of psychosis (28). For example, individuals in the traumatic psychosis subgroup may develop a voice that resembles a flashback in an auditory modality, but the initial presentation in this subgroup is more like typical PTSD symptoms. Flashbacks and nightmares, resulting in insomnia and increased arousal, are followed by psychotic symptoms overtly linked to the trauma. For example, vulnerability to developing psychosis in this subgroup (e.g., perceptual phenomena) can be a result of prolonged exposure to threatening stimuli and extreme hypervigilance, perhaps *via* sleep deprivation associated with these symptoms.

Individuals in this subgroup would be expected to respond to expert CBT directly targeting the PTSD. For example, use of the cognitive model of PTSD (23) is crucial for introducing the link between past and current experiences and hence creating a rationale for trauma-focused intervention as well as quickly establishing triggers and maintenance factors in the current environment. In line with evidence-based practice for PTSD (29), both trauma-focused CBT (TF-CBT) and eye movement desensitization and reprocessing (EMDR) are viable and involve work on emotional hotspots (such as shame and anger) along with cognitive restructuring or imaginal reliving.

SUBGROUP 4: PSYCHOSIS-INDUCED PTSD

The final subgroup relates to the triggering of PTSD as a result of acute psychosis (30). This could be owing to loss of insight, leading to high levels of perceived threat and conviction in distressing delusional beliefs. It could also relate to previous traumas that have been suppressed, where re-traumatization occurs. For example, a person on an inpatient ward who tried to abscond believing that the nursing staff were planning to castrate him, resulted in a nurse grabbing hold of him and pulling down his trousers for the purposes of rapid tranquilization. This acted to confirm his beliefs that he was going to be castrated. If the same person had experienced sexual trauma or abuse, this could result in re-traumatization through activation of existing beliefs. Both might have resulted in PTSD. Although re-traumatization is possible in this subgroup, this is different to the triggers described in the traumatic psychosis subgroup, as the crucial trigger here is the episode of psychosis, which predates PTSD symptoms. It is crucial that PTSD is detected and managed, but quite often this is not the case and a lack of understanding can act as a powerful maintenance factor for chronicity and relapse to occur. For example, individuals may become mistrustful of their own self-awareness and ability to cope, often owing to a later acknowledgment that they themselves had no insight into their own deterioration of mental state during the initial psychotic episode. This can be a powerful maintaining factor in subsequent episodes owing to high threat sensitivity for perceptual/psychotic phenomena.

In addition to TF-CBT for PTSD, there also needs to be a strong emphasis on making sense of, and understanding, the experiences of psychosis in the context of the person's life. Some psychoeducation around hypervigilance would also be important, in the context of monitoring bodily experiences and interpreting these in a particular way (e.g., as in health anxiety). This should help to inform a robust relapse plan that emphasizes a balance between recognizing signs of relapse, but also being aware of hypervigilance to threat and the impact that this can have on misinterpretation of bodily experiences.

SUMMARY AND FUTURE DIRECTIONS

Four subgroups of traumatic psychosis have been briefly described in relation to mechanisms of action and recommended intervention modalities, based on clinical practice and the available literature. This paper supports the argument that schizophrenia should be explored in a symptom-specific way, given the varying symptom presentations and multifactorial means of understanding the trajectories of trauma and psychosis. It is clear that this is more complex than the initial conceptualization of traumatic psychosis. This paper intended to provide a summary, and hence further research is needed to understand other clinical presentations. Although this paper discussed subgroups in the context of schizophrenia spectrum disorders, it is not implied that these presentations are limited to such, given the presentation of psychosis across diagnostic categories. Also, it is not always intuitive or possible to consider these subgroups as discrete categories. However, the nature and timing of the trauma, and initial symptom presentation can be a means of identifying these subgroups and guiding treatment.

By developing further subdivisions of psychosis based on potential mechanisms of trigger, these categories are formulation driven, which is beneficial for informing evidence-based interventions, as demonstrated in this paper. There are many pioneering approaches beyond the scope of this paper that may provide efficacy in managing trauma and perceptual phenomena, which should be considered further. These include EMDR, method of levels, acceptance and commitment therapy, compassion-focused therapy, dialectical behavioral therapy, and imagery reprocessing.

AUTHOR CONTRIBUTIONS

We confirm that all authors contributed equally to the writing of this manuscript.

REFERENCES

1. Kraepelin E. *Psychiatrie. Ein Lehrbuch für Studirende und Aerzte. Fünfte, vollständig umgearbeitete Aufl age.* Leipzig: Barth (1896).
2. American Psychiatric Association. *Diagnostic and Statistical Manual of Mental Disorders.* 5th ed. Arlington, VA: American Psychiatric Publishing (2013).
3. Heckers S, Barch DM, Bustillo J, Gaebel W, Gur R, Malaspina D, et al. Structure of the psychotic disorders classification in DSM-V. *Schizophr Res* (2013) 150(1):11–4. doi:10.1016/j.schres.2013.04.039
4. Cooke A, Basset T, Bentall R, Boyle M, Cupitt C, Dillon J, et al. *Understanding Psychosis and Schizophrenia.* London: British Psychological Society (2014).
5. Callcott P, Turkington D. CBT for traumatic psychosis. In: Larkin W, Morrison AP, editors. *Trauma and Psychosis: New Directions for Theory and Therapy.* UK: Routledge (2006). p. 222–38.
6. Kingdon DG, Turkington D. *Cognitive Therapy of Schizophrenia.* London: The Guilford Press (2005).
7. Read J, Agar K, Argyle N, Aderhold V. Sexual and physical abuse during childhood and adulthood as predictors of hallucinations, delusions and thought disorder. *Psychol Psychother* (2003) 76(1):1–22. doi:10.1348/14760830260569210
8. Arseneault L, Cannon M, Fisher HL, Polanczyk G, Moffitt TE, Caspi A. Childhood trauma and children's emerging psychotic symptoms: a genetically sensitive longitudinal cohort study. *Am J Psychiatry* (2011) 168(1):65–72. doi:10.1176/appi.ajp.2010.10040567
9. Fisher HL, Jones PB, Fearon P, Craig TK, Dazzan P, Morgan K, et al. The varying impact of type, timing and frequency of exposure to childhood adversity on its association with adult psychotic disorder. *Psychol Med* (2010) 40(12):1967–78. doi:10.1017/S0033291710000231
10. Janssen I, Krabbendam L, Bak M, Hanssen M, Vollebergh W, Graaf RD, et al. Childhood abuse as a risk factor for psychotic experiences. *Acta Psychiatrica* (2004) 109(1):38–45. doi:10.1046/j.0001-690X.2003.00217.x
11. Alemany S, Arias B, Aguilera M, Villa H, Moya J, Ibanez MI, et al. Childhood abuse, the BDNF-Vall66Met polymorphism and adult psychotic-like experiences. *Br J Psychiatry* (2011) 199(1):38–42. doi:10.1192/bjp.bp.110.083808
12. McGowan PO, Sasaki PA, D'Alessio AC, Dymov S, Labonte B, Szyf M, et al. Epigenic regulation of the glucocorticoid receptor in human brain associates with childhood abuse. *Nat Neurosci* (2009) 12:342–8. doi:10.1038/nn.2270
13. Varese F, Smeets F, Drukker M, Lieverse R, Lataster T, Viechtbauer W, et al. Childhood adversities increase the risk of psychosis: a meta-analysis of patient-control, prospective- and cross-sectional cohort studies. *Schizophr Bull* (2012) 38(4):661–71. doi:10.1093/schbul/sbs050
14. Ellasson JW, Ross CA. Childhood trauma and psychiatric symptoms. *Psychol Rep* (1997) 80:447–50. doi:10.2466/pr0.1997.80.2.447
15. Bentall RP, Wickham S, Shevlin M, Varese F. Do specific early life adversities lead to specific symptoms of psychosis? A study from the 2007 the Adult Psychiatric Morbidity Study. *Schizophr Bull* (2012) 38(4):734–40. doi:10.1093/schbul/sbs049
16. Shevlin M, Dorahy M, Adamson G. Childhood traumas and hallucinations: an analysis of the National Comorbidity Study. *J Psychiatr Res* (2007) 41(3–4):222–8. doi:10.1016/j.jpsychires.2006.03.004
17. Waters F, Collerton D, Ffytche DH, Jardri R, Pins D, Dudley R, et al. Visual hallucinations in the psychosis spectrum and comparative information from neurodegenerative disorders and eye disease. *Schizophr Bull* (2014) 40(4):S233–45. doi:10.1093/schbul/sbu036
18. Turkington D, Spencer H, Jassal I, Cummings A. Cognitive behaviour therapy for the treatment of delusional systems. *Psychosis* (2015) 7:48–62. doi:10.1080/17522439.2014.899385

19. Brabban A, Turkington D. The search for meaning: detecting congruence between life events, underlying schema and psychotic symptoms. In: Morrison AP, editor. *A Casebook of Cognitive Therapy for Psychosis*. Hove: Brunner-Routledge (2002). p. 59–75.
20. Romme M. Metaphors and emotions. In: Romme M, Escher S, Dillon J, Corstens D, Morris M, editors. *Living with Voices: 50 Stories of Recovery*. Herefordshire, UK: PCCS Books Ltd (2009). p. 63–72.
21. Hassan AN, De Luca V. The effect of lifetime adversities on resistance to antipsychotic treatment in schizophrenia patients. *Schizophr Res* (2015) 161:496–500. doi:10.1016/j.schres.2014.10.048
22. Callcott P, Dudley R, Standart S, Freeston M, Turkington D. Treating trauma in people with first-episode psychosis using cognitive behavioural therapy. In: Hagen R, Turkington D, Berge T, Grawe RW, editors. *CBT for Psychosis: A Symptom Based Approach*. London: Routledge (2011). p. 175–92.
23. Ehlers A, Clark DM. A cognitive model of posttraumatic stress disorder. *Behav Res Ther* (2000) 38:319–45. doi:10.1016/S0005-7967(99)00123-0
24. Sekar A, Bialas AR, de Rivera H, Davis A, Hammond TR, Kamitaki N, et al. Schizophrenia risk from complex variation of complement component 4. *Nature* (2016) 530(7589):177–83. doi:10.1038/nature16549
25. Mueser KT, Rosenberg SD, Goodman LA, Trumbetta SL. Trauma, PTSD, and the course of severe mental illness: an interactive model. *Schizophrenia Res* (2002) 53:123–43. doi:10.1016/S0920-9964(01)00173-6
26. Read PL, Anthony JC, Breslau N. Incidents of drug problems in young adults exposed to trauma and posttraumatic stress disorder: do early life experiences and predispositions matter? *Arch Gen Psychiatry* (2007) 64(12):1435–42. doi:10.1001/archpsyc.64.12.1435
27. Maslow AH. *Motivation and Personality*. New York: Harper and Row (1954).
28. Romme MAJ, Escher S. Hearing voices in patients and non-patients. In: Romme MAJ, editor. *Understanding Voices: Coping with Auditory Hallucinations and Confusing Realities*. Gloucester, UK: Handsell Publications (1996). p. 9–21.
29. NICE. *Post-Traumatic Stress Disorder (PTSD): The Management of PTSD in Adults and Children in Primary and Secondary Care*. NICE Clinical Guideline 26 (2005). Available from: http://guidance.nice.org.uk/CG26
30. McGorry PD, Chanen A, McCarthy E, Van Riel R, Singh BS. Posttraumatic stress disorder following recent onset psychosis: an unrecognized post psychotic syndrome. *J Nerv Ment Dis* (1991) 179(5):253–8. doi:10.1097/00005053-199105000-00002

Posttraumatic Growth in Psychosis

Yael Mazor[1], Marc Gelkopf[1], Kim T. Mueser[2] and David Roe[1]*

[1] Faculty of Social Welfare and Health Sciences, Department of Community Mental Health, University of Haifa, Haifa, Israel,
[2] Department of Occupational Therapy, Psychology, and Psychiatry, Boston University Center for Psychiatric Rehabilitation, Boston, MA, USA

Edited by:
Mark A. Elliott,
National University of Ireland Galway, Ireland

Reviewed by:
Christine M. Falter,
University of Cologne, Germany
Omar Mothersill,
National University of Ireland Galway, Ireland

****Correspondence:***
Yael Mazor
yael.mazor@gmail.com

Objective: Recent research has shown high rates of exposure to trauma among people with serious mental illness (SMI). In addition, studies suggest that psychosis and mental illness-related experiences can be extremely traumatic. While some individuals develop full blown PTSD related to these experiences, it has been noted that some may also experience posttraumatic growth (PTG). However, few studies have examined PTG as a possible outcome in people who have experienced psychosis.

Method: To further understand the relationships between psychosis and PTG, 121 participants were recruited from community mental health rehabilitation centers and administered trauma and psychiatric questionnaires.

Results: High levels of traumatic exposure were found in the sample. Regarding our main focus of study, we observed that people who endured psychosis can experience PTG, and that PTG is mediated by meaning making and coping self-efficacy (CSE) appraisal. Psychotic symptoms were found to be a major obstacle to meaning making, CSE, and PTG, whereas negative symptoms were found to be significantly related to PTG when mediated by meaning making and CSE.

Conclusion: The current research provides preliminary evidence for potential role of meaning making and CSE as mediators of PTG in the clinical, highly traumatized population of people with SMI who have experienced psychosis. This may have both research as well as clinical practice relevance for the field of psychiatric rehabilitation.

Keywords: posttraumatic growth, psychosis, psychopathological symptoms, meaning making, coping self-efficacy

INTRODUCTION

Research has suggested that psychosis and mental illness-related experiences can be extremely traumatic (1–3). As in the case of traumatic life events in non-clinical populations (4), psychosis could theoretically also lead to posttraumatic growth (PTG). PTG consists of five facets of growth: appreciation of life, relating to others, new found possibilities in life (for example, a new career pursuit following trauma), personal strength, and spiritual change (5, 6). PTG occurs after a trauma, which may have significant negative impact, but at the same time be the starting point of an emotional and behavioral rebuilding process, through PTG (7). The promotion of PTG may contribute to the treatment of people who experienced massive traumas such as people with serious mental illness (SMI) who have endured psychotic symptoms. Although multiple studies have found that traumas are frequent and repetitive experiences in these individuals (8, 9), and qualitative studies on the experiences of recovery have reported elements of growth in this population (10, 11), only few have explored the possibility of PTG in people with SMI who have experienced psychosis.

Psychotic symptoms are a common feature of SMI, most prominent in schizophrenia, but frequently present in other disorders as well, such as bipolar disorder and major depression. Individuals who have experienced psychosis are also more likely to have been exposed to trauma (12) and are more vulnerable to developing posttraumatic symptomatology (8, 13–16). The impact of exposure to traumatic events has been found to worsen the characteristic symptoms of SMI, such as grandiose or paranoid delusions, hallucinations, anxiety, and depression and to contribute to general psychopathology (e.g., depression, anxiety, impaired social judgment, etc.) in psychiatric disorders such as cognitive deficits, risk taking behaviors, and the experience of psychosis itself (8, 17–20). A possible explanation to the adverse impact of traumatic exposure on SMI symptoms is the "social defeat hypothesis of Schizophrenia" (21). This approach suggests that long-term exposure to the experience of social defeat or exclusion can lead to the sensitization of the mesolimbic dopamine system, whereby exposure to a given stimulus (e.g., stressor), may result in an increased response to subsequent exposures. Continuous humiliation and seclusion, which are inherent in childhood traumas, such as abuse, can indeed result in feelings of social defeat, and therefore repeated traumatic exposure may be one of the reasons of the aggravation of SMI symptoms (12).

Psychopathological symptoms can appear in the form of both positive and negative symptoms. Positive (or psychotic) symptoms can be experienced as severely traumatic on account of reality distortions such as delusions and hallucinations (3, 22–25), and can contain adverse and frightening, and potentially traumatic content.

Negative symptoms could also contribute to the traumatic experiencing of psychosis. These symptoms manifest in a lack of energy, drive, and interest, which are caused by a basic inhibition in motivation (26–28). Amotivation is one of the negative symptom groups and is specifically relevant to the possible traumatic sequelae of psychosis. These include anhedonia, lack of social drive and social isolation, and treatment non-adherence (8, 29, 30). This chain of events might elevate the risk for relapse and indirectly lead to traumatic experiences that are part of psychosis (3, 8).

Alongside, the adverse consequences of psychopathological symptoms are the unique outcome of coping with adversity (31), namely, PTG. PTG manifests itself after trauma through one's thought processes, emotions, and behaviors, and it may include both a constructive and an illusory aspect (32). PTG is facilitated by the reduction of emotional distress associated with traumatic experiences, which allows ruminations to transform into deliberate thinking about the trauma and its aftermath. As a result, people may feel that they have changed positively following their traumatic experience (31, 33). In addition, PTG can also express itself as concrete actions whereby people act in new and different ways in the face of trauma (34, 35). Although traumatic experiences are common in people who have experienced psychosis—studies have suggested that up to 98% of people who experienced psychosis were exposed to prior trauma (36), only a few studies investigated PTG in this population (37–39). Thus, we still lack the understanding of what might facilitate PTG in these individuals.

One important factor that may contribute to the development of PTG is coping self-efficacy (CSE), which has been found to be positively correlated with PTG (40). CSE is the perceived or appraised ability to manage one's personal functioning and environmental demands following traumatic or stressful events, through cognitive processes and changes in one's belief system (41, 42). These processes can provide a sense of control and actual control in the face of traumatic adversity, reducing vulnerability to being overwhelmed by helplessness (12, 43) CSE includes three dimensions: (a) self-appraisal of coping capabilities; (b) transformative actions [e.g., the ability to change or maintain one's coping style when faced with different challenges (43)]; and (c) thought control efficacy (i.e., the sense of control people have over their thoughts, and their ability not to be influenced continuously by cognitive intrusions). Research suggests that the ability to accept situations that cannot be changed is a major aspect in adaptation to uncontrollable events, and that the reappraisal of coping in a more positive light is one path to PTG (32, 44). An important question is whether individuals who experience psychosis and therefore might suffer from stereotyped thinking, delusions, preoccupation, and lack of insight, might be hampered in their ability to develop self-appraisals, transformative actions, and the belief in one's ability to control one's thoughts (i.e., CSE), and therefore possibly PTG.

Another major factor that is both protective and facilitative of PTG is meaning making. The need to search for meaning is a basic human tendency (45), which may be activated after the violation of basic life assumptions regarding oneself and the world following trauma (46–49). Definitions and measures of meaning making vary throughout theories (50); however, all theoreticians agree that meaning is a crucial component in confronting adversity and promoting growth (51). The inability to find meaning in life after encountering adverse situations can result in extreme distress (45). Studies show that individuals with SMI are capable of searching for and finding meaning (11, 52). For example, Piltch (53) described her recovery process from major depression, in which finding meaningful roles and activities (i.e., parenthood and acquiring a profession), was facilitative not only of recovery, but also had elements that can otherwise be described as PTG. However, as psychiatric symptoms may affect meaning making processes (54–56), we do not know if it affects PTG in individuals who have experienced psychosis. We therefore posed the question of whether PTG is contingent upon meaning making and CSE in people who experienced psychosis.

Trauma, although excruciating, may set in motion a process of rebuilding and positive change (i.e., PTG). However, yet to be thoroughly investigated is the possibility of PTG in individuals who experienced psychosis. To address this issue, we conducted a study to examine the extent to which PTG occurs and to assess the possible mediating effect of CSE and meaning making processes, in such individuals with SMI. We examined the relationships between positive psychotic symptoms, negative symptoms, general psychopathology, and PTG, and hypothesized that:

(a) Positive psychotic symptoms (such as conceptual disorganization and suspicion/persecution), negative symptoms, and general symptoms will be negatively correlated with meaning making processes, CSE, and PTG.
(b) CSE and meaning making processes will be positively correlated with PTG and mediate the relationship between positive psychotic symptoms, negative symptoms, general psychopathological symptoms, and PTG in people who have experienced psychosis.

MATERIALS AND METHODS

Participants

One hundred and twenty-one participants were recruited from community mental health rehabilitation services of the Israeli Ministry of Health. To be eligible for the study, participants had to meet Israeli criteria for having a "psychiatric disability" severe enough to compromise at least 40% of one's functioning. This is determined by a committee, including a psychiatrist and recognized by National Insurance Institute regulations. The last registry hospital discharge diagnosis of schizophrenia, of whom all Israeli rehab service users are part of, has acceptable sensitivity and specificity assessed against research diagnosis (57); has acceptable stability over time (58); and captured over 90% of cases with schizophrenia disorders based on research criteria in a community sample (59). Inclusion criteria were: men and women over the age of 18, who had been psychiatrically hospitalized in the past, had experienced psychotic symptoms according to their clinicians and corroborated by the Positive and Negative Syndrome Scale (PANSS) [(60) –see measures] clinical interview (administered by the first author) and were eligible to sign an informed consent.

Potential participants were referred to the study by mental health professionals in the rehabilitation services. Participants who wished to take part and met the inclusion criteria contacted the researcher and signed an informed consent form.

Participants completed the questionnaires and were administered the PANSS clinical interview, after which they were paid for their participation. Data were collected by the first author between May 2014 and October 2014. The study protocol was reviewed and approved by the University of Haifa ethics board.

Measures

Demographic Data

Factors such as gender, age, education, and marital status were queried.

Clinical History

Diagnosis and time since last hospitalization were determined by psychiatrists and other mental health professionals during the intake procedure.

Traumatic History

The Trauma History Screen [THS (61)] is an 18-item instrument used to screen lifetime trauma history. The THS examines high magnitude stressors (HMS), traumatic stressors (TS), and persisting posttraumatic distress, which refers to sudden events that have been found to cause extreme distress. Items include natural disasters, interpersonal traumas, military trauma, etc. For each potentially traumatic event on the scale, participants indicated whether they had ever experienced it in a binary (yes/no) format. The THS has been found to be reliable and have good psychometric properties (61). The THS was translated into Hebrew, back translated, with any language discrepancies resolved by a third bilingual person with trauma expertise. Three psychosis-related items were added, namely: "Have you ever experienced psychosis?" "Have you been psychiatrically hospitalized?" and "Do you suffer from serious mental illness?"

Positive, Negative, and General Symptoms

The PANSS (60) is a semi-formalized 30-item interview used to assess affective, motor, cognitive, perceptual, attentional, integrative, and interactive functions in individuals with SMI. The PANSS measures three domains: positive symptoms (7 items; e.g., hallucinations, delusions), negative symptoms (7 items; e.g., blunted affect, social withdrawal), and general symptoms (16 items; e.g., depression, anxiety). The symptoms are assessed on a 7-point scale that represents the severity of psychopathology from 1 (*absent*) to 7 (*extreme*). The summations of ratings range from 7 to 49 for the positive and negative scales and from 16 to 112 for the general symptoms scale. The reliability and validity of the PANSS in Hebrew are well established (62, 63). The internal consistency of the PANSS in the present sample was good ($\alpha = 0.86$). The PANSS interviews were administered by the first author, an experienced mental health professional, after extensive clinical training on the scale.

Posttraumatic Growth Inventory (PTGI)

The PTGI (5) is a 21-item scale that assesses positive changes occurring in response to major adversities. The PTGI is scored on a 6-point Likert scale, from 0 ("*I did not experience this change as a result of my crisis*") to 5 ("*I experienced this change to a very great extent as a result of my crisis*"). The Hebrew PTGI showed good psychometric properties (64, 65) and was successfully used in previous studies (66). Cronbach's α for the PTGI factors in the present sample was good to excellent (range $\alpha = 0.84–0.92$). In the current research, one question was added in which participants were asked to name the traumatic event to which they referred regarding their PTG. PTG summation of ratings range from 0 to 105. A cutoff point regarding PTG level was determined as follow: scores of 45 and below represented none to low PTG levels, whereas scores of 46 and above represented medium to very high PTG levels.

Coping Self-Efficacy

The CSE Scale (67) is a 26-item scale that assesses the respondent's confidence in performing coping behaviors when faced with life challenges and is constructed from three facets: (a) problem-focused coping; (b) ability to stop unpleasant emotions and thoughts, and (c) ability to get support from family and friends. The CSE is scored on a 10-point scale from 0 ("*cannot do it at* all") to 10 ("*certain I can do it when faced with challenges*"). The CSE has been used in several studies worldwide (68, 69) and has been translated and back translated into Hebrew and English. The internal consistency of the CSE in the present study was excellent ($\alpha = 0.93$).

Meaning in Life

The Meaning in Life Questionnaire [MLQ (51)] is a 10-item scale that was used to identify meaning making processes; namely, the presence of meaning and the search for meaning, on a scale from1 ("*absolutely untrue*") to 7 ("*absolutely true*"). The MLQ was used in a variety of studies (70, 71) and was translated and back translated into Hebrew and English. Cronbach's α for the MLQ total score was excellent ($\alpha = 0.90$).

Data Analyses

The study hypotheses about mediation were examined regarding (a) PANSS positive, negative, and general symptoms as the independent variable (IV), meaning making processes (MLQ) and CSE as mediators, and post-traumatic growth inventory (PTGI) as the dependent variable (DV). Mediation was examined with Preacher and Hayes' (72, 73) bootstrapping procedures (MEDIATE, SPSS22.0). To avoid the inflation of alpha due to multiple analyses, the Bonferroni criterion was applied for each table, resulting in a cutoff of $p = 0.008$ ($0.05/6 = 0.008$). Due to high inter-correlations between the MLQ factors ($r = 0.59$, $p < 0.001$) and between the CSE factors ($r = 0.62$–0.80, $p < 0.001$), total scores of MLQ and CSE factors were used. Due to moderate inter-correlations between the PANSS factors ($r = 0.53$–0.65, $p < 0.001$), the total score was used in the main analyses. For exploratory purposes, in the final part of the study, the three factors were used, each in a separate analysis. Moderate to high inter-correlations were found between the PTGI factors as well ($r = 0.30$–0.67, $p < 0.001$), but because this measure was the DV, each factor was used separately. To understand the nature of marginal relationships found between MLQ and PANSS positive symptoms, the MLQ was split at the median and the PANSS positive symptom factor was split into three equal groups, which were analyzed using a chi-square test.

RESULTS

Descriptive Information

Table 1 summarizes the demographic, clinical, and trauma characteristics of the study sample. The participants were an average of 43.8-years old (SD = 11.8). Most of them had schizophrenia or schizoaffective disorder. Over half of the participants (57%, based upon the traumatic history screen) had previous traumatic experiences; two thirds (66.2%) reported events that caused extreme distress, and 47.1% of participants reported exposure to continuous TS. The most common HMS were psychiatric hospitalization (90.1%) and psychotic symptoms (90.9%).

Correlational Analyses

To assess the relationships between the study variables, Pearson correlations were performed, which are presented in **Table 2.**

TABLE 1 | Participants' demographic and clinical characteristics ($N = 121$).

Variable	*n*	%
Gender		
Male	56	46.3
Female	65	53.7
Diagnosis		
Schizophrenia and schizoaffective	95	78.5
Bipolar with past psychotic symptoms	9	7.4
Personality or affective disorders with psychotic symptoms	17	14.1
Family status		
Single	70	57.9
Divorced/separated/widowed	32	26.5
Married/living in couple relationship	19	15.6
Children		
No children	82	67.8
With children	39	32.2
Housing status		
Lives independently	24	19.8
Lives with family	37	30.6
Rehabilitation housing services in the community	60	49.6
Employment status		
Not working	33	27.3
Working in community rehabilitation factories	88	72.7
Psychiatric hospitalization		
Were psychiatrically hospitalized	119	98.3
No hospitalization	2	1.7
Time since last psychiatric hospitalization		
Less than 1 year	15	12.4
1–5 years	48	39.7
More than 5 years	28	23.1
More than 10 years	24	19.8
Did not answer	6	5.0
Traumatic history (including multiple experiences)		
Experienced more than five high magnitude stressors	106	87.5
Experienced sexual abuse as a child	31	25.6
Experienced violence as a child	47	39.7
Experienced a sudden death/loss of a loved one	81	66.9

Higher PTG was generally related to lower PANSS scores and to higher meaning making and CSE scores. This was found for PTG total scores, as well as for most subscales, except for some of the relationships between PTG and PANSS positive symptoms. In addition, higher PANSS scores were related to lower meaning making and CSE scores, whereas higher meaning making and higher CSE were interrelated. An exception was the marginal correlation between meaning making and PANSS positive symptoms ($p = 0.076$; subsequent lowest p value was.081). Correlations between age, years of education, time of hospitalization, and the total PTGI score were not significant, nor were gender differences on any of the measures. Family status had low variance; therefore, analyses were conducted without the control of background variables.

To understand the nature of the marginal relationship between meaning making (MLQ) and PANSS positive symptoms, MLQ was split at the median [at score 47 (range 10–70)] and PANSS positive symptoms were split into three equal groups [at scores 16 and 21 (range 9–32)] and analyzed

TABLE 2 | Means, SDs, and correlations of the research variables, subscale scores ($N = 121$).

Variable, M (SD)	PTGI relation with others	PTGI new possibilities	PTGI personal strength	PTGI spiritual change	PTGI appreciation of life	PANSS total	PANSS positive symptoms	PANSS negative symptoms	PANSS general psychopathology	Meaning total (Meaning in Life Questionnaire)	Coping self-efficacy (CSE) total
PTGI total score 61.16 (21.87)	0.89***	0.86***	0.81***	0.62***	0.78***	−0.38***	−0.20*	−0.38***	−0.36***	0.68***	0.66***
PTGI relation with others 19.91 (*7.98*)		0.67***	0.64***	0.49***	0.61***	−0.41***	−0.26**	−0.42***	−0.34***	0.58***	0.56***
PTGI new possibilities 14.99 (*6.42*)			0.60***	0.48***	0.61***	−0.31***	−0.15	−0.33***	−0.28**	0.61***	0.62***
PTGI personal strength 12.45 (*4.58*)				0.40***	0.65***	−0.28**	−0.16	−0.20*	−0.31***	0.47***	0.54***
PTGI spiritual change 4.86 (*3.41*)					0.30***	−0.21*	−0.05	−0.24**	−0.20*	0.50***	0.35**
PTGI appreciation of life 8.96 (*4.31*)						−0.28**	−0.12	−0.25**	−0.29***	0.55***	0.54***
PANSS total 84.20 (19.33)							0.76***	0.86***	0.91***	−0.39***	−0.40***
PANSS positive symptoms 18.79 (*5.08*)								0.53***	0.57***	−0.16	−0.21*
PANSS negative symptoms 23.73 (*7.61*)									0.65***	−0.34***	−0.31***
PANSS general psychopathology 41.68 (*9.76*)										−0.43***	−0.45***
Meaning total (MLQ) 45.54 (*14.57*)											0.74***
CSE total 139.80 (*50.64*)											

PTGI, Posttraumatic Growth Inventory; PANSS, Positive and Negative Syndrome Scale.
*p < 0.05.
**p < 0.01.
***p < 0.001.

TABLE 3 | Mediation analyses for Meaning in Life Questionnaire total, Positive and Negative Syndrome Scale total, and Posttraumatic Growth Inventory (total and its five dimensions) scores ($N = 121$).

Dependent variable (DV)	Independent variable (IV)	Mediator	IV to mediator	Mediator to DV	Mediation effect	Z
			B (SE)	B (SE)	B (SE)	
PTGI total	PANSS total	MLQ total	−0.29*** (0.06)	0.93*** (0.11)	−0.27 (0.07)	4.02***
PTGI relations with others total				0.09** (0.03)	−0.08 (0.02)	3.60***
PTGI new possibilities total				0.25*** (0.03)	−0.07 (0.02)	3.97***
PTGI personal strength total				0.14*** (0.03)	−0.04 (0.01)	3.07**
PTGI spiritual change total				0.12*** (0.02)	−0.03 (0.01)	3.89***
PTGI appreciation of life total				0.15*** (0.02)	−0.05 (0.01)	3.40***

** $p < 0.01$, *** $p < 0.001$.

TABLE 4 | Mediation analyses for Positive and Negative Syndrome Scale total, coping self-efficacy total, and Posttraumatic Growth Inventory (total and its five dimensions) scores ($N = 121$).

Dependent variable (DV)	Independent variable (IV)	Mediator	IV to mediator	Mediator to DV	Mediation effect	Z
			B (SE)	B (SE)	B (SE)	
PTGI total	PANSS total	CSE total	−1.05*** (0.22)	0.26*** (0.03)	−0.27 (0.08)	3.53***
PTGI relations with others total				0.07*** (0.01)	−0.08 (0.02)	3.33***
PTGI new possibilities total				0.07*** (0.01)	−0.08 (0.02)	3.85***
PTGI personal strength total				0.05*** (0.01)	−0.05 (0.02)	2.93**
PTGI spiritual change total				0.02** (0.01)	−0.02 (0.01)	2.88**
PTGI appreciation of life total				0.04*** (0.01)	−0.05 (0.02)	2.83**

** $p < 0.01$, *** $p < 0.001$.

TABLE 5 | Mediation analyses for the dimensions of Positive and Negative Syndrome Scale, Meaning in Life Questionnaire total, coping self-efficacy total, and Posttraumatic Growth Inventory total ($N = 121$).

Dependent variable (DV)	Independent variable (IV)	Mediator	IV to mediator	Mediator to DV	Mediation effect	Z
			B (SE)	B (SE)	B (SE)	
PTGI total	PANSS positive symptoms total	MLQ total	−0.46 (0.26)	0.99*** (0.10)	−0.46 (0.27)	1.71
		CSE total	−2.08 (0.89)	0.28*** (0.03)	−0.58 (0.28)	2.09
	PANSS negative symptoms total	MLQ total	−0.64*** (0.17)	0.93*** (0.11)	−0.60 (0.17)	3.62***
		CSE total	−2.06*** (0.58)	0.26*** (0.03)	−0.53 (0.17)	3.13**
	PANSS general psychopathology total	MLQ total	−0.64*** (0.12)	0.96*** (0.11)	−0.61 (0.13)	4.77***
		CSE total	−2.32*** (0.43)	0.27*** (0.03)	−0.62 (0.15)	4.08***

** $p < 0.01$, *** $p < 0.001$.

using a chi-square test. Results showed that among those with low positive symptoms, 62% reported high MLQ, whereas among those with high positive symptoms, only 29% reported high MLQ. Among those with moderate positive symptoms, 55% reported high MLQ [$\chi^2(2) = 9.17$, Cramer's $V = 0.275$, $p = 0.010$].

To explore which positive symptoms were most strongly related to PTG, we computed the correlation between the severity of positive PANSS items and the MLQ. Conceptual disorganization (PANSS positive, item #2) was negatively correlated to meaning in life ($r_p = -0.26$, $p = 0.004$) (i.e., higher conceptual disorganization was related to lower MLQ). Moreover, suspicion/persecution (PANSS positive, item #6) was negatively related to MLQ ($r_p = -0.18$, $p = 0.05$), whereas grandiosity (PANSS positive, item #5) was positively related to MLQ ($r_p = 0.18$, $p = 0.04$). The other correlations between the individual positive symptoms and MLQ total score were not significant.

Mediation Analyses

To assess the mediating role of meaning in life (MLQ) and CSE between the PANSS (IV) and PTGI (DV), mediation bootstrapping procedures were used, as mentioned above in the analytical strategy section. As the inter-correlations between the dimensions of PANSS were high ($r = 0.53$–0.65, $p < 0.001$), we first assessed the mediated relationships with the five PTGI dimensions as the outcomes, and the PANSS total score as the IV. That is to say, mediation was examined for (a) PANSS total score, MLQ total score, and PTGI and its dimensions (**Table 3**), and (b) PANSS total score, CSE total score, and PTGI and its dimensions (**Table 4**). Due to the theoretical importance of PANSS dimensions, they were examined separately, with MLQ total score and CSE total score. This time, only the PTGI total score was used to avoid redundancy (**Table 5**).

Results of the role of MLQ regarding the relationship between PANSS total and PTGI total and its dimensions showed that MLQ mediated the relationship between the PANSS total score and the PTGI total score and its dimensions. In other words, less severe symptoms on the PANSS were associated with higher meaning making (MLQ total score), which in turn were related to a higher PTG on the PTGI.

Results regarding the mediating role of CSE total on PANSS total and PTGI total and dimensions showed that more severe symptoms on the PANSS were related to lower CSE on the CSE, which in turn were related to a lower level of PTG.

Finally, results showed that both MLQ and CSE mediated the relationship between PANSS negative symptoms and PANSS general psychopathology, and PTGI (see **Table 5**). Results also showed that lower scores on PANSS negative symptoms and PANSS general symptoms were related to higher MLQ scores and higher CSE scores, which were then related to higher PTGI total scores. However, mediation was not significant for PANSS positive symptoms and PTGI total score.

DISCUSSION

In the current study, 80% of participants indicated medium to very high levels of PTG. The mean score on overall PTG was moderately high (M = 63), which is consistent with PTG scores in other populations such as earthquake survivors (74), bereaved parents (75), and women with breast cancer (76). Greater severity across all symptoms (positive, negative, and general psychopathological symptoms) was associated with worse CSE, less meaning making, and less PTG. One possible explanation for these associations may be that distress and distraction, which is associated with the above said symptoms, can thwart coping efforts and the ability to develop meaning from experiences, thus hamper PTG. Further findings, consistent with our hypotheses, indicated that CSE and meaning mediated the adverse impact of negative symptoms and general symptoms on PTG among people with SMI who have experienced psychosis. In addition, screening for traumatic history elicited elevated levels of traumatic exposure and cumulative trauma; 87.5% indicated experiencing more than five HMS during their lives, 25.6% experienced sexual abuse as children, and 39.7% experienced violence as children. These elevated levels of traumatic exposure replicate previous research suggesting high levels of trauma exposure in SMI (9, 77, 78).

As hypothesized, positive symptoms had a significant negative relationship with CSE and PTG. This may be explained by the cognitive impairments that often accompany psychotic symptoms (79), which might be caused by aberrant assignment of salience to external objects and internal representations (54, 80–82). Indeed, reality distortions and conceptual disorganization might hamper cognitive processing (e.g., thoughtful reflection and awareness) and cause higher levels of distress alongside distressing reappraisal processes, which might lead to the development of less effective coping means (50, 83–85). The accompanying distress might also elevate the feelings of uncontrollability and arousal that are inherent to psychotic symptoms (86–88), and further affect the appraisal of coping efficacy, actual coping (42, 89, 90), and possibly PTG. Another possible explanation for the negative relationship between positive symptoms, CSE and PTG, can stem from a neurocognitive perspective regarding deficits in executive function, which lead to passive avoidant coping strategies (89, 91) and can thus hamper both CSE and PTG. Finally, dopaminergic transmission dysfunction in the prefrontal cortex in schizophrenia and its grave effect on cognitive impairments (such as difficulties in working memory and decision making) (80), may also contribute to poor CSE appraisal and difficulties in experiencing PTG.

As hypothesized, positive symptoms had a significant negative relationship with meaning. This is consistent with previous studies reporting maladaptive processes of misplaced meaning and inaccurate interpretation of external and internal stimulus in psychosis (92, 93). Positive symptoms such as reality distortion and conceptual disorganization could hamper normal emotional processes that allow people to find meaning following adversity. Normal emotional processing is composed, in part, of self-regulation of emotional disturbances (e.g., anxiety, depression, etc.). When hampered, difficulties in meaning making might develop and subsequently hinder PTG. As witnessed by the negative correlation found between conceptual disorganization and meaning making, cognitive disorganization (as manifested by confusion, distress, and elevated levels of emotional stress reactivity) might also affect the emotional and cognitive ability to engage in meaning making (54–56). However, one positive symptom was found to have positive relationship with meaning (i.e., grandiosity; PANSS positive, item #5). This raises two possibilities. First, high levels of grandiosity, such as the belief that one has special powers or abilities, or is famous or very accomplished, may be associated with a sense of discovery and relief that incorporates meaning and the experience of PTG, irrespective of the reality of those beliefs, reflecting the possible illusory part of PTG. The illusory part of PTG may thus be conceptualized as a component of PTG that helps people counterbalance their emotional distress in the face of trauma (32). Alternatively, high levels of grandiosity may merely reflect the psychotic symptoms these people still experience and not PTG.

The results of this study offer support for our hypothesis that negative symptoms and general psychopathological symptoms are negatively correlated with meaning, CSE, and PTG. The relationship between negative symptoms and meaning making may be explained by deficits inherent in negative symptoms, such as lack of motivation (28), over estimation of effort required to achieve goals, and the anticipation of negative outcomes (94, 95). These deficits, in turn, might lead to a lack in drive and energy to commence meaning making processes and thus might hamper PTG. Next, consistent with the literature (90, 96) and as mentioned above, higher levels of negative symptoms were linked to lower CSE levels. This might be because individuals with psychotic disorders have difficulty in anticipating pleasure (97, 98). This deficit in anticipatory pleasure might hamper people's ability to motivate themselves toward beneficial coping actions, thereby hampering CSE. This is in line with studies showing that people with psychosis perceive threats as less controllable, and that higher levels of negative as well as positive symptoms are linked to more dysfunctional coping strategies (86, 99, 100), which might hinder PTG. Additionally, the negative correlations found between general psychopathological symptoms and meaning making, CSE and PTG, are in accordance with studies that found that higher levels of symptoms were related to higher distress levels, which could hinder the ability to appraise coping abilities and find meaning in people who experienced psychosis (90, 101, 102), and therefore impede PTG.

Finally, our findings offer support for the hypothesis that CSE and meaning making mediate the adverse impact of negative symptoms and general symptoms on PTG among people who have experienced psychosis. This is consistent with PTG literature, which suggests that a certain level of distress (which might be caused by both negative as well as general psychopathological symptoms, as mentioned above) is needed to embark on the journey of meaning making and PTG (31). On the other hand, this may not be the case when extreme or persistent levels of distress are evident, as might be seen in our findings regarding positive symptoms, namely that meaning making and CSE did not mediate the adverse impact of positive symptoms on PTG. This might be due to the potentially adverse consequences of positive symptoms on cognitive and emotional processes (3, 36, 82), which could hamper meaning making, CSE, and ultimately PTG. In addition, the lack of mediation effect may be due to differences among participants regarding when psychotic symptoms were experienced (i.e., currently or in the past), thus effecting the ability to experience PTG.

A number of practice and policy-related implications can be drawn from the current study, including the importance of addressing traumatic exposure phenomena in rehabilitation programs for people with SMI who have experienced psychosis. Indeed, there is a lack of knowledge and treatment for individuals with SMI who also suffer from high levels of trauma exposure accompanied with a potential for re-traumatization due to psychosis itself. Considering the high levels of comorbidity found in this population extant, psychiatric interventions are not adequate for the treatment of the traumatic aspects of their illnesses. On the other hand, our findings suggest that even when facing high levels of symptoms individuals with SMI can experience PTG, contingent upon their ability to engage in meaning making processes and positively appraise their coping abilities. Hence, we suggest that greater emphasis should be placed on teaching these individuals more effective coping strategies, along with both broadening the perspective of recovery in mental health rehabilitation to PTG, and developing interventions promoting meaning making.

Although the current study has a number of strengths, including well-established assessment tools and a good sample size, it has some limitations. First, external validity might be limited due to the selection process. Indeed, participation was voluntary and participants were solely from rehabilitation centers in the community, which might both bias and limit the generalizability of our sample. Second, this study was cross-sectional and thus does not allow tracking of PTG development over time. We therefore recommend recruiting a large sample for longitudinal studies in the field of psychosis and PTG, specifically regarding the dynamics of positive psychotic symptoms and PTG. Finally, since the current study is exploratory in nature, the findings provide only preliminary data regarding mediational effects and further study of longitudinal data is needed to confirm it.

ETHICS STATEMENT

The study protocol was reviewed and approved by the University of Haifa ethics board. One hundred and twenty-one participants were recruited from community mental health rehabilitation services of the Israeli Ministry of Health (MOH). To be eligible for the study, participants had to meet Israeli criteria for having a "psychiatric disability" severe enough to compromise at least 40% of one's functioning. This is determined by a committee, including a psychiatrist, and recognized by National Insurance Institute regulations. The last registry hospital discharge diagnosis of schizophrenia, of whom all Israeli rehab service users are part of, has acceptable sensitivity and specificity assessed against research diagnosis (57); has acceptable stability over time (58); and captured over 90% of cases with schizophrenia disorders based on research criteria in a community sample (59). Inclusion criteria were: men and women over the age of 18, who had been psychiatrically hospitalized in the past, had experienced psychotic symptoms according to their clinicians and corroborated by the PANSS [(60), see measures] clinical interview (administered by the first author), and were eligible to sign an informed consent. Potential participants were referred to the study by mental health professionals in the rehabilitation services. Participants who wished to take part and met the inclusion criteria contacted the researcher, and signed an informed consent form. Participants completed the questionnaires and were administered the PANSS clinical interview, after which they were paid for their participation. Data were collected by the first author between May 2014 and October 2014. The study protocol was reviewed and approved by the University of Haifa ethics board. Additional considerations: persons with severe mental illness.

AUTHORS NOTE

This paper is part of the first author's requirements to attain a Ph.D. degree.

AUTHOR CONTRIBUTIONS

YM: head researcher; substantial contributor to the conception and design of the work; responsible for the acquisition, analysis, and interpretation of data; revising the work critically for important intellectual content; approved final version for publication; agreeing to be accountable for all aspects of the work. MG: advisor; substantial contributor to the conception and design of the work; responsible for the analysis and interpretation of data; drafting and revising the work critically for important intellectual content; approved final version for publication; agreeing to be accountable for all aspects of the work. KM: substantial contributor to the conception and design of the work; responsible for the analysis and interpretation of data; revising the work critically for important intellectual content; approved final version for publication; agreeing to be accountable for all aspects of the work. DR: advisor; substantial contributor to the conception and design of the work; responsible for the analysis and interpretation of data; drafting and revising the work critically for important intellectual content; approved final version for publication; agreeing to be accountable for all aspects of the work.

ACKNOWLEDGMENTS

The authors thank the Laszlo N. Tauber Foundation for its generous scholarship support. The authors also thank to "Shekulo Tov" rehabilitation organization and "Consumers as providers" organization for their assistance in recruiting participants.

REFERENCES

1. Berry K, Ford S, Jellicoe-Jones L, Haddock G. PTSD symptoms associated with the experience of psychosis and hospitalization: review of literature. *Clin Psychol Rev* (2013) 33:526–38. doi:10.1016/j.cpr.2013.01.011
2. Gelkopf M, Roe D, Werbloff N, Ohayon Hasson I, Mueser K, Caspi A, et al. The prevalence of full and partial PTSD among people with severe mental illness in Israel. *J Nerv Ment Dis* (2013) 201:244–50. doi:10.1097/NMD.0b013e3182848d1e
3. Mueser KT, Lu W, Rosenberg SD, Wolfe R. The trauma of psychosis: post-traumatic stress disorder and recent onset psychosis. *Schizophr Res* (2010) 116:217–27. doi:10.1016/j.schres.2009.10.025
4. Pooley JA, Cohen L, O'Connor M, Taylor M. Posttraumatic stress and posttraumatic growth and their relationship to coping and self-efficacy in Northwest Australian cyclone communities. *Psychol Trauma* (2013) 5(4):392. doi:10.1037/a0028046
5. Tedeschi RG, Calhoun LG. The posttraumatic growth inventory: measuring the positive legacy of trauma. *J Trauma Stress* (1996) 9:455–71. doi:10.1007/BF02103658
6. Tedeschi RG, Calhoun LG. Posttraumatic growth: conceptual foundations and empirical evidence. *Psychol Inq* (2004) 15:1–18. doi:10.1207/s15327965pli1501_01
7. Calhoun LG, Tedeschi RG. The foundations of posttraumatic growth: new considerations. *Psychol Inq* (2004) 15:93–102. doi:10.1207/s15327965pli1501_03
8. Mueser KT, Rosenberg SD, Goodman LA, Trumbetta SL. Trauma, PTSD, and the course of severe mental illness: an interactive model. *Schizophr Res* (2002) 53:123–43. doi:10.1016/S0920-9964(01)00173-6
9. Mueser KT, Salyers MP, Rosenberg SD, Goodman LA, Essock SM, Osher FC, et al. Interpersonal trauma and posttraumatic stress disorder in patients with severe mental illness: demographic, clinical, and health correlates. *Schizophr Bull* (2004) 30:45–57. doi:10.1093/oxfordjournals.schbul.a007067
10. Davidson L, Borg M, Marin I, Topor A, Mezzina R, Sells D. Processes of recovery in serious mental illness: findings from a multinational study. *Am J Psychiatr Rehabil* (2005) 8(3):177–201. doi:10.1080/15487760500339360
11. Roe D, Chopra M. Beyond coping with serious mental illness: toward personal growth. *Am J Orthopsychiatry* (2003) 73:334–44. doi:10.1037/0002-9432.73.3.334
12. Selten JP, van der Ven E, Rutten BP, Cantor-Graae E. The social defeat hypothesis of schizophrenia: an update. *Schizophr Bull* (2013) 39(6):1180–6. doi:10.1093/schbul/sbt134
13. Bendall S, McGorry P, Krstev H. The trauma of being psychotic. In: Larkin W, Morrison AP, editors. *Trauma and Psychosis: New Directions for Theory and Therapy*. East Sussex: Routledge (2006). p. 58–74.
14. Morrison A, Read J, Turkington D. Trauma and psychosis: theoretical and clinicalimplications. *Acta Psychiatr Scand* (2005) 112(5):327–9. doi:10.1111/j.1600-0447.2005.00644.x
15. Priebe S, Broker M, Gunkel S. Involuntary admission and posttraumatic stress disorder symptoms in schizophrenia patients. *Compr Psychiatry* (1998) 39:220–4. doi:10.1016/S0010-440X(98)90064-5
16. Shelvin M, Houston JE, Dorahy MJ, Adamson G. Cumulative traumas and psychosis: an analysis of the national comorbidity survey and the British psychiatric morbidity survey. *Schizophr Bull* (2008) 34:193–9. doi:10.1093/schbul/sbm069
17. Goodman LA, Rosenberg SD, Mueser KT, et al. Physical and sexual assault history in women with serious mental illness: prevalence, correlates, treatment, and future research directions. *Schizophr Bull* (1997) 23:685–96. doi:10.1093/schbul/23.4.685
18. Kilcommons A, Morrison AP. Relationships between trauma and psychosis: an exploration of cognitive and dissociative factors. *Acta Psychiatr Scand* (2005) 112:351–9. doi:10.1111/j.1600-0447.2005.00623.x
19. Penn DL, Corrigan PW, Bentall RP, Racenstein JM, Newman L. Social cognition in schizophrenia. *Psychol Bull* (1997) 121:114–32. doi:10.1037/0033-2909.121.1.114
20. Sherrer M. The role of cognitive appraisal in adaptation to traumatic stress in adults with serious mental illness: a critical review. *Trauma Violence Abuse* (2011) 12:151–67. doi:10.1177/1524838011404254
21. Selten JP, Cantor-Graae E. Hypothesis: social defeat is a risk factor for schizophrenia? *Br J Psychiatry Suppl* (2007) 51():s9–12. doi:10.1192/bjp.191.51.s9
22. American Psychiatric Association, Task Force on DSM-IV. *Diagnostic and Statistical Manual of Mental Disorders: DSM-IV*. Washington, DC: American Psychiatric Pub Inc. (1994).
23. American Psychiatric Association. *DSM 5*. Arlington, VA: American Psychiatric Association (2013).
24. Freeman D, Fowler D. Routes to psychotic symptoms: trauma, anxiety and psychosis-like experiences. *Psychiatry Res* (2009) 169(2):107–12. doi:10.1016/j.psychres.2008.07.009
25. Lysaker PH, LaRocco VA. The prevalence and correlates of trauma-related symptoms in schizophrenia spectrum disorder. *Compr Psychiatry* (2008) 49(4):330–4. doi:10.1016/j.comppsych.2007.12.003
26. Bleuler E. *Dementia Praecox or the Group of Schizophrenias*. Oxford, England: International Universities Press (1950).
27. Heerey EA, Gold JM. Patients with schizophrenia demonstrate dissociation between affective experience and motivated behavior. *J Abnorm Psychol* (2007) 116:268–78. doi:10.1037/0021-843X.116.2.268
28. Myin-Germeys I, Oorschot M, Collip D, Lataster J, Delespaul P, van Os J. Experience sampling research in psychopathology: opening the black box of daily life. *Psychol Med* (2009) 39:1533–47. doi:10.1017/S0033291708004947
29. Fervaha G, Foussias G, Agid O, Remington G. Impact of primary negative symptoms on functional outcomes in schizophrenia. *Eur Psychiatry* (2014) 29(7):449–55. doi:10.1016/j.eurpsy.2014.01.007
30. Foussias G, Remington G. Negative symptoms in schizophrenia: avolition and Occam's razor. *Schizophr Bull* (2010) 36:359–69. doi:10.1093/schbul/sbn094
31. Tedeschi RG, Calhoun LG. *Trauma & Transformation: Growing in the Aftermath of Suffering*. Thousand Oaks, CA: SAGE (1995).
32. Zoellner T, Maercker A. Posttraumatic growth in clinical psychology – a critical review and introduction of a two component model. *Clin Psychol Rev* (2006) 26(5):626–53. doi:10.1016/j.cpr.2006.01.008
33. Tedeschi RG, Calhoun LG, Cann A. Evaluating resource gain: understanding and misunderstanding posttraumatic growth. *Appl Psychol* (2007) 56:396–340. doi:10.1111/j.1464-0597.2007.00299.x
34. Hobfoll SE, Canetti-Nisim D, Johnson RJ. Exposure to terrorism, stress-related mental health symptoms, and defensive coping among Jews and Arabs in Israel. *J Consult Clin Psychol* (2006) 74:207–18. doi:10.1037/0022-006X.74.2.207
35. Hobfoll SE, Tracy M, Galea S. The impact of resource loss and traumatic growth on probable PTSD and depression following terrorist attacks. *J Trauma Stress* (2006) 19:867–78. doi:10.1002/jts.20166
36. Mueser KT, Trumbetta SL, Rosenberg SD, Vidaver R, Goodman LB, Osher FC, et al. Trauma and posttraumatic stress disorder in severe mental illness. *J Consult Clin Psychol* (1998) 66:493–9. doi:10.1037/0022-006X.66.3.493

37. Dunkley JE, Bates GW. Recovery and adaptation after first-episode psychosis: the relevance of posttraumatic growth. *Psychosis* (2015) 7(2):130–40. doi:10.1080/17522439.2014.936027
38. Mapplebeck C, Joseph S, Sabin-Farrell R. An interpretative phenomenological analysis of posttraumatic growth in people with psychosis. *J Loss Trauma* (2015) 20(1):34–45. doi:10.1080/15325024.2013.821375
39. Pietruch M, Jobson L. Posttraumatic growth and recovery in people with first episode psychosis: an investigation into the role of self-disclosure. *Psychosis* (2012) 4(3):213–23. doi:10.1080/17522439.2011.608434
40. Cieslak R, Benight C, Schmidt N, Luszczynska A, Curtin E, Clark RA, et al. Predicting posttraumatic growth among Hurricane Katrina survivors living with HIV: the role of self-efficacy, social support, and PTSD symptoms. *Anxiety Stress Coping* (2009) 22(4):449–63. doi:10.1080/10615800802403815
41. Bandura A. Self-efficacy: toward a unifying theory of behavioral change. *Psychol Rev* (1977) 84:191. doi:10.1037/0033-295X.84.2.191
42. Bandura A. On the functional properties of perceived self-efficacy revisited. *J Manag* (2012) 38:9–44. doi:10.1177/0149206311410606
43. Benight CC, Bandura A. Social cognitive theory of posttraumatic recovery: the role of perceived self-efficacy. *Behav Res Ther* (2004) 42:1129–48. doi:10.1016/j.brat.2003.08.008
44. Prati G, Pietrantoni L. Optimism, social support, and coping strategies as factors contributing to posttraumatic growth: a meta-analysis. *J Loss Trauma* (2009) 14(5):364–88. doi:10.1080/15325020902724271
45. Frankl VE. *Man's Search for Meaning: An Introduction to Logotherapy*. Tel-Aviv: Dvir Publishing House (1963/1970).
46. Herman JL. *Trauma and Recovery*. Tel-Aviv: Basic Books (1992).
47. Janoff-Bulman R. *Shattered Assumptions: Towards a New Psychology of Trauma*. New York: Free Press (1992).
48. Neimeyer RA. *Meaning Reconstruction & the Experience of Loss*. Washington, DC: American Psychological Association (2001).
49. Updegraff JA, Silver RC, Holman EA. Searching for and finding meaning in collective trauma: results from a national longitudinal study of the 9/11 terrorist attacks. *J Pers Soc Psychol* (2008) 95:709–22. doi:10.1037/0022-3514.95.3.709
50. Park CL. Making sense of the meaning literature: an integrative review of meaning making and its effects on adjustment to stressful life events. *Psychol Bull* (2010) 136:257–301. doi:10.1037/a0018301
51. Steger MF, Frazier P, Oishi S, Kaler M. The meaning in life questionnaire: assessing the presence of and search for meaning in life. *J Couns Psychol* (2006) 53:80–93. doi:10.1037/0022-0167.53.1.80
52. Stolovy T, Lev-Wiesel R, Doron A, Gelkopf M. Meaning of life inside the psychiatric hospital: an exploratory study. *J Nerv Ment Dis* (2009) 197:133–5. doi:10.1097/NMD.0b013e3181963ede
53. Piltch CA. The role of self-determination in mental health recovery. *Psychiatr Rehabil J* (2016) 39(1):77. doi:10.1037/prj0000176
54. Lataster T, Valmaggia L, Lardinois M, van Os J, Myin-Germeys I. Increased stress reactivity: a mechanism specifically associated with the positive symptoms of psychotic disorder. *Psychol Med* (2013) 43(07):1389–400. doi:10.1017/S0033291712002279
55. Myin-Germeys I, van Os J, Schwartz JE, Stone AA, Delespaul PA. Emotional reactivity to daily life stress in psychosis. *Arch Gen Psychiatry* (2001) 58(12):1137–44. doi:10.1001/archpsyc.58.12.1137
56. Myin-Germeys I, Nicolson NA, Delespaul PA. The context of delusional experiences in the daily life of patients with schizophrenia. *Psychol Med* (2001) 31(03):489–98. doi:10.1017/S0033291701003646
57. Weiser M, Kanyas K, Malaspina D, Harvey PD, Glick I, Goetz D, et al. Sensitivity of ICD-10 diagnosis of psychotic disorders in the Israeli National Hospitalization Registry compared with RDC diagnoses based on SADS-L. *Compr Psychiatry* (2005) 46(1):38–42. doi:10.1016/j.comppsych.2004.07.016
58. Rabinowitz J, Slyuzberg M, Ritsner M, Mark M, Popper M, Ginath Y. Changes in diagnosis in a 9-year national longitudinal sample. *Compr Psychiatry* (1994) 35(5):361–5. doi:10.1016/0010-440X(94)90276-3
59. Weiser M, Werbeloff N, Dohrenwend BP, Levav I, Yoffe R, Davidson M. Do psychiatric registries include all persons with schizophrenia in the general population? A population-based longitudinal study. *Schizophr Res* (2012) 135(1):187–91. doi:10.1016/j.schres.2011.12.023
60. Kay SR, Fiszbein A, Opler LA. The positive and negative syndrome scale (PANSS) for schizophrenia. *Schizophr Bull* (1987) 13:261–76. doi:10.1093/schbul/13.2.261
61. Carlson EB, Smith SR, Palmieri PA, Dalenberg C, Ruzek JI, Kimerling R, et al. Development and validation of a brief self-report measure of trauma exposure: the Trauma History Screen. *Psychol Assess* (2011) 23:463–77. doi:10.1037/a0022294
62. Barak Y, Shamir E, Weizman R. Would a switch from typical antipsychotics to risperidone be beneficial for elderly schizophrenic patients? A naturalistic, long-term, retrospective, comparative study. *J Clin Psychopharmacol* (2002) 22:115–20. doi:10.1097/00004714-200204000-00003
63. Werner P, Aviv A, Barak Y. Self-stigma, self-esteem and age in persons with schizophrenia. *Int Psychogeriatr* (2008) 20(01):174–87. doi:10.1017/S1041610207005340
64. Laufer A, Solomon Z. Posttraumatic symptoms and posttraumatic growth among Israeli youth exposed to terror incidents. *J Soc Clin Psychol* (2006) 25:429–48. doi:10.1521/jscp.2006.25.4.429
65. Solomon Z, Laufer A. In the shadow of terror: changes in world assumptions in Israeli youth. *J Aggress Maltreat Trauma* (2005) 9:353–64. doi:10.1300/J146v09n03_06
66. Levine SZ, Laufer A, Hamama-Raz Y, Stein E, Solomon Z. Posttraumatic growth in adolescence: examining its components and relationship with PTSD. *J Trauma Stress* (2008) 21:492–6. doi:10.1002/jts.20361
67. Chesney MA, Neilands TB, Chambers DB, Taylor JM, Folkman S. A validity and reliability study of the coping self-efficacy scale. *Br J Health Psychol* (2006) 11:421–37. doi:10.1348/135910705X53155
68. Carrico AW, Chesney MA, Johnson MO, Morin SF, Neilands TB, Remien RH, et al. Randomized controlled trial of a cognitive-behavioral intervention for HIV-positive persons: an investigation of treatment effects on psychosocial adjustment. *AIDS Behav* (2009) 13(3):555–63. doi:10.1007/s10461-008-9429-6
69. Rodkjaer L, Chesney MA, Lomborg K, Ostergaard L, Laursen T, Sodemann M. HIV-infected individuals with high coping self-efficacy are less likely to report depressive symptoms: a cross-sectional study from Denmark. *Int J Infect Dis* (2014) 22:67–72. doi:10.1016/j.ijid.2013.12.008
70. Steger MF, Kashdan TB. Stability and specificity of meaning in life and life satisfaction over one year. *J Happiness Stud* (2007) 8(2):161–79. doi:10.1007/s10902-006-9011-8
71. Steger MF, Owens GP, Park CL. Violations of war: testing the meaning-making model among Vietnam veterans. *J Clin Psychol* (2015) 71(1):105–16. doi:10.1002/jclp.22121
72. Preacher KJ, Hayes AF. SPSS and SAS procedures for estimating indirect effects in simple mediation models. *Behav Res Methods Instrum Comput* (2004) 36(4):717–31. doi:10.3758/BF03206553
73. Preacher KJ, Hayes AF. Asymptotic and resampling strategies for assessing and comparing indirect effects in multiple mediator models. *Behav Res Methods* (2008) 40(3):879–91. doi:10.3758/BRM.40.3.879
74. Chen J, Zhou X, Zeng M, Wu X. Post-traumatic stress symptoms and post traumatic growth: evidence from a longitudinal study following an earthquake disaster. *PLoS One* (2015) 10(6):e0127241. doi:10.1371/journal.pone.0127241
75. Polatinsky S, Esprey Y. An assessment of gender differences in the perception of benefit resulting from the loss of a child. *J Trauma Stress* (2000) 13:709–18. doi:10.1023/A:1007870419116
76. Weiss T. Posttraumatic growth in women with breast cancer and their husbands: an intersubjective validation study. *J Psychosoc Oncol* (2002) 20:65–80. doi:10.1300/J077v20n02_04
77. Lu W, Yanos PT, Silverstein SM, Mueser KT, Rosenberg SD, Gottlieb JD, et al. Public mental health clients with severe mental illness and probable posttraumatic stress disorder: trauma exposure and correlates of symptom severity. *J Trauma Stress* (2013) 26(2):266–73. doi:10.1002/jts.21791
78. Shaw K, McFarlane AC, Bookless C, Air T. The aetiology of postpsychotic posttraumatic stress disorder following a psychotic episode. *J Trauma Stress* (2002) 15:39–47. doi:10.1023/A:1014331211311
79. Keefe RS, Fenton WS. How should DSM-V criteria for schizophrenia include cognitive impairment? *Schizophr Bull* (2007) 33(4):912–20. doi:10.1093/schbul/sbm046
80. Howes OD, Kapur S. The dopamine hypothesis of schizophrenia: version III—the final common pathway. *Schizophr Bull* (2009) 35(3):549–62. doi:10.1093/schbul/sbp006

81. Kapur S. Psychosis as a state of aberrant salience: a framework linking biology, phenomenology, and pharmacology in schizophrenia. *Am J Psychiatry* (2003) 160(1):13–23. doi:10.1176/appi.ajp.160.1.13
82. Smeets F, Lataster T, Dominguez MD, Hommes J, Lieb R, Wittchen HU, et al. Evidence that onset of psychosis in the population reflects early hallucinatory experiences that through environmental risks and affective dysregulation become complicated by delusions. *Schizophr Bull* (2012) 38(3):531–42. doi:10.1093/schbul/sbq117
83. Creswell JD, Lam S, Stanton AL, Taylor SE, Bower JE, Sherman DK. Does self-affirmation, cognitive processing, or discovery of meaning explain cancer-related health benefits of expressive writing? *Pers Soc Psychol Bull* (2007) 33(2):238–50. doi:10.1177/0146167206294412
84. Ehlers A, Clark DM. Predictors of chronic posttraumatic stress disorder: trauma memories and appraisals. In: Rothbaum BO, editor. *Pathological Anxiety: Emotional Processing in Etiology and Treatment, (pp. 39–55)*. New York, NY: Guilford Press (2006). p. 272.
85. Rachman S. Emotional processing, with special reference to post-traumatic stress disorder. *Int Rev Psychiatry* (2001) 13(3):164–71. doi:10.1080/09540260120074028
86. Berry K, Barrowclough C, Byrne J, Purandare N. Coping strategies and social support in old age psychosis. *Soc Psychiatry Psychiatr Epidemiol* (2006) 41(4):280–4. doi:10.1007/s00127-005-0023-1
87. Horan WP, Blanchard JJ. Neurocognitive, social, and emotional dysfunction in deficit syndrome schizophrenia. *Schizophr Res* (2003) 65(2):125–37. doi:10.1016/S0920-9964(02)00410-3
88. Morrison AP, Wells A. A comparison of metacognitions in patients with hallucinations, delusions, panic disorder, and non-patient controls. *Behav Res Ther* (2003) 41(2):251–6. doi:10.1016/S0005-7967(02)00095-5
89. Lysaker PH, Clements CA, Wright DE, Evans J, Marks KA. Neurocognitive correlates of helplessness, hopelessness, and well-being in schizophrenia. *J Nerv Ment Dis* (2001) 189(7):457–62. doi:10.1097/00005053-200107000-00007
90. Lysaker PH, Davis LW, Lightfoot J, Hunter N, Stasburger A. Association of neurocognition, anxiety, positive and negative symptoms with coping preference in schizophrenia spectrum disorders. *Schizophr Res* (2005) 80(2):163–71. doi:10.1016/j.schres.2005.07.005
91. Lysaker PH, Bryson GJ, Marks K, Greig TC, Bell MD. Coping style in schizophrenia: associations with neurocognitive deficits and personality. *Schizophr Bull* (2004) 30(1):113–21. doi:10.1093/oxfordjournals.schbul.a007056
92. Galdos M, Simons C, Fernandez-Rivas A, Wichers M, Peralta C, Lataster T, et al. Affectively salient meaning in random noise: a task sensitive to psychosis liability. *Schizophr Bull* (2011) 37(6):1179–86. doi:10.1093/schbul/sbq029
93. Morrison AP. The interpretation of intrusions in psychosis: an integrative cognitive approach to hallucinations and delusions. *Behav Cogn Psychother* (2001) 29(03):257–76. doi:10.1017/S1352465801003010
94. Juckel G, Schlagenhauf F, Koslowski M, Filonov D, Wüstenberg T, Villringer A, et al. Dysfunction of ventral striatal reward prediction in schizophrenic patients treated with typical, not atypical, neuroleptics. *Psychopharmacology* (2006) 187(2):222–8. doi:10.1007/s00213-006-0405-4
95. Simon JJ, Biller A, Walther S, Roesch-Ely D, Stippich C, Weisbrod M, et al. Neural correlates of reward processing in schizophrenia – relationship to apathy and depression. *Schizophr Res* (2010) 118(1):154–61. doi:10.1016/j.schres.2009.11.007
96. Macdonald EM, Pica S, McDonald S, Hayes RL, Baglioni AJ Jr. Stress and coping in early psychosis: role of symptoms, self-efficacy, and social support in coping with stress. *Br J Psychiatry* (1998) 172:122–7.
97. Gard DE, Kring AM, Gard MG, Horan WP, Green MF. Anhedonia in schizophrenia: distinctions between anticipatory and consummatory pleasure. *Schizophr Res* (2007) 93(1):253–60. doi:10.1016/j.schres.2007.03.008
98. Foussias G, Agid O, Fervaha G, Remington G. Negative symptoms of schizophrenia: clinical features, relevance to real world functioning and specificity versus other CNS disorders. *Eur Neuropsychopharmacol* (2014) 24(5):693–709. doi:10.1016/j.euroneuro.2013.10.017
99. Horan WP, Ventura J, Mintz J, Kopelowicz A, Wirshing D, Christian-Herman J, et al. Stress and coping responses to a natural disaster in people with schizophrenia. *Psychiatry Res* (2007) 151(1):77–86. doi:10.1016/j.psychres.2006.10.009
100. Phillips LJ, Francey SM, Edwards J, McMurray N. Strategies used by psychotic individuals to cope with life stress and symptoms of illness: a systematic review. *Anxiety Stress Coping* (2009) 22(4):371–410. doi:10.1080/10615800902811065
101. Jimeno Bulnes N, Jimeno Valdes A, Aragón ML, Fernández L. Psychopathological verbal expression of self-perceived stress in three groups of psychotic patients. *Psychopathology* (1997) 30(1):39–48. doi:10.1159/000285027
102. Ritsner M, Modai I, Ponizovsky A. Assessing psychological distress in psychiatric patients: validation of the Talbieh Brief Distress Inventory. *Compr Psychiatry* (2002) 43(3):229–34. doi:10.1159/000285027

5

Can We Use an Interventionist-Causal Paradigm to Untangle the Relationship between Trauma, PTSD and Psychosis?

Rachel M. Brand[1,2*], *Susan L. Rossell*[1,2,3], *Sarah Bendall*[4,5] *and Neil Thomas*[1,2]

[1] *Centre for Mental Health, Swinburne University, Hawthorn, VIC, Australia,* [2] *The Voices Clinic, Monash Alfred Psychiatry Research Centre, Alfred Hospital and Monash University Central Clinical School, Melbourne, VIC, Australia,* [3] *Psychiatry, St. Vincent's Hospital, Fitzroy, VIC, Australia,* [4] *Orygen: The National Centre of Excellence in Youth Mental Health, Parkville, VIC, Australia,* [5] *The Centre for Youth Mental Health, The University of Melbourne, Parkville, VIC, Australia*

Keywords: trauma, psychosis, posttraumatic stress disorder, schizophrenia, causal, methodology

Edited by:
Kate Hardy,
Stanford University, USA

Reviewed by:
Craig Steel,
University of Reading, UK

****Correspondence:***
Rachel M. Brand
rbrand@swin.edu.au

There is mounting evidence that exposure to traumatic or adverse life-events is associated with increased risk of psychosis (Read et al., 2001; Bendall et al., 2008, 2010; Read and Bentall, 2012). However, to inform treatment and prevention, it is necessary to go beyond association to understand *how* traumatic experiences may lead to the development of psychotic symptoms. In this paper, we argue that doing so requires the identification of biological, psychological and social processes that may be involved in the observed trauma–psychosis relationship, and determining which are causally related. We propose that this can be done in conjunction with focused intervention procedures that may test theoretical mechanisms, in parallel with piloting potential components of therapeutic interventions.

A recent proliferation of research has examined a broad range of factors as putative causal mechanisms. One important strand of this research has drawn on the particular relationship between trauma, posttraumatic stress disorder (PTSD) and psychosis. PTSD is one of the most rigorously researched sequelae of trauma exposure and is, by definition, caused by traumatic events. There are high rates of comorbidity between PTSD and psychosis (Kilcommons and Morrison, 2005; Sareen et al., 2005; Anketell et al., 2010), and PTSD is a risk factor in the subsequent development of psychosis (Okkels et al., 2017). This relationship may provide an insight into the mechanisms through which trauma exposure can lead to the emergence and maintenance of psychosis.

To make causal inferences regarding these putative mechanisms, the literature needs to move beyond establishing association to experimental studies in which trauma exposure, PTSD symptoms or causal mechanisms involved in PTSD, are subject to controlled manipulations. However, there are feasibility and ethical issues in this undertaking and we therefore propose that a research paradigm referred to as the "interventionist-causal" approach offers a critical way forward. We pay particular attention to trauma-related psychological mechanisms, with a view that a more sophisticated understanding of the causal role of these mechanisms will lead to much needed improvements in psychological interventions for psychosis (Freeman, 2011; Thomas et al., 2014). While identifying causal mechanisms is not the only way of addressing recovery, this process of intervention development can add value to broader intervention approaches. Indeed, this process has been helpful in refining and improving the efficacy of psychological interventions for anxiety (Clark, 2004).

MECHANISMS LINKING PTSD AND PSYCHOSIS

Mueser et al. (2002) proposed that PTSD symptomatology itself mediates the relationship between trauma exposure and the course of serious mental illness, particularly schizophrenia. Whilst not commenting on whether PTSD plays a casual role in the development of psychosis, this theory places PTSD symptomatology centrally in understanding the exacerbation of psychotic symptoms.

Morrison (2003) went further, proposing that rather than being separate, psychotic symptoms and PTSD fall on a continuum of trauma-related reactions and are caused and maintained by similar psychological mechanisms. Researchers have since further elucidated psychological mechanisms involved in specific symptoms of psychosis that may be shared with those involved in PTSD. The correlation between posttraumatic intrusions and hallucinations in trauma-affected populations (Gracie et al., 2007; Alsawy et al., 2015; Ayub et al., 2015) and the fact that the content of hallucinations often have thematic or direct links with trauma content (Read et al., 2003; Hardy et al., 2005; Corstens and Longden, 2013; McCarthy-Jones et al., 2014) has led to the proposal that some hallucinations may in fact be a form of posttraumatic intrusion. Contemporary psychological theories of PTSD conceptualize the nature of cognitive processing during traumatic events to be central to the development of posttraumatic intrusions (Ehlers and Clark, 2000; Brewin, 2001; Brewin et al., 2010). Shifts in information-processing style during traumatic events are posited to lead to trauma memories that are de-contextualized, fragmented, dominated by sensory information, and sensitive to involuntary priming. The nature of cognitive processing during traumatic events has also been implicated in the development of hallucinations in the general population (Geddes et al., 2016) and in people high in schizotypy (Steel et al., 2005).

Dissociation, another psychological process implicated in PTSD, has also been linked to hallucinations following trauma. Indeed, many researchers propose that hallucinations are dissociative phenomena (Moskowitz and Corstens, 2007; Longden et al., 2012). Dissociation is correlated with hallucinatory experiences (Pilton et al., 2015), mediates the relationship between childhood trauma and hallucinations (Perona-Garcelán et al., 2012; Varese et al., 2012) and predicts hallucinations in the flow of daily life (Varese et al., 2011).

Hallucinations are not the only psychotic symptom that has been linked to PTSD symptoms and related mechanisms. Associations between delusional beliefs and PTSD symptoms have been observed following traumatic events (Freeman et al., 2011; Ayub et al., 2015) and the same cognitive factors have been found to predict both paranoia and PTSD following a physical assault (Freeman et al., 2013). Research has been more equivocal with regards to negative symptoms (Lysaker and Larocco, 2008; Strauss et al., 2011) but it has been suggested that these can be manifestations of the avoidance of traumatic memories (Stampfer, 1990; McGorry, 1991; Morrison, 2003).

In summary, there is evidence of a close relationship between PTSD and psychotic experiences, but questions remain regarding whether PTSD symptomatology itself represents a casual mechanism in the development or maintenance of psychosis, or whether shared mechanisms underpin the causal relationships between trauma and both PTSD and psychosis outcomes. Establishing causal inferences regarding psychological mechanisms involved in psychosis is, of course, complex. Symptoms are likely to be caused by multiple mechanisms and each mechanism is likely only to contribute to the probability of a symptom occurring. Nonetheless, identifying the potential role of each PTSD-related psychological mechanism in the development and maintenance of psychosis will inform more evidence-driven and targeted psychological interventions for trauma-related psychoses. A particularly tantalizing aspect of the relationship between PTSD and psychosis is that there are already well-established, effective treatments for PTSD. If psychological mechanisms involved in PTSD do play a causal role in psychotic experiences, this would open up promising new treatments for psychotic symptoms.

BEYOND ASSOCIATION TO IDENTIFYING CAUSAL MECHANISMS

In order to establish the causal role of candidate mechanisms, certain criteria must be met. Despite a lack of consensus on the precise definition of causality, epidemiologists have outlined the essential properties of causal relationships; namely, that there is an association between the variables, that the cause temporally precedes the effect, that change in the putative causal variable leads to change in the outcome, and that spurious, confounding variables in this relationship are controlled for (also referred to as sole plausibility) (Reininghaus et al., 2016).

Thus far, research in the field has predominantly involved cross-sectional studies that examine associations between trauma, PTSD, psychosis, and putative shared mechanisms. Cross-sectional studies are, however, limited in drawing causal inferences, since it is not possible to robustly establish temporal relationships and sole plausibility. There are also examples of prospective studies in the area, which have built on these cross-sectional associations by establishing temporal ordering (Okkels et al., 2017). However, prospective studies can be time intensive and still do not offer control over extraneous variables to establish sole plausibility. Observational studies that observe natural fluctuations in putative mechanisms and how these interact with symptoms have also made recent valuable additions to the literature, particularly with the use of mobile technology in ecological momentary assessment studies (e.g., Varese et al., 2011). Yet, without controlled manipulation of variables it is again difficult to establish sole plausibility (Reininghaus et al., 2016).

We argue that what is now needed are experimental approaches using controlled manipulations of trauma exposure, PTSD symptoms, or putative shared casual mechanisms and an assessment of the impact of these manipulations on psychotic symptoms. There have been initial examples of this in the use of the analog trauma paradigm, in which trauma exposure is experimentally manipulated (with the presentation of a distressing film) and outcomes examined (e.g., Marks et al., 2012). There are, however, challenges in the design and execution of these studies in trauma-affected and psychosis populations, possibly explaining why the majority of these studies have thus far been conducted with non-clinical samples. In clinical groups, there are ethical and clinical issues with introducing trauma exposure as an independent variable, or with inducing controlled increases in PTSD symptoms.

TABLE 1 | Putative causal mechanisms involved in both PTSD and psychosis and interventions with which the interventionist-causal paradigm can be used to examine causality.

Putative mechanism	Intervention
Trauma memory processing	Imaginal exposure, EMDR
Negative posttraumatic beliefs	Trauma-focused cognitive therapy, cognitive processing therapy
Dissociation	Cognitive behavioral interventions for dissociation
Posttraumatic avoidance	*In vivo* and imaginal exposure

AN INTERVENTIONIST-CASUAL PARADIGM FOR THE INVESTIGATION OF THE RELATIONSHIP BETWEEN TRAUMA, PTSD AND PSYCHOSIS

We propose that an alternative experimental model that holds promise in moving past this methodological impasse is the interventionist-causal paradigm. In this approach, causation is substantiated by controlled manipulation of the hypothesized causal mechanism and examination of the subsequent effect on the symptom of interest (Kendler and Campbell, 2009). In psychiatry research this can be accomplished using interventions proposed to act on causal mechanisms, establishing their effect on these mechanisms when compared with a control intervention to minimize other confounding variables, and observing the impact on the symptoms of interest. If this chain of causality can be established, then causal inferences regarding the mechanisms in question may be confirmed. In practice, this looks like a randomized controlled trial of an intervention, but as well as establishing treatment efficacy, we use this paradigm to further our understanding of causal mechanisms. An interventionist-causal paradigm has been previously noted for its use in understanding causal mechanisms in psychosis (Freeman, 2011; Garety and Freeman, 2013; Reininghaus et al., 2016). An attractive aspect of this model is that the experimental intervention is one that is designed to reduce problematic causal processes and thus (hypothetically) improve symptom outcomes of interest. This is well aligned with the ethos of the fields of clinical psychology and psychiatry.

The well-developed PTSD treatment literature gives us a head start in terms of assessing the causal role of PTSD symptomatology itself in psychotic experiences using the interventionist-causal model. Treatments that are already known to be effective in reducing PTSD symptoms, such as prolonged exposure, trauma focused CBT and Eye Movement Desensitization and Reprocessing therapy (EMDR) (Bisson et al., 2007), can be delivered to people with psychosis in controlled studies and the effects on both PTSD symptoms and psychotic symptoms established. Approaches to date using these treatments for people experiencing psychosis have focused on treating comorbid PTSD symptoms, demonstrating the safety of using such interventions and some positive effects on PTSD symptoms, particularly for EMDR and prolonged exposure (van den Berg et al., 2015), but less so for cognitive restructuring (Steel et al., 2017). There is, however, limited data on the impact of these interventions on psychotic symptoms.

Additionally, the putative shared mechanisms involved in both PTSD and psychosis can be subject to interventionist-causal enquiry using specific components of psychological interventions, ascertaining that they act on a mechanism of interest, and observing the effect on psychotic symptoms. This is somewhat more complex, since literature regarding the mechanisms of action of psychological treatments remains in its infancy, however the interventionist-causal model is well placed to deal with this complexity in separating specific mechanisms of action and their relationship to treatment outcomes. A promising example of this, a pilot trial of a brief CBT intervention for depersonalization in psychosis, is currently underway (Farrelly et al., 2016). We propose that this paradigm now needs to be extended to the multitude of other potential casual mechanisms implicated in PTSD and psychosis. **Table 1** outlines interventions or intervention components that may be explored in an interventionist-causal model to explicate the casual role of these mechanisms.

In summary, we believe that interventionist-causal models offer a crucial next step in untangling the relationship between trauma, PTSD and psychosis. Importantly, the paradigm offers a way of extending our understanding beyond that of association, into establishing causal inferences. In addition, research of this nature can establish individual treatment components, acting on specific causal mechanisms, which can effectively be used to treat psychotic experiences in those who have experienced trauma.

AUTHOR CONTRIBUTIONS

RB drafted the original manuscript and conceived of the idea for the content. NT contributed to conception of the ideas in the article and revised the manuscript. SB and SR revised the final manuscript and advised on content.

REFERENCES

Alsawy, S., Wood, L., Taylor, P. J., and Morrison, A. P. (2015). Psychotic experiences and PTSD: exploring associations in a population survey. *Psychol. Med.* 45, 2849–2859. doi: 10.1017/S003329171500080X

Anketell, C., Dorahy, M. J., Shannon, M., Elder, R., Hamilton, G., Corry, M., et al. (2010). An exploratory analysis of voice hearing in chronic PTSD: potential associated mechanisms. *J. Trauma Dissoc.* 11, 93–107. doi: 10.1080/15299730903143600

Ayub, M., Saeed, K., Kingdon, D., and Naeem, F. (2015). Rate and predictors of psychotic symptoms after Kashmir earthquake. *Eur. Arch. Psychiatry Clin. Neurosci.* 265:471. doi: 10.1007/s00406-014-0561-1

Bendall, S., Jackson, H., and Hulbert, C. (2010). Childhood trauma and psychosis: review of the evidence and directions for psychological interventions. *Aust. Psychol.* 45, 299–306. doi: 10.1080/00050060903443219

Bendall, S., Jackson, H. J., Hulbert, C. A., and McGorry, P. D. (2008). Childhood trauma and psychotic disorders: a systematic, critical review of the evidence. *Schizophr. Bull.* 34, 568–579. doi: 10.1093/schbul/sbm121

Bisson, J. I., Ehlers, A., Matthews, R., Pilling, S., Richards, D., and Turner, S. (2007). Psychological treatments for chronic post-traumatic stress disorder. Systematic review and meta-analysis. *Br. J. Psychiatry* 190, 97–104. doi: 10.1192/bjp.bp.106.021402

Brewin, C. R. (2001). A cognitive neuroscience account of posttraumatic stress disorder and its treatment. *Behav. Res. Ther.* 39, 373–393. doi: 10.1016/S0005-7967(00)00087-5

Brewin, C. R., Gregory, J. D., Lipton, M., and Burgess, N. (2010). Intrusive images in psychological disorders: characteristics, neural mechanisms, and treatment implications. *Psychol. Rev.* 117, 210–232. doi: 10.1037/a0018113

Clark, D. M. (2004). Developing new treatments: on the interplay between theories, experimental science and clinical innovation. *Behav. Res. Ther.* 42, 1089–1104. doi: 10.1016/j.brat.2004.05.002

Corstens, D., and Longden, E. (2013). The origins of voices: links between life history and voice hearing in a survey of 100 cases. *Psychosis* 5, 270–285. doi: 10.1080/17522439.2013.816337

Ehlers, A., and Clark, D. M. (2000). A cognitive model of posttraumatic stress disorder. *Behav. Res. Ther.* 38, 319–345. doi: 10.1016/S0005-7967(99)00123-0

Farrelly, S., Peters, E., Azis, M., David, A., and Hunter, E. C. (2016). A brief CBT intervention for depersonalisation/derealisation in psychosis: study protocol for a feasibility randomised controlled trial. *Pilot Feasibil. Stud.* 2:47. doi: 10.1186/s40814-016-0086-7

Freeman, D. (2011). Improving cognitive treatments for delusions. *Schizophr. Res.* 132, 135–139. doi: 10.1016/j.schres.2011.08.012

Freeman, D., McManus, S., Brugha, T., Meltzer, H., Jenkins, R., and Bebbington, P. (2011). Concomitants of paranoia in the general population. *Psychol. Med.* 41, 923–936. doi: 10.1017/S0033291710001546

Freeman, D., Thompson, C., Vorontsova, N., Dunn, G., Carter, L. A., Garety, P., et al. (2013). Paranoia and post-traumatic stress disorder in the months after a physical assault: a longitudinal study examining shared and differential predictors. *Psychol. Med.* 43, 2673–2684. doi: 10.1017/S0033291713 00038X

Garety, P. A., and Freeman, D. (2013). The past and future of delusions research: from the inexplicable to the treatable. *Br. J. Psychiatry* 203, 327–333. doi: 10.1192/bjp.bp.113.126953

Geddes, G., Ehlers, A., and Freeman, D. (2016). Hallucinations in the months after a trauma: an investigation of the role of cognitive processing of a physical assault in the occurrence of hallucinatory experiences. *Psychiatry Res.* 246, 601–605. doi: 10.1016/j.psychres.2016.10.081

Gracie, A., Freeman, D., Green, S., Garety, P. A., Kuipers, E., Hardy, A., et al. (2007). The association between traumatic experience, paranoia and hallucinations: a test of the predictions of psychological models. *Acta Psychiatr. Scand.* 116, 280–289. doi: 10.1111/j.1600-0447.2007.01011.x

Hardy, A., Fowler, D., Freeman, D., Smith, B., Steel, C., Evans, J., et al. (2005). Trauma and hallucinatory experience in psychosis. *J. Nerv. Ment. Dis.* 193, 501–507. doi: 10.1097/01.nmd.0000172480.56308.21

Kendler, K. S., and Campbell, J. (2009). Interventionist causal models in psychiatry: repositioning the mind-body problem. *Psychol. Med.* 39, 881–887. doi: 10.1017/S0033291708004467

Kilcommons, A. M., and Morrison, A. P. (2005). Relationships between trauma and psychosis: an exploration of cognitive and dissociative factors. *Acta Psychiatr. Scand.* 112, 351–359. doi: 10.1111/j.1600-0447.2005.00623.x

Longden, E., Madill, A., and Waterman, M. G. (2012). Dissociation, trauma, and the role of lived experience: toward a new conceptualization of voice hearing. *Psychol. Bull.* 138, 28–76. doi: 10.1037/a0025995

Lysaker, P. H., and Larocco, V. A. (2008). The prevalence and correlates of trauma-related symptoms in schizophrenia spectrum disorder. *Compr. Psychiatry* 49, 330–334. doi: 10.1016/j.comppsych.2007.12.003

Marks, E. M., Steel, C., and Peters, E. R. (2012). Intrusions in trauma and psychosis: information processing and phenomenology. *Psychol. Med.* 42, 2313–2323. doi: 10.1017/S0033291712000505

McCarthy-Jones, S., Trauer, T., MacKinnon, A., Sims, E., Thomas, N., and Copolov, D. L. (2014). A new phenomenological survey of auditory hallucinations: evidence for subtypes and implications for theory and practice. *Schizophr. Bull.* 40, 231–235. doi: 10.1093/schbul/sbs156

McGorry, P. (1991). Negative symptoms and PTSD. *Aust. N.Z. J. Psychiatry* 25, 12–13.

Morrison, A. P., Frame L., Larkin, W. (2003). Relationships between trauma and psychosis: a review and integration. *Br. J. Clin. Psychol.* 42, 331–353. doi: 10.1348/014466503322528892

Moskowitz, A., and Corstens, D. (2007). Auditory hallucinations: psychotic symptom or dissociative experience? *J. Psychol. Trauma* 6, 35–63. doi: 10.1300/J513v06n02_04

Mueser, K. T., Rosenberg, S. D., Goodman, L. A., and Trumbetta, S. L. (2002). Trauma, PTSD, and the course of severe mental illness: an interactive model. *Schizophr. Res.* 53, 123–143. doi: 10.1016/S0920-9964(01) 00173-6

Okkels, N., Trabjerg, B., Arendt, M., and Pedersen, C. B. (2017). Traumatic stress disorders and risk of subsequent schizophrenia spectrum disorder or bipolar disorder: a nationwide cohort study. *Schizophr. Bull.* 43, 180–186. doi: 10.1093/schbul/sbw082

Perona-Garcelán, S., Carrascoso-López, F., García-Montes, J. M., Ductor-Recuerda, M. J., López Jiménez, A. M., Vallina-Fernández, O. et al. (2012). Dissociative experiences as mediators between childhood trauma and auditory hallucinations. *J. Trauma. Stress*, 25, 323–329. doi: 10.1002/jts.21693

Pilton, M., Varese, F., Berry, K., and Bucci, S. (2015). The relationship between dissociation and voices: a systematic literature review and meta-analysis. *Clin. Psychol. Rev.* 40, 138–155. doi: 10.1016/j.cpr.2015.06.004

Read, J., Agar, K., Argyle, N., and Aderhold, V. (2003). Sexual and physical abuse during childhood and adulthood as predictors of hallucinations, delusions and thought disorder. *Psychol. Psychother.* 76(Pt 1), 1–22. doi: 10.1348/14760830260569210

Read, J., and Bentall, R. (2012). Negative childhood experiences and mental health: theoretical, clinical and primary prevention implications. *Br. J. Psychiatry* 200, 89–91. doi: 10.1192/bjp.bp.111.096727

Read, J., Perry, B. D., Moskowitz, A., and Connolly, J. (2001). The contribution of early traumatic events to schizophrenia in some patients: a traumagenic neurodevelopmental model. *Psychiatry* 64, 319–345. doi: 10.1521/psyc.64.4.319.18602

Reininghaus, U., Depp, C. A., and Myin-Germeys, I. (2016). Ecological interventionist causal models in psychosis: targeting psychological mechanisms in daily life. *Schizophr. Bull.* 42, 264–269. doi: 10.1093/schbul/sbv193

Sareen, J., Cox, B. J., Goodwin, R. D., and Asmundson, G. (2005). Co-occurrence of posttraumatic stress disorder with positive psychotic symptoms in a nationally representative sample. *J. Trauma. Stress* 18:313. doi: 10.1002/jts.20040

Stampfer, H. G. (1990). "Negative symptoms": a cumulative trauma stress disorder? *Aust. N.Z. J. Psychiatry* 24, 516–528. doi: 10.3109/00048679009062908

Steel, C., Fowler, D., and Holmes, E. A. (2005). Trauma-related intrusions and psychosis: an information processing account. *Behav. Cogn. Psychother.* 33, 139. doi: 10.1017/S1352465804001924

Steel, C., Hardy, A., Smith, B., Wykes, T., Rose, S., Enright, S., et al. (2017). Cognitive-behaviour therapy for post-traumatic stress in schizophrenia. A randomized controlled trial. *Psychol. Med.* 47, 43–51. doi: 10.1017/S0033291716002117

Strauss, G. P., Duke, L. A., Ross, S. A., and Allen, D. N. (2011). Posttraumatic stress disorder and negative symptoms of schizophrenia. *Schizophr. Bull.* 37, 603–610. doi: 10.1093/schbul/sbp122

Thomas, N., Hayward, M., Peters, E., van der Gaag, M., Bentall, R. P., Jenner, J., et al. (2014). Psychological therapies for auditory hallucinations (voices): current status and key directions for future research. *Schizophr. Bull.* 40, S202–S212. doi: 10.1093/schbul/sbu037

van den Berg, D. P. G., de Bont, P. A. J. M., van der Vleugel, B. M., de Roos, C., de Jongh, A., Van Minnen, A., et al. (2015). Prolonged exposure vs eye movement desensitization and reprocessing vs waiting list for posttraumatic stress disorder in patients with a psychotic disorder. *JAMA Psychiatry* 72:259. doi: 10.1001/jamapsychiatry.2014.2637

Varese, F., Barkus, E., and Bentall, R. P. (2012). Dissociation mediates the relationship between childhood trauma and hallucination-proneness. *Psychol. Med.* 42, 1025–1036. doi: 10.1017/S0033291711001826

Varese, F., Udachina, A., Myin-Germeys, I., Oorschot, M., and Bentall, R. P. (2011). The relationship between dissociation and auditory verbal hallucinations in the flow of daily life of patients with psychosis. *Psychosis* 3, 14–28. doi: 10.1080/17522439.2010.548564

6

Early Psychosis and Trauma-Related Disorders: Clinical Practice Guidelines and Future Directions

Casey A. Cragin[1], Martha B. Straus[1], Dawn Blacker[2], Laura M. Tully[3] and Tara A. Niendam[3]*

[1] Department of Clinical Psychology, Antioch University New England, Keene, NH, USA, [2] CAARE Diagnostic and Treatment Center, Department of Pediatrics, University of California, Davis, Sacramento, USA, [3] UC Davis Imaging Research Center, Department of Psychiatry and Behavioral Sciences, University of California, Davis, Sacramento, USA

Edited by:
Kate Hardy,
Stanford University, USA

Reviewed by:
Craig Steel,
University of Reading, UK
Sara Freedman,
Bar-Ilan University, Israel

****Correspondence:***
Casey A. Cragin
ccragin@antioch.edu

Despite high rates of trauma-related disorders among individuals with early psychosis, no clinical practice guidelines for the treatment of comorbid early psychosis and trauma-related disorders exist to date. Indeed, the routine exclusion of individuals with past and current psychosis from participation in trauma research and practice has limited the accumulation of research that could support such clinical practice guidelines. While preliminary research evidence suggests that traditional, evidence-based treatments for trauma-related disorders can be safely and effectively employed to reduce symptoms of posttraumatic stress and chronic psychosis, it remains unclear whether such treatments are appropriate for individuals in the early stages of psychotic illness. Clinical experts (N = 118) representing 121 early psychosis programs across 28 states were surveyed using the expert consensus method. Forty-nine clinical experts responded and reached consensus on 46 of 49 expert consensus items related to the treatment of comorbid early psychosis and trauma-related disorders. Conjoint or family therapy and individual therapy were rated as treatment approaches of choice. Anxiety or stress management and psychoeducation were rated as treatment interventions of choice for addressing both trauma symptoms and psychotic symptoms. In addition, case management was rated as a treatment intervention of choice for addressing psychotic symptoms. No consensus was reached on expert consensus items regarding the appropriateness of a parallel treatment approach exposure interventions for addressing psychotic symptoms, or sensorimotor or movement interventions for addressing trauma symptoms. In areas where expert consensus exists and is supported by current research, preliminary clinical practice guidelines for the treatment of comorbid early psychosis and trauma-related disorders are offered. In areas where expert consensus does not exist, recommendations for future research are offered. The results of this study are intended to serve as a launching point for scientists and practitioners interested in advancing appropriate treatment for high-risk and underserved individuals with comorbid early psychosis and trauma-related disorders.

Keywords: early psychosis, trauma, posttraumatic stress disorder, clinical practice guidelines, expert consensus method

INTRODUCTION

Rates of PTSD among individuals in the early stages of psychotic illness are high: in a study of Cincinnati psychiatric services, nearly 23% of first episode psychosis individuals presented with comorbid PTSD (1) versus an estimated 15% lifetime prevalence in individuals with chronic psychotic illness (2–4) and 6.8% prevalence in the general population (5). These high rates of comorbidity have prompted research on the effectiveness of interventions for comorbid psychosis and PTSD, with recent conceptual frameworks posing a reciprocal relationship between trauma and psychosis in the context of the cognitive model (6, 7). Empirically supported treatments for PTSD predominantly include trauma-focused treatments that provide direct exposure to traumatic events in order to combat the role of avoidance in the maintenance of PTSD (8, 9). Findings suggest these traditional evidence-based treatments for trauma-related disorders can be safely and effectively employed to reduce symptoms of posttraumatic stress and chronic psychosis (3, 10–12); however, it remains unclear whether such treatments are appropriate for individuals with early psychosis (i.e., within the first 5 years of illness onset). The early stages of psychotic illness are a critical period for intervention. With onset typically occurring between 15 and 25 years of age, psychosis symptoms disrupt important developmental trajectories in social, academic, and vocational domains. Combined with high rates of relapse (13) and comorbid trauma-related disorders (1), early intervention using evidence-based practices is necessary to prevent a long-term trajectory of accumulating disability (14). Yet, despite the burgeoning number of early psychosis treatment programs across the United States (15, 16), no clinical practice guidelines for treating comorbid early psychosis and trauma-related disorders currently exist.

The effect of exposure interventions on PTSD symptoms in adults with PTSD and chronic psychotic disorders has been explored in four studies to date. In an open trial study of 20 adults with PTSD and either schizophrenia or schizoaffective disorder, Frueh and colleagues (10) found cognitive behavioral therapy (CBT) that included imaginal exposure interventions integrated with treatment-as-usual (TAU) approaches significantly decreased PTSD symptoms and anger, as well as increased general mental health, compared to TAU alone. In another open pilot trial, van den Berg and van der Gaag (12) found eye movement desensitization and reprocessing (EMDR) plus TAU significantly decreased posttraumatic stress symptoms, psychotic symptoms (i.e., auditory verbal hallucinations and delusions), and other psychiatric symptoms (i.e., depression and anxiety), as well as increased self-esteem, after treatment compared to TAU alone. Similarly, in a within-group controlled study, de Bont and colleagues (3) found both prolonged exposure (PE) and EMDR decreased PTSD severity and diagnosis. Subsequently, in a randomized control trial, van den Berg and colleagues (17) found both PE and EMDR significantly decreased PTSD symptoms and diagnosis compared to waiting list (WL); however, PE, but not EMDR, resulted in full remission of PTSD compared to WL.

Two randomized control trials (RCTs) have examined the effect of CBT that did not include exposure interventions on PTSD symptoms in adults with PTSD and schizophrenia-spectrum disorders. Mueser and colleagues (11) found CBT integrated with TAU significantly decreased PTSD, mood, and anxiety symptoms, negative trauma-related cognitions, other psychiatric symptoms, and health-related concerns compared to TAU alone. Additionally, CBT participants endorsed increased knowledge of PTSD and client-case manager working alliance. The observed effects were significantly more robust for individuals with severe PTSD compared to those with mild or moderate PTSD. More recently, Steel and colleagues (18) found CBT without exposure, conducted in the context of TAU, did not significantly decrease trauma-related cognitions, severity of PTSD symptoms, positive symptoms of psychosis, severity of hallucinations and delusions, depression, or anxiety, or increase functioning or quality of life. Steel and colleagues concluded that exposure interventions focused on processing emotions related to traumatic memories may be needed in order for CBT to be effective in individuals with comorbid PTSD and psychotic disorders. Both studies also recommended future research include exposure interventions in treatment protocols in order to increase their effectiveness.

Collectively, these findings demonstrate that CBT, PE, and EMDR can be employed safely and effectively to reduce both PTSD and psychotic symptoms in adults with comorbid chronic psychosis and PTSD (3, 10–12); however, the inclusion of exposure interventions may result in more robust effects compared to non-exposure interventions in this population. There is, however, no available literature to guide the treatment of comorbid early psychosis and trauma-related disorders. As a result, additional research is needed to clarify which treatments are appropriate for individuals in the early stages of psychotic illness.

The Current Study

Well-constructed clinical practice guidelines have the potential to improve the consistency, efficiency, value, and outcome of health care, as well as to empower patients and practitioners to make more informed health-care decisions, protecting both parties from the negative influences of uncertainty and antiquity; however, poorly constructed clinical practice guidelines have the potential to reduce the quality, efficiency, availability, and flexibility of health care (19). It is, therefore, important to use empirical methods to promote guideline development, ideally rooted in a strong foundation of carefully conducted RCTs on multiple large, independent, well-defined samples; however, RCTs often require years to conduct and the adoption of original research into clinical practice can take up to two decades (20); other methods can be used to generate preliminary guidelines and inform clinical practice in the interim.

One such method is the expert consensus method, which is designed to allow researchers to collect consensus evidence in cases where the outcome literature is unclear, incomplete, or absent, and must be supplemented with expert opinion (21). The expert consensus method has been used to develop clinical practice guidelines for dementia (22), obsessive–compulsive disorder (23), bipolar disorder (24), schizophrenia (25), PTSD (9), and complex PTSD (26). Here, we use the expert consensus method to develop preliminary clinical practice guidelines as a first step toward addressing the needs of individuals with comorbid early psychosis and trauma-related disorders.

We conducted a survey of clinical experts responsible for overseeing the clinical services provided in early psychosis programs across the United States. This survey elicited their expert opinions about treatment appropriateness for individuals with comorbid early psychosis and trauma-related disorders. In areas where expert consensus existed and was supported by current research, preliminary clinical practice guidelines for comorbid early psychosis and trauma-related disorders are offered. In areas where expert consensus does not exist, recommendations for future research are offered. The results of this study are intended to serve as a launching point for scientists and practitioners interested in advancing appropriate treatment for high-risk and underserved individuals with comorbid early psychosis and trauma-related disorders. To this end, the current study is designed to address the following research questions:

1. Which treatment modalities (e.g., individual therapy, conjoint or family therapy, consultation) are most appropriate for individuals with comorbid early psychosis and trauma-related disorders?
2. Which treatment approaches (e.g., single-diagnosis, sequenced, parallel, or integrated) are most appropriate?
3. Which treatment interventions are most appropriate for addressing psychotic symptoms? For treating trauma symptoms?
4. Is trauma-focused treatment appropriate? If so, under what clinical and psychosocial conditions (e.g., stage of psychosis, current psychosocial context, past psychosocial context)?
5. Should treatment modalities, approaches, or interventions be modified based on the individual's developmental level (e.g., under age 18 or over age 25)? If so, how?
6. What are the barriers to treating comorbid early psychosis and trauma-related disorders in early psychosis programs?
7. How can the treatment of comorbid early psychosis and trauma-related disorders in early psychosis programs be improved?

MATERIALS AND METHODS

Participants

Participants included clinical directors or persons in comparable positions responsible for overseeing the clinical services of early psychosis programs in the United States. Given the specialized nature of evidence-based care for early psychosis populations (14), these individuals were presumed to have the knowledge and experience needed to offer expert clinical opinions about the treatment of individuals with comorbid early psychosis and trauma-related disorders in the United States. There were no *a priori* exclusion criteria for this study.

Procedures

Early psychosis program directories, located through an Internet search and consultation with experts in the field, were reviewed in order to identify potential recruitment sites (15, 16, 27, 28). This resulted in the identification of 121 early psychosis programs across 28 states (see Supplementary Material). Clinical directors or persons in comparable positions were identified for all 121 early psychosis programs in the United States. In some cases, one person fulfilled this role at multiple early psychosis programs. As a result, the total number of prospective participants ($N = 118$) was slightly lower than the total number of early psychosis programs ($N = 121$). No early psychosis programs or prospective participants were excluded.

Participants were recruited *via* email, including a brief description of the study and a link to the anonymous online survey. No identifying information was collected or attached to survey responses to allow the participants to respond as honestly as possible. Reminder emails were sent to all prospective participants 2 and 4 weeks after the initial recruitment email. Participants were offered two optional participation incentives: optional entry into a raffle for one of four $25 Amazon gift cards and optional receipt of study results. In order to ensure that survey responses remained anonymous, prospective participants were instructed to opt-in to one or both optional participation incentives by emailing the principle investigator with "RAFFLE" and/or "RESULTS" in the subject line. This study was reviewed and approved by the Institutional Review Board (IRB) of Antioch University New England (AUNE). The IRB of AUNE granted this study exempt status under 45 CFR 46.101(b)(2) exemption from 45 CFR part 46 requirements.

Measure

Participants completed an anonymous 15–20 min online survey, administered *via* the Qualtrics secure web-based platform. The online survey contained 24–30 questions (the exact number varied depending on six conditional response questions) about participant characteristics, program characteristics, and expert consensus questions regarding modalities, approaches, interventions, treatments, developmental considerations, treatment barriers, and treatment improvements. Definitions of key terms and interventions were provided. See Supplementary Material for the complete survey and definitions.

The expert consensus questions were modeled after prior studies (22, 26, 29). Participants were instructed to use a 9-point scale to rate the appropriateness of modalities, approaches, interventions, and treatments. Scores in the 7–9 range indicate a degree of appropriateness, scores in the 4–6 range indicate a degree of equivocal opinion, and scores in the 1–3 range indicate a degree of inappropriateness with the following anchors: 9 = extremely appropriate: your modality, approach, intervention, or treatment of choice (TOC) (you may have more than one per question); 7–8 = appropriate: a first-line modality, approach, intervention, or treatment you would often use; 4–6 = equivocal: a second-line modality, approach, intervention, or treatment you would sometimes use (e.g., after first-line modalities, approaches, interventions, or treatments failed); 2–3 = usually Inappropriate: at most, a third-line modality, approach, intervention, or treatment you would rarely use; and 1 = extremely inappropriate: a modality, approach, intervention, or treatment you would never use.

Data Analysis

Expert consensus data were analyzed using procedures identical to those described in Frances and colleagues (29). First, the mean and confidence interval (95%) was calculated for each expert consensus item. The confidence interval for each expert consensus item was used to assign a categorical rating based on the range into which the lowest confidence limit (LCL) fell. A categorical rating of first-line was assigned to modalities, approaches, interventions, and treatments with a LCL that fell into the 6.50–9.00 range; a categorical rating of second-line was assigned to modalities, approaches, interventions, and treatments with a LCL that fell into the 3.50–6.49 range; and a categorical rating of third-line was assigned to modalities, approaches, interventions, and treatments with a LCL that fell into the 1.00–3.49 range. The distribution of responses for each expert consensus item was then analyzed for consensus. The categorical ratings for each expert consensus item were coded (i.e., first-line = 1, second-line = 2, and third-line = 3), and a non-parametric chi-square test was conducted for each expert consensus item in order to determine whether or not expert consensus existed. Consensus was defined as when the response distribution of categorical ratings was statistically different from chance ($p \leq 0.05$) (29). Finally, expert consensus items rated a 9 by 50% or more of participants were determined to represent a TOC for modalities, approaches, interventions, and treatments. Participant and program characteristics data are reported in Supplementary Material. Qualitative data were analyzed using a general inductive approach (30).

RESULTS

Online survey responses were collected from June 27 to August 5, 2016. Of the 118 clinical experts invited to participate, 66 (56%) responded. Seventeen (26%) of the 66 responses were omitted due to discontinuation of the survey prior to reaching the expert consensus items. The remaining 49 (42%) survey responses were included and analyzed to yield the following results.

Quantitative Results

Participant Characteristics

Twenty-six (53%) participants identified a master's degree and 23 (47%) identified a doctorate or professional degree as their highest level of completed education. Forty-three (88%) participants reported providing treatment to individuals with early psychosis and 35 (71%) reported providing treatment to individuals with comorbid early psychosis and trauma-related disorders in the last 12 months. Forty-nine (100%) participants reported receiving formal training or supervised clinical experience in the treatment of early psychosis: 35 (73%) reported receiving both formal training and supervised clinical experience, while 13 (27%) reported receiving formal training only. Thirty-nine (80%) participants reported also receiving formal training or supervised clinical experience in the treatment of trauma-related disorders: 23 (62%) reported receiving both formal training and supervised clinical experience, while 11 (30%) reported receiving formal training only and 3 (8%) reported receiving supervised clinical experience only. See Supplementary Material for specific early psychosis and trauma treatments in which participants reported receiving formal training and supervised clinical experience.

Program Characteristics

Participants represented early psychosis programs from 18 states (see Supplementary Material). Twenty-eight (57%) programs were based in the community, 11 (22%) programs were based in a university, and 2 (4%) programs were based in a hospital. The remaining 8 (16%) programs were based in a combination of community, hospital, or university settings. Thirty-eight (95%) programs served clients under age 18 and 28 (70%) served clients over age 25. Forty-two (86%) participants reported that their programs offered coordinated specialty care for early psychosis, the primary evidence-based model for outpatient treatment of early psychosis (14). See Supplementary Material for types of services offered.

Forty-eight (98%) programs provided staff members with formal training or supervised clinical experience in the treatment of early psychosis: 39 (85%) provided staff members with both formal training and supervised clinical experience, while 5 (11%) provided formal training only and 2 (4%) provided supervised clinical experience only. Twenty-three (47%) programs also provided staff members with formal training or supervised clinical experience in the treatment of trauma-related disorders: 33 (68%) provided staff members with both formal training and supervised clinical experience, while 7 (14%) provided formal training only and 9 (18%) provided supervised clinical experience only. See Supplementary Material for early psychosis and trauma treatments in which programs provided formal training and supervised clinical experience.

Treatment Modalities

Participants were asked to rate the appropriateness of individual therapy (i.e., seeing client alone), consultation (i.e., seeing family members or support persons alone), and conjoint or family therapy (i.e., seeing client and family members or support persons together) for clients aged 18–25 with comorbid early psychosis and trauma-related disorders. Conjoint or family therapy (LCL = 7.98), individual therapy (LCL = 7.73), and consultation (LCL = 6.87) were all rated as first-line treatment modalities. Conjoint or family therapy (TOC = 57.14%) and individual therapy (TOC = 53.06%), however, were rated as the treatments of choice. See **Table 1** for expert consensus ratings of treatment modalities.

Treatment Approaches

Participants were asked to rate the appropriateness of single-diagnosis (i.e., treating either early psychosis or trauma-related disorder only), sequenced (i.e., treating early psychosis before treating trauma-related disorder or *vice versa*), parallel (i.e., different providers treating early psychosis and trauma-related disorder at the same time), and integrated (i.e., the same provider treating early psychosis and trauma-related disorder at the same time) treatment approaches for clients aged 18–25 with comorbid early psychosis and trauma-related disorders. Integrated treatment (LCL = 8.10) was rated as a first-line treatment approach. Sequenced treatments, beginning with either the treatment of

TABLE 1 | Expert consensus ratings of treatment modalities and approaches.

				Expert ratings								
				Treatment of choice (TOC)		1st line		2nd line		3rd line		Total
	Lowest confidence limit (LCL)	M	SD	%	N	%	N	%	N	%	N	N
Modality												
Conjoint/family therapy	7.98[b]	8.31	1.14	57.14[a]	28	95.91	47	2.04	1	2.04	1	49
Individual therapy	7.73[b]	8.12	1.36	53.06[a]	26	91.83	45	6.12	3	2.04	1	49
Consultation	6.87[b]	7.39	1.81	30.61	15	79.59	39	14.28	7	6.12	3	49
Approach												
Integrated	7.40[b]	7.88	1.63	45.83	22	85.42	41	10.41	5	4.16	2	48
Sequenced[EP]	5.52[c]	6.04	1.79	4.17	2	41.67	20	54.16	26	4.16	2	48
Sequenced[TRD]	4.11[c]	4.73	2.14	2.08	1	20.83	10	50.00	24	29.16	14	48
Single-diagnosis[EP]	2.92[d]	3.52	2.08	2.08	1	10.41	5	33.33	16	56.25	27	48
Single-diagnosis[TRD]	2.60[d]	3.19	2.04	0.00	0	8.33	4	31.24	15	60.42	29	48
Parallel	4.29[nc]	5.00	2.46	6.25	3	31.25	15	41.67	20	27.09	13	48

[a]*TOC.*
[b]*First-line.*
[c]*Second-line.*
[d]*Third-line.*
[nc]*No consensus.*
[EP]*Early psychosis.*
[TRD]*Trauma-related disorder.*

early psychosis (LCL = 5.52) or the treatment of the trauma-related disorder (LCL = 4.11), were rated as second-line treatment approaches. Single-diagnosis treatments, only treating early psychosis (LCL = 2.92) or the trauma-related disorder (LCL = 2.60), were rated as third-line treatment approaches. No consensus was reached on the appropriateness of parallel treatment. See **Table 1** for expert consensus ratings of treatment approaches.

Treatment Interventions

Participants were asked to rate the appropriateness of treatment interventions for addressing either psychotic symptoms or trauma symptoms for clients aged 18–25 with comorbid early psychosis and trauma-related disorders. These various treatment interventions are often components of broader treatment protocols for early psychosis and/or trauma-related disorders. See Supplementary Material for definitions of interventions.

Psychotic Symptoms

Anxiety or stress management (LCL = 8.10), psychoeducation (LCL = 7.97), cognitive restructuring (LCL = 7.48), case management (LCL = 7.43), interpersonal effectiveness (LCL = 7.16), meditation or mindfulness (LCL = 6.66), and emotion-focused (LCL = 6.52) interventions were rated as first-line treatment interventions for addressing psychotic symptoms. Anxiety or stress management (TOC = 73.91%), psychoeducation (TOC = 73.91%), and case management (TOC = 50.00%) interventions were rated as treatment interventions of choice. Sensorimotor or movement (LCL = 4.86) and bilateral stimulation (LCL = 4.00) interventions were rated as second-line treatment interventions. No consensus was reached on the appropriateness of exposure interventions for addressing psychotic symptoms. See **Table 2** for expert consensus ratings of treatment interventions for addressing psychotic symptoms.

Trauma Symptoms

Anxiety or stress management (LCL = 8.13), psychoeducation (LCL = 7.78), meditation or mindfulness (LCL = 7.45), cognitive restructuring (LCL = 7.42), interpersonal effectiveness (LCL = 6.99), emotion-focused (LCL = 6.98), and case management (LCL = 6.81) interventions were rated as first-line treatment interventions for addressing trauma symptoms. Anxiety or stress management (TOC = 68.89%) and psychoeducation (TOC = 61.36%) interventions were rated as treatments of choice. Exposure (LCL = 6.00) and bilateral stimulation (LCL = 4.69) interventions were rated as second-line treatment interventions. No consensus was reached on the appropriateness of sensorimotor or movement interventions for addressing trauma symptoms. See **Table 2** for expert consensus ratings of treatment interventions for trauma symptoms.

Trauma-Focused Treatment

Trauma-focused treatment addresses exposure to traumatic events directly by asking clients to recall or encounter thoughts, images, feelings, or situations related to traumatic events. Participants were asked to rate the appropriateness of trauma-focused treatment for clients aged 18–25 with comorbid early psychosis and trauma-related disorders overall, at each stage of psychosis, and under specific current and past clinical and psychosocial conditions. Given that participants were previously asked to rate various treatment interventions that are often components of specific trauma-focused treatments, here, participants were asked to rate the appropriateness of trauma-focused treatment in general. Overall, trauma-focused treatment (LCL = 6.97) was rated as a

TABLE 2 | Expert consensus ratings of interventions to address psychotic symptoms and trauma symptoms.

				Expert ratings									
				TOC		1st line		2nd line		3rd line		Total
	LCL	M	SD	%	N	%	N	%	N	%	N	N
Psychotic symptoms												
Anxiety/stress management	8.10[b]	8.48	1.26	73.91[a]	34	95.65	44	2.17	1	2.17	1	46
Psychoeducation	7.97[b]	8.39	1.41	73.91[a]	34	89.13	41	8.70	4	2.17	1	46
Cognitive restructuring	7.48[b]	7.89	1.37	42.22	19	84.44	38	13.33	6	2.22	1	45
Case management	7.43[b]	7.89	1.54	50.00[a]	23	82.61	38	13.04	6	4.35	2	46
Interpersonal effectiveness	7.10[b]	7.60	1.45	32.56	14	79.07	34	18.61	8	2.33	1	43
Meditation/mindfulness	6.66[b]	7.18	1.74	31.11	14	68.80	31	26.66	12	4.44	2	45
Emotion-focused	6.52[b]	7.00	1.58	15.91	7	61.36	27	36.36	16	2.27	1	44
Sensorimotor/movement	4.86[c]	5.50	2.10	9.09	4	29.54	13	54.55	24	15.92	7	44
Bilateral stimulation	4.00[c]	4.60	1.91	4.76	2	9.52	4	69.04	29	21.42	9	42
Exposure	4.54[nc]	5.30	2.49	11.63	5	32.56	14	44.18	19	23.26	10	43
Trauma symptoms												
Anxiety/stress management	8.13[b]	8.49	1.18	68.89[a]	31	95.55	43	2.22	1	2.22	1	45
Psychoeducation	7.78[b]	8.20	1.41	61.36[a]	27	88.63	39	9.09	4	2.27	1	44
Meditation/mindfulness	7.45[b]	7.91	1.51	45.45	20	84.09	37	13.64	6	2.27	1	44
Cognitive restructuring	7.42[b]	7.83	1.32	42.86	18	85.72	36	11.90	5	2.38	1	42
Interpersonal effectiveness	6.99[b]	7.48	1.57	30.95	13	78.57	33	19.04	8	2.38	1	42
Emotion-focused	6.98[b]	7.40	1.35	20.93	9	74.42	32	25.58	11	0.00	0	43
Case management	6.81[b]	7.30	1.60	30.23	13	72.09	31	23.26	10	4.65	2	43
Exposure	6.00[c]	6.57	1.82	19.05	8	52.38	22	42.86	18	4.76	2	42
Bilateral stimulation	4.69[c]	5.44	2.30	12.82	5	30.77	12	53.85	21	15.38	6	39
Sensorimotor/movement	5.27[nc]	5.98	2.27	14.29	6	45.25	19	38.09	16	16.66	7	42

[a]*TOC.*
[b]*First-line.*
[c]*Second-line.*
[nc]*No consensus.*

first-line treatment for clients aged 18–25 with early psychosis and comorbid trauma-related disorders. See **Table 3** for expert consensus ratings of trauma-focused treatment.

Stage of Psychosis

Stages of psychosis included genetic risk and deterioration (i.e., family history of psychosis and decline in functioning without attenuated or threshold psychotic symptoms), ultra-high or clinical high risk (i.e., attenuated psychotic symptoms), first-episode psychosis (i.e., onset of threshold psychotic symptoms less than 5 years ago), and established or chronic psychosis (i.e., onset of threshold psychotic symptoms more than 5 years ago). Trauma-focused treatment (LCL = 6.97) was rated as a first-line treatment for clients at all stages of psychosis: first-episode psychosis (LCL = 7.21), genetic risk and deterioration (LCL = 7.19), chronic or established psychosis (LCL = 7.14), and ultra-high risk or clinical high risk (LCL = 7.07). See **Table 3** for expert consensus ratings of trauma-focused treatment at each stage of psychosis.

Current Clinical and Psychosocial Conditions

Trauma-focused treatment was rated as a first-line treatment for clients with current attenuated or residual psychotic symptoms (LCL = 7.12). It was rated as a second-line treatment for clients with current comorbid personality disorders (LCL = 6.29), other comorbid psychiatric disorders (LCL = 6.35), low involvement of family members or support persons (LCL = 6.09), and significant life stressors (LCL = 6.00). See **Table 3** for expert consensus ratings of trauma-focused treatment given current conditions.

Past Clinical and Psychosocial Conditions

Trauma-focused treatment was rated as a first-line treatment for clients with a history of multiple traumas (LCL = 6.99), single trauma (LCL = 6.71), and long-duration psychotic symptoms (LCL = 6.69). It was rated as a second-line treatment for clients with a history of poor functioning (LCL = 6.49) and severe psychotic symptoms (LCL = 6.37), as well as a history of hospitalization (LCL = 5.95), substance use (LCL = 6.34), non-suicidal self-injury (LCL = 6.38), high suicide risk (LCL = 5.54), and high violence risk (LCL = 5.14). See **Table 3** for expert consensus ratings of trauma-focused treatment given past conditions.

Qualitative Results

Developmental Considerations

Because the expert consensus items asked specifically about clients aged 18–25, participants who reported serving clients under age 18 or over age 25 were asked if and how the appropriateness of modalities, approaches, interventions, or treatments differ for these other age groups. Of those participants who reported serving clients under age 18 and over age 25, respectively, 19 (50%) and 6 (21%) agreed that the appropriateness of modalities,

TABLE 3 | Expert consensus ratings of trauma-focused treatment.

				Expert ratings								
				TOC		1st line		2nd line		3rd line		Total
	LCL	M	SD	%	*N*	%	*N*	%	*N*	%	*N*	*N*
Overall												
Trauma-focused treatment	6.97[a]	7.54	1.80	41.46	17	78.04	32	19.52	8	2.44	1	41
Stage of psychosis												
First-episode psychosis	7.21[a]	7.70	1.54	45.00	18	77.5	31	20.00	8	2.50	1	40
Genetic risk and deterioration	7.19[a]	7.70	1.60	35.00	14	87.5	35	10.00	4	2.50	1	40
Chronic/established psychosis	7.14[a]	7.65	1.59	35.00	14	87.5	35	10.00	4	2.50	1	40
Ultra-high risk/ clinical high risk	7.07[a]	7.58	1.57	32.50	13	80	32	17.5	7	2.50	1	40
Current condition												
Attenuated or residual psychotic symptoms	7.12[a]	7.59	1.42	35.14	13	78.38	29	21.62	8	0.00	0	37
Other comorbid psychiatric disorder	6.35[b]	6.95	1.79	24.32	9	64.86	24	29.73	11	5.40	2	37
Comorbid personality disorder	6.29[b]	6.95	1.96	24.32	9	64.86	24	29.73	11	5.40	2	37
Low involvement of support persons	6.09[b]	6.73	1.92	29.73	11	54.06	20	40.55	15	5.41	2	37
Significant life stressors	6.00[b]	6.73	2.19	32.43	12	59.46	22	27.03	10	13.51	5	37
Past condition												
Multiple traumas	6.99[a]	7.63	1.94	42.11	16	86.84	33	7.89	3	5.26	2	38
Single trauma	6.71[a]	7.42	2.16	42.11	16	84.21	32	7.89	3	7.89	3	38
Long-duration symptoms	6.69[a]	7.25	1.65	22.22	8	74.99	27	22.22	8	2.78	1	36
Poor functioning	6.49[b]	7.05	1.68	21.62	8	67.57	25	29.73	11	2.7	1	37
Non-suicidal self-injury	6.38[b]	6.97	1.79	18.92	7	67.57	25	27.03	10	5.41	2	37
Severe symptoms	6.37[b]	7.03	1.95	22.22	8	69.45	25	25	9	5.56	2	36
Substance use	6.34[b]	6.89	1.66	18.92	7	62.16	23	35.14	13	2.7	1	37
Hospitalization	5.95[b]	6.72	2.28	27.78	10	63.89	23	25.01	9	11.12	4	36
High suicide risk	5.54[b]	6.32	2.36	24.32	9	48.65	18	37.83	14	13.52	5	37
High violence risk	5.14[b]	6	2.58	16.22	6	54.06	20	27.04	10	18.92	7	37

[a]*First-line.*
[b]*Second-line.*

approaches, interventions, or treatments differs for the specified age group.

Family Involvement

Participants acknowledged both the ethical (e.g., consent) and supportive functions of the family, noting that they work harder to engage family members in treatment in general and in decision-making specifically when working with clients under age 18. One participant, for example, noted the increased importance of family consent and engagement for clients with comorbid early psychosis and trauma-related disorders due to the perception of "increased risk with trauma treatment." In cases where family involvement is low, another participant reported wanting "to ensure the individual had [...] other identified support persons." For clients over age 25, participants noted alternative support persons like close friends or partners might be more apt to be involved in treatment than members of the client's family of origin.

Modification of Treatment Materials or Interventions

Participants noted the importance of "using age appropriate materials, language, and consideration of developmental tasks." Participants noted cognitive interventions might be less appropriate or require additional assessment or modification for clients under age 18 compared to older clients. In addition, participants noted the importance of skill building for clients under age 18. For example, one participant responded, "Ensure [the] young person has skills to manage [a] potential increase in symptoms prior to commencing trauma work."

Treatment Barriers

Participants were also asked if they were aware of any barriers their early psychosis programs encountered in attempting to treat clients with comorbid early psychosis and trauma-related disorders and, if so, to describe those barriers. Twenty-eight (78%) participants reported being aware of such barriers.

Differentiating Trauma Exposure from Psychotic Experiences

Participants noted high endorsement of traumatic events and other stressful life experiences or difficulty determining whether traumatic events and other stressful life experiences were real or delusional. In addition, participants reported difficulty determining how to handle reports of the first episode of psychosis as a traumatic event. Participants described attempts to overcome these barriers by focusing on educating clients about stressful experiences in general and helping clients develop and utilize strategies to cope with stressful experiences in lieu of educating clients specifically about trauma or helping clients to directly process the reported traumatic events. One participant noted that inclusion of collateral information can help to clarify the validity of the experiences that are being reported.

Symptom Interference and Exacerbation

One participant, for example, noted impairment associated with either early psychosis or trauma-related disorders can impede recovery from the other disorder. This participant described trauma as a major source of stress that can worsen psychotic symptoms. Another participant noted that psychotic symptoms interfere with the processing of traumatic events, especially in cases where the first episode of psychosis was experienced as traumatic.

Inadequate Training and Supervision

One participant noted that programmatic training, as well as available tools and interventions, focus only on early psychosis treatment despite a clearly identified need to be able to integrate early psychosis and trauma treatment. This participant also noted individual efforts to obtain training in trauma treatments on the part of clinicians have not been effective due to a lack of structured supervision and technical support. Another participant noted programmatic efforts to provide training in trauma treatments have not been effective due to a lack of available funding.

Discomfort Treating Both Trauma and Psychosis

Some participants reported not treating clients with comorbid trauma-related disorders due to specializing in early psychosis. In contrast, one participant noted clients are often misdiagnosed in the community as a result of practitioners specializing in trauma treatment incorrectly conceptualizing psychotic symptoms as trauma symptoms. Another participant noted difficulty identifying referral sites that are comfortable providing both early psychosis and trauma treatment.

Improving Treatment

Finally, participants were asked to provide any additional information they thought would help to improve the treatment of clients with comorbid early psychosis and trauma-related disorders. Eleven (22%) participants offered such suggestions.

Increase Training in Trauma Assessment and Treatment

Participants suggested increased training in trauma assessment and treatment would improve the treatment of clients with comorbid early psychosis and trauma-related disorders. For example, one participant noted, "We have addressed a lot of training but never trained in the context of comorbidity with trauma and psychosis." Another participant suggested "early identification of trauma or stressful experiences using a[n] evidence-based scale to evaluate need for further treatment."

Increase Trauma Research and Treatment Planning Guidance

Participants also suggested increased trauma research in general and related to treatment planning in particular. For example, one participant responded, "I wish that there were more data comparing treatments to guide decisions about what treatment options would be best for a specific individual." Another participant noted a need for greater consistency in how trauma-related disorders are treated in early psychosis programs; however, participants noted that research-based treatment protocols would also need to allow treatment to be tailored to client symptoms and client and family preferences.

Increase Funding for Multidisciplinary Programs

Finally, participants suggested increased funding for programs that treat clients with a wider range of presenting problems including early psychosis, rather than for programs that specialize in treating early psychosis only, would improve the treatment of clients with comorbid early psychosis and trauma-related disorders.

DISCUSSION

With the growing number of early psychosis programs in the United States and abroad, this study represents an essential first step toward addressing the needs of individuals with comorbid early psychosis and trauma-related disorders. The development of clinical practice guidelines has been limited historically by the routine exclusion of individuals with past and present psychosis from participation in trauma research and practice (31–33), as well as trauma symptoms not being adequately addressed in psychosis research and practice. Using a comprehensive online survey of clinical experts who are responsible for overseeing the clinical services provided in early psychosis programs, we investigated the current opinions and intervention practices that are guiding the treatment of individuals with comorbid early psychosis and trauma-related disorders in the United States. Based on these responses and preliminary evidence that traditional evidence-based treatments for trauma-related disorders can be safely and effectively employed to reduce symptoms of posttraumatic stress and chronic psychosis (3, 10–12), we offer preliminary clinical practice guidelines and recommendations for future research.

Preliminary Clinical Practice Guidelines and Suggestions for Future Research

Selecting a Treatment Modality

More than half of the clinical experts surveyed in this study rated conjoint or family therapy and individual therapy as their treatment modalities of choice when working with individuals with comorbid early psychosis and trauma-related disorders. This suggests that practitioners should see the client and family members or alternative support persons together with client consent or see the client alone at the start of treatment. This is consistent with current treatment guidelines for psychosis, which support the use of individualized and integrated family interventions (34–36). Additionally, the clinical experts surveyed in this study believed involving family members in the client's treatment is particularly important for individuals under age 18; however, practitioners should also consider the benefits of involving alternative support persons, such as friends or romantic partners, when other family involvement is low or when treating individuals over age 25.

Consultation with family or support persons (without the client present) was also rated as a first-line treatment modality. In cases in which conjoint or family therapy or individual therapy is ineffective, seeing family members or alternative support persons alone with client consent could be an appropriate alternative treatment modality. Family members often experience significant burden when caring for individuals with serious mental illness (37). Therefore, family support may be helpful in protecting the family system if the client refuses to engage; however, current practice models suggest that engagement of family alone would likely not be sufficient in promoting recovery in the client (38).

Selecting a Treatment Approach

Integrated treatment was rated as a first-line treatment approach and sequenced treatments were rated as second-line treatment approaches for the treatment of comorbid early psychosis and trauma-related disorders. The first-line rating of an integrated treatment approach is somewhat surprising given that inadequate training and supervision, as well as inadequate institutional and financial support, were cited as barriers to integrated treatment in these open response data. Integrated treatment may represent the ideal approach that clinical experts recognize as most appropriate and often strive to provide even if they are ill equipped to do so. Funding should be provided to develop innovative programs that strive to address the complex needs of the early psychosis population through staff training and additional program supports.

The second-line rating of sequenced treatment approaches is consistent with participants' report that the exacerbation of early psychosis by a comorbid trauma-related disorder, or visa versa, is a potential barrier to treatment. Clinical experts gave examples of psychotic symptoms interfering with or worsening as a result of treatment of a comorbid trauma-related disorder, as well as the traumatic nature of psychotic symptoms for some clients interfering with treatment of early psychosis. In such cases, sequenced treatment (i.e., treating the exacerbating disorder first in part or in entirety) may be more appropriate than integrated treatment. Practitioners who elect to use a sequenced treatment approach, however, should clearly delineate the client's treatment goals and carefully monitor client progress in the initial phase of treatment. A sequenced approach carries with it the risk that treatment will ultimately focus disproportionately on a single-diagnosis if the provider never feels the client is stable enough to shift to the second phase of treatment (39). Importantly, single-diagnosis treatment was rated as a third-line treatment approach, indicating that the clinical experts surveyed in this study believe that treating only early psychosis or only a trauma-related disorder when both conditions are present is inappropriate.

No consensus was reached regarding the appropriateness of a parallel treatment approach. This is consistent with current recommendations that suggest coordinating parallel treatment by different providers, often in different treatment settings, may fail to address the overlapping aspects of the comorbid psychiatric conditions or work at cross-purposes (39). Parallel treatment may, however, have merits in addressing barriers related to practitioner discomfort treating both trauma and early psychosis. Successful parallel treatment may be possible in the context of the early psychosis coordinated specialty care model, in which multiple practitioners from different specialties work together as a team to address the various needs of early psychosis clients (14). If practitioners specializing in the treatment of trauma-related disorders were added to these multidisciplinary teams, clients could access appropriate treatment for trauma-related disorders without compromising their access to evidence-based early psychosis care. In addition, working within a multidisciplinary team with specialty in early psychosis care would likely increase the competence and comfort of these trauma specialists with treating clients with early psychosis.

Selecting Treatment Interventions to Address Psychotic and Trauma Symptoms

First-line treatment interventions for addressing both psychotic and trauma symptoms included: anxiety or stress management, psychoeducation, case management, cognitive restructuring, emotion-focused interventions, interpersonal effectiveness, and meditation or mindfulness interventions. Bilateral stimulation was rated as a second-line treatment intervention for addressing both psychotic and trauma symptoms. When addressing trauma symptoms in the context of psychosis, exposure interventions were rated as second-line interventions. Sensorimotor or movement interventions were also rated as second-line treatment interventions for addressing psychotic symptoms.

Based on these ratings and consistent with evidence-based cognitive behavioral models for treating psychosis (35, 40) and PTSD (8, 9), we make the following recommendations. Practitioners should begin by providing psychoeducation about early psychosis and trauma. This should include descriptions of psychotic and trauma symptoms and information about treatment rationale and efficacy in order to help the client and their support persons understand the client's problems as surmountable over time with appropriate treatment. Practitioners should then use anxiety and stress management interventions to help individuals develop coping skills to reduce stress and stress-related difficulties. Throughout treatment, practitioners should also provide case management to coordinate services and identify resources needed by the client. Finally, practitioners should select from first-line interventions (e.g., cognitive restructuring, emotion-focused, interpersonal effectiveness, and meditation or mindfulness) to address any residual psychotic and trauma symptoms.

Using Trauma-Focused Treatments and Exposure

Clinical experts surveyed here rated trauma-focused treatment (i.e., treatments that address exposure to traumatic events directly by asking individuals to recall or encounter thoughts, images, feelings, or situations related to traumatic events) as a first-line treatment for individuals aged 18–25 with comorbid early psychosis and trauma-related disorders in general and at all stages of psychosis. Trauma-focused treatment was rated as a first-line treatment for individuals presenting with current attenuated or residual psychotic symptoms, as well as a history of both single and multiple traumas and long-duration psychotic symptoms.

Furthermore, trauma-focused treatment was rated as a second-line treatment for individuals presenting with additional comorbidities and complexities, including: comorbid personality disorders, low involvement of support persons, significant life stressors, as well as a history of poor functioning, severe psychotic symptoms, substance use, non-suicidal self-injury, high suicide risk, high violence risk, and/or hospitalization. This indicates that the clinical experts surveyed in this study believe trauma-focused treatment may be appropriate for such individuals if more appropriate alternatives, not explored in this study, have failed. Notably, there were no current or past conditions for which trauma-focused treatment was rated as inappropriate. Practitioners should, therefore, diligently monitor areas of risk when utilizing trauma-focused treatment with individuals with comorbid early psychosis and trauma-related disorders; however, these risk factors should not be viewed as contraindications for trauma-focused treatment.

These findings contradict the experts' ratings of exposure and bilateral stimulation, two interventions considered to be key components of trauma-focused treatments, as second-line interventions. It may be the case that clinical experts believe trauma-focused treatments that include interventions of choice (e.g., psychoeducation, anxiety, and stress management) and first-line interventions (e.g., cognitive restructuring, emotional-focused) before or in addition to exposure, for example, are more appropriate for individuals with comorbid early psychosis and trauma-related disorders than exposure interventions alone. Conversely, clinical experts may worry about the possible negative impact of exposure interventions on the recovery process, such as the exacerbation of psychotic symptoms, and may hesitate to use them. To date, the positive effect of exposure interventions on chronic psychotic symptoms in adults has been reported as effective in one published study (12), and two other studies have noted that the exclusion of exposure may have decreased the observed effectiveness of their treatment protocols (11, 18).

Exposure interventions are a primary component of all cognitive and behavioral interventions, including cognitive behavioral therapy for psychosis (CBTp), the early psychosis treatment in which participants received and programs provided training and supervision most often. It is possible that clinical experts are not utilizing recommended exposure components of CBTp in their practice despite evidence that doing so is beneficial, which is a phenomenon commonly seen in trauma treatment as well (31). It is also possible that clinical experts are utilizing exposure interventions without recognizing they are doing so, including psychoeducation about psychotic or trauma symptoms and behavioral experiments. This study asked participants to rate the appropriateness of component interventions, as opposed to combinations of interventions, in order to guide the composition of treatment for comorbid early psychosis and trauma-related disorders. Had participants been asked to consider the use of exposure in the context of broader treatment approaches (e.g., CBT), they might have responded more favorably to exposure interventions.

While the clinical experts surveyed in this study were unable to agree on the appropriateness of exposure interventions for addressing psychotic symptoms in individuals with comorbid trauma-related disorders, they agreed that exposure interventions are appropriate for addressing trauma symptoms in this population when first-line interventions have proved to be ineffective. Nonetheless, because exposure is such an important part of trauma treatment, expert attitudes toward exposure therapy for this population merit greater exploration. Research is needed to determine whether practitioners are either not utilizing or not recognizing their use of exposure interventions. Similarly, future studies should determine which exposure interventions are considered most appropriate when treating individuals with early psychosis in general, versus individuals with comorbid early psychosis and trauma-related disorders in particular.

Using Sensorimotor and Movement Interventions to Address Trauma Symptoms

Sensorimotor and movement interventions were included in the current study to reflect the wide range of evidence-based interventions used in clinical practice, despite not being included in the expert consensus study of PTSD conducted over a decade ago (9) and being rated as second-line treatment interventions in the expert consensus study of complex PTSD. Sensorimotor and movement interventions are used to assist individuals with trauma-related disorders regulate their autonomic nervous system, think more clearly, and derive information from emotional states more accurately by processing dissociated, incomplete, or ineffective sensorimotor reactions (e.g., trauma-related images, sounds, smells, and physical sensations) (41). Individuals with early psychosis are frequently vulnerable to excessive autonomic arousal in response to stress (42) and may misinterpret anomalous cognitive or perceptual experiences resulting in emotional arousal and behavioral withdrawal (7) secondary to trauma exposure (43). While mind-body interventions, like sensorimotor and movement interventions, are important to contemporary trauma treatment, their utility for the treatment of psychosis alone has not been well investigated (44). The experts' rating of these approaches as second-line for the treatment of psychotic symptoms may represent growing interest in the integration of mind-body practices into psychosis care, but more well-controlled studies are needed before conclusions can be drawn (45). Currently, these approaches are not seen as core interventions for individuals with psychosis (34). Therefore, additional research is needed to determine whether sensorimotor and movement interventions could be beneficial for individuals with only early psychosis, as well as for individuals with comorbid early psychosis and trauma-related disorders.

Understanding Reports of Trauma in the Context of Psychosis

Open response data indicated that practitioners are often concerned about the validity of high rates of trauma exposure and other stressful life experiences reported by individuals with comorbid early psychosis and comorbid trauma-related disorders, particularly when trauma-related content is mixed with delusional content. As a result, clinical experts surveyed in this study reported program-wide efforts to address this issue by focusing on psychoeducation about stress in general and on developing and using coping skills to manage stress in daily life rather than providing psychoeducation about trauma and processing traumatic events. Auditory hallucinations and non-bizarre delusions of guilt, paranoia, or persecution occur in up to 40% of individuals with severe PTSD (46, 47). The content of these psychotic symptoms are often, though not always, trauma-related (48), and the relationship between trauma and psychosis is extraordinarily complex both causally and diagnostically (42, 43). Future research should aim to provide clearer guidance on how to safely and effectively address the mixture of trauma-related content and the content of delusions/hallucinations in treatment. In the meantime, practitioners should obtain collateral information to understand the temporal relationship between reported traumatic events and psychotic symptom development and conceptualize psychotic symptoms with trauma-related content as an indication that trauma-focused treatment, including psychoeducation about trauma, may be appropriate.

Limitations

A limitation of all studies utilizing the expert consensus method is that the opinion of experts may be wrong (29). As a result, it is recommended that practitioners consider the results of this study in conjunction with the results of existing and emerging literature on the treatment of comorbid early psychosis and trauma-related disorders. In addition, the outcomes associated with implementation of these preliminary clinical practice guidelines should be evaluated to determine whether they are efficacious and effective.

Additionally, the survey utilized in this study was anonymous to encourage participants to respond as honestly as possible about their personal and programmatic clinical decision-making and intervention practices in the course of treating individuals with comorbid early psychosis and trauma-related disorders. As a result, we were not able to evaluate potential differences between those individuals who were contacted and responded versus those who did not respond.

Finally, the response rate for this study (42%) is lower than the typical response rates of other expert consensus method studies; however, the number of participants included in this study ($N = 49$) is comparable (29). While the expert consensus method is appropriate for use with clinical experts, it has been used primarily with preselected groups of research experts, which tends to increase the response rate (29). To yield the larg est possible sample of respondents for this study, we consulted multiple published resources and available clinical and research experts and invited individuals from across the United States to participate. As research in this area increases, future endeavors to develop more comprehensive practice guidelines should include clinical and research experts in psychosis, as well as trauma, treatment to incorporate a variety of perspectives and sources of knowledge.

CONCLUSION

This study addresses a gap in the existing outcome literature on the treatment of comorbid early psychosis and trauma-related disorders by supplementing it with consensus evidence obtained from a national survey of clinical experts. The clinical experts reached consensus on 46 (94%) of the 49 expert consensus items. In areas where expert consensus existed, preliminary clinical practice guidelines for comorbid early psychosis and trauma-related disorders were offered. Recommendations for future research were also proposed in areas in which expert consensus did not exist.

Perhaps most important is what this study did not find: the clinical experts surveyed in this study did *not* rate the use of trauma-focused treatment, or any component intervention including exposure interventions, as inappropriate for individuals with comorbid early psychosis and trauma-related disorders under any condition. In contrast, the clinical experts agree that not treating early psychosis and trauma-related disorders when both conditions are present is inappropriate. As a result, practitioners should use existing research evidence, clinical expertise and judgment, and client preferences and values to treat comorbid early psychosis and trauma-related disorders in individuals presenting with both conditions (49).

AUTHOR CONTRIBUTIONS

CC contributed to conception and design of the study, acquired, analyzed, and interpreted these data, and drafted and revised the manuscript. MS, DB, and LT contributed to conception and design of the study, as well as to revisions of the manuscript. TN contributed to conception and design of the study, acquisition and interpretation of these data, and revisions of the manuscript. All authors approved the final version of the manuscript to be published. In addition, all authors agreed to be accountable for all aspects of the work, including ensuring that all questions related to the accuracy and integrity of the work are appropriately investigated and resolved.

ACKNOWLEDGMENTS

The content of this article first appeared in the dissertation of the first author (CC), submitted in partial fulfillment for the degree of Doctor of Psychology in the Department of Clinical Psychology at Antioch University New England. The authors thank William Slammon, Ph.D., Adjunct Faculty at Antioch University New England, for his feedback on the conception and design of the study provided as a dissertation committee member. The authors also thank Divya Kumar, Junior Specialist at the UC Davis Imaging Research Center, for assistance with managing data collection.

REFERENCES

1. Strakowski SM, Keck PE Jr, McElroy SL, Lonczak HS, West SA. Chronology of comorbid and principal syndromes in first-episode psychosis. *Compr Psychiatry* (1995) 36(2):106–12. doi:10.1016/S0010-440X(95)90104-3
2. Achim AM, Maziade M, Raymond E, Olivier D, Merette C, Roy M-A. How prevalent are anxiety disorders in schizophrenia? A meta-analysis and critical review on a significant association. *Schizophr Bull* (2011) 37(4):811–21. doi:10.1093/schbul/sbp148
3. de Bont PAJM, van Minnen A, de Jongh A. Treating PTSD in patients with psychosis: a within-group controlled feasibility study examining the efficacy and safety of evidence-based PE and EMDR protocols. *Behav Ther* (2013) 44:717–30. doi:10.1016/j.beth.2013.07.002

4. Grubaugh AL, Zinzow HM, Paul L, Egede LE, Frueh BC. Trauma exposure and posttraumatic stress disorder in adults with severe mental illness: a critical review. *Clin Psychol Rev* (2011) 31(6):883–99. doi:10.1016/j.cpr.2011.04.003
5. Kessler RC, Berglund P, Demler O, Jin R, Merikangas KR, Walters EE. Lifetime prevalence and age-of-onset distributions of DSM-IV disorders in the national comorbidity survey replication. *Arch Gen Psychiatry* (2005) 62(6):593–602. doi:10.1001/archpsyc.62.6.593
6. Ehlers A, Clark DM. A cognitive model of posttraumatic stress disorder. *Behav Res Ther* (2000) 38:319–45. doi:10.1016/S0005-7967(99)00123-0
7. Morrison AP, Frame L, Larkin W. Relationships between trauma and psychosis: a review and integration. *Br J Clin Psychol* (2003) 42:331–53. doi:10.1348/014466503322528892
8. Cohen JA, Bukstein O, Walter H, Benson SR, Chrisman A, Farchione TR, et al. Practice parameters for the assessment and treatment of children and adolescents with posttraumatic stress disorder. *J Am Acad Child Adolesc Psychiatry* (2010) 49(4):414–30. doi:10.1016/j.jaac.2009.12.020
9. Foa EB, Davidson JRT. The expert consensus guideline series: treatment of posttraumatic stress disorder. *J Clin Psychiatry* (1999) 60(16):3–76.
10. Frueh BC, Grubaugh AL, Cusack KJ, Kimble MO, Elhai JD, Knapp RG. Exposure-based cognitive behavioral treatment of PTSD in adults with schizophrenia or schizoaffective disorder: a pilot study. *J Anxiety Disord* (2009) 23(5):665–75. doi:10.1016/j.janxdis.2009.02.005
11. Mueser KT, Rosenberg SD, Xie H, Jankowski MK, Bolton EE, Lu W, et al. A randomized control trial of cognitive-behavioral treatment of posttraumatic stress disorder in severe mental illness. *J Consult Clin Psychol* (2008) 76(2):259–71. doi:10.1037/0022-006X.76.2.259
12. van den Berg DPG, van der Gaag M. Treating trauma in psychosis with EMDR: a pilot study. *J Behav Ther Exp Psychiatry* (2012) 43:664–71. doi:10.1016/j.jbtep.2011.09.011
13. Eisner E, Drake R, Barrowclough C. Assessing early signs of relapse in psychosis: review and future directions. *Clin Psychol Rev* (2013) 33(5):637–53. doi:10.1016/j.cpr.2013.04.001
14. Heinssen RK, Goldstein AB, Azrin ST. *Evidence-Based Treatments for First Episode Psychosis: Components of Coordinated Specialty Care*. National Institute of Mental Health (2014). Available from: http://www.nimh.nih.gov/health/topics/schizophrenia/raise/nimh-white-paper-csc-for-fep_147096.pdf
15. Program Directory of Early Psychosis Intervention Programs. *Foundation for Excellence in Mental Health Care [Internet]*. (2015). Available from: http://www.mentalhealthexcellence.org/wp-content/uploads/2013/08/Early-Psychosis-Intervention-Directory-011015.pdf
16. Program Directory of Early Psychosis Intervention Program. *Stanford Medicine [Internet]*. (2016). Available from: https://med.stanford.edu/content/dam/sm/peppnet/documents/PEPPNET_directory.html
17. van den Berg DPG, de Bont PAJM, van der Vleugel BM, de Roos C, de Jongh A, Van Minnen A, et al. Prolonged exposure vs eye movement desensitization and reprocessing vs waiting list for posttraumatic stress disorder in patients with a psychotic disorder: a randomized clinical trial. *JAMA Psychiatry* (2015) 3:259–67. doi:10.1001/jamapsychiatry.2014.2637
18. Steel C, Hardy A, Smith B, Wykes T, Rose S, Enright S, et al. Cognitive-behaviour therapy for post-traumatic stress in schizophrenia. A randomized controlled trial. *Psychol Med* (2017) 47:43–51. doi:10.1017/S0033291716002117
19. Woolf SH, Grol R, Hutchinson A, Eccles M, Grimshaw J. Clinical guidelines: potential benefits, limitations, and harms of clinical guidelines. *BMJ* (1999) 318:527–30. doi:10.1136/bmj.318.7182.527
20. *Translating Research into Practice (TRIP)-II: Fact Sheet*. Rockville, MD: Agency for Healthcare Research and Quality (2001). Available from: http://archive.ahrq.gov/research/findings/factsheets/translating/tripfac/trip2fac.html
21. Kahn DA, Docherty JP, Carpenter D, Frances A. Consensus methods in practice guideline development: a review and description of a new method. *Psychopharmacol Bull* (1997) 33(4):631–9.
22. Alexopoulous GS, Jeste DV, Chung H, Carpenter D, Ross R, Docherty JP. The expert consensus guideline series. Treatment of dementia and its behavioral disturbances: methods, commentary, and summary. *Postgrad Med* (2005):6–22.
23. Frances A, Docherty JP, Kahn DA. Treatment of obsessive-compulsive disorder. *J Clin Psychiatry* (1997) 58(4):5–72.
24. Sachs GS, Printz DJ, Kahn DA, Carpenter D, Docherty JP. The expert consensus guideline series: medication treatment of bipolar disorder. *Postgrad Med* (2000):1–104.
25. McEvoy JP, Scheifler PL, Frances A. The expert consensus guideline series: treatment of schizophrenia. *J Clin Psychiatry* (1999) 60(11):4–80.
26. Cloitre M, Courtois CA, Charuvastra A, Carapezza R, Stolbach BC, Green BL. Treatment of complex PTSD: results of the ISTSS expert clinician survey on best practices. *J Trauma Stress* (2011) 24(6):615–27. doi:10.1002/jts.20697
27. Worldwide Early Diagnosis & Treatment Centers for Psychosis & Schizophrenia. (2010). Available from: http://www.schizophrenia.com/earlypsychosis.htm
28. Early Psychosis Treatment Program (U.S.). (2014). Available from: https://www.thenationalcouncil.org/topics/first-episode-psychosis/
29. Frances A, Kahn DA, Carpenter D, Ross R, Docherty JP. The expert consensus practice guideline project: a new method of establishing best practice. *J Pract Psychiatr Behav Health* (1996) 2:295–306.
30. Thomas DR. A general inductive approach for analyzing qualitative evaluation data. *Am J Eval* (2006) 27(2):237–46. doi:10.1177/1098214005283748
31. Becker C, Zayfert C, Anderson E. A survey of psychologists' attitudes towards and utilization of exposure therapy for PTSD. *Behav Res Ther* (2004) 42:277–92. doi:10.1016/S0005-7967(03)00138-4
32. Litz BT, Blake DD, Gerardi RG, Keane TM. Decision making guidelines for the use of direct therapeutic exposure in the treatment of post-traumatic stress disorder. *Behav Ther* (1990) 13(4):91–3.
33. Ronconi JM, Shiner B, Watts BV. Inclusion and exclusion criteria in randomized control trials of psychotherapy for PTSD. *J Psychiatr Pract* (2014) 20(1):25–37. doi:10.1097/01.pra.0000442936.23457.5b
34. Dixon LB, Dickerson F, Bellack AS, Bennett M, Dickinson D, Goldberg RW, et al. The 2009 schizophrenia PORT psychosocial treatment recommendations and summary statements. *Schizophr Bull* (2010) 36(1):48–70. doi:10.1093/schbul/sbp115
35. Dixon LB, Goldman HH, Bennett ME, Wang Y, McNamara KA, Mendon SJ, et al. Implementing coordinated specialty care for early psychosis: the RAISE connection program. *Psychiatr Serv* (2015) 66(7):691–8. doi:10.1176/appi.ps.201400281
36. Ince P, Haddock G, Tai S. A systematic review of the implementation of recommended psychological interventions for schizophrenia: rates, barriers, and improvement strategies. *Psychol Psychother* (2016) 89(3):324–50. doi:10.1111/papt.12084
37. Awad AG, Voruganti LN. The burden of schizophrenia on caregivers: a review. *Pharmacoeconomics* (2008) 26(2):149–62. doi:10.2165/00019053-200826020-00005
38. Dixon L. Providing services to families of persons with schizophrenia: present and future. *J Ment Health Policy Econ* (1999) 2(1):3–8. doi:10.1002/(SICI)1099-176X(199903)2:1<3::AID-MHP31>3.0.CO;2-0
39. Mueser KT, Noordsy DL, Drake RE, Fox L. *Integrated Treatment for Dual Disorders: A Guide to Effective Practice*. New York, NY: The Guilford Press (2003).
40. Morrison AP, Renton JC, Dunn H, Williams S, Bentall RP. *Cognitive Therapy for Psychosis: A Formulation-Based Approach*. New York, NY: Brunner-Routledge (2004).
41. Ogden P, Minton K. Sensorimotor psychotherapy: one method for processing traumatic memory. *Traumatology* (2000) 6(3):149–73. doi:10.1177/153476560000600302
42. Walker EF, Diforio D. Schizophrenia: a neural diathesis-stress model. *Psychol Rev* (1997) 104(4):667–85. doi:10.1037/0033-295X.104.4.667
43. Read J, Fosse R, Moskowitz A, Perry B. The traumagenic neurodevelopmental model of psychosis revisited. *Neuropsychiatry* (2014) 4(1):65–79. doi:10.2217/npy.13.89
44. Jadidi J, Mirshoja MS. The impact of the sensory integration approach on positive and negative symptoms in a patient with non-paranoid schizophrenia: a case report. *Middle East J Rehabil Health* (2016) 3(2):e33275. doi:10.17795/mejrh-33275
45. Helgason C, Sarris J. Mind-body medicine for schizophrenia and psychotic disorders: a review of the evidence. *Clin Schizophr Relat Psychoses* (2013) 7(3):138–48. doi:10.3371/CSRP.HESA.020813

46. David D, Kutcher GS, Jackson EI, Mellman TA. Psychotic symptoms in combat-related posttraumatic stress disorder. *J Clin Psychiatry* (1999) 60(1):29–32. doi:10.4088/JCP.v60n0106
47. Hamner MB, Frueh C, Ulmer HG, Huber MG, Twomey BS, Tyson C, et al. Psychotic features in chronic posttraumatic stress disorder and schizophrenia. *J Nerv Ment Dis* (2000) 188(4):217–21. doi:10.1097/00005053-200004000-00004
48. Hamner MB, Frueh BC, Ulmer HG, Arana GW. Psychotic features and illness severity in combat veterans with chronic posttraumatic stress disorder. *Biol Psychiatry* (1999) 45(7):846–52. doi:10.1016/S0006-3223(98)00301-1
49. Melchert TM. *Biopsychosocial Practice: A Science-Based Framework for Behavioral Health Care*. Washington, DC: American Psychological Association (2015).

7

Longitudinal Associations between Posttraumatic Stress Disorder Severity and Personality Disorder Features among Female Rape Survivors

Michelle J. Bovin[1,2], Erika J. Wolf[1,2] and Patricia A. Resick[3]*

[1] VA National Center for PTSD, Boston, MA, USA, [2] Boston University School of Medicine, Boston, MA, USA, [3] Duke University Medical Center, Durham, NC, USA

Edited by:
Kate Hardy,
Stanford University, USA

Reviewed by:
Diane Carol Gooding,
University of Wisconsin-Madison, USA
Yuqing Zhang,
Chinese Academy of Sciences, China
Jennie Kuckertz,
University of California San Diego, USA

***Correspondence:**
Michelle J. Bovin
michelle.bovin@va.gov

This study evaluated how change in posttraumatic stress disorder (PTSD) symptoms was associated with residualized change in comorbid personality disorder (PD) features and *vice versa* over the course of 5–10 years. The sample was comprised of 79 female rape survivors who met criteria for PTSD and who were a part of a larger study examining the effects of trauma-focused therapy. PTSD was assessed with the fourth edition of the *Diagnostic and Statistical Manual of Mental Disorders* (DSM-IV) version of the Clinician-Administered PTSD Scale [CAPS-IV (1)] and PD features were assessed with the DSM-IV dimensional PD scales on the Schedule for Non-adaptive and Adaptive Personality [SNAP (2)]. PTSD symptom severity and PD features were assessed at baseline and between 5 and 10 years after completing treatment. Multiple regression analyses revealed that PTSD symptom change was related to residualized change in PD severity for paranoid, schizotypal, antisocial, borderline, avoidant, and dependent PD (βs ranged from −0.23 to −0.33; all $ps < 0.05$). In addition, for borderline and antisocial PDs, longitudinal stability of the PD was attenuated among those with greater PTSD symptom improvement (i.e., the relationship between these PDs over time was altered as a function of PTSD symptom change; βs ranged from −0.27 to −0.29; all $ps < 0.05$). Similarly, change in severity of paranoid, schizotypal, antisocial, avoidant, and obsessive–compulsive (OC) PD was associated with residualized change in PTSD symptoms (βs ranged from −0.32 to −0.41; all $ps < 0.05$), and the longitudinal stability of PTSD was attenuated as a product of change in OC PD ($\beta = -0.27$; $p < 0.02$). These findings suggest that these two sets of disorders may impact one another substantially, altering the course of even chronic, characterological conditions. This carries important clinical implications for the treatment of both PTSD and PDs.

Keywords: PTSD, personality disorders, trauma, longitudinal, rape

INTRODUCTION

Posttraumatic stress disorder (PTSD) is highly comorbid with a range of other mental health disorders. In fact, Brown et al. (3) found that of the anxiety and mood disorders, PTSD had the highest prevalence and most diverse pattern of comorbid psychopathology. Similarly, in the National Comorbidity Study, Kessler et al. (4) found that PTSD was associated with increased odds of being diagnosed with a mood disorder, an anxiety disorder, alcohol/drug abuse or dependence, and conduct disorder (4). More recent research has identified a link between psychosis and PTSD, with estimates suggesting that the prevalence of PTSD in people with psychotic disorders ranges from 12 to 29% (5, 6).

Posttraumatic stress disorder is also highly comorbid with many personality disorders (PDs). In a national epidemiological survey, Pietrzak et al. (7) found that 50% of individuals with PTSD also met criteria for at least one PD. Further, in a sample of male combat Veterans with PTSD, Dunn and her colleagues (8) found that more than 45% met criteria for at least one PD, and more than 16% met criteria for two or more PDs.

Traditionally, PDs have been conceptualized as stable and unresponsive to treatment. According to the fourth edition of the *Diagnostic and Statistical Manual of Mental Disorders* [DSM-IV (9); the version of the manual most relevant to this manuscript, although this definition has been preserved in DSM-5], a PD is "an enduring pattern of inner experience and behavior that ... is *pervasive and inflexible* ... is *stable over time*, and leads to distress or impairment," [p. 629; italics added (9)]. Recent studies have offered greater optimism about the course of PDs, suggesting that PD features can improve both over time and in response to treatment (10, 11). Consistent with this, in a study designed to examine the association between PTSD treatment and change in PDs, Markowitz and his colleagues (12) found that after a short course of trauma-focused therapy, 43% of participants lost their PD diagnosis by the end of treatment. There was no association between PTSD change and PD change explicitly, which they hypothesized could be due to a limited sample size (only 35 participants had a PD at baseline), the range of PDs excluded (i.e., participants who met criteria for borderline, antisocial, schizoid, and schizotypal PD at baseline), and/or the broad level of PD improvement. However, they did find that 56% of patients with PTSD and a comorbid PD who responded to the intervention [i.e., ≥30% Clinician-Administered PTSD Scale (CAPS) improvement] lost their PD diagnosis by the 26-week follow-up. Because of the small sample size and range of PDs excluded, it is unclear whether Markowitz et al.'s results generalize to the full range of PDs or if differential patterns of co-occurring change might emerge across specific PDs.

In addition to the limited body of research focused on how PTSD change affects PDs over time, a similarly small number of studies have examined the comparable question regarding how PDs might affect PTSD change over time. The studies that do exist have focused on the predictive value of PDs at baseline on PTSD change; in general, they have suggested that PDs do not interfere with changes in PTSD [e.g., Ref. (13, 14)]. However, these studies have not tended to evaluate how PD *change* (as opposed to baseline PD features) may relate to PTSD change over time.

Despite the lack of empirical attention, there is reason to suspect co-occurring change in PTSD and PDs. Research has suggested that PTSD and PDs may share an underlying vulnerability that may contribute to both disorders. Specifically, trait negative emotionality (NEM; reflecting a tendency toward negative affect and generalized distress that is rooted in temperament) has been identified as the primary risk factor for the development of PTSD and its comorbidities [e.g., Ref. (15–17)], and may underlie a range of posttraumatic psychopathology (18), including PDs (19). Therefore, it is possible that co-occurring symptom reductions in PTSD and PD could arise from decreases in this shared underlying vulnerability. It is also possible that in response to trauma, repeated victimization, and avoidant behavior, people develop overgeneralized patterns of behavior and thinking that is diagnosed as a PD (20), but may more accurately reflect trauma-related psychopathology.

The purpose of this study was to examine how changes in PTSD and PD severity covary over time. To investigate this question, we conducted secondary data analyses on existing data from a treatment trial conducted by Resick et al. (21), comparing cognitive processing therapy (CPT) and prolonged exposure (PE) for the treatment of chronic PTSD in female rape survivors. We examined the baseline data from the trial as well as the long-term follow-up (LTFU) data collected 5–10 years after treatment (22). Previously published research from this trial found that PTSD symptoms decreased significantly as the result of trauma-focused therapy (21), and therefore, this dataset provided an excellent opportunity to examine the covariation of change in PTSD severity and PDs. We hypothesized that PD features would decrease in severity (as operationalized by a residualized change score variable, see below) among those with the greatest PTSD change (e.g., co-occurring symptom amelioration), and that the longitudinal stability of PD features would be attenuated in individuals who experienced the greatest amount of PTSD symptom improvement. That is, PD features, which are traditionally thought to be stable and intractable (9), may become less stable given PTSD symptom improvement. With respect to the related question of how PD changes are associated with PTSD changes, we similarly hypothesized that reductions in PD severity would predict decreases in PTSD severity (again operationalized as a residualized change score) and that the longitudinal stability of PTSD severity (23, 24) would be attenuated in individuals who experienced the greatest amount of PD symptom improvement. We did not make specific hypotheses about differential patterns of change as a function of each specific PD, but generally thought that PDs with greater saturation with underlying NEM would evidence the greatest co-occurring change.

PARTICIPANTS AND METHODS

Participants

Participants had experienced at least one completed rape and met full DSM-IV PTSD criteria. Treatment trial exclusion criteria included current substance dependence, illiteracy, suicidal/homicidal intent or parasuicidal behavior, psychosis, involvement in an abusive relationship, and being stalked. There were 171 participants in the original intent-to-treat sample. Of these, 79 participants had complete data on all variables of interest for this study. Participants who were excluded from the current study did not differ from those included on age ($t = 0.33$; $p > 0.05$), education ($t = 0.32$; $p > 0.05$), race ($\chi^2 = 3.05$; $p > 0.05$), or baseline PTSD severity or PD scores (all *ts* < 1.86; all *ps* > 0.05). The 79 participants ranged in age from 18 to 55 years (M = 31.7; SD = 9.6); 70% self-reported as Caucasian, 27% African-American, and 3% other. Participants reported 10–24 years of education (M = 14.3; SD = 2.3). Of the 79 included participants, 38 were randomly assigned to receive CPT and 41 to PE. This was a highly traumatized sample. In addition to experiencing at least one completed rape, the prevalence of additional trauma exposure in the sample was as follows: 39% (*n* = 31) reported childhood sexual abuse; 24% (*n* = 29) witnessed or learned of a criminal or vehicular homicide of a close friend or family member; 15% (*n* = 12) reported being the victim of attempted murder; 18% (*n* = 14) reported being robbed; 21% (*n* = 17) reported being kidnapped; 19% (*n* = 15) reported serious physical assault; and 53% (*n* = 42) reported experiencing at least one other rape (in addition to the index event).

Procedure

Data for the current study were collected as part of a larger randomized controlled trial (21). All participants received either CPT or PE. Approximately 5–10 years later (M = 6.03 years, SD = 0.93 years), participants were re-contacted and asked to complete the same measures as at baseline. Institutional Review Board approval was secured for all phases of the study.

Measures

The Clinician-Administered PTSD Scale for DSM-IV [CAPS-IV (1)] is a reliable and valid structured diagnostic interview that assesses DSM-IV PTSD severity and diagnosis. For each symptom, a clinician rates two dimensions, frequency and intensity, on separate five-point scales; these scales can be combined across items to form a total PTSD severity score, which was used in this study. Interrater reliability for total PTSD symptom severity was 0.97 for baseline and 0.94 for LTFU.

The Schedule for Non-adaptive and Adaptive Personality [SNAP (2)] is a personality inventory comprised of validity scales, temperament and trait scales, and 13 PD scales with dichotomous (diagnostic) and dimensional scoring options. Ten scales reflect DSM-IV PD criteria. The dimensional scores for these 10 PD scales were used in analyses because prior work suggests that they are internally consistent and relate well to interview-based PD assessments; the dichotomous scores show weaker associations with these assessments (2, 25). Further, the long-term rank-order stability (i.e., correlation) of the dimensional scores is strong [mean 2-year PD severity correlation = 0.69 (26)], even with declining group mean levels over time, suggesting that these scales tend to be stable and reliable over time. We also chose to focus on the dimensional scores rather than the diagnostic scores because this approach is more aligned with research supporting the dimensionality of PDs (25, 27, 28).

At the LTFU visit, we assessed additional treatment completed after the trial with a single yes/no question: "Have you received more therapy since you completed our program?"

Data Analysis

First, we examined group mean changes for PDs and PTSD by comparing baseline and LTFU SNAP and CAPS scores using paired-sample *t*-tests. In addition, we conducted correlational analyses to examine how PD feature scores at each time point were associated with each other as well as with the CAPS severity scores at both time points.

To test our first hypothesis, that individuals who experienced improvement in PTSD symptoms also demonstrated reductions in PD features, we ran 10 hierarchical multiple regression analyses (1 for each PD). Each regression had five steps with the LTFU PD score as the dependent variable and the following variables entered into each step of the equation as predictors: (1) SNAP baseline PD score; (2) treatment completer status (0 = *did not complete treatment*; 1 = *completed treatment*); (3) CAPS change score (baseline-LTFU); (4) interaction of baseline PD × CAPS change; and (5) additional treatment received after study completion (0 = *no additional treatment received*; 1 = *additional treatment received*). In these analyses, the dependent variable is an index of residualized change in each PD. Residualized change scores (29, 30) are common in the research literature [e.g., Ref. (31–34)]. They reflect residual variance in the dependent variable that is not predicted by the same variable measured at an earlier time point. In other words, when there is either positive or negative residual variance in the dependent variable, this reflects increased or decreased level of the dependent variable, respectively.

Step 1 allowed for evaluation of the longitudinal stability of the PD features and controlled for baseline PD scores in subsequent steps, with a positive sign indicating that higher PD feature scores at baseline were associated with higher PD feature scores at LTFU. Step 2 controlled for the effect of treatment completion to separate variance associated with therapy completion from that associated with symptom change. Treatment completion was entered at Step 2 because we wanted to first account for variance attributable to completion of the study and then determine the extent to which PTSD symptom change accounted for additional variance beyond that attributable to simply completing the study. For this step, a negative sign indicated that completer status was associated with decreases in PD at LTFU. Step 3 tested the main effect of PTSD change on residualized change in LTFU PD features. In other words, this step examined if greater PTSD symptom improvement was associated with less PD severity at LTFU when baseline levels of the PD were held constant at the sample mean. For this step, a negative sign indicated that more PTSD symptom reduction was associated with lower LTFU PD feature scores. Step 4 tested if PTSD change moderated the relationship between baseline and LTFU PD scores. That is, this step examined if the longitudinal stability of PDs was attenuated among those with the greatest PTSD symptom improvement. This step effectively begins to look at subgroups within the sample by examining if there are different slopes for the longitudinal PD association as a function of degree of PTSD change. A negative sign for this step suggested that the stability of the LTFU PD was attenuated as a product of greater PTSD reduction. Step 5 tested whether additional treatment received after the treatment phase of the study added additional variance to the model. This was entered as the last step to reflect the temporal ordering of the variables since this variable captured variance from the end of the treatment trial to the LTFU. For this step, a positive sign indicated that individuals engaged in additional treatment after the trial phase of the study had higher LTFU PD feature scores.

We followed the same analytic approach to test our second and complementary hypothesis, that individuals who demonstrate a reduction in PD features also demonstrate decreases in PTSD symptoms (as indexed by residualized change scores), in 10 hierarchical multiple regression analyses (one for each PD). As before, each regression had five steps: (1) CAPS baseline severity score; (2) treatment completer status; (3) PD change score (baseline-LTFU); (4) interaction of baseline CAPS × PD change; and (5) additional treatment received after study completion. Interpretation of these regression coefficients mirrored those described above, with the exception being that these related to LTFU PTSD scores (not PDs).

For both sets of analyses, we used Holm (35) correction for the overall *F*-test to protect against type I error given the 10 regressions (one for each PD) conducted in each set of analyses. Effect size was evaluated by calculating Cohen's (36) f^2 (0.02 = small, 0.15 = medium, 0.35 = large). Prior to conducting hypothesis testing, we centered all predictors included in interaction terms to avoid concerns related to multicollinearity and inflated standardized effect size estimates.

RESULTS

Descriptive statistics for the CAPS and PD scales, and *t*-tests examining group mean changes over time, are presented in **Table 1**. Correlational analyses are presented in **Table 2**. Before proceeding with our planned analyses, we explored the potential effect of treatment type. We compared means for the two treatments at baseline and LTFU; participants who received CPT versus PE did not differ on baseline (all $ts < 1.90$; all $ps > 0.15$) or LTFU (all $ts < 1.70$; all $ps > 0.05$) CAPS or PD scores in these 79 subjects. Therefore, we collapsed the data across treatment type for all subsequent analyses.

TABLE 1 | Baseline and LTFU posttraumatic stress disorder symptom severity scores and personality disorder feature scores.

Variable	Time point				*t*-Test *t* (df)
	Baseline		LTFU		
	(*n* = 79)				
	M	SD	M	SD	
CAPS	77.15	19.61	26.33	24.31	17.40 (78)**
SNAP					
Paranoid	13.77	4.89	8.79	5.59	9.18 (78)**
Schizoid	7.10	3.17	5.70	3.40	4.26 (78)**
Schizotypal	12.19	4.29	8.32	4.94	7.46 (78)**
Antisocial	8.97	5.44	7.57	5.25	3.04 (78)**
Borderline	11.81	4.85	8.24	5.83	6.06 (78)**
Histrionic	8.94	4.19	7.67	3.69	3.43 (78)**
Narcissistic	9.30	3.92	7.27	3.67	5.18 (78)**
Avoidant	11.11	3.76	8.33	4.48	5.86 (78)**
Dependent	9.89	4.68	6.35	4.16	7.81 (78)**
OC	12.85	3.23	10.81	3.74	5.62 (78)**

LTFU, long-term follow-up; CAPS, Clinician-Administered PTSD Scale; SNAP, Schedule for Non-adaptive and Adaptive Personality; OC, obsessive–compulsive.
$^{**}p < 0.01$.

Predicting LTFU PDs

Next, we evaluated if change in PTSD severity was associated with residualized change in PD features in 10 separate regressions. For all regressions, the overall *F*-test met the adjusted Holm criterion for statistical significance (all $ps < 0.005$). In each equation, baseline PD significantly predicted LTFU PD with large effect sizes (all ($f^2 > 0.30$; **Table 3**), indicating substantial stability. Completion of treatment added a small amount of incremental variance to the prediction of residualized change in LTFU paranoid ($f^2 = 0.06$), schizotypal ($f^2 = 0.05$), and obsessive–compulsive (OC) PD ($f^2 = 0.04$; **Table 3**), suggesting that completing a course of trauma-focused therapy was associated with decreased PD features at LTFU. Change in CAPS scores added significant incremental variance to the prediction of LTFU paranoid ($f^2 = 0.09$), schizotypal ($f^2 = 0.12$), antisocial ($f^2 = 0.05$), borderline ($f^2 = 0.06$), avoidant ($f^2 = 0.09$), and dependent PD ($f^2 = 0.09$; **Table 3**), suggesting that PTSD symptom reductions were associated with residualized change (reductions) in these PDs (and similarly, PTSD symptom increases were associated with PD increases).

The interaction between baseline PD features and CAPS change added incremental variance in Step 4 to the prediction of LTFU antisocial ($f^2 = 0.09$) and borderline PD ($f^2 = 0.07$; **Table 3**). To depict these interactions, we plotted the association between PD at baseline and LTFU as a function of change in CAPS. Degree of CAPS change was defined by a median split on the CAPS difference score for the purposes of the figures (**Figures 1** and **2**). These figures show that participants with greater decreases on the CAPS evidenced sharper declines in PD features over time (i.e., the substantial stability of PD features evident from the results of Step 1 of the equation was attenuated for individuals who achieved greater PTSD improvement). These figures also show the stability (i.e., slope) of borderline and antisocial PD change as a function of CAPS change in comparison to the average stability of these PDs over time (shown in red). Results indicated that additional treatment after completion of the study treatment protocol resulted in small but significant increases in variance explained in LTFU schizotypal ($f^2 = 0.04$) and borderline PD ($f^2 = 0.03$; **Table 3**), such that participants who sought additional treatment had higher LTFU PD scores than those who did not.

In summary, this set of analyses revealed that greater PTSD symptom improvement was associated with greater residualized change (symptom improvement) in paranoid, schizotypal, antisocial, borderline, avoidant, and dependent PDs. Further, results revealed that for borderline and antisocial PD, the stability of the PD was not uniform across subjects, but rather, there were different slopes for the longitudinal PD association that differed by the degree of PTSD change.

Predicting LTFU PTSD

We next evaluated if change in PD features was associated with residualized change (e.g., improvements) in PTSD severity in

TABLE 2 | Correlations between baseline and LTFU posttraumatic stress disorder symptom severity scores and personality disorder scores (n = 79).

Variable	CAPS-IV	Paranoid	Schizoid	Schizotypal	Antisocial	Borderline	Histrionic	Narcissistic	Avoidant	Dependent	OC
CAPS-IV		0.37**	0.22	0.42**	0.25*	0.28*	0.15	0.22	0.28*	0.30**	0.19
Paranoid	0.14		0.62**	0.87**	0.51**	0.70**	0.15	0.58**	0.72**	0.44**	0.59**
Schizoid	−0.10	0.22		0.69**	0.27*	0.37*	−0.34**	0.18	0.76**	0.05	0.35*
Schizotypal	0.13	0.68**	0.47**		0.52**	0.68**	0.08	0.55**	0.74**	0.42**	0.53**
Antisocial	0.15	0.29**	−0.04	0.42**		0.72**	0.50**	0.58**	0.25*	0.51**	0.24*
Borderline	0.36**	0.42**	0.01	0.48**	0.64**		0.35**	0.57**	0.53**	0.66**	0.49**
Histrionic	0.26*	0.16	−0.46**	0.06	0.51**	0.46**		0.55**	−0.24*	0.37**	0.15
Narcissistic	0.01	0.45**	−0.11	0.43**	0.58**	0.46**	0.60**		0.21	0.36**	0.52**
Avoidant	0.09	0.47**	0.70**	0.49**	−0.04	0.22*	−0.44**	−0.10		0.33**	0.48**
Dependent	0.35**	0.12	−0.32**	0.08	0.17	0.49**	0.39**	0.05	0.02		0.21
OC	0.10	0.53**	0.26**	0.34**	0.03	0.27*	−0.06	0.21	0.52**	−0.05	

The lower triangle reflects correlations from baseline assessments and the upper triangle reflects correlations from the LTFU assessments. LTFU, long-term follow-up; OC, obsessive–compulsive; CAPS-IV, Clinician-Administered PTSD Scale for DSM-IV.

*$p < 0.05$.

**$p < 0.001$.

10 separate regressions.[1] Five of the overall F-tests did not meet the Holm criterion for statistical significance and were therefore not interpreted.[2] In each of the five equations that were interpretable (i.e., those involving paranoid, schizotypal, antisocial, avoidant, and OC PD), baseline CAPS significantly predicted LTFU CAPS (f^2 = 0.06; **Table 4**). By contrast, completion of treatment, entered in Step 2, did not add significant incremental value to any of the models (all $ps > 0.05$). However, changes in all five of these PDs (all $f^2 > 0.10$) added significant incremental variance to the prediction of LTFU CAPS. These results suggest that in these five analyses, PD change covaried with residualized PTSD change.

The interaction between baseline CAPS and change in OC PD features (f^2 = 0.07) added significant incremental variance to the prediction of LTFU CAPS (**Table 4**). To depict this interaction, we plotted the association between baseline and LTFU PTSD symptom severity as a function of change in OC PD. Degree of PD change was defined for the purposes of the figure, by a median split on the OC PD difference score (**Figure 3**). The figure shows that individuals with greater decreases on OC PD evidenced greater residualized change (e.g., sharper declines) in PTSD severity over time. Specifically, the association between baseline and LTFU CAPS was attenuated for those who demonstrated the greatest OC PD improvement. The differential strength of association between PTSD at baseline and LTFU as a function of OC PD change can be viewed in contrast to the average stability of PTSD over time (shown by the red line in **Figure 3**). Results from Step 5 of the equations indicated that receiving additional treatment after completion of the study treatment protocol did not improve prediction of LTFU CAPS severity in any of the models (**Table 4**).

In summary, this set of analyses revealed that decreases in features of paranoid, schizotypal, antisocial, avoidant, and OC PD were associated with greater residualized change (decreased severity) in PTSD. Beyond this, the average stability of PTSD symptoms over time was altered as a function of the degree of change in OC PD features, with subjects who showed greater decreases in this PD also demonstrating reduced PTSD stability over time.

DISCUSSION

To our knowledge, the current study is the first to examine associations between PTSD and PD symptom change over the long-term and to do so for all 10 DSM-IV PDs. To explore these associations, we conducted two sets of analyses. Our first set of analyses examined how change in PTSD severity was associated with residualized change in PD severity. We found that change in PTSD severity correlated with PD scores at LTFU for six of the PDs (paranoid, schizotypal, antisocial, borderline, avoidant, and dependent), even after controlling for baseline levels of these PDs. This association implies that PTSD change was associated with residualized change in these six PDs such that improvements in PTSD covaried with reductions in each PD. This extends the work of Markowitz et al. (12) in that our results suggest that PTSD change is associated with PD change, and that participation in trauma-focused therapy is associated with decreases across a range of PDs (i.e., lower scores than what would be predicted based on baseline level of PD). These findings are particularly important because the treatments given were brief with only 13 hours of therapist contact in total conducted twice a week.

Interestingly, five of the six PDs (paranoid, schizotypal, antisocial, borderline, and dependent) that were significantly associated with change in PTSD severity in this study have been previously shown to be strongly related to trait NEM (19). The sixth PD, avoidant PD, is thought to have equivalent associations with NEM and trait positive emotionality [PEM; i.e., a tendency towards positive affect and social closeness (25)]. This suggests

[1] An initial examination of the data suggested the existence of a number of potential outliers. We tested for multivariate outliers using leverage tests and found that five participants had leverage values that were more than 2 SDs above the mean. These five participants were therefore excluded from all subsequent analyses.

[2] For these analyses, the most significant test needed to surpass adjusted $p < 0.005$ (0.05/10) and the least significant test needed to surpass $p < 0.05$ (0.05/1). Overall model p-values for histrionic, narcissistic, dependent, borderline, and schizoid PDs did not meet these thresholds, though results are reported in **Table 4** for completeness. For the remaining five analyses, the overall model surpassed the intervening adjusted p-value thresholds (all $ps < 0.004$).

TABLE 3 | Hierarchical linear regression analyses predicting change in PD features as a function of change in posttraumatic stress disorder.

PD	Predictor				
	Step 1 **Baseline PD**	**Step 2** **Tx completer**	**Step 3** **CAPS Δ**	**Step 4** **Baseline PD × CAPS Δ**	**Step 5** **Additional Tx**
Paranoid					
ΔR^2	0.34**	0.06**	0.09**	0.01	0.01
β	0.58**	−0.24**	−0.29**	−0.08	0.19
B (SE)	0.67 (0.11)	−2.83 (1.06)	−0.06 (0.02)	−0.00 (0.00)	1.29 (0.98)
(CI)	(0.46–0.88)	(−4.94 to −0.72)	(−0.10 to −0.03)	(−0.01 to 0.00)	(−0.66 to 3.23)
Schizoid					
ΔR^2	0.36**	0.02	0.03	0.01	0.00
β	0.60**	−0.15	−0.16	−0.11	0.05
B (SE)	0.65 (0.10)	−1.06 (0.66)	−0.02 (0.01)	−0.00 (0.00)	0.36 (0.63)
(CI)	(0.45–0.84)	(−2.36 to 0.25)	(−0.04 to 0.00)	(−0.01 to 0.00)	(−0.90 to 1.62)
Schizotypal					
ΔR^2	0.26**	0.04*	0.11**	0.02	0.04*
β	0.51**	−0.22*	−0.33**	−0.14	0.20*
B (SE)	0.59 (0.11)	−2.25 (1.04)	−0.06 (0.02)	−0.01 (0.00)	2.04 (0.90)
(CI)	(0.36–0.81)	(−4.31 to −0.19)	(−0.10 to −0.03)	(−0.02 to 0.00)	(0.25–3.83)
Antisocial					
ΔR^2	0.50**	0.01	0.05**	0.08**	0.01
β	0.71**	−0.12	−0.23**	−0.29**	0.08
B (SE)	0.68 (0.08)	−1.29 (0.91)	−0.05 (0.02)	−0.01 (0.00)	0.89 (0.82)
(CI)	(0.52–0.84)	(−3.11 to 0.53)	(−0.08 to −0.02)	(−0.02 to −0.01)	(−0.75 to 2.52)
Borderline					
ΔR^2	0.28**	0.02	0.06**	0.07**	0.03*
β	0.53**	−0.13	−0.25**	−0.27**	0.19*
B (SE)	0.64 (0.12)	−1.59 (1.19)	−0.06 (0.02)	−0.01 (0.01)	2.27 (1.07)
(CI)	(0.41–0.87)	(−3.96 to 0.79)	(−0.10 to −0.01)	(−0.02 to −0.01)	(0.14–4.41)
Histrionic					
ΔR^2	0.44**	0.01	0.00	0.00	0.00
β	0.66**	−0.10	−0.03	0.04	−0.03
B (SE)	0.58 (0.08)	−0.75 (0.67)	−0.00 (0.01)	0.00 (0.00)	−0.26 (0.70)
(CI)	(0.43–0.73)	(−2.08 to 0.58)	(−0.03 to 0.02)	(−0.01 to 0.01)	(−1.65 to 1.12)
Narcissistic					
ΔR^2	0.33**	0.00	0.03	0.01	0.00
β	0.58**	−0.05	−0.18	0.07	0.07
B (SE)	0.54 (0.09)	−0.40 (0.73)	−0.03 (0.01)	0.00 (0.00)	0.51 (0.75)
(CI)	(0.37–0.71)	(−1.85 to 1.04)	(−0.05 to 0.00)	(−0.00 to 0.01)	(−0.99 to 2.01)
Avoidant					
ΔR^2	0.24**	0.01	0.08**	0.02	0.01
β	0.49**	−0.11	−0.29**	−0.15	0.12
B (SE)	0.58 (0.12)	−1.06 (0.95)	−0.05 (0.02)	−0.01 (0.01)	1.14 (0.88)
(CI)	(0.34–0.82)	(−2.95 to 0.84)	(−0.08 to −0.02)	(−0.02 to 0.00)	(−0.63 to 2.90)
Dependent					
ΔR^2	0.35**	0.03	0.09**	0.00	0.01
β	0.59**	−0.16	−0.30**	−0.05	0.08
B (SE)	0.53 (0.08)	−1.39 (0.80)	−0.05 (0.01)	−0.00 (0.00)	0.65 (0.74)
(CI)	(0.36–0.69)	(−2.98 to 0.20)	(−0.08 to −0.02)	(−0.01 to 0.00)	(−0.83 to 2.13)
OC					
ΔR^2	0.34**	0.04*	0.02	0.00	0.01
β	0.58**	−0.19*	−0.14	−0.01	0.08
B (SE)	0.67 (0.11)	−1.53 (0.73)	−0.02 (0.01)	0.00 (0.00)	0.63 (0.72)
(CI)	(0.46–0.88)	(−2.98 to −0.07)	(−0.05 to 0.01)	(−0.01 to 0.01)	(−0.80 to 2.06)

PD, personality disorder; CAPS, Clinician-Administered PTSD Scale; Tx, treatment; OC, obsessive–compulsive; ΔR^2, R-squared change; β, standardized beta; B, unstandardized beta; CI, 95% confidence interval for B. All overall F-tests were significant using Holm's adjusted p-value thresholds (all Fs > 8.47; all ps < 0.001).
For illustrative purposes, only the final variable added to each step is displayed in the table. The dependent variable for each regression was the respective long-term follow-up PD feature score. PDs are listed in the first column, as opposed to the top row (which might be more typical) due to space considerations.
$^*p < 0.05$.
$^{**}p < 0.01$.

that the co-occurring reductions in PTSD symptom severity and these five PDs may be related to more general decreases in trait NEM which would be expected to broadly influence the expression and severity of these disorders. By contrast, three of the four PDs that were not predicted by changes in PTSD severity (schizoid, histrionic, and narcissistic PD) are most strongly

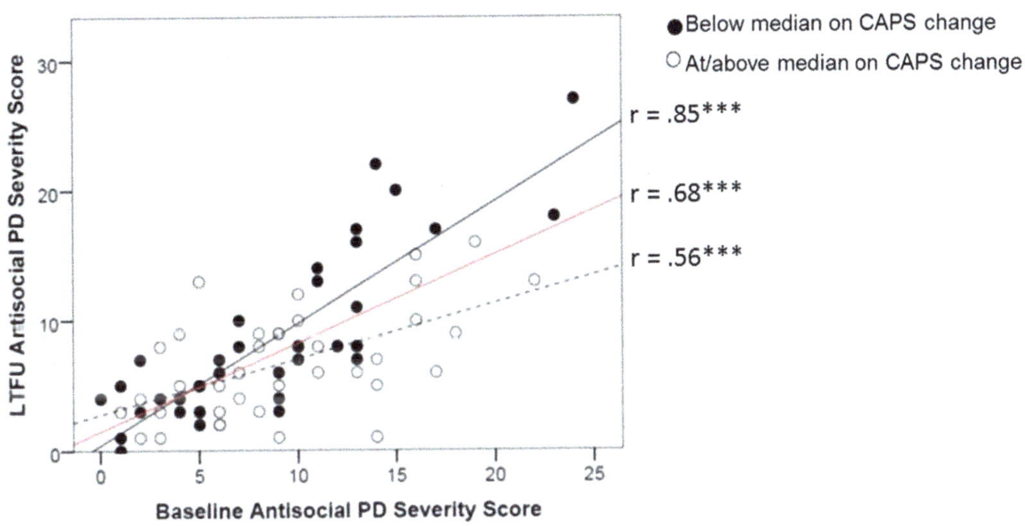

FIGURE 1 | **Change in mean raw antisocial PD score from baseline to LTFU as a function of improvement in CAPS score from baseline to LTFU.** Degree of improvement on the CAPS was defined by a median split on the baseline minus LTFU difference score (median CAPS change score = 50). The red line reflects the average stability for this PD for the sample. CAPS, Clinician-Administered PTSD Scale; PD, personality disorder; LTFU, long-term follow-up. [+]$p < 0.10$; [*]$p < 0.05$; [**]$p < 0.01$; [***]$p < 0.001$.

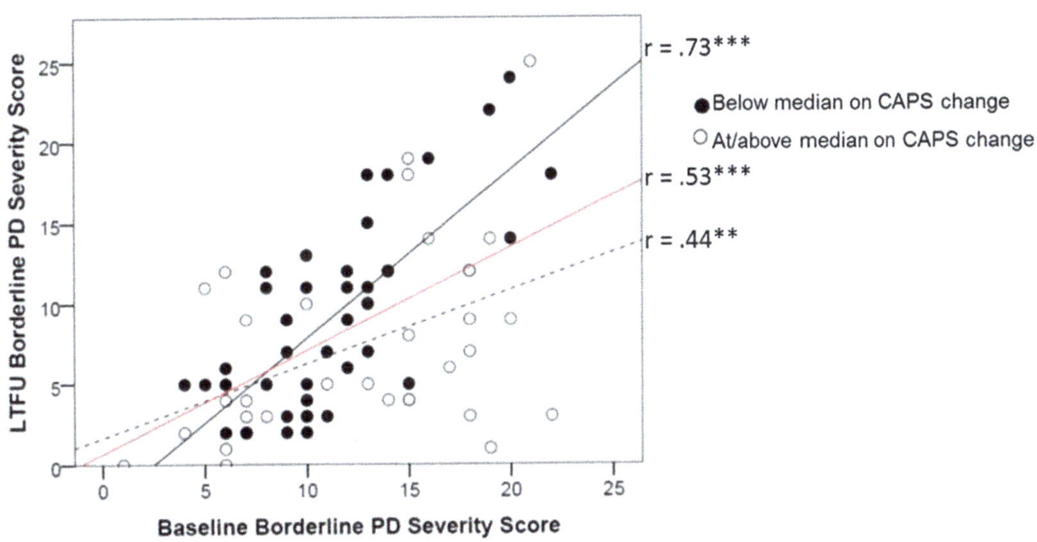

FIGURE 2 | **Change in mean raw borderline PD score from baseline to LTFU as a function of improvement in CAPS score from baseline to LTFU.** Degree of improvement on the CAPS was defined by a median split on the baseline minus LTFU difference score (median CAPS change score = 50). The red line reflects the average stability for this PD for the sample. CAPS, Clinician-Administered PTSD Scale; PD, personality disorder; LTFU, long-term follow-up. [+]$p < 0.10$; [*]$p < 0.05$; [**]$p < 0.01$; [***]$p < 0.001$.

associated with PEM. Though speculative, this may imply that reductions in NEM (e.g., perhaps in response to treatment) have a greater generalized impact on symptom improvements; while by contrast, PEM, which is orthogonal to NEM (37) may be unchanged as a function of treatment. Reduced NEM may be a mechanism responsible for decreases in both PTSD and the six PDs that were associated with PTSD change.

Our results further suggest that the longitudinal stability of both antisocial and borderline PD features was attenuated in individuals who experienced the greatest amount of PTSD symptom improvement. Interestingly, both of these PDs load strongly on the latent dimension of "externalizing" (18). Externalizing disorders are associated with impulse control problems (38, 39). Externalizing PDs are associated with difficulty controlling

TABLE 4 | Hierarchical linear regression analyses predicting change in posttraumatic stress disorder severity as a function of change in PD features.

	Predictor				
PD	**Step 1 Baseline CAPS**	**Step 2 Tx completer**	**Step 3 PD Δ**	**Step 4 Baseline CAPS × PD Δ**	**Step 5 Additional Tx**
Paranoid					
ΔR^2	0.053*	0.036	0.16***	0.027	0.0020
β	0.23*	−0.19	−0.41***	−0.17	−0.041
B (SE)	0.26 (0.13)	−8.23 (4.93)	−1.71 (0.45)	−0.038 (0.024)	−1.69 (4.46)
(CI)	(0.001–0.51)	(−18.06 to 1.59)	(−2.60 to −0.82)	(−0.086 to 0.010)	(−10.59 to 7.22)
Schizoid[a]					
ΔR^2	0.053*	0.036	0.062*	0.018	0.000
β	0.23*	−0.19	−0.25*	−0.15	0.001
B (SE)	0.26 (0.13)	−8.23 (4.93)	−1.74 (0.77)	−0.056 (0.045)	0.049 (4.74)
(CI)	(0.001–0.51)	(−18.06 to 1.59)	(−3.28 to −0.20)	(−0.15 to 0.035)	(−9.4 to 9.5)
Schizotypal					
ΔR^2	0.053*	0.036	0.15***	0.014	0.006
β	0.23*	−0.19	−0.40***	−0.14	−0.083
B (SE)	0.26 (0.13)	−8.23 (4.93)	−1.74 (0.46)	−0.028 (0.024)	−3.45 (4.64)
(CI)	(0.001–0.51)	(−18.06 to 1.59)	(−2.66 to −0.82)	(−0.76 to 0.020)	(−12.71 to 5.81)
Antisocial					
ΔR^2	0.053*	0.036	0.13***	0.005	0.003
β	0.23*	−0.19	−0.36***	−0.077	−0.056
B (SE)	0.26 (0.13)	−8.23 (4.93)	−1.76 (0.53)	−0.017 (0.027)	−2.32 (4.66)
(CI)	(0.001–0.51)	(−18.06 to 1.59)	(−2.81 to −0.71)	(−0.070 to 0.036)	(−11.61 to 6.97)
Borderline[a]					
ΔR^2	0.053*	0.036	0.050*	0.016	0.002
β	0.23*	−0.19	−0.23*	−0.14	−0.043
B (SE)	0.26 (0.13)	−8.23 (4.93)	−0.88 (0.44)	−0.028 (0.025)	−1.77 (4.99)
(CI)	(0.001–0.51)	(−18.06 to 1.59)	(−1.75 to −0.009)	(−0.078 to 0.022)	(−11.73 to 8.18)
Histrionic[a]					
ΔR^2	0.053*	0.036	0.001	0.012	0.000
β	0.23*	−0.19	0.027	−0.11	−0.001
B (SE)	0.26 (0.13)	−8.23 (4.93)	0.18 (0.79)	−0.044 (0.046)	−0.044 (4.98)
(CI)	(0.001–0.51)	(−18.06 to 1.59)	(−1.39 to 1.76)	(−0.14 to 0.048)	(−9.98 to 9.89)
Narcissistic[a]					
ΔR^2	0.053*	0.036	0.027	0.030	0.000
β	0.23*	−0.19	−0.16	−0.17	0.011
B (SE)	0.26 (0.13)	−8.23 (4.93)	−1.01 (0.69)	−0.054 (0.035)	0.45 (4.81)
(CI)	(0.001–0.51)	(−18.06 to 1.59)	(−2.39 to 0.37)	(−0.13 to 0.016)	(−9.16 to 10.05)
Avoidant					
ΔR^2	0.053*	0.036	0.12*	0.027	0.001
β	0.23*	−0.19	−0.35*	−0.18	−0.039
B (SE)	0.26 (0.13)	−8.23 (4.93)	−1.72 (0.54)	−0.050 (0.032)	−1.63 (4.70)
(CI)	(0.001–0.51)	(−18.06 to 1.59)	(−2.80 to −0.65)	(−0.11 to 0.014)	(−11.00 to 7.74)
Dependent[a]					
ΔR^2	0.053*	0.036	0.013	0.057*	0.001
β	0.23*	−0.19	−0.13	−0.25*	0.036
B (SE)	0.26 (0.13)	−8.23 (4.93)	−0.65 (0.64)	−0.07 (0.032)	1.50 (4.88)
(CI)	(0.001–0.51)	(−18.06 to 1.59)	(−1.94 to 0.63)	(−0.13 to −0.005)	(−8.24 to 11.24)
OC					
ΔR^2	0.053*	0.036	0.094**	0.065*	0.000
β	0.23*	−0.19	−0.32**	−0.27*	0.013
B (SE)	0.26 (0.13)	−8.23 (4.93)	−1.99 (0.70)	−0.085 (0.035)	0.53 (4.58)
(CI)	(0.001–0.51)	(−18.06 to 1.59)	(−3.40 to −0.59)	(−0.16 to −0.015)	(−8.61 to 9.67)

PD, personality disorder; CAPS, Clinician-Administered PTSD Scale; Tx, treatment; OC, obsessive–compulsive; ΔR^2, R-squared change; β, standardized beta; B, unstandardized beta; CI, 95% confidence interval for B.

For illustrative purposes, only the final variable added to each step is displayed in the table. The dependent variable for each regression was long-term follow-up CAPS score.

[a]The overall F-tests for these five analyses were not significant after applying the adjusted Holm p-value threshold; therefore, results of these analyses are not interpreted in the manuscript.

$^{*}p < 0.05$.

$^{**}p < 0.001$.

$^{***}p < 0.001$.

impulses toward aggressive, reckless, and dangerous behavior, and this type of behavior may perpetuate stress and lead to chronic PTSD symptoms. Given this, our finding that symptoms of these two PDs were attenuated in those with PTSD symptom reductions highlights the critical importance of treating PTSD even in the context of these particularly impairing comorbidities.

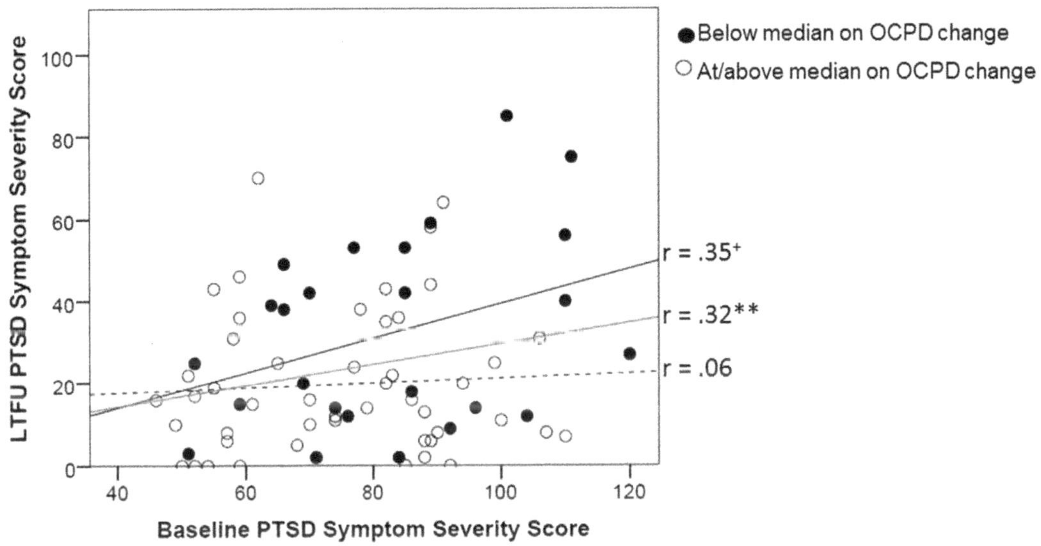

FIGURE 3 | Change in mean raw CAPS score from baseline to LTFU as a function of improvement in OC PD score from baseline to LTFU. Degree of improvement on OC PD was defined by a median split on the baseline minus LTFU difference score (median OC PD change score = 1). OC, obsessive–compulsive; CAPS, Clinician-Administered PTSD Scale; PD, personality disorder; LTFU, long-term follow-up. $^{+}p < 0.10$; $^{*}p < 0.05$; $^{**}p < 0.01$; $^{***}p < 0.001$.

Clinicians who view comorbid borderline and antisocial PD as contraindications for PTSD treatment may want to consider re-evaluating this stance.

Our second set of analyses explored how changes in PD severity might longitudinally relate to PTSD severity. For these analyses, we expected PTSD severity to evidence residualized decreases in association with decreases in PD severity, and that the longitudinal stability of PTSD severity would be attenuated in individuals who experienced the greatest amount of PD symptom improvement. Consistent with predictions, PTSD severity at LTFU was associated with changes in five PDs (paranoid, schizotypal, antisocial, avoidant, OC PD), at mean levels of baseline PTSD severity. Again, because paranoid, schizotypal, and antisocial PD are strongly associated with NEM (25), and both avoidant and OC PD are equally associated with NEM and PEM (25), these findings potentially provide additional support to the conjecture that NEM may be a mechanism responsible for change in both PTSD and these PDs. Our finding that change in OC PD was associated with attenuated longitudinal stability of PTSD symptoms is an intriguing one. One possible explanation for this may be that reductions in rigidity, a hallmark feature of OC PD, may be associated with improved cognitive flexibility, which would be expected to aide in the ability to reappraise negative trauma-related cognitions. This may be one pathway by which changes in this PD relate to residualized changes in PTSD.

The consistent association between change in PTSD and change in PDs observed in this study suggests that these two sets of disorders may be associated with one another in a more fundamental way than originally thought. It is possible that PDs may develop out of trauma exposure and PTSD symptoms. For example, assault survivors may believe that they are at fault for being assaulted and that they are incapable of making good decisions; in turn, they may become dependent upon others to make decisions for them and may develop dependent PD. Similarly, assault survivors may believe that it is not safe to trust anyone; this may develop into paranoid PD. The PD features may therefore partially represent trauma-related biases and overgeneralized schemas [sometimes referred to as overaccomodation (20, 40)], which is targeted in CPT. In this study of women with an index rape trauma, a large number had also experienced childhood abuse. Such abuse, early in personality development, could result in PTSD symptoms, as well as emotions, behaviors, and styles of relating to others that become seemingly entrenched and characterological. Therefore, trauma may be a risk factor linking PTSD and PD comorbidity, which implies that treating trauma and associated symptoms may reduce severity of both sets of disorders.

Our findings may also be relevant to individuals suffering from comorbid PTSD and psychotic symptoms. Traditionally, patients with comorbid PTSD and psychosis are not provided trauma-focused therapy (41, 42) due to the argument that treatment of PTSD in patients with psychotic symptoms is contraindicated [e.g., Ref. (41)]. Research suggests that schizoid, schizotypal, and paranoid PD may all be on the "schizophrenic spectrum" (43) and as a result, we were particularly intrigued by evidence in this study that change in these PDs was associated with change in PTSD and *vice versa*. Specifically, our results suggested that changes in PTSD were associated with both LTFU paranoid and schizotypal PD scores, even after controlling for baseline levels of these PDs. This implies that PTSD treatment in those with psychotic-spectrum disorders [i.e., paranoid, schizotypal, and schizoid PD (27, 28)] is not contraindicated, and further, that such treatment may assist in reducing symptoms of both disorders. In addition, our finding that change in these PDs also affects residualized change in PTSD severity, and that individuals who demonstrate larger decreases in paranoid and schizoid PD also demonstrate larger decreases in

PTSD symptoms, suggests that targeting psychotic-like features in therapy may also reduce PTSD symptoms.

Like all studies, the current study was not without limitations. First, the study was limited in that our analyses were based on data from only two widely spaced time points (5–10 years apart). Therefore, it is unclear whether unmeasured intervening factors affected the results, although our follow-up analyses further suggest that our results cannot be explained completely by additional therapy received after the completion of trauma-focused therapy. Nevertheless, future studies should replicate these analyses with multiple time points, including an earlier follow-up, to more fully evaluate the association between PTSD and PDs. Second, with only two equally spaced data points, we could not fully examine potential reciprocal or bidirectional associations in the data or examine if change in PTSD symptoms had a greater effect on PDs relative to the effects of change in PDs on subsequent PTSD symptoms. For this reason, we conducted parallel sets of analyses for PTSD and PDs, but we are limited in our ability to draw clear causal inferences. Third, this study examined a relatively small number of women who had experienced at least one rape (although they were a severely traumatized sample). To examine if the results are generalizable to other PTSD populations, future investigations should examine whether men and patients exposed to other kinds of trauma demonstrate the same pattern of results. Finally, although we included a self-report measure of PDs that has demonstrated high construct validity with interview measures in the assessment of PDs, we did not use an interview measure designed to diagnose PDs. Future studies should use structured diagnostic interviews to assess PDs and determine if results generalize to diagnostic threshold-level PDs.

In conclusion, the current study suggests that changes in PTSD are associated with changes in a range of PDs, and conversely, changes in a number of PDs are associated with changes in PTSD symptom severity over time. Our findings raise the possibility of a shared underlying mechanism driving the covariation of change: NEM. These results have important clinical implications, in that they suggest that therapeutic efforts to reduce one set of these disorders may impact the symptomotology of the other. This runs counter to the common conceptualization that PDs are intractable and that they are contraindications for trauma-focused PTSD treatment. Thus, results provide confidence that even severe psychopathology and comorbidity may be meaningfully ameliorated, thereby reducing the considerable personal, societal, and financial burden of these disorders. Because there are short, evidence-based protocols for PTSD available, this may be the best place to start.

ETHICS STATEMENT

This study was carried out in accordance with the recommendations of Institutional Review Board of both the University of Missouri-St. Louis and the VA Boston Healthcare System, with written informed consent from all subjects. All subjects gave written informed consent in accordance with the Declaration of Helsinki. The protocol was approved by both IRBs.

AUTHOR CONTRIBUTIONS

MB, EW, and PR all made substantial contributions to the conception of the work; all contributed to drafting the work, revising it critically, and provided final approval of the version to be published; all agreed to be accountable for all aspects of the work in ensuring that questions related to accuracy or integrity of any part of the work are appropriately investigated and resolved. PR acquired the data, and MB and EW were responsible for analysis and interpretation.

REFERENCES

1. Blake DD, Weathers FW, Nagy LM, Kaloupek DG, Gusman FD, Charney DS, et al. The development of a clinician-administered PTSD scale. *J Trauma Stress* (1995) 8:1. doi:10.1002/jts.2490080106
2. Clark LA. *Schedule for Nonadaptive and Adaptive Personality. Manual for Administration, Scoring, and Interpretation*. Minneapolis, MN: University of Minnesota Press (1996).
3. Brown TA, Di Nardo PA, Lehman CL, Campbell LA. Reliability of DSM-IV anxiety and mood disorders: implications for the classification of emotional disorders. *J Abnorm Psychol* (2001) 110:1. doi:10.1037/0021-843X.110.1.49
4. Kessler RC, Sonnega A, Bromet E, Hughes M, Nelson CB. Posttraumatic stress disorder in the national comorbidity survey. *Arch Gen Psychiatry* (1995) 52:12. doi:10.1001/archpsyc.1995.03950240066012
5. Achim AM, Maziade M, Raymond E, Olivier D, Mérette C, Roy MA. How prevalent are anxiety disorders in schizophrenia? A meta-analysis and critical review on a significant association. *Schizophr Bull* (2011) 37:4. doi:10.1093/schbul/sbp148
6. Buckley PF, Miller BJ, Lehrer DS, Castle DJ. Psychiatric comorbidities and schizophrenia. *Schizophr Bull* (2009) 35:2. doi:10.1093/schbul/sbn135
7. Pietrzak RH, Goldstein RB, Southwick SM, Grant BF. Personality disorders associated with full and partial posttraumatic stress disorder in the U.S. population: results from wave 2 of the national epidemiologic survey on alcohol and related conditions. *J Psychiatr Res* (2011) 45:5. doi:10.1016/j.jpsychires.2010.09.013
8. Dunn NJ, Yanasak E, Schillaci J, Simotas S, Rehm LP, Souchek J, et al. Personality disorders in veterans with posttraumatic stress disorder and depression. *J Trauma Stress* (2004) 17:1. doi:10.1023/B:JOTS.0000014680.54051.50
9. American Psychiatric Association. *Diagnostic and Statistical Manual of Mental Disorders*. 4th ed. Washington, DC: American Psychiatric Association (1994).
10. Gunderson JG, Stout RL, McGlashan TH, Shea MT, Morey LC, Grilo CM, et al. Ten-year course of borderline personality disorder: psychopathology and function from the collaborative longitudinal personality disorders study. *Arch Gen Psychiatry* (2011) 68:8. doi:10.1001/archgenpsychiatry.2011.37
11. Linehan MM, Comtois K, Murray AM, Brown MZ, Gallop RJ, Heard HL, et al. Two-year randomized controlled trial and follow-up of dialectical behavior therapy vs therapy by experts for suicidal behaviors and borderline personality disorder. *Arch Gen Psychiatry* (2006) 63:7. doi:10.1001/archpsyc.63.7.757

12. Markowitz JC, Petkova E, Biyanova T, Ding K, Suh EJ, Neria Y. Exploring personality diagnosis stability following acute psychotherapy for chronic posttraumatic stress disorder. *Depress Anxiety* (2015) 32:12. doi:10.1002/da.22436
13. Clarke SB, Rizvi SL, Resick PA. Borderline personality characteristics and treatment outcome in cognitive-behavioral treatments for PTSD in female rape victims. *Behav Ther* (2008) 39:72–8. doi:10.1016/j.beth.2007.05.002
14. Walter KH, Bolte TA, Owens GP, Chard KM. The impact of personality disorders on treatment outcome for veterans in a posttraumatic stress disorder residential treatment program. *Cognit Ther Res* (2012) 36:576. doi:10.1007/s10608-011-9393-8
15. Miller MW, Greif JL, Smith AA. Multidimensional personality questionnaire profiles of veterans with traumatic combat exposure: externalizing and internalizing subtypes. *Psychol Assess* (2003) 15(2):205–15. doi:10.1037/1040-3590.15.2.205
16. Miller MW, Kaloupek DG, Dillon AL, Keane TM. Externalizing and internalizing subtypes of combat-related PTSD: a replication and extension using the PSY-5 scales. *J Abnorm Psychol* (2004) 113:4. doi:10.1037/0021-843X.113.4.636
17. Wolf EJ, Miller MW, Harrington KM, Reardon A. Personality-based latent classes of posttraumatic psychopathology: personality disorders and the internalizing/externalizing model. *J Abnorm Psychol* (2012) 121:256–62. doi:10.1037/a0023237
18. Miller MW, Wolf EJ, Rearson A, Greene A, Ofrat S, McInerney S. Personality and the latent structure of PTSD comorbidity. *J Anxiety Disord* (2012) 26:5. doi:10.1016/j.janxdis.2012.02.016
19. Wolf EJ, Harrington KM, Miller MW. Psychometric properties of the Schedule for Nonadaptive and Adaptive Personality in a PTSD sample. *Psychol Assess* (2011) 23:4. doi:10.1037/a0023985
20. Resick PS, Monson CM, Chard KM. *Cognitive Processing Therapy for PTSD: A Comprehensive Manual.* New York, NY: The Guilford Press (2017).
21. Resick PA, Nishith P, Weaver TL, Astin MC, Feuer CA. A comparison of cognitive-processing therapy with prolonged exposure and a waiting condition for the treatment of chronic posttraumatic stress disorder in female rape victims. *J Consult Clin Psychol* (2002) 70:4. doi:10.1037/0022-006X.70.4.867
22. Resick PA, Williams LF, Suvak MK, Monson CM, Gradus JL. Long-term outcomes of cognitive-behavioral treatments for posttraumatic stress disorder among female rape survivors. *J Consult Clin Psychol* (2012) 80:2. doi:10.1037/a0026602
23. Perkonigg A, Pfister H, Stein MB, Höfler M, Lieb R, Maercker A, et al. Longitudinal course of posttraumatic stress disorder and posttraumatic stress disorder symptoms in a community sample of adolescents and young adults. *Am J Psychiatry* (2005) 162:1320–7. doi:10.1176/appi.ajp.162.7.1320
24. Sadeh N, Miller MW, Wolf EJ, Harkness KL. Negative emotionality and disconstraint influence PTSD symptom course via exposure to new major adverse life events. *J Anxiety Disord* (2015) 20:7. doi:10.1016/j.janxdis.2015.01.003
25. Wolf EJ, Miller MW, Brown TA. The structure of personality disorders in individuals with posttraumatic stress disorder. *Personal Disord* (2011) 2:4. doi:10.1037/a0023168
26. Samuel DB, Hopwood CJ, Ansell EB, Morey LC, Sanislow CA, Markowitz JC, et al. Comparing the temporal stability of self-report and interview assessed personality disorder. *J Abnorm Psychol* (2011) 120:3. doi:10.1037/a0022647
27. Keyes KM, Eaton NR, Krueger RF, Skodol AE, Wall MM, Grant B, et al. Thought disorder in the meta-structure of psychopathology. *Psychol Med* (2013) 43:8. doi:10.1017/S0033291712002292
28. Markon KE. Modeling psychopathology structure: a symptom-level analysis of axis I and II disorders. *Psychol Med* (2010) 40(2):273–88. doi:10.1017/S0033291709990183
29. Allison PD. Change scores as dependent variables in regression analysis. *Sociol Methodol* (1990) 20:93–114. doi:10.2307/271083
30. Shutz RW. Analyzing change. In: Safrit MK, Wood TM, editors. *Measurement Concepts in Physical Education and Exercise Science.* Champaign, IL: Human Kinetics Books (1989). p. 207–28.
31. Kendall PC, Cummings CM, Villabø MA, Narayanan MK, Treadwell K, Birmaher B, et al. Mediators of change in the child/adolescent anxiety multimodal treatment study. *J Consult Clin Psychol* (2016) 84(1):1–14. doi:10.1037/a0039773
32. Blair C, Raver CC, Berry DJ; Family Life Project Investigators. Two approaches to estimating the effects of parenting on the development of executive function in early childhood. *Dev Psychol* (2014) 50(2):554–65. doi:10.1037/a0033647
33. Miller YD, Trost SG, Brown WJ. Mediators of physical activity behavior change among women with young children. *Am J Prev Med* (2002) 23(2 Suppl):98–103. doi:10.1016/S0749-3797(02)00484-1
34. Blatt SJ, Sanislow CA III, Zuroff DC, Pilkonis PA. Characteristics of effective therapists: further analyses of data from the National Institute of Mental Health Treatment of Depression Collaborative Research Program. *J Consult Clin Psychol* (1996) 64(6):1276–84. doi:10.1037/0022-006X.64.6.1276
35. Holm S. A simple sequentially rejective multiple test procedure. *Scand J Statist* (1979) 6:65–70.
36. Cohen J. A power primer. *Psychol Bull* (1992) 112:155–9. doi:10.1037/0033-2909.112.1.155
37. Tellegen A, Waller NC. Exploring personality through test construction: development of the multidimensional personality questionnaire. In: Boyle GJ, Matthews G, Saklofska DH, editors. *The SAGE Handbook of Personality Theory and Assessment: Vol. 2. Personality Measurement and Testing.* Thousand Oaks, CA: SAGE (2008). p. 261–92.
38. Achenbach TM, Edelbrock CS. The classification of child psychopathology: a review and analysis of empirical efforts. *Psychol Bull* (1978) 6:1275–301. doi:10.1037/0033-2909.85.6.1275
39. Achenbach TM, Edelbrock CS. Psychopathology of childhood. *Annu Rev Psychol* (1984) 35:227–56. doi:10.1146/annurev.ps.35.020184.001303
40. Resick PA, Monson CM, Chard KM. *Cognitive Processing Therapy: Veteran/Military Version: Therapist's Manual.* Washington, DC: Department of Veterans Affairs (2014).
41. Becker CB, Zayfert C, Anderson E. A survey of psychologists' attitudes towards and utilization of exposure therapy for PTSD. *Behav Res Ther* (2004) 42:3. doi:10.1016/S0005-7967(03)00138-4
42. Ronconi JM, Shiner B, Watts BV. Inclusion and exclusion criteria in randomized controlled trials of psychotherapy for PTSD. *J Psychiatr Pract* (2014) 20:1. doi:10.1097/01.pra.0000442936.23457.5b
43. Wei Y, Zhang T, Chow A, Tang Y, Xu L, Dai Y, et al. Co-morbidity of personality disorder in schizophrenia among psychiatric outpatients in China: data from epidemiologic survey in a clinical population. *BMC Psychiatry* (2016) 16:244. doi:10.1186/s12888-016-0920-8

8

Integrated Trauma-Focused Cognitive-Behavioural Therapy for Post-traumatic Stress and Psychotic Symptoms: A Case-Series Study Using Imaginal Reprocessing Strategies

Nadine Keen[1,2]*, Elaine C. M. Hunter[1,2] and Emmanuelle Peters[2,1]

[1] South London and Maudsley NHS Foundation Trust, Psychological Interventions Clinic for outpatients with Psychosis (PICuP), London, United Kingdom, [2] Department of Psychology, Institute of Psychiatry, Psychology and Neuroscience, King's College London, United Kingdom

Edited by:
Kim T. Mueser,
Boston University, United States

Reviewed by:
Dean McKay,
Fordham University, United States
Mahesh Menon,
University of British Columbia, Canada
Giancarlo Dimaggio,
Centro di Terapia Metacognitiva Interpersonale, Italy

****Correspondence:***
Nadine Keen
nadine.1.keen@kcl.ac.uk,
nadine.keen@slam.nhs.uk

Despite high rates of trauma in individuals with psychotic symptoms, post-traumatic stress symptoms are frequently overlooked in clinical practice. There is also reluctance to treat post-traumatic symptoms in case the therapeutic procedure of reprocessing the trauma exacerbates psychotic symptoms. Recent evidence demonstrates that it is safe to use reprocessing strategies in this population. However, most published studies have been based on treating post-traumatic symptoms in isolation from psychotic symptoms. The aims of the current case series were to assess the acceptability, feasibility, and preliminary effectiveness of integrating cognitive-behavioural approaches for post-traumatic stress and psychotic symptoms into a single protocol. Nine participants reporting distressing psychotic and post-traumatic symptoms were recruited from a specialist psychological therapies service for psychosis. Clients were assessed at five time points (baseline, pre, mid, end of therapy, and at 6+ months of follow-up) by an independent assessor on measures of current symptoms of psychosis, post-traumatic stress, emotional problems, and well-being. Therapy was formulation based and individualised, depending on presenting symptoms and trauma type. It consisted of five broad, flexible phases, and included imaginal reprocessing strategies (reliving and/or rescripting). The intervention was well received, with positive post-therapy feedback and satisfaction ratings. Unusually for this population, no-one dropped out of therapy. Post therapy, all but one (88% of participants) achieved a reliable improvement compared to pre-therapy on at least one outcome measure: post-traumatic symptoms (63%), voices (25%), delusions (50%), depression (50%), anxiety (36%), and well-being (40%). Follow-up assessments were completed by 78% (n = 7) of whom 86% (n = 6) maintained at least one reliable improvement. Rates of improvements following therapy (average of 44% across measures post therapy; 32% at follow-up) were over twice those found during the waiting list period (19%). No participant indicated a reliable worsening of any symptoms during or after therapy. The study shows that an integrative therapy incorporating reprocessing strategies was an acceptable and feasible intervention for this small sample, with promising effectiveness. A randomised controlled trial is warranted to test the efficacy of the intervention for this population.

Keywords: psychosis, trauma, post-traumatic stress disorder, trauma-focused cognitive-behavioural therapy for psychosis, psychological intervention, reprocessing, imaginal exposure

INTRODUCTION

There are very high rates of trauma in individuals presenting with psychotic symptoms. In their review of more than 40 studies (1), Grubaugh et al. found rates of 49–100% (depending on population and methods of assessment), with 75–98% of those exposed to trauma reporting multiple traumas. Post-traumatic stress symptoms are reported in approximately 33% of people with psychosis, and 12.5% of patients with a psychotic disorder meet criteria for a diagnosis of post-traumatic stress disorder (PTSD) (2). Post-traumatic symptoms are frequently intertwined with psychotic symptoms (3, 4), with an overlap between symptoms such as hallucinations and trauma sequelae such as dissociation (5, 6). Recent theoretical models have identified underlying factors through which trauma is related to the development and maintenance of positive symptoms (7), with specific mechanisms linking different types of adversity with hallucinations and with delusions (8, 9). It is suggested that there is a direct link between the re-experiencing and arousal symptoms of PTSD, such as intrusions ("flashbacks"), and both the occurrence and content of hallucinations (9). Dissociative processes and disrupted contextual integration at the time of the trauma leave an individual vulnerable to experiencing anomalous experiences. If the trauma-memory-related intrusion is, for example, of the abuser, in combination with high levels of arousal, this may be experienced as an auditory hallucination of the voice of the abuser in individuals with an information processing style prone to weakened contextual integration (10). Further, interpersonal traumas lead to maladaptive schema and appraisals of self and others, predisposing to paranoia and delusional beliefs (11, 12). Maladaptive schema about self and others are also closely related to the concept of metacognitive capacity (13), i.e., an integrated representation of the self and others, which is suggested to be a foundation for resilience (14). Both individuals with psychosis and with PTSD show poor metacognitive mastery, which is further associated with greater distress and hyperarousal in PTSD patients (15), suggesting that a limited understanding of mental states, especially others' emotions (16), may be another possible shared mechanism between psychotic and post-traumatic stress symptoms.

The presence of PTSD symptoms results in worse outcomes and long-term distress for many clients with trauma histories, including a poorer response to antipsychotic medication and more severe psychotic symptoms (17), higher rates of emotional disorders, substance abuse, self-harm, and suicide; and increased and longer-term use of services (1). Thus, a failure to treat trauma sequelae is costly to both service users and the National Health Service (NHS). Despite this, in clinical practice, PTSD symptoms are usually overlooked in such clients (18). Service users (19–21) have long campaigned to have professionals recognise the central role of trauma in people's lives, and that the impact of trauma is not treated by antipsychotic medication alone. However, despite these calls, the psychological effects of trauma in those with psychotic symptoms are often not treated in mainstream services. Encouragingly, however, in the UK, the National Institute for Health and Care Excellence (NICE) (22) have, for the first time, recommended that people presenting with a first episode of psychosis in early interventions for psychosis (EIP) services should be assessed for a history of trauma and PTSD, and that NICE guidelines for PTSD (23) should be followed in those showing signs of PTSD.

Although cognitive-behavioural therapy (CBT) is recommended for both psychosis [CBT for psychosis: CBTp (22), and for PTSD (trauma-focused CBT, tf-CBT) (23)], evidence is lacking on specific, integrated tf-CBT for psychosis (tf-CBTp). CBTp does not focus directly on trauma sequelae, and therapists are often reluctant to treat PTSD symptoms due to concerns that the experiential reprocessing of trauma may exacerbate psychotic symptoms (24, 25). Consequently, this leads to people with psychotic symptoms failing to access trauma-based therapies, and/or therapists choosing modes of therapy for the trauma that exclude imaginal reprocessing techniques, which may mean that the treatment is not optimally effective. Similarly, these concerns have excluded people with psychosis (both current of a history of psychosis) from all prominent PTSD trials (26). Encouragingly however, three recent reviews (27, 28), including a Cochrane review (29), have found that there is some good quality, albeit limited, evidence to suggest that trauma-focused psychological therapies can be safe and efficacious in individuals with psychosis. Until recently, most of the studies of trauma-focused therapy in psychosis consisted of case studies (30–33), open trials (34, 35), pilot studies (36), and small-scale randomised controlled trials (RCTs) (37–39). Overall, the results are promising in terms of reduction in post-traumatic symptoms. Nevertheless, some of these studies have been in clients with "severe mental illness (SMI)" with mixed diagnosis samples, where the majority did not have psychotic disorders (39), or samples who did not necessarily present with current psychotic symptoms (38). More recently, there have been two larger-scale RCTs of trauma-focused therapy in psychosis samples. The largest was carried out in the Netherlands, and found large effect sizes for both exposure (0.78) and EMDR (0.65) on PTSD symptoms, with 57% in the exposure treatment group ($N = 53$) and 60% in the EMDR treatment group ($N = 55$) achieving a loss of PTSD diagnosis compared to 6% of the waiting list group ($N = 47$) (40). Furthermore, treatment effects were maintained 6 months later for both treatment groups. This promising outcome contrasts with the findings from a recent RCT in the UK (41), which, despite showing that tf-CBT was safe and feasible, found no differences between the therapy and treatment-as-usual (TAU) groups on PTSD outcomes. One possible explanation for these discrepancies in results is that the latter trial, unlike the Dutch study, did not include a direct memory reprocessing element in the therapy protocol but focused instead on cognitive restructuring alone.

It is, therefore, an exciting time for the development of interventions for post-traumatic stress in people presenting with psychotic symptoms. However, there is a still a lack of consensus as to the best and safest approach (e.g., cognitive restructuring versus more directive imaginal reprocessing methods such as EMDR, exposure, or re-scripting) for this vulnerable client group. In addition, there has been mixed implementation across the studies on the use of a stabilisation or preparatory phase prior to beginning the trauma-focused components of the intervention. The debate over the safety and tolerability of exposure-based PTSD therapies is not limited to those with psychotic symptoms. Therapists have long had reservations about exposure-based therapies in terms of their potential to destabilise clients (24, 25, 42), and indeed some studies have found that even during beneficial exposure-based interventions clients can experience initial worsening of PTSD symptoms, physical symptoms of anxiety, and emotional exhaustion (43–45). Thus, whilst exposure-based treatment for PTSD is effective, it can also be distressing and difficult for clients to undertake. Nevertheless, a recent review suggests that there is insufficient evidence to support a phase-based treatment approach to complex PTSD, i.e., specifically in relation to a stabilisation phase, and that its inclusion may in itself act as a delay or barrier to intervention targeting the trauma (46). Importantly, in the Dutch trial, which did not include a stabilisation phase, there were no occurrences of severe adverse events and PTSD symptom exacerbation induced by the intervention at the end of treatment or at follow-up, or of psychotic symptom exacerbation or increased suicidality (40, 47). Nevertheless, as psychotic symptom exacerbation was only measured after the first two exposure sessions (47), and current psychotic symptoms were only present in 55% of their sample, additional research is needed to build on this evidence base to gain clarity regarding the safety and efficacy of implementing exposure-based interventions within this population.

In addition, most of the studies to date have treated post-traumatic symptoms in isolation from psychotic symptoms. This may be reflective of the fact that RCTs, whilst clearly the gold standard in informing evidenced-based practice, are often required to have strict exclusion criteria, pre-defined primary outcomes, and a focus on one underlying mechanism. It is perhaps unsurprising then that despite promising outcomes in terms of PTSD symptoms, there are inconsistent results in terms of whether (and which) psychotic symptoms improve following therapy (36, 48). In clinical practice, this may pose an issue for clients whose primary goal is to address their psychotic symptoms (e.g., to reduce compliance with commanding voices) even though post-traumatic symptoms may be fuelling these, or clients who initially present and seek help for a "psychotic" explanation of their difficulties (i.e., the persecutor is following me and trying to kill me) as opposed to a "trauma" explanation (i.e., I am experiencing flashbacks of the persecutor assaulting me). This perhaps highlights the need for "practice-based evidence" integrating treatment approaches for post-traumatic stress and psychotic symptoms, and which can be tailored to the individual needs and goals of the client, in addition to the evidence base from RCTs.

The aims of the current study were to assess the acceptability, feasibility, and preliminary effectiveness of integrating current cognitive-behavioural approaches for post-traumatic stress and psychotic symptoms into a single protocol, within a routine clinical service. The therapy protocol included exposure-based reprocessing strategies since, particularly in view of recent trials (40, 41), this is likely to be a crucial mode of action in the treatment of PTSD. The protocol also includes a stabilisation phase because (1) although emotional arousal is key in exposure therapy, high levels of affect arousal in the absence of effective coping strategies may trigger information processing difficulties and psychotic symptoms (49) and (2) clinically we have found the stabilisation phase helpful in fostering an initial sense of hope and control over symptoms, and in enhancing engagement and increasing trust in the therapist. The study reports the outcomes of nine consecutive clients, obtained as part of the service's routine assessments at baseline, pre-therapy, mid-therapy, post-therapy, and at a minimum of 6-month follow-up. The study aimed to explore changes on a range of meaningful clinical outcomes, namely measures of post-traumatic stress, psychosis symptoms, affective problems, and emotional well-being, following receipt of tf-CBTp.

MATERIALS AND METHODS

Service Setting

These data were collected at the Psychological Interventions Clinic for outpatients with Psychosis (PICuP), based in South London and Maudsley (SLaM) NHS Foundation Trust. PICuP is a stand-alone psychological therapies clinic offering CBTp for outpatients with distressing positive symptoms of psychosis (regardless of diagnosis), or with emotional difficulties in the context of a history of psychosis. Therapists liaise closely with care coordinators in recovery multidisciplinary teams, but are not part of the team, or with general practitioners (GPs) if the person is held in primary care; they do not prescribe medication or care coordinate/case manage. Further information about the service setting, therapy and supervision structures, population characteristics, and clinical outcomes can be found in the study by Peters et al. (50).

Ethical Approval

Ethical approval for the use of outcome data from the PICuP Clinic was obtained by the London-Dulwich Research Ethics Committee (Reference 15/LO/1831), and all participants gave written informed consent for their clinical data to be used in research studies.

Design

A single case-series A–B design was used with five assessments (baseline, pre-intervention, mid-intervention, post-intervention, and follow-up).

Participants

Nine participants were recruited from consecutive referrals to PICuP according to the following criteria: (1) the presence of at least one current psychotic symptom [as identified by the Psychotic Symptom Rating Scales (PSYRATS) (51) at the assessment stage]; (2) reporting distressing post-traumatic stress symptoms [scores in the moderate or above range (≥11) on the Post-traumatic Diagnostic Scale (PDS) (52)]; (3) willingness to address trauma sequelae in therapy.

The sample consisted of five (56%) men and four (44%) women, with a mean age of 37 years [standard deviation (SD) = 11.34; range 17–52]. Participants were from several ethnic backgrounds with over three-quarters (n = 7; 78%) from Black and Minority Ethnic (BME) groups. Seventy-eight percent (n = 7) were single. A substantial majority (n = 8; 89%) were unemployed. All participants were prescribed anti-psychotic medication. Five participants (56%) had a primary schizophrenia spectrum diagnosis (ICD-10 F20–F29), two (22%) had a primary diagnosis of PTSD (F43.1), and two (22%) had a primary diagnosis of severe depressive episode with psychotic features (F32.3). Two patients (22%) also had secondary PTSD diagnoses. The four patients with non-schizophrenia primary diagnoses did not differ from the rest of the sample in terms of presenting symptoms, and all reported persecutory delusions and hallucinations (three with command hallucinations, and three with hallucinations in multiple modalities; **Table 1**).

Measures

The assessments consisted of a battery of measures assessing current symptoms of psychosis, post-traumatic stress, affective problems, and general well-being. The choice of routine outcome measures selected by the service is reflective of the wide range of problems held by many clients attending PICuP, and the individualized nature of therapy and people's goals (50, 53). Pragmatic considerations typical of routine clinical services, such as financial constraints or trust-wide initiatives, led to the discontinuation of some measures [Beck Depression Inventory (BDI) and Beck Anxiety Inventory (BAI) (54, 55)], and the introduction of others (Clinical Outcomes in Routine Evaluation-10; CORE-10 (56); and Depression Anxiety Stress Scales (DASS) (57)). Hence, some participants in this study completed different measures for their affective problems and only 67% completed the CORE-10 (56).

The Post-traumatic Diagnostic Scale (52)

The PDS was used as a self-report screen of post-traumatic stress symptoms severity. The measure includes 17 items rated on a 4-point ordinal scale (0–3); yielding total symptom scores ranging between 0 and 51. It has been shown to have high internal consistency, test–re-test reliability, and high diagnostic validity when compared to the Structured Clinical Interview for DSM IV, and good sensitivity and specificity (52).

Psychotic Symptom Rating Scales (51)

This scale is a semi-structured clinician administered interview assessing the severity of 11 dimensions (frequency, duration, location, loudness, beliefs about origin, negative content, distress, disruption to life, and control) of auditory hallucinations and six dimensions (preoccupation, conviction, distress, and disruption to life) of delusions via 5-point ordinal scales (0–4). Evaluation of the PSYRATS-delusion and hallucination scales indicates good inter-rater reliability (51) and concurrent validity with the Positive and Negative Syndromes Scale (58). Total scores range between 0 and 44 for auditory hallucinations and 0 and 24 for delusions.

Beck Depression Inventory (55) and Beck Anxiety Inventory (54)

Twenty-one-item self-report questionnaires assessing symptoms of depression and anxiety, respectively, over the past week (BAI) or 2 weeks (BDI-II) (possible range 0–63).

Depression Anxiety Stress Scales-21 (57)

Twenty-one-item self-report questionnaire assessing symptoms of depression, anxiety, and stress, over the past week (range of 0–42 for each subscale). For the purpose of this study, only the depression and anxiety subscales are reported, as an alternative to the BDI-II and BAI.

Clinical Outcomes in Routine Evaluation-10 (56)

Ten-item-self-report questionnaire assessing emotional well-being. The CORE-10 generates a total distress score, based on each item being rated from 0 to 4, with total scores ranging from 0 (low) to 40 (severe).

Satisfaction with Therapy Questionnaire (STQ) (59)

An amended service-specific 22-item version of the STQ (60) was administered at the end of therapy to obtain further data regarding the acceptability of the intervention. The STQ is an adaptation of Beck et al.'s (59) Patient's Report of Therapy Session and was first used to assess satisfaction with CBTp by Kuipers et al. (61). The measure asks about progress and satisfaction with therapy, and also includes specific items assessing clients' beliefs in the extent to which they gained CBT skills and knowledge, perceptions of the usefulness of homework tasks set, and ratings of their therapist's attributes. Items are scored on a scale ranging from 1 to 5, with higher scores corresponding to higher satisfaction and a score of 3 reflecting a neutral or uncertain response (e.g., unsure, no progress, and indifferent). The adapted STQ has been used with clients with psychosis in a number of other studies (61, 62).

Procedure

Participants were assessed at five different time points on all measures as part of the routine outcome assessments for the clinic (50):

- Baseline—when first referred to the service, before going on the waiting list.
- Pre-therapy – just before starting therapy after having been on the waiting list for a median of 3 months after the baseline assessment (range 0–5 months).
- Mid-therapy—median of 5 months into therapy (range 2–7 months).
- Post-therapy—median of 22 months after starting therapy (range 8–35 months); assessments were carried out within a few days or weeks of finishing therapy (range 0–58 days; median = 7 days).

TABLE 1 | Summary of trauma type, PTSD, psychotic symptoms, target hotspot and associated memory, and key tf-CBTp interventions.

Participant (diagnosis)	Trauma type	Psychotic symptoms	Target hotspot and associated memory	Key tf-CBTp; phase 4 intervention
P1 *Primary*: unspecified non-organic psychosis *Secondary*: PTSD	Childhood; multiple Sought asylum in the UK	Auditory command hallucinations Visual hallucinations Paranoia	Witnessing murder of childhood friend; childhood physical abuse; held captive and tortured	Cognitive restructuring Reliving with CR Imagery rescripting (for nightmares and visions)
P2 *Primary*: schizophrenia *Secondary*: severe depressive episode with psychotic symptoms	Adult; single event	Auditory command hallucinations Persecutory beliefs	Living in conflict zone and held at gunpoint by terrorists	Cognitive restructuring Reliving with CR
P3 *Primary*: other non-organic psychotic disorder *Secondary*: PTSD	Childhood; multiple Sought asylum in the UK	Auditory hallucinations Visual, tactile, and olfactory hallucinations Persecutory beliefs	Living in conflict zone (civil war/genocide); parents killed. Held captive and gang raped; witnessed murder of grandfather	Cognitive restructuring Imagery rescripting
P4 *Primary*: unspecified non-organic psychosis *Secondary*: none	Childhood; single event	Auditory command hallucinations Visual and tactile hallucinations Persecutory beliefs	Rape in childhood	Cognitive restructuring Imagery rescripting for trauma event and visual hallucinations Schema work
P5 *Primary*: PTSD *Secondary*: emotionally unstable personality disorder	Adult; multiple	Auditory command hallucinations Visual, olfactory, and tactile hallucinations Persecutory beliefs	Several rapes and extreme physical assaults (long-term domestic violence); stillbirth of child	Cognitive restructuring Reliving with CR for trauma events Imagery rescripting for visual, olfactory tactile, and hallucinations
P6 *Primary*: severe depressive episode with psychotic symptoms *Secondary*: none	Childhood; single event	Auditory hallucinations Persecutory beliefs	Physical and emotional abuse	Imagery rescripting Schema work
P7 *Primary*: schizophrenia *Secondary*: severe depressive episode with psychotic symptoms	Adult; single event	Auditory hallucinations Visual, tactile, and olfactory hallucinations Persecutory beliefs	Being threatened with a knife	Cognitive restructuring reliving with CR
P8 *Primary*: PTSD *Secondary*: severe depressive episode with psychotic symptoms	Adult; multiple Sought asylum in the UK	Commanding voices Visual and tactile hallucinations Persecutory beliefs	Long-term imprisonment with physical and sexual torture. Witnessing murder in prison	Cognitive restructuring reliving with CR Imagery rescripting
P9 *Primary*: severe depressive episode with psychotic symptoms *Secondary*: none	Childhood; multiple	Auditory command hallucinations Visual and tactile hallucinations Persecutory beliefs	Repeated childhood physical abuse	Cognitive restructuring Imagery rescripting for trauma events, visual and tactile hallucinations, and nightmares

- Follow-up—median of 9 months after finishing therapy (range 5–18 months).

There were two exceptions to this: clients did not complete the second assessment (pre-therapy) if the waiting list was ≤2 weeks, and the PDS (52) was only administered at pre-, post-, and follow-up assessments; both to minimize client burden. For the purpose of this study, mid-therapy scores are not reported.

Independent assessors (assistant psychologists trained in administering all the measures) conducted the assessments [NB: at both the pre-therapy assessment and end-of-therapy assessment four participants (Ps 4, 5, 7, and 8 and Ps 1, 2, 5, and 8, respectively) declined to complete the PDS with the assistant psychologist but agreed to complete it with their therapist]. Assessments lasted between 45 and 90 min and could be conducted over more than one session if necessary. Demographic information from participants was collected at the baseline assessment.

Therapy

All clients were offered approximately 9 months of therapy, although in practice duration of therapy was flexible, according to the clinical need (see Results). Whilst clients were in therapy with PICuP, they continued to receive routine mental health care from their recovery team (such as medication and appointments with care coordinators; $n = 6$), or their GP ($n = 3$) if they had been discharged from their team, but they did not receive other psychosocial interventions.

Therapy was usually delivered in weekly or fortnightly 60–90-min sessions. The integrated tf-CBTp therapy protocol is outlined in **Figure 1**, with five phases. Therapy was conducted in a flexible style with an emphasis on engagement and building a good therapeutic relationship. Although we have manualised our approach in this study, to maintain a consistent approach, in practice therapy is pragmatic in that it is adapted to the individual and their changing needs, with clinicians able to shift between stages of therapy according to clinical need. Similarly, therapy speed and progression are tailored to the individual to ensure that any changes in psychotic experiences are addressed as they arise.

Therapists consisted of two senior clinical psychologists [first (Nadine Keen) and second (Elaine C. M. Hunter) author] and one clinical psychologist (MS) supervised by Elaine C. M. Hunter. Nadine Keen and Elaine C. M. Hunter had extensive experience of delivering CBT interventions for both PTSD and for psychosis, and developed the current protocol integrating therapeutic procedures for post-traumatic and psychotic symptoms. Cases were discussed in fortnightly peer supervision groups, and MS received extra weekly individual supervision.

Phase 1: Assessment, Engagement, and Goal-Setting

A thorough assessment and the establishment of clients' goals are key in determining how best to offer help. A combination of questionnaires and clinical interview is essential to maximise data gathering. Although questionnaires can feel impersonal, they are often helpful at the outset as they can feel less intrusive and normalising for clients who may be shame prone, and so clients may disclose information that otherwise they might be reluctant to say directly to their clinician. From the outset, all symptoms are framed as understandable reactions to overwhelming traumatic events and the therapist provides psychoeducation to facilitate this. To facilitate trust, engagement, and a sense of safety, a non-colluding, non-confrontational therapeutic style is required, using the client's own terminology (63, 64). Strategies such as the symbolic panic button and having periods free from trauma/symptom discussion, to help the client work within their therapeutic "window of tolerance," are further used as a means of sharing power and giving the client some control over the process of therapy (65). It is important to be mindful of the potential for exacerbation of affect, post-traumatic or psychotic symptoms (e.g., voices commenting, paranoia, dissociation, and flashbacks), so the pace may need to be slow with frequent checking out and reassurance. This needs to be carefully balanced with not colluding with any understandable avoidance of traumatic or affect-laden topics.

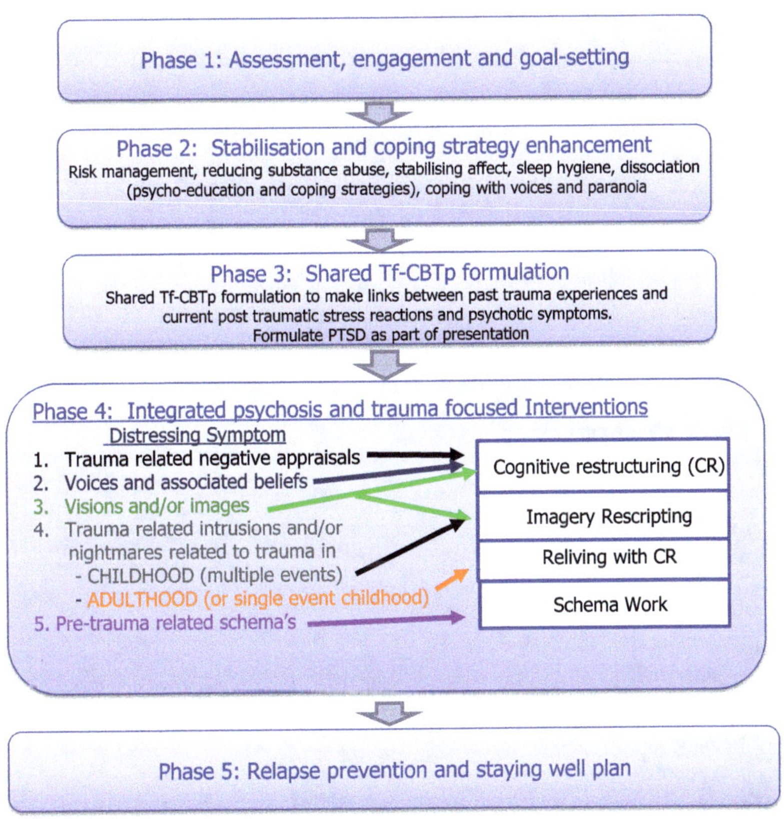

FIGURE 1 | Integrated trauma and psychosis intervention protocol.

Phase 2: Stabilisation and Coping Strategy Enhancement

Risks of psychosis exacerbations are minimised by the inclusion of a stabilisation, coping, and affect management phase that also targets psychotic symptoms prior to trauma-focused work. Although there is debate about the inclusion of this phase (46), we find it helpful in fostering an initial sense of hope and control over symptoms, and in enhancing engagement and increasing trust in the therapist. Developing control is also helpful for the subsequent, shared formulation phase, as gaining control over some symptoms can provide evidence to support a trauma-based understanding of their experiences [e.g., "if grounding strategies stop the 'attacks' (i.e. somatic flashbacks) then perhaps these might be flashbacks rather than the abuser attacking me again"], and hence provides the rationale for trauma-focused interventions. Strategies employed during this phase will depend on the client's specific presentation, needs, and goals but may include: managing and reducing risk; anxiety management (e.g., controlled breathing and special place imagery); grounding strategies; coping with voices, paranoia and other anomalous experiences; sleep hygiene and CBT strategies for depression.

Phase 3: Shared tf-CBTp Formulation

By this time, the therapist may have already shared simple cognitive-behavioural maintenance vicious cycles for mood, anxiety, post-traumatic, and/or psychotic symptoms, but the aim in this study is to develop a shared formulation (template in **Figure 2**) helping the client to make links between their past traumatic event(s) and their current post-traumatic and psychotic symptoms. This enables possible reformulation of the client's current difficulties as understandable responses to trauma and provides further rationale for the trauma-focused interventions. We found that changes in symptom attribution in themselves can lead to a reduction in distress. For example, P1 said he was relieved and preferred to believe the alternative explanation that his nightmares were likely caused by "unprocessed memories" of his traumatic experiences, as opposed to his original belief that they were the Devil reminding him that he was guilty of the murder of his friend. Timelines and formulation letters can also be helpful here to facilitate the contextualisation of clients' experiences/memories and to help make links between particular events and experiences.

Phase 4: Integrated Psychosis and Trauma-Focused Interventions

In this phase, the psychotic and post-traumatic stress-focused interventions are listed by symptom in **Figure 1** to help guide the choice of specific trauma-focused interventions. This will be guided by the formulation as well as the client's goals and what is most distressing for them. Since trauma-related intrusions and/or nightmares are the hallmark symptoms of PTSD, we propose that the exposure element of phase 4 is an *essential* ingredient of the protocol [either imagery rescripting as described by Arntz and Weertman (68, 69) or reliving with cognitive restructuring

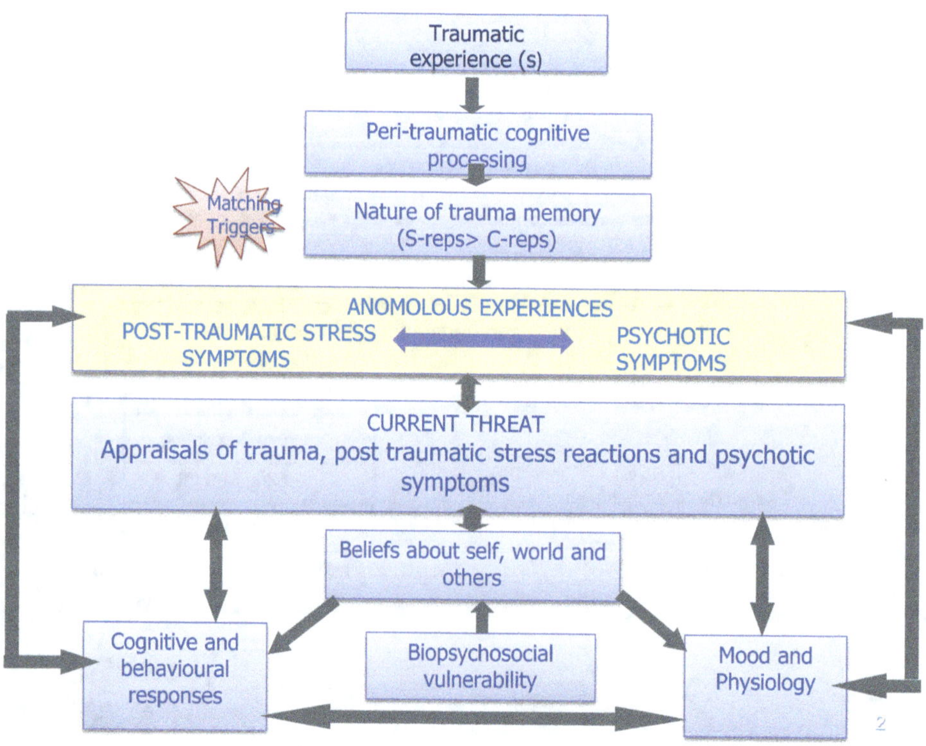

FIGURE 2 | Integrated model of trauma and psychosis [adapted from models in Ref. (3, 66, 67)].

as described by Grey et al. (70) or nightmare rescripting followed the protocol described by Sheaves et al. (71), adapted from Nappi et al. (72)]. All clients in this case series received and completed some form of exposure in their treatment (**Table 1**) which was preceded either by:

(1) Cognitive restructuring ($N = 8$): to reappraise negative psychosis and trauma-related appraisals including peri-traumatic hotspots (e.g., I am going to die) and/or post-traumatic appraisals (e.g., the voices tell me it was my fault, therefore it must be).
(2) Schema work ($N = 1$). when the peri traumatic appraisal(s) (e.g., I am responsible) are rooted in congruent pre-existing schemas (which by their nature are rigid to change), it might be necessary to use more schema-focused strategies to facilitate the re-appraisal process.

Phase 5: Staying Well and Relapse Prevention

This phase involves the development of a relapse prevention and staying well plan, which includes a summary of key techniques and strategies learnt, as well as what to do if one faces a set-back.

Statistical Analysis

Mean and SD are presented, and the Reliable Change Index (RCI) (73) was used as a marker of reliable change in symptoms for individual participants. Reliable change refers to the extent to which change between intervention time points falls beyond what would be expected on the basis of measurement variability. The equation uses reliability of the measure itself [using the internal consistency method for clinical populations (74), as well as a the measure of the variance of the sample (SD)]. The reliable change criterion is 1.96 times the standard error of the difference (75). If the participant falls beyond the reliable change criteria specified, it can be concluded with 95% certainty that they have shown a statistically reliable change in score, rather than that change occurring due to chance.

For the majority of measures (PDS, PSYRATS for voices and beliefs, DASS, CORE-10), the SDs and reliability scores for each measure were calculated in the software package SPSS (version 21) from baseline scores from the PICuP database ($N = 627$) of all clients seen in the service between 2003 and 2015. For the BDI and BAI, it was not possible to calculate the reliability using this method as individual item scores were not available and reliability scores were based on the data produced in a previous study (76).

Group statistics (such as paired *t*-tests) were not carried out as the sample was too small for meaningful analyses at the group level, and to minimise the number of analyses reported, bearing in mind six measures were used across three time periods [waiting list (five measures only), post-therapy; follow-up].

RESULTS

Baseline Clinical Characteristics

At baseline, all participants presented with current auditory hallucinations and over half ($n = 5$; 56%) experienced command hallucinations. The majority ($n = 7$; 78%) also experienced hallucinations in other modalities (tactile, visual, somatic, or olfactory). Seventy-eight percent ($n = 7$) experienced delusions, all of which were persecutory in nature. Seventy-eight percent ($n = 7$) were in the severe or extremely severe range for depression [>28 on the BDI-II (55) or ≥28 on the DASS-21 (57)] and 89% ($n = 8$) were in the severe or extremely severe range for anxiety [>25 on the BAI (54) or ≥15 on the DASS-21 (57)]. Of the six participants who completed the CORE-10 (56), 67% ($N = 4$) fell in the moderate-to-severe or severe range for emotional well-being.

Pre therapy, 67% ($N = 6$) were in the severe range for post-traumatic stress symptoms (≥36 on the PDS (52)). Seventy-eight percent ($n = 7$) had experienced multiple traumas, 56% ($n = 5$) had experienced childhood trauma, and 33% ($n = 3$) were refugees and had sought asylum in the UK due to their traumatic experiences. **Table 1** summarises the trauma type, PTSD and psychotic symptoms, target hotspot and associated memory, and key tf-CBTp interventions, for each of the participants.

Therapy and Assessment Attrition

None of the participants dropped out of therapy. There was considerable variation across individuals in the length of therapy (median number of months = 22; range = 8–35 months) and number of sessions received (median number. of sessions = 41; range = 25–66). Towards the end of therapy, sessions were often tapered down to fortnightly, then monthly, hence prolonging therapy. Of note, one participant (P5), who received 42 sessions of the tf-CBTp protocol, also had further 82 sessions for a range of other, complex presenting difficulties, relating to secondary diagnoses of emotionally unstable personality disorder and obsessive–compulsive disorder, multiple physical health problems including frontal lobe damage following a stroke, and ongoing social needs.

Two clients (22%; P1 and P8) did not complete the baseline assessment because the waiting list was under 2 weeks. All participants (100%) completed the pre-therapy assessment, and eight participants (89%) completed an end-of-therapy assessment. The participant (P4) who did not complete an end-of-therapy assessment completed a follow-up assessment, therefore, permitting a comparison of between pre-therapy and follow-up. Seven participants (78%) completed their follow-up assessment. One participant (P1) did not attend his follow-up appointment due to physical health issues, and one participant (P5) was not offered a follow-up because she was seen for therapy prior to this becoming a routine assessment point in the service (note that participant numbers were allocated alphabetically rather than according to referral time point). In addition, two participants did not complete measures of post-traumatic symptoms (P2 and P7), depression (P3 and P7), or anxiety (P3 and P7) at follow-up. As only seven participants experienced delusions, only 78% of the sample completed the PSYRATS-delusions (51). Only 67% ($n = 6$) completed the CORE-10 (56) as this measure was introduced in the service after three participants had already started therapy. A summary of mean data for each of the measures at each assessment point is presented in **Table 2** and shown graphically

TABLE 2 | Mean scores (SD; *n*) for outcomes at the four time points.

Measure	Time point			
	Initial	Pre-therapy	Post-therapy	Follow-up
PDS	Not administered	37.22 (8.94; *n* = 9)	23.38 (12.40; *n* = 8)	23.60 (11.61; *n* = 5)
PSYRATS—delusions	16.17 (3.87; *n* = 6)	13.57 (5.44; *n* = 7)	8.33 (9.09; *n* = 6)	10.14 (8.51; *n* = 7)
PSYRATS—voices	31.71 (6.73; *n* = 7)	29.56 (6.73; *n* = 9)	20.50 (10.97; *n* = 8)	24.29 (10.06; *n* = 7)
BDI-II	41.83 (10.53; *n* = 6)	34.50 (18.60; *n* = 6)	24.80 (19.84; *n* = 5)	23.00 (19.47; *n* = 3)
BAI	37.67 (16.71; *n* = 6)	32.33 (19.05; *n* = 6)	21.40 (15.64; *n* = 5)	20.33 (21.94; *n* = 3)
DASS—depression	16 (*n* = 1)	28.00 (19.29; *n* = 3)	18.00 (10.00; *n* = 3)	19.00 (18.38; *n* = 2)
DASS—anxiety	18 (*n* = 1)	30.67 (9.02; *n* = 3)	24.67 (11.72; *n* = 3)	9.00 (7.07; *n* = 2)
CORE-10	21.25 (7.37; *n* = 4)	20.33 (6.77; *n* = 6)	14.60 (8.32; *n* = 5)	13.80 (8.96; *n* = 5)

PDS, Post-traumatic Diagnostic Scale; PSYRATS, Psychotic Symptoms Rating Scale; BDI-II, Beck Depression Inventory-II; BAI, Beck Anxiety Inventory; DASS-21, Depression Anxiety Stress Scales-21; CORE-10, Clinical Outcomes in Routine Evaluation-10.

in **Figure 3**. Individual scores on measures at each assessment point is shown in **Figure 4**, and a summary of changes across each phase (waiting list; pre- to post-therapy; pre-therapy to follow-up) for each measure is provided in **Table 3**.

Changes during the Waiting List Period

Data were not available for the PDS for this period. Data were also not available on other measures for the two clients (P1 and P8) who only completed a pre-therapy assessment. Means for the other seven individuals remained comparable [PSYRATS-voices; well-being (CORE-10)] or reduced marginally [PSYRATS-delusions; depression (BDI-II); anxiety (BAI)] for the majority of measures whilst participants were on the waiting list. The means remained in the severe or extremely severe ranges for depression and anxiety, and moderate to severe for emotional well-being. None of the seven participants showed a reliable improvement on PSYRATS-voices, as evidenced by the RCI. One (17%) of the six participants with delusions, and one (25%) of the four participants who completed the CORE-10, showed a reliable improvement (with 95% confidence) in delusions and well-being, respectively. Two (29%) of the seven participants showed a reliable improvement on depression and one (14%) of the seven showed a reliable improvement on anxiety (**Table 3**). One participant (14%) showed a reliable worsening of anxiety whilst on the waiting list. No further reliable changes were found.

Changes during Therapy

Post-traumatic Symptoms

The overall mean for the group on the PDS fell from the "severe" range at pre-therapy to the "moderate-to-severe" range post therapy, which was maintained at follow-up. In terms of individual scores on the PDS, all participants completing pre- and post-assessments (*n* = 8) had lower scores post therapy, and 63% (*n* = 5) of these showed reliable improvements. No participants showed any symptom deterioration at the end of therapy compared to pre-therapy. Five (56%) participants completed the PDS at follow-up. Of these, four participants (80%) showed improvements compared to pre-therapy, one of whom (20%) showed a reliable improvement. One (20%) participant's score on the PDS at follow-up had returned to the same level as their score pre therapy (despite showing a non-reliable improvement between pre- and post-therapy). No participants showed a worsening of post-traumatic symptoms at follow-up compared to pre-therapy.

Auditory Hallucinations

The overall mean for the group on the PSYRATS-voices was reduced at both post-therapy and follow-up compared to pre-therapy. Scores between pre- and post-therapy decreased in five (63%) of the eight participants who completed their post-therapy assessment, of whom two (25%) participants showed reliable improvements in their voices. Seven participants (78%) completed the PSYRATS-voices at follow-up. Of these, 29% (*n* = 2) showed reliable improvements at follow-up compared to pre-therapy. Fifty-seven percent (*n* = 4) showed a worsening in their voices, although none of these indicated reliable changes.

Delusions

Compared to pre-therapy, the overall mean for the group on the PSYRATS-delusions was reduced at both post-therapy and follow-up. Of the seven participants experiencing delusions, six (86%) completed the PSYRATS-delusions post therapy, and scores between pre- and post-therapy decreased in four (67%) of these, of whom three (50%) showed reliable improvements. There were no other reliable changes. All participants who experienced delusions (*n* = 7) completed this measure at follow-up. Of these, 43% (*n* = 3) showed reliable improvements in their delusion scores at follow-up compared to pre-therapy, with no other reliable changes.

Depression

The overall mean for the group on measures of depression fell from the severe and extremely severe ranges [on the BDI-II (*n* = 5) and DASS-depression (*n* = 3), respectively] to the moderate range, which was maintained at follow-up. Of the eight people completing their post-therapy assessment, all but one participant (*n* = 7) improved on their depression score between pre- and post-therapy, four (50%) of whom indicated reliable improvements. Five participants (56%) completed a depression measure at follow-up. Of these, 80% (*n* = 4) showed improvements in their depression scores at follow-up compared to pre-therapy, 40% (*n* = 2) of whom showed reliable improvements, with no other reliable changes.

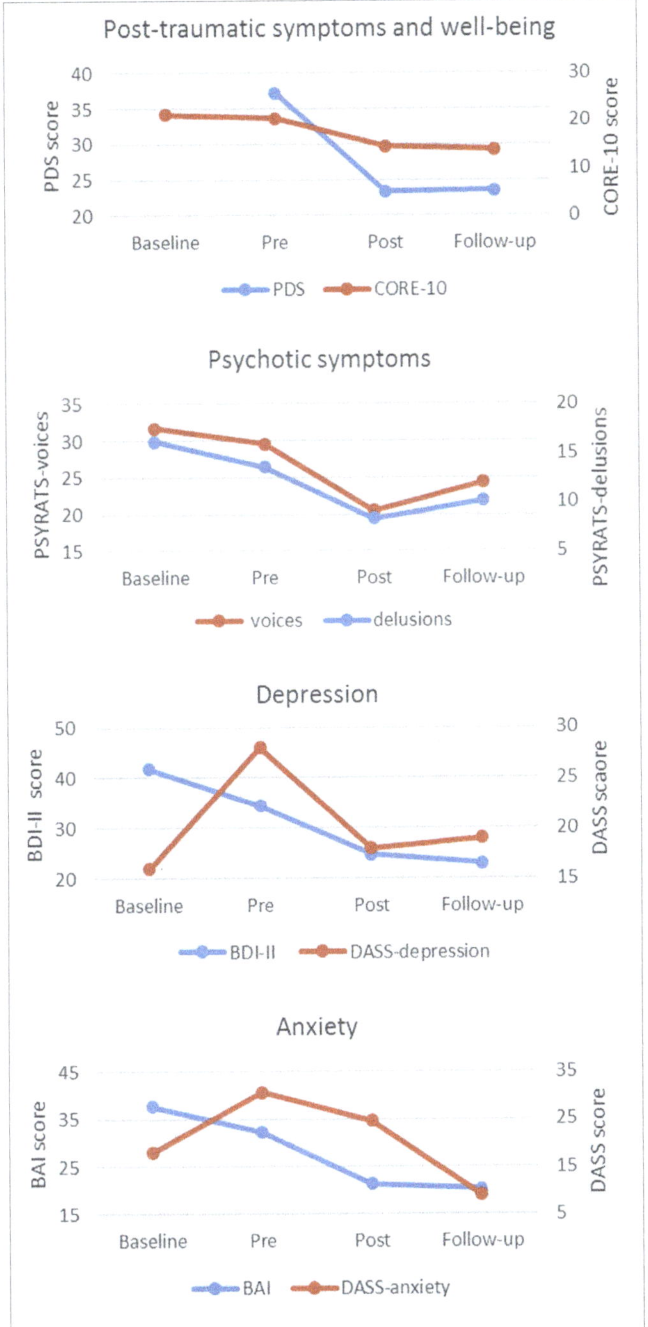

FIGURE 3 | **Mean scores on outcome measures across time points.**

Anxiety

Eight participants (89%) completed an anxiety measure at the end of therapy. The overall mean for the group on the BAI fell from the severe range pre therapy to the moderate range post therapy ($n = 5$). This was maintained at follow-up ($n = 3$). For those who completed the DASS-anxiety ($n = 3$), the overall mean scores reduced at the end of therapy compared to pre-therapy but remained in the extremely severe range. At follow-up, however, the mean for the DASS-anxiety fell to being in the mild range ($n = 2$). Sixty-three percent ($n = 5$) of participants' anxiety improved between pre- and post-therapy, 36% ($n = 3$) of whom indicated reliable improvements. There were no other reliable changes. Five participants (56%) completed an anxiety measure at follow-up. Of these, 100% ($n = 5$) showed improvements in their anxiety at follow-up compared to pre-therapy, 40% ($n = 2$) of whom showed reliable improvements.

Emotional Well-being

Five participants (83%) completed the CORE-10 at the end of therapy. The overall mean for the group on the CORE-10 ($n = 5$) fell from the moderate-to-severe range at pre-therapy to the mild range at the end of therapy. This was maintained at follow-up. Four participants (80%) improved on their emotional well-being score between pre- and post-therapy, and 40% ($n = 2$) indicated reliable improvements. There were no other reliable changes. Five participants (83%) completed the CORE-10 at follow-up. Of these, 80% ($n = 4$) showed a reduction in their well-being score at follow-up compared to pre-therapy, one of whom (20%) showed a reliable improvement, with no other reliable changes.

Summary of Change across All Symptom Measures

Visual comparison of the means between pre-therapy and the end of therapy for the whole group indicated that overall the sample showed a trend for improved scores on all symptom measures, which appeared to be maintained at 6-month follow-up (**Table 3**; **Figure 3**). At the end of therapy, all but one client (88%) achieved a reliable improvement on at least one symptom measure; 75% on at least two symptom measures; and 50% on at least three symptom measures. Of those who completed a follow-up assessment, 86% ($n = 6$) indicated at least one reliable improvement at follow-up, with 43% ($n = 3$) exhibiting a reliable change on at least two symptoms measures. No participants indicated a reliable worsening of their symptoms at either time point. One participant (14%) indicated a reliable worsening in their anxiety whilst on the waiting list. In terms of individual change scores, depending on outcome measure, there was a reduction of between 60–100% of scores from pre to post therapy, and between 29–100% of scores from pre-therapy to follow up. Reliable change was found on between 25–63% (average 44%) of scores at post therapy and between 20–43% (average 32%) of scores at follow up. This compared to a reduction in 29–75% of individual change scores in the waiting list period, with 0–29% (average 19%) of scores showing reliable improvement.

Participant Feedback Regarding Satisfaction with Therapy

All participants ($n = 9$) completed the STQ (59) either at the end of therapy ($n = 8$) or at follow-up (P4). Overall, 78% ($n = 7$) were "very satisfied" and 22% ($n = 2$) were "satisfied" with the therapy they received. Eighty-nine percent ($n = 8$) rated that they felt they had made "a lot of progress" in therapy and one participant (11%) felt they had made "a little progress." All participants (100%) rated that they had "a lot" of trust in their therapist; 89% felt "very understood" by their therapist; 11% ($n = 1$) felt "fairly understood" by their therapist. Eighty-nine percent ($n = 8$)

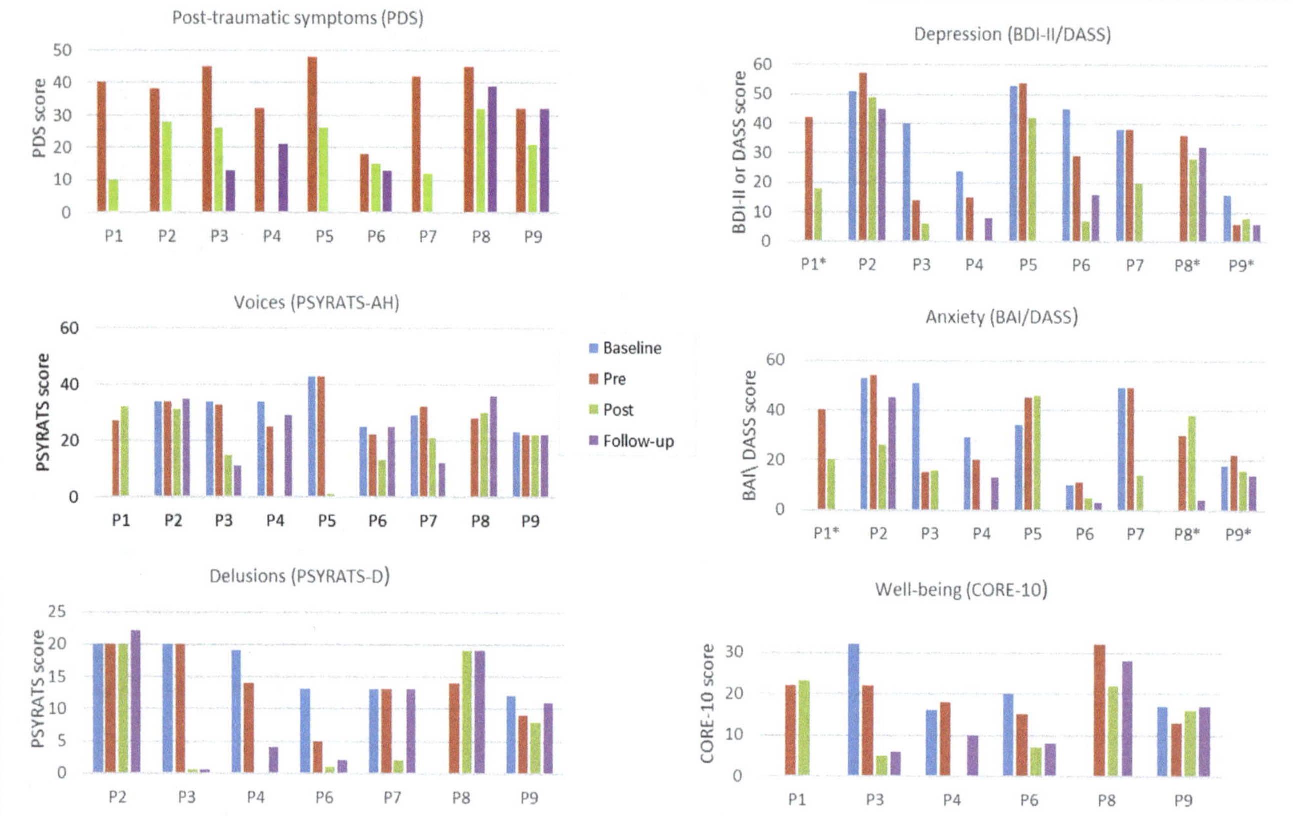

FIGURE 4 | Individual scores across time points. Key: P, participant; * completed DASS-depression/anxiety. Missing data: Post-traumatic symptoms: baseline (all), post-therapy (P4), follow-up (P1, P2, P5, P7); Voices: baseline (P1, P8), post-therapy (P4), follow-up (P1, P5); Delusions: baseline (P8), post-therapy (P4); Depression: baseline (P1, P8), post-therapy (P4), follow-up (P1, P3, P5, P7); Anxiety: baseline (P1, P8), post-therapy (P4), follow-up (P1, P3, P5, P7); Well-being (not completed by P2, P5, and P7 at any time point): baseline (P1, P8), post-therapy (P4), follow-up (P1).

endorsed that they either "strongly agreed" or "agreed" that they had achieved a better understanding of the development of their problems and 78% ($n = 7$) endorsed that they "strongly agreed" they had achieved a better understanding of their experiences. Eighty-nine percent ($n = 8$) rated that they "strongly agreed" that they had gained methods and techniques to cope with their problems. Sixty-seven percent ($n = 6$) and 33% ($n = 3$) rated that tasks between sessions were "very helpful" or "slightly helpful," respectively. Selected verbatim comments from the nine participants regarding the intervention are presented in **Table 4**.

DISCUSSION

This case-series study demonstrated that it is safe, feasible, and acceptable to integrate current cognitive-behavioural approaches for post-traumatic stress and psychotic symptoms into a single protocol, in individuals with current distressing symptoms of psychosis and post-traumatic stress presenting to a psychological therapies service. All participants completed therapy, and no adverse outcomes in terms of reliable worsening of symptoms, relapse, or hospital admissions occurred as a result of the intervention. Satisfaction ratings were very high, and all but one client (88%) achieved a reliable improvement on at least one symptom measure post therapy.

Visual examination of the group means showed a trend for improved scores across all symptoms, both at the end of therapy and at the 6+ months of follow-up. In terms of individual change scores, it is very encouraging that a substantial majority showed improvements on each of the symptom measures, with approximately one-third of the participants indicating reliable changes on each of the measures at each time point. Rates of improvements following therapy were twice those found during the waiting list period, for those outcomes where waiting list data were available (i.e., all measures except PDS (52)). The greatest improvement noted was on post-traumatic symptoms, in which all clients showed improved scores, with 63% indicating a reliable change. These promising findings provide some support for the view that the inclusion of direct memory reprocessing strategies is necessary to address post-traumatic symptoms.

Whilst these results are encouraging, it is important to note that the mean PDS score was still in the moderate-to-severe range post therapy and at follow-up (as compared to being in the severe range pre therapy). Nevertheless, it is worth bearing in mind that this was a very complex sample with the majority (78%) presenting with multiple complex traumas (e.g., participant 2 experienced long-term imprisonment with physical and sexual torture, and participant 3 was living in conflict zone (civil war and genocide) during which her parents were killed. She was then held captive,

TABLE 3 | Change scores for each participant's outcome measures across phases.

Measures (reliable change criterion for each measure)	Post-traumatic symptoms		Voice symptom levels			Delusion symptom levels			Depression			Anxiety			Emotional well-being		
	PDS		PSYRATS			PSYRATS			BDI			BAI; RCI = 8.83[a]			CORE		
	Reliable Change Index (RCI) = 12.96[a]		RCI = 9.76[a]			RCI = 7.40[a]			DASS			DASS-A*; RCI = 18.38[a]			RCI = 9.34[a]		
Time point	Pre-therapy–post-therapy	Pre-therapy–follow-up	Baseline–pre-therapy	Pre-therapy–post-therapy	Pre-therapy–follow-up	Baseline–pre-therapy	Pre-therapy–post-therapy	Pre-therapy–follow-up	Baseline–pre-therapy	Pre-therapy–post-therapy	Pre-therapy–follow-up	Baseline–pre-therapy	Pre-therapy–post-therapy	Pre-therapy–follow-up	Baseline–pre-therapy	Pre-therapy–post-therapy	Pre-therapy–follow-up
P1*	↓30	m	m	↑5	m	NA	NA	NA	m	↓24	m	m	↓20	m	m	↑1	m
P2	↓10	m	↔	↓3	↑1	↔	↔	↑2	↑6	↓8	↓12	↑1	↓18	↓9	m	m	m
P3	↓19	↓32	↓1	↓18	↓22	↔	↓20	↓20	↓26	↓8	m	↓36	↑1	m	↓10	↓17	↓16
P4	m	↓11	↓9	m	↑4	↓4	m	↓10	↓9	m	↓7	↓9	m	↓7	↑2	m	↓8
P5	↓22	m	↔	↓43	m	NA	NA	NA	↑1	↓12	m	↑11	↑1	m	m	m	m
P6	↓3	↓5	↓3	↓9	↑3	↓8	↓12	↓11	↓16	↓22	↓13	↑1	↓6	↓8	↓5	↓8	↓7
P7	↓30	m	↑3	↓9	↓20	↔	↓11	↔	↔	↓18	m	↔	↓35	m	m	m	m
P8*	↓13	↓6	m	↓2	↑8	m	↑5	↑5	m	↓8	↓4	m	↑8	↓26	m	↓10	↓4
P9*	↓11	↔	↓1	↔	↔	↑3	↓1	↑2	↓10	↑2	↔	↑4	↓6	↓6	↓4	↑3	↑4
	8 improved (5 reliably)	4 improved (1 reliably) 1 remained the same	4 improved 2 remained the same 1 worsened	5 improved (2 reliably) 1 remained the same 2 worsened	2 improved (reliably) 1 remained the same 4 worsened	3 improved (1 reliably) 3 remained the same	4 improved (3 reliably) 1 remained the same 1 worsened	3 improved (reliably) 1 remained the same; 3 worsened	4 improved (2 reliably) 1 remained the same 2 worsened	7 improved (4 reliably) 1 worsened	4 improved (2 reliably) 1 remained the same	2 improved (reliably) 1 remained the same 3 worsened	5 improved (3 reliably) 3 worsened	5 improved (2reliably)	3 improved (1 reliably) 1 worsened	3 improved (2 reliably) 2 worsened	4 improved (1 reliably) 1 worsened

*These 3 participants (P1, P8 and P9) completed the DASS-anxiety/depression as opposed to the BAI/BDI-II.

[a]RCI scores correspond to the score which had to be exceeded for a reliable change to be obtained for each particular measure.

Numeric figure represents change in score on each measure. Figures in red represent reliable change scores. ↓, improvement; ↔, no change; ↑, worsening; NA, non-applicable; m, missing.

TABLE 4 | Examples of participant comments on their response to the tf-CBTp intervention.

Selected comments from participants
"It was like being woken from a lifelong coma—I can actually start to live again."
"I feel more in control. I still hear the voices but I don't have to do what they say. I don't feel I'm back there again. They are just memories from the past."
"I never thought I would be able to say the words 'It's not my fault' but I have learnt to, and I believe it. I can now move forward."
"If you don't talk about it, the root of the trauma is still there, it just keeps coming back and you end up in repeated vicious cycles. I wouldn't be here today if I wasn't referred...not only did it help me recover but it was educational and empowering."
"I think if more people were offered trauma focused therapy there would be less mad people, or at least, less people thinking that they are mad."
"I could write a book about my experience of therapy and I would definitely refer a friend."
"Things I found helpful included: imagery rescripting, cross examination of evidence and alternative explanation of beliefs."

gang raped, and witnessed the murder of grandfather). Over half (56%) had experienced childhood trauma, and a third (33%) were refugees (who in addition to their index trauma had additionally experienced the trauma of living in conflict zones and having to relocate to the UK). The majority of the clients had ongoing social needs, multiple diagnoses, and high levels of baseline depression and anxiety (78 and 89% scoring in the severe or extremely severe range for depression and anxiety, respectively). Given these profiles, it is perhaps understandable that many clients had some residual post-traumatic symptoms post therapy (albeit much reduced).

In terms of impact on voices, the majority of participants indicated improved scores but only a minority improved reliably post therapy (25%) or at follow-up (29%). It is worth noting that in this sample, individuals' voices were very severe, with over half (56%) experiencing distressing command hallucinations associated with risky compliance behaviours. Greater improvements were seen for delusions, with approximately half indicating reliable improvement post therapy (50%) or at follow-up (43%). This change may be explained by the fact that the therapy protocol included re-formulating distressing delusional beliefs (e.g., the Devil is suffocating me at night) as understandable reactions to traumatic experiences (e.g., feeling suffocated is a flashback to my abuser who reminds me of the Devil), hence potentially providing alternative, less distressing explanations for clients' delusional beliefs (77). These results are consistent with the findings from the Dutch trial, where changes were found for paranoid thoughts but not hallucinations (48), although fewer of their patients presented with voices than paranoia at baseline, which may have skewed their results. Impact on affect and emotional well-being was also encouraging, and most people indicated improved scores on measures of depression, anxiety, and well-being with 50, 36, and 40% indicating reliable changes on these, respectively, many of whom maintained their scores, or at least showed some improvement at follow-up (40, 40, and 20%, respectively).

It should be noted that the intervention was long (median 41 sessions) and included a stabilisation phase, unlike in the Dutch trial (40). Clinically, it was felt that the stabilisation phase was necessary to build coping strategies, foster a sense of control, and trust in the therapist, and to provide a rationale for the trauma-focused phase of the therapy. Indeed, client feedback was positive with regard to this (e.g., "I understood why it kept coming back and by learning to control the visions I felt more empowered to tackle it head on" [P7]). This supports previous findings within the PTSD literature that therapeutic alliance during the first phase of treatment predicts successful reduction of PTSD symptoms during exposure therapy in the second phase (78). Furthermore, for the majority of the clients, there were ongoing social issues (e.g., immigration, housing, and ongoing domestic violence) that needed to be addressed prior to some clients feeling able to commence the trauma-focused phase of the treatment. As therapists were often the only mental health professionals involved in the client's care, it frequently became therapists' responsibility to address these issues, and, therefore, the length of therapy should be interpreted in this context. Further, given that the NICE guidelines recommend (even when treated in isolation) at least 12 sessions for PTSD, with more for complex PTSD or multiple traumas (23), and at least 16 for psychosis (22) and for severe depression (79), in addition to the recent finding that 25 sessions is the optimal dose for CBT for psychosis (80), 41 sessions is perhaps understandable for this very complex client group. However, whether the stabilisation phase is necessary remains an empirical question that needs to be tested. Consideration will need to be taken with regard to different service contexts, and how some may be better equipped than others to provide holistic care (i.e., in some community teams, e.g., care coordinators may be able to provide stabilisation strategies alongside a therapist doing the trauma-focused work).

Overall, these findings support the emerging evidence base in this area (27–29) and suggest that an integrated approach, targeting both psychotic and post-traumatic symptoms, can have a positive impact not only on positive symptoms of psychosis and post-traumatic symptoms but also on depression, anxiety, and emotional well-being for some clients. The results should be interpreted within the context of a number of strengths and limitations.

Strengths

The study has good ecological validity in that the sample was representative of the heterogeneity and complexity of individuals presenting with distressing post-traumatic stress and psychotic symptoms in the clinic, unlike RCTs that have been criticized on the basis of strict inclusion criteria, and which include individuals without current psychotic symptoms.

The intervention was well received by participants. A number of key factors were likely involved in keeping people engaged in therapy. First, we recruited only individuals who expressed willingness in addressing their trauma sequelae. Many individuals are highly avoidant of discussing their trauma, and ascertaining readiness for therapy is crucial. Second, the therapy adhered to the central tenets and values of CBTp (64, 81): much emphasis was given to engagement and a good therapeutic relationship; therapy was collaborative, with active participation from the client who is seen as an expert in his or her experiences, and had a normalizing philosophy; it was geared towards achieving the person's personal valued goal(s) and based on an individualized, shared formulation, which provided a rationale for trauma-focused interventions; emotional processes were fully integrated within the formulation of psychotic and post-traumatic stress symptoms, and addressed in therapy, not just as the sequelae, but in terms of their role in the formation, trigger, and maintenance of symptoms; paramount importance was given to maintaining the person's self-esteem, empowering and providing hope, and promoting recovery-oriented values (82). Third, we felt the stabilisation stage was helpful in preparing the client for the exposure work ahead, providing hope, trust and optimism, and minimising the risk of exacerbations of psychotic symptoms. Fourth, trauma exposure was conducted within the client's therapeutic "window of tolerance," in that the client was in control of the amount and duration of direct PTSD exposure they could manage within the therapy sessions. This is likely to have been a key factor in minimising dropouts in the therapy process. Finally, the flexible and pragmatic nature of the protocol meant that the intervention was tailored to the needs and goals of the individual, and targeted psychotic and post-traumatic symptoms in an integrated, rather than isolated, fashion. Other groups, such as Lysaker and Dimaggio, have also recommended the use of integrated approaches for people with psychosis, rather than developing new schools of treatment, which promote guided discovery to foster an increased awareness of mental phenomena and making sense of what is happening in one's own mind and the minds of others (i.e., targeting metacognitive capacity, a potential common mechanism in post-traumatic and psychotic symptoms), to move meaningfully towards recovery (83).

The use of independent assessors, rather than outcomes being elicited by the therapists themselves, is a further strength, although a number of participants only agreed to complete the PDS with their therapists. The availability of data from five assessment points, including during a waiting list period, meant that this could serve as a control for each participant, and allowed 6+ months of follow-up for 78% of participants.

Limitations

The study design was limited by the small number of participants, although a sample size of nine is acceptable for a case series. Nevertheless, we were unable to report group statistics, or to investigate potential differences between those who showed improvements on specific outcomes and those who did not. Unfortunately, there were no data available for the PDS during the waiting list period. This means that it is not possible to draw firm conclusions regarding the impact of the intervention on post traumatic symptoms. There were also missing data for some clients on certain measures or at particular time points. Due to service changes, two different measures were used for different clients to assess depression (BDI-II and DASS) and anxiety (BDI and DASS). The PDS has been shown to have a tendency to overdiagnose PTSD (84). The Clinician-Administered PTSD Scale for Schizophrenia (CAPS-S) (85) would have been a more robust, albeit more time-consuming measure. Moreover, as this is a new therapy protocol, which was being developed and elaborated over time, there were no adherence or competence ratings obtained for the therapy delivered. Also, given this was a pragmatic study in which the protocol employed a range of techniques designed to be tailored to the clients' needs and goals, the key mechanism of change remains unclear. A further limitation was that all therapists were experienced in the delivery of this work and had assured protected time for the delivery of the therapy and attendance at supervision, free from competing demands of multidisciplinary team work. It would be important to ascertain whether it would be feasible to implement this in an NHS setting with therapists with a range of experiences, and in a range of settings.

CONCLUSION

This study has important implications for the psychological treatment of post-traumatic stress symptoms in people presenting with psychotic symptoms. First, it builds on emerging evidence that treating post-traumatic symptoms through the use of imaginal reprocessing strategies is safe, acceptable, and feasible in this population. It also supports van den Berg et al.'s (40) assertion that there does not appear to be any justification for excluding people with current psychotic symptoms from trauma-focused interventions. Furthermore, it suggests that an integrated approach, targeting both psychotic and post-traumatic symptoms, can have a positive impact not only on positive symptoms of psychosis and post-traumatic symptoms but also on depression, anxiety, and well-being. An RCT is now warranted to test the efficacy of the intervention for this population. It will be important for future studies to also report on functional gains such as change in employment status or number of health care visits, as well as outcomes such as quality of life and social functioning.

ETHICS STATEMENT

Ethical approval for the use of outcome data from the PICuP Clinic was obtained by the London-Dulwich Research Ethics Committee (Reference 15/LO/1831), and all participants gave written informed consent for their clinical data to be used in research studies.

AUTHOR CONTRIBUTIONS

NK: made substantial contributions to the design of the work; participated in the acquisition, analysis, and interpretation of the data; delivered the therapy for several participants ($n = 6$) in the study; took the lead for drafting and revising the manuscript; gave final approval of the version to be published; agreed to be accountable for all aspects of the work in ensuring the questions related to the accuracy or integrity of any part of the work. EH: made substantial contributions to the design of the work and the acquisition of data; delivered the therapy for participants ($n = 2$) in the study; supervised the delivery of therapy for one other case; made substantial contributions towards drafting and revising the manuscript; gave final approval of the version to be published; agreed to be accountable for all aspects of the work. EP: made substantial contributions to the conception or design of the work; participated in the analysis and interpretation of the data for the work; made substantial contributions to drafting and revising the manuscript; gave final approval of the version to be published; agreed to be accountable for all aspects of the work.

ACKNOWLEDGMENTS

We are very grateful to Professor Tony Morrison for generously allowing us to adapt his formulation and for firing our interest in this area. We would also like to thank the Assistant Psychologists (Lisa Grünwald, Zara Kanji, Bina Sharma, Jenny Beardwood, Annabel Broyd, Rosanna Michalczuk, Philip Milner, Rebecca Ison, and Eleanor Parker) who skilfully administered the assessments and Malcolm Scoales for the excellent therapy he provided to one of the clients in this case series. Mostly, we are very grateful to the participants attending the PICuP within SLaM NHS Foundation Trust who courageously committed to the therapy and allowed us to share their experience of therapy. Open access for this article was funded by King's College London.

REFERENCES

1. Grubaugh AL, Zinzow HM, Paul L, Egede LE, Frueh BC. Trauma exposure and posttraumatic stress disorder in adults with severe mental illness: a critical review. *Clin Psychol Rev* (2011) 31(6):883–99. doi:10.1016/j.cpr.2011.04.003
2. Achim AM, Maziade M, Raymond E, Olivier D, Merette C, Roy MA. How prevalent are anxiety disorders in schizophrenia? A meta-analysis and critical review on a significant association. *Schizophr Bull* (2011) 37(4):811–21. doi:10.1093/schbul/sbp148
3. Morrison AP, Frame L, Larkin W. Relationships between trauma and psychosis: a review and integration. *Br J Clin Psychol* (2003) 42:331–53. doi:10.1348/014466503322528892
4. van der Vleugel BM, van den Berg DPG, Staring ABP. Trauma, psychosis, post-traumatic stress disorder and the application of EMDR. *Riv Psichiatr* (2012) 47(2):33–8. doi:10.1708/1071.11737
5. Renard SB, Huntjens RJC, Lysaker PH, Moskowitz A, Aleman A, Pijnenborg GHM. Unique and overlapping symptoms in schizophrenia spectrum and dissociative disorders in relation to models of psychopathology: a systematic review. *Schizophr Bull* (2017) 43(1):108–21. doi:10.1093/schbul/sbw063
6. Pilton M, Varese F, Berry K, Bucci S. The relationship between dissociation and voices: a systematic literature review and meta-analysis. *Clin Psychol Rev* (2015) 40:138–55. doi:10.1016/j.cpr.2015.06.004
7. Read J, Perry BD, Moskowitz A, Connolly J. The contribution of early traumatic events to schizophrenia in some patients: a traumagenic neurodevelopmental model. *Psychiatry* (2001) 64(4):319–45. doi:10.1521/psyc.64.4.319.18602
8. Bentall RP, Wickham S, Shevlin M, Varese F. Do specific early-life adversities lead to specific symptoms of psychosis? A study from the 2007 the Adult Psychiatric Morbidity Survey. *Schizophr Bull* (2012) 38(4):734–40. doi:10.1093/schbul/sbs049
9. Hardy A, Emsley R, Freeman D, Bebbington P, Garety PA, Kuipers EE, et al. Psychological mechanisms mediating effects between trauma and psychotic symptoms: the role of affect regulation, intrusive trauma memory, beliefs, and depression. *Schizophr Bull* (2016) 42:S34–43. doi:10.1093/schbul/sbv175
10. Steel C, Fowler D, Holmes EA. Trauma-related intrusions and psychosis: an information processing account. *Behav Cogn Psychoth* (2005) 33(2):139–52. doi:10.1017/S1352465804001924
11. Gracie A, Freeman D, Green S, Garety PA, Kuipers E, Hardy A, et al. The association between traumatic experience, paranoia and hallucinations: a test of the predictions of psychological models. *Acta Psychiatr Scand* (2007) 116(4):280–9. doi:10.1111/j.1600-0447.2007.01011.x
12. Lovatt A, Mason O, Brett C, Peters E. Psychotic-like experiences, appraisals, and trauma. *J Nerv Ment Dis* (2010) 198(11):813–9. doi:10.1097/NMD.0b013e3181f97c3d
13. Dimaggio G, Lysaker PH. *Metacognition and Severe Adult Mental Disorders*. Florence, USA: Taylor and Francis (2010).
14. Lysaker PH, Vohs JL, Ballard R, Fogley R, Salvatore G, Popolo R, et al. Metacognition, self-reflection and recovery in schizophrenia. *Future Neurol* (2012) 8(1):103–15. doi:10.2217/fnl.12.78
15. Lysaker PH, Dimaggio G, Wickett-Curtis A, Kukla M, Luedtke B, Vohs J, et al. Deficits in metacognitive capacity are related to subjective distress and heightened levels of hyperarousal symptoms in adults with posttraumatic stress disorder. *J Trauma Dissociation* (2015) 16(4):384–98. doi:10.1080/15299732.2015.1005331
16. Lysaker PH, Gumley A, Brune M, Vanheule S, Buck KD, Dimaggio G. Deficits in the ability to recognize one's own affects and those of others: associations with neurocognition, symptoms and sexual trauma among persons with schizophrenia spectrum disorders. *Conscious Cogn* (2011) 20(4):1183–92. doi:10.1016/j.concog.2010.12.018
17. Hassan AN, De Luca V. The effect of lifetime adversities on resistance to antipsychotic treatment in schizophrenia patients. *Schizophr Res* (2015) 161(2–3):496–500. doi:10.1016/j.schres.2014.10.048
18. de Bont PAJM, van den Berg DPG, van der Vleugel BM, de Roos C, de Jongh A, van der Gaag M, et al. Predictive validity of the Trauma Screening Questionnaire in detecting post-traumatic stress disorder in patients with psychotic disorders. *Br J Psychiatry* (2015) 206(5):408–16. doi:10.1192/bjp.bp.114.148486
19. Dillon J. The personal is the political. In: Rapley M, Moncrieff J, Dillon J, editors. *De-Medicalizing Misery: Psychiatry, Psychology and the Human Condition*. Basingstoke, England: Palgrave MacMillan (2011). p. 141–57.
20. Coleman R. *Recovery: An Alien Concept?*. Fife, Scotland: P&P Press (2011).
21. Longden E. *Learning from the Voices in My Head*. New York, NY: TED Books (2013).
22. NICE. *Psychosis and Schizophrenia in Adults: Treatment and Management*. London: National Institute for Health and Care Excellence (2014).
23. NICE. *Post-Traumatic Stress Disorder (PTSD): The Management of PTSD in Adults and Children in Primary and Secondary Care*. London: Gaskell Press (2005).
24. Gairns S, Alvarez-Jimenez M, Hulbert C, McGorry P, Bendall S. Perceptions of clinicians treating young people with first-episode psychosis for post-traumatic stress disorder. *Early Interv Psychia* (2015) 9(1):12–20. doi:10.1111/eip.12065
25. Becker CB, Zayfert C, Anderson E. A survey of psychologists' attitudes towards and utilization of exposure therapy for PTSD. *Behav Res Ther* (2004) 42(3):277–92. doi:10.1016/S0005-7967(03)00138-4
26. Ronconi JM, Shiner B, Watts BV. Inclusion and exclusion criteria in randomized controlled trials of psychotherapy for PTSD. *J Psychiatr Pract* (2014) 20(1):25–37. doi:10.1097/01.pra.0000442936.23457.5b
27. Sin J, Spain D. Psychological interventions for trauma in individuals who have psychosis: a systematic review and meta-analysis. *Psychosis* (2016) 9(1):67–81. doi:10.1080/17522439.2016.1167946
28. Swan S, Keen N, Reynolds N, Onwumere J. Psychological interventions for post-traumatic stress symptoms in psychosis: a systematic review. *Front Psychol* (2017) 8:341. doi:10.3389/fpsyg.2017.00341
29. Sin J, Spain D, Furuta M, Murrells T, Norman I. Psychological interventions for post-traumatic stress disorder (PTSD) in people with severe mental illness. *Cochrane Database Syst Rev* (2017) 1:CD011464. doi:10.1002/14651858.CD011464.pub2
30. Kevan IM, Gumley AI, Coletta V. Post-traumatic stress disorder in a person with a diagnosis of schizophrenia: examining the efficacy of psychological intervention using single N methodology. *Clin Psychol Psychot* (2007) 14(3):229–43. doi:10.1002/cpp.534
31. Hamblen JL, Jankowski MK, Rosenberg SD, Mueser KT. Cognitive-behavioral treatment for PTSD in people with severe mental illness: three case studies. *Am J Psychiatr Rehabil* (2004) 7(2):147–70. doi:10.1080/15487760490476192
32. Callcott P, Standart S, Turkington D. Trauma within psychosis: using a CBT model for PTSD in psychosis. *Behav Cogn Psychoth* (2004) 32(2):239–44. doi:10.1017/S1352465804001249
33. Kayrouz R, Vrklevski LP. Fatal torment – from psychosis-driven index offence to trauma: a case study in forensic psychotherapy, trauma therapy and matricide. *Australas Psychiatry* (2015) 23(1):54–8. doi:10.1177/1039856214563850

34. Frueh BC, Grubaugh AL, Cusack KJ, Kimble MO, Elhai JD, Knapp RG. Exposure-based cognitive-behavioral treatment of PTSD in adults with schizophrenia or schizoaffective disorder: a pilot study. *J Anxiety Disord* (2009) 23(5):665–75. doi:10.1016/j.janxdis.2009.02.005
35. Lu W, Fite R, Kim E, Hyer L, Yanos PT, Mueser KT, et al. Cognitive-behavioral treament of PTSD in severe mental illness: pilot study replication in an ethnically diverse population. *Am J Psychiatr Rehabil* (2009) 12:73–91. doi:10.1080/15487760802615863
36. van den Berg DPG, van der Gaag M. Treating trauma in psychosis with EMDR: a pilot study. *J Behav Ther Exp Psychiatry* (2012) 43(1):664–71. doi:10.1016/j.jbtep.2011.09.011
37. Bernard M, Jackson C. Written emotional disclosure following first episode psychosis: effects on symptoms of PTSD. *Schizophr Res* (2006) 86:S45–S. doi:10.1016/S0920 9964(06)70134-7
38. Jackson C, Trower P, Reid I, Smith J, Hall M, Townend M, et al. Improving psychological adjustment following a first episode of psychosis: a randomised controlled trial of cognitive therapy to reduce post psychotic trauma symptoms. *Behav Res Ther* (2009) 47(6):454–62. doi:10.1016/j.brat.2009.02.009
39. Mueser KT, Rosenberg SD, Xie H, Jankowski MK, Bolton EE, Lu W, et al. A randomized controlled trial of cognitive-behavioral treatment for posttraumatic stress disorder in severe mental illness. *J Consult Clin Psychol* (2008) 76(2):259–71. doi:10.1037/0022-006X.76.2.259
40. van den Berg DPG, de Bont PAJM, van der Vleugel BM, de Roos C, de Jongh A, Van Minnen A, et al. Prolonged exposure vs eye movement desensitization and reprocessing vs waiting list for posttraumatic stress disorder in patients with a psychotic disorder a randomized clinical trial. *JAMA Psychiatry* (2015) 72(3):259–67. doi:10.1001/jamapsychiatry.2014.2637
41. Steel C, Hardy A, Smith B, Wykes T, Rose S, Enright S, et al. Cognitive-behaviour therapy for post-traumatic stress in schizophrenia. A randomized controlled trial. *Psychol Med* (2017) 47(1):43–51. doi:10.1017/S0033291716002117
42. Frueh BC, Cusack KJ, Grubaugh AL, Sauvageot JA, Wells C. Clinicians' perspectives on cognitive-behavioral treatment for PTSD among persons with severe mental illness. *Psychiat Serv* (2006) 57(7):1027–31. doi:10.1176/ps.2006.57.7.1027
43. Hundt NE, Barrera TL, Arney J, Stanley MA. "It's worth it in the end": veterans' experiences in prolonged exposure and cognitive processing therapy. *Cognit Behav Prac* (2017) 24(1):50–57. doi:10.1016/j.cbpra.2016.02.003
44. Shearing V, Lee D, Clohessy S. How do clients experience reliving as part of trauma-focused cognitive behavioural therapy for posttraumatic stress disorder? *Psychol Psychother* (2011) 84(4):458–72. doi:10.1111/j.2044-8341.2010.02012.x
45. Vincent F, Jenkins H, Larkin M, Clohessy S. Asylum-seekers' experiences of trauma-focused cognitive behaviour therapy for post-traumatic stress disorder: a qualitative study. *Behav Cogn Psychother* (2013) 41(5):579–93. doi:10.1017/S1352465812000550
46. de Jongh A, Resick PA, Zoellner LA, van Minnen A, Lee CW, Monson CM, et al. Critical analysis of the current treatment guidelines for complex PTSD in adults. *Depress Anxiety* (2016) 33(5):359–69. doi:10.1002/da.22469
47. van den Berg DP, de Bont PA, van der Vleugel BM, de Roos C, de Jongh A, van Minnen A, et al. Trauma-focused treatment in PTSD patients with psychosis: symptom exacerbation, adverse events, and revictimization. *Schizophr Bull* (2016) 42(3):693–702. doi:10.1093/schbul/sbv172
48. de Bont PA, van den Berg DP, van der Vleugel BM, de Roos C, de Jongh A, van der Gaag M, et al. Prolonged exposure and EMDR for PTSD v. a PTSD waiting-list condition: effects on symptoms of psychosis, depression and social functioning in patients with chronic psychotic disorders. *Psychol Med* (2016) 46(11):2411–21. doi:10.1017/S0033291716001094
49. O'Driscoll C, Mason O, Brady F, Smith B, Steel C. Process analysis of trauma-focused cognitive behavioural therapy for individuals with schizophrenia. *Psychol Psychother* (2016) 89(2):117–32. doi:10.1111/papt.12072
50. Peters E, Crombie T, Agbedjro D, Johns LC, Stahl D, Greenwood K, et al. The long-term effectiveness of cognitive behavior therapy for psychosis within a routine psychological therapies service. *Front Psychol* (2015) 6:1658. doi:10.3389/fpsyg.2015.01658
51. Haddock G, McCarron J, Tarrier N, Faragher EB. Scales to measure dimensions of hallucinations and delusions: the psychotic symptom rating scales (PSYRATS). *Psychol Med* (1999) 29(4):879–89. doi:10.1017/S0033291799008661
52. Foa EB, Cashman L, Jaycox L, Perry K. The validation of a self-report measure of posttraumatic stress disorder: the Posttraumatic Diagnostic Scale. *Psychol Assess* (1997) 9(4):445–51. doi:10.1037/1040-3590.9.4.445
53. Peters E, Landau S, McCrone P, Cooke M, Fisher P, Steel C, et al. A randomised controlled trial of cognitive behaviour therapy for psychosis in a routine clinical service. *Acta Psychiatr Scand* (2010) 122(4):302–18. doi:10.1111/j.1600-0447.2010.01572.x
54. Beck AT, Steer RA. *Beck anxiety Inventory Manual*. San Antonio, TX: Psychological Corporation (1990).
55. Beck AT, Steer RA, Brown GK. *Beck Depression Inventory*. 2nd ed. San Antonio, TX: Psychological Corporation (1996).
56. Barkham M, Bewick BM, Mullin T, Gilbody S, Connell J, Cahill J, et al. The CORE-10: a short measure of psychological distress for routine use in the psychological therapies. *Counsell Psychother* (2013) 13(1):3–13. doi:10.1080/14733145.2012.729069
57. Lovibond PF, Lovibond SH. The structure of negative emotional states – comparison of the Depression Anxiety Stress Scales (DASS) with the beck depression and anxiety inventories. *Behav Res Ther* (1995) 33(3):335–43. doi:10.1016/0005-7967(94)00075-U
58. Drake R, Haddock G, Tarrier N, Bentall R, Lewis S. The Psychotic Symptom Rating Scales (PSYRATS): their usefulness and properties in first episode psychosis. *Schizophr Res* (2007) 89(1–3):119–22. doi:10.1016/j.schres.2006.04.024
59. Beck AT, Wright FD, Newman CF, Liese BS. *Cognitive Therapy of Substance Abuse*. New York, NY: Guildford Press (1993).
60. Lawlor C, Sharma B, Khondoker M, Peters E, Kuipers E, Johns L. Service user satisfaction with cognitive behavioural therapy for psychosis: associations with therapy outcomes and perceptions of the therapist. *Br J Clin Psychol* (2016) 56:84–102. doi:10.1111/bjc.12122
61. Kuipers E, Garety P, Fowler D, Dunn G, Bebbington P, Freeman D, et al. London East Anglia randomised controlled trial of cognitive-behavioural therapy for psychosis is 1. Effects of the treatment phase. *Brit J Psychiatry* (1997) 171:319–27. doi:10.1192/bjp.171.4.319
62. Miles H, Peters E, Kuipers E. Service-user satisfaction with CBT for psychosis. *Behav Cogn Psychother* (2007) 35(1):109–16. doi:10.1017/S1352465806003158
63. Johns L, Jolley S, Keen N, Peters E. CBT for people with psychosis. In: Grey N, Whittington A, editors. *How to Become a More Effective CBT Therapist Developing Metya-Competence in Clinical Practice*. Chichester: Wiley-Blackwell (2013). p. 191–207.
64. Morrison AP. A manualised treatment protocol to guide delivery of evidence-based cognitive therapy for people with distressing psychosis: learning from clinical trials. *Psychosis* (2017) 1–11. doi:10.1080/17522439.2017.1295098
65. Meaden A, Keen N, Aston R, Barton K, Bucci S. *Working with Command Hallucinations: An Advanced Practical Companion*. London: Routledge (2013).
66. Ehlers A, Clark DM. A cognitive model of posttraumatic stress disorder. *Behav Res Ther* (2000) 38(4):319–45. doi:10.1016/S0005-7967(99)00123-0
67. Brewin CR, Dalgleish T, Joseph S. A dual representation theory of post-traumatic stress disorder. *Psychol Rev* (1996) 103(4):670–86. doi:10.1037/0033-295X.103.4.670
68. Arntz A, Weertman A. Treatment of childhood memories: theory and practice. *Behav Res Ther* (1999) 37(8):715–40. doi:10.1016/S0005-7967(98)00173-9
69. Weertman A, Arntz A. Effectiveness of treatment of childhood memories in cognitive therapy for personality disorders: a controlled study contrasting methods focusing on the present and methods focusing on childhood memories. *Behav Res Ther* (2007) 45(9):2133–43. doi:10.1016/j.brat.2007.02.013
70. Grey N, Young K, Holmes E. Cognitive restructuring within reliving: a treatment for peritraumatic emotional "hotspots" in posttraumatic stress disorder. *Behav Cogn Psychother* (2002) 30(1):37–56. doi:10.1017/S1352465802001054
71. Sheaves B, Onwumere J, Keen N, Stahl D, Kuipers E. Nightmares in patients with psychosis: the relation with sleep, psychotic, affective, and cognitive symptoms. *Can J Psychiatry* (2015) 60(8):354–61.
72. Nappi CM, Drummond SPA, Hall JMH. Treating nightmares and insomnia in posttraumatic stress disorder: a review of current evidence. *Neuropharmacology* (2012) 62(2):576–85. doi:10.1016/j.neuropharm.2011.02.029
73. Jacobson NS, Truax P. Clinical-significance – a statistical approach to defining meaningful change in psychotherapy-research. *J Consult Clin Psychol* (1991) 59(1):12–9. doi:10.1037/0022-006X.59.1.12

74. Martinovich Z, Saunders S, Howard KI. Some comments on "assessing clinical significance". *Psychother Res* (1996) 6(2):124–32. doi:10.1080/10503309612331331648
75. Evans C, Margison F, Barkham M. The contribution of reliable and clinically significant change methods to evidence-based mental health. *Evid Based Mental Health* (1998) 1:70–2. doi:10.1136/ebmh.1.3.70
76. Morris EMJ, Garety P, Peters E. Psychological flexibility and nonjudgemental acceptance in voice hearers: relationships with omnipotence and distress. *Aust N Z J Psychiatry* (2014) 48(12):1150–62. doi:10.1177/0004867414535671
77. Freeman D, Garety PA, Fowler D, Kuipers E, Bebbington PE, Dunn G. Why do people with delusions fail to choose more realistic explanations for their experiences? An empirical investigation. *J Consult Clin Psychol* (2004) 72(4):671–80. doi:10.1037/0022-006X.72.4.671
78. Cloitre M, Stovall-McClough KC, Miranda R, Chemtob CM. Therapeutic alliance, negative mood regulation, and treatment outcome in child abuse-related posttraumatic stress disorder. *J Consult Clin Psychol* (2004) 72(3): 411–6. doi:10.1037/0022-006X.72.3.411
79. NICE. *Depression in Adults: Recognition and Management*. London: National Institute for Health and Care Excellence (2009).
80. Lincoln TM, Jung E, Wiesjahn M, Schlier B. What is the minimal dose of cognitive behavior therapy for psychosis? An approximation using repeated assessments over 45 sessions. *Eur Psychiatry* (2016) 38:31–9. doi:10.1016/j.eurpsy.2016.05.004
81. Morrison AP, Barratt S. What are the components of CBT for psychosis? A Delphi Study. *Schizophr Bull* (2010) 36(1):136–42. doi:10.1093/schbul/sbp118
82. Brabban A, Byrne R, Longden E, Morrison AP. The importance of human relationships, ethics and recovery-orientated values in the delivery of CBT for people with psychosis. *Psychosis* (2016) 1–10. doi:10.1080/17522439.2016.1259648
83. Lysaker PH, Dimaggio G. Metacognitive capacities for reflection in schizophrenia: implications for developing treatments. *Schizophr Bull* (2014) 40(3):487–91. doi:10.1093/schbul/sbu038
84. Griffin MG, Uhlmansiek MH, Resick PA, Mechanic MB. Comparison of the posttraumatic stress disorder scale versus the clinician-administered posttraumatic stress disorder scale in domestic violence survivors. *J Trauma Stress* (2004) 17(6):497–503. doi:10.1007/s10960-004-5798-4
85. Gearon JS, Bellack AS, Tenhula WN. Preliminary reliability and validity of the Clinician-Administered PTSD Scale for schizophrenia. *J Consult Clin Psychol* (2004) 72(1):121–5. doi:10.1037/0022-006X.72.1.121

9

Dopamine Rebound-Excitation Theory: Putting Brakes on PTSD

*Jason C. Lee[1], Lei Philip Wang[1,2] and Joe Z. Tsien[1]**

[1] Department of Neurology, Brain and Behavior Discovery Institute, Medical College of Georgia, Augusta University, Augusta, GA, USA, [2] Department of Psychiatry, Medical College of Georgia, Augusta University, Augusta, GA, USA

Edited by:
Kim T. Mueser,
Boston University, USA

Reviewed by:
Mark Dust,
Claremont Graduate University, USA
Henry W. Chase,
University of Pittsburgh, USA

***Correspondence:**
Joe Z. Tsien
jtsien@augusta.edu

It is not uncommon for humans or animals to experience traumatic events in their lifetimes. However, the majority of individuals are resilient to long-term detrimental changes turning into anxiety and depression, such as post-traumatic stress disorder (PTSD). What underlying neural mechanism accounts for individual variability in stress resilience? Hyperactivity in fear circuits, such as the amygdalar system, is well-known to be the major pathophysiological basis for PTSD, much like a "stuck accelerator." Interestingly, increasing evidence demonstrates that dopamine (DA) – traditionally known for its role in motivation, reward prediction, and addiction – is also crucial in regulating fear learning and anxiety. Yet, how dopaminergic (DAergic) neurons control stress resilience is unclear, especially given that DAergic neurons have multiple subtypes with distinct temporal dynamics. Here, we propose the *Rebound-Excitation Theory*, which posits that DAergic neurons' rebound-excitation at the termination of fearful experiences serves as an important "brake" by providing intrinsic safety-signals to fear-processing neural circuits in a spatially and temporally controlled manner. We discuss how DAergic neuron rebound-excitation may be regulated by genetics and experiences, and how such physiological properties may be used as a brain-activity biomarker to predict and confer individual resilience to stress and anxiety.

Keywords: stress resilience, post-traumatic stress disorder, fear memory, dopamine, fear generalization

In describing emotions as natural selection traits, Darwin observed that fear is universal across multiple species (1). Despite its biological importance, fear can become dysregulated, such that an otherwise harmless situation or neutral cue can later trigger an unreasonable and exaggerated fearful response, resulting in psychiatric disorders, such as anxiety disorders, panic attacks, and post-traumatic stress disorders (PTSD) (2). PTSD patients exhibit avoidance behaviors, hypervigilance, and sleep disturbance. They also experience persistent negative mood and flashbacks about the traumatic event (3). Investigation into the fear circuit has revealed that PTSD could arise due to enhanced fear-learning or fear-sensitization (4, 5), reduced or delayed fear extinction (6, 7), or impaired safety-learning processes (8–10). One key criterion for PTSD diagnosis is the exposure to a traumatic or stressful event. However, it is well-known that only a small percentage of individuals develop PTSD following trauma or stressors (11). What are the neural mechanisms responsible for the inter-individual variability in stress resilience?

Indeed, the interest in stress resilience has increased in recent years. Several genetic studies have identified potential molecular contributors to stress resilience involving neural circuits, such as the serotoninergic circuit and hypothalamic–pituitary–adrenal axis (12–17). Interestingly, resilience and susceptibility to a stressor, such as using social defeat protocols in rodents, have also been attributed to the mesolimbic dopamine (DA) circuit (18). However, how dopaminergic (DAergic) neural activities on a network level contribute to resilience or susceptibility remains unclear. Here, we wish to propose the *Rebound-Excitation Theory*, which posits that the DAergic neuromodulatory circuit generates spatially and temporally precise safety signals upon the termination of fearful stimuli, which act as important innate brakes on fear signals in the brain. Importantly, this intrinsic rebound-excitation signal can be modified by repeated exposure to aversive experiences, as well as by associative safety-signal learning via pairing with conditioned stimulus (CS, such as a neutral tone), via NMDA receptors on DAergic neurons.

DA CIRCUIT DIVERSITY AND COMPLEXITY

DAergic neurons are well-known to subserve a wide range of biological functions, such as learning and memory (19), motivation (20, 21), reward prediction error (22, 23), salience and valence (24, 25), addiction (26, 27), and wanting (28, 29). Recently, a growing body of evidence suggests that DA may also play a crucial role in regulating fear memory and behaviors (30–34). Micro-dialysis and fast-scan cyclic voltammetry studies have also shown that DA concentrations change in DAergic projection areas, such as the nucleus accumbens (NAc), in response to aversive stimuli (32, 35). Moreover, *in vivo* electrophysiological studies in rodents and monkeys have also reported heterogeneous DAergic responses to aversive events (24, 36–43). However, understanding how DAergic neurons subserve fear processing is proving to be a difficult task. For instance, DAergic neurons exhibit both tonic and burst type firing modes (44–46), both of which exert distinct DA release profiles that act on separate DA receptor populations (47). Moreover, DAergic neurons are diverse in nature and can be classified by multiple criteria, such as anatomical locations (48), input-projections (49–52), distinct response dynamics to rewards, and aversive stimuli (25, 43, 53). Adding more dimensions to the circuit complexity, DAergic firing exhibits temporal and spatial dynamics that must also be taken into consideration. For example, multi-phasic temporal dynamics in DAergic neurons have been reported in studies using unexpected (unconditioned) aversive stimuli (40, 53). Consistent with such complex dynamics, we recently described computational classifications of DAergic subtypes based on their distinct inter-spike-interval dynamics (54). Such classifications were further verified by optogenetic methods (54). In addition, downstream targets receiving DAergic projections can send feedback projections to modulate DA activities (55–57). Likewise, local controls of DAergic activities by GABAergic neurons can further add to the complexity of DA signal regulation (58–60).

REBOUND-EXCITATION THEORY

In order to understand the role that DAergic neurons play in processing traumatic experiences, the aforementioned DA circuit complexity necessitates the need to systematically compare and contrast how distinct subpopulations of DAergic neurons respond to emotionally traumatizing events. Emerging evidence clearly suggests that DAergic neurons readily respond to aversive stimuli, including air-puffs to the eyelids of monkeys, or administering bitter tastant quinine in awake rats or tail pinches or foot-shocks to anesthetized rats. However, how the same DAergic neurons respond to a variety of fearful stimuli has rarely been investigated. Thus, the tuning properties of distinct DAergic neuron subtypes remain unclear. Moreover, anesthetized states examined in some of the literature could alter the hedonic state of the stimuli and thus the neural responsivities (61, 62). Furthermore, while negative stimuli – such as air-puffs to the eye or administration of quinine to the mouth, or tail pinch under anesthetized state – are aversive in nature, they are not appropriate as PTSD-inducing models.

To specifically examine how DAergic neurons respond to traumatic fear in real-life events, we used laboratory versions of fearful unconditioned stimuli (US) (such as an earthquake, free fall, or foot-shocks) that induce profound fear memory and rapid cardiac responses in freely behaving mice (63). Combined with pharmacological and optogenetic methods, chronic *in vivo* recordings of VTA DAergic neural activities in freely behaving mice have shown two major types of DAergic neuron responses: fear-inhibited and fear-excited DAergic neurons (40). Notably, we observed that many aversive-inhibited DAergic neurons show phasic rebound-excitation responses at the offset of unexpected aversive stimuli (40) (**Figure 1**). This unique response pattern to fearful US has lent us the idea that offset phasic rebound-excitation of this particular sub-population of DAergic neurons may act as a critical safety signal to encode the termination of a fearful event. The signal strength of this phasic DA release, time-locked to the termination of fearful events, will exert immediate as well as long-term changes in downstream targets, thereby setting up the different thresholds for each individual's resilience to stress and anxiety.

TESTING THE REBOUND-EXCITATION THEORY EXPERIMENTALLY

The *Rebound-Excitation Theory* predicts that attenuation or lack of rebound safety signals following fearful stimuli leads to stress susceptibility, whereas strong rebound safety signals confer stress resilience. Furthermore, the *Rebound-Excitation Theory* predicts that a rebound safety signal is likely to be evolutionarily conserved across multiple species and is subject to modulation via experience-dependent synaptic plasticity. One of the most powerful ways to study stress resilience is to directly examine individual stress response variability following a stressor (64). As a result, testing for rebound-excitation in human PTSD vs. trauma resilient populations could prove invaluable. However, present imaging techniques, such as functional magnetic resonance imaging (fMRI) and EEG, have limited temporal and spatial resolution, which makes rebound-excitation study in humans difficult. This may change with development of transformative BRAIN technologies in future.

On the other hand, large-scale *in vivo* electrophysiological recordings in freely behaving laboratory animals now allows single neural unit activity to be accessed in real time with high temporal and spatial resolution (65). In addition, reliable identification of DAergic neuron subtypes can be achieved by using optogenetics and computational analysis (54). Therefore, initial efforts to test the *Rebound-Excitation Theory* may be fruitful in animal models. Much like that of the human population, a fraction of wild-type

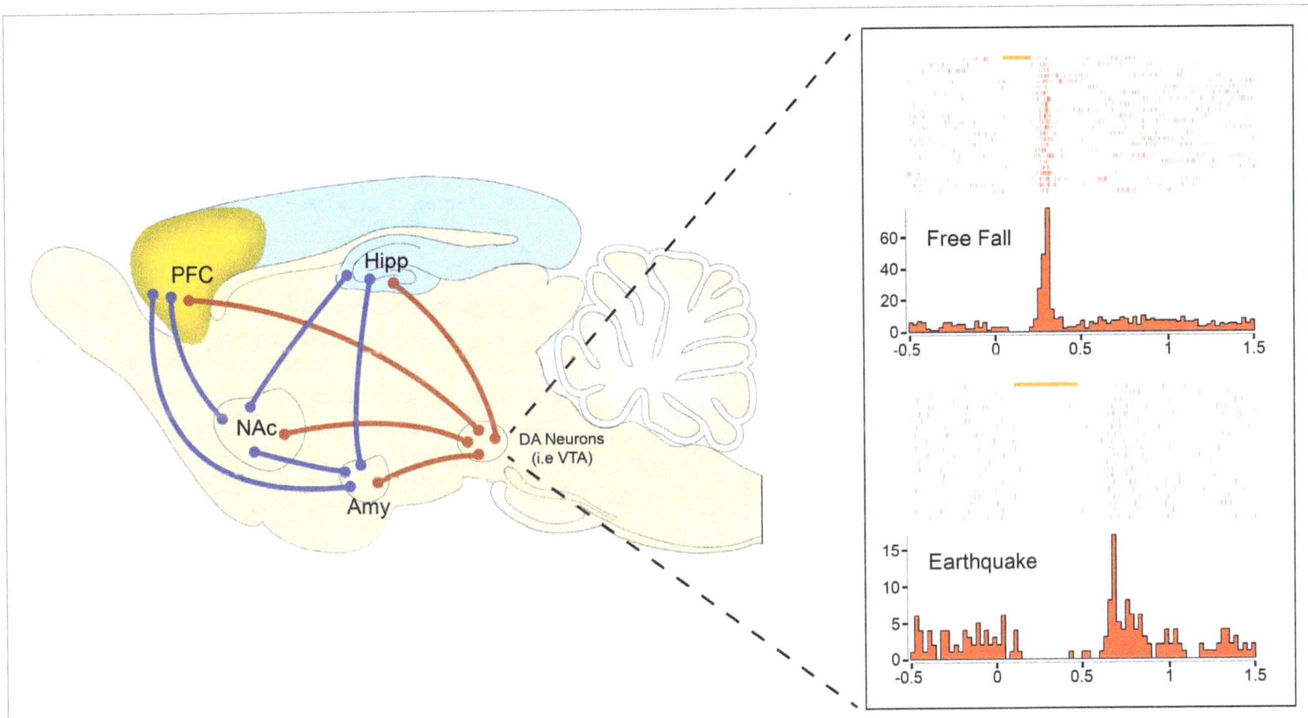

FIGURE 1 | Representative amygdalar fear circuits (blue) with DA circuit (red) involvement. DA units showing rebound-excitation to two distinct types of fearful stimuli: free fall (top) and earthquake (bottom). Rebound-excitation occurs at the termination of fearful stimuli and is proposed to serve as an innate safety signal to modulate fear-related learning and behaviors by broadcasting to downstream targets such as the amygdala (Amy), nucleus accumbens (NAc), prefrontal cortex (PFC), or hippocampus (Hipp).

laboratory animals are known to be more susceptible to stressors than others (17, 66, 67). Thus, the *Rebound-Excitation Theory* can be initially tested by screening and comparing DA rebound-excitation in stress-susceptible vs. stress-resilient animals.

Genetic manipulation in laboratory animals that alters rebound-excitation safety signals can also be useful. For example, we have produced DA neuron-specific NMDA receptor knockout (DA-NR1-KO) mice (68) and have shown that the NMDA receptors in DAergic neurons play a critical and specific role in regulating phasic firing patterns of the DAergic neurons (69). Given the reported excessive fear generalization in this mutant model (41), this knockout model offers a rare opportunity to examine the circuitry dynamics by which DAergic neuron NMDA receptors modulate rebound-excitation safety signals and fear behaviors. This mouse model can also be used to test whether repeated exposure to aversive US may enhance rebound-excitation-based safety-signals in normal animals vs. little or no enhancement effect on PTSD-sensitive models.

TARGETS AND ACTIONS OF DAergic NEURON REBOUND-EXCITATION

What are the potential mechanisms through which DA rebound-excitation safety signals alleviate fear and fear overgeneralization? In general, this innate safety signal can come from three major sources of regulation: (1) the intrinsic DAergic neuron properties, such as ion channels and receptor compositions that produce rebound phasic firings; (2) downstream targets that detect and process DAergic neuron rebound excitation; and (3) cortical and subcortical feedback to the DA circuits.

Obviously, DAergic neurons' safety signals may directly modulate downstream targets' neural and biochemical activities. Phasic firing by DAergic neurons can result in robust DA release (70, 71), leading to the elevation of DA in a variety of neural circuits [i.e., the prefrontal cortex (PFC), striatum, amygdala, hippocampus, etc.]. For example, DA is known to induce short-lived excitatory responses via D1 receptors in downstream neurons (72). The time window in which DA mediates structural changes, such as dendritic spine enlargement is also precise, in the range of seconds or less (0.3–2 s) (73). Furthermore, manipulating DAergic firing has been shown to produce acute behavioral changes (74, 75). Moreover, DA is known to be involved in the induction and maintenance of long-term potentiation (LTP) in the amygdala and hippocampus, respectively (76, 77). DAergic neurons are well-known to project to the PFC, which is important for processing emotional information (78). For example, we recently showed that neurons in the anterior cingulate cortex exhibited diverse responses in response to traumatizing events, such as mild blast events, which mimicked the combat experiences of war fighters when witnessing an explosion of a road-side bomb (79). Importantly, we showed that robust-pattern reverberation occurs frequently in the ACC of blast-exposed animals (79). Pattern reverberation is a process by which real-time memory patterns and traces are replayed shortly after emotionally charged, episodic events (80, 81). DA rebound-excitation may modulate pattern reverberation of fearful memories in downstream targets, such as the ACC and hippocampus. Abnormal pattern reverberation due to alteration in DA rebound-excitation may manifest as PTSD symptoms, such as flashbacks. Effects of DA rebound-excitation on real-time memory traces can be examined using large-scale recording and decoding methods (80, 82). In addition, a DA signal may modulate adult neurogenesis in the dentate gyrus (83–86), which has been linked to stress and depressive behaviors (87, 88), as well as to reduced clearance of fear memory traces (89).

Furthermore, changes in rebound-excitation-based intrinsic safety signals can likely manifest at multiple circuit levels given the DA circuit complexity. For instance, dysregulation from upstream DAergic afferent inputs (90) may alter rebound-excitation safety signals, perhaps by influencing local GABAergic control within the VTA. Dysfunction in feedback control from cortical and subcortical sites (55–57) may also cause pathological alterations in rebound-excitation and fear-related behaviors. This can be highly interesting because cortical and subcortical inputs to DAergic neurons can serve as an important mechanism to create Pavlovian learning paradigms under which associative safety-learning can occur. This would enable a set of Pavlovian neural substrates – which have been extensively studied under Prediction Error theory and temporal difference (TD) models – to be recruited to generate CS/US pairing-triggered safety-learning signal (which is distinct from the innate rebound-excitation-mediated safety signals as we described here). Moreover, abnormal expression of DA receptors or mutations in DA receptors' intracellular signal transduction may lead to instances in which the rebound-excitation of DAergic neurons is intact but is unable to activate downstream targets.

Another possible physiological effect of DA is to regulate neural network synchronization and oscillation. Neural synchronization and oscillation are thought to be an important mechanism by which networks of neurons coordinate their activities in a temporally meaningful pattern to generate cognition, perception, and behaviors (91–93). One study examining cortical input to the hippocampus and Schaffer-collateral found that DA can modulate the excitatory drive onto pyramidal and GABAergic interneurons (94). Additionally, therapeutic dosage of DA agonist levodopa has been shown to cause the frequency synchronization between the globus pallidus and subthalamic nucleus to shift from low frequency (<30 Hz) to high frequency (~70 Hz) (95). Moreover, recent studies using neuroimaging techniques, such as magnetoencephalography (MEG) and functional magnetic resonance imaging (fMRI), have found irregular network synchrony and oscillations in PTSD patients (96, 97). Therefore, rebound-excitation of DAergic neurons on modulating fear circuits should be investigated at multiple levels.

REBOUND-EXCITATION THEORY OFFERS A NEW APPROACH TO STUDY PTSD

The *Rebound-Excitation Theory* predicts that rebound-excitation consistency across multiple fearful experiences may, in part, account for inter-individual variability in stress resilience. We have previously observed rebound-excitation to be similar between distinct fearful events (40). Therefore, a stress resilience index may be constructed by accessing rebound-excitation in individual subjects, and such a resilience index may serve as a useful predictor in clinical settings to screen individuals that may be stress-susceptible. Indeed, we have recently developed fear resistance indices in mice based on inter-individual variability in cardiac responses [heart rate variability (HRV)] across multiple fearful experiences (63). Given that PTSD patients had abnormal HRV (98), in the future, it will be of great interest to study the correlation between inter-individual variability of rebound-excitation signals and HRV. Such potential correlation may provide a mechanistic framework to examine predictive values of HRV in the human population.

Moreover, the proposed theory should open new avenues to develop novel therapeutic strategies for studying and treating PTSD. For instance, DA burst firing has been shown to increase at the onset and offset of voluntary exercises (39). Therefore, exercise with an appropriate time regimen might be explored as a way to improve behavioral therapy. In fact, exercises can enhance neurogenesis in the hippocampus (99), a process linked with reducing depression (88, 100, 101). It is encouraging that a pilot study in an adolescent with PTSD showed that aerobic exercises reduced the symptoms of PTSD (102). Rebound-excitation signals can also be used as a brain-activity biomarker to screen novel compounds for their *in vivo* drug efficacies in preclinical PTSD research.

In literature, external CS (such as a neutral tone) have been used to create Pavlovian association and turning CS into the predictive safety-learning cues about signaling the absence of fearful US in animal models (8, 10, 103–106). This powerful associative learning process utilized Pavlovian conditioning paradigms by repeated pairing of CS with US. Interestingly, PSTD models and patients exhibit impaired ability to suppress fear response even in the presence of conditioned safety-learning cues, despite they can learn normally in Pavlovian fear conditioning (9). This suggests that PTSD deficit was not a result of simple failure in associative learning, but rather specific defects in generating innate safety signals as well as prediction errors based on extinction or discrimination learning. It further highlights the need to differentiate the neural mechanisms underlying conditioned safety-learning of external neutral cues vs. the safety signals derived from DA rebound excitation. It would be of great interest to examine how DAergic neuron rebound excitation signal interacts and influences external safety-learning process, or vice versa, and whether such associative dynamics can be further modeled by prediction error based on TD learning model (23, 107). Because real-life traumatic events rarely occurred by the predictive CS, DA rebound-excitation theory now offers a novel approach to analyzing innate DA safety signal in response to unpredictable US, thereby leading explanation as to how the brain can taper down the otherwise excessive neural trace reverberation that typically followed upon fear experiences (79–82).

This critical distinction between the proposed rebound-excitation theory and TD model should and can be tested experimentally; for example, DAergic neuron rebound-excitation should be observed upon US stimulation alone without repeated CS/US pairing. Rebound-excitation signals the termination of the aversive US itself. As a result, variations in stimulus durations can be used, together with repeated trials, to further define dynamic modulation of its rebound responses, in a similar way that TD learning model and prediction error theory have been examined. Because repetition of aversive US can lead to varying degrees of behavioral habituation or sensitization, we postulate that the repeated presentation of US over trials will lead to stronger DAergic neuron rebound-excitation signal in PTSD-resilient animals vs. diminished rebound-excitation in PTSD-prone animals, and this process should be dependent on the NMDA receptors of the DAergic neurons. It is conceivable that this intrinsic safety signal based on DAergic neuron rebound-excitation is advantageous for an organism's overall survival given the unpredictability of aversive stimuli in nature in terms of types, duration, as well as intensity. Defects in this innate safety-signal due to genetic mutations in the relevant circuits can make the animals vulnerable to PTSD and impair safety-learning in general. Better understanding of both the innate safety-signaling mechanisms, gene mutations, and Pavlovian condition-based safety-learning mechanisms can lead to novel insights to PTSD pathogenesis.

In summary, the proposed *Rebound-Excitation Theory* specifies that DAergic neurons generate intrinsic safety signals at the termination of unconditioned fearful events in a spatially and temporally precise manner. Impairment in the production and reception of this safety signal constitutes a potentially genetic defect in the brake on the fear system. Restoration of this rebound-excitation signal may offer a much-needed new avenue for developing pharmacological and behavioral therapeutic strategies to treat psychiatric disorders.

AUTHOR CONTRIBUTIONS

JL and JT developed the idea and worked with LW. JL generated the figure with input from LW and JT. JL, LW, and JT co-wrote the article.

ACKNOWLEDGMENTS

This work is supported by a NIH grant (R01NS079774). We would like to thank Sandra Jackson for proof-reading.

REFERENCES

1. Darwin C. *The Expression of Emotions in Man and Animals*. Chicago, IL: Chicago Press. (1965)
2. Mahan AL, Ressler KJ. Fear conditioning, synaptic plasticity and the amygdala: implications for posttraumatic stress disorder. *Trends Neurosci* (2012) 35(1):24–35. doi:10.1016/j.tins.2011.06.007
3. American Psychiatric Association. *Diagnostic and Statistical Manual of Mental Disorders*. Washington, DC: American Psychiatric Association (2013).
4. Rosen JB, Schulkin J. From normal fear to pathological anxiety. *Psychol Rev* (1998) 105(2):325–50. doi:10.1037/0033-295X.105.2.325
5. Rau V, DeCola JP, Fanselow MS. Stress-induced enhancement of fear learning: an animal model of posttraumatic stress disorder. *Neurosci Biobehav Rev* (2005) 29(8):1207–23. doi:10.1016/j.neubiorev.2005.04.010
6. Rothbaum BO, Davis M. Applying learning principles to the treatment of post-trauma reactions. *Ann N Y Acad Sci* (2003) 1008:112–21. doi:10.1196/annals.1301.012
7. Blechert J, Michael T, Vriends N, Margraf J, Wilhelm FH. Fear conditioning in posttraumatic stress disorder: evidence for delayed extinction of autonomic, experiential, and behavioural responses. *Behav Res Ther* (2007) 45(9):2019–33. doi:10.1016/j.brat.2007.02.012
8. Jovanovic T, Norrholm SD, Fennell JE, Keyes M, Fiallos AM, Myers KM, et al. Posttraumatic stress disorder may be associated with impaired fear inhibition: relation to symptom severity. *Psychiatry Res* (2009) 167(1–2):151–60. doi:10.1016/j.psychres.2007.12.014
9. Jovanovic T, Kazama A, Bachevalier J, Davis M. Impaired safety signal learning may be a biomarker of PTSD. *Neuropharmacology* (2012) 62(2):695–704. doi:10.1016/j.neuropharm.2011.02.023
10. Kazama AM, Schauder KB, McKinnon M, Bachevalier J, Davis M. A novel AX+/BX- paradigm to assess fear learning and safety-signal processing with repeated-measure designs. *J Neurosci Methods* (2013) 214(2):177–83. doi:10.1016/j.jneumeth.2013.01.022
11. Kessler RC, Sonnega A, Bromet E, Hughes M, Nelson CB. Posttraumatic stress disorder in the National Comorbidity Survey. *Arch Gen Psychiatry* (1995) 52(12):1048–60. doi:10.1001/archpsyc.1995.03950240066012
12. Zhou Z, Zhu G, Hariri AR, Enoch MA, Scott D, Sinha R, et al. Genetic variation in human NPY expression affects stress response and emotion. *Nature* (2008) 452(7190):997–1001. doi:10.1038/nature06858
13. Polanczyk G, Caspi A, Williams B, Price TS, Danese A, Sugden K, et al. Protective effect of CRHR1 gene variants on the development of adult depression following childhood maltreatment: replication and extension. *Arch Gen Psychiatry* (2009) 66(9):978–85. doi:10.1001/archgenpsychiatry.2009.114
14. Stein MB, Campbell-Sills L, Gelernter J. Genetic variation in 5HTTLPR is associated with emotional resilience. *Am J Med Genet B Neuropsychiatr Genet* (2009) 150B(7):900–6. doi:10.1002/ajmg.b.30916
15. Murrough JW, Charney DS. The serotonin transporter and emotionality: risk, resilience, and new therapeutic opportunities. *Biol Psychiatry* (2011) 69(6):510–2. doi:10.1016/j.biopsych.2011.01.019
16. Ressler KJ, Mercer KB, Bradley B, Jovanovic T, Mahan A, Kerley K, et al. Posttraumatic stress disorder is associated with PACAP and the PAC1 receptor. *Nature* (2011) 470(7335):492–7. doi:10.1038/nature09856
17. Cohen H, Liu T, Kozlovsky N, Kaplan Z, Zohar J, Mathe AA. The neuropeptide Y (NPY)-ergic system is associated with behavioral resilience to stress exposure in an animal model of post-traumatic stress disorder. *Neuropsychopharmacology* (2012) 37(2):350–63. doi:10.1038/npp.2011.230
18. Krishnan V, Han MH, Graham DL, Berton O, Renthal W, Russo SJ, et al. Molecular adaptations underlying susceptibility and resistance to social defeat in brain reward regions. *Cell* (2007) 131(2):391–404. doi:10.1016/j.cell.2007.09.018
19. Grecksch G, Matties H. The role of dopaminergic mechanisms in the rat hippocampus for the consolidation in a brightness discrimination. *Psychopharmacology (Berl)* (1981) 75(2):165–8. doi:10.1007/BF00432180
20. Wise RA. Dopamine, learning and motivation. *Nat Rev Neurosci* (2004) 5(6):483–94. doi:10.1038/nrn1406
21. Everitt BJ, Robbins TW. Neural systems of reinforcement for drug addiction: from actions to habits to compulsion. *Nat Neurosci* (2005) 8(11):1481–9. doi:10.1038/nn1579
22. Schultz W. Predictive reward signal of dopamine neurons. *J Neurophysiol* (1998) 80(1):1–27.
23. Schultz W. Updating dopamine reward signals. *Curr Opin Neurobiol* (2013) 23(2):229–38. doi:10.1016/j.conb.2012.11.012
24. Matsumoto M, Hikosaka O. Two types of dopamine neuron distinctly convey positive and negative motivational signals. *Nature* (2009) 459(7248):837–41. doi:10.1038/nature08028
25. Bromberg-Martin ES, Matsumoto M, Hikosaka O. Dopamine in motivational control: rewarding, aversive, and alerting. *Neuron* (2010) 68(5):815–34. doi:10.1016/j.neuron.2010.11.022
26. Grace AA. The tonic/phasic model of dopamine system regulation and its implications for understanding alcohol and psychostimulant craving. *Addiction* (2000) 95(Suppl 2):S119–28. doi:10.1046/j.1360-0443.95.8s2.1.x
27. Volkow ND, Fowler JS, Wang GJ, Baler R, Telang F. Imaging dopamine's role in drug abuse and addiction. *Neuropharmacology* (2009) 56(Suppl 1):3–8. doi:10.1016/j.neuropharm.2008.05.022
28. Berridge KC. Food reward: brain substrates of wanting and liking. *Neurosci Biobehav Rev* (1996) 20(1):1–25. doi:10.1016/0149-7634(95)00033-B

29. Berridge KC, Robinson TE, Aldridge JW. Dissecting components of reward: 'liking', 'wanting', and learning. *Curr Opin Pharmacol* (2009) 9(1):65–73. doi:10.1016/j.coph.2008.12.014
30. Nader K, LeDoux J. The dopaminergic modulation of fear: quinpirole impairs the recall of emotional memories in rats. *Behav Neurosci* (1999) 113(1):152–65. doi:10.1037/0735-7044.113.1.152
31. Pezze MA, Feldon J. Mesolimbic dopaminergic pathways in fear conditioning. *Prog Neurobiol* (2004) 74(5):301–20. doi:10.1016/j.pneurobio.2004.09.004
32. Roitman MF, Wheeler RA, Wightman RM, Carelli RM. Real-time chemical responses in the nucleus accumbens differentiate rewarding and aversive stimuli. *Nat Neurosci* (2008) 11(12):1376–7. doi:10.1038/nn.2219
33. Fadok JP, Dickerson TM, Palmiter RD. Dopamine is necessary for cue-dependent fear conditioning. *J Neurosci* (2009) 29(36):11089–97. doi:10.1523/JNEUROSCI.1616-09.2009
34. Abraham AD, Neve KA, Lattal KM. Dopamine and extinction: a convergence of theory with fear and reward circuitry. *Neurobiol Learn Mem* (2014) 108:65–77. doi:10.1016/j.nlm.2013.11.007
35. Young AM. Increased extracellular dopamine in nucleus accumbens in response to unconditioned and conditioned aversive stimuli: studies using 1 min microdialysis in rats. *J Neurosci Methods* (2004) 138(1–2):57–63. doi:10.1016/j.jneumeth.2004.03.003
36. Ungless MA, Magill PJ, Bolam JP. Uniform inhibition of dopamine neurons in the ventral tegmental area by aversive stimuli. *Science* (2004) 303(5666):2040–2. doi:10.1126/science.1093360
37. Brischoux F, Chakraborty S, Brierley DI, Ungless MA. Phasic excitation of dopamine neurons in ventral VTA by noxious stimuli. *Proc Natl Acad Sci U S A* (2009) 106(12):4894–9. doi:10.1073/pnas.0811507106
38. Mileykovskiy B, Morales M. Duration of inhibition of ventral tegmental area dopamine neurons encodes a level of conditioned fear. *J Neurosci* (2011) 31(20):7471–6. doi:10.1523/JNEUROSCI.5731-10.2011
39. Wang DV, Tsien JZ. Conjunctive processing of locomotor signals by the ventral tegmental area neuronal population. *PLoS One* (2011) 6(1):e16528. doi:10.1371/journal.pone.0016528
40. Wang DV, Tsien JZ. Convergent processing of both positive and negative motivational signals by the VTA dopamine neuronal populations. *PLoS One* (2011) 6(2):e17047. doi:10.1371/journal.pone.0017047
41. Zweifel LS, Fadok JP, Argilli E, Garelick MG, Jones GL, Dickerson TM, et al. Activation of dopamine neurons is critical for aversive conditioning and prevention of generalized anxiety. *Nat Neurosci* (2011) 14(5):620–6. doi:10.1038/nn.2808
42. Cohen JY, Haesler S, Vong L, Lowell BB, Uchida N. Neuron-type-specific signals for reward and punishment in the ventral tegmental area. *Nature* (2012) 482(7383):85–8. doi:10.1038/nature10754
43. Fiorillo CD, Yun SR, Song MR. Diversity and homogeneity in responses of midbrain dopamine neurons. *J Neurosci* (2013) 33(11):4693–709. doi:10.1523/JNEUROSCI.3886-12.2013
44. Grace AA, Bunney BS. The control of firing pattern in nigral dopamine neurons: burst firing. *J Neurosci* (1984) 4(11):2877–90.
45. Grace AA. Phasic versus tonic dopamine release and the modulation of dopamine system responsivity: a hypothesis for the etiology of schizophrenia. *Neuroscience* (1991) 41(1):1–24. doi:10.1016/0306-4522(91)90196-U
46. Johnson SW, Seutin V, North RA. Burst firing in dopamine neurons induced by N-methyl-D-aspartate: role of electrogenic sodium pump. *Science* (1992) 258(5082):665–7. doi:10.1126/science.1329209
47. Richfield EK, Penney JB, Young AB. Anatomical and affinity state comparisons between dopamine D1 and D2 receptors in the rat central nervous system. *Neuroscience* (1989) 30(3):767–77. doi:10.1016/0306-4522(89)90168-1
48. Dahlstroem A, Fuxe K. Evidence for the existence of monoamine-containing neurons in the central nervous system. I. Demonstration of monoamines in the cell bodies of brain stem neurons. *Acta Physiol Scand Suppl* (1964) 232:231–55.
49. Swanson LW. The projections of the ventral tegmental area and adjacent regions: a combined fluorescent retrograde tracer and immunofluorescence study in the rat. *Brain Res Bull* (1982) 9(1–6):321–53. doi:10.1016/0361-9230(82)90145-9
50. Lammel S, Hetzel A, Hackel O, Jones I, Liss B, Roeper J. Unique properties of mesoprefrontal neurons within a dual mesocorticolimbic dopamine system. *Neuron* (2008) 57(5):760–73. doi:10.1016/j.neuron.2008.01.022
51. Lammel S, Ion DI, Roeper J, Malenka RC. Projection-specific modulation of dopamine neuron synapses by aversive and rewarding stimuli. *Neuron* (2011) 70(5):855–62. doi:10.1016/j.neuron.2011.03.025
52. Beier KT, Steinberg EE, DeLoach KE, Xie S, Miyamichi K, Schwarz L, et al. Circuit architecture of VTA dopamine neurons revealed by systematic input-output mapping. *Cell* (2015) 162(3):622–34. doi:10.1016/j.cell.2015.07.015
53. Fiorillo CD, Song MR, Yun SR. Multiphasic temporal dynamics in responses of midbrain dopamine neurons to appetitive and aversive stimuli. *J Neurosci* (2013) 33(11):4710–25. doi:10.1523/JNEUROSCI.3883-12.2013
54. Li M, Zhao F, Lee J, Wang D, Kuang H, Tsien JZ. Computational classification approach to profile neuron subtypes from brain activity mapping data. *Sci Rep* (2015) 5:12474. doi:10.1038/srep12474
55. Gariano RF, Groves PM. Burst firing induced in midbrain dopamine neurons by stimulation of the medial prefrontal and anterior cingulate cortices. *Brain Res* (1988) 462(1):194–8. doi:10.1016/0006-8993(88)90606-3
56. Lisman JE, Grace AA. The hippocampal-VTA loop: controlling the entry of information into long-term memory. *Neuron* (2005) 46(5):703–13. doi:10.1016/j.neuron.2005.05.002
57. Gao M, Liu CL, Yang S, Jin GZ, Bunney BS, Shi WX. Functional coupling between the prefrontal cortex and dopamine neurons in the ventral tegmental area. *J Neurosci* (2007) 27(20):5414–21. doi:10.1523/JNEUROSCI.5347-06.2007
58. Steffensen SC, Svingos AL, Pickel VM, Henriksen SJ. Electrophysiological characterization of GABAergic neurons in the ventral tegmental area. *J Neurosci* (1998) 18(19):8003–15.
59. Carr DB, Sesack SR. Projections from the rat prefrontal cortex to the ventral tegmental area: target specificity in the synaptic associations with mesoaccumbens and mesocortical neurons. *J Neurosci* (2000) 20(10):3864–73.
60. Tan KR, Yvon C, Turiault M, Mirzabekov JJ, Doehner J, Labouebe G, et al. GABA neurons of the VTA drive conditioned place aversion. *Neuron* (2012) 73(6):1173–83. doi:10.1016/j.neuron.2012.02.015
61. Koulchitsky S, De Backer B, Quertemont E, Charlier C, Seutin V. Differential effects of cocaine on dopamine neuron firing in awake and anesthetized rats. *Neuropsychopharmacology* (2012) 37(7):1559–71. doi:10.1038/npp.2011.339
62. McCutcheon JE, Ebner SR, Loriaux AL, Roitman MF. Encoding of aversion by dopamine and the nucleus accumbens. *Front Neurosci* (2012) 6:137. doi:10.3389/fnins.2012.00137
63. Liu J, Wei W, Kuang H, Tsien JZ, Zhao F. Heart rate and heart rate variability assessment identifies individual differences in fear response magnitudes to earthquake, free fall, and air puff in mice. *PLoS One* (2014) 9(3):e93270. doi:10.1371/journal.pone.0093270
64. Yehuda R, Flory JD, Southwick S, Charney DS. Developing an agenda for translational studies of resilience and vulnerability following trauma exposure. *Ann N Y Acad Sci* (2006) 1071:379–96. doi:10.1196/annals.1364.028
65. Lin L, Chen G, Xie K, Zaia KA, Zhang S, Tsien JZ. Large-scale neural ensemble recording in the brains of freely behaving mice. *J Neurosci Methods* (2006) 155(1):28–38. doi:10.1016/j.jneumeth.2005.12.032
66. Cao JL, Covington HE III, Friedman AK, Wilkinson MB, Walsh JJ, Cooper DC, et al. Mesolimbic dopamine neurons in the brain reward circuit mediate susceptibility to social defeat and antidepressant action. *J Neurosci* (2010) 30(49):16453–8. doi:10.1523/JNEUROSCI.3177-10.2010
67. Taliaz D, Loya A, Gersner R, Haramati S, Chen A, Zangen A. Resilience to chronic stress is mediated by hippocampal brain-derived neurotrophic factor. *J Neurosci* (2011) 31(12):4475–83. doi:10.1523/JNEUROSCI.5725-10.2011
68. Wang LP, Li F, Shen X, Tsien JZ. Conditional knockout of NMDA receptors in dopamine neurons prevents nicotine-conditioned place preference. *PLoS One* (2010) 5(1):e8616. doi:10.1371/journal.pone.0008616
69. Wang LP, Li F, Wang D, Xie K, Wang D, Shen X, et al. NMDA receptors in dopaminergic neurons are crucial for habit learning. *Neuron* (2011) 72(6):1055–66. doi:10.1016/j.neuron.2011.10.019
70. Gonon FG. Nonlinear relationship between impulse flow and dopamine released by rat midbrain dopaminergic neurons as studied by in vivo electrochemistry. *Neuroscience* (1988) 24(1):19–28. doi:10.1016/0306-4522(88)90307-7
71. Chergui K, Suaud-Chagny MF, Gonon F. Nonlinear relationship between impulse flow, dopamine release and dopamine elimination in the rat brain in vivo. *Neuroscience* (1994) 62(3):641–5. doi:10.1016/0306-4522(94)90465-0

72. Gonon F. Prolonged and extrasynaptic excitatory action of dopamine mediated by D1 receptors in the rat striatum in vivo. *J Neurosci* (1997) 17(15):5972–8.
73. Yagishita S, Hayashi-Takagi A, Ellis-Davies GC, Urakubo H, Ishii S, Kasai H. A critical time window for dopamine actions on the structural plasticity of dendritic spines. *Science* (2014) 345(6204):1616–20. doi:10.1126/science.1255514
74. Tye KM, Mirzabekov JJ, Warden MR, Ferenczi EA, Tsai HC, Finkelstein J, et al. Dopamine neurons modulate neural encoding and expression of depression-related behaviour. *Nature* (2013) 493(7433):537–41. doi:10.1038/nature11740
75. Gunaydin LA, Grosenick L, Finkelstein JC, Kauvar IV, Fenno LE, Adhikari A, et al. Natural neural projection dynamics underlying social behavior. *Cell* (2014) 157(7):1535–51. doi:10.1016/j.cell.2014.05.017
76. Frey U, Schroeder H, Matthies H. Dopaminergic antagonists prevent long-term maintenance of posttetanic LTP in the CA1 region of rat hippocampal slices. *Brain Res* (1990) 522(1):69–75. doi:10.1016/0006-8993(90)91578-5
77. Bissiere S, Humeau Y, Luthi A. Dopamine gates LTP induction in lateral amygdala by suppressing feedforward inhibition. *Nat Neurosci* (2003) 6(6):587–92. doi:10.1038/nn1058
78. Bush G, Luu P, Posner MI. Cognitive and emotional influences in anterior cingulate cortex. *Trends Cogn Sci* (2000) 4(6):215–22. doi:10.1016/S1364-6613(00)01483-2
79. Xie K, Kuang H, Tsien JZ. Mild blast events alter anxiety, memory, and neural activity patterns in the anterior cingulate cortex. *PLoS One* (2013) 8(5):e64907. doi:10.1371/journal.pone.0064907
80. Lin L, Osan R, Shoham S, Jin W, Zuo W, Tsien JZ. Identification of network-level coding units for real-time representation of episodic experiences in the hippocampus. *Proc Natl Acad Sci U S A* (2005) 102(17):6125–30. doi:10.1073/pnas.0408233102
81. Chen G, Wang LP, Tsien JZ. Neural population-level memory traces in the mouse hippocampus. *PLoS One* (2009) 4(12):e8256. doi:10.1371/journal.pone.0008256
82. Zhang H, Chen G, Kuang H, Tsien JZ. Mapping and deciphering neural codes of NMDA receptor-dependent fear memory engrams in the hippocampus. *PLoS One* (2013) 8(11):e79454. doi:10.1371/journal.pone.0079454
83. Baker SA, Baker KA, Hagg T. Dopaminergic nigrostriatal projections regulate neural precursor proliferation in the adult mouse subventricular zone. *Eur J Neurosci* (2004) 20(2):575–9. doi:10.1111/j.1460-9568.2004.03486.x
84. Hoglinger GU, Rizk P, Muriel MP, Duyckaerts C, Oertel WH, Caille I, et al. Dopamine depletion impairs precursor cell proliferation in Parkinson disease. *Nat Neurosci* (2004) 7(7):726–35. doi:10.1038/nn1265
85. Kippin TE, Kapur S, van der Kooy D. Dopamine specifically inhibits forebrain neural stem cell proliferation, suggesting a novel effect of antipsychotic drugs. *J Neurosci* (2005) 25(24):5815–23. doi:10.1523/JNEUROSCI.1120-05.2005
86. Takamura N, Nakagawa S, Masuda T, Boku S, Kato A, Song N, et al. The effect of dopamine on adult hippocampal neurogenesis. *Prog Neuropsychopharmacol Biol Psychiatry* (2014) 50:116–24. doi:10.1016/j.pnpbp.2013.12.011
87. Schloesser RJ, Manji HK, Martinowich K. Suppression of adult neurogenesis leads to an increased hypothalamo-pituitary-adrenal axis response. *Neuroreport* (2009) 20(6):553–7. doi:10.1097/WNR.0b013e3283293e59
88. Snyder JS, Soumier A, Brewer M, Pickel J, Cameron HA. Adult hippocampal neurogenesis buffers stress responses and depressive behaviour. *Nature* (2011) 476(7361):458–61. doi:10.1038/nature10287
89. Feng R, Rampon C, Tang YP, Shrom D, Jin J, Kyin M, et al. Deficient neurogenesis in forebrain-specific presenilin-1 knockout mice is associated with reduced clearance of hippocampal memory traces. *Neuron* (2001) 32(5):911–26. doi:10.1016/S0896-6273(01)00523-2
90. Geisler S, Zahm DS. Afferents of the ventral tegmental area in the rat-anatomical substratum for integrative functions. *J Comp Neurol* (2005) 490(3):270–94. doi:10.1002/cne.20668
91. Singer W. Neuronal synchrony: a versatile code for the definition of relations? *Neuron* (1999) 24(1):49–65,111–125.
92. Varela F, Lachaux JP, Rodriguez E, Martinerie J. The brainweb: phase synchronization and large-scale integration. *Nat Rev Neurosci* (2001) 2(4):229–39. doi:10.1038/35067550
93. Buzsaki G, Draguhn A. Neuronal oscillations in cortical networks. *Science* (2004) 304(5679):1926–9. doi:10.1126/science.1099745
94. Ito HT, Schuman EM. Frequency-dependent gating of synaptic transmission and plasticity by dopamine. *Front Neural Circuits* (2007) 1:1. doi:10.3389/neuro.04.001.2007
95. Brown P, Oliviero A, Mazzone P, Insola A, Tonali P, Di Lazzaro V. Dopamine dependency of oscillations between subthalamic nucleus and pallidum in Parkinson's disease. *J Neurosci* (2001) 21(3):1033–8.
96. Cohen JE, Shalev H, Admon R, Hefetz S, Gasho CJ, Shachar LJ, et al. Emotional brain rhythms and their impairment in post-traumatic patients. *Hum Brain Mapp* (2013) 34(6):1344–56. doi:10.1002/hbm.21516
97. Dunkley BT, Doesburg SM, Jetly R, Sedge PA, Pang EW, Taylor MJ. Characterising intra- and inter-intrinsic network synchrony in combat-related post-traumatic stress disorder. *Psychiatry Res* (2015) 234(2):172–81. doi:10.1016/j.pscychresns.2015.09.002
98. Tan G, Dao TK, Farmer L, Sutherland RJ, Gevirtz R. Heart rate variability (HRV) and posttraumatic stress disorder (PTSD): a pilot study. *Appl Psychophysiol Biofeedback* (2011) 36(1):27–35. doi:10.1007/s10484-010-9141-y
99. van Praag H, Kempermann G, Gage FH. Running increases cell proliferation and neurogenesis in the adult mouse dentate gyrus. *Nat Neurosci* (1999) 2(3):266–70. doi:10.1038/6368
100. Sahay A, Scobie KN, Hill AS, O'Carroll CM, Kheirbek MA, Burghardt NS, et al. Increasing adult hippocampal neurogenesis is sufficient to improve pattern separation. *Nature* (2011) 472(7344):466–70. doi:10.1038/nature09817
101. Hill AS, Sahay A, Hen R. Increasing adult hippocampal neurogenesis is sufficient to reduce anxiety and depression-like behaviors. *Neuropsychopharmacology* (2015) 40(10):2368–78. doi:10.1038/npp.2015.85
102. Newman CL, Motta RW. The effects of aerobic exercise on childhood PTSD, anxiety, and depression. *Int J Emerg Ment Health* (2007) 9(2):133–58.
103. Jovanovic T, Norrholm SD, Blanding NQ, Davis M, Duncan E, Bradley B, et al. Impaired fear inhibition is a biomarker of PTSD but not depression. *Depress Anxiety* (2010) 27(3):244–51. doi:10.1002/da.20663
104. Christianson JP, Jennings JH, Ragole T, Flyer JG, Benison AM, Barth DS, et al. Safety signals mitigate the consequences of uncontrollable stress via a circuit involving the sensory insular cortex and bed nucleus of the stria terminalis. *Biol Psychiatry* (2011) 70(5):458–64. doi:10.1016/j.biopsych.2011.04.004
105. Christianson JP, Fernando AB, Kazama AM, Jovanovic T, Ostroff LE, Sangha S. Inhibition of fear by learned safety signals: a mini-symposium review. *J Neurosci* (2012) 32(41):14118–24. doi:10.1523/JNEUROSCI.3340-12.2012
106. Fernando AB, Mar AC, Urcelay GP, Dickinson A, Robbins TW. Avoidance behavior: a free-operant lever-press avoidance task for the assessment of the effects of safety signals. *Curr Protoc Neurosci* (2015) 70:1–12. doi:10.1002/0471142301.ns0832s70
107. Glimcher PW. Understanding dopamine and reinforcement learning: the dopamine reward prediction error hypothesis. *Proc Natl Acad Sci U S A* (2011) 108(Suppl 3):15647–54. doi:10.1073/pnas.1014269108

10

Motivational and Behavioral Activation as an Adjunct to Psychiatric Rehabilitation for Mild to Moderate Negative Symptoms in Individuals with Schizophrenia

Kee-Hong Choi, Eunju Jaekal and Ga-Young Lee*

Department of Psychology, Korea University, Seoul, Republic of Korea

Edited by:
Kim T. Mueser,
Boston University, USA

Reviewed by:
Ryan Balzan,
Flinders University, Australia
Daniel Fulford,
Boston University, USA

****Correspondence:***
Kee-Hong Choi
keehongchoi@gmail.com

Few psychosocial approaches address the negative symptoms of schizophrenia, which shares common features with depression and anxiety. Behavioral activation (BA) is effective for addressing depression and anxiety in adults with various mental disorders. Motivational interviewing (MI) has been successfully applied to address ambivalence or lack of motivation toward treatment. Motivational and behavioral activation (mBA) has been developed by incorporating the core principles from BA and MI with recent findings on the negative symptoms of schizophrenia. In this study, we aimed to examine the feasibility and preliminary efficacy of mBA in a non-randomized controlled pilot study that included individuals with schizophrenia with mild to moderate negative symptoms receiving psychiatric rehabilitation. A total of 73 individuals with schizophrenia were recruited. Forty-seven of the participants who met the study inclusion and exclusion criteria were assigned to either an mBA + usual psychiatric rehabilitation group (mBA) or a usual psychiatric rehabilitation only group (treatment as usual, TAU). Administering mBA to individuals with schizophrenia with mild to moderate negative symptoms was feasible in a community mental health setting. Relative to TAU, mBA was associated with large effects in reducing negative symptoms measured using the Positive and Negative Syndrome Scale (PANSS) and the Brief Negative Symptom Scale (BNSS). However, after considering PANSS cognitive deficits and marital status as covariates due to significant differences in their baseline levels, the treatment effects on the BNSS were partially observed. In addition, participants in the mBA group showed improved verbal learning and memory compared with those in the TAU group. In individuals with schizophrenia receiving the usual forms of psychiatric rehabilitation in a community mental health setting, mBA appears to offer a promising adjunctive approach for addressing mild to moderate negative symptoms. Further investigations are needed to replicate the current findings in a randomized controlled trial.

Keywords: behavioral activation, motivational interviewing, psychosocial intervention, negative symptoms, schizophrenia

INTRODUCTION

Many individuals with schizophrenia experience negative symptoms, which are a key determinant of poor functioning and quality of life (Pogue-Geile and Harrow, 1985; Rabinowitz et al., 2012). Negative symptoms can persist even in individuals who participate in the usual forms of psychiatric rehabilitation offered in the community (Buchanan, 2007). Both clinicians and participants would benefit from a psychosocial treatment approach that targets persistent negative symptoms and can easily be delivered in community mental health settings. However, the majority of psychosocial interventions focus primarily on positive symptoms (Breier et al., 1991; Milev et al., 2005). Few studies have reported the efficacy of psychosocial treatments for negative symptoms (Dobson et al., 1995; Rector and Beck, 2001; Tarrier et al., 2004; Kurtz and Mueser, 2008; Staring et al., 2013; Velligan et al., 2015), and the estimated effect size reported in a recent meta-analysis was small and inconsistent across studies (Velthorst et al., 2015). Another meta-analysis indicates that social skills training had small to moderate effects ($d = 0.40$; 95% CI = 0.19, 0.61) on negative symptoms; although, the benefits only appear to be stable for younger patients with schizophrenia or in studies of greater design quality (Kurtz and Mueser, 2008). Most recently, Velligan et al. (2015) reported potential treatment gains using comprehensive psychosocial treatments for those who have persistent and clinically significant negative symptoms. Thus, the effective and cost-efficient treatment of negative symptoms is a high priority when developing interventions.

A two-factor model of negative symptoms describing experiential (avolition, asociality, and anhedonia) and emotional expressive impairments (alogia and flat affect) has been shown to better explain the heterogeneity of negative symptoms in schizophrenia than a single factor model (Horan et al., 2011; Kirkpatrick et al., 2011; Jang et al., 2016a). Due to the establishment of a vicious cycle between the two distinct but related domains of negative symptoms, individuals with schizophrenia not only exhibit low base rates of behavior and have reduced rates of positive reinforcement from the environment (Silverstein, 2010), but also lack the opportunity to identify, estimate the effort required, and pursue their own values and goals (Gold et al., 2008, 2013; Strauss et al., 2011).

Even though cognitive behavioral therapy for psychosis (CBT-p) and CBT for negative symptoms (CBT-n) take comprehensive approaches to addressing diverse problems including positive symptoms, depressive symptoms, dysfunctional beliefs (e.g., defeatist beliefs), and negative symptoms (Morrison and Barratt, 2010; Grant et al., 2012; Staring et al., 2013), we aimed to exclusively target a two-factor model of negative symptoms using the core principles of behavioral activation (BA) and motivational interviewing (MI).

BA is an evidence-based treatment option for depression (Cuijpers et al., 2007; Mazzucchelli et al., 2009), and might be a treatment option for negative symptoms. BA may interrupt the vicious cycle by assisting individuals with schizophrenia to reconnect with positive experiences using daily activity monitoring, values and goals assessment, and goal-led activity scheduling. More importantly, BA would be a cost-efficient option for both clinicians and individuals with schizophrenia mainly due to its concise structure and principles (Porter et al., 2004; Ekers et al., 2011). Porter et al. (2004) suggested that group-format BA is a viable and effective adjunct to the usual treatment conducted in community mental health settings for depressed clients. Ekers et al. (2011) demonstrated that generic mental health professionals without expertise in psychotherapy could deliver BA in an effective manner.

Recent neuroscience data indicate that individuals with schizophrenia have an intact capacity for experiencing here-and-now pleasure, but experience difficulty recalling and predicting pleasure (i.e., retrospective and prospective hedonia) with aberrant attentional deficits to pleasurable stimuli (Strauss and Gold, 2012; Jang et al., 2016b,c). Thus, it is speculated that daily activity monitoring would help to allocate attention to meaningful and pleasant daily activities that individuals with schizophrenia have had in the recent past. At the beginning of each session, there is an additional opportunity to recall and share the participant's pleasurable activities in the past week without looking at their monitoring form. This was used to enhance the participant's retrospective hedonic experience. Assessments of one's own values and goals and implementation of value/goal-led activities would help to link here-and-now pleasure with the prediction of pleasure for prospective hedonistic experiences. Given the difficulties that individuals with schizophrenia have in goal-setting and planning, several goal domains (i.e., interpersonal, educational, vocational, independent living, etc.) were provided to them in printed form. Specific activities (i.e., less than 5) under each goal domain were also provided in a summarized form so that participants could voluntarily choose among the options. Therapists also encouraged the participants to link each activity with their own goals, and encouraged moving slowly to the other goals and activities that they had not yet explored. During this process, given the motivational deficits of individuals with schizophrenia, MI becomes a core principle and is the core method used (McCambridge and Strang, 2003).

Several adjustments were made to the original BA. These included simplification of treatment materials (e.g., monitoring and scheduling forms) and terms, providing greater structure for every session, minimizing the number of forms to be completed during the session, minimizing homework activities, developing strategies to remember core activities (i.e., monitoring and activating activities), slowing the pace of conversation, and greater repetition for those with cognitive impairments.

Recent meta-analysis indicates that social skills training is associated with some improvement in negative symptoms (Kurtz and Mueser, 2008). In each session, brief components of social skills training that could be delivered in the context of the motivational and behavioral activation (mBA) group session [i.e., speaking loud enough to be heard, practicing (half) smiles while talking about pleasant events, listening to others, and providing feedback to others] were incorporated to target emotional expressivity (e.g., vocal expression, expressive gestures, facial expression, quantity of speech). The clinicians then provide consistent positive feedback whenever the participants display emotional expressivity (Supplementary Table S2).

After the incorporation of these adjustments, BA could assist individuals with schizophrenia to recall and monitor pleasurable and goal-directed activities in the past and to plan and implement a future schedule. Given extensive data supporting the efficacy of behaviorally oriented approaches in psychiatric rehabilitation (e.g., contingency management) for individuals with schizophrenia with various levels of functioning (Porter et al., 2004; Ekers et al., 2011; Granholm et al., 2015; Murphy et al., 2015), BA would be feasible and beneficial for individuals with schizophrenia with mild to moderate negative symptoms. Mairs et al. (2011) reported in a small-sample pilot case study that BA exhibited a large effect and appeared to be a promising approach for treating the negative symptoms of schizophrenia.

To target motivational deficits or ambivalence toward treatment, MI has recently been successfully combined with various interventions such as cognitive remediation (Rüsch and Corrigan, 2002; Steinberg et al., 2004; Fiszdon et al., 2016), and has demonstrated synergistic effects. Likewise, MI is incorporated into BA to better understand the relationships between ambivalence about change and each participant's goals, values, and resistance. It is carried out by expressing empathy, rolling with resistance, supporting self-efficacy, and developing discrepancy whenever necessary (Miller and Rollnick, 2002). MI is a particularly important component when assisting the participant in his/her search for their own goals/values, potential barriers and concerns, and for evaluating and establishing solutions and plans (McCambridge and Strang, 2003). Since BA and MI share common aspects (e.g., searching for values/goals and planning for behavioral changes), MI is not only well integrated into BA, but is expected to further help to deliver the core components of BA to individuals with schizophrenia with motivational deficits or ambivalence toward behavioral change.

With these theories and findings in mind, we have developed the mBA Program as an adjunct to psychiatric rehabilitation for individuals with schizophrenia with mild to moderate negative symptoms. This is a brief manual-based psychological approach that incorporates BA principles and MI components targeting a two-factor model of negative symptoms.

For Stage I-A of intervention development, as suggested by Onken et al. (2014), the authors translated and modified the Brief Behavioral Activation Treatment for Depression (BATD) manual by Lejuez et al. (2001) and evaluated its feasibility in eight community-dwelling individuals with schizophrenia with mild to moderate negative symptoms using a 12-session group format (Choi et al., 2014), with a low dropout rate ($n = 1$, employed). Following Stage I-A, the authors incorporated feedback from participants and clinicians, and the program was revised accordingly, with the BATD manual being simplified to a 10-session group format (Choi et al., 2014). With these revisions, the mBA program was finally established for a Stage I-B pilot trial.

We hypothesized that the mBA program would be feasible and tolerable to individuals with schizophrenia with mild or moderate negative symptoms participating in community-based psychiatric rehabilitation. In addition, it was hypothesized that the mBA group would have lower levels of negative symptoms compared with the treatment as usual (TAU) group. Lastly, given that extensive research supports the link between negative symptoms, daily functioning, and cognitive impairments (Green, 1996; Velligan et al., 1997; Green et al., 2000; Foussias and Remington, 2010), and the mBA program includes repetitive practice of attending and recalling one's own activities and planning, we explored whether mBA was associated with recovery in neurocognition.

MATERIALS AND METHODS

Participants

Seventy-three participants were recruited from community mental health centers and day hospitals from September 2012 until January 2015. Inclusion criteria for the participants were as follows (Buchanan, 2007): (1) a primary diagnosis of schizophrenia or schizoaffective disorder, (2) aged between 18 and 65 at the time of pre-testing, (3) mild to moderate negative symptoms [greater than 3 on at least two negative symptom items from the Positive and Negative Syndrome Scale (PANSS)], and (4) stably prescribed psychotropic medications for at least the previous 6 months. Exclusion criteria included (1) a history of organic brain syndrome, seizures, or traumatic brain injury, (2) current comorbid disorders such as mental retardation, or current alcohol or other substance abuse/dependence, (3) more than moderate positive symptoms (greater than 4 on PANSS positive symptom items), (4) more than mild depressive symptoms (greater than 3 on PANSS depressive symptom items), (5) receiving psychological services that include behavioral activation components, and (6) risk of self-harming or homicide. There were no differences in demographic variables between the two groups, except for marital status and baseline PANSS cognitive symptoms (**Table 1**), which were included as covariates in subsequent analyses (**Table 1**).

Procedures

The participants in this pilot study were recruited from various community mental health centers located in urban areas in South Korea. Prior to pre-treatment assessment, all participants provided informed consent. Local Institutional Review Boards approved this study. After the pre-treatment assessment, 47 participants who met study inclusion criteria were allocated to either the mBA ($n = 23$) or the TAU group ($n = 24$) (**Figure 1**) based on negative symptom scores. Group allocation was made alternately from active group to control group, and thus the most subjects were assigned to the active group or the control group based on their interest to participate in the current study after having received information on the study. Regardless of the allocated group, participants attended the centers for psychiatric rehabilitation program. About 10 weeks after completing the mBA program, the post-treatment assessment was administered to mBA and TAU groups over similar time frames. Of the 49 participants, one participant (of 23) in the treatment group was dropped due to job conflicts, while five participants (of 24) in the control group were dropped for reasons such as hospitalization, service refusal, and losing contact.

TABLE 1 | Baseline characteristics of participants.

	Treatment group (n = 23)	Control group (n = 24)	t or χ^2
Age, *M* (*SD*)	40.43 (11.72)	44.38 (10.77)	−1.20
Age of onset, *M* (*SD*)	24.22 (7.03)	24.29 (8.39)	−0.03
Years of education, *M* (*SD*)	12.04 (2.67)	11.21 (3.58)	0.90
Gender, *n* (%)			
Men	11 (47.83)	12 (50.00)	0.02
Women	12 (52.17)	12 (50.00)	
Marital status, *n* (%)			
Married	1 (4.35)	9 (37.50)	11.05**
Single	18 (78.26)	8 (33.33)	
Divorced/other	4 (17.39)	7 (29.17)	
Medication, *n* (%)	23 (100.00)	24 (100.00)	–
PANSS, *M* (SD)			
Negative	18.17 (3.66)	18.38 (4.21)	−0.17
Excitement	6.52 (1.93)	6.83 (2.06)	−0.54
Cognitive	11.22 (2.56)	13.08 (3.36)	−2.14*
Positive	8.57 (2.76)	8.46 (3.48)	0.12
Depression	9.52 (2.76)	9.17 (3.12)	0.41
Total	68.26 (9.86)	69.67 (14.13)	−0.39

*$p < 0.05$; **$p < 0.01$.

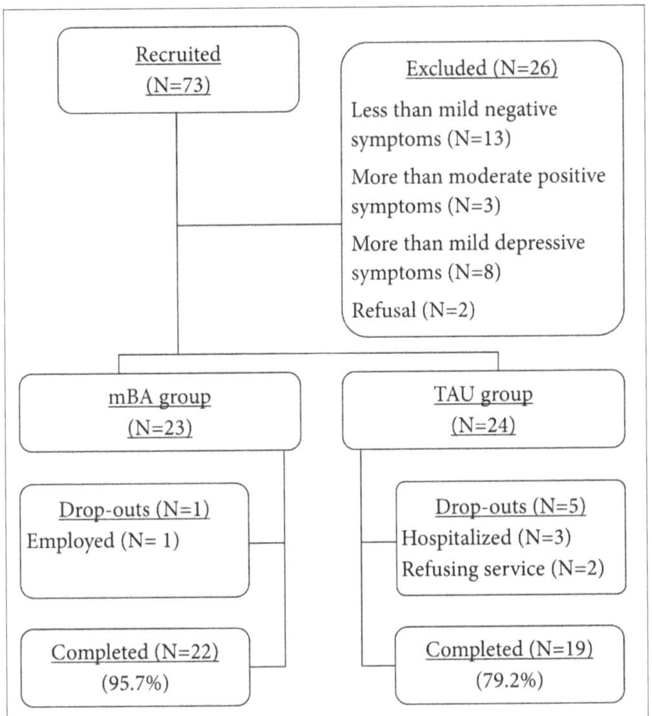

FIGURE 1 | Flow chart of participants.

Motivational and Behavioral Activation

The mBA program for negative symptoms was provided by the researchers in our team. Fidelity was assessed with a random visit (92.31%; Supplementary Table S1). Participants received ten 60- to 70-minute group sessions either once or twice weekly. The main purpose of mBA was to increase the level of routine and social activities that participants identified as pleasurable, meaningful, and valuable. Specifically, mBA assisted participants (1) to monitor daily activities in the previous week, (2) to set goals, (3) to identify and plan daily activities that fit their own goals, (4) to administer their own goal-led activities, and (5) to identify and address barriers to achieving their goal-led activities. Throughout the mBA program, participants were expected to practice (1) goal setting, (2) monitoring of activities and remembering pleasurable and meaningful activities, (3) goal-led activity planning, and (4) problem-solving skills. Therapists were expected to persistently use MI techniques such as employing open-ended questions, using positive feedback, reflection, and summarizing the participant's words, especially for participants with ambivalence or lack of motivation toward the treatment. In addition to target emotional expressivity in the context of mBA, brief components of social skills training [i.e., speaking loud enough to be heard, practicing (half) smiles while talking about pleasant events, listening to others, and providing feedback to others] were practiced in each session. The content of each session of mBA is presented in Supplementary Table S2.

Measures

Participants each completed a semi-structured interview-based psychiatric symptom assessment, self-report questionnaires for motivation, and brief neurocognitive assessment batteries. All interviews were conducted by licensed clinical psychologists and clinical psychology graduate students who obtained satisfactory intra-class correlations (ICCs).

Psychiatric Symptoms

The PANSS (Kay et al., 1987) was administered to evaluate the severity of psychiatric symptoms. Each item was scored on a 1 (absent symptom) to 7 (extreme symptom) Likert scale. Five factor scores were calculated for the PANSS, i.e., Negative symptoms, Excitement, Cognition, Positive symptoms, and Depression (Bell et al., 1994; Lindenmayer et al., 1994, 1995). In the current study, Cronbach's α for each subscale was as follows: Negative symptoms = 0.87, Excitement = 0.64, Cognition = 0.69, Positive symptoms = 0.70, and Depression = 0.67. ICCs for each subscale were as follows: Negative symptoms = 0.93, Excitement = 0.69, Cognition = 0.95, Positive symptoms = 0.98, Depression = 0.50.

The Brief Negative Symptom Scale (BNSS) is a semi-structured clinical interview that measures the severity of negative symptoms in schizophrenia and schizoaffective disorder (Kirkpatrick et al., 2011). The BNSS was based on a two-factor model of negative symptoms, consisting of experiential impairment (anhedonia, asociality, and avolition) and expressive impairment (alogia and blunted affect) (Horan et al., 2011; Strauss et al., 2012). Thirteen items, each ranging from absence of symptom (0) to extremely severe symptom (6) in motivation–pleasure and emotional expressivity subscales, were assessed over a time period of 1 week. Since the BNSS was translated into Korean and was available after the initiation of this trial, we obtained BNSS data from thirty participants (n = 14 for mBA, n = 16 for TAU). In the current study, Cronbach's α for the motivation–pleasure subscale was 0.93 and for the emotional expressivity subscale was 0.86. ICCs for each subscale were as follows: motivation–pleasure = 0.68, emotional expressivity = 0.89.

Neurocognitive Function

The Korean Auditory Verbal Learning Test (K-AVLT) was designed to evaluate short-term memory, auditory verbal memory, and learning strategies (Rey, 1964). Cheong et al. (1999) revised and validated the Korean version. After listening to 15 words presented verbally, participants were asked to complete free recall trials immediately and after a 30-minute delay, and a recognition trial.

Trail Making Test A and B (TMT-A, B) are included in the Halstead–Reitan neuropsychological test battery (Reitan, 1992). In part A, subjects were asked to sequentially connect dispersed digits (1–25) to measure psychomotor speed and attention. In part B, subjects were required to connect 15 digits and 14 letters alternately in ascending order, to measure executive function related to frontal lobe activity such as mental flexibility and visuospatial working memory. Times to complete the tasks and the number of errors constituted the test scores. If subjects exceeded 90 s in part A or 300 s in B, the data were excluded from the analysis.

The Coding (CD) subtest in the Wechsler Adult Intelligence Scale–Fourth Edition (WAIS-IV; Wechsler, 2008; Hwang et al., 2012) was used to measure visual-motor coordination, persistence of concentration, and short-term visual memory. Subjects were required to copy as many symbols as possible within 120 s using a key. Total scores were based on the number of correctly matched items.

Premorbid Intelligence Quotients

To estimate premorbid IQ, the Information subtest (IN) in the K-WAIS-IV (Hwang et al., 2012) was administered. Items covered a range of common, realistic, and general knowledge. Premorbid intelligence was estimated using an algorithm from the Korea Premorbid Intelligence Estimate for the WAIS-IV (KPIE-IV; Kim et al., 2015).

RESULTS

Feasibility

Dropout rates (4.35% for mBA vs. 20.83% for TAU) were similar between the mBA and the TAU groups ($\chi^2 = 2.87$, $p = 0.09$), indicating that mBA would be tolerable and feasible to administer to individuals with schizophrenia with mild to moderate negative symptoms participating in the usual psychiatric rehabilitation services.

Effects of mBA on Psychiatric Symptoms

We conducted repeated-measures ANOVAs for negative symptom scores and other psychiatric symptoms (i.e., positive, depressive, cognitive, and excitement symptoms) measured using the PANSS and the BNSS, with treatment and control groups as the between-subjects factor (mBA vs. TAU) and time as the within-subjects factor (pre- and post-) (**Table 2**). These analyses revealed no significant main effect of group on any PANSS subscale except for the negative scale, $F_{(1,39)} = 4.15$, $p < 0.05$, and cognitive scale, $F_{(1,39)} = 23.87$, $p < 0.001$. There were significant interaction effects of group by time on scores for the negative symptoms subscale, $F_{(1,39)} = 10.10$, $p < 0.01$, cognitive symptoms subscale, $F_{(1,39)} = 10.45$, $p < 0.01$, and depression subscale, $F_{(1,39)} = 10.99$, $p < 0.01$ (**Table 2**). The findings indicate that participants in the mBA improved their negative, cognitive, and depressive symptoms compared to those in the TAU group. Even after considering baseline PANSS cognitive symptoms or marital status as a covariate, all of the significant findings reported above were maintained.

In addition, there was no significant main effect of group on the BNSS score. However, there were significant interaction effects of group by time on the motivation and pleasure subscale, $F_{(1,28)} = 4.72$, $p < 0.05$, and emotional expressivity subscale, $F_{(1,28)} = 4.35$, $p < 0.05$ (**Table 2**). The findings indicate that participants in the mBA group improved their BNSS subscale scores when compared to those in the TAU group. However, after considering baseline PANSS cognitive symptoms as a covariate, the treatment effect on BNSS motivation and pleasure subscales disappeared ($p = 0.12$). To consider marital status as a covariate, we examined the study hypotheses only using participants who were single. Using these participants, the treatment effects on the BNSS subscales disappeared ($n = 11$ for mBA; $n = 5$ for TAU).

To delineate the significant interaction effects, we calculated a partial eta-squared measure of effect size for use in ANOVA (Cohen, 1988; Miles and Shevlin, 2001) with general rules of thumb for the magnitude of the effect sizes, i.e., small (∼0.01), medium (∼0.06), and large (∼0.14). The effect sizes for the treatment group were mostly large for the above-mentioned negative symptoms, cognition, and depressive symptoms in the PANSS and BNSS (**Table 2**).

Effects of mBA on Neurocognitive Function

We conducted repeated-measures ANOVAs on neurocognitive function with the treatment and control groups as the between-subjects factor (Group) and time (pre-, post-) as the within-subjects factor (**Table 3**). The analyses revealed no significant main effect of group on neurocognitive function. There was a significant interaction effect of group by time on the K-AVLT total score, $F_{(1,39)} = 5.37$, $p < 0.01$ (**Table 2**). The effect size for the treatment group on the K-AVLT total score was medium (**Table 3**).

DISCUSSION

We have developed a manual-based brief psychosocial intervention that incorporates the core principles of BA and MI with recent findings on negative symptoms to target the two-factor components of negative symptoms in schizophrenia. The current study is the first to investigate the feasibility and efficacy of mBA as an adjunct to psychiatric rehabilitation for individuals with schizophrenia with mild to moderate negative

TABLE 2 | Effects of mBA on psychiatric symptoms.

Measure	Group	Pre	Post	Main effect		Interaction effect	Effect Size
		M (SD)	*M (SD)*	Group *F*	Time *F*	Group × time *F*	Partial η^2
PANSS[a]							
Negative	Treatment	18.05 (3.70)	14.09 (4.74)	4.15*	12.49**	10.10**	0.21
	Control	18.79 (4.50)	18.58 (5.07)				
Excitement	Treatment	6.50 (1.97)	6.55 (2.13)	0.48	0.48	0.33	0.01
	Control	6.63 (1.80)	7.11 (2.05)				
Cognitive	Treatment	11.36 (2.52)	9.82 (2.68)	23.87***	0.21	10.45**	0.21
	Control	13.00 (3.04)	15.05 (3.24)				
Positive	Treatment	8.68 (2.77)	9.00 (3.34)	0.01	3.15	1.60	0.04
	Control	7.90 (2.94)	9.63 (3.42)				
Depression	Treatment	9.59 (2.81)	8.96 (2.79)	0.75	3.56	10.99**	0.22
	Control	8.90 (3.36)	11.21 (3.87)				
BNSS[c]							
Motivation and pleasure	Treatment	21.29 (8.67)	16.86 (7.86)	1.07	3.56	4.72*[a]	0.14
	Control	21.69 (7.60)	22.00 (7.53)				
Emotional expressivity	Treatment	18.50 (5.97)	15.29 (7.17)	0.12	0.84	4.35*[b]	0.14
	Control	17.13 (8.35)	18.38 (7.36)				

*$p < 0.05$; **$p < 0.01$; ***$p < 0.001$.*
[a] *After considering baseline PANSS cognitive symptoms as a covariate, the treatment effect on the BNSS motivation and pleasure subscale disappeared ($p = 0.12$).*
[b] *The treatment effect on the BNSS subscales disappeared ($n = 11$ for mBA, $n = 5$ for TAU) when examining the study hypotheses only using participants with single marital status.*
[c] *BNSS sample size ($n = 14$ for mBA, $n = 16$ for TAU).*

symptoms, compared with TAU. In accordance with Onken et al. (2014), the current study is considered to be Stage I-B of an intervention development process.

The results indicate that the dropout rate for mBA was minimal compared with TAU (4.35% for mBA; 20.83% for TAU). This may support its feasibility for community dwelling individuals with schizophrenia. Velligan et al. (2015) reported a dropout rate of 34.6% in their recent randomized controlled trial (RCT) of the MOtiVation and Enhancement (MOVE) program conducted over 9 months. Given that the MOVE trial targeted persistent and clinically significant negative symptoms in a comprehensive manner over a longer treatment period, it is speculated that the concise structure of mBA (e.g., principles and techniques), the shorter treatment duration, and the participant characteristics (mild to moderate negative symptoms, regular participation in psychiatric rehabilitation program) would permit greater treatment survival rates. Even though a 10-session time frame is quite challenging for tackling negative symptoms, the repetition of exercises and gradual addition of treatment components across sessions appeared to provide enough opportunities for gaining treatment effects. Another possible reason for the differential drop-out rates between the mBA and TAU groups may be the potential extraneous variable affecting the allocation of the participants, as this was a non-randomized trial and the mBA and TAU groups were formed alternately. Thus, in this procedure, participants might have known the group they were allocated to prior to group allocation. This may have resulted in selection bias; for example, participants who had greater motivation for change may have been more likely to be assigned to the mBA group than the TAU group.

To examine the potential impacts of different demographic characteristics (i.e., marital status) and psychiatric conditions (i.e., PANSS cognitive impairments factor) on drop-out rates, we compared those who dropped out to those who did not drop-out in terms of demographic and symptom variables. There were no differences in age, gender, age of onset, years of education, and PANSS subscales. The only observed difference was in marital status ($\chi^2 = 10.755$, $p = 0.005$). Interestingly, none of the single participants dropped out of either group. Even though marital status was not related to the primary study findings, a future study should examine the relationship between marital status and drop-out rates in the mBA.

As hypothesized, mBA was associated with large treatment effects on negative symptoms, cognition, and depressive symptoms in the PANSS and the BNSS emotional expressivity subscale even after considering the PANSS cognitive factor. It is notable that the large effects gained within a shorter period (10 weeks) were comparable with those of other approaches conducted over a longer period (Kurtz and Mueser, 2008; Velligan et al., 2015; Velthorst et al., 2015). It is speculated that the comparable treatment gains might be attributable to the sample characteristic (mild to moderate negative symptoms) and/or treatment characteristics explicitly targeting a two-factor theory of negative symptoms.

After considering the PANSS cognitive factor, the treatment effects on the BNSS emotional expressivity were maintained but motivation and pleasure subscales disappeared. Since the BNSS was administered to a subsample of the study participants ($n = 14$ for mBA and $n = 16$ for TAU), this finding should be cautiously interpreted because of its lack of power in detecting

TABLE 3 | Effects of mBA on neurocognitive function.

Measure	Group	Pre	Post	Main effect		Interaction effect	Effect size
		M (SD)	*M (SD)*	Group *F*	Time *F*	Group × time *F*	Partial η^2
Coding	Treatment	34.37 (7.73)	37.42 (8.85)	0.18	12.18**	0.00	0.00
	Control	35.45 (8.70)	38.53 (8.06)				
Digit span	Treatment	44.05 (10.18)	44.42 (9.60)	1.11	4.05	2.50	0.07
	Control	39.49 (10.37)	42.56 (8.75)				
K-AVLT total	Treatment	28.95 (13.19)	41.21 (16.44)	2.16	14.30**	5.37*	0.13
	Control	28.11 (10.79)	31.05 (11.24)				
TMT-A	Treatment	38.18 (11.76)	43.28 (10.26)	0.39	7.82**	0.02	0.00
	Control	35.74 (16.87)	40.34 (16.83)				
TMT-B	Treatment	39.46 (15.65)	41.82 (16.53)	2.10	0.03	0.43	0.01
	Control	32.21 (22.39)	30.79 (24.27)				

*$p < 0.05$; **$p < 0.01$.

potential therapeutic benefits. However, there are several possible interpretations. First, it is speculated that the PANSS cognitive factor might share common aspects (e.g., cognitive deficits) with motivation and pleasure (Bell et al., 1994; Foussias et al., 2014), rather than with emotional expressivity. Thus, in future studies, cognitive symptoms of allocated participants should be counter-balanced. Second, to target emotional expressivity, mBA incorporated brief components of social skills training [e.g., speaking loud enough to be heard, practicing (half) smiles while talking about pleasant events, listening to others, providing feedback to others, clinician's positive and corrective feedback], of which repetitive practice in the context of BA group session may result in robust improvement on the BNSS emotional expressivity, even after considering cognitive symptoms. To clarify whether mBA would lead to incremental benefits beyond social skills training on the two distinct factors of negative symptoms, mBA should be compared with social skills training in a future study.

In addition, even though we recruited participants with mild to moderate negative symptoms and less-than-mild depressive symptoms to avoid comorbidity between negative symptoms and depressive symptoms, mBA was associated with improvement in depressive symptoms. Given that this is a preliminary study with limitations regarding the investigation of underlying mechanisms, common aspects between negative symptoms and depressive symptoms affected by mBA should be explored in a future study.

However, the current findings were gained from a Stage I-B pilot trial, and thus should be replicated in an RCT trial.

Interestingly, even though it was not specifically predicted, mBA was associated with a medium effect on verbal learning and memory measured by the K-AVLT total score. Even though this finding should be interpreted cautiously due to the absence of *a priori* hypothesis testing, it can be speculated that verbal learning and memory might mediate the treatment gains from mBA as they have functional implications in individuals with schizophrenia (Green et al., 2000) and depression (Clark et al., 2009). A future study should determine whether treatment components of the mBA (e.g., recalling pleasurable and meaningful activities) are related to improvements in verbal learning and memory.

Several limitations should be noted. With a non-RCT, the causality of mBA on outcome variables should not be assumed and needs to be replicated in a future RCT study. Second, the PANSS negative symptoms factor was used as an inclusion criterion for mild to moderate negative symptoms in the current study. However, the PANSS is often regarded as an inadequate measure of negative symptoms, especially for experiential negative symptoms. Although in our data, the PANSS negative symptom factor scores at baseline were strongly correlated with the BNSS motivation and pleasure subscale scores ($r = 0.727$, $p < 0.001$), in future trials of mBA, study inclusion criteria should be revised to assess for the primary target of mBA. Third, the current study did not include follow-up assessments. Thus, a future study needs to evaluate whether the treatment gains reported in the current study are maintained. Fourth, it should be determined whether the 10-session format is sufficient for mastery of the core treatment components by individuals with schizophrenia with mild to moderate negative symptoms. Even though the major purpose of the current study was to prove the concept and evaluate the preliminary efficacy, future trials should evaluate whether longer treatment sessions produce larger treatment gains. Finally, clinicians have reported that MI is a critical component while they are assisting and encouraging participants to search for their own goals/values, to link each activity with their own goals, and to encourage moving slowly to other unexplored goals and activities. However, there were no specific measures regarding these factors included in the study design. Thus, in a future study, specific scales (e.g., the Stage of Change Readiness and Treatment Engagement Scale) should be included to examine these phenomena.

Despite the limitations mentioned above, the current findings support the notion that mBA would be a promising adjunctive approach to the usual psychiatric rehabilitation services delivered in community mental health settings for addressing mild to moderate negative symptoms in individuals with schizophrenia. As a next step (Stage II), RCT trials should replicate the current findings to confirm the causality of mBA in improving mild to moderate negative symptoms. We believe that the current findings will facilitate the development of an effective psychosocial treatment for individuals with schizophrenia with mild to moderate negative symptoms who participate in community based psychiatric rehabilitation services.

AUTHOR CONTRIBUTIONS

K-HC designed the study and supervised overall research processes including assessment, data management, supervision of the research assistants, and wrote the first draft of the manuscript. EJ performed statistical analyses. EJ and G-YL conducted psychological assessment, diagnostic interviewing and psychiatric symptom ratings. All authors revised subsequent drafts of the manuscript. All authors contributed to and have approved the final manuscript.

ACKNOWLEDGMENTS

We would like to thank the participants and the staff at community mental health centers.

REFERENCES

Bell, M. D., Lysaker, P. H., Beam-Goulet, J. L., Milstein, R. M., and Lindenmayer, J.-P. (1994). Five-component model of schizophrenia: assessing the factorial invariance of the positive and negative syndrome scale. *Psychiatry Res.* 52, 295–303. doi: 10.1016/0165-1781(94)90075-2

Breier, A., Schreiber, J. L., Dyer, J., and Pickar, D. (1991). National Institute of Mental Health longitudinal study of chronic schizophrenia: prognosis and predictors of outcome. *Arch. Gen. Psychiatry* 48, 239–246. doi: 10.1001/archpsyc.1991.01810270051007

Buchanan, R. W. (2007). Persistent negative symptoms in schizophrenia: an overview. *Schizophr. Bull.* 33, 1013–1022. doi: 10.1093/schbul/sbl057

Cheong, S. S., Woo, J. M., Kim, E., Yeon, B. K., and Hong, K. S. (1999). Development of Korean auditory verbal learning test. *J. Korean Neuropsychiatr. Assoc.* 38, 1016–1025. doi: 10.3233/JAD-2012-120079

Choi, H. I., Song, M. J., Jekal, E., and Choi, K. H. (2014). Psychosocial approaches to negative symptoms of schizophrenia: a comprehensive systematic review. *Korean J. Psychol. Gen.* 33, 875–902.

Clark, L., Chamberlain, S. R., and Sahakian, B. J. (2009). Neurocognitive mechanisms in depression: implications for treatment. *Annu. Rev. Neurosci.* 32, 57–74. doi: 10.1146/annurev.neuro.31.060407.125618

Cohen, J. (1988). *Statistical Power Analysis for the Behavioral Sciences*, 2nd Edn. Mahwah, NJ: Erlbaum.

Cuijpers, P., Van Straten, A., and Warmerdam, L. (2007). Behavioral activation treatments of depression: a meta-analysis. *Clin. Psychol. Rev.* 27, 318–326. doi: 10.1016/j.cpr.2006.11.001

Dobson, D. J., McDougall, G., Busheikin, J., and Aldous, J. (1995). Effects of social skills training and social milieu treatment on symptoms of schizophrenia. *Psychiatr. Serv.* 46, 376–380. doi: 10.1176/ps.46.4.376

Ekers, D., Richards, D., McMillan, D., Bland, J. M., and Gilbody, S. (2011). Behavioural activation delivered by the non-specialist: phase II randomised controlled trial. *Br. J. Psychiatry* 198, 66–72. doi: 10.1192/bjp.bp.110.079111

Fiszdon, J. M., Kurtz, M. M., Choi, J., Bell, M. D., and Martino, S. (2016). Motivational interviewing to increase cognitive rehabilitation adherence in schizophrenia. *Schizophr. Bull.* 42, 327–334. doi: 10.1093/schbul/sbv143

Foussias, G., Agid, O., Fervaha, G., and Remington, G. (2014). Negative symptoms of schizophrenia: clinical features, relevance to real world functioning and specificity versus other CNS disorders. *Eur. Neuropsychopharmacol.* 24, 693–709. doi: 10.1016/j.euroneuro.2013.10.017

Foussias, G., and Remington, G. (2010). Negative symptoms in schizophrenia: avolition and Occam's razor. *Schizophr. Bull.* 36, 359–369. doi: 10.1093/schbul/sbn094

Gold, J. M., Strauss, G. P., Waltz, J. A., Robinson, B. M., Brown, J. K., and Frank, M. J. (2013). Negative symptoms of schizophrenia are associated with abnormal effort-cost computations. *Biol. Psychiatry* 74, 130–136. doi: 10.1016/j.biopsych.2012.12.022

Gold, J. M., Waltz, J. A., Prentice, K. J., Morris, S. E., and Heerey, E. A. (2008). Reward processing in schizophrenia: a deficit in the representation of value. *Schizophr. Bull.* 34, 835–847. doi: 10.1093/schbul/sbn068

Granholm, E., Holden, J. L., Sommerfeld, D., Rufener, C., Perivoliotis, D., Mueser, K., et al. (2015). Enhancing assertive community treatment with cognitive behavioral social skills training for schizophrenia: study protocol for a randomized controlled trial. *Trials* 16:438. doi: 10.1186/s13063-015-0967-8

Grant, P. M., Huh, G. A., Perivoliotis, D., Stolar, N. M., and Beck, A. T. (2012). Randomized trial to evaluate the efficacy of cognitive therapy for lowfunctioning patients with schizophrenia. *Arch. Gen. Psychiatry* 69, 121–127. doi: 10.1001/archgenpsychiatry.2011.129

Green, M. F. (1996). What are the functional consequences of neurocognitive deficits in schizophrenia? *Am. J. Psychiatry* 153, 321–330. doi: 10.1176/ajp.153.3.321

Green, M. F., Kern, R. S., Braff, D. L., and Mintz, J. (2000). Neurocognitive deficits and functional outcome in schizophrenia: are we measuring the "right stuff"? *Schizophr. Bull.* 26, 119–136. doi: 10.1093/oxfordjournals.schbul.a033430

Horan, W. P., Kring, A. M., Gur, R. E., Reise, S. P., and Blanchard, J. J. (2011). Development and psychometric validation of the Clinical Assessment Interview for Negative Symptoms (CAINS). *Schizophr. Res.* 132, 140–145. doi: 10.1016/j.schres.2011.06.030

Hwang, S. T., Kim, J. H., Park, K. B., Chey, J. Y., and Hong, S. H. (2012). *Korean Wechsler Adult Intelligence Scale-Fourth Edition guideline of description and interpretation.* Daegu: Korea Psychology.

Jang, S. K., Choi, H. I., Park, S., Jaekal, E., Lee, G. Y., Cho, Y. I., et al. (2016a). A two-factor model better explains heterogeneity in negative symptoms: evidence from the Positive and Negative Syndrome Scale. *Front. Psychol.* 7:707. doi: 10.3389/fpsyg.2016.00707

Jang, S. K., Kim, S., Kim, C. Y., Lee, H. S., and Choi, K. H. (2016b). Attentional processing of emotional faces in schizophrenia: evidence from eye tracking. *J. Abnorm. Psychol.* 125, 894–906. doi: 10.1037/abn0000198

Jang, S. K., Park, S. C., Lee, S. H., Cho, Y. S., and Choi, K. H. (2016c). Attention and memory bias to facial emotions underlying negative symptoms of schizophrenia. *Cogn. Neuropsychiatry* 21, 45–59. doi: 10.1080/13546805.2015.1127222

Kay, S. R., Fiszbein, A., and Opfer, L. A. (1987). The positive and negative syndrome scale (PANSS) for schizophrenia. *Schizophr. Bull.* 13, 261–276. doi: 10.1093/schbul/13.2.261

Kim, S. G., Lee, E. H., Hwang, S. T., Park, K. B., Chey, J. Y., Hong, S. H., et al. (2015). Estimation of K-WAIS-IV Premorbid Intelligence in South Korea: development of the KPIE-IV. *Clin. Neuropsychol.* 29, 19–29. doi: 10.1080/13854046.2015.1072248

Kirkpatrick, B., Strauss, G. P., Nguyen, L., Fischer, B. A., Daniel, D. G., Cienfuegos, A., et al. (2011). The brief negative symptom scale: psychometric properties. *Schizophr. Bull.* 37, 300–305. doi: 10.1093/schbul/sbq059

Kurtz, M. M., and Mueser, K. T. (2008). A meta-analysis of controlled research on social skills training for schizophrenia. *J. Consult. Clin. Psychol.* 76, 491–504. doi: 10.1037/0022-006X.76.3.491

Lejuez, C. W., Hopko, D. R., and Hopko, S. D. (2001). A brief behavioral activation treatment for depression. Treatment manual. *Behav. Modif.* 25, 255–286. doi: 10.1177/0145445501252005

Lindenmayer, J. P., Bernstein-Hyman, R., and Grochowski, S. (1994). A new five factor model of schizophrenia. *Psychiatr. Q.* 65, 299–322. doi: 10.1007/BF02354306

Lindenmayer, J. P., Grochowski, S., and Hyman, R. B. (1995). Five factor model of schizophrenia: replication across samples. *Schizophr. Res.* 14, 229–234. doi: 10.1016/0920-9964(94)00041-6

Mairs, H., Lovell, K., Campbell, M., and Keeley, P. (2011). Development and pilot investigation of behavioral activation for negative symptoms. *Behav. Modif.* 35, 486–506. doi: 10.1177/0145445511411706

Mazzucchelli, T., Kane, R., and Rees, C. (2009). Behavioral activation treatments for depression in adults: a meta-analysis and review. *Clin. Psychol. Sci. Pract.* 16, 383–411. doi: 10.1111/j.1468-2850.2009.01178.x

McCambridge, J., and Strang, J. (2003). Development of a structured generic drug intervention model for public health purposes: a brief application of motivational interviewing with young people. *Drug Alcohol Rev.* 22, 391–399. doi: 10.1080/09595230310001613903

Miles, J., and Shevlin, M. (2001). *Applying Regression and Correlation: A Guide for Students and Researchers*. London: Sage Publications.

Milev, P., Ho, B. C., Arndt, S., and Andreasen, N. C. (2005). Predictive values of neurocognition and negative symptoms on functional outcome in schizophrenia: a longitudinal first-episode study with 7-year follow-up. *Am. J. Psychiatry* 162, 495–506. doi: 10.1176/appi.ajp.162.3.495

Miller, W. R., and Rollnick, S. (2002). *Motivational Interviewing: Preparing People for Change*, 2nd Edn. New York, NY: Guilford.

Morrison, A. P., and Barratt, S. (2010). What are the components of CBT for psychosis? A Delphi study. *Schizophr. Bull.* 36, 136–142. doi: 10.1093/schbul/sbp118

Murphy, S. M., McDonell, M. G., McPherson, S., Srebnik, D., Angelo, F., Roll, J. M., et al. (2015). An economic evaluation of a contingency-management intervention for stimulant use among community mental health patients with serious mental illness. *Drug Alcohol Depend.* 153, 293–299. doi: 10.1016/j.drugalcdep.2015.05.004

Onken, L. S., Carroll, K. M., Shoham, V., Cuthbert, B. N., and Riddle, M. (2014). Reenvisioning clinical science: unifying the discipline to improve the public health. *Clin. Psychol. Sci.* 2, 22–34. doi: 10.1177/2167702613497932

Pogue-Geile, M. F., and Harrow, M. (1985). Negative symptoms in schizophrenia: their longitudinal course and prognostic importance. *Schizophr. Bull.* 11, 427–439. doi: 10.1093/schbul/11.3.427

Porter, J. F., Spates, C. R., and Smitham, S. (2004). Behavioral activation group therapy in public mental health settings: a pilot investigation. *Prof. Psychol. Res. Pract.* 35, 297–301. doi: 10.1037/0735-7028.35.3.297

Rabinowitz, J., Levine, S. Z., Garibaldi, G., Bugarski-Kirola, D., Berardo, C. G., and Kapur, S. (2012). Negative symptoms have greater impact on functioning than positive symptoms in schizophrenia: analysis of CATIE data. *Schizophr. Res.* 137, 147–150. doi: 10.1016/j.schres.2012.01.015

Rector, N. A., and Beck, A. T. (2001). Cognitive behavioral therapy for schizophrenia: an empirical review. *J. Nerv. Ment. Dis.* 189, 278–287. doi: 10.1097/00005053-200105000-00002

Reitan, R. M. (1992). *Trail Making Test: Manual for Administration and Scoring*. Mesa, AZ: Reitan Neuropsychology Laboratory.

Rey, A. (1964). *The Clinical Examination in Psychology*. Paris: Press Universitaire de France.

Rüsch, N., and Corrigan, P. W. (2002). Motivational interviewing to improve insight and treatment adherence in schizophrenia. *Psychiatr. Rehabil. J.* 26, 23–32. doi: 10.2975/26.2002.23.32

Silverstein, S. M. (2010). Bridging the gap between extrinsic and intrinsic motivation in the cognitive remediation of schizophrenia. *Schizophr. Bull.* 36, 949–956. doi: 10.1093/schbul/sbp160

Staring, A. B., ter Huurne, M. A. B., and van der Gaag, M. (2013). Cognitive Behavioral Therapy for negative symptoms (CBT-n) in psychotic disorders: a pilot study. *J. Behav. Ther. Exp. Psychiatry* 44, 300–306. doi: 10.1016/j.jbtep.2013.01.004

Steinberg, M. L., Ziedonis, D. M., Krejci, J. A., and Brandon, T. H. (2004). Motivational interviewing with personalized feedback: a brief intervention for motivating smokers with schizophrenia to seek treatment for tobacco dependence. *J. Consult. Clin. Psychol.* 72, 723–728. doi: 10.1037/0022-006X.72.4.723

Strauss, G. P., Frank, M. J., Waltz, J. A., Kasanova, Z., Herbener, E. S., and Gold, J. M. (2011). Deficits in positive reinforcement learning and uncertainty-driven exploration are associated with distinct aspects of negative symptoms in schizophrenia. *Biol. Psychiatry* 69, 424–431. doi: 10.1016/j.biopsych.2010.10.015

Strauss, G. P., and Gold, J. M. (2012). A new perspective on anhedonia in schizophrenia. *Am. J. Psychiatry* 169, 364–373. doi: 10.1176/appi.ajp.2011.11030447

Strauss, G. P., Keller, W. R., Buchanan, R. W., Gold, J. M., Fischer, B. A., McMahon, R. P., et al. (2012). Next-generation negative symptom assessment for clinical trials: validation of the Brief Negative Symptom Scale. *Schizophr. Res.* 142, 88–92. doi: 10.1016/j.schres.2012.10.012

Tarrier, N., Lewis, S., Haddock, G., Bentall, R., Drake, R., Kinderman, P., et al. (2004). Cognitive-behavioural therapy in first-episode and early schizophrenia. *Br. J. Psychiatry* 184, 231–239. doi: 10.1192/bjp.184.3.231

Velligan, D. I., Mahurin, R. K., Diamond, P. L., Hazleton, B. C., Eckert, S. L., and Miller, A. L. (1997). The functional significance of symptomatology and cognitive function in schizophrenia. *Schizophr. Res.* 25, 21–31. doi: 10.1016/S0920-9964(97)00010-8

Velligan, D. I., Roberts, D., Mintz, J., Maples, N., Li, X., Medellin, E., et al. (2015). A randomized pilot study of MOtiVation and Enhancement (MOVE) Training for negative symptoms in schizophrenia. *Schizophr. Res.* 165, 175–180. doi: 10.1016/j.schres.2015.04.008

Velthorst, E., Koeter, M., van der Gaag, M., Nieman, D. H., Fett, A. K., Smit, F., et al. (2015). Adapted cognitive–behavioural therapy required for targeting negative symptoms in schizophrenia: meta-analysis and meta-regression. *Psychol. Med.* 45, 453–465. doi: 10.1017/S0033291714001147

Wechsler, D. (2008). *Wechsler Adult Intelligence Scale*, 4th Edn. San Antonio, TX: Pearson.

11

Identifying Electrophysiological Prodromes of Post-traumatic Stress Disorder

Chao Wang[1,2], *Michelle E. Costanzo*[2,3], *Paul E. Rapp*[1]*, *David Darmon*[1,2], *Kylee Bashirelahi*[1,2], *Dominic E. Nathan*[1,2,4], *Christopher J. Cellucci*[5], *Michael J. Roy*[3] and *David O. Keyser*[1]

[1] *Traumatic Injury Research Program, Department of Military and Emergency Medicine, Uniformed Services University of the Health Sciences, Bethesda, MD, USA,* [2] *The Henry M. Jackson Foundation for the Advancement of Military Medicine, Inc., Bethesda, MD, USA,* [3] *Department of Medicine and Center for Neuroscience and Regenerative Medicine, Uniformed Services University of the Health Sciences, Bethesda, MD, USA,* [4] *Graduate School of Nursing, Uniformed Services University of the Health Sciences, Bethesda, MD, USA,* [5] *Aquinas LLC, Berwyn, PA, USA*

Edited by:
Kim T. Mueser,
Boston University, USA

Reviewed by:
Jonathan K. Wynn,
University of California Los Angeles, USA
Takako Mitsudo,
Kyushu University, Japan

***Correspondence:**
Paul Rapp
paul.rapp@usuhs.edu

The objective of this research project is the identification of a physiological prodrome of post-traumatic stress disorder (PTSD) that has a reliability that could justify preemptive treatment in the sub-syndromal state. Because abnormalities in event-related potentials (ERPs) have been observed in fully expressed PTSD, the possible utility of abnormal ERPs in predicting delayed-onset PTSD was investigated. ERPs were recorded from military service members recently returned from Iraq or Afghanistan who did not meet PTSD diagnostic criteria at the time of ERP acquisition. Participants ($n = 65$) were followed for up to 1 year, and 7.7% of the cohorts ($n = 5$) were PTSD-positive at follow-up. The initial analysis of the receiver operating characteristic (ROC) curve constructed using ERP metrics was encouraging. The average amplitude to target stimuli gave an area under the ROC curve of greater than 0.8. Classification based on the Youden index, which is determined from the ROC, gave positive results. Using average target amplitude at electrode Cz yielded Sensitivity = 0.80 and Specificity = 0.87. A more systematic statistical analysis of the ERP data indicated that the ROC results may simply represent a fortuitous consequence of small sample size. Predicted error rates based on the distribution of target ERP amplitudes approached those of random classification. A leave-one-out cross validation using a Gaussian likelihood classifier with Bayesian priors gave lower values of sensitivity and specificity. In contrast with the ROC results, the leave-one-out classification at Cz gave Sensitivity = 0.65 and Specificity = 0.60. A bootstrap calculation, again using the Gaussian likelihood classifier at Cz, gave Sensitivity = 0.59 and Specificity = 0.68. Two provisional conclusions can be offered. First, the results can only be considered preliminary due to the small sample size, and a much larger study will be required to assess definitively the utility of ERP prodromes of PTSD. Second, it may be necessary to combine ERPs with other biomarkers in a multivariate metric to produce a prodrome that can justify preemptive treatment.

Keywords: post-traumatic stress disorder, prodromes, event-related potentials, delayed onset, traumatic brain injury, P300

INTRODUCTION

Historically, psychiatric practice has been reactive rather than preemptive. It has been recognized that a transition to preemptive psychiatry requires the identification of prodromes of psychiatric disorders that have a predictive reliability that justifies intervention in the absence of a fully expressed disorder. A prodrome is not a risk factor. A prodrome is a physiological change antecedent to a full expression of the disorder. Costello and Angold (1) provide the following definition: "... a prodrome is a premonitory manifestation of the disease. It is not a characteristic of the individual or their environment or a causal agent of the disease. A prodromal symptom may or may not continue to be manifest once the full disease appears. Conversely, the same disease may or may not manifest prodromal symptoms in different episodes." Emerging genetic, epigenetic, and psychophysiological technologies offer the possibility of identifying prodromes or combinations of prodromes (where a combination of metrics may improve specificity) that can warrant preemptive treatment (2, 3). Prior research has investigated prodromes of several psychiatric disorders including psychosis (4–7), depression (8), autism (9, 10), dementia (11), alcoholism and substance abuse (1, 12), and post-traumatic stress disorder [PTSD (13–15)].

The objective of this research project is the identification of a physiological prodrome of PTSD that has a reliability that could justify preemptive treatment in the sub-syndromal state. The search for statistically reliable prodromes requires two things: a sub-syndromal period where physiological changes prior to the disease onset have been initiated, and a measure that can quantify these changes. In the ideal case, a third element can facilitate the search for prodromes: the identification of an at-risk population because an enriched population (a population where incidence is higher than the general population) will increase the statistical likelihood of identifying a prodrome. In this contribution, we address a specific question: can event-related potentials identify individuals at risk of delayed-onset PTSD? As preceding questions we must ask whether an at-risk population can be identified and if there is evidence indicating that PTSD can, in some instances, present with delayed onset? It is the period between trauma exposure and the presentation of a fully expressed PTSD that provides the window of opportunity for preemptive treatment.

Can a PTSD At-Risk Group Be Identified?

Military deployment is a risk factor for PTSD. The reported incidence of PTSD in veterans varies greatly between studies. A critical review found that PTSD incidence in US Iraq veterans ranges from 4 to 17% (16). Reports of the incidence of PTSD in the general population are similarly varied, but the National Comorbidity Survey Replication Study (17, 18) estimated the lifetime prevalence of PTSD in adult Americans to be 6.8%. Current past year prevalence was estimated at 3.5%. This suggests that military service members (SMs) who have returned from deployment will provide a statistically enriched population increasing the likelihood of identifying prodromes of PTSD. When making this observation, it is recognized that it is possible that military-related PTSD and PTSD in civilian populations may have distinct pathophysiological etiologies. This would potentially limit the general utility of results obtained with a military population.

Can PTSD Present with Delayed Onset?

Meta-analysis indicates that approximately 25% of PTSD cases present with delayed onset, where delayed onset is defined as meeting diagnostic criteria after a sub-syndromal or asymptomatic period of at least 6 months after the precipitating traumatic event (19, 20). In a military population, Grieger et al. (21) found that the majority of individuals PTSD-positive 7 months after serious combat injury did not meet diagnostic threshold at 1 month post-injury. In cases of PTSD following mild traumatic brain injury (TBI), the fraction of cases presenting with delayed onset can be higher. Bryant et al. (22) found that of those who met PTSD criteria at 24 months following a TBI, 44.1% reported no PTSD at 3 months. The analysis of Smid et al. (20) and Andrews et al. (19) indicates that PTSD can present after a symptom-free period, but it has been found to be more likely after a period of sub-syndromal PTSD in which two or three of the symptom clusters are endorsed (22). The factors contributing to delayed-onset PTSD in the absence of mild TBI are incompletely understood (15). On reviewing the trajectories of full and sub-syndromal PTSD, Bryant et al. (22) reached the following conclusions: "The present study demonstrates longitudinally that there is not a linear relationship between acute trauma response and long-term PTSD and highlights that PTSD levels fluctuate markedly in the initial years after trauma exposure. This pattern can explain the modest predictive capacity of acute markers to identify subsequent PTSD status. The complexity of these trajectories is further indicated by the delayed occurrence of PTSD responses, which appears to result from a combination of the immediate stress response and cumulative stress in the aftermath of the trauma." These clinical observations further encourage the search for reliable physiological prodromes of PTSD.

Is There a Prior Literature Reporting Alterations of Event-Related Potentials in Fully Expressed PTSD?

As noted above, an additional requirement in the search for prodromes is the identification of a measure that can quantify physiological changes antecedent to disease onset. This search can be informed by asking whether there are markers that show alteration in the fully expressed disease, since it seems possible that these alterations may have begun prior to reaching diagnostic threshold. In the specific context of this investigation, this question becomes is there a prior literature showing abnormalities in event-related potentials in PTSD patients? An examination of the prior literature summarized in **Table 1** suggests that event-related potentials can be altered in the fully expressed PTSD state.

The divergence of electrophysiological results across studies is consistent with the emerging understanding that PTSD is not a discrete clinical entity and that different pathophysiological processes may be active in different individuals. The results do, however, suggest that alterations of brain electrical behavior can be associated with the disorder. As indicated in **Table 1**, alterations in P300 are most frequently reported.

There is an emerging understanding of the neurological origin of the empirical results reported in **Table 1** that suggests why alterations of P300 may be associated with both fully expressed PTSD and the sub-syndromal state. P300 has been hypothesized

TABLE 1 | Studies reporting ERP abnormalities in PTSD-positive participants.

Study	Reported observation(s)
Araki et al. (23)	Lower amplitude ERPs at Pz in an auditory oddball task
Blomhoff et al. (24)	Amplitudes to emotionally related words were significantly related to CAPS scores
Charles et al. (25)	P300 amplitude lower in PTSD-positive participants
Felmingham et al. (26)	Auditory oddball, PTSD positive participants show the following
	Target stimuli: reduced P200 amplitude, reduced P300 amplitude, increased N200 amplitude, increased N200 latency, increased P300 latency
	Standard stimuli: reduced P200 amplitude
Ghisolfi et al. (27)	PTSD positive participants showed auditory P50 sensory gating deficits
Hansenne (28)	Literature review includes PTSD
Javanbakht et al. (29)	Literature review of 36 studies. Increased P300 response to trauma-related stimuli. P50 studies suggest impaired gating
Johnson et al. (30)	P300a, P300b amplitudes larger with trauma related stimuli
	P300b small with neutral stimuli
	P300 working memory amplitudes smaller
Karl et al. (31)	Reduced P50 suppression
	Increase P300 amplitude to trauma-related stimuli
Kimble et al. (32)	Significant P300 amplitude enhancements to distracting stimuli
Kimble et al. (33)	Larger frontal, smaller central, and parietal CNVs
McFarlane et al. (34)	Delayed N200 P300 elicited by target and distracter tones indistinguishable
Metzger et al. (35)	Parietal P300 amplitude to target tones were smaller in unmedicated PTSD positive participants
Metzger et al. (36)	Modified Stroop task for personal traumatic, personal positive, and neutral words. PTSD-positive participants have reduced and delayed P300 across word type
Metzger et al. (37)	Contrary to previous results, the PTSD group had larger P300b amplitude and increased P200 amplitude/intensity slopes
Neylan et al. (38)	Impaired P50 gating to non-startle trauma-neutral auditory stimuli
Neylan et al. (39)	Nine of 24 P300 measures were significantly less predictable over time in the PTSD-positive group
Shu et al. (40)	mTBI only compared against mTBI + PTSD, larger emotional face processing ERPs in mTBI + PTSD
Shu et al. (41)	mTBI only compared against mTBI + PTSD, larger inhibitory processing ERPs in mTBI + PTSD
Shucard et al. (42)	PTSD group has longer P300 latency to NoGo stimuli and greater P300 amplitude to irrelevant non-target stimuli

CAPS, Clinician-Administered PTSD Scale; CNV, contingent negative variation; ERP, event-related potential.

to reflect neural activity associated with attention and subsequent memory processing (43), with larger P300 amplitude associated with greater attentional resources employed in the task (44, 45). The prior studies with PTSD positive participants reporting reduced P300 amplitude to target stimuli in the PTSD group compared to the control group, suggest impairment of attentional processes which is consistent with clinical observation. In addition, a meta-analysis examining ERP components and PTSD revealed that the P300 amplitude may also be sensitive to contextual cues such that information processing is modulated based on the situation and environment (31). These dynamics are consistent with functional changes of two reported neural generators of the P300 (46, 47): the anterior cingulate cortex (ACC) and the hippocampus, which are also altered in individuals with PTSD (48). The ACC is critical to attentional processing and fear inhibition (49, 50) and the hippocampus is involved in memory and contextual representations (51). Araki et al. (23) revealed that lower P300 amplitude in patients with PTSD was associated with smaller ACC volume, which linked the P300 abnormality to underlying brain morphological abnormality.

It should be recognized that the results in **Table 1** were obtained from participants who were diagnostically PTSD-positive at the time of recording. The question of the utility of ERPs as a predictor of a transition to PTSD is not addressed by these studies, but these studies do suggest that altered ERPs may be present in the subsyndromal state. This possibility is investigated in this study. The study was sponsored by the Department of Defense to investigate the utility of using a reduced montage that could be implemented in a military field hospital environment. Event-related potentials can be elicited by visual, auditory, somatosensory, and olfactory stimuli, with visual and auditory stimuli being the most commonly used. Hearing and vision can be compromised after blast exposure, but visual disturbances typically resolve faster. We therefore used visual stimuli in this study. As indicated in **Table 1**, several ERP components [P50, P200, N200, and contingent negative variation (CNV)] can be altered in PTSD-positive participants. Typically, however, the P300 is the most robust component. Since the object of this research program is the development of a robust technology that can be implemented in an austere medical environment, we focused on the P300.

METHODS

Subjects

We recruited 85 military SMs within 2 months of their return from an Operation Enduring Freedom (OEF)/Operation Iraqi Freedom (OIF) deployment of at least 3 months' duration in either Iraq or Afghanistan. The Clinician-Administered PTSD Scale (CAPS) (52) and the PTSD Checklist-Military Version (PCL-M) (53) were administrated to assess PTSD. Patient Health Questionnaire-9 (PHQ-9) (54) and the International Classification of Diseases, 10th Clinical Modification (ICD-10) criteria for postconcussional syndrome (PCS) were administrated to determine the presence of depression and PCS, respectively. Exclusion criteria included a history of head injury resulting in loss of consciousness for 60 min or more; a current Glasgow Coma Scale less than 13; visual acuity lower than 20/100 after correction; psychosis; active suicidal, or homicidal ideation; pregnancy; a diagnosis of PCS according ICD-10, PHQ-9 score greater than or equal to 10; and a PCL-M score greater than or equal to 50, or a diagnosis of PTSD made by an experienced psychologist using the CAPS based on the

DSM-IV criteria. All subjects provided written informed consent in accordance with the protocol approved by institutional review boards at Uniformed Services University, Walter Reed National Military Medical Center, and the National Institutes of Health.

Out of the 85 participants, 8 were excluded after baseline assessment: 2 for PCL-M $\geq$50, 2 for PHQ-9 scores $\geq$10, and 4 for problems with electroencephalogram (EEG) recording. Among the remaining 77 participants, 65 completed at least one follow-up psychological evaluation (52 at 3 months, 33 at 6 months, and 53 at 12 months). On serial follow-up evaluations, 5 of the 65 participants developed PTSD as determined by PCL-M scores (4 PTSD, 1 PTSD with depression). We therefore separated the 65 participants into 5 cases (referred to as Converters, mean age 35.6 $\pm$ 6.2 years, 4 men and 1 woman) and 60 controls (referred to as Stables, mean age 30.5 $\pm$ 8.0 years, 54 men and 6 women). The 5 Converters and 60 Stables are the final set of subjects in this study. In this paper, we focus on electrophysiological data from baseline assessment as we are trying to identify neural markers that predict the development of PTSD.

All participants in the group of 65 were exposed to relatively severe traumatic experiences. The types of index trauma reported by those who developed PTSD included experiencing a base attack (e.g., mortar or rocket fire, $n=1$), engaging in combat-related violence (e.g., firefights, hit by improvised explosive device, IED, killing enemy, $n=2$), witnessing combat-related violence (e.g., watching truck in convoy hit by an IED, witnessing death $n=1$), and deployment bullying and abuse ($n=1$). Those who did not develop PTSD also reported experiencing base attacks ($n=24$), engaging in combat-related violence ($n=23$), and witnessing combat-related violence ($n=13$). Two factors, however, preclude a meaningful search for correlations between ERP abnormalities and cause of trauma. The first is the small size of the study population. The second would be applicable even in a larger study. Many, if not most of these participants have received multiple traumas from many causes.

Electrophysiological Recording

A visual oddball task was performed by subjects in an acoustically and electrically shielded room. Visual stimuli were presented by a digital tachistoscope of our own design and construction. The tachistoscope is a 5 $\times$ 5 square array of yellow, light-emitting diodes. Each diode is 1 cm in diameter. Given spacing between LEDs, the array is 6 cm $\times$ 6 cm. The standard visual stimulus was a vertical stimulus which consists of the five vertical center line LEDs illuminated simultaneously for 40 ms. The target visual stimulus was a horizontal stimulus which is composed of the five horizontal center line LEDs illuminated simultaneously for 40 ms. Each subject received 125 stimuli in total, of which about 21% (26 $\pm$ 1 trials) were target and 79% (99 $\pm$ 1 trials) were standard stimuli. The subjects were instructed to maintain a silent count of the number of target stimulus presentations and to report their count at the end. The inter-stimulus onset time was varied randomly between 1.4 and 1.8 s. The number of trials in the current study is sufficient to elicit a valid P300 response. For example, a classic P300 study by Pollich et al. (55) used 25 target trials. Cohen and Polich (56) found that the P300 stabilized with approximately 20 trials.

The scalp EEG was recorded using the EPA6 amplifier (Sensorium Inc.) and the Grass electrodes (Natus Neurology Inc.) at Fz, Cz, Pz, Oz, C3, and C4 according to the standard 10-20 electrode system, with linked earlobes as reference and a forehead ground. Electrode impedances were maintained under 5 kΩ. EOG was recorded from two electrodes placed below and above the right eye. The sampling rate was 2,048 Hz, and the analog filter band-pass was 0.02–500 Hz.

Data Processing of Electrophysiological Data

Data processing was performed offline using custom scripts written in MATLAB (www.mathworks.com). Channels contaminated by artifacts were removed from analysis. This resulted in one Fz channel (from the Stable group) and four Oz channels (one from the Converter group and three from the Stable group) being removed. EOG artifacts were corrected by using a regression approach (57). The data after EOG correction were high-pass filtered at 0.5 Hz, low-pass filtered at 50 Hz, and down sampled to 256 Hz. The analysis period was -200 to 1,000 ms where time zero denotes stimulus onset. Trials with peak potentials exceeding 75 μV or exhibiting abnormal trends were excluded from ERP averaging. The overall trial rejection rate was 4.84%. Target trials and standard trials were averaged separately. P300 amplitude was measured as the voltage of the largest positive peak of target ERP within 250–500 ms. P300 latency was measured as the time from stimulus onset to the maximum positive amplitude within 250–500 ms.

Statistical Analyses

Differences between groups in demographics, psychological measures, and task performance (accuracy of target count) were examined by Student's t-tests if data are numerical or Fisher's exact tests if data are categorical. Because the Oz channel was lost in some recordings (including one in the Converter group), the statistical analysis is limited to Fz, Cz, Pz, C3, and C4 electrode sites. Group differences in P300 amplitude and latency at each electrode site were tested by Student's t-tests. Correlations between P300 amplitude and the psychological measures were examined by Pearson's correlation coefficient. p-Values less than 0.05 were considered statistically significant.

To examine the efficacy of using P300 amplitude as the predictor for PTSD, we performed several statistical analyses including approximate classification error rate, receiver operating characteristic (ROC) curve, leave-one-out cross validation, and bootstrapping. The detailed mathematical methods and equations can be found in the Mathematical Appendices.

RESULTS

Subject Characteristics and Baseline Psychological Measures

The subject characteristics and baseline psychological measures were summarized in **Table 2**. Age, gender, handedness, and history of mild TBI (mTBI) were not significantly different between the Converter and Stable groups. At the baseline assessment, the

TABLE 2 | Subject characteristics and baseline psychological measures.

Variable	Converter ($n=5$)		Stable ($n=60$)		Group comparison[a]		
	Mean	SD	Mean	SD	df	*t*-Value	*p*-Value
Age	35.6	6.2	30.5	8.0	63	1.37	0.18
Gender, male/female	4/1		54/6				0.36
Handedness, R/L	5/0		55/5				0.66
History of mTBI < 10 years, yes/no	2/3		18/42				0.33
Clinician-Administered PTSD Scale total	30.6	15.4	18.7	12.5	63	2.02	0.047
Patient Health Questionnaire-9 score	5.2	2.3	2.5	2.3	62	2.51	0.015
PTSD Checklist-Military Version (PCL-M) score	33.4	11.0	25.9	7.4	63	2.10	0.040

[a] *Fisher's exact tests were used for gender, handedness, and history of mTBI. Student's t-tests were used for other variables.*

Converter group reported significantly higher CAPS, PHQ-9, and PCL-M scores than the Stable group.

Behavioral Data

The accuracy of target count at baseline assessment was not significantly different between Converters and Stables. For Converters, the mean accuracy of target count was 93.1% (SD 5.0%) and for Stables the mean accuracy was 97.4% (SD 5.5%) The difference was not statistically significant ($t=1.70$, df $=63$, $p=0.095$).

P300 Data: Amplitude and Latencies of Averaged Responses

We computed the approximate signal-to-noise ratios (SNRs) for both target and standard trials within the P300 time window for each subject. The SNR was calculated from the power of the ERP during the P300 window (300–400 ms) minus the power of the ERP during baseline (−200 to 0 ms) and then divided by the power of the ERP during baseline window. The mean SNR for single subject ERP for target trials at Pz is 145 (21.6 dB). The mean SNR for single subject ERP for standard trials at Pz is 87 (19.4 dB).

The P300 waveforms of average responses to standard stimuli do not have a well-defined single peak that can provide a unique amplitude and latency measure that can be incorporated into statistical analysis. Statistical analysis is therefore limited to the average responses to target stimuli where well-defined P300 waveforms make precise measurements possible. **Figure 1** displays the grand average ERPs in response to target and standard stimuli at the six electrodes in Converters and Stables. Because the Oz channel was lost in some recordings, the statistical analysis is further limited to Fz, Cz, Pz, C3, and C4 electrode sites. We found that for all these electrode sites, the P300 amplitude was significantly smaller ($p<0.05$) for the Converter group compared to the Stable group. The P300 latency was not significantly different ($p>0.05$) between the two groups. The statistical results for each electrode were summarized in **Table 3**. We also explored the correlation between the P300 amplitudes and the psychological measures (CAPS, PHQ-9, and PCL-M) across subjects. No significant correlations were found ($p>0.05$).

DIAGNOSTIC VALIDITY

Approximate Classification Error Rate

As summarized in **Table 3**, there was a statistically significant difference in the target amplitude between the participants who remained PTSD-negative throughout the study and those who became PTSD-positive. A statistically significant between-group separation does not, however, establish the efficacy of these measures as predictors. The most commonly applied quantitative measure of between-group separation is the *t*-test. As shown in **Table 3**, a naive calculation (a two-tailed *t*-test that assumes unequal variances) suggests a significant separation between the two participant groups. Two essential observations should be made. First, the asymptotic assumptions of the *t*-test cannot be meaningfully satisfied when $N_C=5$. Second, a separation of means, which is what the *t*-test assesses, does not of itself ensure a successful classification even in those instances where the assumptions of the test are satisfied. An estimate of classification error rates can be made by again assuming normality of the two populations. The equations used are given in the Mathematical Appendices. This estimate often results in a substantial under estimate of the true error rate. This is particularly true when population numbers are small (58). The results shown in **Table 3** show that application of this admittedly optimistic error rate estimate predicts that using target amplitude results in unacceptable classification error rates of $P_{ERROR}=0.29$ to $P_{ERROR}=0.32$, where it should be remembered that random assignment results in a 0.50 error if we assume that the two populations occur in equal proportions. This negative conclusion will be supported by the more reliable empirical determinations of classification error. It should be noted, however, that the error rates are different between the amplitudes and latencies, namely approximately 30% for the amplitudes and 50% for the latencies.

ROC Curve

Prediction using prodromes can be treated as a diagnostic problem in which the disease-positive state corresponds to being a member of the group that becomes PTSD positive. Calculation of the ROC curve is a commonly employed method for characterizing a diagnostic classification. The first row of **Table 4** shows the area under the curve (AUC), for the electrophysiological measures. The mathematical methods used to determine the AUC and its confidence intervals are given in the Mathematical Appendices. A value of AUC >0.5 indicates better than random assignment. The P300 amplitude at Cz showed the highest predictive power, with an AUC of 0.85 (confidence interval of [0.67, 0.94]). The ROC curve of the P300 amplitude at Cz is shown in **Figure 2**. While the values of the AUC are encouraging, the very large confidence intervals diminish confidence in the result.

Diagnostic Efficacy and Determination of the Diagnostic Cut Score

The results of a diagnostic calculation (and by implication for the present context the identification of a prodrome) can be expressed in the canonical four element diagnostic matrix: true positive, false positive, false negative, and true negative. There is

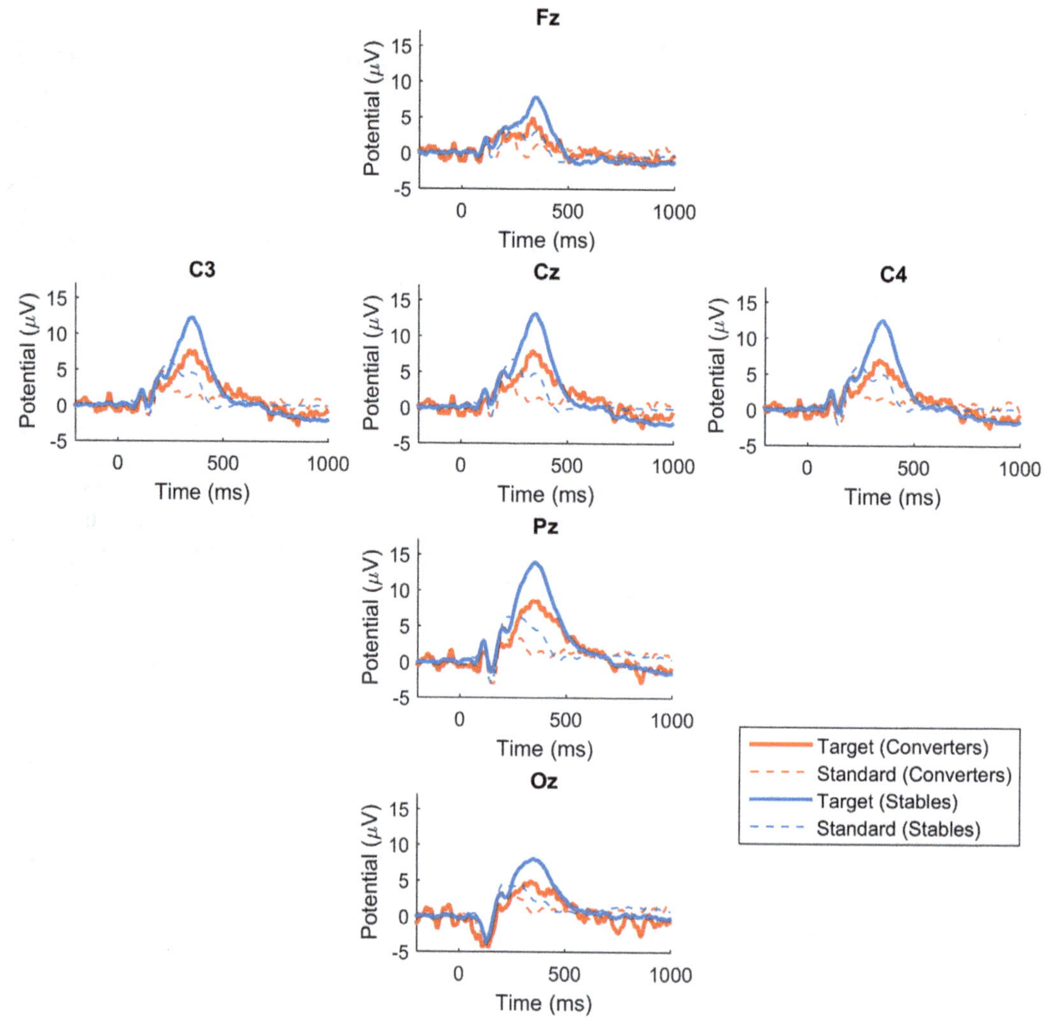

FIGURE 1 | P300 waveforms in converters and stables. Grand average ERPs in response to target and standard stimuli at the six electrodes. Blue lines represent waveforms for Stables. Red lines represent waveforms for Converters.

TABLE 3 | Baseline results from participants who remained PTSD-negative for one year after enrollment ($N = 60$) and those who converted to PTSD-positive ($N = 5$).

	Baseline scores individuals	Baseline scores individuals	Between-group separation	P_{ERROR}
	PTSD-negative at 1 year stables	PTSD-positive at 1 year converters	T-test, two-tailed, unequal variance	Equal priors
	$N = 60$ ($N = 59$ for Fz)	$N = 5$	*p*	
Average Fz amplitude response to target stimulus (μV)	9.87 ± 4.25	5.98 ± 2.38	0.0157	0.3193
Average Cz amplitude response to target stimulus (μV)	15.48 ± 5.45	9.71 ± 2.65	0.0038	0.2937
Average Pz amplitude response to target stimulus (μV)	16.18 ± 5.27	11.13 ± 3.71	0.0338	0.3130
Average C3 amplitude response to target stimulus (μV)	14.52 ± 5.16	9.34 ± 2.54	0.0054	0.3032
Average C4 amplitude response to target stimulus (μV)	14.72 ± 5.23	9.07 ± 2.67	0.0046	0.2898
Average Fz latency response to target stimulus (ms)	356.2 ± 43.8	357.0 ± 57.2	0.9760	0.4963
Average Cz latency response to target stimulus (ms)	359.7 ± 39.0	357.3 ± 57.6	0.9235	0.4868
Average Pz latency response to target stimulus (ms)	360.5 ± 42.4	374.2 ± 58.6	0.6345	0.4377
Average C3 latency response to target stimulus (ms)	359.4 ± 37.3	352.3 ± 68.2	0.8291	0.4646
Average C4 latency response to target stimulus (ms)	355.2 ± 36.9	355.5 ± 60.3	0.9928	0.4987

TABLE 4 | Area under the receiver operating curve and measures of diagnostic efficacy computed using the smallest value of threshold giving the maximum value of the Youden index.

Measure	Average Fz amplitude response to target stimulus	Average Cz amplitude response to target stimulus	Average Pz amplitude response to target stimulus	Average C3 amplitude response to target stimulus	Average C4 amplitude response to target stimulus
Area under the curve	0.7864 [0.5616, 0.8960]	0.8533 [0.6708, 0.9347]	0.7833 [0.4737, 0.9108]	0.8233 [0.6170, 0.9185]	0.8433 [0.5980, 0.9390]
Max Youden Index	0.5763	0.6667	0.5500	0.6000	0.7000
T_{MAX} (μV)	9.0140	10.4186	12.1866	12.4016	9.1688
Diagnostic accuracy	0.6094	0.8615	0.7538	0.6308	0.8923
Sensitivity	1.0000	0.8000	0.8000	1.0000	0.8000
Specificity	0.5763	0.8667	0.7500	0.6000	0.9000
Positive likelihood ratio	2.3600	6.0000	3.2000	2.5000	8.0000
Negative likelihood ratio	0.0000	0.2308	0.2667	0.0000	0.2222
Diagnostic odds ratio	Undefined	26.0000	12.0000	Undefined	36.0000

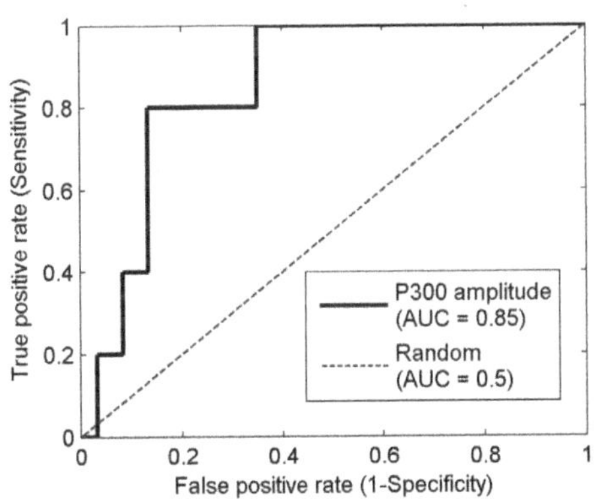

FIGURE 2 | The receiver operating characteristic (ROC) curve of the P300 amplitude at Cz. Horizontal axis is the false positive rate (1-specificity) which equals the number of false positive divided by the sum of false positive and true negative. Vertical axis is the true positive rate (sensitivity) which equals the number of true positives divided by the sum of true positive and false negative. The solid line represents the ROC curve for using the P300 amplitude at Cz as the diagnostic test. The dashed line represents the ROC curve for a random test.

no single fully satisfactory summary measure for characterizing the diagnostic matrix. Each has advantages and limitations. The limitations are particularly evident in studies like this one where disease prevalence is low. We will therefore examine six common measures of diagnostic efficacy: diagnostic accuracy, sensitivity, specificity, the positive likelihood ratio, the negative likelihood ratio, and the diagnostic odds ratio. Their definitions are given in the Mathematical Appendices.

The values of elements in the diagnostic matrix, and therefore measures of diagnostic efficacy like sensitivity and specificity, are critically dependent on the cut score used to assign individuals to the disease-positive and disease-negative groups. The choice of the cut value is therefore a central problem in the implementation of a diagnostic procedure. As outlined in the Mathematical Appendices, more than one candidate procedure has been proposed. In the calculations summarized in **Table 4**, the diagnostic threshold was determined by the value of threshold that gave the maximum value of *J*, the Youden index (59). The value of sensitivity, specificity, and other measures of diagnostic efficacy reported in **Table 4** are the values obtained when the threshold was set to the smallest value of threshold giving the maximum *J*. Because the results of **Table 3** indicate that target latencies cannot discriminate between-group means, the analysis is limited to target amplitudes.

Leave-One-Out Cross Validation

The results presented in **Table 4** are encouraging particularly in the cases of average Cz amplitude and average C4 amplitude which give sensitivity and specificity values in excess of 0.8. Measures of diagnostic efficacy obtained by examination of the ROC can be misleadingly optimistic if sample sizes are small. A fast, albeit imperfect, reality check can be implemented by a leave-one-out cross validation. In this calculation, one of the values is removed from the sample. A between-group classifier is constructed from the remaining data, and the omitted value is classified. It is then replaced. Another value is removed and classified. This procedure continues to exhaustion and the classification results are used to populate the diagnostic matrix (true positive, false positive, false negative, true negative). The measures of diagnostic efficacy introduced in the previous section are then calculated.

In order to implement a leave-one-out cross validation the choice of classifier must be addressed. In these calculations, a classifier based on Gaussian populations with prior probabilities was used. The mathematical structure of the classifier is given in the Mathematical Appendices. Two sets of prior probabilities were considered. In the first set of calculations, equal priors were used. In the second, it was supposed that the prior probability of delayed-onset PTSD was 0.25 which is the value derived from a review of the clinical literature (19, 20).

With both sets of prior probabilities, the sensitivity and specificity values are considerably less encouraging (**Table 5**). In the previous calculations, the sensitivity and specificity obtained at Cz are 0.80 and 0.87, respectively. In the leave-one-out calculation using equal priors, the corresponding values are 0.60 and 0.65. Similarly, the previous sensitivity and specificity results obtained at C4 were 0.80 and 0.90, respectively. The leave-one-out values with equal priors are 0.80 and 0.62. This divergence counsels interpretive caution when evaluating the results summarized in **Table 3**.

Populating the Diagnostic Matrix by Bootstrapping

A deficiency of the results presented in the previous section is immediately apparent on examining **Table 5**. The sensitivities

TABLE 5 | Classification based on average target amplitudes determined by a leave-one-out calculation.

Measure	Average Fz amplitude response to target stimulus	Average Cz amplitude response to target stimulus	Average Pz amplitude response to target stimulus	Average C3 amplitude response to target stimulus	Average C4 amplitude response to target stimulus
Prior probabilities, $P_s = 0.5$, $P_c = 0.5$					
Number of true positives	4	3	4	3	4
Number of false positives	25	21	25	24	23
Number of false negatives	1	2	1	2	1
Number of true negatives	34	39	35	36	37
Diagnostic accuracy	0.5938	0.6462	0.6000	0.6000	0.6308
Sensitivity	0.8000	0.6000	0.8000	0.6000	0.8000
Specificity	0.5763	0.6500	0.5833	0.6000	0.6167
Prior probabilities, $P_s = 0.75$ $P_c = 0.25$					
Number of true positives	0	1	0	1	3
Number of false positives	6	7	3	7	8
Number of false negatives	5	4	5	4	2
Number of true negatives	53	53	57	53	52
Diagnostic accuracy	0.8281	0.8308	0.8769	0.8308	0.8462
Sensitivity	0.0000	0.2000	0.0000	0.2000	0.6000
Specificity	0.8983	0.8833	0.9500	0.8833	0.8667

TABLE 6 | Classification based on average target amplitudes determined by a bootstrap calculation.

Measure	Average Fz amplitude response to target stimulus	Average Cz amplitude response to target stimulus	Average Pz amplitude response to target stimulus	Average C3 amplitude response to target stimulus	Average C4 amplitude response to target stimulus
Prior probabilities $P_s = 0.5$, $P_c = 0.5$					
Diagnostic accuracy	0.6288 [0.4348, 0.8261]	0.6719 [0.4500, 0.8621]	0.6087 [0.3333, 0.8462]	0.6431 [0.4500, 0.8261]	0.6954 [0.4286, 0.9091]
Sensitivity	0.6236 [0.0000, 1.0000]	0.5916 [0.0000, 1.0000]	0.6835 [0.0000, 1.0000]	0.5790 [0.0000, 1.0000]	0.6746 [0.0000, 1.0000]
Specificity	0.6325 [0.4118, 0.9048]	0.6802 [0.4211, 0.9444]	0.6068 [0.3158, 0.9444]	0.6513 [0.4211, 0.8846]	0.6996 [0.3913, 1.0000]
Positive likelihood ratio	1.6108 [0.4423, 3.2051]	1.8999 [0.5882, 4.6667]	1.6975 [0.3333, 3.8182]	1.5957 [0.4058, 3.3409]	2.6276 [0.7667, 7.0000]
Negative likelihood ratio	0.6720 [0.2174, 1.3889]	0.6592 [0.2121, 1.2857]	0.6695 [0.2069, 1.8254]	0.6992 [0.2114, 1.4457]	0.5572 [0.2100, 1.1613]
Diagnostic odds ratio	3.7930 [0.3176, 11.9231]	4.3037 [0.4667, 15.6154]	4.0970 [0.2000, 13.8889]	3.9384 [0.2870, 13.8889]	5.9901 [0.6863, 19.8000]
Prior probabilities $P_s = 0.75$, $P_c = 0.25$					
Diagnostic accuracy	0.8282 [0.6364, 0.9583]	0.8159 [0.6400, 0.9545]	0.8647 [0.6818, 0.9615]	0.8023 [0.6190, 0.9565]	0.8562 [0.7143, 0.9583]
Sensitivity	0.1533 [0.0000, 1.0000]	0.3104 [0.0000, 1.0000]	0.1481 [0.0000, 1.0000]	0.2175 [0.0000, 1.0000]	0.3513 [0.0000, 1.0000]
Specificity	0.8887 [0.6667, 1.0000]	0.8622 [0.6667, 1.0000]	0.9269 [0.7200, 1.0000]	0.8542 [0.6522, 1.0000]	0.9030 [0.7273, 1.0000]
Positive likelihood ratio	4.0682 [0.5778, 12.5000]	3.3854 [0.6786, 12.0000]	5.5863 [0.7407, 15.7500]	3.0264 [0.4902, 12.0000]	4.9856 [0.9286, 16.5000]
Negative likelihood ratio	0.8286 [0.2949, 1.1667]	0.7378 [0.2660, 1.1111]	0.7963 [0.2805, 1.0811]	0.8170 [0.2838, 1.2069]	0.6722 [0.2000, 1.0135]
Diagnostic odds ratio	6.1093 [0.4921, 19.8000]	6.6509 [0.6104, 29.4000]	8.6072 [0.6863, 39.0000]	5.1757 [0.4026, 23.4000]	10.2212 [0.9184, 43.0000]

and specificities are reported without confidence intervals. This deficiency can be addressed with a bootstrap calculation. The procedure is outlined in the Mathematical Appendices. Two thousand bootstrap samples were used to estimate the bootstrapped distribution. The results are shown in **Table 6**. The confidence intervals provide an essential clarification to the preceding results. The sample size precludes a dispositive response to the hypothesis that the amplitudes of average ERPs can serve as a predictor of delayed-onset PTSD.

The confidence intervals reported for sensitivity values, [0,1] in all cases, are particularly telling. The definition of sensitivity is

$$\text{Sensitivity} = \text{True Positive Ratio} = \frac{N_{\text{TP}}}{N_{\text{TP}} + N_{\text{FN}}}$$

where N_{TP} is the number of true positives and N_{FN} is the number of false negatives. There are only five elements in the Converter set, and two of these elements are used to build the classifier. Therefore, N_{TP} is frequently zero, giving Sensitivity $= 0$. Similarly, if in other cases $N_{\text{TP}} \neq 0$ and $N_{\text{FN}} = 0$ giving Sensitivity $= 1$ as another frequent value. This results in a bootstrapped confidence interval of [0,1].

DISCUSSION

In this analysis, the identification of individuals who will present delayed-onset PTSD is treated as a diagnostic process where the diagnostic groups are Converters (those who present delayed-onset PTSD) and Stables (those who do not). Sensitivity values based on average target stimulus amplitude range from 0.58 to 0.68. Specificity values range from 0.61 to 0.70, suggesting that event-related potentials may be helpful in identifying at-risk individuals.

The results in this study can only be considered preliminary due to the small sample size of Converters. The limitations of the sample size are indicated by the calculations presented in **Table 6.** Suppose the objective is to know sensitivity to an accuracy of ± 0.1

with 95% confidence. A calculation given in the Mathematical Appendices indicates that $N \geq 185$ is required, where it must be emphasized that this N is the number of Converters. If Converters are 10% of the population, then the projected requirement is for 1,850 participants in the study. The implications of this simple calculation extend beyond the study of PTSD and generalize to all of neuropsychiatry where conversion rates even in enriched populations are low. Large participant numbers will be required. Additionally, by definition, the search for prodromes requires a longitudinal study extended, perhaps, over a period of years. The challenges of supporting and implementing very large longitudinal studies are formidable.

Further limitations should be acknowledged. Electrophysiological abnormalities associated with neuropsychiatric disorders are non-specific. For example, in addition to PTSD, alterations in EEG synchronization have been observed in AD/HD, alcohol abuse, alexithymia, autism, bipolar disorder, dementia, depression, migraine, multiple sclerosis, Parkinson's disease, TBI, schizophrenia, and other psychotic disorders (60). The potential loss of electrophysiological specificity is particularly likely in a military population where PTSD is often associated with TBI and is comorbid with depression and substance abuse. Additionally, medications can alter event-related potentials and will complicate diagnosis based on ERPs.

Statistical identification of individuals who will present with PTSD might, however, be improved by two extensions to the present analysis. First, the analysis of ERPs reported here was limited to calculation of average ERPs. More recently, developed methods of analysis, for example, information dynamics (61) and network analysis of brain electrical activity (62) might improve results. Second, specificity and sensitivity may be improved by combining electrophysiological measures with other biomarkers and clinical information. Incorporating scores from psychological questionnaires with electrophysiological results in a multivariate discrimination would be an obvious possibility. The psychological measures including CAPS, PHQ-9, and PCL-M scores showed significant difference between Stables and Converters at the baseline assessment, but none of the scores significantly correlated with the P300 amplitude. The discordance between neural responses and self-reported symptoms may be partially a consequence of psychological defensive denial (63, 64). Some SMs recruited in this study may deny the presence of their PTSD symptoms due to military training or concerns that this may jeopardize their job, promotion, and self-image. This defensive denial may be softened after a prolonged period. Consistent with this possibility, a review by Andrews et al. (19) reported that most delayed-onset PTSD cases occurred in military samples rather than in civilian samples. If this is the case, objective biomarkers would be fundamentally more favorable than self-report psychological measures in identifying SMs at risk of PTSD.

While additional forms of electrophysiological analysis in combination with other classes of data may improve the likelihood of success, this will not eliminate the previously documented requirement for large sample sizes in a longitudinal study. Such detection would be critical to the military because early intervention to prevent PTSD has revealed a critical window for fear activation and extinction of conditioned responses related to traumatic memories (65).

ETHICS STATEMENT

This research protocol was approved by the Institutional Review Board of the Uniformed Services University and by the Institutional Review Board of the Walter Reed National Military Medical Center. All participants gave written informed consent in accordance with the Declaration of Helsinki.

AUTHOR CONTRIBUTIONS

CW performed the analysis of the event-related potentials and the preliminary statistical analysis. MC screened participants for eligibility and conducted the psychological assessments. PR performed the literature search, statistical analysis, and wrote the final drafts of the paper. DD participated in developing and implementing the statistical analysis plan. KB and DN obtained the electrophysiological data. CC designed and built the ERP acquisition system. MR participated in the design of the investigation. DK lead the research effort and participated in acquisition of the electrophysiological data.

ACKNOWLEDGMENTS

We would like to acknowledge support from the Uniformed Services University, the Defense Medical Research and Development Program and the Center for Neuroscience and Regenerative Medicine. The Opinions and assertions contained herein are the private opinions of the authors and are not to be construed as official or reflecting the views of the United States Department of Defense.

REFERENCES

1. Costello EJ, Angold A. Developmental transitions to psychopathology: are there prodromes of substance use disorder? *J Child Psychol Psychiatry* (2010) 51(4):526–32. doi:10.1111/j.1469-7610.2010.02221.x
2. Insel TR. The arrival of preemptive psychiatry. *Early Interv Psychiatry* (2007) 1(1):5–6. doi:10.1111/j.1751-7893.2007.00017.x
3. Insel TR. From prevention to preemption: a paradigm shift in psychiatry. *Psychiatric Times* (2008) 25(9):13.
4. Addington J, Cadenhead KS, Cornblatt BA, Mathalon DH, McGlashan TH, Perkins DO, et al. North American prodrome longitudinal study (NADLS2): overview and recruitment. *Schizophr Res* (2012) 142(1–3):77–82. doi:10.1016/j.schres.2012.09.012
5. Murphy JR, Rawdon C, Kelleher I, Twomey D, Markey PS, Cannon M, et al. Reduced duration mismatch negativity in adolescents with psychotic symptoms: further evidence for mismatch negativity as a possible biomarker for vulnerability to psychosis. *BMC Psychiatry* (2013) 13(1):1. doi:10.1186/1471-244X-13-45

6. Clark SR, Schubert KL, Baune BT. Towards indicated prevention of psychosis: using probabilistic assessments of transition risk in psychosis prodrome. *J Neural Transm* (2015) 122(1):155–69. doi:10.1007/s00702-014-1325-9
7. Joa I, Gisselgård J, Brønnick K, McGlashan T, Olav J. Primary prevention of psychosis through interventions in the symptomatic prodromal stage, a pragmatic Norwegian ultra high risk study. *BMC Psychiatry* (2015) 15:89. doi:10.1186/s12888-015-0470-5
8. Kovacs M, Lopez-Duran N. Prodromal symptoms and atypical affectivity as predictors of major depression in juveniles: implications for prevention. *J Child Psychol Psychiatry* (2010) 51(4):472–96. doi:10.1111/j.1469-7610.2010.02230.x
9. Osterling J, Dawson G. Early recognition of children with autism: a study of first birthday home videotapes. *J Autism Dev Disord* (1994) 24(3):247–57. doi:10.1007/BF02172225
10. Bosl W, Tierney A, Tager-Flusberg H, Nelson C. EEG complexity as a biomarker for autism spectrum disorder risk. *BMC Med* (2011) 9:18. doi:10.1186/1741-7015-9-18
11. Riley KP, Snowdon DA, Desrosiers MF, Markesbery WR. Early life linguistic ability, late life cognitive function and neuropahthology. Findings from the Nun Study. *Neurobiol Aging* (2005) 26(3):341–3. doi:10.1016/j.neurobiolaging.2004.06.019
12. Petit G, Cimochowska A, Kornreich C, Hanak C, Verbanck P, Campanella S. Neurophysiological correlates of response inhibition predict relapse in detoxified alcoholic patients: some preliminary evidence from event-related potentials. *Neuropsychiatr Dis Treat* (2014) 10:1025–37. doi:10.2147/NDT.S61475
13. Karstoft K-I, Galatzer-Levy IR, Statnikov A, Li Z, Shalev AY; Members of Jerusalem Trauma Outreach and Prevention Study (J-TOPS) Group. Bridging a translational gap: using machine learning to improve the prediction of PTSD. *BMC Psychiatry* (2015) 15:30. doi:10.1186/s12888-015-0399-8
14. Smid GE. *Deconstructing Delayed Onset Posttraumatic Stress Disorder [Dissertation]*. Utrecht: University of Utrecht (2011).
15. Smid GE, van der Velden PG, Gersone BPR, Kleber RJ. Late-onset posttraumatic stress disorder following a disaster: a longitudinal study. *Psychol Trauma* (2012) 4(3):312–22. doi:10.1037/a0023868
16. Richardson LK, Frueh BC, Acierno R. Prevalence estimates of combat-related PTSD: a critical review. *Aust N Z J Psychiatry* (2011) 44(1):4–19. doi:10.3109/00048670903393597
17. Kessler RC, Berglund P, Demler O, Jin R, Merikangas KR, Walters EE. Lifetime prevalence and age-of-onset distributions of DSM-IV disorders in the National Comorbidity Survey Replication. *Arch Gen Psychiatry* (2005) 62(6):593–602. doi:10.1001/archpsyc.62.6.593
18. Kessler RC, Chiu WT, Demler O, Merikangas KR, Walters EE. Prevalence, severity and comorbidity of 12-month DSM_V disorders in the National Comorbidity Survey Replication. *Arch Gen Psychiatry* (2005) 62(6):617–26. doi:10.1001/archpsyc.62.6.593
19. Andrews B, Brewin CR, Philpott R, Stewart L. Delayed-onset posttraumatic stress disorder: a systematic review of the evidence. *Am J Psychiatry* (2007) 164:1319–26. doi:10.1176/appi.ajp.2007.06091491
20. Smid GE, Mooven TT, van der Mast RC, Gersons BP, Kleber RJ. Delayed posttraumatic stress disorder: systematic review, meta-analysis and meta-regression analysis of prospective studies. *J Clin Psychiatry* (2009) 70(11):1572–82. doi:10.4088/JCP.08r04484
21. Grieger TA, Cozza SJ, Ursano RJ, Hoge C, Martinez PE, Engel CC, et al. Posttraumatic stress disorder and depression in battle-injured soldiers. *Am J Psychiatry* (2006) 163:1777–83. doi:10.1176/ajp.2006.163.10.1777
22. Bryant RA, O'Donnell ML, Creamer M, McFarlane AC, Silove D. A multisite analysis of the fluctuating course of posttraumatic stress disorder. *JAMA Psychiatry* (2013) 70(8):839–46. doi:10.1001/jamapsychiatry.2013.1137
23. Araki T, Kasai K, Yamasue H, Kato N, Kudo N, Ohtani T, et al. Association between lower P300 amplitude and smaller anterior cingulate cortex volume in patients with posttraumatic stress disorder: a study of victims of Tokyo subway sarin attack. *Neuroimage* (2005) 25:43–50. doi:10.1016/j.neuroimage.2004.11.039
24. Blomhoff S, Reinvang I, Malt UF. Event-related potentials to stimuli with emotional impact in posttraumatic stress patients. *Biol Psychiatry* (1998) 44(10):1045–53. doi:10.1016/S0006-3223(98)00058-4
25. Charles G, Hansenne M, Ansseau M, Pichot W, Machowski R, Schittecatte M, et al. P300 in posttraumatic stress disorder. *Neuropsychobiology* (1995) 32(2):72–4. doi:10.1159/000119216
26. Felmingham KL, Bryant RA, Kendall C, Gordon E. Event-related potential dysfunction in posttraumatic stress disorder: the role of numbing. *Psychiatry Res* (2002) 109:171–9. doi:10.1016/S0165-1781(02)00003-3
27. Ghisolfi ES, Margis R, Becker J, Zanardo AP, Strimitzer IM, Lara DR. Impaired P50 sensory gating in post-traumatic stress disorder secondary to urban violence. *Int J Psychophysiol* (2004) 51(3):209–14. doi:10.1016/j.ijpsycho.2003.09.002
28. Hansenne M. Event-related brain potentials in psychopathology: clinical and cognitive perspectives. *Psychol Belg* (2006) 46(1–2):5–36. doi:10.5334/pb-46-1-2-5
29. Javanbakht A, Liberzon I, Amirsadri A, Gjini K, Boutros NN. Event-related potential studies of post-traumatic stress disorder: a critical review and synthesis. *Biol Mood Anxiety Disord* (2011) 1:5. doi:10.1186/2045-5380-1-5
30. Johnson JD, Allana TN, Medlin MD, Harris EW, Karl A. Meta-analytic review of P3 components in posttraumatic stress disorder and their clinical utility. *Clin EEG Neurosci* (2013) 44(2):112–34. doi:10.1177/1550059412469742
31. Karl A, Malta LS, Maercker A. Meta-analytic review of event-related potential studies in post-traumatic stress disorder. *Biol Psychol* (2006) 71:123–47. doi:10.1016/j.biopsycho.2005.03.004
32. Kimble M, Kaloupek D, Kaufman M, Deldin P. Stimulus novelty differentially affects attentional allocation in PTSD. *Biol Psychiatry* (2000) 47:880–90. doi:10.1016/S0006-3223(99)00258-9
33. Kimble M, Ruddy K, Deldin P, Kaufman M. A CNV-distraction paradigm in combat veterans with posttraumatic stress disorder. *J Neuropsychiatry Clin Neurosci* (2004) 16:102–8. doi:10.1176/jnp.16.1.102
34. McFarlane AC, Weber DL, Clark CR. Abnormal stimulus processing in posttraumatic stress disorder. *Biol Psychiatry* (1993) 34:311–20. doi:10.1016/0006-3223(93)90088-U
35. Metzger LJ, Orr SP, Lasko NB, Pitman RK. Auditory event related potentials to tone stimuli in combat-related posttraumatic stress disorder. *Biol Psychiatry* (1997) 42:1006–15. doi:10.1016/S0006-3223(97)00138-8
36. Metzger LT, Orr SP, Lasko NB, McNally RJ, Pitman RK. Seeking the source of emotional Stroop interference effects in PTSD: a study of P3a to traumatic words. *Integr Physiol Behav Sci* (1997) 32(1):43–51. doi:10.1007/BF02688612
37. Metzger LJ, Carson MA, Paulus LA, Lasko NB, Paige SR, Pitman RK, et al. Event related potentials to auditory stimuli in female Vietnam nurse veterans with posttraumatic stress disorder. *Psychophysiology* (2002) 39(1):49–63. doi:10.1111/1469-8986.3910049
38. Neylan TC, Fletcher DJ, Lenoci M, McCallin K, Weiss DS, Schoenfeld FB, et al. Sensory gating in chronic posttraumatic stress disorder: reduced auditory p50 suppression in combat veterans. *Biological Psychiatry* (1999) 46(12):1656–64. doi:10.1016/S0006-3223(99)00047-5
39. Neylan TC, Jasiukaitis PA, Lenoci M, Scott JC, Metzler TJ, Weiss DS, et al. Temporal instability of auditory and visual event-related potentials in posttraumatic stress disorder. *Biol Psychiatry* (2003) 53:216–25. doi:10.1016/S0006-3223(02)01450-6
40. Shu I-W, Onton JA, Prabhakar N, O'Connell RM, Simmons AN, Matthews SC. Combat veterans with PTSD after mild TBI exhibit greater ERPs from posterior-medial cortical areas while appraising facial features. *J Affect Disord* (2014) 155:234–40. doi:10.1016/j.jad.2013.06.057
41. Shu I-W, Onton JA, O'Connell RM, Simmons AN, Matthews SC. Combat veterans with comorbid PTSD and mild TBI exhibit a greater inhibitory processing ERP from the dorsal anterior cingulate cortex. *Psychiatr Res Neuroimaging* (2014) 224(1):58–66. doi:10.1016/j.pscychresns.2014.07.010
42. Shucard JL, McCabe DC, Szymanski H. An event-related potential study of attention deficits in posttraumatic stress disorder during auditory and visual Go/NoGo continuous performance tasks. *Biol Psychol* (2008) 79(2):223–33. doi:10.1016/j.biopsycho.2008.05.005
43. Polich J. Updating P300: an integrative theory of P3a and P3b. *Neurophysiol Clin* (2007) 118(10):2128–48. doi:10.1016/j.clinph.2007.04.019
44. Isreal JB, Chesney GL, Wickens CD, Donchin E. P300 and tracking difficulty: evidence for multiple resources in dual-task performance. *Psychophysiology* (1980) 17:259–73. doi:10.1111/j.1469-8986.1980.tb00146.x
45. Kramer AF, Wickens CD, Donchin E. Processing of stimulus properties: evidence for dual-task integrality. *J Exp Psychol Hum Percept Perform* (1985) 11:393–408.
46. Mulert C, Pogarell O, Juckel G, Rujescu D, Giegling I, Rupp D, et al. The neural basis of the P300 potential. Focus on the time-course of the underlying

cortical generators. *Eur Arch Psychiatry Clin Neurosci* (2004) 254(3):190–8. doi:10.1007/s00406-004-0469-2
47. Picton T. The P300 wave of the human event-related potential. *J Clin Neurophysiol* (1992) 9:456–79. doi:10.1097/00004691-199210000-00002
48. Shin LM, Rauch SL, Pitman RK. Amygdala, medial prefrontal cortex and hippocampal function in PTSD. *Ann N Y Acad Sci* (2006) 1079:67–79. doi:10.1196/annals.1364.007
49. Bush G, Luu P, Posner MI. Cognitive and emotional influences in the anterior cingulate cortex. *Trends Cogn Sci* (2000) 4(6):215–22. doi:10.1016/S1364-6613(00)01483-2
50. Jovanovic T, Norrholm SD. Neural mechanisms of impaired fear inhibition in posttraumatic stress disorder. *Front Behav Neurosci* (2011) 5:44. doi:10.3389/fnbeh.2011.00044
51. Maren S, Phan KL, Liberzon I. The contextual brain: implications for fear conditioning, extinction and psychopathology. *Nat Rev Neurosci* (2013) 14:417–28. doi:10.1038/nrn3492
52. Weathers FW, Keane TM, Davidson RJ. Clinician-administered PTSD scale: a review of the first ten years of research. *Depress Anxiety* (2001) 13:132–56. doi:10.1002/da.1029
53. Forbes D, Creamer M, Biddle D. The validity of the PTSD checklist as a measure of symptomatic change in combat-related PTSD. *Behav Res Ther* (2001) 39:977–86. doi:10.1016/S0005-7967(00)00084-X
54. Spitzer RL, Kroenke D, Williams JBW; The Patient Health Questionnaire Primary Care Study Group. Validation and utility of a self-report version of PRIME-MD: the PHQ primary care study. *J Am Med Assoc* (1999) 282(18):1737–44. doi:10.1001/jama.282.18.1737
55. Pollich J, Ellerson PC, Cohen J. P300, stimulus intensity, modality and probability. *Int J Psychophysiol* (1996) 23(1–2):55–62. doi:10.1016/0167-8760(96)00028-1
56. Cohen J, Polich J. On the number of trials needed for P300. *Int J Psychophysiol* (1997) 25(3):249–55. doi:10.1016/S0167-8760(96)00743-X
57. Croft RJ, Barry RJ. EOG correction: a new perspective. *Electroencephalogr Clin Neurophysiol* (1998) 107(6):387–94. doi:10.1016/S0013-4694(98)00086-8
58. Rapp PE, Cellucci CJ, Keyser DO, Gilpin AMK, Darmon DM. Statistical issues in TBI clinical studies. *Front Neurol* (2013) 4:177. doi:10.3389/fneur.2013.00177
59. Youden D. Index for rating diagnostic tests. *Cancer* (1950) 3:32–5. doi:10.1002/1097-0142(1950)3:1<32::AID-CNCR2820030106>3.0.CO;2-3
60. Rapp PE, Keyser DO, Albano AM, Hernandez R, Gibson D, Zambon R, et al. Traumatic brain injury detection using electrophysiological methods. *Front Hum Neurosci* (2015) 9:11. doi:10.3389/fnhum.2015.00011
61. Darmon D. Specific differential entropy rate estimation for continuous-valued time series. *Entropy* (2016) 18:190. doi:10.3390/e18050190
62. Smith Bassett D, Bullmore E. Small-world brain networks. *Neuroscientist* (2006) 12(6):512–23. doi:10.1177/1073858406293182
63. Shedler J, Mayman M, Manis M. The illusion of mental health. *Am Psychol* (1993) 48(11):1117–31. doi:10.1037/0003-066X.48.11.1117
64. Orr SP, Roth WT. Psychophysiological assessment: clinical applications for PTSD. *J Affect Disord* (2000) 61(3):225–40. doi:10.1016/S0165-0327(00)00340-2
65. Rothbaum BO, Kearns MC, Price M, Malcoun E, Davis M, Ressler KJ, et al. Early intervention may prevent the development of posttraumatic stress disorder: a randomized pilot civilian study with modified prolonged exposure. *Biol Psychiatry* (2012) 72(11):957–63. doi:10.1016/j.biopsych.2012.06.002
66. Böhning D, Holling H, Patilea V. A limitation of the diagnostic odds ratio in determining an optimal cut-off value for a continuous diagnostic test. *Stat Methods Med Res* (2011) 20(5):541–50. doi:10.1177/0962280210374532
67. Efron B. Better bootstrap confidence intervals. *J Am Stat Assoc* (1987) 82:171–200. doi:10.1080/01621459.1987.10478410
68. Efron B, Tibshirani R. Bootstrap methods for statistical errors: confidence intervals and other measures of statistical accuracy. *Stat Sci* (1986) 1(1):54–75 doi:10.1214/ss/1177013815
69. Efron B, Tibshirani R. *An Introduction to the Bootstrap*. London: Chapman and Hall (1993).
70. Glas AS, Lijmer JG, Prins MH, Bonse GJ, Bussuyt PM. The diagnostic odds ratio: a single indicator of test performance. *J Clin Epidemiol* (2003) 56(11):1129–35. doi:10.1016/S0895-4356(03)00177-X
71. Hanley JA, McNeil BJ. A method of comparing the areas under receiver operating characteristic curves derived from the same cases. *Radiology* (1983) 148:839–42. doi:10.1148/radiology.148.3.6878708
72. Hoeffding W. Probability inequalities for sums of bounded random variables. *J Am Stat Assoc* (1963) 58(301):13–30. doi:10.1080/01621459.1963.10500830
73. Jiang W, Varma S, Simon R. Calculating confidence intervals for prediction error microarray classification using resampling. *Stat Appl Genet Mol Biol* (2008) 7(1):8. doi:10.2202/1544-6115.1322
74. Krazanowski W, Hand DJ. *ROC Curves for Continuous Data*. Roca Raton, FL: Chapman Hall/CRC (2009).
75. Lachenbruch PA. *Discriminant Analysis*. New York, NY: Hafner Press (1975).
76. Pepe MS. *Statistical Evaluation of Medical Tests or Classification and Prediction*. Oxford: Oxford University Press (2003).
77. Pepe MS, Janes H, Longton G, Leisenring W, Newcomb P. Limitations of the odds ratio in gauging the performance of a diagnostic, prognostic or screening marker. *Am J Epidemiol* (2004) 159(9):882–90. doi:10.1093/aje/kwh101
78. Portney LG, Watkins MP. *Foundations of Clinical Research. Applications to Practice*. 3rd ed. Upper Saddle River, NJ: Prentice Hall Health (2009).
79. Wasserman L. *All of Statistics: A Concise Course in Statistical Inference*. New York, NY: Springer (2010).
80. Zou KH, Hall WJ, Shapiro DE. Smooth non-parametric receiver operating characteristic (ROC) curves for continuous diagnostic tests. *Stat Med* (1997) 16:2143–56.

MATHEMATICAL APPENDICES

Estimating Classification Error (Contents of Table 3)

For the case of a single discriminating variable, the Group A–Group B between-group Mahalanobis distance is

$$D^2_{\mathrm{A,B}} = \frac{(\hat{\mu}_{\mathrm{A}} - \hat{\mu}_{\mathrm{B}})^2}{\hat{\sigma}^2_{\mathrm{AB}}},$$

$$\hat{\sigma}^2_{\mathrm{AB}} = \frac{(N_{\mathrm{A}} - 1)\hat{\sigma}^2_{\mathrm{A}} + (N_{\mathrm{B}} - 1)\hat{\sigma}^2_{\mathrm{B}}}{N_{\mathrm{A}} + N_{\mathrm{B}} - 2},$$

$\hat{\mu}_{\mathrm{A}}$ is the Group A sample mean, and $\hat{\sigma}_{\mathrm{A}}$ is the Group A sample SD. $\hat{\mu}_{\mathrm{B}}$ and $\hat{\sigma}_{\mathrm{B}}$ are defined analogously. $P_{\mathrm{ERROR}}(G_{\mathrm{A}}, G_{\mathrm{B}})$ is the error rate for the optimal classifier under the assumption of normality for the two populations and provides an estimate classification error when only means and SDs are known. It can give a serious underestimate of true classification error. This is especially true if group population numbers are low or the assumption of normality is violated. When full data sets are available, an empirical calculation of error rate is preferred *via* either cross-validation or bootstrapping. Let ρ_{A} and ρ_{B} be prior probabilities of Group A and Group B membership. $P_{\mathrm{ERROR}}(G_{\mathrm{A}}, G_{\mathrm{B}})$ is given by

$$P_{\mathrm{ERROR}}(G_{\mathrm{A}}, G_{\mathrm{B}}) = \rho_{\mathrm{A}}\Phi\left\{-\frac{1}{2}\sqrt{D^2_{\mathrm{A,B}}} + \frac{1}{\sqrt{D^2_{\mathrm{A,B}}}}\log_e\left(\frac{\rho_{\mathrm{B}}}{\rho_{\mathrm{A}}}\right)\right\}$$
$$+ \rho_{\mathrm{B}}\Phi\left\{-\frac{1}{2}\sqrt{D^2_{\mathrm{A,B}}} - \frac{1}{\sqrt{D^2_{\mathrm{A,B}}}}\log_e\left(\frac{\rho_{\mathrm{B}}}{\rho_{\mathrm{A}}}\right)\right\}$$

where $\Phi(x)$ is the cumulative distribution function for a standard normal random variable (75). For the case of equal priors, the expression reduces to

$$P_{\mathrm{ERROR}}(G_{\mathrm{A}}, G_{\mathrm{B}}) = 1 - \Phi\left(\frac{\sqrt{D^2_{\mathrm{A,B}}}}{2}\right) = \Phi\left(\frac{-\sqrt{D^2_{\mathrm{A,B}}}}{2}\right).$$

Receiver Operating Characteristic Curve (Contents of Table 4)

The area under an empirical receiver operating characteristic curve is equal to the Mann–Whitney U statistic [Ref. (74), p. 65 following from a proof on p. 27] and thus the Mann–Whitney U statistic provides an estimator for the population level AUC. Random assignment results in AUC = 0.5. The following notation is introduced:

N_S number of longitudinally stable participants
N_C number of converter participants
S_i observed value for the i-th stable participant
C_j observed value for the j-th converter participant.

$$\widehat{\mathrm{AUC}} = \frac{1}{N_C N_S}\sum_{i=1}^{N_S}\sum_{j=1}^{N_C}\left\{I(C_j < S_i) + \frac{1}{2}I(C_j = S_i)\right\}$$

where $I(Z) = 1$ if argument Z is true. It is important to note that "less than" used in this application, contra textbooks where "greater than" appears, because in this analysis a participant is classed as positive if the observed value is less than the threshold value.

There are several estimates of the variance of the AUC [listed on p. 67 of Ref. (74)]. We use here the expression in Hanley and McNeil (71).

$$s^2(\widehat{\mathrm{AUC}}) = \frac{1}{N_S N_C}\left\{\widehat{\mathrm{AUC}}(1 - \widehat{\mathrm{AUC}}) + (N_C - 1)(Q_1 - \widehat{\mathrm{AUC}^2})\right.$$
$$\left. + (N_S - 1)(Q_2 - \widehat{\mathrm{AUC}^2})\right\}$$

As in the equation for AUC, the definition of Q_1 and Q_2 uses "less than" rather than "greater than" because a participant is classed as a positive if the measure value is below threshold rather than greater than threshold. Q_1 is the proportion of all possible triples composed of two sampled members from the Converter group and one from the Stable group where the two Converter scores are less than the Stable score

$$Q_1 = \frac{1}{N_S N_C N_C}\sum_{i=1}^{N_S}\sum_{j=1}^{N_C}\sum_{k=1}^{N_C} I(C_j < S_i)I(C_k < S_i)$$

Q_2 is the proportion of all possible triples composed on one member from the Converter group and two members from the Stable group where the Converter score is less than both scores from the Stable group.

$$Q_2 = \frac{1}{N_C N_S N_S}\sum_{i=1}^{N_C}\sum_{j=1}^{N_S}\sum_{k=1}^{N_S} I(C_i < S_j)I(C_i < S_k)$$

An expression for confidence intervals has been constructed by (80), where with confidence $1 - \alpha$, the true AUC lies in the interval given by

$$1 - (1 - \widehat{\mathrm{AUC}})\exp\left\{\pm z_{1-\alpha/2}\sqrt{s^2(\widehat{\mathrm{AUC}})}/(1 - \widehat{\mathrm{AUC}})\right\},$$

where $z_{1-\alpha/2}$ is the $1 - \alpha/2$ quantile of a standard normal random variable. Under this transformation/inverse transformation, the upper and lower confidence intervals are always in the interval [0,1].

An analysis of the ROC can be used to determine the optimal cutoff value for a continuous, dichotomous diagnostic test. Glas et al. (70) have endorsed the diagnostic odds ratio as a single indicator of test performance and proposed using its maximum to determine the cutoff value. Pepe et al. (76) have argued against this practice and have provided examples that identify limitations of the odds ratio. A fundamental limitation is immediately apparent on examining the equation below for the ratio. It is undefined if the number of false positive or the number of false negatives is 0. Böhning et al. (66) have continued the analysis and recommend using the maximum value of the Youden index (59) as an alternative indicator of the best cutoff value. The Youden index, also called the Youden J statistic is

$$J = \text{Sensitivity} + \text{Specificity} - 1.$$

It is reported as a function of threshold, and the recommended value of threshold is the lowest threshold value giving the maximum of J.

Measures of Diagnostic Efficacy (Contents of Table 4)

Dichotomous diagnosis (two possible outcomes, disease positive and disease negative), using a single continuous variable is considered here. The diagnostic utility of the measure and classifier combination is investigated by first populating the diagnostic matrix and then computing standard measures of diagnostic efficacy. Six measures are considered here diagnostic accuracy, sensitivity, specificity, positive likelihood ratio, negative likelihood ratio, and the diagnostic odds ratio, where it should be recognized that no single measure of diagnostic effectiveness provides a complete assessment of a measure's ability to classify participants (76). Additional measures are presented in Pepe (76) and in Portney and Watkins (78).

	Disease present	Disease absent
Test positive	True positive N_{TP}	False positive N_{FP}
Test negative	False negative N_{FN}	True negative N_{TN}

$$\text{Diagnostic Accuracy} = (N_{\text{TP}} + N_{\text{TN}})/(N_{\text{TP}} + N_{\text{FP}} + N_{\text{FN}} + N_{\text{TN}})$$

$$\text{Sensitivity} = \text{True Positive Fraction} = \frac{N_{\text{TP}}}{N_{\text{TP}} + N_{\text{FN}}}$$

$$\text{Specificity} = \text{True Negative Fraction} = \frac{N_{\text{TN}}}{N_{\text{TN}} + N_{\text{FP}}}$$

$$\begin{aligned}\text{Positive Likelihood Ratio} = \text{LR+} &= \frac{\text{True Positive Fraction}}{\text{False Positive Fraction}}\\ &= \left(\frac{N_{\text{TP}}}{N_{\text{TP}} + N_{\text{FN}}}\right)\Big/\left(\frac{N_{\text{FP}}}{N_{\text{FP}} + N_{\text{TN}}}\right)\\ &= \frac{\text{Sensitivity}}{1 - \text{Specificity}}\end{aligned}$$

$$\begin{aligned}\text{Negative Likelihood Ratio} = \text{LR}- &= \frac{\text{False Negative Fraction}}{\text{True Negative Fraction}}\\ &= \left(\frac{N_{\text{FN}}}{N_{\text{FN}} + N_{\text{TP}}}\right)\Big/\left(\frac{N_{\text{TN}}}{N_{\text{TN}} + N_{\text{FP}}}\right)\\ &= \frac{1 - \text{Sensitivity}}{\text{Specificity}}\end{aligned}$$

$$\begin{aligned}\text{Diagnostic Odds Ratio} = \text{DOR} &= \frac{\text{LR+}}{\text{LR}-} = \left(\frac{N_{\text{TP}} \cdot N_{\text{TN}}}{N_{\text{FP}} \cdot N_{\text{FN}}}\right)\\ &= \left(\frac{\text{Sensitivity}}{1 - \text{Sensitivity}}\right)\left(\frac{\text{Specificity}}{1 - \text{Specificity}}\right)\end{aligned}$$

Classification Based on Gaussian Likelihood and Bayesian Priors (Contents of Table 5)

The classifier is constructed from a single continuous variable, in this case the amplitude of the average response to the target stimulus. $\{S_j\}_{j=1}^{N_S}$ is the set of values obtained from clinically stable participants. $\hat{\mu}_S$ is the sample mean and $\hat{\sigma}_S$ is the corresponding SD. $\{C_j\}_{j=1}^{N_c}$ is the set of values obtained from participants who became PTSD-positive and has mean $\hat{\mu}_C$ and SD $\hat{\sigma}_C$. Let x denote the value of the measure obtained from the individual who is to be classified. The group specific density function for clinically stable participants is

$$f_S(x) = \frac{1}{\left(2\pi\hat{\sigma}_S^2\right)^{1/2}} \exp\left\{-\frac{1}{2}(x - \hat{\mu}_S)^2/\hat{\sigma}_S^2\right\}$$

$f_C(x)$ is defined analogously. The posterior probabilities of group membership are

$$P(G = S|x)\frac{\rho_S f_S(x)}{\rho_S f_S(x) + \rho_C f_C(x)}$$

and

$$P(G = C|x)\frac{\rho_C f_C(x)}{\rho_S f_S(x) + \rho_C f_C(x)}$$

where ρ_S and ρ_C are the prior probabilities of membership in the healthy or disease-positive groups. The participant presenting measure equal to x is classified into the group with the higher posterior probability.

Populating the Diagnostic Matrix with a Bootstrap Estimator (Contents of Table 6)

A bootstrap (67) can be used to determine the value of the diagnostic metrics, and the corresponding confidence intervals. The procedure used here is similar to the bootstrap cross validation scheme for small sample sizes implemented by Jiang et al. (73). A procedure for finding the best estimate of Sensitivity from the available data is described here. The procedure immediately generalizes to other measures of diagnostic efficacy.

As before, this presentation describes a dichotomous classification using a single continuous variable between two groups, clinically stable participants and participants presenting delayed onset PTSD. $\{S_j\}_{j=1}^{N_S}$ is the set of values of this measure obtained from clinically stable participants. There are N_S elements. $\{C_j\}_{j=1}^{N_c}$ is the set of values obtained from participants who convert to the PTSD-positive state. There are N_C values. A single iteration of the bootstrap proceeds as follows:

1. $N_C + N_S$ elements are drawn randomly with replacement from the combined set $\{S_j\}_{j=1}^{N_S} \cup \{C_j\}_{j=1}^{N_c}$. This set of randomly drawn elements is denoted by $\{B_j\}_{j=1}^{N_S+N_C}$, the bootstrap sample. Typically, the bootstrap sample will contain repeated values. It is possible that the bootstrap sample does not contain an element from either set $\{S_j\}_{j=1}^{N_S}$ or set $\{C_j\}_{j=1}^{N_c}$. If this

occurs, this iteration of the bootstrap is ignored. Additionally, depending on the classifier used, a minimum number of distinct values from $\{S_j\}_{j=1}^{N_S}$ and $\{C_j\}_{j=1}^{N_c}$ will be required to construct the classifier. For example, the classifier based on Gaussian population densities will require at least two distinct elements from each set. If this minimum requirement is not satisfied this iteration of the bootstrap is ignored and the process returns to the beginning of Step 1. Also, if there is not at least one element of $\{S_j\}_{j=1}^{N_S}$ and one element of $\{C_j\}_{j=1}^{N_c}$ in the set of elements that will be classified, the randomization is rejected and the process returns to the beginning of Step 1.

2. The class membership of each element of $\{B_j\}_{j=1}^{N_S+N_C}$ is known. Use $\{B_j\}_{j=1}^{N_S+N_C}$ to construct a classifier.
3. Use this classifier to classify all members of the combined set $\{S_j\}_{j=1}^{N_S} \cup \{C_j\}_{j=1}^{N_C}$ not in $\{B_j\}_{j=1}^{N_S+N_C}$, namely $\{\{S_j\}_{j=1}^{N_S} \cup \{C_j\}_{j=1}^{N_C}\}\backslash\{B_j\}_{j=1}^{N_S+N_C}$. The results of this classification are used to calculate N_{TP}, N_{FP}, N_{FP}, N_{TN} specific to this bootstrap sample. Though in the general case, it is possible, but unlikely, that $\{\{S_j\}_{j=1}^{N_S} \cup \{C_j\}_{j=1}^{N_C}\}\backslash\{B_j\}_{j=1}^{N_S+N_C}$ is the null set, this will not occur in the present application because of the constraints on the randomization put in place in Step 1.
4. Sensitivity and other measures of diagnostic efficacy for this iteration of the bootstrap are then calculated using standard formulas.

This process is repeated until N_B values of Sensitivity are obtained. This may require more than N_B iterations of the bootstrap if the requirements of the random sample outlined in Step 1 are not met.

The average value of sensitivity, computed from the N_B successful iterations of the bootstrap is the best available estimate from $\{S_j\}_{j=1}^{N_S}$ and $\{C_j\}_{j=1}^{N_c}$. The confidence interval of sensitivity can be determined from the distribution of the N_B values of sensitivity. For example, suppose that sensitivities are calculated from 2,000 bootstrap samples and suppose that the 95% confidence interval is to be determined. Rank order the values of sensitivity. The lower bound of the confidence interval is the 50th element, and the upper bound is element 1950th.

This leaves the specification of N_B as an open question. This is not a question that has a single answer (68, 69). The required number of iterations will depend on what is being estimated and the properties of the underlying distribution. A convention in the community regards $N_B = 1{,}000$ as a lower bound. As an operational suggestion the estimate of sensitivity, for $N_B = 1{,}000$ and $N_B = 2{,}000$ can be compared. N_B should be large enough to give a stable value of sensitivity. $N_B = 2{,}000$ was used in these calculations.

This is a constrained randomization. At least two distinct elements of each class (Stables and Converters) must be in the set used to construct the classifier (the Training Set, $\{B_j\}_{j=1}^{N_S+N_C}$). At least one element of each class must be in the set that is classified (the Testing Set $=$ $\{S_j\}_{j=1}^{N_S} \cup \{C_j\}_{j=1}^{N_C}\backslash\{B_j\}_{j=1}^{N_S+N_C}$). Because at least one element of $\{C_j\}_{j=1}^{N_c}$ is classified, there will be at least one true positive (a converter assigned into the converter group) or one false negative (a converter classified into the stable group). Sensitivity may be 0 ($N_{TP} = 0$), but it will not be singular because $N_{TP} + N_{FN} \neq 0$. Because there are only five elements of $\{C_j\}_{j=1}^{N_c}$ and two are used to build the classifier, N_{TP} is, however, frequently 0, and Sensitivity $= 0$ is therefore a frequent result from an iteration of the bootstrap. Additionally in many other cases, $N_{TP} \neq 0$, but $N_{FN} = 0$ giving Sensitivity $= 1$. This explains the confidence interval of [0,1].

Because at least one element of $\{S_j\}_{j=1}^{N_S}$ will be classified, there is at least one true negative or one false positive. Therefore, since $N_{TN} + N_{FP} \neq 0$, specificity will be defined at each iteration of the bootstrap. In contrast with Sensitivity, because $\{S_j\}_{j=1}^{N_S}$ is a much larger set, Specificity typically shows values different from 0 to 1.

The positive likelihood ratio is undefined if Specificity is equal to 1. As noted in the preceding paragraph this is unlikely, but it is possible. The negative likelihood ratio is undefined if Specificity is equal to 1. This frequently occurs with these data. The diagnostic odds ratio is undefined if either Specificity or Sensitivity is equal to 1. Glas et al. [(70), p. 1131] suggests adding 0.5 to all four elements of the diagnostic matrix in those applications where undefined values of the diagnostic ratios are likely to occur. This was done in these calculations.

Sample Size Requirements for Measures of Diagnostic Efficacy

Sample size requirements for sensitivity and specificity assessments can be computed using an argument based on Hoeffding's inequality [(72, 79), p. 65]. If α is the significance level for a confidence interval of length 2Δ, we require

$$\alpha \leq 2e^{-2N\Delta^2}$$

giving

$$N \geq \frac{-\ln(\alpha/2)}{2\Delta^2}$$

The sample size required for a ± 0.1 sensitivity estimate with 95% ($\alpha = 0.05$) confidence is seen to be $N \geq 185$. It should be stressed that this is an estimate of sensitivity. N in this equation is the number of individuals in the sample who are disease positive. If the prevalence of the disorder in the enrollment population is 10%, then an enrollment $\geq$1,850 is required.

12

Pathways from Trauma to Psychotic Experiences: A Theoretically Informed Model of Posttraumatic Stress in Psychosis

Amy Hardy[1,2]*

[1] *Institute of Psychiatry, Psychology & Neuroscience, King's College London, London, UK,* [2] *Psychosis Clinical Academic Group, South London and Maudsley NHS Foundation Trust, London, UK*

Edited by:
Kate Hardy,
Stanford University, USA

Reviewed by:
Faye Katherine Doell,
Centre for Addiction and Mental Health, Canada
Mahesh Menon,
University of British Columbia, Canada

***Correspondence:**
Amy Hardy
amy.hardy@kcl.ac.uk

In recent years, empirical data and theoretical accounts relating to the relationship between childhood victimization and psychotic experiences have accumulated. Much of this work has focused on co-occurring Posttraumatic Stress Disorder or putative causal mechanisms in isolation from each other. The complexity of posttraumatic stress reactions experienced in psychosis remains poorly understood. This paper therefore attempts to synthesize the current evidence base into a theoretically informed, multifactorial model of posttraumatic stress in psychosis. Three trauma-related vulnerability factors are proposed to give rise to intrusions and to affect how people appraise and cope with them. First, understandable attempts to survive trauma become habitual ways of regulating emotion, manifesting in cognitive-affective, behavioral and interpersonal responses. Second, event memories, consisting of perceptual and episodic representations, are impacted by emotion experienced during trauma. Third, personal semantic memory, specifically appraisals of the self and others, are shaped by event memories. It is proposed these vulnerability factors have the potential to lead to two types of intrusions. The first type is anomalous experiences arising from emotion regulation and/or the generation of novel images derived from trauma memory. The second type is trauma memory intrusions reflecting, to varying degrees, the retrieval of perceptual, episodic and personal semantic representations. It is speculated trauma memory intrusions may be experienced on a continuum from contextualized to fragmented, depending on memory encoding and retrieval. Personal semantic memory will then impact on how intrusions are appraised, with habitual emotion regulation strategies influencing people's coping responses to these. Three vignettes are outlined to illustrate how the model accounts for different pathways between victimization and psychosis, and implications for therapy are considered. The model is the first to propose how emotion regulation and autobiographical memory may lead to a range of intrusive experiences in psychosis, and therefore attempts to explain the different phenomenological associations observed between trauma and intrusions.

However, it includes a number of novel hypotheses that require empirical testing, which may lead to further refinement. It is anticipated the model will assist research and practice, in the hope of supporting people to manage the impact of victimization on their lives.

Keywords: trauma, psychosis, posttraumatic stress, emotion regulation, perceptual memory, episodic memory, personal semantic memory, intrusions

INTRODUCTION

It seems obvious that what happens in our lives has the potential to shape how we are. And yet, for so long in mental healthcare, the life stories of people with psychosis have been neglected. A wealth of empirical evidence now questions this position, highlighting the significant impact that traumatic events[1], particularly childhood victimization, can have on people's difficulties (Morgan and Gayer-Anderson, 2016). The challenge, therefore, is to reduce the impact of adversity on the lives of people with psychosis. Necessary steps include a focus on prevention, and a humane approach to identification, safeguarding and redress (Read and Bentall, 2012). Alongside this, effective interventions are needed to support people to manage the consequences of victimization and move on in life. The development of trauma-focused therapy for psychosis is dependent on an evidence-based understanding of the pathways from trauma to psychotic experiences. This understanding can then be used to highlight targets and strategies for intervention, in line with the interventionist causal model (Kendler and Campbell, 2009). But this is no easy task. The diverse phenomenology of psychosis indicates these pathways are complex; they will vary from person to person and fluctuate over time. Nonetheless, progress is being made in identifying possible underlying mechanisms and theoretical models have been proposed.

This paper outlines a multifactorial model that aims to integrate existing accounts, drawing on cognitive-behavioral, attachment and neuropsychological perspectives of psychosis and PTSD. Within the model, these accounts are viewed as complimentary, in that both cognitive-behavioral and attachment approaches highlight the importance of internal representations of experience, the meaning derived from these experiences, the ways emotions are regulated, and how these mechanisms interact with neuropsychological processes. A central role is therefore proposed for autobiographical memory and trauma-related emotion regulation strategies in shaping the phenomenology of intrusive imagery, subsequent appraisals and coping responses. Evidence and accounts of the relationships between trauma and psychosis will first be briefly reviewed, then the new model of posttraumatic stress in psychosis described. Three vignettes, based on clinical experience, will be discussed in relation to the model to illustrate the possible ways psychological posttraumatic stress processes may play a role in psychosis. Implications for intervention indicated by the model will be reflected on, together with methodological challenges and directions for future research.

[1]Trauma, traumatic events and traumatic experiences are used interchangeably. The considerable debate regarding the definition of traumatic stressors is acknowledged and beyond the scope of this article (Friedman et al., 2011). For the purposes of this paper, a broad definition of traumatic events is employed, defined as any event(s) the individual perceives as involving a significant physical and/or psychological threat to the self.

RELATIONSHIPS BETWEEN TRAUMA AND PSYCHOSIS

The relationship between trauma and psychosis is now well established. Higher rates of childhood victimization and Posttraumatic Stress Disorder (PTSD, DSM 5, American Psychiatric Association, 2013) are reported across the spectrum of psychosis compared to the general population, although findings vary depending on the population sampled and methodology used (Kessler et al., 2005; Achim et al., 2011; Matheson et al., 2013; Kraan et al., 2015; Steel et al., 2017a). The most robust study of PTSD prevalence estimated 16% of people with schizophrenia-spectrum diagnoses meet diagnostic criteria (de Bont et al., 2015). This is of relevance to mental healthcare as co-occurring PTSD and psychosis appear to be associated with worse clinical and functional outcomes, and difficulties with engagement, adherence, and treatment response (Schneeberger et al., 2014; Hassan and De Luca, 2015; Mondelli et al., 2015; Trotta et al., 2015; Seow et al., 2016).

Given the higher incidence of trauma in psychosis, research has considered whether victimization may play a causal role in psychotic experiences, at least for some people. Demonstrating the causality of trauma in psychosis is methodologically complex and research is in its infancy. However, preliminary findings are in line with the proposal that victimization does have a causal effect. Prospective, case-control, and epidemiological studies support an association, and dose-response relationships and mediation by plausible mechanisms have been demonstrated (Hill, 1965; Varese et al., 2012b; Kelleher et al., 2013; Alsawy et al., 2015; Hardy et al., 2016; Amanuel et al., 2017; McGrath et al., 2017).

A key controversy is whether victimization has a generic impact on mental health outcomes or if there is some degree of specificity between certain trauma types and symptoms of psychosis (Bentall et al., 2014; van Nierop et al., 2014a, 2015; van Dam et al., 2015). The latter hypothesis is based on the possibility that some events may have a greater propensity to trigger particular psychological mechanisms. For example, it has been found that childhood sexual abuse is associated with voices, whereas emotional abuse and neglect are related to paranoia, with the former at least partially accounted for by emotion regulation and the latter by beliefs about the self and others (Sitko et al., 2014; Hardy et al., 2016; Wickham and Bentall, 2016). However, a consensus on the debate has yet to be reached and further investigation is needed.

From a symptom-specific perspective, the association between victimization and positive symptoms has been more established than for negative symptoms (Bentall et al., 2014). Relationships between trauma and negative symptoms are feasible, given the proposal they represent a response to the psychologically overwhelming trauma of psychosis, together with the phenomenological overlap between them and the avoidance and numbing symptoms of PTSD (Stampfer, 1990). However, current findings are equivocal (Resnick et al., 2003; Lysaker and Larocco, 2008; Vogel et al., 2013, van Dam et al., 2015). Future work in the area will benefit from adopting a symptom-specific dimensional approach to assessment, distinguishing experiential from expressive negative symptoms (Kirkpatrick et al., 2011).

The findings of studies examining the specificity of the impact of trauma on psychosis will depend on the analytic approach employed, whether the relationships within victimization types and psychosis outcomes are considered, and if other difficulties, such as depression, are viewed as co-occurring mental health outcomes or mechanisms by which psychosis may arise. The debate is further complicated by the phenomenological overlap in traumagenic mental health problems, and that psychotic experiences, such as voices and paranoia, are relatively common in other diagnoses, including depression, bipolar affective disorder, PTSD and personality disorder (Johnson et al., 1991; Brewin and Patel, 2010; Schroeder et al., 2013; Cloitre et al., 2014; McCarthy-Jones and Longden, 2015; Geddes et al., 2016; Palmier-Claus et al., 2016; Kelleher and DeVylder, 2017; Okkels et al., 2017). Adopting a transdiagnostic, network analytic approach, examining potential causal systems of interacting symptoms, to understand the interplay between victimization, posttraumatic stress reactions and psychosis seems a promising way forward (Looijesetijn et al., 2015; Isvoranu et al., 2016, 2017).

CURRENT UNDERSTANDING OF THE RELATIONSHIP BETWEEN TRAUMA AND PSYCHOSIS

Seminal cognitive behavioral models of psychosis addressed how trauma might shape beliefs, intrusions, appraisals and coping responses (Garety et al., 2001; Morrison, 2001). Central to these models is the proposal that the triggering of a biopsychosocial vulnerability gives rise to sensory-perceptual intrusions, which leads to a search for meaning (Maher, 1974). It is these attributions of meaning that result in psychotic experiences, which are then maintained by attempts to cope. For example, if a person's childhood is characterized by physical abuse and strict religious observance, they may develop beliefs that spiritual entities are very powerful and that others will harm them. If they then experience a mugging, leading to distress and disrupted sleep, this could trigger an intrusion of a threatening voice saying 'you're going to get it'. In this context, it is understandable they might interpret the voice as a sign of persecution by evil spirits. This could then lead to hypervigilance, rumination and interpersonal avoidance, which may paradoxically perpetuate hearing voices through attentional focus, confirmatory bias and reduced opportunities to feel safe around others. Whilst the Garety et al. (2001) and Morrison (2001) models have been highly influential in research and practice, they arguably do not consider in detail the processes that may give rise to intrusions occurring in the context of trauma.

Morrison et al. (2003) further expanded these accounts, outlining three routes between trauma and psychosis: trauma may lead to psychosis, psychosis and related experiences can themselves give rise to PTSD, and that psychosis and PTSD may lie on a spectrum of shared reactions to trauma. They propose an integrative model of the spectrum of trauma reactions, emphasizing how the interpretation of intrusions determines the subsequent labeling of difficulties as PTSD or psychosis, and their consequences. In turn, appraisals of intrusions may be influenced by memory processes, dissociation and, schematic and metacognitive beliefs about intrusive experiences and coping responses. To return to the above example, if the person recognized the voice content as being related to what the perpetrator said during the mugging, the intrusion might instead be appraised as trauma-related. In this case, it would be viewed as a memory-based re-experiencing characteristic of PTSD instead of an externally attributed voice reflective of psychosis. A strength of this integrative model is in highlighting the potential spectrum from posttraumatic stress to psychosis. However, it does not consider in detail the diverse phenomenology of intrusions in psychosis and adopts a somewhat categorical approach to the appraisal of intrusions (i.e., that they will be attributed to either PTSD or psychosis). Whilst memory is mentioned as a potential process that might impact intrusions and how they are explained, the specific ways in which memory might shape intrusions and their interpretations is not explored.

Another important account, by Mueser et al. (2002), views PTSD and psychosis as distinct entities, and adopts a pragmatic position emphasizing how their symptoms may directly and indirectly interact to exacerbate each other. The model is descriptively useful at a symptom level, although unlike the previously mentioned models does not comment on the causal mechanisms that may give rise to PTSD and psychosis. Since these initial proposals, a number of theorists (Steel et al., 2005; Fowler et al., 2006; Longden et al., 2011; Read et al., 2014; Barker et al., 2015; Berry and Bucci, 2015) and empirical studies have added additional insights. A range of specific processes have been highlighted in recent literature, including stress sensitivity, dissociation, attachment styles, social defeat, trauma-related beliefs, contextual integration, and intrusive memories (e.g., Gracie et al., 2007; Varese et al., 2012a; Sitko et al., 2014; Alsawy et al., 2015; Geddes et al., 2016; Jaya et al., 2016; Valmaggia et al., 2016; Bucci et al., 2017). Broadly speaking, the processes implicated relate to (1) attempts to regulate emotion and survive trauma, (2) the storage and retrieval of trauma memories and (3) the meaning derived from these memories in the form of schema, beliefs or appraisals. However, this work has not yet been synthesized into a multifactorial model.

In real world settings, the lack of integration of these findings into a coherent framework is problematic, because people with psychosis and clinicians are faced with trying to understand and manage a complex and diverse array of posttraumatic stress reactions. Rates of diagnostic PTSD in psychosis are relatively modest and do not account for the full range of posttraumatic reactions that people experience. There is also variability in the extent to which psychotic experiences appear objectively or subjectively related to traumatic events, and this variation requires explanation. For example, people sometimes report their psychosis is unrelated to their trauma history, even though to others there may appear to be links between them. Further, people's difficulties may lend themselves to distinct intervention approaches if they arise from different underlying mechanisms. A model integrating the current literature is clearly needed to address these practical and conceptual challenges, which can then guide formulation and intervention.

A MODEL OF POSTTRAUMATIC STRESS IN PSYCHOSIS

Drawing on the accounts outlined above and more recent findings in the area, a model of posttraumatic stress in psychosis will be described, based on cognitive-behavioral, attachment and neuropsychological perspectives of psychosis and PTSD. Specifically, trauma-related emotion regulation strategies and autobiographical memory are proposed to shape the phenomenology of intrusive imagery and subsequent appraisals and coping responses (see **Figure 1**). Distressing emotions are not explicitly named in the model as they are viewed as interwoven in all of the implicated processes, given the well-established role of emotional experience as a precursor to, part of and consequence of psychosis and PTSD (Birchwood, 2003; Freeman and Garety, 2003; Kessler et al., 2011; Fowler et al., 2012; Okkels et al., 2017).

Vulnerability Factors

It is proposed in the model that one or more of three trauma-related vulnerability factors (i.e., emotion regulation, event memory (including perceptual and episodic memory representations) and personal semantic memory) give rise to a range of sensory-perceptual involuntary intrusions, and shape the appraisals of these and the subsequent coping responses. The theoretical basis for the vulnerability factors will first be described, with evidence for their impact on psychosis detailed in the "Intrusions," "Appraisals," and "Coping" Sections.

Emotion Regulation

The first psychological vulnerability factor proposed to lead to the development and maintenance of trauma-related psychosis consists of the ways in which people regulate emotions associated with threat resulting from traumatic events. Read et al. (2014) propose exposure to childhood victimization results in neurodevelopmental changes such as hyperactivity of the hypothalamic-pituitary-adrenal (HPA) axis. This leaves people vulnerable to understandable but unhelpful ways of regulating stress, which may then contribute to psychosis. We respond to threat with varying degrees of sympathetic (i.e., fight and flight) and parasympathetic (i.e., flag and faint) nervous system activation (the defense cascade), depending on the nature of the event and the individual (Schauer and Elbert, 2010). In the context of repeated childhood victimization, people may repeatedly oscillate through cycles of these reactions such that their response to the world is increasingly mediated by defense cascade responses. Dissociative detachment or 'shutting down' may be the most likely way of surviving inescapable threat, leading to the parasympathetic system being more persistently activated (Brown, 2006). These protective responses may therefore become habitual means of regulating emotion. In this sense, they can be viewed as attempts to survive extreme circumstances where fundamental developmental needs are not met (e.g., for safety, connection and autonomy) (Young et al., 2003).

The defense cascade is primarily conceptualized as reflecting cognitive-affective and behavioral responses. However, it is proposed that when these emotion regulation strategies become implicit ways of regulating threat, they will also show themselves in how the person relates to others (Bowlby, 1969, 1973). Parallels can therefore be drawn between emotion regulation and attachment styles (Hesse, 2008). For example, sympathetic nervous system activation could result in anger or fear, with congruent cognitive processing (e.g., hypervigilance and threat-focused reasoning), and aggressive, dependent or actively avoidant behavior and relating styles (Bartholomew and Horowitz, 1991). In contrast, dissociative detachment response (ranging from emotional numbing to more intense experiences of derealization and depersonalization) and interpersonal passivity may be manifestations of parasympathetic nervous system activity (Brown, 2006; Vogel et al., 2013). Thus, childhood victimization may result in increased or reduced stress sensitivity, or fluctuations between the two (Main and Hesse, 1990). As will be described in detail in the Sections on "Intrusions" and "Coping," these strategies can paradoxically increase an individual's sense of threat by impacting on intrusions and coping responses, thereby perpetuating psychosis.

Event Memory

The second vulnerability factor is memory for victimization events, which forms part of the autobiographical memory system[2]. In this model, autobiographical memory is defined as memory relating to life experiences that contributes to a person's sense of self and includes three levels of representation. *Personal semantic memory* consists of abstracted meaning about the self, others and the world, which is derived from specific episodic memories and general sociocultural knowledge. *Episodic memory* consists of declarative, contextualized and allocentric event representations that can be manipulated, and voluntarily and involuntarily retrieved. *Perceptual memory* consists of

[2]Different, albeit overlapping, conceptualizations of autobiographical memory have been proposed in the literature, with debate over the precise mechanisms involved (Conway and Pleydell-Pearce, 2000; Baddley, 2001; Brewin, 2001, 2014; Conway, 2001, 2005, 2009; Tulving, 2002, 2005; Brewin et al., 2010; Prebble et al., 2013). For the purposes of this model and ease of understanding, a pragmatic conceptualization is adopted. This is done with the acknowledgment that some theorists have used different terminology to describe the referenced concepts.

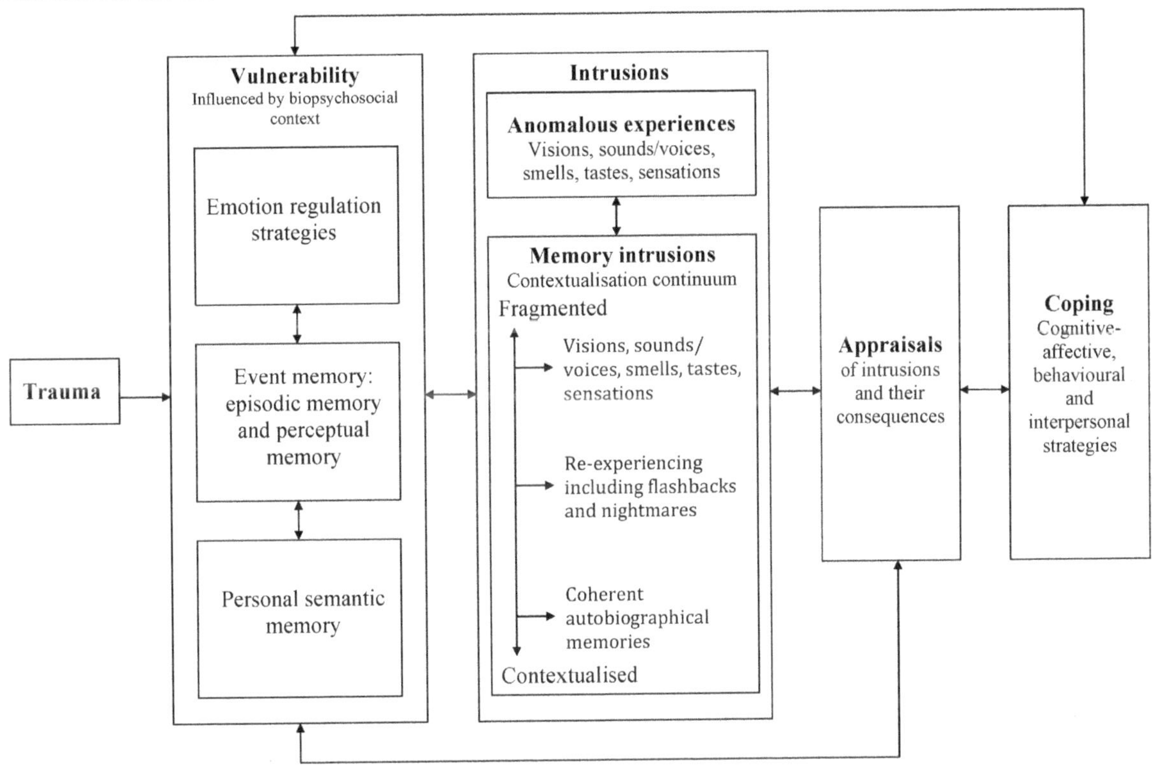

FIGURE 1 | A model of posttraumatic stress in psychosis.

detailed, egocentric, viewpoint dependent representations of sensory-perceptual stimuli experienced during events. Perceptual memory is held to be inaccessible to intentional retrieval independent of episodic or personal semantic memory representations but may, under certain conditions, be involuntarily recalled. Perceptual and episodic representations are relevant to understanding the storage and retrieval of event memory, and will be considered below, with the role of personal semantic memory as a vulnerability factor outlined in the next section.

So, how do we store and recall memory for events, and how do emotions experienced during trauma impact on event memory? Memory researchers propose that long-term memory for specific, everyday events is primarily a function of episodic memory, processed in the structures of the medial temporal lobe, including the hippocampus, and prefrontal areas (Tulving et al., 1991; Conway and Pleydell-Pearce, 2000; Brewin, 2001, 2014; Conway, 2001, 2005, 2009; Brewin et al., 2010). When an event is experienced, sensory-perceptual stimuli (including emotions, sights, sounds, sensations, tastes and smells) are initially encoded in perceptual memory through subcortical structures such as the amygdala. This encoding is then converted into a more abstract representation in episodic memory, consisting of a contextual representation of spatio-temporal information (of when and where stimuli were experienced), which in turn is integrated into personal semantic memory.

In everyday situations, the sensory-perceptual information in perceptual memory fades once it has been represented in episodic memory, and becomes relatively inaccessible. However, the event memory is still available for voluntary retrieval. When a person tries to recollect what happened, a search leads to the activation of the abstract representation in episodic memory, which then reconstructs the associated perceptual representation. This memory will be experienced as sufficiently vivid to conjure a sense of recollection, but less intensely than when the event actually happened, so it is perceived as a past experience. For example, if someone is asked what happened on a recent shopping trip, this will trigger an iterative search of his or her memory until the specific episodic representation of the event is identified. The abstract, episodic representation will then be used to reconstruct the perceptual experiences associated with the shopping trip so the person can recollect what happened.

Critical to understanding the role of victimization in psychosis is the proposal that, in the context of increased emotion, representations in perceptual memory may be encoded in greater detail than usual (Ehlers and Clark, 2000; Hackmann and Holmes, 2004; Brewin et al., 2010). The consequence of this is that when the episodic memory is later retrieved, the sensory-perceptual stimuli present at the time of the event (stored in perceptual memory) will be experienced more intensely than if encoded under less emotional conditions. For example, if a person accidentally urinated in public during a shopping trip, the anxiety and shame experienced as a result would be encoded in detail in their perceptual memory. When the memory is recalled it would still be experienced as a past recollection, but the detailed perceptual representation would result in the emotions felt at the time being acutely experienced in the present moment.

Further, cognitive-behavioral models of PTSD propose that, under conditions of extreme emotion, the episodic processing of information may also change. The encoding of contextualized representations is inhibited (also known as C-reps, arising from conceptual processing; Ehlers and Clark, 2000; Brewin et al., 2010) and, instead, stimuli are encoded in even greater detail in perceptual memory (also known as sensory representations, or S-reps, driven by data driven processing; Ehlers and Clark, 2000; Brewin et al., 2010). This has an evolutionary advantage as it supports faster processing of information and activation of survival responses, and also ensures detailed information about threat is available after danger has passed, when important learning can be integrated into memory (LeDoux, 1998).

However, event memories encoded under conditions of extreme emotion are retrieved differently from less emotional memories. First, given their reduced contextualization in episodic memory, perceptual memories are highly vulnerable to being directly retrieved by internal or external stimuli reminiscent of the highly arousing event. When this happens, they will be experienced (to a greater or lesser extent) as vivid and occurring in the 'here and now'. This type of memory retrieval therefore reflects the hallmark re-experiencing symptoms of PTSD. Second, intentional recall of events is impaired, as the associated episodic memory has not been fully elaborated, particularly for moments of highest arousal during events (known as hotspots, Grey and Holmes, 2008). Thus, if a person experienced intense arousal due to witnessing a violent, armed robbery during a shopping trip, the episodic encoding of this event would be inhibited, whilst the storage of sensory-perceptual experiences would be enhanced. This would mean the person would have difficulty intentionally recalling a coherent account of the robbery, particularly peripheral details. They would also be vulnerable to experiencing intrusions, for example, of seeing people bleeding and feeling very scared, triggered by reminders of the event (e.g., going shopping, seeing men, ruminating about how they could have been killed). Intrusions encoded under circumstances of extreme emotion can become less intrusive if people are able to experience their memories, so the perceptual representations fade and become integrated into episodic memory. However, if people avoid their memory intrusions, the contextualization of episodic memory is prevented and involuntary intrusions will be maintained.

Habitual emotion regulation strategies related to persistent victimization may be particularly problematic for the storage and retrieval of distressing events. Whilst these strategies may be protective during trauma, they may exacerbate disruptions in episodic memory processing. If persistent, they will then prevent the contextual elaboration of perceptual memories into episodic memory representations, leading to intrusion maintenance. Indeed, Steel et al. (2005) and Fowler et al. (2006) argue that people affected by psychosis may have a weakened ability to integrate contextual information, possibly due to enhanced stress sensitivity. This is likely to further disrupt memory processing and the contextualization of perceptual representations in episodic memory (Read et al., 2014). People with a vulnerability to psychosis may therefore have perceptual memories that are even more fragmented from episodic memory. Plausibly, contextual representations could be absent at storage or retrieval such that the involuntary retrieval of perceptual memory is experienced with no awareness of its association to a past traumatic event. In this circumstance, the witness to the armed robbery who experiences intrusions of people bleeding and feeling scared may view these, not as memories, but as a premonition of a future attack. The potential role of extremely decontextualized memory intrusions in psychosis will be explored further in the Section "Intrusions: Memory Intrusions."

Personal Semantic Memory

The third vulnerability factor for trauma-related psychosis is personal semantic memory, which reflects autobiographical knowledge that is abstracted from a specific time or place, and is likely mediated by the neocortex (Prebble et al., 2013). Personal semantic memory can therefore be viewed as reflecting the beliefs, schemas or appraisals implicated in cognitive-behavioral models of psychosis and PTSD, which can maintain problematic event memory representations (Ehlers and Clark, 2000; Garety et al., 2001; Morrison, 2001; Brewin et al., 2010). Alternatively, the cognitive-affective representations of the self and others in personal semantic memory also have parallels with the internal working models outlined by attachment theory (Bowlby, 1969, 1973). Personal semantic memory is derived from both episodic memories and broader sociocultural knowledge, and in this sense may be a proximal cognitive-affective mechanism by which risk factors associated with social defeat impact on psychosis (Selten et al., 2016). Personal semantic memory can be retrieved in concordance with or in isolation from episodic and perceptual memories; meaning it may be activated as abstract knowledge divorced from event content or in parallel with event memories to produce a rich, autobiographical experience.

Conway and Pleydell-Pearce (2000), Conway (2001, 2005, 2009), and Conway et al. (2004) propose personal semantic memory is categorically organized into general events, life periods and life stories, and may be particularly derived from key self-referent or self-defining episodic memories (Singer and Salovey, 1993). It is part of a self-memory system (SMS) dependent on frontotemporal regions of the brain. The SMS consists of personal semantic memory and a working self. The working self is a goal-orientated conductor of memory storage and retrieval that organizes both personal semantic and episodic memory in line with goals, to support problem solving and planning. The activity of the working self dynamically leads to and is shaped by personal semantic memory to derive an abstracted representation of the self and world. In this regard, personal semantic memory is held to be particularly central to a coherent sense of self (James, 1890; Prebble et al., 2013). A key function of the working self is to maintain correspondence and coherence between internal and external reality, and current goals. It therefore modifies memory encoding and retrieval to meet these needs. As stability of the SMS is prioritized this potentially gives rise to distortions in memory, as representations are modified to be congruent with the goals of the working self. The SMS thus has a key role in the reconstructive nature of memory. It may account for modifications in memory over time, as it transforms to fit with the person's current goals or concerns (Conway and Loveday, 2015).

Childhood victimization will understandably shape personal semantic memory and the working self. Given these systems are resistant to change, they therefore provide a means through which victimization can have a pervasive impact on how people experience and interpret the world. A threat-focused SMS will give rise to congruent storage and recall of event memories. For example, a person who has the appraisal 'I am bad' represented in their personal semantic memory, based on memories of what their abusers said about them, would be more likely to retrieve episodic and perceptual representations in line with this appraisal, and to store aspects of new experiences which are consistent with this view of themselves.

Intrusions

It is proposed that the trauma-related vulnerability factors outlined above are likely to give rise to certain types of intrusive imagery that, dependent on how they are appraised and responded to, may then lead to psychosis. The importance of imagery in understanding mental wellbeing, including psychosis, has long been recognized (Beck, 1970; Lang, 1977; Garety et al., 2001; Morrison, 2001; Hackmann and Holmes, 2004). Images are defined as "contents of consciousness that possess sensory qualities as opposed to those that are purely verbal or abstract" (Hackmann et al., 1998, p. 301) and can occur in any sensory modality. They are experienced "on a continuum from the near veridical reconstruction in the mind of a real event to the construction of an entirely hypothetical situation" (Martin and Williams, 1990, p. 268), and in this sense may be past or future orientated. Intrusive imagery is common, and so is viewed as a normative process, with distress and functional impact determined by responses to it (Hirsch and Holmes, 2007; Brewin et al., 2010). Transdiagnostically, it appears people usually experience a relatively small number of recurrent images, they tend to be thematically linked to people's concerns, and associations with specific adverse events may not be recognized until people are encouraged to consider any links (Hackmann and Holmes, 2004). In the context of psychosis, the most studied type of imagery is voice hearing, although hallucinations in other modalities and multimodal experiences also occur and are increasingly subject to investigation (McCarthy-Jones et al., 2012; Woods et al., 2015). Other studies have noted that images are often associated with psychotic experiences, although there has been relatively little investigation of their phenomenology and relationship to memory (Morrison et al., 2002; Schulze et al., 2013; Ison et al., 2014; Sheaves et al., 2015). In this model of posttraumatic stress in psychosis, two types of trauma-related intrusive imagery will be considered. Anomalous experience intrusions influenced by emotion regulation strategies and autobiographical memory, and trauma memory intrusions arising from varying degrees of retrieval of personal semantic, episodic and perceptual memory representations. It is suggested that intrusions are likely to trigger each other, and so may act synergistically in the development and maintenance of psychosis.

Intrusions: Anomalous Experiences

The first type of intrusions, anomalous experiences, are proposed to arise through a number of putative pathways, involving emotion regulation (i.e., hyperarousal and dissociation) and representations in autobiographical memory. The rationale for and evidence for each of these will be considered.

In relation to hyperarousal, a hypervigilance subtype of voice hearing has been previously proposed (McCarthy-Jones et al., 2012, 2014; Garwood et al., 2015) and within this model is viewed as linked to the sensitization of the sympathetic nervous system following childhood victimization. Understandable hypervigilance to danger may result in a reduced threshold for threat detection in environmental noise (e.g., perceiving background sounds of people talking or traffic as a sign of danger), leading to intrusions of anomalous experiences. Previous evidence has focused on threatening content arising from the external environment, although it seems feasible this process could also relate to internal stimuli, such as detecting intrusions of somatic pain or felt-sense presences (McCarthy-Jones et al., 2014). In line with a role for trauma-related hypervigilance in anomalous experiences, Hardy et al. (2016) found posttraumatic hyperarousal mediated the association between childhood sexual abuse and voices in 228 people with relapsing psychosis. However, this study was cross-sectional and therefore the temporal association between hypervigilance and voices was not established.

Dissociative detachment is also proposed as a driver of anomalous experience intrusions. Habitual dissociation in an attempt to manage threat may paradoxically give rise to intrusive experiences. This is because it has a detrimental impact on the integration of sensory-perceptual processes, and so may result in intrusions into consciousness (Brown, 2006). The role of dissociation in intrusive anomalous experiences is supported by observed correlations between depersonalization/derealization and hallucinatory experiences (Vogel et al., 2011; Alderson-Day et al., 2014; Pilton et al., 2015), its mediation of the relationship between childhood trauma and hallucinations (Perona-Garcelán et al., 2012; Varese et al., 2012a; Hardy et al., 2016) and its prediction of hallucinations in the flow of daily life (Udachina et al., 2014).

The final way in which anomalous experience intrusions are proposed to arise is through the impact of autobiographical memory and the working self on current and future-orientated imagery (Brewin et al., 2010). It is proposed that autobiographical memory representations of childhood victimization may indirectly shape anomalous experiences, as the working self draws on personal semantic, episodic or perceptual memory representations to generate novel imagery. This will be affectively and/or perceptually congruent with the underlying representations. For example, a person who has been the victim of past harassment may experience an intrusive image of being humiliated at an upcoming social event. The perceptual qualities of this image (sensation of cheeks flushing, tension and physiological arousal) together with the associated appraisal (others will judge me) will be shaped by their personal semantic and event memories, even though the person may not have an explicit awareness of the link between this image and their past experiences.

Novel images generated from the working self and autobiographical memory representations will be shaped by victimization experiences and in this regard may map onto the inner speech subtype of voices proposed by McCarthy-Jones et al. (2012) and McCarthy-Jones et al. (2014). Evidence in support of this mechanism comes from studies finding that the autobiographical context of intrusions can be present without subjective awareness, and the observation that hallucinatory content is often thematically linked with victimization and personal goals, suggesting a possible influence of autobiographical memory representations and the working self (Hardy et al., 2005; Corstens and Longden, 2013; McCarthy-Jones et al., 2014; Varese et al., 2016).

Finally, it is also important to note that all anomalous experience intrusions may, if sufficiently arousing, be encoded as a long lasting memory representation and potentially intrude through the mechanisms outlined below. For example, a person who was neglected and bullied may be hypervigilant for threat and have an appraisal "I am dirty" in their personal semantic memory. This could lead to the generation of novel olfactory and auditory imagery in the form of the smell of feces and a voice saying, "you smell so bad, no one wants to know you." The distress associated with this experience could lead to disruptions in autobiographical memory processing, with the perceptual representation stored in detail and the contextual, episodic representation inhibited, so the memory of the voice and the smell could later be involuntarily re-experienced.

Intrusions: Memory Intrusions

The second type of intrusions proposed to result from the trauma-related vulnerability factors are those arising from the direct retrieval of autobiographical memories. These are hypothesized to fall along a continuum of contextual integration. The position of intrusions is relatively rather than absolutely defined. For the purposes of the model, three distinct positions along the continuum are highlighted, although there will be variation within these positions as to the degree of contextualization experienced for any given intrusion. The positions range from fully contextualized memory intrusions, to those lacking in contextual integration (as is observed in the re-experiencing symptoms of PTSD), to at the extreme end, severely decontextualized memories that may be particularly characteristic of psychosis.

It is emphasized that, at this time, the continuum is speculative. It is not clear whether such a continuum exists or, rather, whether memory intrusions may be more accurately conceptualized categorically, experienced either as occurring in the 'here and now' or as past memories (Brewin et al., 2010). However, this dimensional approach to intrusions may better reflect the dynamic and reconstructive nature of memory, including how intrusions can be experienced with varying degrees of awareness of their link to past events. The mechanisms by which each of the three hypothesized types of memory intrusion arises will be considered below.

Contextualized memory intrusions

Intrusions of emotionally salient, contextualized memories may occur through two routes (Brewin et al., 2010). First, perceptual memories formed by emotionally arousing experiences may be retrieved by emotional or sensory cues, and given a context by corresponding information in episodic memory. Alternatively, a top–down process may occur when episodic memories are triggered with their associated perceptual memory. For example, if a person is dwelling on thoughts of being worthless, they might involuntarily remember a time when they failed. The contextual specifics of this event would be retrieved from episodic memory (being expelled from school), together with the corresponding perceptual memory of the stimuli present during the time (sinking sensation in stomach, welling up and sadness). Intrusions arising from this mechanism do not represent a shift in the nature of memory processing, but rather the impact of emotion on the storage and retrieval across the whole autobiographical memory system. There has been relatively little naturalistic investigation of this type of memory intrusion in psychosis, however, indirect support for the presence of this mechanism comes from findings indicating intrusive, coherent memories occur transdiagnostically and are likely to arise in the context of verbal, depressive rumination (Pearson et al., 2008; Brewin et al., 2010).

Re-experiencing memory intrusions

Re-experiencing memory intrusions, the 'hallmark' symptoms of PTSD, arise in the context of disruptions to the storage of event memory, as previously outlined. Detailed encoding in perceptual memory, coupled with inhibition of episodic representations, will increase the likelihood of representations of stimuli present at the time of trauma being triggered by associated cues (Brewin et al., 2010; Brewin, 2014). When people experience this type of intrusion, memory retrieval occurs, at least to some degree, in isolation from broader autobiographical recollection and the episodic grounding of events, such that they are experienced with a sense of occurring in the 'here and now' (Brown, 2006). However, the contextual, episodic representation is not entirely inaccessible, so this type of intrusion will still be experienced as linked to the associated event. Support for the role of re-experiencing in psychosis comes from findings indicating increased rates of PTSD in psychosis compared to the general population (de Bont et al., 2015), results from a non-clinical study that re-experiencing may partially account for the association between childhood sexual abuse and hallucinations (Gracie et al., 2007), and an association between posttraumatic intrusions and hallucinations in a large-scale population survey (Alsawy et al., 2015).

Fragmented memory intrusions

The final type of intrusions highlighted on the contextualisation continuum are fragmented sensory-perceptual experiences arising from perceptual memory representations. Together with the proposed anomalous experience intrusions, these memory intrusions are those that are most likely to reflect the hallucinatory imagery characteristic of psychosis. The theoretical basis for this type of intrusion, as highlighted earlier, is the proposal that people with psychosis may have a weakened ability to integrate contextual information, possibly linked to the sensitization of threat regulation (Steel et al., 2005; Fowler et al., 2006; Waters et al., 2006). Previous investigations of this hypothesis have highlighted that people high in schizotypy report more frequent, distressing intrusions after watching a traumatic film and following a road traffic accident (Holmes and Steel, 2004; Steel et al., 2008), and that there may be an association between contextual memory ability and intrusions in people high in psychosis proneness (Glazer et al., 2013). Steel and colleagues' proposal therefore focuses on how contextual integration difficulties increase intrusion frequency, with other factors (e.g., paranormal beliefs) determining the appraisal of these intrusions and whether they lead to psychosis.

This new model takes the contextual integration hypothesis a step further to propose perceptual memory intrusions may occur in the absence of any episodic context, such that they are experienced as occurring in the 'here and now' with no recollection of their link to past trauma. In this case, it is the intrusion itself that will manifest as a hallucinatory, psychotic experience, regardless of how it is appraised. Nonetheless, this type of intrusion seems likely to compel the person to attribute it externally. For example, if a person experiences an intrusion of vaginal pain with no recollection of its association to the pain experienced during a rape, it makes sense they appraise this as an experience of being raped in the present moment by an evil spirit. It is acknowledged that investigating this hypothesis is methodologically fraught, as by definition these fragments of memory will not be viewed as linked to memory, which makes assessment of them difficult. Further, such intrusions may be phenomenologically impossible to distinguish from the intrusive anomalous experiences outlined earlier.

However, there are some preliminary indications that this type of memory intrusion may exist. First, this intrusion type has some parallels with a previously proposed dissociative autobiographical subtype of voice hearing, whereby people report experiencing voices (not memories) that replay previously experienced content (McCarthy-Jones et al., 2014). Further, studies demonstrating links between the content of trauma and voices are possibly in line with the involuntary retrieval of perceptual memories shaping psychosis (Hardy et al., 2005; Read et al., 2005; Corstens and Longden, 2013; McCarthy-Jones et al., 2014). A recently completed study also found that self-reported fragmentation of intrusive memories was positively associated with the severity of hallucinations, but not paranoia, in a small sample of people with psychosis (Marsh-Picksley et al., in preparation). Whilst very tentative, this study is the first to indicate that fragmentation of perceptual memory intrusions may impact on psychosis. Further, anecdotal evidence suggests that people may recognize their intrusions as memory-related only after having the opportunity to reflect on and contextualize episodic memories for the associated events. For example, a threatening voice saying 'I'm going to have you' being recognized, following trauma-focused exposure therapy, as linked to what was said during a sexual assault, when previously it had not been perceived as memory-based.

Appraisals

In line with cognitive-behavioral models of psychosis and PTSD, the way in which people appraise their experience of intrusions will determine their consequences (Ehlers and Clark, 2000; Garety et al., 2001; Morrison, 2001). Within this model, it is proposed that appraisals will particularly be influenced by personal semantic memory and the goals of the working self. Appraisals of intrusions will therefore be consistent with and play a role in maintaining representations of the self and others in personal semantic memory. Appraisals can be primary (i.e., interpretations of the intrusion) and secondary (i.e., the implications of the interpretation). For example, a whispering voice may be interpreted as a sign of persecution by the devil (primary) that the person views himself or herself as being too weak to cope with (secondary). Both of these appraisals will be shaped by personal semantic memory, such as, the person believing they are evil and incompetent. Evidence supporting the role of personal semantic memory in psychosis comes from studies investigating trauma-related beliefs and schema, social defeat and attachment. Research has found that trauma is associated with negative beliefs about the self, world and others in psychosis, and these at least partially account for the relationship with paranoia in non-clinical, clinical and epidemiological samples (Kilcommons and Morrison, 2005; Gracie et al., 2007; Kilcommons et al., 2008; Geddes et al., 2016; Hardy et al., 2016; Jaya et al., 2016; Wickham and Bentall, 2016).

Other work has investigated the concept of social defeat, often assessed by measures of appraisals, which within this model are viewed as being derived from representations in personal semantic memory. For example, van Nierop et al. (2014b) in a large epidemiological study found social defeat mediated the relationship between childhood trauma, the extended psychosis phenotype and clinically significant psychosis. Similarly, Valmaggia et al. (2016) demonstrated the prospective impact of social defeat on paranoia in people at Ultra High Risk for psychosis compared to a control group. UHR participants reported higher levels of social defeat appraisals, and following exposure to a virtual social interaction environment reported more paranoia than controls, predicted by baseline levels of social defeat. Given social defeat is viewed as being shaped by previous events, this study suggests people's interpretation of experiences within the virtual environment was influenced by appraisals stored in their personal semantic memory.

As noted previously, attachment styles can be viewed as reflecting representations of self and others in personal semantic memory. Insecure attachment, and particularly disorganized attachment, is associated with childhood victimization, and more severe psychotic experiences (Gumley et al., 2014; Korver-Nieberg et al., 2014; van Dam et al., 2014; Wickham et al., 2015; Bucci et al., 2017). Findings highlighting the role of attachment styles in psychosis are therefore arguably consistent with the view that appraisals in personal semantic memory shape interpretations of intrusions to give rise to psychotic experiences. A final piece of evidence comes from a trial that found trauma-focused interventions aiming to update threat-related information in traumatic event memory reduced paranoia as well as re-experiencing symptoms (van den Berg et al., 2015). This finding is therefore in line with the view that paranoid appraisals arise from autobiographical memory, and that modifying these representations will improve paranoia.

Coping

Building on the proposal that habitual emotional regulation strategies can arise in response to victimization, this section will review how these strategies may, in turn, impact on coping with intrusions and appraisals. As noted previously, these strategies may relate to activation or deactivation of arousal, and manifest cognitive-affectively, behaviorally or interpersonally. In relation to the role of hyperarousal, is well established that stress sensitivity is associated with psychosis (DeVylder et al., 2016). Further, associations between childhood trauma and negative reactivity to daily stressors have been found, together with links to more severe positive symptoms (Glaser et al., 2006; Lataster et al., 2010; Lardinois et al., 2011). More recently, people with psychosis and a history of childhood trauma reported experiencing elevated stress sensitivity and paranoia compared to controls when in a virtual reality social environment (Veling et al., 2016). Other findings in support of the role of hyperarousal include studies demonstrating threat-focused processing in psychosis in the context of childhood victimization. For example, Bendall et al. (2013) found that people with a history of trauma demonstrated selective attention to threatening stimuli compared to controls. The previously mentioned findings by Hardy et al. (2016), that hyperarousal mediated the association between childhood sexual abuse and voices are also in line with this hypothesis. However, the cross-sectional design meant it was not possible to identify whether hyperarousal acted as a precursor to intrusions and/or as a coping response to intrusions and appraisals.

Indirect support for the role of trauma-related emotion regulation in psychosis also comes from findings highlighting the role of sleep disruption and rumination in psychosis. These have both been implicated as maintenance factors in posttraumatic stress difficulties, as they may perpetuate problematic autobiographical memory representations and exacerbate intrusions (Ehlers and Clark, 2000; Williams et al., 2007; Brewin et al., 2010; Freeman and Garety, 2014; Ricarte et al., 2017). Substance use is another potential coping strategy, and interactions have been found between childhood victimization, cannabis use and the odds of experiencing psychosis (Morgan et al., 2014). Fast thinking habits, or rapid reasoning, may also reflect a way of coping with threatening intrusions and appraisals, and could be associated with hyperaroused emotional regulation (Garety and Hardy, 2017). However, an association between fast thinking and emotion in psychosis has not been demonstrated, although this may be due to assessments lacking ecological validity (Freeman et al., 2008).

All the previously reviewed studies highlighting a role for attachment styles and dissociation in psychosis are also consistent with the hypothesized role of emotion regulation in coping with psychosis. For example, insecure anxious and avoidant styles may be linked to threat-focused coping, and disorganized attachment may be particularly associated with dissociation as a coping response (Braehler et al., 2013; van Dam et al., 2014; Bucci et al., 2017). Powers et al. (2016) reported that avoidance and numbing mediated the relationship between childhood trauma and psychosis in a large sample, after controlling for demographic variables and trauma exposure. Finally, it is noted that avoidant coping may also manifest as experiential negative symptoms (such as anhedonia, avolition and asociality) as people withdraw in an attempt to cope with their psychotic experiences (Raffard et al., 2010).

PATHWAYS FROM VICTIMIZATION TO PSYCHOSIS: VIGNETTES

To illustrate the model, three vignettes will briefly be described, based on clinical cases modified to ensure confidentiality. They aim to highlight different pathways between victimization and psychosis that anecdotally appear common in clinical practice. They are not intended to reflect discrete categories or subtypes. Whilst it is plausible that subtypes of trauma-related psychosis do exist, further empirical work is needed to investigate this hypothesis. Each person's situation has been simplified, with a particular focus on the intrusions that appear to be playing a key role in driving their difficulties. The terminology in the formulations has been adapted from **Figure 1** to highlight how the model can be modified to a person's understanding of their situation.

Tanya (see Figure 2)

Tanya described feeling very low and ashamed, as she believed others did not want her around because she was a waste of space. She reported things had always been this way, as growing up she did not fit in at home or school. Tanya said she intentionally made herself small so that others did not notice her, and became increasingly detached to the extent she felt numb and not human. It did not appear that she had experienced any periods of extreme arousal (e.g., characterized by overwhelming fear, horror or helpless) during her traumatic events of being excluded, although they had understandably triggered strong emotions of anxiety and shame. She reported being able to clearly recollect the most difficult events, with vivid impressions of what happened.

When around others, Tanya experienced them looking away from her and would be reminded of times when people had treated her similarly in the past. She also reported often hearing the voice of her dad criticizing what she was doing. Tanya described how these experiences confirmed her longstanding belief that people did not want her around because she was a waste of space, and that she did not think that things would ever change. She reported withdrawing and drinking alcohol excessively. She said she often ruminated on how much she had failed, and described a persistent, critical internal dialog.

In terms of formulating Tanya's difficulties, it appears her early experiences gave rise to a pervasive avoidant style of relating to herself and others. This may have provided some protection from people and the intensity of her internal distress. She was able to

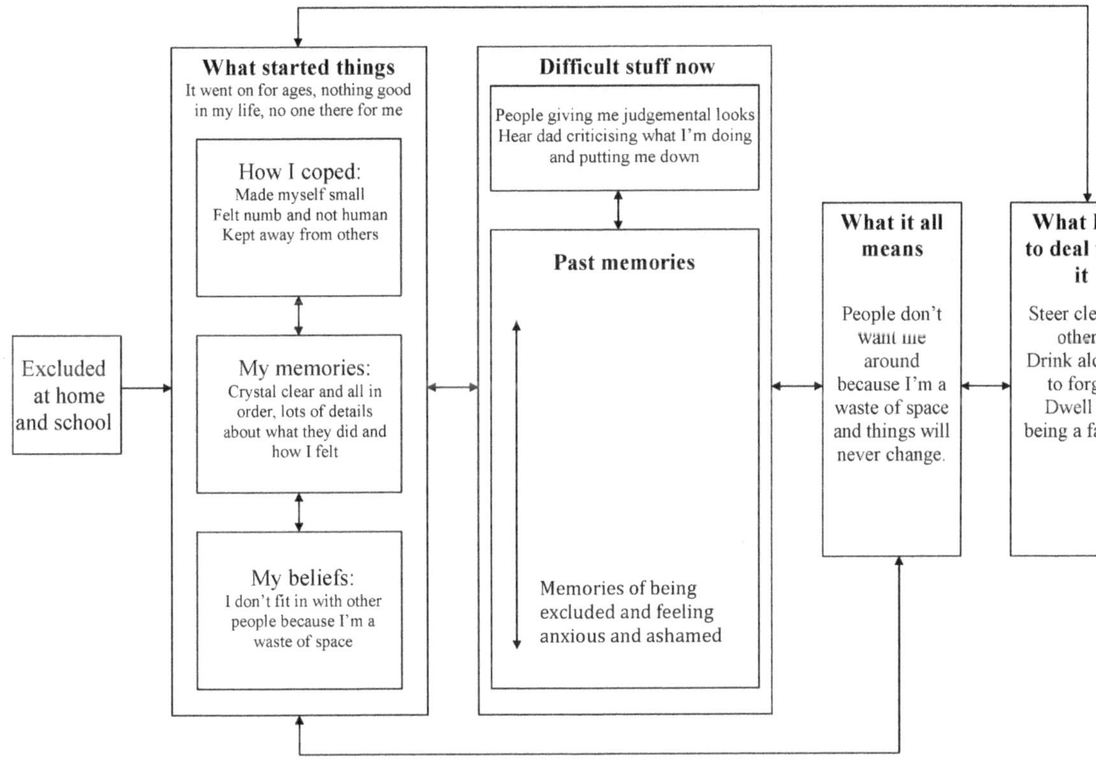

FIGURE 2 | Posttraumatic stress in psychosis model: Tanya's formulation.

coherently describe her past memories, with no avoidance, and did not report experiencing extreme arousal at the time of these events. This suggests her traumatic experiences had not been of sufficient intensity to disrupt contextual memory processing. Instead, she reported contextualized episodic memories, with vivid perceptual representations of what she had experienced at the time. The meaning of these experiences, that she was a waste of space had been ingrained in her personal semantic memory, and she was not able to recollect any alternative self-images.

In the context of this vulnerability, she was hypothesized to have both anomalous experience and trauma memory intrusions. The anomalous experiences took the form of perceiving others to be giving her judgmental looks and hearing a critical voice of her dad. It can be speculated that these experiences may have arisen from dissociative detachment and novel images generated from her autobiographical memory, in interaction with ambiguous stimuli in the environment (e.g., people looking at her). Memories of being excluded could have generated anomalous internal experiences of perceiving others looking at her judgmentally and a critical, derogatory voice. The salience of these experiences may have been further magnified by her persistent dissociation. The anomalous experience intrusions may have triggered and/or been exacerbated by intrusions of contextualized memories, such that Tanya would often have vivid recollections of the most difficult times from her past.

Understandably, these intrusions appeared to confirm her appraisal, represented in personal semantic memory, of herself as a waste of space. Further, her secondary appraisal, that things would never change, was in line with her lack of self-efficacy. Her coping responses were shaped by how she had learnt to survive growing up, with avoidance and rumination dominating, which in turn maintained her difficulties.

The formulation indicates that recommended cognitive-behavioral strategies may be of benefit, including developmental and maintenance formulations, psychoeducation, normalization, modifying coping, cognitive reappraisal, behavioral experiments and imagery modification (Morrison, 2017). In addition, the model specifically highlights the importance of addressing the impact of past ways of coping and memory recall on current problems. Following this, it appears imagery modification purely aiming to elaborate contextual representations in Tanya's episodic memory, as in traditional exposure approaches, may not be helpful because her memory is already contextualized (Foa et al., 2007). Instead, it may be more useful to focus on developing new episodic representations of her intrusive memories, using techniques such as competitive memory training and imagery rescripting (Steel et al., 2015; Morina et al., 2017).

Further, whilst simple imagery transformations could be used to modify Tanya's memory (e.g., imagining a time when she felt excluded disappearing or a negative outcome happening to those who left her out) it is possible that imagery modification may be more potent if the transformation addresses representations in both her event and personal semantic memory. This could involve, for example, having a trusted older adult enter the memory to remind her that she is lovable and worthwhile, even if others have not cared for her as they should. Given Tanya's prolonged attachment difficulties, she may need support to notice or develop alternative experiences that can be drawn on when updating memories and images. Limited re-parenting and empathic confrontation, together with support to live a valued life through social inclusion, may assist with developing these new perspectives (Young et al., 2003).

Kobe (see Figure 3)

Kobe reported his main difficulty was people staring and whispering about him. He explained how it was just him and his mother growing up, who hurt him by making them have sexual contact. Kobe said he would shut off during this abuse and pretend it was not happening. He lived in fear of it happening again and was always on the look out for ways to avoid it or escape. Kobe described how he was quite confused about some of what happened, and his memories from that period of his life were different to later times. He indicated how he always knew what happened was his fault as he was dirty.

Kobe said he could tell from others' stares and whispers that they were disgusted by him and knew what happened. He also reported experiencing flashbacks and nightmares of being sexually abused. Kobe further described having a very scary experience of hearing his mum's voice saying 'be a good boy' and feeling very spacey. He interpreted these experiences as confirmation that everyone knew about and was judging him for this past, and that his life had been ruined and he could not cope. He described how he protected himself by trying not to think about the past, having radar out for signs that people knew him, and shutting down.

A preliminary understanding of Kobe's difficulties suggests he tried to cope with the abuse by alternating between being hypervigilant for signs that an assault would happen, and being dissociatively detached when it did and feeling shut off. Kobe's confused intentional recall of the abuse suggests that his perceptual memory encoding could have been enhanced, with his episodic processing of events inhibited, due to the understandable extreme arousal he would have experienced. This would have meant that his memories for the assaults were poorly contextualized and vulnerable to being triggered by associated stimuli. It may be that Kobe's shutting off during assaults, and being hypervigilant at other times, further exacerbated the lack of episodic processing. His perceptual memories might have then been even more fragmented from their episodic context. Kobe's main appraisals of his experiences, represented in his personal semantic memory, were that he was dirty, it was his fault, and others would judge him negatively for what happened.

Against this background of vulnerability factors, Kobe had anomalous experience intrusions of people staring and whispering about him, possibly driven by hypervigilance. He was constantly alert for signs that people would know what had happened, so would likely have a lower threshold for detecting stimuli consistent with his fears. Kobe also experienced trauma memory intrusions in the form of flashbacks and nightmares of abuse, which made sense given the lack of contextualization of his trauma memory. The intrusive voice and spacey sensation Kobe experienced might have been manifestations of perceptual memories that were very fragmented from their episodic context, given they had content which appeared directly related to the abuse but were not experienced as arising from memory. Kobe experienced these intrusions not as posttraumatic stress difficulties but as further confirmation of others' judging him for his past, in line with his appraisals in personal semantic memory. His tricks to stay safe would likely further perpetuate his difficulties. He constantly tried to suppress his intrusions, was alert and experienced dissociative detachment. This made it difficult for him to elaborate and contextualize his traumatic memories, to have the opportunity to evaluate the validity of his internal experiences and appraisals through developing safer relationships with others, and to consider other possible explanations for what might be happening.

As with Tanya, recommended cognitive-behavioral approaches for psychosis may support Kobe in managing his difficulties. However, in contrast to Tanya, his formulation suggests memory exposure is indicated, with the aim of elaborating and updating episodic memories so the perceptual representations are less likely to intrude. Possible techniques include narrative exposure therapy, prolonged exposure, reliving with restructuring, and eye movement desensitization and reprocessing therapy (Shapiro, 2001; Ehlers et al., 2005; Foa et al., 2007; Schauer et al., 2011). However, to date, little is known about the comparable effectiveness of these approaches in psychosis, and what factors, if any, should moderate intervention choice. It is also not clear whether exposure itself is sufficient to update the memory, or whether further cognitive or experiential reappraisal may be required.

A further dilemma in working with Kobe is how and when to introduce memory-focused interventions. Best practice guidelines recommend that trauma-focused therapy be offered. However, targeting past memories may not be a priority for Kobe. His main concern is people judging him negatively, even though the formulation suggests elaborating his memory may have a beneficial effect on his fears about others. As with any therapy, an open and transparent discussion of intervention options (including their pros and cons) is indicated to support Kobe in identifying his preferred approach. This would also involve developing a rationale for memory work that fitted within Kobe's belief system. For example, framing the aim of exposure as being to minimize the impact of the past memories on him, so he might be more able to focus on managing his current difficulties with others.

Mo (See Figure 4)

Mo's main concern was about being persecuted by the spiritual mafia. He explained he was brought up in a children's home where he frequently experienced violent assaults. Mo said he coped by having a shield on which meant he was not bothered much by what was happening, although he also learnt to have his guard up and was alert to signs of things kicking off. Mo was dismissive when asked about his experiences, and said he did not have much memory of what happened. However, he was clear that he had learnt early in life that the world wants to ruin him. He indicated that he now heard and saw shadowy figures shouting

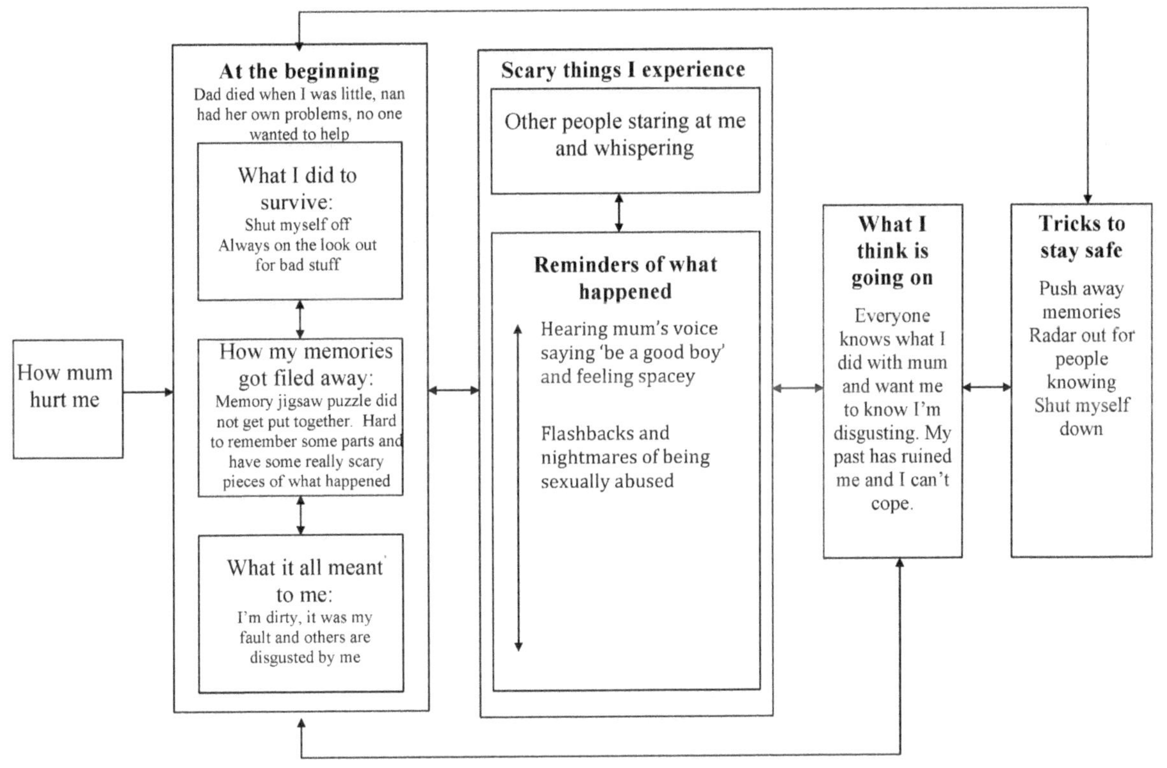

FIGURE 3 | Posttraumatic stress in psychosis model: Kobe's formulation.

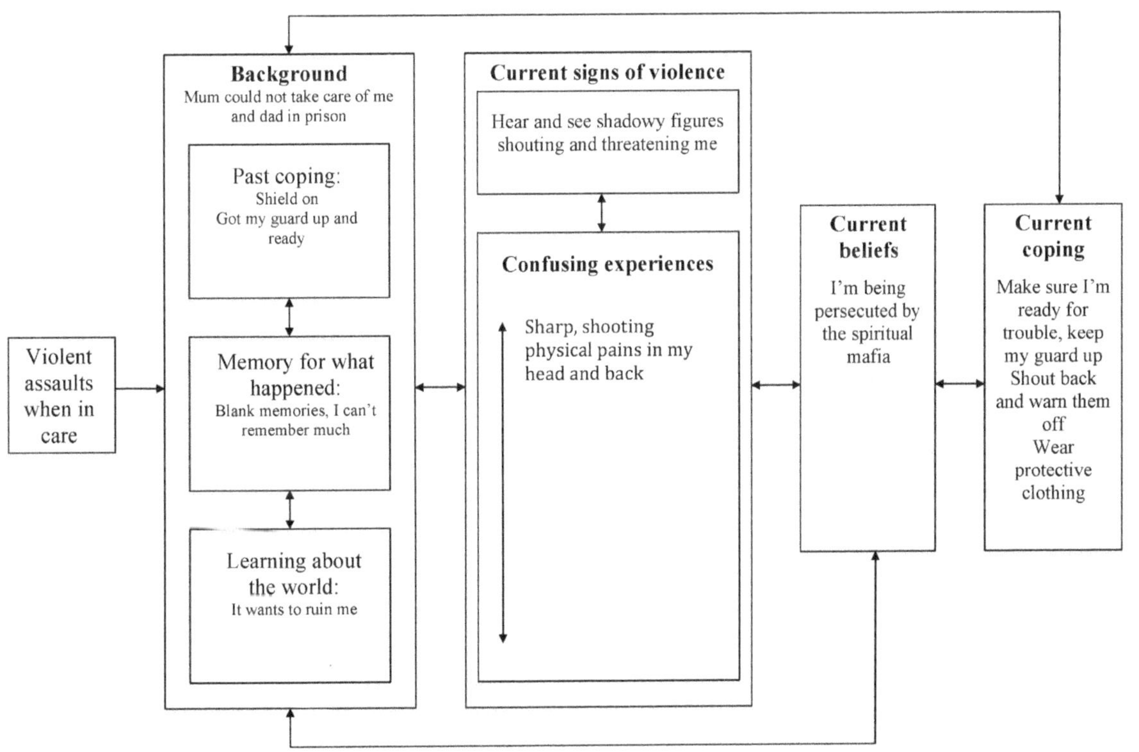

FIGURE 4 | Posttraumatic stress in psychosis model: Mo's formulation.

and being threatening, which would sometimes be accompanied by physical pains. Mo described how he knew the spiritual mafia was persecuting him, as he was cursed and it made sense others would continue to assault him. He described how he still coped by having his guard up, being alert to signs of trouble, and trying to fight back. He also reported wearing protective clothing to reduce the likelihood of the spirits being able to hurt him.

In terms of understanding Mo's difficulties, his shield could be viewed as an extreme form of dissociative detachment, as he reported little or no emotional response to the assaults. He also appeared to have become hyperviglance to threat, which could reflect a sensitization to stress. Intriguingly, Mo reported very little recollection of what had happened to him in the past. It is difficult to establish the extent to which this reflected an avoidance of memory retrieval and/or the nature of the underlying memory representation for what happened. It is possible that a shutting down of attention during the assaults meant that his episodic encoding of them was significantly limited such that he did have significantly impaired voluntary retrieval for the events. However, given the nature of what happened, he would have likely had at least some detailed perceptual representations of the assaults. Mo's appraisal of his early experiences, represented in personal semantic memory, was that he knew the world wanted to ruin him.

Mo reported no memory intrusions, although he did have multimodal experiences of shadowy threatening figures and experienced intrusive pain. Establishing the mechanisms underlying these experiences is difficult, and alternative hypotheses should be considered. However, the shadowy threatening figures appear more thematically as opposed to directly related to previous assaults (as the content of what they said reflected current not past concerns) and he described them as being adult figures, not children or young adults. It is therefore hypothesized that these intrusive images might have arisen from his emotion regulation strategies of having his shield up and being on guard, together with his working self and autobiographical memory representations generating novel images that were thematically congruent with his previous experiences. However, it is noted that these intrusions could also arise from involuntary recall of memories modified over successive retrieval attempts, in line with the goals of his working self to be alert for danger.

In contrast, it is speculated that the somatic pain Mo experienced could be a very fragmented intrusion arising from perceptual memories of what he experienced during past assaults. Given his report of his trauma memories, it is potentially feasible that this perceptual memory fragment was so decontextualized when intruding it had no grounding episodic context. As with Tanya and Kobe, Mo's appraisal of his intrusions was shaped by his personal semantic memory (i.e., that others want to harm him) and the anomalous nature of his intrusions, such that he viewed them as being a spiritual attack by the mafia. Trying to cope with this meant he was in a persistently hyperaroused state, increasing the likelihood of him noticing any possible threats, maintaining his appraisal of others in personal semantic memory, and preventing any possibility to reflect on his past.

Therapeutically, it is difficult to know whether trauma-focused interventions would be helpful for Mo. He reported no distressing impact of trauma although at the same time his current concerns appeared to be a mirror to his past. As with Tanya and Kobe, conventional cognitive-behavioral techniques targeting his appraisals and coping may help him in developing a sense of safety in life. In addition, at least some psychoeducation about trauma and its consequences appears indicated. This could include tentative exploration of Mo's thoughts about whether this information is relevant to his situation and, if he wishes to pursue further, shared formulation about the ways his past may contribute to his current difficulties. It of course should be respected that Mo and others may never be willing or able to address their experiences of victimization, and other approaches can be effectively used to support moving on in life. Nonetheless, it is suggested it is helpful to hold trauma-related hypotheses in mind and ensure people are aware of the option of trauma-focused therapy, should they wish to pursue this in the future.

CLINICAL IMPLICATIONS

A key implication of this model is that trauma and posttraumatic stress processes should be assessed in psychosis. However, evidence suggests routine assessment is rare in mental health services (de Bont et al., 2015; Brooker et al., 2016). This is particularly concerning in the UK, where it is recommended in best practice guidelines (National Institute for Health and Care Excellence [NICE], 2014). Improving practice requires the development of a trauma-informed service culture, clinicians having a biopsychosocial model of psychosis, skills training, and supervision of assessment and follow-up (Walters et al., 2016).

It is also important to recognize that assessment of posttraumatic stress in psychosis is complex. People often have a multitude of trauma, posttraumatic stress and psychosis experiences, with varying etiological origins. It can also be hard to disentangle types of memory encoding and retrieval, and establish whether difficulties are indeed trauma-related. Memory representations, posttraumatic stress reactions and psychosis will also change over time, influenced by a range of factors (particularly the reconstructive nature of trauma memory) and the potential to identify any links between them will oscillate accordingly. In addition, it is obviously not possible to directly assess stored memory representations; they can only be inferred from people's report of intrusions and their voluntary recall. People's reports will also be moderated by their ability to reflect on their memory processes and links with prior difficulties, which is a complex metacognitive task (McCarthy-Jones et al., 2014). Progress in the area will be supported by the development of more sensitive tools for assessing trauma memories (Brewin, 2015; Ford, 2016).

In terms of formulation, clinicians are encouraged to use the model flexibly and adapt to each individual. It is emphasized that in practice it would not be recommended, unless there is a clear preference from the person, to collaboratively discuss all aspects of the formulation given its complexity. Instead, the model is intended to guide clinicians in highlighting potential directions for collaborative micro-formulation and intervention. People may not find it helpful to differentiate intrusion types and in which case intrusions should be formulated generally, as in existing cognitive-behavioral formulations of psychosis (Garety et al., 2001; Morrison, 2001). The therapist, however, can hold in mind hypotheses about the distinct mechanisms contributing to different intrusions, and implications for intervention.

The model suggests trauma-focused therapy for psychosis should target emotion regulation and autobiographical memory. This proposal is consistent with protocols for cognitive-behavior therapy for psychosis and PTSD, given their focus on modifying coping, and understanding and contextualizing beliefs through experiential learning (e.g., Fowler et al., 1995; Ehlers and Clark, 2008; Morrison, 2017). This model builds on these approaches to emphasize the developmental context of coping mechanisms and indicates memory interventions should be prioritized, at least for some people. Further, as highlighted by the vignettes above, it suggests that different interventions should be used depending on the nature of people's intrusions and the hypothesized mechanisms driving them.

However, it may also be the case that the precise form of memory modification is less relevant. Instead, the key mechanism of change could be to develop alternative memory representations, through whatever means, that have the retrieval advantage over distressing representations (Brewin, 2006). For example, there are indications that imagery rescripting may be beneficial in PTSD, even though it does not involve fully recontextualising the perceptual memory representation, and instead focuses on encoding a new, less distressing representation (Morina et al., 2017). Interestingly, two recent trials of trauma-focused therapy for PTSD in psychosis found that exposure and EMDR, but not cognitive restructuring, were effective in reducing posttraumatic stress. This suggests the importance of accessing and experientially modifying event memories, not just focusing on appraisals in personal semantic memory (van den Berg et al., 2015; Steel et al., 2017b).

Another intervention consideration is whether trauma memories themselves need to be targeted or if it may be beneficial to engender ways of relating to internal experiences or memory retrieval that naturalistically support helpful processing. For example, initial findings suggest mindfulness or memory specificity training may reduce difficulties in people with experience of childhood trauma and current depression, and in PTSD, although to date this has not been robustly evaluated in psychosis (Hitchcock et al., 2016; Kuyken et al., 2016). An alternative approach would be to focus on emotion regulation. Learning new ways to manage threat may have a beneficial impact on memory representations, intrusions and appraisals. For example, third wave approaches including dialectic behavior therapy, mindfulness, acceptance and commitment therapy and compassion-focused therapy could be of value (Linehan, 1993; Mayhew and Gilbert, 2008; Morris et al., 2013). Further research is required to identify the effectiveness of these approaches, and what works best for whom.

Regardless of the specific cognitive-behavioral techniques used, as with any psychological therapy, a safe, secure and validating therapeutic relationship is essential, and the importance of humane values is emphasized (Brabban et al., 2016). Indeed, non-specific factors in the therapeutic relationship may be particularly valuable in providing an alternative experience to how people were treated in the past, and memories of this may usefully moderate threat-focused representations. Finally, whilst the model outlined here has focused on psychological mechanisms, the social context in which difficulties occur and the immense value of social and societal interventions is acknowledged. The social consequences of victimization, in terms of ongoing experiences of inequality and discrimination, are well documented and can of course significantly impede people's potential to move on in their lives (Gilbert et al., 2010; Metzler et al., 2016). Addressing these consequences (including broader societal attitudes and responses to victimization) is essential and could, indirectly, have a beneficial impact on the posttraumatic stress processes outlined in the model.

FUTURE RESEARCH

To date, there has been relatively little investigation of the posttraumatic stress processes implicated in the model and clearly further work is needed to investigate the hypothesized causal pathways. A strength of the model is its mechanism-focused conceptualization, meaning it can cut across diagnostic boundaries. Whilst the focus in this article has been on psychosis, the model could potentially be used to formulate other posttraumatic stress presentations where intrusions are viewed as playing a causal role in maintaining distress. The model also has a developmental emphasis, with a focus on childhood trauma. However, it is recognized that trauma may occur later in life and/or be related to experiences of psychosis. The mechanisms described could be applicable to trauma occurring at any life stage.

The methodological challenges of researching the area are significant. It is ethically and legal complex and costly to conduct methodologically robust, prospective studies, and many studies use a cross-sectional design and relatively small samples. The complexity of pathways to psychosis, and the heterogeneity of psychosis itself, also clouds research endeavors. In addition to assessment issues raised previously, concerns have been highlighted regarding the reliability of trauma reports in psychosis. However, comparable reliability has been found to general population samples and obstacles to disclosure mean that false negatives are more of an issue (Hardt and Rutter, 2004; Fisher et al., 2011). A further concern is that subjective reports of intrusions may not accurately assess involuntary retrieval. Avoidance of trauma memory may distort people's responses, and people may not be aware of intrusions when they are triggered. Whilst ethically contentious, it could be preferable to evoke intrusions under experimental conditions or to develop new techniques for *in vivo* investigation. Greater clarity and consensus in operationalizing and assessing dimensions of voluntary and involuntary memory retrieval, such as fragmentation and coherence, will also support progress in the field.

A possible starting point for developing our understanding of the pathways from trauma to psychosis could include detailed phenomenological assessment of involuntary and voluntary recall of traumatic memories, and other intrusions. For example, the model predicts more incoherent voluntary recall would be related to increasingly fragmented, vivid and frequent intrusions, which could manifest as hallucinatory experiences. Moving beyond diagnostic boundaries to focus on the causal interplay between specific posttraumatic processes and symptoms is also a useful direction for future research. Experience Sampling Methodology, whilst not without its limitations, may also be a more promising route to investigating the ways in which the implicated processes interact in real-world settings, and potentially provide a means to deliver intervention prompts (e.g., to support people in responding helpfully to intrusions) (Reininghaus et al., 2015).

CONCLUSION

In conclusion, a multifactorial model of posttraumatic stress in psychosis has been outlined, drawing on current theoretical accounts and empirical evidence. Emotion regulation and autobiographical memory (including perceptual, episodic and personal semantic representations) are hypothesized to lead to the development and maintenance of intrusions, appraisals and coping responses in psychosis. Two types of intrusive experiences are proposed to account for the diversity of phenomenological links between trauma and intrusions. First, anomalous experience intrusions, driven by emotion regulation and the generation of novel images from autobiographical memory, may explain experiences which appear unrelated to or which only thematically mirror trauma history. Second, trauma memory intrusions may be retrieved at any point along a continuum of contextualization, with recollections ranging from coherent memories to very fragmented intrusions. Given the extent of their fragmentation, the latter are unlikely to be perceived as arising from memory events even if they seem objectively linked. The reconstructive nature of memory is emphasized, as stored representations may be modified over time depending on the goals of the working self. It is highlighted that at this stage the model is speculative, and robust empirical designs are needed to elucidate the mechanisms by which victimization impacts on psychotic experiences. However, it is hoped that the model may contribute to supporting people with psychosis and clinicians in understanding the sometimes overwhelming and complex difficulties that they face. In healthcare services, our role is to get better at recognizing when people have experienced trauma, assisting them in making sense of their problems and providing the support they need to move on in their lives.

AUTHOR CONTRIBUTIONS

AH had sole responsibility for the development and writing of the manuscript.

ACKNOWLEDGMENTS

I would like to express my gratitude to the researchers whose work inspired this paper, particularly the Psychosis Research Partnership, and to the people with psychosis, clinicians and researchers I have worked with for the helpful discussions that shaped my ideas. Additional thanks goes to Philippa Garety and Thomas Ward for their insightful comments on an earlier draft of the manuscript.

REFERENCES

Achim, A. M., Maziade, M., Raymond, E., Olivier, D., Merette, C., and Roy, M. A. (2011). How prevalent are anxiety disorders in schizophrenia? A meta-analysis and critical review on a significant association. *Schizophr. Bull.* 37, 811–821. doi: 10.1093/schbul/sbp148

Alderson-Day, B., McCarthy-Jones, S., Bedford, S., Collins, H., Dunne, H., Rooke, C., et al. (2014). Shot through with voices: dissociation mediates the relationship between varieties of inner speech and auditory hallucination proneness. *Conscious. Cogn.* 27, 288–296. doi: 10.1016/j.concog.2014.05.010

Alsawy, S., Wood, L., Taylor, P. J., and Morrison, A. P. (2015). Psychotic experiences and PTSD: exploring associations in a population survey. *Psychol. Med.* 45, 2849–2859. doi: 10.1017/S003329171500080X

Amanuel, A. A., Kisely, S., Scott, J. G., Williams, G., Clavarino, A., Stathearn, L., et al. (2017). Childhood maltreatment and young adulthood hallucinations, delusional experiences, and psychosis: a longitudinal study. *Schizophr. Bull.* doi: 10.1093/schbul/sbw175 [Epub ahead of print].

American Psychiatric Association (2013). *Diagnostic and Statistical Manual of Mental Disorders*, 5th Edn. Washington, DC: American Psychiatric Association. doi: 10.1176/appi.books.9780890425596

Baddley, A. D. (2001). Is memory still working? *Am. Psychol.* 56, 851–864.

Barker, V., Gumley, A., Schwannauer, M., and Lawrie, S. (2015). An integrated biopsychosocial model of childhood maltreatment and psychosis. *Br. J. Psychiatry* 206, 177–180. doi: 10.1192/bjp.bp.113.143578

Bartholomew, K., and Horowitz, L. M. (1991). Attachment styles among young adults: a test of a four category model. *J. Pers. Soc. Psychol.* 61, 226–244. doi: 10.1037/0022-3514.61.2.226

Beck, A. T. (1970). Role of fantasies in psychotherapy and psychopathology. *J. Nerv. Ment. Dis.* 150, 3–17. doi: 10.1097/00005053-197001000-00002

Bendall, S., Hulbert, C. A., Alvarez-Jimenez, M., Allott, K., McGorry, P. D., and Jackson, H. J. (2013). Testing a model of the relationship between childhood sexual abuse and psychosis in a first-episode psychosis group: the role of hallucinations, delusions, posttraumatic intrusions, and selective attention. *J. Nerv. Ment. Dis.* 201, 941–947. doi: 10.1097/NMD.0000000000000033

Bentall, R., de Sousa, P., Varese, F., Wickham, S., Sitko, K., Haarmans, M., et al. (2014). From adversity to psychosis: pathways and mechanisms from specific adversities to specific symptoms. *Soc Psychiatry Psychiatr. Epidemiol.* 49, 1011–1022. doi: 10.1007/s00127-014-0914-0

Berry, K., and Bucci, S. (2015). What does attachment theory tell us about working with distressing voices? *Psychosis* 8, 60–71. doi: 10.1080/17522439.2015.1070370

Birchwood, M. (2003). Pathways to emotional dysfunction in first-episode psychosis. *Br. J. Psychiatry* 182, 373–375. doi: 10.1192/bjp.182.5.373

Bowlby, J. (1969). *Attachment and Loss*. New York, NY: Basic Books.

Bowlby, J. (1973). *Attachment and Loss: Separation*, Vol. 2. New York, NY: Basic Books.

Brabban, A., Byrne, R., Longden, E., and Morrison, A. P. (2016). The importance of human relationships, ethics and recovery-orientated values in the delivery of CBT for people with psychosis. *Psychosis*. doi: 10.1080/17522439.2016.1259648 [Epub ahead of print].

Braehler, C., Valiquette, L., Holowka, D., Malla, A. K., Joober, R., Ciampi, A., et al. (2013). Childhood trauma and dissociation in first-episode psychosis, chronic schizophrenia and community controls. *Psychiatry Res.* 210, 36–42. doi: 10.1016/j.psychres.2013.05.033

Brewin, C. R. (2001). A cognitive neuroscience account of posttraumatic stress disorder and its treatment. *Behav. Res. Ther.* 39, 373–393. doi: 10.1016/S0005-7967(00)00087-5

Brewin, C. R. (2006). Understanding cognitive behavior therapy: a retrieval competition account. *Behav. Res. Ther.* 44, 765–784. doi: 10.1016/j.brat.2006.02.005

Brewin, C. R. (2014). Episodic memory, perceptual memory, and their interaction: foundations for a theory of posttraumatic stress disorder. *Psychol. Bull.* 140, 69–97. doi: 10.1037/a0033722

Brewin, C. R. (2015). Re-experiencing traumatic events in PTSD: new avenues in research on intrusive memories and flashbacks. *Eur. J. Psychotraumatol.* 6:27180. doi: 10.3402/ejpt.v6.27180

Brewin, C. R., Gregory, J. D., Lipton, M., and Burgess, N. (2010). Intrusive images in psychological disorders: characteristics, neural mechanism, and treatment implications. *Psychol. Rev.* 117, 210–232. doi: 10.1037/a0018113

Brewin, C. R., and Patel, T. (2010). Auditory pseudohallucinations in United Kingdom war veterans and civilians with posttraumatic stress disorder. *J. Clin. Psychiatry* 71, 419–425. doi: 10.4088/JCP.09m05469blu

Brooker, C. G. D., Brown, K. T., and Kennedy, A. (2016). Sexual violence and abuse and the care programme approach. *Br. J. Psychiatry* 209, 359–360. doi: 10.1192/bjp.bp.116.186122

Brown, R. J. (2006). Different types of "dissociation" have different psychological mechanisms. *J. Trauma. Dissociation.* 7, 7–28. doi: 10.1300/J229v07n04_02

Bucci, S., Emsley, R., and Berry, K. (2017). Attachment in psychosis: a latent profile analysis of attachment styles and association with symptoms in a large psychosis cohort. *Psychiatry Res.* 247, 243–249. doi: 10.1016/j.psychres.2016.11.036

Cloitre, M., Garvert, D. W., Weiss, B., Carlson, E. B., and Bryant, R. A. (2014). Distinguishing PTSD, complex PTSD, and borderline personality disorder: a latent class analysis. *Eur. J. Psychotraumatol.* 5:25097. doi: 10.3402/ejpt.v5.25097

Conway, M. A. (2001). Sensory-perceptual episodic memory and its context: autobiographical memory. *Philos. Trans. R. Soc. Lond. B Biol. Sci.* 356, 1375–1384. doi: 10.1098/rstb.2001.0940

Conway, M. A. (2005). Memory and the self. *J. Mem. Lang.* 53, 594–628. doi: 10.1016/j.jml.2005.08.005

Conway, M. A. (2009). Episodic memories. *Neuropsychologia* 47, 2305–2313. doi: 10.1016/j.neuropsychologia.2009.02.003

Conway, M. A., and Loveday, C. (2015). Remembering, imagining, false memories and personal meanings. *Consious. Cogn.* 33, 574–581. doi: 10.1016/j.concog.2014.12.002

Conway, M. A., Meares, K., and Standart, S. (2004). Images and goals. *Memory* 12, 525–531. doi: 10.1080/09658210444000151

Conway, M. A., and Pleydell-Pearce, C. W. (2000). The construction of autobiographical memories in the self-memory system. *Psychol. Rev.* 107, 261–288. doi: 10.1037/0033-295x.107.2.261

Corstens, D., and Longden, E. (2013). The origins of voices: links between life histories and voice hearing in a survey of 100 cases. *Psychosis* 5, 270–285. doi: 10.1080/17522439.2013.816337

de Bont, P. A., van den Berg, D. P., van der Vleugel, B. M., de Roos, C., de Jongh, A., van der Gaag, M., et al. (2015). Predictive validity of the Trauma Screening Questionnaire in detecting posttraumatic stress disorder in patients with psychotic disorders. *Br. J. Psychiatry.* 206, 408–416. doi: 10.1192/bjp.bp.114.148486

DeVylder, J. E., Koyanagi, A., Unick, J., Oh, H., Nam, B., and Stickley, A. (2016). Stress sensitivity and psychosis experiences in 39 low and middle-income countries. *Schizophr. Bull.* 42, 1353–1362. doi: 10.1093/schbul/sbw044

Ehlers, A., and Clark, D. (2008). Posttraumatic stress disorder: the development of effective psychological treatments. *Nord. J. Psychiatry* 62(Suppl. 47), 11–18. doi: 10.1080/08039480802315608

Ehlers, A., and Clark, D. M. (2000). A cognitive model of posttraumatic stress disorder. *Behav. Res. Ther.* 38, 319–345. doi: 10.1016/S0005-7967(99)00123-0

Ehlers, A., Clark, D. M., Hackmann, A., McManus, G., and Fennell, M. (2005). Cognitive therapy for PTSD: development and evaluation. *Behav. Res. Ther.* 43, 413–431. doi: 10.1016/j.brat.2004.03.006

Fisher, H. L., Craig, T. K., Fearon, P., Morgan, K., Dazzan, P., Lappin, J., et al. (2011). Reliability and comparability of psychosis patients' retrospective reports of childhood abuse. *Schizophr. Bull.* 37, 546–553. doi: 10.1093/schbul/sbp103

Foa, E. B., Hembree, E. A., and Rothbaum, B. O. (2007). *Prolonged Exposure Therapy for PTSD: Emotional Processing of Traumatic Experiences, Therapist Guide.* Oxford: Oxford University Press. doi: 10.1093/med:psych/9780195308501.001.0001

Ford, M. (2016). Current approaches to studying hallucinations: overcoming barriers to progress. *Schizophr. Bull.* 43, 21–23. doi: 10.1093/schbul/sbw149

Fowler, D., Freeman, D., Steel, C., Hardy, A., Smith, B., Hackman, C., et al. (2006). "The catastrophic interaction hypothesis: How do stress, trauma, emotion and information processing abnormalities lead to psychosis?," in *Trauma and Psychosis: New Directions for Theory and Therapy*, eds W. Larkin and A. P. Morrison (Hove: Routledge), 101–134.

Fowler, D., Garety, P., and Kuipers, E. (1995). *Cognitive Behaviour Therapy for Psychosis: Theory and Practice.* London: Wiley.

Fowler, D., Hodgekins, J., Garety, P., Freeman, D., Kuipers, E., Dunn, G., et al. (2012). Negative cognition, depressed mood, and paranoia: a longitudinal pathway analysis using structured equation modeling. *Schizophr. Bull.* 38, 1063–1073. doi: 10.1093/schbul/sbr019

Freeman, D., and Garety, P. (2014). Advances in understanding and treating persecutory delusions: a review. *Soc. Psychiatry Psychiatr. Epidemiol.* 49, 1179–1189. doi: 10.1007/s00127-014-0928-7

Freeman, D., and Garety, P. A. (2003). Connecting neurosis and psychosis: the direct influence of emotion on delusions and hallucinations. *Behav. Res. Ther.* 41, 923–947. doi: 10.1016/S0005-7967(02)00104-3

Freeman, D., Pugh, K., and Garety, P. A. (2008). Jumping to conclusions and paranoid ideation in the general population. *Schizophr. Res.* 103, 254–260. doi: 10.1016/j.schres.2008.03.020

Friedman, M. J., Resick, P. A., Bryant, R. A., and Brewin, C. R. (2011). Considering PTSD for DSM-5. *Depress Anxiety* 28, 750–769. doi: 10.1002/da.20767

Garety, P. A., and Hardy, A. (2017). The clinical relevance of appraisals of psychotic experiences. *World Psychiatry* 16, 140–141. doi: 10.1002/wps.20408

Garety, P. A., Kuipers, E., Fowler, D., Freeman, D., and Bebbington, P. E. (2001). A cognitive model of the positive symptoms of psychosis. *Psychol. Med.* 31, 189–195. doi: 10.1017/S0033291701003312

Garwood, L., Dodgson, G., Bruce, V., and McCarthy-Jones, S. (2015). A preliminary investigation into the existence of a hypervigilance subtype of auditory hallucination in people with psychosis. *Behav. Cogn. Psychother.* 43, 52–62. doi: 10.1017/S1352465813000714

Geddes, G., Ehlers, A., and Freeman, D. (2016). Hallucinations in the months after a trauma: an investigation of the role of cognitive processing of a physical assault in the occurrence of hallucinatory experiences. *Psychiatry Res.* 246, 601–605. doi: 10.1016/j.psychres.2016.10.081

Gilbert, L. K., Breiding, M. J., Merrick, M. T., Thompson, W. W., Ford, D. C., Dhingra, S. S., et al. (2010). Childhood adversity and adult chronic disease: an update from ten states and the District of Columbia. *Am. J. Prev. Med.* 48, 345–349. doi: 10.1016/j.amepre.2014.09.006

Glaser, J. P., van Os, J., Portegijs, P. J. M., and Myin-Germeys, I. (2006). Childhood trauma and emotional reactivity to daily stress in adult frequent attenders of general practitioners. *J. Psychosom. Res.* 61, 229–236. doi: 10.1016/j.jpsychores.2006.04.014

Glazer, D. A., Mason, O., King, J. A., and Brewin, C. R. (2013). Contextual memory, psychosis-proneness, and experience of intrusive imagery. *Cogn. Emot.* 27, 150–157. doi: 10.1080/02699931.2012.683850

Gracie, A., Freeman, D., Green, S., Garety, P. A., Kuipers, E., Hardy, A., et al. (2007). The association between traumatic experience, paranoia and hallucinations: a test of the predictions of psychological models. *Acta Psychiatr. Scand.* 116, 280–289. doi: 10.1111/j.1600-0447.2007.01011.x

Grey, N., and Holmes, E. A. (2008). "Hotspots" in trauma memories in the treatment of post-traumatic stress disorder: a replication. *Memory* 16, 788–796. doi: 10.1080/09658210802266446

Gumley, A., Taylor, H. E., Schwannauer, M., and Macbeth, A. (2014). A systematic review of attachment and psychosis: measurement, construct validity and outcomes. *Acta Psychiatr. Scand.* 129, 257–274. doi: 10.1111/acps.12172

Hackmann, A., and Holmes, E. (2004). Reflecting on imagery: a clinical perspective and overview of a special issue of memory on mental imagery and memory in psychopathology. *Memory* 12, 389–402. doi: 10.1080/09658210444000133

Hackmann, A., Surawy, C., and Clark, M. (1998). Seeing yourself through others' eyes: a study of spontaneously occurring images in social phobia. *Behav. Cogn. Psychother.* 26, 3–12. doi: 10.1017/S1352465898000022

Hardt, J., and Rutter, M. (2004). Validity of adult retrospective reports of adverse childhood experiences: review of the evidence. *J. Child Psychol. Psychiatry* 45, 260–273. doi: 10.1111/j.1469-7610.2004.00218.x

Hardy, A., Emsley, R., Freeman, D., Bebbington, P., Garety, P. A., Kuipers, E. E., et al. (2016). Psychological mechanisms mediating effects between trauma and psychotic symptoms: the role of affect regulation, intrusive trauma memory, beliefs, and depression. *Schizophr. Bull.* 42(Suppl.), S34–S43. doi: 10.1093/schbul/sbv175

Hardy, A., Fowler, D., Freeman, D., Smith, B., Steel, C., Evans, J., et al. (2005). Trauma and hallucinatory experience in psychosis. *J. Nerv. Ment. Dis.* 193, 501–507. doi: 10.1097/01.nmd.0000172480.56308.21

Hassan, A. N., and De Luca, V. (2015). The effect of lifetime adversities on resistance to antipsychotic treatment in schizophrenia patients. *Schizophr. Res.* 161, 496–500. doi: 10.1016/j.schres.2014.10.048

Hesse, E. (2008). "The adult attachment interview: protocol, method of analysis, and empirical studies," in *Handbook of Attachment: Theory, Research and Clinical Implications*, 2nd Edn, eds J. Cassidy and P. R. Shaver (New York, NY: Guilford Press).

Hill, A. B. (1965). The environment and disease: Association or causation? *Proc. R. Soc. Med.* 58, 295–300.

Hirsch, C. R., and Holmes, E. A. (2007). Mental imagery in anxiety disorders. *Psychiatry* 6, 161–165. doi: 10.1016/j.mppsy.2007.01.005

Hitchcock, C., Werner-Seidler, A., Blackwell, S. E., and Dalgleish, T. (2016). Autobiographical episodic memory-based training for the treatment of mood, anxiety and stress-related disorders: a systematic review and meta-analysis. *Clin. Psychol. Rev.* 52, 92–107. doi: 10.1016/j.cpr.2016.12.003

Holmes, E. A., and Steel, C. (2004). Schizotypy: a vulnerability factor for traumatic intrusions. *J. Nerv. Ment. Dis.* 192, 28–34. doi: 10.1097/01.nmd.0000105997.28152.4b

Ison, R., Medoro, L., Keen, N., and Kuipers, E. (2014). The use of rescripting imagery for people with psychosis who hear voices. *Behav. Cogn. Psychother.* 42, 129–142. doi: 10.1017/S135246581300057X

Isvoranu, A. M., Borsboom, D., van Os, J., and Guloksuz, S. (2016). A network approach to environmental impact in psychotic disorders: brief theoretical framework. *Schizophr. Bull.* 42, 870–873. doi: 10.1093/schbul/sbw049

Isvoranu, A. M., van Borkulo, C. D., Boyette, L. L., Wigman, J. T. W., Vinkers, C. H., Borsboom, D., et al. (2017). A network approach to psychosis: pathways between childhood trauma and psychotic symptoms. *Schizophr. Bull.* 43, 187–196. doi: 10.1093/schbul/sbw055

James, W. (1890). *Principles of Psychology*. New York, NY: Holt. doi: 10.1037/11059-000

Jaya, E. S., Ascone, L., and Lincoln, T. M. (2016). Social adversity and psychosis: the mediating role of cognitive vulnerability. *Schizophr. Bull.* 43, 557–565. doi: 10.1093/schbul/sbw104

Johnson, J., Horwath, E., and Weissman, M. M. (1991). The validity of major depression with psychotic features based on a community study. *Arch. Gen. Psychiatry* 48, 1075–1081. doi: 10.1001/archpsyc.1991.01810360039006

Kelleher, I., and DeVylder, J. E. (2017). Hallucinations in borderline personality disorder and common mental disorders. *Br. J. Psychiatry* 210, 230–231. doi: 10.1192/bjp.bp.116.185249

Kelleher, I., Keeley, H., Corcoran, P., Ramsay, H., Wasserman, C., and Carli, V. (2013). Childhood trauma and psychosis in a prospective cohort study: cause, effect and directionality. *Am. J. Psychiatry* 170, 734–741. doi: 10.1176/appi.ajp.2012.12091169

Kendler, K. S., and Campbell, J. (2009). Interventionist causal models in psychiatry: repositioning the mind-body problem. *Psychol. Med.* 39, 881–887. doi: 10.1017/S0033291708004467

Kessler, R. C., Berglund, P., Demler, O., Jin, R., Merikangas, K. R., and Walters, E. E. (2005). Lifetime prevalence and age of-onset distributions of DSM-IV disorders in the National Comorbidity Survey Replication. *Arch. Gen. Psychiatry* 62, 593–602. doi: 10.1001/archpsyc.62.6.593

Kessler, R. C., Ormel, J., Petukhova, M., McLaughlin, K. A., Green, J. G., and Russo, L. J. (2011). Development of lifetime comorbidity in the WHO World Mental (WMH) Surveys. *Arch. Gen. Psychiatry* 68, 90–100. doi: 10.1001/archgenpsychiatry.2010.180

Kilcommons, A. M., and Morrison, A. P. (2005). Relationships between trauma and psychosis: an exploration of cognitive and dissociative factors. *Acta Psychiatr. Scand.* 112, 351–359. doi: 10.1111/j.1600-0447.2005.00623.x

Kilcommons, A. M., Morrison, A. P., Knight, A., and Lobban, F. (2008). Psychotic experiences in people who have been sexually abused. *Soc. Psychiatry Psychiatr. Epidemiol.* 43, 602–611. doi: 10.1007/s00127-007-0303-z

Kirkpatrick, B., Strauss, G. P., Nguyen, L., Fischer, B. A., Daniel, D. G., Cienfuegos, A., et al. (2011). The brief negative symptom scale: psychometric properties. *Schizophr. Bull.* 37, 300–305. doi: 10.1093/schbul/sbq059

Korver-Nieberg, N., Berry, K., Meijer, C. J., and de Haan, L. (2014). Adult attachment and psychotic phenomenology in clinical and non-clinical samples: a systematic review. *Psychol. Psychother.* 87, 127–154. doi: 10.1111/papt.12010

Kraan, T., Velhorst, E., Smit, F., de Haan, L., and van der Gaag, M. (2015). Trauma and recent life events in individuals at ultra high risk for psychosis: review and meta-analysis. *Schizophr. Res.* 161, 143–149. doi: 10.1016/j.schres.2014.11.026

Kuyken, W., Warren, F. C., Taylor, R. S., Whalley, B., Crane, C., Bondolfi, G., et al. (2016). Efficacy of mindfulness-based cognitive therapy in prevention of depressive relapse: an individual patient data meta-analysis from randomized trials. *JAMA Psychiatry* 73, 565–574. doi: 10.1001/jamapsychiatry.2016.0076

Lang, P. J. (1977). Imagery in therapy: an information processing analysis of fear. *Behav. Ther.* 8, 862–886. doi: 10.1016/S0005-7894(77)80157-3

Lardinois, M., Lataster, T., Mengelers, R., van Os, J., and Myin-Germeys, I. (2011). Childhood trauma and increased stress sensitivity in psychosis. *Acta Psychiatr. Scand.* 123, 28–35. doi: 10.1111/j.1600-0447.2010.01594.x

Lataster, T., Dina, C., Lardinois, M., Valmaggia, L., Van Os, J., and Myin-Germeys, I. (2010). On the pathway from stress to psychosis. *Schizophr. Res.* 117:182. doi: 10.1016/j.schres.2010.02.224

LeDoux, J. (1998). *The Emotional Brain: The Mysterious Underpinnings of Emotional Life*. New York, NY: Simon and Schuster.

Linehan, M. (1993). *Cognitive-Behavioral Treatment of Borderline Personality Disorder*. New York, NY: Guildford Press.

Longden, E., Madill, A., and Waterman, M. G. (2011). Dissociation, trauma, and the role of lived experience: toward a new conceptualization of voice hearing. *Psychol. Bull.* 138, 28–76. doi: 10.1037/a0025995

Looijesetijn, J., Dirk Blom, J., Aleman, A., Hoek, H. W., and Goekoop, R. (2015). An integrated network model of psychotic symptoms. *Neurosci. Biobehav. Rev.* 59, 238–250. doi: 10.1016/j.neubiorev.2015.09.016

Lysaker, P. H., and Larocco, V. A. (2008). The prevalence and correlates of trauma-related symptoms in schizophrenia-spectrum disorder. *Compr. Psychiatry* 49, 330–334. doi: 10.1016/j.comppsych.2007.12.003

Maher, B. A. (1974). Delusional thinking and perceptual disorder. *J. Individ. Psychol.* 30, 98–113.

Main, M., and Hesse, E. (1990). "Parents' unresolved traumatic experiences are related to infant disorganized attachment status: Is frightened or frightening parental behavior the linking mechanism?," in *Attachment in the Preschool Years*, eds M. Greenberg, D. Cicchetti, and E. M. Cummings (Chicago, IL: University of Chicago Press), 161–182.

Martin, M., and Williams, R. (1990). "Imagery and emotion: clinical and experimental approaches," in *Imagery: Current Developments*, eds P. Hampson, P. J. Marks, F. David, and J. T. E. Richardson (Florence, KY: Taylor & Francis), 268–306.

Matheson, S. L., Shepherd, A. M., Pinchbeck, R. M., Laurens, K. R., and Carr, V. J. (2013). Childhood adversity in schizophrenia: a systematic meta-analysis. *Psychol. Med.* 43, 225–238. doi: 10.1017/S0033291712000785

Mayhew, S. L., and Gilbert, P. (2008). Compassionate mind training with people who hear malevolent voices: a case series report. *Clin. Psychol. Psychother.* 15, 113–138. doi: 10.1002/cpp.566

McCarthy-Jones, S., and Longden, E. (2015). Auditory verbal hallucinations in schizophrenia and post-traumatic stress disorder: common phenomenology, common cause, common interventions? *Front. Psychol.* 6:1071. doi: 10.3389/fpsyg.2015.01071

McCarthy-Jones, S., Thomas, N., Strauss, C., Dodgson, G., Jones, N., Woods, A., et al. (2014). Better than mermaids and stray dogs? Subtyping auditory verbal hallucinations and its implications for research and practice. *Schizophr. Bull.* 40(Suppl. 4), S275–S284. doi: 10.1093/schbul/sbu018

McCarthy-Jones, S., Trauer, T., Mackinnon, A., Sims, E., Thomas, N., and Copolov, D. L. (2012). A new phenomenological survey of auditory hallucinations: evidence for subtypes and implications for theory and practice. *Schizophr. Bull.* 40, 231–235. doi: 10.1093/schbul/sbs156

McGrath, J., McLaughlin, K. A., Saha, S., Aguilar-Gaxiola, S., Al-Hamzawi, A., Alonso, J., et al. (2017). The association between childhood adversities and subsequent first onset of psychotic experiences: a cross-national analysis of 23,998 respondents from 17 countries. *Psychol. Med.* 47, 1230–1245. doi: 10.1017/S0033291716003263

Metzler, M., Merrick, M., Klevens, J., Ports, K. A., and Ford, D. (2016). Adverse childhood experiences and life opportunities: shifting the narrative. *Child. Youth Serv. Rev.* 72, 141–149. doi: 10.1016/j.childyouth.2016.10.021

Mondelli, V., Ciufolini, S., Belvederio, M. M., Bonaccorso, S., Di Forti, M., Giordano, A., et al. (2015). Cortisol and inflammatory biomarkers predict poor treatment response in first episode psychosis. *Schizophr. Bull.* 41, 1162–1170. doi: 10.1093/schbul/sbv028

Morgan, C., and Gayer-Anderson, C. (2016). Childhood adversities and psychosis: evidence, challenges, implications. *World Psychiatry* 15, 93–102. doi: 10.1002/wps.20330

Morgan, C., Reininghaus, U., Reichenberg, A., Frissa, S., SELCoH study team, Hotopf, M., et al. (2014). Adversity, cannabis use and psychotic experiences: evidence of cumulative and synergistic effects. *Br. J. Psychiatry* 204, 346–353. doi: 10.1192/bjp.bp.113.134452

Morina, N., Lancee, J., and Arntz, A. (2017). Imagery rescripting as a clinical intervention for aversive memories: a meta-analysis. *J. Behav. Ther. Exp. Psychiatry* 55, 6–15. doi: 10.1016/j.jbtep.2016.11.003

Morris, E. M. J., Johns, L. C., and Oliver, J. E. (2013). *Acceptance and Commitment Therapy and Mindfulness for Psychosis.* London: Wiley-Blackwell. doi: 10.1002/9781118499184

Morrison, A. P. (2001). The interpretation of intrusions in psychosis: an integrative approach to hallucinations and delusions. *Behav. Cogn. Psychother.* 29, 257–276. doi: 10.1017/S1352465801003010

Morrison, A. P. (2017). A manualised treatment protocol to guide delivery of evidence-based cognitive therapy for people with distressing psychosis: learning from clinical trials. *Psychosis.* doi: 10.1080/17522439.2017.1295098 [Epub ahead of print].

Morrison, A. P., Beck, A., Glentworth, D., Dunn, H., Reid, G., Larkin, W., et al. (2002). Imagery and psychotic symptoms: a preliminary investigation. *Behav. Res. Ther.* 40, 1053–1062.

Morrison, A. P., Frame, L., and Larkin, W. (2003). Relationships between trauma and psychosis: a review and integration. *Br. J. Clin. Psychol.* 42, 331–353. doi: 10.1348/014466503322528892

Mueser, K. T., Rosenberg, S. D., Goodman, L. A., and Trumbetta, S. L. (2002). Trauma, PTSD, and the course of severe mental illness: an interactive model. *Schizophr. Res.* 53, 123–143. doi: 10.1016/S0920-9964(01)00173-6

National Institute for Health and Care Excellence [NICE] (2014). *Psychosis and Schizophrenia in Adults: Prevention and Management. NICE Guideline (CG178).* London: National Institute for Health and Care Excellence.

Okkels, N., Trabjerg, B., Arendt, M., and Pedersen, C. B. (2017). Traumatic stress disorders and risk of subsequent schizophrenia spectrum disorder or bipolar disorder: a nationwide cohort study. *Schizophr. Bull.* 43, 180–186. doi: 10.1093/schbul/sbw082

Palmier-Claus, J. E., Berry, K., Bucci, S., Mansell, W., and Varese, F. (2016). Relationship between childhood adversity and bipolar affective disorder: systematic review and meta-analysis. *Br. J. Psychiatry* 209, 454–459. doi: 10.1192/bjp.bp.115.179655

Pearson, M., Brewin, C. R., Rhodes, J., and McCarron, G. (2008). Frequency and nature of rumination in chronic depression: a preliminary study. *Cogn. Behav. Ther.* 37, 160–168. doi: 10.1080/16506070801919224

Perona-Garcelán, S., Carrascoso-Lopez, F., Garcia-Montes, J. M., Ductor-Recuerda, M. J., Jimenez, A. M. L., Vallina-Fernandez, O., et al. (2012). Dissociative experiences as mediators between childhood trauma and auditory hallucinations. *J. Trauma. Stress* 25, 323–329. doi: 10.1002/jts.21693

Pilton, M., Varese, F., Berry, K., and Bucci, S. (2015). The relationship between dissociation and voices: a systematic literature review and meta-analysis. *Clin. Psychol. Rev.* 40, 138–155. doi: 10.1016/j.cpr.2015.06.004

Powers, A., Fani, N., Cross, D., Ressler, K. J., and Bradley, B. (2016). Childhood trauma, PTSD, and psychosis: findings from a highly traumatized, minority sample. *Child Abuse Negl.* 58, 111–118. doi: 10.1016/j.chiabu.2016.06.015

Prebble, S. C., Addis, D. R., and Tippett, L. J. (2013). Autobiographical memory and sense of self. *Psychol. Bull.* 139, 815–840. doi: 10.1037/a0030146

Raffard, S., D'Argembeau, A., Lardi, C., Bayard, S., Boulenger, J. P., and van der Linden, M. (2010). Narrative identity in schizophrenia. *Conscious. Cogn.* 19, 328–340. doi: 10.1016/j.concog.2009.10.005

Read, J., and Bentall, R. P. (2012). Negative childhood experiences and mental health: theoretical, clinical and primary prevention implications. *Br. J. Psychiatry* 200, 89–91. doi: 10.1192/bjp.bp.111.096727

Read, J., Fosse, R., Moskowitz, A., and Perry, B. (2014). The traumagenic neurodevelopmental model of psychosis revisited. *Neuropsychiatry* 4, 65–79. doi: 10.2217/npy.13.89

Read, J., van Os, J., Morrison, A. P., and Ross, C. A. (2005). Childhood trauma, psychosis and schizophrenia: a literature review with theoretical and clinical implications. *Acta Psychiatr. Scand.* 112, 330–350. doi: 10.1111/j.1600-0447.2005.00634.x

Reininghaus, U., Depp, C. A., and Myin-Germeys, I. (2015). Ecological interventionist causal models in psychosis: targeting psychological mechanisms in daily life. *Schizophr. Bull.* 42, 264–269. doi: 10.1093/schbul/sbv193

Resnick, S. G., Bond, G. R., and Mueser, K. T. (2003). Trauma and posttraumatic stress disorder in people with schizophrenia. *J. Abnorm. Psychol.* 112, 415–423. doi: 10.1037/0021-843X.112.3.415

Ricarte, J. J., Ros, L., Latorre, J. M., and Watkins, E. (2017). Mapping autobiographical memory in schizophrenia: clinical implications. *Clin. Psychol. Rev.* 51, 96–108. doi: 10.1016/j.cpr.2016.11.004

Schauer, M., and Elbert, T. (2010). Dissociation following traumatic stress: etiology and treatment. *Z. Psychol.* 218, 109–127. doi: 10.1027/0044-3409/a000018

Schauer, M., Neuner, F., and Elbert, T. (2011). *Narrative Exposure Therapy: A Short-term Treatment for Traumatic Stress Disorders*, 2nd Edn. Gottingen: Hogrefe.

Schneeberger, A. R., Muenzenmaier, K., Castille, D., Battaglia, J., and Link, B. (2014). Use to psychotropic medication groups in people with severe mental illness and stressful childhood experiences. *J. Trauma. Dissociation* 15, 494–511. doi: 10.1080/15299732.2014.903550

Schroeder, K., Fisher, H. L., and Schafer, I. (2013). Psychotic symptoms in patients with borderline personality disorder: prevalence and clinical management. *Curr. Opin. Psychiatry* 26, 113–119. doi: 10.1097/YCO.0b013e32835a2ae7

Schulze, K., Freeman, D., Green, C., and Kuipers, E. (2013). Intrusive mental imagery in patients with persecutory delusions. *Behav. Res. Ther.* 51, 7–14. doi: 10.1016/j.brat.2012.10.002

Selten, J. P., van Os, J., and Cantor-Graae, E. (2016). The social defeat hypothesis of schizophrenia: issues of measurement and reverse causality. *World Psychiatry* 15, 294–295. doi: 10.1002/wps.20369

Seow, L. S., Ong, C., Mahesh, M. V., Sagayadevan, V., Shafie, S., Chong, S. A., et al. (2016). A systematic review on comorbid post-traumatic stress disorder in schizophrenia. *Schizophr. Res.* 176, 441–451. doi: 10.1016/j.schres.2016.05.004

Shapiro, F. (2001). *Eye Movement Desensitization and Reprocessing: Basic Principles, Protocols and Procedures*, 2nd Edn. New York, NY: Guilford Press.

Sheaves, B., Onwumere, J., Keen, N., Stahl, D., and Kuipers, E. (2015). Nightmares in patients with psychosis: the relation with sleep, psychotic, affective and cognitive symptoms. *Can. J. Psychiatry* 60, 354–361.

Singer, J. A., and Salovey, P. (1993). *The Remembered Self: Emotion and Memory in Personality.* New York, NY: Free Press.

Sitko, K., Bentall, R. P., Shevlin, M., O'Sullivan, N., and Sellwood, W. (2014). Associations between specific psychotic symptoms and specific childhood adversities are mediated by attachment styles: an analysis of the National Comorbidity Survey. *Psychiatry Res.* 217, 202–209. doi: 10.1016/j.psychres.2014.03.019

Stampfer, H. G. (1990). "Negative symptoms": A cumulative stress disorder? *Aust. N. Z. J. Psychiatry* 24, 516–528. doi: 10.3109/00048679009062908

Steel, C., Doukani, A., and Hardy, A. (2017a). The PCL as a brief screen for posttraumatic stress disorder within schizophrenia. *Int. J. Psychiatry Clin. Pract.* 2, 1–3. doi: 10.1080/13651501.2016.1271897

Steel, C., Fowler, D., and Holmes, E. A. (2005). Traumatic intrusions in psychosis: an information processing account. *Behav. Cogn. Psychother.* 33, 139–152. doi: 10.1017/S1352465804001924

Steel, C., Hardy, A., Smith, B., Wykes, T., Rose, S., Enright, S., et al. (2017b). Cognitive-behaviour therapy for post-traumatic stress in schizophrenia: a randomized controlled trial. *Psychol. Med.* 47, 43–51. doi: 10.1017/S0033291716002117

Steel, C., Mahmood, M., and Holmes, E. A. (2008). Positive schizotypy and trait dissociation as vulnerability factors for post-traumatic distress. *Br. J. Clin. Psychol.* 47, 245–249. doi: 10.1348/014466507X255276

Steel, C., van der Gaag, M., Korrelboom, K., Simon, J., Phiri, P., Baksh, F., et al. (2015). A randomised controlled trial of positive memory training for the treatment of depression within schizophrenia. *BMC Psychiatry* 15:85. doi: 10.1186/s12888-015-0453-6

Trotta, A., Murray, R. M., and Fisher, H. L. (2015). The impact of childhood adversity on the persistence of psychotic symptoms: a systematic review and meta-analysis. *Psychol. Med.* 45, 2481–2498. doi: 10.1017/S0033291715000574

Tulving, E. (2002). Episodic memory: from mind to brain. *Annu. Rev. Psychol.* 53, 1–25. doi: 10.1146/annurev.psych.53.100901.135114

Tulving, E. (2005). "Episodic memory and autonoesis: uniquely human?," in *The Missing Link in Cognition*, eds H. S. Terrace and J. Metcalfe (Oxford: Oxford University Press), 3–56.

Tulving, E., Hayman, C. A., and Macdonald, C. A. (1991). Long-lasting perceptual priming and semantic learning in amnesia: a case experiment. *J. Exp. Psychol. Learn. Mem. Cogn.* 17, 595–617. doi: 10.1037/0278-7393.17.4.595

Udachina, A., Varese, F., Myin-Germeys, I., and Bentall, R. P. (2014). The role of experiential avoidance in paranoid delusions: an experience sampling study. *Br. J. Clin. Psychol.* 54, 422–432. doi: 10.1111/bjc.12054

Valmaggia, L. R., Day, F., Garety, P., Freeman, D., Antley, A., Slater, M., et al. (2016). Social defeat predicts paranoid appraisals in people at high risk for psychosis. *Schizophr. Res.* 168, 16–22. doi: 10.1016/j.schres.2015.07.050

van Dam, D. S., Korver-Nieberg, N., Velthorst, E., Meijer, C. J., and de Haan, L. (2014). Childhood maltreatment, adult attachment and psychotic symptomatology: a study in patients, siblings and controls. *Soc. Psychiatry Psychiatr. Epidemiol.* 11, 1759–1767. doi: 10.1007/s00127-014-0894-0

van Dam, D. S., van Nierop, M., Viechtbauer, W., Velthorst, E., van Winkel, R., Group investigators, et al. (2015). Childhood abuse and neglect in relation to the presence and persistence of psychotic and depressive symptomatology. *Psychol. Med.* 45, 1363–1377. doi: 10.1017/S0033291714001561

van den Berg, D. P. G., de Bont, P. A., van der Vleugel, B. M., de Roos, C., de Jongh, A., van Minnen, A., et al. (2015). Prolonged exposure vs eye movement desensitization and reprocessing vs waiting list for posttraumatic stress disorder in patients with a psychotic disorder: a randomized clinical trial. *JAMA Psychiatry* 72, 259–267. doi: 10.1001/jamapsychiatry.2014.2637

van Nierop, M., Lataster, T., Smeets, F., Gunther, N., van Zelst, C., de Graaf, R., et al. (2014a). Psychopathological mechanisms linking childhood traumatic experiences to risk of psychotic symptoms: analysis of a large, representative population-based sample. *Schizophr. Bull.* 40(Suppl. 2), S123–S130. doi: 10.1093/schbul/sbt150

van Nierop, M., van Os, J., Gunther, N., de Graaf, R., ten Have, M., van Dorsselaer, S., et al. (2014b). Does social defeat mediate the association between childhood trauma and psychosis? *Acta Psychiatr. Scand.* 129, 467–476. doi: 10.1111/acps.12212

van Nierop, M., Viechbauer, W., Gunther, N., van Zeist, C., de Graaf, R., Ten Have, M., et al. (2015). Childhood trauma is associated with a specific admixture of affective, anxiety, psychosis symptoms cutting across traditional diagnostic boundaries. *Psychol. Med.* 45, 1277–1288. doi: 10.1017/S003329171400 2372

Varese, F., Barkus, E., and Bentall, R. P. (2012a). Dissociation mediates the relationship between childhood trauma and hallucination-proneness. *Psychol. Med.* 42, 1025–1036. doi: 10.1017/S0033291711001826

Varese, F., Smeets, F., Drukker, M., Lieverse, R., Lataster, T., Viechtbauer, W., et al. (2012b). Childhood adversities increase the risk of psychosis: a meta-analysis of patient-control, prospective- and cross-sectional cohort studies. *Schizophr. Bull.* 38, 661–671. doi: 10.1093/schbul/sbs050

Varese, V., Tai, S. J., Pearson, L., and Mansell, W. (2016). Thematic associations between personal goals and clinical and non-clinical voices (auditory verbal hallucinations). *Psychosis* 8, 12–22. doi: 10.1080/17522439.2015.1040442

Veling, W., Counotte, J., Pot-Kolder, R., van Os, J., and van der Gaag, M. (2016). Childhood trauma, psychosis liability and social stress reactivity: a virtual reality study. *Psychol. Med.* 46, 3339–3348. doi: 10.1017/S0033291716002208

Vogel, M., Braungardt, T., Grabe, H. J., Schneider, W., and Klauer, T. (2013). Detachment, compartmentalization, and schizophrenia: linking dissociation and psychosis by subtype. *J. Trauma. Dissociation* 14, 273–287. doi: 10.1080/15299732.2012.724760

Vogel, M., Meier, J., Gronke, S., Waage, M., Schneider, W., Freyberger, H. J., et al. (2011). Differential effects of childhood abuse and neglect: mediation by posttraumatic distress in neurotic disorder and negative symptoms in schizophrenia? *Psychiatry Res.* 189, 121–127. doi: 10.1016/j.psychres.2011.01.008

Walters, S., Hogg, L., and Gillmore, C. (2016). Evaluation of a tailored training programme to improve the assessment and treatment of trauma in an Early Intervention in Psychosis (EIP) service. *Psychosis* 8, 226–237. doi: 10.1080/17522439.2015.1131324

Waters, F. A. V., Badcock, J. C., Michie, P. T., and Mayberry, M. T. (2006). Auditory hallucinations in schizophrenia: intrusive thoughts and forgotten memories. *Cogn. Neuropsychiatry* 11, 65–83. doi: 10.1080/13546800444000191

Wickham, S., and Bentall, R. P. (2016). Are specific early-life adversities associated with specific symptoms of psychosis? A patient study considering just world beliefs as a mediator. *J. Nerv. Ment. Dis.* 204, 606–613. doi: 10.1097/NMD.0000000000000511

Wickham, S., Sitko, K., and Bentall, R. P. (2015). Insecure attachment is associated with paranoia but not hallucinations in psychotic patients: the mediating role of negative self-esteem. *Psychol. Med.* 45, 1495–1507. doi: 10.1017/S0033291714002633

Williams, J. M. G., Barnhofer, T., Crane, C., Hermans, D., Raes, F., Watkins, E., et al. (2007). Autobiographical memory specificity and emotional disorder. *Psychol. Bull.* 133, 122–148. doi: 10.1037/0033-2909.133.1.122

Woods, A., Jones, N., Alderson-Day, B., Callard, F., and Fernyhough, C. (2015). Experiences of hearing voices: analysis of a novel phenomenological survey. *Lancet Psychiatry* 2, 323–331. doi: 10.1016/S2215-0366(15)00006-1

Young, J. E., Klosko, J. S., and Weishaar, M. E. (2003). *Schema Therapy: A Practitioners Guide.* New York, NY: Guilford Press.

13

Psychological Interventions for Post-traumatic Stress Symptoms in Psychosis

Sarah Swan[1]*, *Nadine Keen*[1,2], *Nicola Reynolds*[1,2] *and Juliana Onwumere*[1,2]

[1] *South London and Maudsley NHS Foundation Trust, London, UK,* [2] *Department of Psychology, Institute of Psychiatry, Psychology and Neuroscience, King's College London, London, UK*

Edited by:
Kate Hardy,
Stanford University, USA

Reviewed by:
Sally E. Riggs,
NYC CBTp, USA
Richard James Brown,
University of Manchester, UK

***Correspondence:**
Sarah Swan
sarah.swan@slam.nhs.uk

Individuals with severe mental health problems, such as psychosis, are consistently shown to have experienced high levels of past traumatic events. They are also at an increased risk of further traumatisation through victimization events such as crime and assault. The experience of psychosis itself and psychiatric hospitalization have also been recognized to be sufficiently traumatic to lead to the development of post-traumatic stress (PTS) symptoms. Rates of post-traumatic stress disorder (PTSD) are elevated in people with psychosis compared to the general population. The current guidance for the treatment of PTSD is informed by an evidence base predominately limited to populations without co-morbid psychiatric disorders. The systematic review therefore sought to present the current available literature on the use of psychological treatments targeting PTS symptoms in a population with a primary diagnosis of a psychotic disorder. The review aimed to investigate the effect of these interventions on PTS symptoms and also the effect on secondary domains such as psychotic symptoms, affect and functioning. Fifteen studies were identified reporting on cognitive behavior therapy, prolonged exposure, eye movement desensitisation and reprocessing and written emotional disclosure. The review provides preliminary support for the safe use of trauma-focused psychological interventions in groups of people with severe mental health problems. Overall, the interventions were found to be effective in reducing PTS symptoms. Results were mixed with regard to secondary effects on additional domains. Further research including studies employing sufficiently powered methodologically rigorous designs is indicated.

Keywords: psychosis, SMI, trauma, post-traumatic stress disorder, PTSD, therapy, psychological intervention

INTRODUCTION

For the majority of individuals in the general adult population, one traumatic experience is likely to occur within their lifetime (Frans et al., 2005; Breslau, 2009). The associated distress is mostly short-lived and diminishes of its own accord (Bisson, 2007). For a proportion, however, distress can continue and symptoms of post-traumatic stress (PTS) can develop. A PTS response is characterised by a number of core symptoms including: intrusive or re-experiencing symptoms such as flashbacks and nightmares; persistent cognitive and/or behavioural avoidance;

negative changes to cognition and affect, and a marked increase in arousal and reactivity such as hypervigiliance and exaggerated startle (American Psychiatric Association, 2013). Post-traumatic stress disorder (PTSD) is diagnosed when a person presents with a combination of symptoms from these core symptom groups, typically within the context of increased distress and disturbance to functioning. Approximately 3% of the general adult population is estimated to have PTSD and an additional 3.6% are thought to experience PTS symptoms which do not meet full diagnostic criteria for a diagnosis of PTSD i.e., sub-threshold (McLaughlin et al., 2015). The diagnosis is associated with significant disturbance to occupational and social functioning (Karam et al., 2014), increased substance misuse (Bisson, 2007), higher suicidality (Sareen et al., 2007) and increased health and social service use (Atwoli et al., 2015).

PTSD is highly co-morbid with other psychiatric diagnoses (Greene et al., 2016) and the co-occurrence of PTS symptoms and more severe mental health difficulties is an area of increasing interest. Individuals with psychosis, in particular, are consistently shown to have experienced high levels of trauma (Lommen and Restifo, 2009; Varese et al., 2012). This group also have an increased risk of continued exposure to traumatic events. Rates of victimisation have been reported to be between 2.3 and 140.4 times higher in people with severe mental illness (SMI) than in the general population; with this vulnerability thought to arise from their current mental state and associated social context such as poverty, homelessness, and social isolation (Maniglio, 2009). There has also been an increasing recognition of the traumatising effects of psychiatric hospitalisation and psychotic symptoms. Significant numbers of individuals with psychosis are shown to develop a PTS response to symptoms of psychosis or hospital experiences severe enough to meet diagnostic criteria for PTSD (Berry et al., 2013). Experiences such as being given medication against one's will, being detained under the Mental Health Act (1983, as amended in 2007) (Tarrier et al., 2007) and threatening auditory hallucinations (Beattie et al., 2009) can lead to PTS symptoms. Following the latest changes to PTSD diagnostic criteria in DSM-V (American Psychiatric Association, 2013), in which the stressor criterion A2: "*the person's response involved intense fear, helplessness or horror*" was removed, controversy remains over whether hospitalisation or symptom related experiences can be sufficiently categorised within the trauma criterion (Jackson et al., 2004). However, the debate regarding DSM changes to criterion A remains outside the scope of this review; for further discussion see published works e.g., Friedman et al. (2011) and Karam et al. (2010). Regardless of this debate, given the high exposure to traumatic events that people with severe mental health problems typically have endured, it is unsurprising that the prevalence of PTS symptoms in this group is higher than that of the general population (Mueser et al., 2002).

The finding that a substantial proportion of people with psychosis and other severe mental health problems can present with PTS symptoms is of growing importance in clinical settings. In the recently updated treatment guidance on psychosis and schizophrenia from the National Institute for Health and Care Excellence (NICE) (National Institute for Health and Care Excellence, 2014), it is acknowledged that individuals are likely to have experienced trauma through events related to the development of psychosis and/or trauma as a direct result of the psychosis itself. Consequently the guidance calls for all service users to be routinely assessed for PTS symptoms. Screening for secondary co-morbid mental health difficulties is of particular importance due to the associated poorer outcome for individuals with multiple mental health difficulties (Buckley et al., 2009). For individuals with psychosis and co-morbid PTSD specifically, there is a positive correlation with increased cognitive, affective and behaviour disturbance (Seedat et al., 2003), reduced quality of life and greater acute service use (Grubaugh et al., 2011). There are also the implications of cost related directly to service use and the wider economic burden incurred through loss of ability to work and welfare (Insel, 2008).

The NICE clinical guidance for PTSD management (National Institute for Health and Care Excellence, 2005) recommends the use of trauma-focused cognitive behaviour therapy (TF-CBT) and TF-CBT and/or eye movement desensitisation and reprocessing (EMDR) as the first line treatment for PTS symptoms present for less than 3 months and those present for longer periods, respectively. The evidence base for the efficacy of TF-CBT and EMDR in reducing PTS symptoms is well established within an adult population (Bisson and Andrew, 2005). As with many intervention outcome trials, strict inclusion criteria are often employed to achieve a homogenous group in an attempt to reduce variance or confounding factors that may arise in an increasingly heterogeneous sample (Green, 2006). In practice, trials tend to include participants with a sole diagnosis of PTSD, with co-morbidity an exclusion criterion. Diagnosis of a psychotic condition is the most common exclusion criterion within many randomised controlled clinical trials (de Bont et al., 2013a). Though the co-occurrence of PTS symptoms and psychosis is emerging as a relatively common phenomenon, the evidence base is mostly limited to individuals without co-morbid conditions. Where the evidence base and clinical guidance is orientated to single morbidity, practitioners are placed in a position where they must rely upon their clinical judgement in treatment decision making (Hughes et al., 2013). It thus follows that mental health professionals are arguably faced with the difficulty of having to infer whether the generally recommended trauma treatments are appropriate for individuals with psychosis. This is further complicated by the fact that therapists are often reluctant to treat PTS symptoms due to concerns that the experiential reprocessing of trauma may exacerbate psychotic symptoms (Becker et al., 2004; Gairns et al., 2015).

The review therefore seeks to complement the existing trauma intervention literature (e.g., Bisson and Andrew, 2005; Mabey and Servellen, 2014; Sin and Spain, 2016) by presenting the breadth of current evidence for the use of psychological interventions targeting PTS symptoms within people with a primary diagnosis of psychosis. The systematic review will seek to address the following questions: (i) what are the psychological interventions with published data on their use to treat PTS symptoms in people with psychosis; (ii) how effective are these treatments in treating PTS symptoms; and (iii) how effective are these treatments in bringing about change in co-morbid psychiatric symptoms or secondary domains (i.e., psychosis, depression, anxiety, functioning).

METHODS

Criteria and Definitions

Study Inclusion

Studies were selected for consideration in the review if they presented outcome data on the effect of one or more psychological interventions targeting PTS symptoms in adults with psychosis. Studies employing a randomised controlled trial design, non-randomised controlled, un-controlled, case series and single n methodology were included. Studies were required to be published in peer reviewed journals with the abstract and content written in English. Studies which did not report on a measure of PTS symptoms were excluded.

Population

Studies for inclusion were required to present data on individuals over the age of 16 years old with a primary diagnosis of a psychotic disorder (including schizophrenia and related disorders, schizoaffective disorder, non-organic psychoses according to either DSM or ICD criteria). Studies were not restricted to those reporting on homogenous psychosis populations. Studies could be included if they reported on a mixed SMI group as long as they included individuals with psychosis. Such studies were included due to the limited evidence base and the authors' intention to provide a representative reflection of the emerging evidence. Studies were not excluded if the population had additional co-morbid disorders, such as depression, anxiety or Axis II diagnoses.

Studies were required to include a population as outlined above with: (i) an additional co-morbid diagnosis of PTSD, according to DSM or ICD criteria; or (ii) the presence of PTS symptoms as indicated by standardised measures. The studies for consideration were not limited on the basis of PTS symptom severity, duration or nature of the traumatic event. Regarding the latter, the index traumatic event could include the experience of symptoms of psychosis or events relating to hospitalisation in addition to more "traditional" notions of a traumatic event as defined by diagnostic criteria.

Psychological Intervention

Psychological interventions were defined for this review as any non-pharmacological treatment specifically aiming to target psychological processes implicated in contributing to symptoms of psychological distress. Treatments were required to be based on psychological theories or models of psychopathology and/or include a clearly defined protocol of treatment (including behavioural, cognitive or other psychotherapeutic techniques) or a theoretical hypothesis for treatment efficacy. An intervention could be delivered within an inpatient or community setting, individually or in a group and be therapist or non-therapist led.

Search

Procedure

The search methods employed to identify potentially relevant studies according to the inclusion criteria and definitions involved the computerised searching of four widely used electronic databases: Embase, PsychINFO, MEDLINE, and Web of Science. Advanced keyword search strategy was conducted by combining the following terms: ("psychosis" OR "psychotic disorder" OR "schizophren*") AND ("ptsd" OR "trauma*" OR "post trauma*" OR "post-trauma*" OR "life event" OR "acute stress") AND ("counsel*" OR "psychological therapy" OR "psychotherapy" OR "talking therapy" OR "intervention"). Regarding the PTS search, a broad selection of terms were included to reflect the heterogeneous use of terminology within the literature, where a number of different descriptors are often employed to describe the same phenomenon.

Additional identification of potential studies was conducted through manual screening of relevant reviews, personal communication with study authors and searching of reference lists of the articles selected for inclusion in the review.

Screening Methodology

Records generated from the electronic search were exported to bibliographic software and duplicates removed electronically. A second screening was conducted manually to remove remaining duplicate records. Articles were chosen for inclusion by firstly screening the titles, and then by reviewing abstracts of titles deemed potentially relevant. Full text articles were then sourced for potentially relevant records and read in full to determine if the study met the full review inclusion criteria. All stages of screening were undertaken independently by the authors. In cases where there was a disagreement, discussion between the authors took place until consensus was reached.

Quality Assessment

Study quality was assessed using the Clinical Trial Assessment Measure (CTAM) (Tarrier and Wykes, 2004). This quality assessment tool is designed to consider the key methodological and design factors within psychotherapeutic intervention trials in mental health research. The assessment tool includes 15 items, falling under six methodological categories: sample size/method of recruitment, treatment allocation, assessment of outcome, control groups, treatment description and analysis. The measure has been used within reviews of psychological interventions (Gregg and Tarrier, 2007; Tarrier et al., 2008) and in reviews specifically within psychosis (Tarrier and Wykes, 2004; Wykes et al., 2008, 2011).

RESULTS

Search Results

A total of 1,949 studies were identified from electronic database searching. Following the removal of duplicate records, 1,477 remained. Records that were not journal articles (i.e., books or book chapters) were then excluded resulting in a pool of 1,218 records which were then screened for eligibility. Full text screening was conducted for 15 articles. At this stage the articles' references were reviewed to identify additional relevant records. Via this method and through direct correspondence with article authors, an additional nine records were identified and full text screened. Fifteen studies were selected to be included in the final review (see **Figure 1** for PRISMA flow diagram) (Moher et al., 2009).

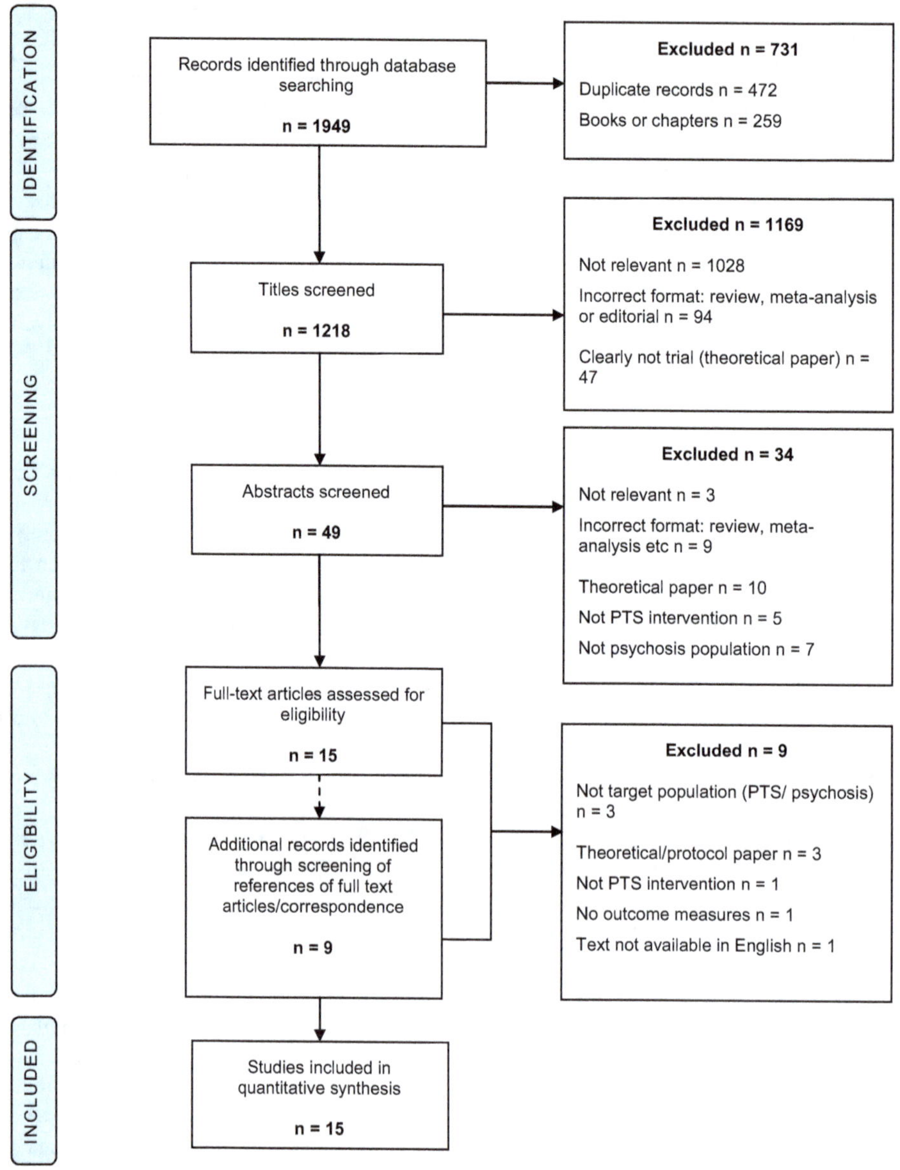

FIGURE 1 | PRISMA flow diagram.

Overview of Included Studies

The studies included in the review varied in study design. Two articles employed single n methodology reporting on a single case study and two studies reported on a case series of two and three participants, respectively. The remaining articles included five un-controlled studies, one non-randomised controlled study and five randomised controlled trials (RCT).

Supplementary Table 1 provides a summary of the characteristics and main findings of each article in the review. Seven studies were conducted in the United States of America (USA), four in the United Kingdom, three in the Netherlands and one in Australia. Eleven studies investigated CBT or a CBT informed intervention e.g., cognitive recovery intervention (CRI), two PE and EMDR, one EMDR alone, and one the use of written emotional disclosure. Twelve studies reported on interventions delivered individually, two via a group format and one study used a mixed group and individual therapy implementation.

Sample Characteristics

The studies reported on a total sample of 585 participants; with the total number of participants per study ranging from 1 to 155. The age of the seven participants in the case studies/series ranged from 31 to 56 years. Of the trial papers, the mean age was 39.7 years (SD 8.5); data were available for 10 of the 11 articles. Fourteen of the studies reported on demographic

TABLE 1 | Primary diagnosis inclusion criteria of included studies.

Study	Primary diagnosis inclusion criteria
Callcott et al., 2004; Hamblen et al., 2004; Kevan et al., 2007; Kayrouz and Vrklevski, 2015	Not applicable as case study/case series
Rosenberg et al., 2004	DSM-IV diagnosis of schizophrenia, schizoaffective disorder, major depression or psychotic disorder not otherwise specified
Bernard et al., 2006; Jackson et al., 2009	ICD-10 diagnosis of schizophrenia, persistent delusional disorders, acute and transient psychotic disorders or schizoaffective disorders (ICD-10 F20, F22, F23, F25)
Mueser et al., 2007	Severe mental illness as defined by DSM-IV Axis I or II disorder and functional impairment with respect to ability to work or care for oneself
Trappler and Newville, 2007; Frueh et al., 2009	DSM-IV diagnosis of schizophrenia or schizoaffective disorder
Mueser et al., 2008; Lu et al., 2009	DSM-IV diagnosis of schizophrenia, schizoaffective disorder, major depression or bipolar disorder
van den Berg and van der Gaag, 2012	Schizophrenia Spectrum Disorder (Diagnostic system not specified)
de Bont et al., 2013a; van den Berg et al., 2015	DSM-IV diagnosis of a psychotic disorder or mood disorder with psychotic features

TABLE 2 | Quality assessment CTAM ratings for papers categorized by study design.

Design	Study	Total CTAM score	Mean Score (SD)
Case study Case series	Callcott et al., 2004	9	11.00 (2.45)
	Hamblen et al., 2004	12	
	Kevan et al., 2007	14	
	Kayrouz and Vrklevski, 2015	9	
Un-controlled study	Rosenberg et al., 2004	28	29.80 (4.27)
	Mueser et al., 2007	34	
	Frueh et al., 2009	34	
	Lu et al., 2009	24	
	van den Berg and van der Gaag, 2012	29	
Controlled study (non-randomised)	Trappler and Newville, 2007	26	n/a
Controlled study (RCT)	Bernard et al., 2006	67	75.20 (15.07)
	Mueser et al., 2008	87	
	Jackson et al., 2009	77	
	de Bont et al., 2013a	54	
	van den Berg et al., 2015	91	
	Grand mean (SD)	39.67 (28.38)	

gender information ($n = 537$); with 59.6% of the sample being female. Eight studies reported on participant ethnicity; where the percentage of non-white participants per study ranged from 0 to 58%. Twelve studies recruited participants from community mental health services, two from inpatient services and one from both community and inpatient services.

Four studies (case studies and case series) did not employ inclusion or exclusion criteria by virtue of the research design. The case studies reported on individuals with a primary diagnosis of paranoid schizophrenia (Kayrouz and Vrklevski, 2015) and schizophrenia (Kevan et al., 2007); where the presence of significant PTS symptoms was confirmed using self report measures. The case series reported on two participants both meeting ICD-10 criteria for schizophrenia and PTSD (Callcott et al., 2004) and on three individuals all meeting DSM-IV criteria for PTSD; one with a primary diagnosis of bipolar affective disorder (BPAD) and two with a diagnosis of schizoaffective disorder (Hamblen et al., 2004). The remaining 11 studies varied in their inclusion criteria regarding primary diagnostic categories (see **Table 1**). The number of participants with a primary diagnosis of a psychotic disorder, as opposed to another diagnosis meeting criteria for SMI such as a mood disorder, ranged from 15.7 to 100% of the sample. Two studies reported solely on participants experiencing a first episode of psychosis (Bernard et al., 2006; Jackson et al., 2009).

Eight of the 11 studies required participants to have a secondary formal diagnosis of PTSD (Rosenberg et al., 2004; Mueser et al., 2007, 2008; Frueh et al., 2009; Lu et al., 2009; de Bont et al., 2013a; van den Berg et al., 2015). In one study it was reported that participants had co-morbid PTSD but it was unclear as to whether this was formally diagnosed or indicated through self-report measures (Trappler and Newville, 2007). Two studies did not stipulate the necessity of a baseline significant presence of PTS symptoms; however trauma-related symptoms were measured and identified as the target of the interventions (Bernard et al., 2006; Jackson et al., 2009).

Description of Interventions

Cognitive Behaviour Therapy (CBT)

CBT interventions targeting PTS symptoms, as described in the literature, have in common four key elements: psycho-education, anxiety management; exposure and cognitive restructuring. The way in which any one of these components is delivered or the extent to which they are emphasised within the intervention varies from one study to another. Four studies in the review described the heterogeneous implementation of a CBT intervention; one study focused on cognitive restructuring following initial written elaboration of trauma memory (Kevan et al., 2007), one study incorporated the use of Smucker's child sexual abuse imagery rescripting (Callcott et al., 2004), one study predominately used exposure preceded by Cloitre's Skill Training in Affect Regulation preparatory work (Trappler and Newville, 2007) and the final study from Kayrouz and Vrklevski (2015) drew on schema therapy ideas.

Six studies reported on the use of a CBT protocol developed specifically for the treatment of PTS symptoms in individuals with SMI (Hamblen et al., 2004; Rosenberg et al., 2004; Mueser et al., 2007, 2008; Frueh et al., 2009; Lu et al., 2009). The main components of the protocol designed by Frueh et al. (2009) were psycho-education, anxiety management, social skills training and exposure therapy. The article described the intervention delivered in a mixed group and individual format over an 11 week period. The exposure element was delivered individually, with the preceding therapy components initially delivered in a group. Four studies used the SMI protocol outlined by Mueser et al. (Lu et al., 2009) which was delivered individually. The protocol summarised an eight stage modular intervention, delivered over 12–16 sessions, broadly grouped into five parts: introduction/engagement, breathing retraining, psycho-education, cognitive restructuring and termination. One study (Mueser et al., 2007) used an adapted version of this protocol delivered in a group over an increased number of sessions.

One of the 11 studies (Jackson et al., 2009) reported on cognitive recovery intervention (CRI); a CBT informed intervention. CRI is a modular protocol based therapy designed to aid psychological recovery and adjustment to first episode psychosis over a period of 6 months (with a maximum of 26 sessions). The three main elements of CRI include engagement/formulation, trauma processing and psychotic illness appraisal (shame, loss, entrapment). Appraisals relating to shame, loss and entrapment have been implicated in the development and maintenance of PTS symptoms (Lu et al., 2009). Hence, cognitive techniques such as developing alternative beliefs are used to challenge and bring about change in these appraisals.

Prolonged Exposure (PE)

Two studies reported on PE (de Bont et al., 2013a; van den Berg et al., 2015). PE is an approach which involves the systematic exposure to previously avoided trauma related stimuli, either via imaginal exposure or *in-vivo* means. Both studies reported on PE delivered in accordance with the manual by Foa et al. (2007), in 90 min sessions. Therapy sessions involved initial case conceptualisation, development of an exposure hierarchy and then repeated exposure within the remaining sessions. In addition, exposure was continued outside of session by listening to audio recordings of the exposure 5 days a week.

Eye Movement Desensitisation and Reprocessing (EMDR)

EMDR was evaluated in three studies (van den Berg and van der Gaag, 2012; de Bont et al., 2013a; van den Berg et al., 2015). All employed the use of the Dutch translation of the standard eight phase EMDR protocol (Shapiro, 2001). Broadly this protocol involves the following: history and treatment planning; preparation of self-control techniques and engagement; assessment and identification of trauma memories; desensitisation including bilateral stimulation typically via visual tracking of the therapist moving their fingers back and forth; installation of positive cognition; body scan; closure involving the implementation of self-control techniques; re-evaluation and review (Menon and Jayan, 2010).

Written Emotional Disclosure

One study (Bernard et al., 2006) reported on the use of written emotional disclosure; where individuals are invited to provide a written account of traumatic experiences. The study used an adapted protocol from Pennebaker and Beall (1986) where participants were asked to write specifically about the experience of psychosis and the related treatment that was perceived as the most stressful and upsetting, doing so for 15 min at three separate time points. The intervention is entirely led by the individual and is not delivered by a therapist.

Outcomes

PTS Symptoms and Trauma Related Measures

For the purpose of this review, measures and results have been categorised into PTSD/ PTS symptoms and measures of all other domains. It should be noted that this is not necessarily the categorisation used within the original articles (for example some studies have included measures of mood as a primary outcome) however to enable clarity in presenting the findings, this crude grouping has been applied and the implications reviewed in the discussion section.

In all 15 studies, the primary outcome was PTSD diagnosis or PTS symptoms. In seven studies (46.7%), where the outcome measure was clinician rated, the Clinician Administered PTSD Scale (CAPS) was used. The remaining eight studies (53.3%) used self-report measures of PTS symptoms (see Supplementary Table 1 for measures used).

Secondary Domains

Eight studies (53.3%) reported on general psychopathology and distress (Callcott et al., 2004; Hamblen et al., 2004; Rosenberg et al., 2004; Trappler and Newville, 2007; Mueser et al., 2008; Frueh et al., 2009; Lu et al., 2009; de Bont et al., 2013a). Ten studies (66.7%) (Callcott et al., 2004; Bernard et al., 2006; Kevan et al., 2007; Mueser et al., 2007, 2008; Frueh et al., 2009; Jackson et al., 2009; Lu et al., 2009; van den Berg and van der Gaag, 2012; Kayrouz and Vrklevski, 2015) reported on symptoms of depression. Four studies included measures of anxiety. Three studies included measures of psychotic symptoms (Callcott et al., 2004; van den Berg and van der Gaag, 2012; de Bont et al., 2013b). Additional secondary outcomes such as recovery style and insight (Bernard et al., 2006), working alliance (Mueser et al., 2008), anger and satisfaction (Frueh et al., 2009), self-esteem (Jackson et al., 2009; van den Berg and van der Gaag, 2012) and social functioning (de Bont et al., 2013a) were included.

Quality Assessment

The outcome of the quality assessment for each study included in the review is presented in **Table 2**. The CTAM total scores ranged from 9 to 91 (with a maximum score of 100). The mean total CTAM score across all studies was 39.67 (SD 28.38). The methodology employed across the studies varied greatly.

The case studies and case series all tended to employ standardised measures and reported on a protocol or described the intervention used in detail. Case studies and case series did not include blinded assessment of outcome and most did not employ statistical methods to evaluate the outcome of the intervention therefore were mostly judged not to have employed appropriate analyses strategies. The five un-controlled studies failed to report on power analyses and had small sample sizes excluding one study. By nature of their design these studies did not include randomisation and were all deemed to use appropriate methods of analysis however the adequate management of drop outs varied. All studies provided a description of the intervention however some studies did not report on adherence to protocol. Of the six controlled studies, half reported on power analyses or included more than 27 participants in each group and all but one involved random group allocation with most describing this process. Of the five RCTs all but one used standardised measures conducted by a blinded independent assessor. There was greater consistency in these studies to use adequate analysis strategies and manage participants that had dropped out in the analysis. All RCTs used and described a protocol driven intervention and reported on therapist adherence.

A CTAM score of 65 or above is considered to be indicative of sound methodological vigour and therefore good quality research with regard to the evaluation of psychological interventions in mental health (Tarrier and Wykes, 2004). Four of the 15 studies (26.67%) in this review scored above this cut off. Given that the review includes two articles employing single n methodology, two studies reporting on a case series and five un-controlled studies the quality scores were predicted to be lower due to the nature of research designs employed.

Findings: PTS and Trauma Related Outcomes

CBT

Four case studies/series reported on CBT delivered individually. The two case studies demonstrated reductions in PTS symptoms following treatment. One case no longer met criteria for PTSD and saw simultaneous reductions in trauma cognitions relative to pre-treatment scores (Kevan et al., 2007) and for the other case PTS scores fell below clinical range (Kayrouz and Vrklevski, 2015). Both cases in Callcott et al. (2004) study demonstrated reductions in symptoms, with one case moving to below clinical range. The same pattern was found for the case series by Hamblen et al. (2004) where two cases no longer met diagnostic criteria for PTSD and gains were maintained at 3 month follow-up. Three additional studies reported on CBT delivered individually and all drew upon a protocol designed specifically for individuals with SMI (Rosenberg et al., 2004; Mueser et al., 2008; Lu et al., 2009). All showed a significant effect of treatment on PTS symptoms.

In an un-controlled pilot study (Rosenberg et al., 2004) 11/12 participants showed a significant reduction in PTS symptoms. For the majority these gains were maintained or further reduced at 3 month follow-up. Significantly fewer participants met diagnostic criteria at follow-up (50%) compared to baseline (100%). Mueser et al. (2008) RCT also showed a significant reduction in symptoms for the CBT group compared to TAU. In their study, CBT proved to be no more effective than TAU in participants no longer meeting diagnostic criteria for a PTSD diagnosis. The study further showed that the effect size of change in PTS symptoms and meeting diagnostic criteria increased for participants with baseline PTS symptoms in the severe range and the effect size greatly reduced for those with a mild to moderate severity. This suggests a greater benefit of treatment for those with more severe symptoms. In keeping with these results, Lu et al. (2009) study conducted with an ethnically diverse sample (58% non-European American) showed significant reductions in PTS symptoms post-treatment and at 3 and 6 month follow-up. There was a significant reduction in the number of participants meeting diagnostic criteria for PTSD across all time points compared to baseline using the PCL. This was also the case for the PDS with comparisons between baseline and at all time points, excluding post-treatment.

Two studies reported on CBT delivered in a group format where treatment effects were demonstrated. Compared to a supportive counselling group, the CBT group saw significant reductions in PTS symptoms post-treatment (Trappler and Newville, 2007). Mueser et al.'s pilot study (Mueser et al., 2008) found significant reductions in PTS symptoms post-treatment and at 3 month follow-up. In this latter study, the number of people meeting PTSD diagnostic criteria was significantly reduced at all time points compared with baseline. On related PTS measures, the Mueser et al. study (Mueser et al., 2008) showed trauma cognitions were significantly reduced post-treatment and at follow-up compared with baseline. Knowledge of PTSD also increased post-treatment but the gains were not maintained at follow up. Frueh et al. study (Frueh et al., 2009) reported on an intervention integrating a mixed group/individually delivered protocol developed specifically for the treatment of PTSD in SMI groups. Results showed that PTS symptoms significantly reduced post-treatment and at 3 month follow-up compared to baseline. Ten of the 13 participants no longer met diagnostic criteria for PTSD at follow-up.

Jackson et al. (2009) study investigating the impact of CRI indicated that participants reported fewer PTS symptoms than the TAU group; with a borderline significant difference between the two groups. Post-treatment and at 12 month follow-up, significantly more participants in the CRI group showed a clinically significant change in PTS symptoms (≥25% reduction from baseline score) than the TAU group. This finding had a small to modest effect size. Baseline level of PTS symptoms predicted post-treatment PTS score, where participants with a higher baseline PTS score benefited most from CRI. A baseline score above clinical cut off on the IES saw a mean reduction of 28 points in comparison to a mean reduction of six points for those scoring below clinical cut off at baseline. Duration of untreated psychosis was also associated with treatment response, where participants with a shorter DUP were seen to benefit most from CRI.

PE

One study compared PE with EMDR using a randomised sample of ten participants with five participants in each group (de Bont et al., 2013b). The pooled treatment results in both intention to treat and completer groups showed self-reported PTS symptoms significantly reduced from pre-treatment through the treatment phase, post-treatment and then at follow-up with large effect size. The CAPS score was also shown to be significantly reduced at follow-up, although yielded borderline significant results at post-treatment. Of the four treatment completers in the PE condition, three no longer met diagnostic criteria for PTSD at post-treatment and this was increased to four participants at 3 month follow-up. When directly comparing PE with the EMDR condition, the findings suggested response to both treatments was comparable. Similarly, the RCT comparing EMDR, PE and waiting list TAU (van den Berg et al., 2015), reporting on a total sample of 155 participants showed that PE (n = 53) was associated with a significant reduction in PTS symptoms compared to waiting list control (n = 47) at post-treatment and at 6 month follow-up. Participants in the PE condition (and EMDR condition) were less likely to meet diagnostic criteria for PTSD post-treatment compared to those in waiting list control condition. Participants in the PE condition were also shown to be more likely to achieve full remission of PSTD symptoms compared with the wait-list control. PE was superior to EMDR in this respect.

EMDR

van den Berg and van der Gaag (2012) conducted a pilot investigation of EMDR, employing an un-controlled study design reporting on 27 participants. Following EMDR, 77.3% of the treatment completers no longer met diagnostic criteria for PTSD. The severity score reduced by 42.4 and 52.6% in intention to treat and completer groups, respectively. Significant improvements in self-reported PTS symptoms were found post-treatment compared to baseline. All significant findings had a large effect size. Similarly the RCT comparing EMDR, PE and waiting list control (van den Berg et al., 2015) showed that EMDR (n = 55), was associated with a significant reduction in PTS symptoms compared to waiting list control at post-treatment and at 6 month follow-up. Participants in the EMDR condition (and PE) were less likely to meet diagnostic criteria for PTSD post-treatment compared to those in waiting-list control condition. The study by de Bont et al. (2013b), with five participants randomised to the EMDR condition, as reported above, demonstrated a significant reduction in self-reported PTS symptoms at pre-treatment through the treatment phase, post-treatment and then at follow-up compared with pre-treatment scores all with a large effect size. Similar reductions in clinician rated PTS scores were too shown. Of the four treatment completers in the EMDR condition, three no longer met diagnostic criteria for PTSD at post-treatment and this was maintained at 3 month follow up.

Written Emotional Disclosure

One RCT (Bernard et al., 2006) investigated the use of written emotional disclosure. The study reported on 23 participants and found a significant reduction in severity of PTS symptoms for the intervention group between baseline and follow-up compared to the control group. Furthermore, significantly more participants in the intervention group (83.3%) reported a reduction in PTS severity compared to the control group (40%). The interaction between group and PTS severity accounted for 17% of the variance, indicating a small effect size. A main effect was found for avoidance symptoms, with lower avoidance ratings found at follow-up compared to baseline. This finding was only found for the intervention group, where a significant avoidance and group interaction was observed. There were no significant effects found for intrusion or arousal symptoms.

Findings: Outcomes in Secondary Domains

CBT

For the studies investigating CBT delivered in an individual format, the case studies/series demonstrated additional improvements in patient reports of self-trust and anxiety (Kayrouz and Vrklevski, 2015), reductions in symptoms of depression (Callcott et al., 2004; Kevan et al., 2007; Kayrouz and Vrklevski, 2015), general psychopathology (Callcott et al., 2004; Hamblen et al., 2004) and negative symptoms of psychosis (Callcott et al., 2004). In keeping with the findings outlined above, there too was a significant reduction in ratings of general psychopathology as measured by the BPRS found at 3 month follow-up but not immediately post-treatment in the pilot study conducted by Rosenberg et al. (2004). Specifically, the affect subscale on the BPRS significantly improved. The study by Lu et al. (2009) too showed significant improvements on the BPRS at 3 and 6 month follow-up, but not at post-treatment. Mueser et al. (2008) also found significant reductions of general psychopathology. Studies reported findings of significantly reduced depression (Mueser et al., 2008; Lu et al., 2009) and anxiety (Mueser et al., 2008). CBT was also associated with reduced health related concerns and improved ratings of the working alliance between the client and case manager (Mueser et al., 2008).

Group CBT appeared to have an impact on general psychopathology (Trappler and Newville, 2007) and on mood, where significant reductions on the BDI were observed post-treatment and at 3 month follow-up compared to baseline (Mueser et al., 2007). CBT delivered initially in a group then exposure delivered in an individual format demonstrated additional gains in ratings of anger and satisfaction post-treatment and at 3 month follow-up compared to baseline ratings (Frueh et al., 2009). General psychopathology also significantly improved at 3 month follow-up compared to baseline. This study found no effect of CBT on symptoms of depression, anxiety or social functioning/engagement. In keeping with these findings, the CRI study showed no significant differences for depression or self-esteem between the CRI treatment condition and TAU (Jackson et al., 2009).

PE

de Bont et al. (2013b) included a measure of general psychopathology and distress (OQ-45) and the pooled treatment results of both PE and EMDR showed a significant reduction in total scores from pre-treatment to post-treatment and follow-up. There was no effect found for social functioning as measured by the social functioning scale (SFS). The pooled results also showed no treatment effect on psychotic symptoms following treatment, however there was a significant reduction in psychosis-prone thinking on the O-life seen pre-treatment to post-treatment; which was not maintained at 3 month follow-up.

EMDR

The van den Berg and van der Gaag (2012) pilot study included secondary outcome measures of psychotic symptoms measured by the PSYRATS and symptoms of paranoia measured by the GPTS. A small significant reduction was found post-treatment on the PSYRATS subscales and total score however there was no significant difference found for paranoia. This is in contrast to the de Bont et al. (2013b) study which as outlined above found no treatment effect on the PSYRATS. A reduction post-treatment was found for psychosis-prone thinking which was not maintained at follow-up.

In the van den Berg et al. study (van den Berg and van der Gaag, 2012), post-treatment there were significant reductions in symptoms of depression and anxiety, and improvements in self esteem compared to baseline for both treatment completers and intention to treat groups. A significant difference was not found for ratings of hopelessness. As above, de Bont (de Bont et al., 2013b) showed a significant reduction in general psychopathology and distress from pre-treatment to post-treatment and follow-up. There was no effect found for social functioning.

Written Emotional Disclosure

Secondary outcome measures included measures of depression, anxiety, recovery style and insight. There were no significant findings with regard to the impact of the intervention on these domains. The results showed a main effect on insight with greater insight seen at follow-up compared with baseline however this did not differ significantly between groups and cannot therefore be interpreted as an effect of the intervention.

DISCUSSION

Summary

What Psychological Interventions Have Published Data?

The review identified 15 studies that had been published in peer reviewed journals reporting on psychological interventions targeting PTS symptoms in psychosis. The studies reported on individual and group interventions employing case studies, case series, un-controlled and controlled designs. More than two thirds of the studies included in the review reported on interventions which were cognitive behaviour therapy (CBT) informed. The review also described the findings of studies investigating eye-movement desensitisation and reprocessing (EMDR), prolonged exposure (PE) and written emotional disclosure.

How Effective Are the Interventions in Reducing PTS Symptoms?

Overall, the studies indicated that psychological interventions are effective in reducing PTS symptoms, as they are shown to be in non-psychosis populations (Bisson and Andrew, 2005). Some studies however, demonstrated a delayed treatment effect with more significant reductions in PTS symptoms occurring following treatment. Some were not superior to TAU in reducing qualifying criteria for PTSD diagnosis, yet they were superior in reducing PTS symptoms. Many of the studies demonstrated maintenance of effect at follow-up comprising varying time points (e.g., 3 or 6 month follow-up). CBT protocols specifically designed for use in SMI populations, CBT used in ethnically diverse samples and CBT delivered in varying formats all demonstrated reduced PTS symptoms post-treatment. Cognitive recovery intervention (CRI) also showed a benefit in reducing PTS symptoms.

It seems important to highlight the heterogeneity of the CBT interventions included in the review. Five studies used a common protocol developed specifically for PTS symptoms within SMI; however the remaining six studies all varied in the degree to which any one aspect of a CBT intervention was prioritised, focused upon or not employed during sessions, with idiosyncratic adaptations for the use in an SMI sample. Although limited in the number of studies reporting on interventions other than CBT, the results for EMDR and PE were shown to be comparably effective in reducing PTS symptoms and associated cognitions. Written emotional disclosure too offered positive findings in terms of reducing PTS symptoms.

Psycho-education, relaxation training, exposure (Frueh et al., 2009) and written trauma elaboration (Kevan et al., 2007) were the treatment components associated with significant changes in PTS symptoms in these studies. Further, PTS symptoms were shown to be mediated by trauma related beliefs (Mueser et al., 2008). This is consistent with studies of trauma focused cognitive behavioural therapy (TF-CBT) in non-psychosis populations, which highlights the modification of trauma-related beliefs as a key mechanism of change (Kleim et al., 2013). Taken together, it would suggest the active treatment components and processes thought to bring about change in "general" PTSD samples might apply to those with a primary diagnosis of psychosis.

How Effective Are the Interventions on Secondary Domains?

For CBT, EMDR, and PE, therapeutic benefits were seen consistently across studies with regard to measures of general psychopathology. Low mood and anxiety was improved following EMDR and PE, however there were mixed findings for CBT. The interventions also had inconsistent effects on psychotic symptoms. EMDR had a positive effect on self-esteem, however CBT did not. CBT was also associated with improvements in self-trust, health concerns, anger, ratings of working alliance and satisfaction. No intervention had an effect on social functioning. Written emotional disclosure was not associated with any secondary improvements in other domains.

Additional Considerations

The studies highlight a number of interesting findings and areas for consideration. Firstly, several studies found CBT to be more effective in reducing PTS symptoms for participants with higher pre-treatment PTS scores; suggesting those with more severe PTS symptoms will benefit most from CBT. Interestingly this is in contrast to the PTSD literature in the general population which shows that high pre-treatment PTS symptoms predicts high PTS symptoms post-treatment (Blanchard et al., 2003).

Homework was also implicated in the effectiveness of the intervention as greater homework completion contributed to improved outcomes for PTS symptoms and other secondary domains including depression and anxiety (Mueser et al., 2008). This is a consistent finding within the psychotherapy literature which sees the completion or engagement in homework tasks having a small to moderate effect size in predicting treatment outcome in CBT trials (Mausbach et al., 2010).

Psychological treatments, like other aspects of health care, need to be efficacious in the treatment of the targeted area of distress/difficulty and also accessible, appropriate and acceptable to the client group (Tarrier et al., 2006). Many of the studies reported on the occurrence of adverse events (e.g., significant increase in symptoms, hospitalisation and suicidality) and numbers of participants withdrawing from the study. A meta-analysis showed the average drop-out rate for trauma focused interventions is 18% (Imel et al., 2013). The drop-out rates of the CBT, PE, and EMDR studies (not including case studies/series) ranged from 14 to 41%. All of the studies with lower retention rates were investigating CBT. It is unclear if CBT is therefore a therapy this population is less able to engage in as there is a lack of data on alternative interventions and therefore direct comparison is currently limited. Written emotional disclosure yielded lower attrition rates with no drop outs in the experimental group. The results suggested that only one participant was lost at follow-up in the control group due to reasons unrelated to the trial. Although only a single study, and therefore with limited generalisability, it raises questions as to the value of non-therapist led interventions. A recent meta-analysis for example has shown a small to moderate effect size for "self help" interventions within psychosis highlighting this as an area for further utilisation and investigation (Scott et al., 2015).

Overall, the treatments presented in this review were reported to be safe to use in a SMI population. It was acknowledged, however, that trauma focused interventions, irrespective of whether the individual has a co-morbid psychosis diagnosis or not, can lead to distress (Devilly and Spence, 1999), and initial worsening of PTSD symptoms, emotional exhaustion and other physical symptoms of anxiety during the exposure phase of the treatment (Shearing et al., 2011; Hundt et al., 2016). No adverse events were reported in the majority of the studies. In a small proportion of cases where symptom exacerbation was reported, the participant either reported it was caused by factors unrelated to the intervention or was associated with the exposure aspects of treatment. In one CBT study however, exposure was not related to any exacerbation of symptoms and there were no drop outs at this stage. Participants expressed high treatment satisfaction and credibility. The majority of drop outs here occurred in the stabilisation phase. There was mixed implementation across the studies as to the use of a stabilisation or preparatory phase prior to beginning the trauma focused components of the intervention. A recent review suggests that there is insufficient evidence to support a phased based treatment approach to complex PTSD, i.e., specifically regarding a stabilisation phase, and that the inclusion of such a phase may in itself act as a delay or barrier to intervention targeting the trauma (De Jongh et al., 2016). It is worth noting however that as psychotic symptom exacerbation was only measured after the first two exposure sessions (van den Berg et al., 2015) further research is required to build on this evidence base regarding the safety and efficacy of treating post-traumatic stress in psychosis.

Placing the Findings in the Current Context

There are a number of findings within the literature that should be noted when considering the evidence relating to trauma-focused psychological interventions in psychosis. One finding is simply the utility and clinical benefit of being able to talk about the difficult experiences one has had. A study investigating the relationship between PTS symptoms arising as a result of first episode psychosis and self-disclosure found fewer PTS symptoms related to increased levels of disclosure about the traumatic experiences (Pietruch and Jobson, 2012). The study highlighted that disclosing and therefore talking about the experience would be beneficial and support recovery. This provides a clinical rationale that health professionals can communicate to individuals when broaching the topic of trauma assessment and treatment. This finding is important in that it provides evidence to counter the belief clinicians often hold that asking clients about traumatic experiences will in some way "make things worse" (Frueh et al., 2006). These types of beliefs have been identified as a common and notable barrier to the development and evaluation of psychological interventions targeting PTS symptoms in SMI groups (Salyers et al., 2004).

Related to encouraging open dialogue about traumatic experiences, there is evidence for the benefit of purely psycho-educational interventions for PTSD. Pratt et al. (2005) provided a three session PTSD psycho-education programme to individuals with primary SMI diagnoses whom all had co-morbid PTSD. The study did not aim to target PTS symptoms; outcomes showed increased knowledge of PTSD and high levels of satisfaction. Importantly, the authors reported many of the participants expressed an increased wish to access an intervention to help with these experiences. Considering that within clinical services, a proportion of service users are often reluctant to engage in psychological therapies (Berry and Haddock, 2008), this finding offers implications for normalisation, education and improving the degree to which interventions are deemed accessible. It must be noted however that this was not formally assessed or followed up in this study. These two findings taken together highlight the potential benefit of greater communication about PTS symptoms and the implications this has not only for engagement in therapies but also directly on recovery and outcome.

Strengths and Limitations

A main strength of the current review is the use of broad search criteria and the inclusion of published articles employing a range of study designs. The use, for example, of a broad trauma search strategy reduced the chance of potentially relevant records not being identified at this stage. Within the current psychosis literature, trauma exposure and symptoms arising as a direct result of these experiences are described heterogeneously. Terms such as trauma, traumatic event and adverse experiences are frequently all used to describe the same concept. Similarly PTSD, PTS symptoms, PTS response and traumatic reaction are also often used interchangeably. Despite the inherent issues arising as a result of a lack of consensus regarding terminology; the review's search methodology was nonetheless reflective of the language within the literature and thus thorough in its efforts to provide an accurate inclusive representation of the current research. The review is inclusive of all relevant findings within the literature independent of study design. In an area of emerging evidence, the exclusion of findings from studies employing less rigorous designs may not provide a comprehensive representation of the available research. The use of the CTAM (Tarrier and Wykes, 2004) has allowed for a transparent account of the evidence base clearly noting the heterogeneity of methodological vigor of the studies presented.

The review however is not without its limitations. The main limitation is, perhaps, simultaneously, also its main strength; the inclusion of un-controlled studies. The use of a controlled study design, in particular RCT, is considered the gold standard of investigating the true efficacy and effectiveness of an intervention (Jones and Podolsky, 2015). On the CTAM, the uncontrolled studies had lower quality ratings than controlled studies. There is evidence to suggest studies with poorer methodology overestimate the magnitude of positive benefits of the intervention; where a significant negative correlation between effect size and CTAM score has been found (Tarrier and Wykes, 2004). It must be noted that the CTAM was not designed to be used to evaluate case studies and therefore it may not have been a tool that accurately measured the quality of this type of study methodology. The lower scores therefore may not necessarily reflect the true quality of this type of research. Case studies by their nature are based on the work completed with people found within routine clinical services, and are therefore representative of the clients the practitioners accessing the research will be exposed to.

Another limitation of the review is the mixed population reported in several studies. The use of mixed samples therefore makes it difficult to infer the effectiveness of these interventions for the psychosis population specifically. Data were rarely stratified by diagnosis and therefore impossible to draw out these particular findings within this review. However, when considering the results of the nine pure psychosis studies, it is encouraging that outcomes suggested a beneficial impact of treatment on symptoms of PTS which provides promising support for use of these interventions in this group.

Clinical and Research Implications

Firstly, the studies included within the review all report on the prevalence of high levels of trauma exposure within individuals with psychosis; which is in keeping with the literature (Bechdolf et al., 2010). The importance of routine trauma assessment and investigation across the illness of the negative sequelae is indicated (Read and Ross, 2003). This idea is consistent with a "screen and treat" methodology employed following the London terrorist bombings in 2005. Using this outreach approach, Brewin et al. (2008) identified significant numbers of people with a traumatic response to the bombings (and offered treatment) in comparison to the very small numbers of people who were referred independently of the screening process. This is of importance especially in the psychosis and SMI population where help seeking can be poor and complicated by other issues such as stigma and fear about the subsequent consequences (Kessler et al., 2001). Engagement and access is an ongoing area that needs to be addressed especially in light of evidence from this review that these individuals can nonetheless engage and benefit from trauma focused interventions such as TF-CBT and EMDR. This is in keeping with the NICE 2005 clinical guidance for the management of PTSD in non-psychosis groups, which recommends these two interventions as the first line treatment options. The review therefore appears to provide support for the applicability of the current PTSD NICE guidance to individuals with co-morbid severe mental health problems.

With NICE guidance for the care of people with experience of psychosis calling for routine screening as standard practice, solutions to overcome the additional impact of barriers at a staff and organisation level must too be sought. A recent study showed that a tailored training programme was successful in increasing staff confidence and knowledge in assessing and treating trauma within psychosis (Berry and Haddock, 2008). It is recommended that all teams employ a proactive informed approach to trauma because although emerging, there is sound evidence for the benefits of psychological interventions within this group.

This review demonstrated the relatively small number of RCTs that have been conducted in the area. Further methodologically vigorous controlled trials investigating the use of psychological interventions are required to be able to draw more solid conclusions about therapy efficacy; mirroring the call for an "*adequately powered, multi-centre RCT*" of a "*CBT based trauma reprocessing intervention*" in the recent NICE guidance. There also remains a need for research that extends targeting PTS symptoms alone. The review shows that the impact of the interventions on symptoms of psychosis is mixed; arguably as these were not the focus of the treatment. It may be interesting however to explore whether current trauma focused approaches can be adapted to optimise treatment gains by integrating components of psychosis focused therapies. Furthermore, new research should be extended beyond CBT as more studies looking at alternative interventions are indicated.

Interestingly, no studies were able to demonstrate functional gains such as change in employment status or number of health care visits. There was also a lack of participant reported outcomes such as measures of quality of life. A focus on both of these domains would be a welcome addition to further research in measuring the subjective impact of the interventions and evaluation of areas of importance for service users. This approach would be consistent with recovery focused services increasingly employed in psychosis (Warner, 2009). It may also provide a more meaningful evidence base that can support therapy engagement.

Trauma arising as a result of psychosis symptoms and hospital experiences is a topic that has received increasing recognition and interest more recently, as it has been shown that a significant number of individuals are meeting criteria for PTSD following these experiences (Berry et al., 2013). In support of this, Bernard and colleagues (Bernard et al., 2006) reported that the majority of their sample in the emotional written disclosure condition wrote about the "*debilitating and threatening effect of positive symptoms* (e.g., voices, delusions, hallucinations and paranoia)" and "*negative experiences such as being sectioned.*" Research with a focus on the development of PTS reactions to psychosis and hospitalisation may help to extend the current understanding about the impact and suitable interventions. Furthermore, studies evaluating interventions specifically targeting these post-psychotic PTS symptoms would be warranted.

CONCLUSIONS

Traumatic experiences are implicated in the development of psychosis conditions and high rates of historical trauma are found in this group. People with psychosis are at higher risk of further trauma exposure. These individuals have greater service use and achieve poorer clinical outcomes including an increased risk of suicidality. There is a fast developing evidence base investigating trauma in psychosis with over 500 articles having been published in the last 5 years. This review presents the current evidence for the use of psychological interventions targeting PTS symptoms in a psychosis population. The review provided encouraging support for the efficacy of CBT, EMDR, PE, and written emotional disclosure suggesting the current NICE guidelines for the management of PTSD are clinically relevant to groups with co-morbid severe mental health difficulties such as psychosis. Although the evidence base has grown, there is a need for further research with a focus on mechanisms of change, patient reported outcomes and trials, particularly other than CBT, and employing rigorous research design within ethnically diverse more representative samples.

AUTHOR CONTRIBUTIONS

SS, NK, NR and JO contributed to the conception, analysis, interpretation, drafting, critical revision and final approval of the manuscript for publication.

REFERENCES

American Psychiatric Association (2013). *Diagnostic and Statistical Manual of Mental Disorders, 5th Edn.* Arlington, VA: American Psychiatric Publishing. doi: 10.1176/appi.books.9780890425596

Atwoli, L., Stein, D. J., Koenen, K. C., and McLaughlin, K. A. (2015). Epidemiology of posttraumatic stress disorder: prevalence, correlates and consequences. *Curr. Opin. Psychiatry* 28, 307–311. doi: 10.1097/YCO.0000000000000167

Beattie, N., Shannon, C., Kavanagh, M., and Mulholland, C. (2009). Predictors of PTSD Symptoms in response to psychosis and psychiatric admission. *J. Nerv. Ment. Dis.* 197, 56–60. doi: 10.1097/NMD.0b013e31819273a8

Bechdolf, A., Thompson, A., Nelson, B., Cotton, S., Simmons, M. B., Amminger, G. P., et al (2010). Experience of trauma and conversion to psychosis in an ultra-high-risk (prodromal) group. *Acta Psychiatr. Scand.* 121, 377–384. doi: 10.1111/j.1600-0447.2010.01542.x

Becker, C. B., Zayfert, C., and Anderson, E. (2004). A survey of psychologists' attitudes towards and utilization of exposure therapy for PTSD. *Behav. Res. Ther.* 42, 277–292. doi: 10.1016/S0005-7967(03)00138-4

Bernard, M., Jackson, C., and Jones, C. (2006). Written emotional disclosure following first-episode psychosis: effects on symptoms of post-traumatic stress disorder. *Br. J. Clin. Psychol.* 45, 403–415. doi: 10.1348/014466505X68933

Berry, K., Ford, S., Jellicoe-Jones, L., and Haddock, G. (2013). PTSD symptoms associated with the experiences of psychosis and hospitalization: a review of the literature. *Clin. Psychol. Rev.* 33, 526–538. doi: 10.1016/j.cpr.2013.01.011

Berry, K., and Haddock, G. (2008). The implementation of the NICE guidelines for schizophrenia: barriers to the implementation of psychological interventions and recommendations for the future. *Psychol. Psychother. Theory Res. Pract.* 81, 419–436. doi: 10.1348/147608308X329540

Bisson, J., and Andrew, M. (2005). Psychological treatment of post-traumatic stress disorder (PTSD). *Cochrane Database Syst. Rev.* 2005:CD003388. doi: 10.1002/14651858.CD003388.pub2

Bisson, J. I. (2007). Post-traumatic stress disorder. *BMJ* 334, 789–793. doi: 10.1136/bmj.39162.538553.80

Blanchard, E. B., Hickling, E. J., Malta, L. S., Jaccard, J., Devineni, T., Veazey, C. H., et al. (2003). Prediction of response to psychological treatment among motor vehicle accident survivors with PTSD. *Behav. Ther.* 34, 351–363. doi: 10.1016/S0005-7894(03)80005-9

Breslau, N. (2009). The epidemiology of trauma, PTSD, and other posttrauma disorders. *Trauma Violence Abuse* 10, 198–210. doi: 10.1177/15248380093 34448

Brewin, C. R., Scragg, P., Robertson, M., Thompson, M., d'Ardenne, P., Ehlers, A., et al. (2008). Promoting mental health following the london bombings: a screen and treat approach. *J. Trauma Stress* 21, 3–8. doi: 10.1002/jts.20310

Buckley, P. F., Miller, B. J., Lehrer, D. S., and Castle, D. J. (2009). Psychiatric comorbidities and schizophrenia. *Schizophr. Bull.* 35, 383–402. doi: 10.1093/schbul/sbn135

Callcott, P., Sally, S., and Douglas, T. (2004). Trauma within psychosis: using a CBT model for PTSD in psychosis. *Behav. Cogn. Psychother.* 32, 239–244. doi: 10.1017/S1352465804001249

de Bont, P. A., van den Berg, D. P., van der Vleugel, B. M., de Roos, C., Mulder, C. L., and Becker, E. S. (2013b). A multi-site single blind clinical study to compare the effects of prolonged exposure, eye movement desensitization and reprocessing and waiting list on patients with a current diagnosis of psychosis and co morbid post traumatic stress disorder: study protocol for the randomized controlled trial Treating Trauma in Psychosis. *Trials* 14:151. doi: 10.1186/1745-6215-14-151

de Bont, P. A., van Minnen, A., and de Jongh, A. (2013a). Treating PTSD in patients with psychosis: a within-group controlled feasibility study examining the efficacy and safety of evidence-based PE and EMDR protocols. *Behav. Ther.* 44, 717–730. doi: 10.1016/j.beth.2013.07.002

De Jongh, A., Resick, P. A., Zoellner, L. A., van Minnen, A., Lee, C. W., Monson, C. M., et al. (2016). Critical analysis of the current treatment guidelines for complex PTSD in adults. *Depress. Anxiety* 33, 359–369. doi: 10.1002/da.22469

Devilly, G. J., and Spence, S. H. (1999). The relative efficacy and treatment distress of EMDR and a cognitive-behavior trauma treatment protocol in the amelioration of posttraumatic stress disorder. *J. Anxiety Disord.* 13, 131–157. doi: 10.1016/S0887-6185(98)00044-9

Foa, E., Hembree, E., and Rothbaum, B. O. (2007). *Prolonged Exposure Therapy for PTSD: Emotional Processing of Traumatic Experiences Therapist Guide: Emotional Processing of Traumatic Experiences Therapist Guide.* Oxford University Press.

Frans, O., Rimmö, P. A., Åberg, L., and Fredrikson, M. (2005). Trauma exposure and post-traumatic stress disorder in the general population. *Acta Psychiatr. Scand.* 111, 291–290. doi: 10.1111/j.1600-0447.2004.00463.x

Friedman, M. J., Resick, P. A., Bryant, R. A., and Brewin, C. R. (2011). Considering PTSD for DSM-5. *Depress. Anxiety* 28, 750–769. doi: 10.1002/da.20767
Emotional Processing of Traumatic Experiences Therapist Guide. Oxford University Press.

Frans, O., Rimmö, P. A., Åberg, L., and Fredrikson, M. (2005). Trauma exposure and post-traumatic stress disorder in the general population. *Acta Psychiatr.*

Scand. 111, 291–290. doi: 10.1111/j.1600-0447.2004.00463.x

Friedman, M. J., Resick, P. A., Bryant, R. A., and Brewin, C. R. (2011). Considering PTSD for DSM-5. *Depress. Anxiety* 28, 750–769. doi: 10.1002/da.20767

Frueh, B. C., Cusack, K. J., Grubaugh, A. L., Sauvageot, J. A., and Wells, C. (2006). Clinicians' perspectives on cognitive-behavioral treatment for PTSD among persons with severe mental illness. *Psychiatr. Serv.* 57, 1027–1031. doi: 10.1176/ps.2006.57.7.1027

Frueh, B., Grubaugh, A. L., Cusack, K. J., Kimble, M. O., Elhai, J. D., and Knapp, R. G. (2009). Exposure-based cognitive-behavioral treatment of PTSD in adults with schizophrenia or schizoaffective disorder: a pilot study. *J. Anxiety Disord.* 23, 665–675. doi: 10.1016/j.janxdis.2009.02.005

Gairns, S., Alvarez-Jimenez, M., Hulbert, C., McGorry, P., and Bendall, S. (2015). Perceptions of clinicians treating young people with first-episode psychosis for post-traumatic stress disorder. *Early Interv. Psychiatry* 9, 12–20. doi: 10.1111/eip.12065

Green, J. (2006). The evolving randomized controlled trial in mental health: studying complexity and treatment process. *Adv. Psychiatr. Treat.* 12, 268–279. doi: 10.1192/apt.12.4.268

Greene, T., Neria, Y., and Gross, R. (2016). Prevalence, detection and correlates of PTSD in the primary care setting: a systematic review. *J. Clin. Psychol. Med. Settings.* 23, 160–180. doi: 10.1007/s10880-016-9449-8

Gregg, L., and Tarrier, N. (2007). Virtual reality in mental health : a review of the literature. *Soc. Psychiatry Psychiatr. Epidemiol.* 42, 343–354. doi: 10.1007/s00127-007-0173-4

Grubaugh, A. L., Zinzow, H. M., Paul, L., Egede, L. E., and Frueh, B. C. (2011). Trauma exposure and posttraumatic stress disorder in adults with severe mental illness: a critical review. *Clin. Psychol. Rev.* 31, 883–899. doi: 10.1016/j.cpr.2011.04.003

Hamblen, J. L., Jankowski, M. K., Rosenberg, S. D., and Mueser, K. T. (2004). Cognitive-behavioral treatment for PTSD in people with severe mental illness: three case studies. *Am. J. Psychiatr. Rehabil.* 7, 147–170. doi: 10.1080/15487760490476192

Hughes, L. D., McMurdo, M. E. T., and Guthrie, B. (2013). Guidelines for people not for diseases: the challenges of applying UK clinical guidelines to people with multimorbidity. *Age Ageing* 42, 62–69. doi: 10.1093/ageing/afs100

Hundt, N. E., Harik, J. M., Barrera, T. L., Cully, J. A., and Stanley, M. A. (2016). Treatment decision-making for posttraumatic stress disorder: the impact of patient and therapist characteristics. *Psychol. Trauma* 8, 728–735. doi: 10.1037/tra0000102

Imel, Z. E., Laska, K., Jakcupcak, M., and Simpson, T. L. (2013). Meta-analysis of dropout in treatments for post-traumatic stress disorder. *J. Consult. Clin. Psychol.* 81, 394–404. doi: 10.1037/a0031474

Insel, T. R. (2008). Assessing the economic costs of serious mental illness. *Am. J. Psychiatry* 165, 663–665. doi: 10.1176/appi.ajp.2008.08030366

Jackson, C., Knott, C., Skeate, A., and Birchwood, M. (2004). The trauma of first episode psychosis: the role of cognitive mediation. *Aust. N. Z. J. Psychiatry* 38, 327–333. doi: 10.1080/j.1440-1614.2004.01359.x

Jackson, C., Trower, P., Reid, I., Smith, J., Hall, M., Townend, M., et al. (2009). Improving psychological adjustment following a first episode of psychosis: a randomized controlled trial of cognitive therapy to reduce post psychotic trauma symptoms. *Behav. Res. Ther.* 47, 454–462. doi: 10.1016/j.brat.2009.02.009

Jones, D. S., and Podolsky, S. H. (2015). The history and fate of the gold standard. *Lancet* 385, 1502–1503. doi: 10.1016/S0140-6736(15)60742-5

Karam, E. G., Andrews, G., Bromet, E., Petukhova, M., Ruscio, A. M., Salamoun, M., et al. (2010). The role of Criterion A2 in the DSM-IV diagnosis of post-traumatic stress disorder. *Biol. Psychiatry* 68, 465–473. doi: 10.1016/j.biopsych.2010.04.032

Karam, E. G., Friedman, M. J., Hill, E. D., Kessler, R. C., McLaughlin, K. A., Petukhova, M., et al. (2014). Cumulative traumas and risk thresholds. 12 month ptsd in the world mental health (Wmh) surveys. *Depress. Anxiety* 31, 130–142. doi: 10.1002/da.22169

Kayrouz, R., and Vrklevski, L. P. (2015). Fatal torment–from psychosis-driven index offence to trauma: a case study in forensic psychotherapy, trauma therapy and matricide. *Australas. Psychiatry* 23, 54–58. doi: 10.1177/1039856214563850

Kessler, R. C., Berglund, P. A., Bruce, M. L., Koch, J. R., Laska, E. M., and Leaf, P. J., et al. (2001). The prevalence and correlates of untreated serious mental illness. *Health Serv. Res.* 36(6 Pt 1):987.

Kevan, I. M., Gumley, A. I., and Coletta, V. (2007). Post-traumatic stress disorder in a person with a diagnosis of schizophrenia: examining the efficacy of psychological intervention using single N methodology. *Clin. Psychol. Psychother.* 14, 229–243. doi: 10.1002/cpp.534

Kleim, B., Grey, N., Wild, J., Nussbeck, F. W., Stott, R., Hackmann, A., et al. (2013). Cognitive change predicts symptom reduction with cognitive therapy for posttraumatic stress disorder. *J. Consult. Clin. Psychol.* 81:383. doi: 10.1037/a0031290

Lommen, M. J. J., and Restifo, K. (2009). Trauma and posttraumatic stress disorder (PTSD) in patients with schizophrenia or schizoaffective disorder. *Commun. Ment. Health J.* 45, 485–496. doi: 10.1007/s10597-009-9248-x

Lu, W., Fite, R., Kim, E., Hyer, L., Yanos, P. T., Mueser, K. T., et al (2009). Cognitive-behavioral treatment of PTSD in severe mental illness: pilot study replication in an ethnically diverse population. *Am. J. Psychiatr. Rehabil.* 12, 73–91. doi: 10.1080/15487760802615863

Mabey, L., and Servellen, G. (2014). Treatment of post-traumatic stress disorder in patients with severe mental illness: a review. *Int. J. Ment. Health Nurs.* 23, 42–50. doi: 10.1111/inm.12007

Maniglio, R. (2009). Severe mental illness and criminal victimization: a systematic review. *Acta Psychiatr. Scand.* 119, 180–191. doi: 10.1111/j.1600-0447.2008.01300.x

Mausbach, B. T., Moore, R., Roesch, S., Cardenas, V., and Patterson, T. L. (2010). The relationship between homework compliance and therapy outcomes: an updated meta-analysis. *Cogn. Ther. Res.* 34, 429–438. doi: 10.1007/s10608-010-9297-z

McLaughlin, K. A., Koenen, K. C., Friedman, M. J., Ruscio, A. M., Karam, E. G., Shahly, V., et al. (2015). Subthreshold posttraumatic stress disorder in the world health organization world mental health surveys. *Biol. Psychiatry* 77, 375–384. doi: 10.1016/j.biopsych.2014.03.028

Menon, S. B., and Jayan, C. (2010). Eye movement desensitization and reprocessing: a conceptual framework. *Indian J. Psychol. Med.* 32, 136–140. doi: 10.4103/0253-7176.78512

Moher, D., Liberati, A., Tetzlaff, J., Altman, D. G., and The PRISMA Group (2009). Preferred reporting items for systematic reviews and meta-analyses: the PRISMA statement. *BMJ* 339:b2535. doi: 10.1136/bmj.b2535

Mueser, K. T., Bolton, E., Carty, P. C., Bradley, M. J., Ahlgren, K. F., Distaso, D. R., et al. (2007). The Trauma Recovery Group: a cognitive-behavioral program for post-traumatic stress disorder in persons with severe mental illness. *Commun. Ment. Health J.* 43, 281–304. doi: 10.1007/s10597-006-9075-2

Mueser, K. T., Rosenberg, S. D., Goodman, L. A., and Trumbetta, S. L. (2002). Trauma, PTSD, and the course of severe mental illness: an interactive model. *Schizophr. Res.* 53, 123–143. doi: 10.1016/S0920-9964(01)00173-6

Mueser, K. T., Rosenberg, S. D., Xie, H., Jankowski, M. K., Bolton, E. E., Lu, W., et al. (2008). A randomized controlled trial of cognitive-behavioral treatment for posttraumatic stress disorder in severe mental illness. *J. Consult. Clin. Psychol.* 76:259. doi: 10.1037/0022-006X.76.2.259

National Institute for Health and Care Excellence (2005). *Post-Traumatic Stress Disorder: Management.* London: National Institute for Health and Care Excellence.

National Institute for Health and Care Excellence (2014). *Psychosis and Schizophrenia in Adults: Treatment and Management.* London: National Institute for Health and Care Excellence.

Pennebaker, J. W., and Beall, S. K. (1986). Confronting a traumatic event: toward an understanding of inhibition and disease. *J. Abnorm. Psychol.* 95, 274–281. doi: 10.1037/0021-843X.95.3.274

Pietruch, M., and Jobson, L. (2012). Posttraumatic growth and recovery in people with first episode psychosis: an investigation into the role of self-disclosure. *Psychosis Psychol. Soc. Integr. Approac.* 4, 213–223. doi: 10.1080/17522439.2011.608434

Pratt, S., Mueser, K. T., Brancato, J., Salyers, M., Jankowski, M. K., and Descamps, M. (2005). Evaluation of a PTSD psychoeducational program for psychiatric inpatients. *J. Ment. Health* 14, 121–127. doi: 10.1080/09638230500066356

Read, J., and Ross, C. A. (2003). Psychological trauma and psychosis: another reason why people diagnosed schizophrenic must be offered psychological therapies. *J. Am. Acad. Psychoanal. Dyn. Psychiatry* 31, 247–268.

Rosenberg, S. D., Mueser, K. T., Jankowski, M., Salyers, M. P., and Acker, K. (2004). Cognitive-behavioral treatment of PTSD in severe mental illness: results of a pilot study. *Am. J. Psychiatr. Rehabil.* 7, 171–186. doi: 10.1080/15487760490476200

Salyers, M. P., Evans, L. J., Bond, G. R., and Meyer, P. S. (2004). Barriers to assessment and treatment of posttraumatic stress disorder and other trauma-related problems in people with severe mental illness: clinician perspectives. *Commun. Ment. Health J.* 40, 17–31. doi: 10.1023/B:COMH.0000015215.45696.5f

Sareen, J., Cox, B. J., Stein, M. B., Afifi, T. O., Fleet, C., and Asmundson, G. J. (2007). Physical and mental comorbidity, disability, and suicidal behavior associated with posttraumatic stress disorder in a large community sample. *Psychosom. Med.* 69, 242–248. doi: 10.1097/PSY.0b013e31803146d8

Scott, A. J., Webb, T. L., and Rowse, G. (2015). Self-help interventions for psychosis: a meta-analysis. *Clin. Psychol. Rev.* 39, 96–112. doi: 10.1016/j.cpr.2015.05.002

Seedat, S., Stein, M. B., Oosthuizen, P. P., Emsley, R. A., and Stein, D. J. (2003). Linking posttraumatic stress disorder and psychosis: a look at epidemiology, phenomenology, and treatment. *J. Nerv. Ment. Dis.* 191, 675–681. doi: 10.1097/01.nmd.0000092177.97317.26

Shapiro, F. (2001). *Eye Movement Desensitization and Reprocessing: Basic Principles, Protocols, and Procedures.* New York, NY: Guilford Press.

Shearing, V., Lee, D., and Clohessy, S. (2011). How do clients experience reliving as part of trauma-focused cognitive behavioral therapy for posttraumatic stress disorder? *Psychol. Psychother. Theory Res. Pract.* 84, 458–475. doi: 10.1111/j.2044-8341.2010.02012.x

Sin, J., and Spain, D. (2016). Psychological interventions for trauma in individuals who have psychosis: a systematic review and meta-analysis. *Psychosis* 67–81. doi: 10.1080/17522439.2016.1167946

Tarrier, N., Khan, S., Cater, J., and Picken, A. (2007). The subjective consequences of suffering a first episode psychosis: trauma and suicide behavior. *Soc. Psychiatry Psychiatr. Epidemiol.* 42, 29–35. doi: 10.1007/s00127-006-0127-2

Tarrier, N., Liversidge, T., and Gregg, L. (2006). The acceptability and preference for the psychological treatment of PTSD. *Behav. Res. Ther.* 44, 1643–1656. doi: 10.1016/j.brat.2005.11.012

Tarrier, N., Taylor, K., and Gooding, P. (2008). Cognitive-behavioral interventions to reduce suicide behavior: a systematic review and meta-analysis. *Behav. Modif.* 32, 77–108. doi: 10.1177/0145445507304728

Tarrier, N., and Wykes, T. (2004). Is there evidence that cognitive behavior therapy is an effective treatment for schizophrenia? A cautious or cautionary tale? *Behav. Res. Ther.* 42, 1377–1401. doi: 10.1016/j.brat.2004.06.020

Trappler, B., and Newville, H. (2007). Trauma healing via cognitive behavior therapy in chronically hospitalized patients. *Psychiatr. Q.* 78, 317–325. doi: 10.1007/s11126-007-9049-8

van den Berg, D. P., and van der Gaag, M. (2012). Treating trauma in psychosis with EMDR: a pilot study. *J. Behav. Ther. Exp. Psychiatry* 43, 664–671. doi: 10.1016/j.jbtep.2011.09.011

van den Berg, D. P. G., de Bont, P. A. J. M., van Der Vleugel, B. M., de Roos, C., de Jongh, A., van Minnen, A., et al. (2015). Prolonged exposure vs eyemovement desensitization and reprocessing vs waiting list for posttraumatic stress disorder in patients with a psychotic disorder: a randomized clinical trial. *JAMA Psychiatry* 72, 259–267. doi: 10.1001/jamapsychiatry.2014.2637

Varese, F., Smeets, F., Drukker, M., Lieverse, R., Lataster, T., Viechtbauer, W., et al. (2012). Childhood adversities increase the risk of psychosis: a meta-analysis of patient-control, prospective-and cross-sectional cohort studies. *Schizophr. Bull.* 38, 661–671. doi: 10.1093/schbul/sbs050

Warner, R. (2009). Recovery from schizophrenia and the recovery model. *Curr. Opin. Psychiatry* 22, 374–380. doi: 10.1097/YCO.0b013e32832c920b

Wykes, T., Huddy, V., Cellard, C., McGurk, S. R., and Czobor, P. (2011). A meta-analysis of cognitive remediation for schizophrenia: methodology and effect sizes. *Am. J. Psychiatry* 168, 472–485. doi: 10.1176/appi.ajp.2010.10060855

Wykes, T., Steel, C., Everitt, B., and Tarrier, N. (2008). Cognitive behavior therapy for schizophrenia: effect sizes, clinical models, and methodological rigor. *Schizophr. Bull.* 34, 523–537. doi: 10.1093/schbul/sbm114

14

Listening and Hearing: A Voice Hearer's Invitation into Relationship

Berta Britz *

Berta Britz Consulting, Havertown, PA, USA

Edited by:
Kim T. Mueser,
Boston University, USA

Reviewed by:
Susana Ochoa,
Parc Sanitari Sant Joan de Déu, Spain
Tanya Luhrmann,
Stanford University, USA

***Correspondence:**
Berta Britz
bbdogfriend@aol.com

Although historically overlooked, empirical links between trauma and psychosis have received growing attention over the past decade. Increasingly, clinical researchers have also zeroed in on the role that distressing or traumatic life events play in the psychosocial formation and maintenance of psychosis. This paper re-locates anomalous experiences in their human contexts, and asks that clinicians and researchers engage with these contexts. The author shares a first person account of her experience changing her relationships with dominance in order to reclaim and accept her human being-ness, a reorientation supported by her involvement in the world hearing voices network movement and community. She calls for mental health systems, providers, and researchers to collaborate with the persons at the center of their work—to dare to listen, hear, and connect for mutual learning, healing, and wholeness. The article concludes with recommendations and a rallying call for services to be made more inclusive and to re-center in meaningful collaboration with people with lived experience. More comprehensive, meaningful, and accountable practices can be co-created when people are met equally as human subjects, both responsible and accountable for change.

Keywords: lived experience, hearing voices, adverse childhood experiences

CONCEPTUAL FRAME

The prevalence of trauma—adverse childhood and adult experiences—in the lives of the people served in the mental health system has been well-established (Álvarez et al., 2011; Larsson et al., 2013). Although, it has been widely acknowledged that providing high quality mental health services requires a trauma informed approach, actual practice is inconsistent, and often absent in clinical work with persons from marginalized and/or under-represented groups (culturally, racially, economically, sexually), including those diagnosed with psychosis (Muskett, 2014; Read et al., 2016). In the area of psychosis specifically, the evidence on more conventional trauma-driven therapeutic approaches such as cognitive behavioral therapy and EMDR for persons with psychosis remains startlingly sparse (Bendall et al., 2010). In contrast, trauma-driven approaches often dominate the landscape of peer-led, peer-informed, and "alternative" approaches to psychosis, including the body of supports and techniques developed within the international hearing voices movement (Longden et al., 2012; Corstens et al., 2014). A core tenet of these latter approaches is that the genesis, messages or content, and phenomenology of voices and unusual beliefs are often, if not always, strongly interconnected with individuals' personal histories and distressing or traumatic life events (Corstens et al., 2014). The hearing voices movement, and allied approaches, strongly encourage the exploration of the meaning of voices and beliefs, and the re-centering of the relationship between the individual and his or her voices/experiences.

Phenomenologically-informed work more broadly attests to the high prevalence of voices and other experiences that are subjectively perceived as rich, meaning-laden, interconnected with life events, and with whom the individual engages as he or she would a person, character, or entity (Woods et al., 2015).

This seeming disconnect between peer-driven approaches and conventional (particularly pharmacotherapy-driven) clinical approaches may stem from the illness-focus and power imbalance in the relationships between clinicians, researchers, and individuals using services. Both clinical service systems and the research that supports them have traditionally strongly marginalized, or outright excluded, the voices and perspectives of persons with lived experience of psychosis (Faulkner and Thomas, 2002; Callard et al., 2012).

Research demonstrates that clinicians often think diagnostically (what's wrong with you?) when approaching clients; however when thinking about their own pain/distress, they think about its context (what's happened to them; Carter et al., 2016; Magliano et al., 2016). Clinical training teaches us to ask and look for presenting problems, focusing on the deficits in the individual or, more rarely, in the family/social system. In typical practice settings in the USA, the structure of the diagnosis, treatment, and documentation upon which payment depends relies on a clinical lens shaped by presuppositions that are illness-focused rather than person-centered, thereby reducing the likelihood of clinicians engaging relationally with the persons they seek to help. The following essay seeks to shift the conventional expert/client perspective to enable a relational lens based in curiosity and listening that values the experiences of both humans at the clinical table.

EXPERIENTIAL LENS

Today I am a woman firmly planted in this world—I belong! Mine has been an odyssey from fear, shame, hopelessness, and "psychosis" to home and liberation. Everything I understand involves relationship to other. The other inside me, the other outside me, the meaning I make and co-create. I am responsible for myself, and I am inextricably connected to my ancestors, my family of origin, the people, and animals I know and have known, nature, community, and Spirit. My experience of disconnect, chaos, and powerlessness, labeled "psychosis," makes sense in the context of those relationships. My journey toward understanding began steeped in fear and terror, fueled by my drive to survive and my thirst for meaning. Like Odysseus I faced opposition and oppression. At times my vessel sank in quicksand, battered by riptides and rocks, I continually emerged to reorient and breathe. In relationship I moved toward healing and wholeness.

I will share my current understanding of how I am becoming whole and its possible relevance to others. I've learned from being part of several communities—the community of voice hearers, Quakers, people working for individual mental health and mental health systems recovery, people working for social and restorative justice and to preserve our planet. I start with my own individual experience of powerlessness and describe the process of moving from aloneness and alienation to connection and love. One of my earliest limiting beliefs was that I was alone and needed to stay that way for my own survival and for the survival of other people. While that might have made a type of sense at adverse times in my early life, it was an anachronistic belief that limited my contacts and possibilities for human connections, learning, and growth over time. As a young child I was afraid of my vulnerability and denied it in order to appear stronger and safer than I felt.

My recovery, my rebirthing, has been a process culminating in my current condition of "emancipation." My emancipation encompasses freedom from old identities forged from fear—my own personal fears and the impact of fear-based interactions with others, especially with others in the mental health/illness systems. I now affirm my birthright as a human being, midwifed by my spiritual, emotional, psychological, and communal relationships with others. I am living into a current freedom to contribute to creating a more just, sustainable community. My current state is a new embodiment of responsibility for myself in relation.

The people I depended on as an infant and young child did and said things that helped as well as harmed me. My early life felt confusing and terrifying, and it was my connection with animals that sustained me. I lacked basic trust and hid my vulnerability.

My identity was forged in powerlessness. My parents tried and failed to save relatives from Nazi concentration camps, and my birth coincided with my mother's grief and rage at the death of her mother. My older brother who had been a caregiver for our maternal grandmother, was reassigned to take care of me, and his care for me included sex. I grew up worshiping my mother and brother, absorbing a mixture of learned helplessness mixed with exceptional power. Surviving was a burden for us all.

When I was an adolescent my disconnection was palpable, and the psychiatric system labeled me psychotic, my voices "auditory hallucinations." My verbalization didn't work; I spoke little and when I did speak or write, it was mixed up. Words meant different things to me. I didn't speak directly—my thoughts and beliefs were dangerous, embodied in terrorizing voices. I connected in code with the people I encountered, and my voices used their own codes to both command and obfuscate. For over 40 years my voices echoed and amplified the harsh and intrusive messages I received in childhood. I believed that I wasn't human. It was declared by my voices and also confirmed and reflected in the objectifying way the psychiatric system conceived and treated me.

I swallowed the beliefs of my voices and the assumptions of the psychiatric system. Whether my badness stemmed from what my voices considered my substance or from psychiatry's ascription of it to my genes and biochemistry, most things were my fault. I felt battered and assaulted by voices and welcomed damage control from medical experts. Terror imprisoned me, and I found belonging and "safety" in hospitals and in psychiatry's dominant message for fixing or at least managing me.

My voices intoned, "You belong in flames. Set yourself on fire." As a toddler I was lifted high in the air and threateningly shown flames in the kitchen incinerator. Throughout my childhood I learned from the stories about Nazi ovens. As a young girl my mother told me that I caused her suffering and illness. Years later my voices said, "All that you touch is tainted." "Stab the eyes, slash the arms." Voices preyed on my fear—claimed to be all powerful and all knowing. They embodied my rage and powerlessness. I was afraid of my voices, afraid of myself. Well-intentioned psychiatrists tried to shut down those voices without considering or acknowledging that the messages might mean something to me. I was told that my experience was not real, and the psychiatric system would help me by annihilating my "symptoms," the messengers. Dominant professionals battled dominant voices, and my relationship with all was subordinate and powerless.

Much treatment unwittingly reenacted hurtful experiences from my childhood. I voluntarily accepted huge doses of neuroleptic medications, but even with that treatment compliance, I acted on the commands of voices to do violence to myself and others. My body was held down, stripped, injected, restrained, and kept in seclusion rooms. I wasn't allowed to use the bathroom and, when in cold wet packs, I had to lay in my urine. At intervals my breathing was monitored, and no one spoke to me for hours. I was denied the experience of being held as a human being and acknowledgment of my right to be. In the 1960's and 1970's I was grateful that the psychiatric system fought to control my dangerousness to protect me and others. I did not want to hurt anyone. I considered psychiatry's aggressive tactics ethically warranted, just as I had accepted the necessity of our country's going to war to fight Nazis.

In the decades that followed, the psychiatric system's solutions for my "behavior" have remained essentially unchanged. They stopped using cold wet packs with me, sometimes provided bedpans, and continued advertising new generations of miracle medications and promising treatments. I have voluntarily used most of their tools. Conventional psychiatry continues to judge my experience as not real. They see my "symptoms" as random, arbitrary effects of neurotransmitters, and genetics, and their well-intentioned goal is my adherence to medication treatment, avoidance of hospitalization, and "maintenance." I no longer accept such invalidation. I have chosen a different path, and my psychiatrist has told me that he expects me to decompensate. If I don't, then the only explanation that his belief system can accommodate is that my diagnosis must have been wrong—wrong for half a century, yet it is I who lack capacity for insight!

He and others in the psychiatric system view me as a defective object to be fixed, and our society has accorded them the role of fixer. Profitmaking and fear-based policies, not scientific rigor or compassion propel our current approach to human suffering. I no longer wear the mantle of "other" as a shackle. I have re-oriented to locate myself, centered to meet, and connect with other humans, nature, and Spirit in respectful relationship. I honor the process of listening, hearing, and expressing together. I don't have solid answers. I have trust that through asking questions with open minds and open hearts, the asking will carry us forward together. Rather than battling pain, fear, and conflict as "other," we can move through the dissonance to seek and co-create multi-dimensional possibilities that include and value all beings, all voices.

It was only after struggling to combat fierce voices for over forty years that I discovered the World Hearing Voices Network Movement. By assertively changing my relationship with my voices, I moved from feeling powerless and disconnected to discovering and affirming their meaning and learning to accept acceptance. Joining the HVNM was not my first liberating experience, but it was qualitatively different from my other healing experience where I had learned that I could live "as-if" I was human. In the 1970's a unique psychologist nurtured me, taught me to show facial expression, to reconnect with common language, and rekindled hope that I could continue growing, learning, even loving. Even in this relationship I learned that to find a place in society, I would need to continue keeping secrets and fight against my anomalous experiences and beliefs. I found meaning working with children who were suffering but learned that I had to conceal my own pain and psychiatric experiences in order to progress through school, training, and professional education. I tried to blend into a system that would view me as "less than human" if I allowed myself to be seen and known. I was incapable of sustaining the contradictory demands of being authentic in relationship with children while denying my deepest self. The harder I tried to suppress my extreme experiences, the more intrusive and overwhelming they became. I accepted disability, hopelessness, and helplessness. Then I stumbled into the Recovery Movement which taught me that I didn't have to conquer my "symptoms" before I could engage in meaningful work. But my subordinate relationship to my voices and beliefs impeded that capacity. When I returned to work in mental health recovery, I still accepted the dominance of my voices and their messages. When I was asked to support another voice hearer, I knew that I must find another approach since mine had not worked. That propelled me to Intervoice and Working to Recovery via the internet, a new medium for me. I connected with experts by training and experts by experience in other countries and connected my local community with them as well. It was in learning and growing together in trainings and in developing Taking Back Our Power Hearing Voices Groups that I grew into my birthright as a human. Finally, I developed my right and responsibility for my own being, belonging, believing, and becoming. I shared my developing agency with others, and we grew together in community. During this time I also grew into my spiritual home with my Quaker Meeting where I realized that moving from "power over" to "power with" was essential, and it led me to recognize "power within." That mutual liberation has continued nurturing me and our local Taking Back Our Power groups and our Hearing Voices Learning Community and Hearing Voices Network.

I know that love helps, and hatred hurts. The major barrier that I've encountered to love has been fear, both individual and societal fear. It has helped me to examine power and powerlessness—actual and perceived. My liberation has involved changing how I relate to "otherness"—the outside world, other cultures, people, adversities, and to my own experience of "otherness"—my voices, visions, anomalous beliefs, fears, and rage—the "other" within and the "other" without. I couldn't make those shifts in my relationships and in my perception of power and powerlessness by myself alone. I needed to do it in relationship, the same way I came into the world at birth, and the same way I developed as a child and adult, even when I considered myself totally alone. Feeling alone relates to presence as well as absence. In recent years, I have learned to meet and engage with "other," to befriend my whole self and open opportunities for building a more compassionate, inclusive community. I believe that a similar process of "being-with" to understand "other" is a process by which we can effect both individual and social change—a way to change our relationships with dominant voices/powers within our cultures, to embrace diversity and take steps toward sustaining our relationships with each other and the planet.

Judi Chamberlin's admonition, "Nothing about us without us" taught me and countless others the importance of finding and using our voice. I have been trying to make sense of my life for as long as I can remember. I have either received, used, provided, or connected with mental health services for over 50 years. Currently I connect with individuals, groups, and systems to promote listening to all experiences and supporting people in lifting their voices to promote mutual understanding and choices for healing and wholeness. When Judi Chamberlin was dying, she wrote that her experience in hospice was the closest to the person-centered "being-with" that she had advocated for in mental health services (Goldberg, 2009). My plea today is for mental health professionals to join in such human accompaniment. We need not wait for hospice: we can create spaces that honor our individual and collective journeys—no matter how painful or frightening. We do this together by practicing presence with courage, curiosity and love.

UNIFYING VISION

Historically, gaps between the experiences of service users and clinicians have all too often led to unnecessary suffering and exclusion, as we see amply illustrated in the history of forced long-term institutionalization, hydrotherapy, involuntary sterilization, and prefrontal lobotomies (Mechanic and Rochefort, 1990; Braslow, 1999). While it is easy to dismiss past practices as naïve and unparalleled in contemporary practice, Braslow (1999) underscores how many of such practices were defended by renowned researchers, including two Nobel laureates in Medicine and the "state of the science" of the day. If randomized controlled trials are one way of working to ensure accountability within systems of care, service user involvement, and leadership is at least as important. Researchers and clinicians, that is, must not only engage with service users' experiences, but collaboratively investigate and interrogate extant understandings of "psychosis" and its causes and origins, practices that support healing, and to deconstruct the power dynamics and hierarchies that continue to dominate the production of knowledge and qualification or disqualification of different forms of experience and expertise (Kalathil and Jones, 2016).

AUTHOR CONTRIBUTIONS

The author confirms being the sole contributor of this work and approved it for publication.

ACKNOWLEDGMENTS

This article was written in relationship and collaboration. Nev Jones provided exceptional and generous expertise by linking relevant research and enabling my perspective to be considered for journal publication. Kate Hardy provided patient, gracious editing essential for completion. I am deeply grateful for their investment in collaboration.

REFERENCES

Álvarez, M. J., Roura, P., Osés, A., Foguet, Q., Sola, J., and Arrufat, F. X. (2011). Prevalence and clinical impact of childhood trauma in patients with severe mental disorders. *J. Nerv. Ment. Dis.* 199, 156–161. doi: 10.1097/NMD.0b013e31820c751c

Bendall, S., Jackson, H. J., and Hulbert, C. A. (2010). Childhood trauma and psychosis: review of the evidence and directions for psychological interventions. *Aust. Psychol.* 45, 299–306. doi: 10.1080/00050060903443219

Braslow, J. T. (1999). History and evidence-based medicine: lessons from the history of somatic treatments from the 1900s to the 1950s. *Ment. Health Serv. Res.* 1, 231–240. doi: 10.1023/A:1022325508430

Callard, F., Rose, D., and Wykes, T. (2012). Close to the bench as well as at the bedside: involving service users in all phases of translational research. *Health Expect.* 15, 389–400. doi: 10.1111/j.1369-7625.2011.00681.x

Carter, L., Read, J., Pyle, M., and Morrison, A. P. (2016). The impact of causal explanations on outcome in people experiencing psychosis: a systematic review. *Clin. Psychol. Psychother.* doi: 10.1002/cpp.2002. [Epub ahead of print].

Corstens, D., Longden, E., McCarthy-Jones, S., Waddingham, R., and Thomas, N. (2014). Emerging perspectives from the Hearing Voices Movement: implications for research and practice. *Schizophr. Bull.* 40, S285–S294. doi: 10.1093/schbul/sbu007

Faulkner, A., and Thomas, P. (2002). User-led research and evidence-based medicine. *Br. J. Psychiatry* 180, 1–3. doi: 10.1192/bjp.180.1.1

Goldberg, C. (2009). *Boston Globe, "A Talk with Judi Chamberlin: Facing Death, A Plea for the Dignity of Psychiatric Patients."* 3-22-2009.

Kalathil, J., and Jones, N. (2016). Unsettling disciplines: madness, identity, research, knowledge. *Philos. Psychiatry Psychol.* 23, 183–188. doi: 10.1353/ppp.2016.0016

Larsson, S., Andreassen, O. A., Aas, M., Røssberg, J. I., Mork, E., Steen, N. E., et al. (2013). High prevalence of childhood trauma in patients with schizophrenia spectrum and affective disorder. *Compr. Psychiatry* 54, 123–127. doi: 10.1016/j.comppsych.2012.06.009

Longden, E., Corstens, D., Escher, S., and Romme, M. (2012). Voice hearing in a biographical context: a model for formulating the relationship between voices and life history. *Psychosis* 4, 224–234. doi: 10.1080/17522439.2011.596566

Magliano, L., Read, J., Rinaldi, A., Costanzo, R., De Leo, R., Schioppa, G., et al. (2016). The influence of causal explanations and diagnostic labeling on psychology students' beliefs about treatments, prognosis, dangerousness and unpredictability in schizophrenia. *Community Ment. Health J.* 52, 361–369. doi: 10.1007/s10597-015-9901-5

Mechanic, D., and Rochefort, D. A. (1990). Deinstitutionalization: an appraisal of reform. *Annu. Rev. Sociol.* 16, 301–327. doi: 10.1146/annurev.so.16.080190.001505

Muskett, C. (2014). Trauma-informed care in inpatient mental health settings: a review of the literature. *Int. J. Ment. Health Nurs.* 23, 51–59. doi: 10.1111/inm.12012

Read, J., Sampson, M., and Critchley, C. (2016). Are mental health services getting better at responding to abuse, assault and neglect? *Acta Psychiatr. Scand.* 134, 287–294. doi: 10.1111/acps.12552

Woods, A., Jones, N., Alderson-Day, B., Callard, F., and Fernyhough, C. (2015). Experiences of hearing voices: analysis of a novel phenomenological survey. *Lancet Psychiatry* 2, 323–331. doi: 10.1016/S2215-0366(15)00006-1

15

Post-traumatic Stress Disorder Symptoms Resulting from Torture and Other Traumatic Events among Syrian Kurdish Refugees in Kurdistan Region, Iraq

Hawkar Ibrahim[1,2]* and *Chiya Q. Hassan*[2]

[1] *Department of Psychology, Clinical Psychology and Psychotherapy, Bielefeld University, Bielefeld, Germany,* [2] *Department of Clinical Psychology, Koya University, Koya, Iraq*

Edited by:
Kim T. Mueser,
Boston University, USA

Reviewed by:
Xiao Zhou,
Tel Aviv University, Israel
Alessandro Pepe,
University of Milano-Bicocca, Italy
Andres Ricardo Schneeberger,
Psychiatrische Dienste Graubuenden,
Switzerland

***Correspondence:**
Hawkar Ibrahim
hawkar@uni-bielefeld.de

Political violence is known to cause psychological distress. There is a large body of empirical studies drawing correlations between war trauma, torture, and post-traumatic stress disorder (PTSD). However, there are few studies on the effects of war-related trauma among Syrian refugees after events following the 'Arab Spring' uprisings between 2010 and 2012. This study examines the association of PTSD symptoms with torture and other traumatic events among Syrian Kurdish refugees living in Kurdistan Region, Iraq. The experiences and PTSD symptoms among 91 Syrian Kurdish refugees in the Arbat camp in the Sulaymaniyah Governorate of the Kurdistan Region of Iraq were assessed using the Harvard Trauma Questionnaire, sections I, IV, and V. Results showed that the estimated levels of PTSD symptoms were high: between 35 and 38%. There were no significant gender differences in the occurrence of PTSD symptoms. However, men reported more general traumatic experiences than women. There were significant positive correlations between PTSD symptoms with traumatic events and torture ($r = 0.500$, $r = 0.366$, respectively). Examining the mental health impact of torture and other traumatic events among refugees has possible implications for organizations managing rehabilitation programs for individuals who have been exposed to traumatic events.

Keywords: PTSD, torture, Kurd, conflict, refugees

INTRODUCTION

Over the past 5 years, the population of Syria has faced numerous civil wars and political conflicts. Thousands of people have died, and millions have fled across the border to Lebanon, Turkey, Jordan, and Iraq, including the semi-autonomous Kurdistan Region of Iraq (KRI). According to official statistics from the United Nations High Commissioner for Refugees (UNHCR) on 31 December 2014, more than 225,000 Syrian refugees have sought refuge in the KRI since the war began. These refugees are dispersed into nine camps in the cities of Erbil, Sulaymaniyah and Duhok (UNHCR and REACH Initiative, 2015). Salman's (2012) assessment of the situation of the Syrian refugees in the KRI found that most of those he interviewed had selected the fled to the KRI instead of to other countries for two main reasons; first the "safety and stability enjoyed by the province," and second for "the fact that people of the province of the same nationality and religion and using the same language" (p. 15).

It is well-known that war in itself can lead to a range of other traumatic experiences, such as witnessing extreme violence, terrorist attacks, kidnappings, torture, separation from one's family and forced migration (Johnson and Thompson, 2008). Studies indicate that most civilian adults and children in war-affected zones, including those in the Middle East, experience at least one traumatic event as a result of war and political conflict (Qouta and El Sarraj, 2004; Khamis, 2005; Fasfous et al., 2013).

Negative mental health consequences of war-related traumatic events are well-documented within current psychological literature. Most studies in post-conflict settings and among war-affected populations indicate a positive association between war trauma and the presence of various mental health disorders. For example, Priebe et al. (2010) examined mental disorders following the war in five countries (Bosnia-Herzegovina, Croatia, Kosovo, the Republic of Macedonia, and Serbia) and found that potentially traumatic experiences during and after the war were associated with higher rates of mood and anxiety disorders. Al-ghzawi et al. (2014) reviewed nine studies related to the impact of war and conflict on mental health among populations in Arab countries. They found a significant impact of war trauma on mental health. In addition, they found that post-traumatic stress disorder (PTSD) was one of the most common psychological complications among war trauma victims. Ayazi et al. (2014) examined the association between exposure to traumatic events and anxiety disorders in the post-conflict setting in South Sudan. They reported that exposure to trauma was significantly associated with diagnoses of anxiety. Similar association was found by Farhood et al. (2013) when they explored the impact of war-related life events on well-being among civilian population in southern Lebanon. More recently, Atwoli et al. (2015) reviewed epidemiological surveys of traumatic events and found high PTSD prevalence rates in post-conflict settings.

In addition to war-related traumatic events, refugees may also experience different types of torture (Gorst-Unsworth and Goldenberg, 1998; Masmas et al., 2008; Heeren et al., 2012; Widmann et al., 2014). In reviewing 40 years of health science research, Green et al. (2010) found that definitions by the World Medical Association and the United Nations were most often utilized in the scientific literature for torture. According to the World Medical Association's Tokyo Declaration, torture is defined as "the deliberate, systematic or wanton infliction of physical or mental suffering by one or more persons acting alone or on the orders of any authority, to force another person to yield information, to make a confession, or for any other reason" (World Medical Association, 1975, p. 1). The United Nations defined torture in article 1.1 of the Convention Against Torture as "any act by which severe pain or suffering, whether physical or mental, is intentionally inflicted on a person for such purposes as obtaining from him or a third person, information or a confession . . ." (Wendland, 2002, p. 23). Many scholars (e.g., Kastrup et al., 1986; Elsass, 1997; Gorman, 2001) have investigated the purposes of torture. They note that the primary aim of torture is not only to obtain information from the victims but also to break down the identities and personalities of those tortured.

Empirical psychological studies in the field of trauma have shown several mental health sequelae of torture. The most frequent psychological disorders among torture survivors were PTSD, generalized anxiety disorder, depression, and somatic disorders (Shrestha et al., 1998; Van Ommeren et al., 2002; Elklit et al., 2012; Tufan et al., 2013). Other psychosocial problems were also mentioned, such as insomnia, isolation, and loneliness (Bolton et al., 2013).

Due to exposure to war trauma, torture and post-migration living difficulties, refugees are more likely to develop mental health disorders (Keller et al., 2006; Schweitzer et al., 2006; Onyut et al., 2009; Badri et al., 2012; Bogic et al., 2012; Aragona et al., 2013).

Alpak et al. (2015) studied trauma and PTSD among Syrian adult refugees in Turkey aged between 18 and 65 years. They found that participants experienced between 0 and 9 traumatic events and PTSD was present in 33.5% of their sample. Naja et al. (2016) interviewed Syrian refugees and found that the prevalence of current depression was 43.9%. More recently, Kazour et al. (2016) examined PTSD among Syrian adult refugees in Lebanon and found 35.4% of lifetime prevalence and 27.2% of point prevalence of PTSD.

Epidemiological studies suggest gender differences in the prevalence of trauma and PTSD. Research suggests that males are more likely to experience traumatic events and that females are more likely to develop PTSD (Keane and Kaloupek, 2002; Kimerling et al., 2007; Wittchen et al., 2009). However, ethnocultural issues may also play a significant role in gender differences. Some studies from Middle Eastern countries have found no gender differences in PTSD (Elbedour et al., 2007; Shaar, 2013). The differences between findings in Middle Eastern and studies carried out in other regions require further attention.

Political violence is known to cause psychological distress, and there is a large body of empirical studies drawing a significant association between war trauma, torture, and PTSD. On the other hand, studies also showed that the traumatized people report positive psychological changes in the aftermath of trauma in their social and personal levels such as well-being, psychological growth, sense of coherence, and adaptive adjustment (Veronese and Pepe, 2015; Sleijpen et al., 2016).

However, cross-cultural studies showed negative impacts of war-related trauma but to date there is limited data on the mental health among Syrian refugees and this represents a serious gap in our knowledge. Our study is part of a larger investigation aimed to see if the expected pattern of war-trauma and the dose-effect model could also be confirmed in this population.

The current study aimed to examine the levels of PTSD symptoms among Kurdish Syrian adult refugees and the relations between torture and traumatic experiences with PTSD symptoms using a quantitative approach. We hypothesize that Kurdish refugees fleeing Syria will experience multiple types of war-related trauma and torture. Furthermore, the study aims to examine gender differences in PTSD symptoms, torture and the experience of traumatic events. We hypothesize that there will be gender differences in frequency of torture, traumatic events, and PTSD.

MATERIALS AND METHODS

Participants

Participants in the research were Syrian Kurdish refugees living in Arbat Camp in Sulaymaniyah Governorate in the KRI. The refugees in this camp originally come from predominantly Kurdish regions of Syria, and fled to the KRI as result of civil war, terrorist attacks, and air strikes. The inclusion criteria for the study were: (1) aged 18 or older; (2) registered as a refugee by UNHCR at least 3 months before the interview. None of the refugees refused to participate in the study. The participants consisted of 100 Syrian Kurdish refugees. Nine participants were excluded from analyses because of missing data. Participants were aged between 18 and 57 years old ($M = 29.91$, $SD = 9.54$). Male participants constituted most of the sample (55%). The majority of the participants (60.4%) were married and 63.7% were unemployed at the time the research was conducted. In terms of education, only 5.5% of participants reported having no formal education. In terms of financial help and mental health services, 80.2% of participants received financial help but only 14.3% received formal mental health services (**Table 1**).

Procedure

Participants were recruited through community leaders in Arbat Camp. The interviews were conducted between January and March, 2014 in their own tents. Due to cultural considerations, verbal rather than written informed consent was obtained. In the local context, signing documents is associated with the bureaucracy of authoritarian states which could have raised suspicions among participants that information may be used for purposes other than scientific research. Moreover, some participants were illiterate. Verbal informed consent was obtained by using a standardized form which included information about voluntary participation, the right to withdraw without negative consequence, confidentiality and ensuring anonymity, reviewing the risks, benefits, and associated information of the study. The verbal consent of each participant was documented by the interviewers. This procedure and the protocols of this research were approved by the Ethical Committee of Koya University. After providing verbal consent, participants were asked to complete a background questionnaire followed by sections I, IV, and V of the Harvard Trauma Questionnaire (HTQ). For illiterate participants, questionnaires were read to them item by item and verbal answers were recorded.

Measures

The Demographic Data Questionnaire consisted of two parts. The first part covered basic demographic variables (e.g., gender, age, marital status, etc.). The second consisted of some specific questions intended to solicit basic information related to refugees and their personal circumstances, such as the number of

TABLE 1 | Characteristics of participants.

Demographics		*N*	%
Gender	Female	40	44.0
	Male	51	56.0
Marital status	Never married	34	37.4
	Currently married	55	60.4
	Divorced	1	1.1
	Separated	1	1.1
Employment status	Employed	33	36.3
	Unemployed	58	63.7
Financial help	Received	73	80.2
	Not received	18	19.8
Mental health services	Received	13	14.3
	Not received	78	85.7
Missing family member or relatives	Yes	71	78.0
	No	20	22.0
Number of family members or relatives missing	Range: 0–25 people. $M = 5.86$, $SD = 6.14$		
Age	Range: 18–57 years old. $M = 29.91$, $SD = 9.54$		
Years of formal education	Range: 0*–19 years. $M = 8.86$, $SD = 3.95$		
Number of children	Range: 0–13. $M = 2.35$, $SD = 2.57$		

**Illiterate and unschooled.*

family members left behind, the date of leaving Syria, and whether they were in receipt of financial help or mental health services.

The HTQ is a self-report checklist designed by the Harvard Program for Refugee Trauma (HPRT) that investigates traumatic events, PTSD symptoms, and torture. There are numerous versions of this questionnaire but the present study used an Arabic version of this questionnaire (sections I, IV, and V) adapted for use by Shoeb et al. (2007) rather than a version using the Kurdish language. The Arabic version of the HTQ was chosen for two reasons; firstly, Arabic is the primary formal language in Syria; and secondly, before the civil war, governmental rules in Syria prohibited Kurds from learning Kurdish or building Kurdish language schools (Human Rights Watch, 1996). As a result, the majority of Syrian Kurds cannot read or write fluently in the Kurdish language.

The first section of the HTQ assesses trauma history before, during and after migration through 42 potentially traumatic events, answered in a "Yes/No" format. The fourth section consists of 45 items describing PTSD symptoms, using a four-point Likert scale rated from 1 (not at all) to 4 (extremely). This section is designed to evaluate different trauma symptoms that people may experience subsequent to hurtful or terrifying events in their lives. The first 16 items were derived from the DSM-IV criteria for PTSD and comprised of three subscales for three separate symptom clusters of PTSD; four items relate to re-experiencing symptoms; five items relate to symptoms of arousal and seven items to symptoms of avoidance. Symptoms scale scores are calculated as the mean score of the items (with a theoretical range of 1–4). The 29 additional symptom items were derived from clinical studies and experience. Generally, this part of the HTQ requests the responder to read each item carefully and decide how much the symptoms bothered them during the past week. The cut-off scores for PTSD diagnosis were greater than 2.5 (a mean score of >2.5). The final section of HTQ named "torture history" consists of 35 potential torture events with "Yes" or "No" answers. The internal consistency of HTQ subscales was shown to be high; the trauma symptoms subscale scored (Cronbach's $\alpha \geq 0.88$) on 16 PTSD items and 0.94 on 45 items, traumatic events (Cronbach's $\alpha = 0.90$) and torture history section (Cronbach's $\alpha = 0.89$).

Data Analysis

All statistical analyses were carried out by using the Statistical Package for the Social Sciences (SPSS) program version 20 for Microsoft Windows. Descriptive statistics (frequencies, means, and standard deviations) were used for analyzing all demographic variables, traumatic events, and PTSD symptoms. The differences between groups were analyzed with the two-tailed t-test. The correlations between the continuous variables were tested with Bivariate-Pearson correlation coefficients. The internal consistency reliability was determined using Cronbach's Alpha. Normality of data was checked using Shapiro-Wilk's test, Kolmogorov–Smirnov's test with histograms and normal Q–Q plots (Ghasemi and Zahediasl, 2012). For adjusting p-value, we used Bonferroni correction (Bland and Altman, 1995). For overall tests (0.003) was set as a significance level for statistical analysis.

RESULTS

PTSD Symptoms

Using the total 45 symptoms items, 35 participants had a mean score greater than 2.5 on HTQ (section V) indicating clinically significant symptomatology. On the first 16 PTSD item subscale of the HTQ, 32 of the participants had a mean score above the cutoff score of 2.5. Thus, the levels of symptoms of PTSD among participants according to established clinical cutoff scores on the HTQ (Arabic version) was between 35.16% (16 items) and 38.46% (45 items) (**Table 2**).

Torture Experience and Other Traumatic Events

Participants reported having experienced between 0 and 29 traumatic events ($M = 11.12$, $SD = 7.37$). Seventy-nine out of the participants reported having experienced at least three traumatic events listed in the first section of the HTQ during or after their migration. The most frequent traumatic events were "forced to flee your country," reported by 79 participants (86.8%), "witnessed shelling, burning, or razing of residential areas or marshlands," reported by 59 participants (64.8%), "confined to home because of chaos and violence outside," reported by 56 participants (61.5%) (**Figure 1**). Regarding experiences of torture, participants reported having been exposed to between 0 and 24 torture events ($M = 4.23$, $SD = 5.21$). Thirty-eight out of the 91 participants reported having experienced at least two events of torture; 38 (41.8%) of participants were exposed to rain or cold, 28 (30.8%) exposed to strong heat, sun, or light and 25 (27.5%) were deprived of food and water (**Figure 2**).

The correlation between PTSD 16 items and 29 items with total 45 items of the HTQ section V were highly significant ($r = 0.72, p = 0.000$; $r = 0.87, p = 0.000$; respectively). As shown in **Table 3**, bivariate correlations showed statistically significant positive correlations between PTSD symptoms, traumatic events and torture ($r = 0.500$, $p = 0.000$; $r = 0.366$, $p = 0.000$; respectively). Similar significant positive relationships were found between each of the three PTSD symptoms clusters (re-experiencing, avoidance and hyperarousal) with traumatic events.

Regarding gender differences in experiencing traumatic events, results showed that male participants had experienced more general traumatic events compared to females ($M = 12.86$ vs. 8.90 events). There were no statistically significant differences found between the genders in experiencing torture (females:

TABLE 2 | Post-traumatic stress disorder (PTSD) symptomatology.

Measures	Cutoff score	*M*	Positive cases	Negative cases
PTSD 16	2.5	2.30	35.16%	64.84%
PTSD 45	2.5	2.25	38.46%	61.54%

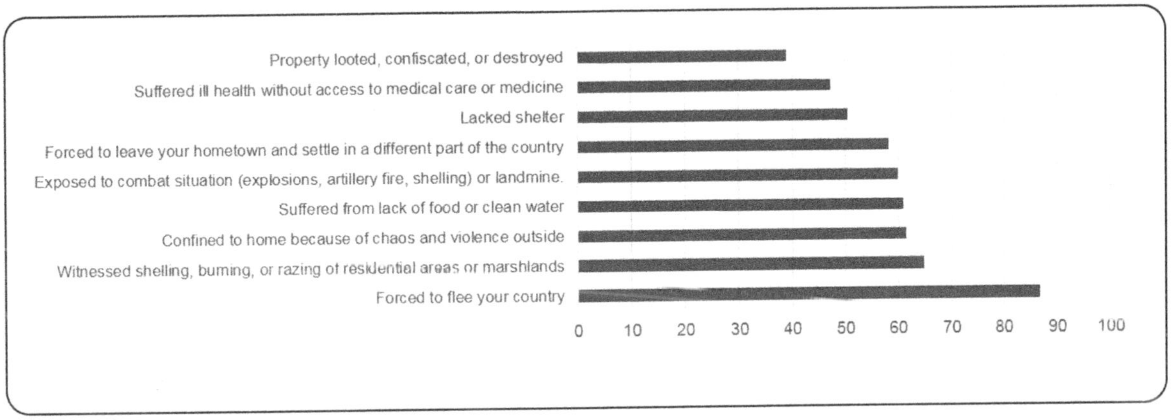

FIGURE 1 | Most frequent traumatic events (%).

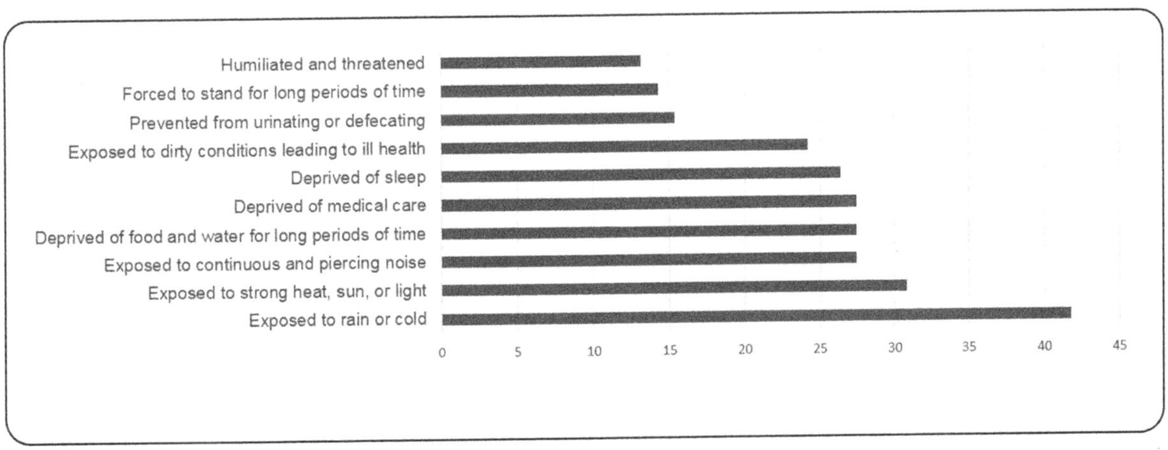

FIGURE 2 | Most frequent torture experiences (%).

TABLE 3 | Bivariate correlations between PTSD symptoms, traumatic events, and torture.

	1	2	3	4	5	6
(1) PTSD	–	0.827**	0.904**	0.917**	0.500**	0.366**
(2) PTSD-RE		–	0.673**	0.624**	0.452**	0.284*
(3) PTSD-AR			–	0.729**	0.360**	0.274
(4) PTSD-AV				–	0.509**	0.389**
(5) Traumatic events					–	0.240
(6) Torture						–

PTSD, PTSD- first sixteen items in section IV of HTQ; PTSD-RE, PTSD-re-experiencing symptoms; PTSD-AR, PTSD-arousal symptoms; PTSD-AV, PTSD-avoidance symptoms.
**p = 0.003; **p < 0.001.*

$M = 4.05$, $SD = 4.55$; male: $M = 4.37$, $SD = 5.71$) two-tailed t-test (equal variances): $t(89) = -0.292$, $p = 0.771$. Similarly, no statistically significant correlation was found between age, traumatic events, and torture ($r = -0.094$, $r = -0.039$, $p > 0.003$).

PTSD Symptoms and Demographics Variables

An exploratory data analysis was conducted to determine if the PTSD scores were normally distributed using the Explore procedure in SPSS Descriptive Statistics. Results from the Shapiro–Wilk's test and Kolmogorov–Smirnov's test along with a visual inspection of their histograms and normal Q–Q plots (Ghasemi and Zahediasl, 2012) showed that the PTSD scores were approximately normally distributed for all variables.

Regarding gender differences in PTSD symptoms, the results from two-tailed t-tests (unequal variances) showed that there were no significant differences in PTSD symptoms between females and males (Females: $M = 2.25$, $SD = 0.589$; Males: $M = 2.34$, $SD = 0.818$), $t(88.420) = -0.620$, $p = 0.537$. In addition, results showed no statistically significant differences of employment status on PTSD symptoms (employed: $M = 2.39$, $SD = 0.145$; unemployed: $M = 2.24$, $SD = 0.654$) two-tailed t-test (equal variances): $t(89) = 0.941$, $p = 0.349$. Similar results were reported in terms of receiving financial help and mental health services. Results from two-tailed t-test showed that there were no significant differences in PTSD symptoms between those refugees who received financial help and mental health services with those who had not received support: [Financial help: $M = 2.26$, $SD = 0.685$; non-financial help: $M = 2.46$, $SD = 0.869$) two-tailed t-test (equal variances): $t(89) = -1.085$, $p = 0.281$]; [mental health services: $M = 2.35$, $SD = 0.7440$; non- mental health services: $M = 2.29$, $SD = 0.725$) two-tailed t-test (equal variances): $t(89) = 0.283$, $p = 0.778$].

Additionally, there was no statistically significant correlation between PTSD symptoms according to age, education, number of children, and number of absent family members (respectively $r = 0.004$, $r = -0.126$, $r = 0.089$, $r = -0.068$, $p = 0.972$, $p = 0.234$, $p = 0.403$, $p = 0.522$).

DISCUSSION

This study examined the prevalence of PTSD symptoms among Syrian Kurdish refugees in association with torture and other traumatic events. Of the total sample, 38.46% reported PTSD symptoms in the clinical range using the 45-item total scale, and 35.16% met criteria on the first 16 symptom items of HTQ using established clinical cut-off scores. This finding is similar to results from a previous study by Alpak et al. (2015) reporting a frequency of PTSD of 33.5% among Syrian refugees in Turkey. It's also in line with finding from meta-analyses, which have documented high levels of PTSD among refugees (Fazel et al., 2005; Bogic et al., 2015).

The results of the present study showed that both the number of traumatic events and instances of torture experienced was positively correlated with PTSD, supporting previous studies that showed similar correlations between traumatic events and PTSD symptoms (Silove et al., 1997; Karunakara et al., 2004; Badri et al., 2012) and between torture and PTSD (Van Ommeren et al., 2001, 2002; Piwowarczyk, 2007; Masmas et al., 2008).

A considerable number of studies have reported that PTSD is more common in women than in men; however, this was not supported by the current study, which found no statistically significant differences in PTSD by gender. Ethnocultural factors may play a significant role in the differences between our results and results from other studies. Most of these studies reported gender differences in PTSD were conducted in Western societies or by Western psychologists/psychiatrists among Kurdish and Arabic population using Western instruments for evaluating trauma and PTSD symptoms without validation. To determine what considered as a traumatic event requires cultural knowledge and awareness because culture plays a significant role in the way people perceive an event as traumatic (von Peter, 2008; Herbert and Forman, 2010). Interestingly, a recent meta-analysis of 10 studies of adolescents in Lebanon in times of civil war found no gender differences in PTSD (Shaar, 2013).

In addition, no gender differences were reported in the number of instances of torture experienced. Tolin and Foa (2006) quantitatively reviewed 25 years of research on sex differences in trauma. They revealed that males report higher levels of exposure to potentially traumatic events. This was supported by the present study showing that the male participants experienced more traumatic events as compared to female participants.

Only 14.3% of participants received mental health services and no significant differences were found between those refugees who received mental health services with those who did not, and this may potentially be attributed to the following two reasons. Firstly, the number of participants who have received mental health services is very small in comparison to those who have not received any mental health services. Secondly, it may potentially be related to the quality of services; because there is a serious lack of psychological services within the KRI. At the current time, there is only one graduate-level clinical psychology program in the whole region.

Several limitations exist in this study. The number of participants was small and only those refugees living in Arbat Camp in Sulaymaniyah Governorate, one of the smaller camps for Syrian refugees in the KRI, were examined. The findings of this study may have also been limited by the instruments used in this study, given that the participants were Syrian Kurdish refugees but the instruments used in this study were presented in the Arabic language. Moreover, there is also the possibility of bias by the participants in responding to the self-reported questionnaires because some of them may have believed that their answers would impact upon the possibility of receiving financial assistance. It was clearly explained to participants that no financial assistance would be provided as a result of their answers, but the possibility exists that some of the results may reflect this bias.

Further research into PTSD among Syrian refugees in the KRI, conducted with a larger sample size, may provide more informative findings. It will be more useful if future studies explore the association between war related events, torture and positive changes after trauma. Additionally, translation of existing trauma questionnaires into the Kurdish language may facilitate interviews and ensure accurate outcomes. Finally, our findings that between 35 and 38% of Syrian refugees are experiencing PTSD symptoms, lend weight to calls for improved mental health services for Syrian Kurdish refugees in the KRI.

CONCLUSION

The results of this study supported findings from the literature about the positive significant association between PTSD symptoms, torture, and other war-related trauma. Our results did not show significant gender differences in the experience of PTSD symptoms. The findings of our study have possible applications for local and international governments, human right and mental health organizations, especially for those who provide psychosocial support programs for Syrian refugees. In addition, the results of our sturdy provide a better understanding of the mental health of Syrian refuges and this will contribute to the cross-cultural understanding of trauma and provide data to expand current models of trauma psychology. Also, such scientific documentation may contribute to increasing awareness of mental health needs and may provide an impetus for supporting expansion of psychological services in KRI and for Syrian refugees.

ETHICS STATEMENT

This procedure and the protocols of this study were approved by the Ethical Committee of Koya University. Due to cultural considerations, verbal rather than written informed consent was obtained by using a standardized form which included information about voluntary participation, the right to withdraw without negative consequence, confidentiality and ensuring anonymity, reviewing the risks, benefits, and associated information of the study.

AUTHOR CONTRIBUTIONS

HI: study conception and design, analysis and interpretation of data, drafting of manuscript, critical revision, and final approval of the version to be published. CH: study design and data collection.

ACKNOWLEDGMENTS

We are grateful to all Syrian Kurdish refugees who participated in this study. We thank Prof. Dr. Frank Neuner in the department of Clinical Psychology and Psychotherapy, Bielefeld University, Germany and Prof. Dr. Sandra Zakowski in the Illinois School of Professional Psychology at Argosy University, Chicago for their comments and helpful advice. We'd like to thanks our dear friend Dr. Joanne Payton from the School of Social Sciences at Cardiff University, UK, for her proofreading. We also acknowledge the financial support of the German Research Foundation (DFG) and the Open Access Publication Fund of Bielefeld University for the article processing charge.

REFERENCES

Al-ghzawi, H. M., ALBashtawy, M., Azzeghaiby, S. N., and Alzoghaibi, I. N. (2014). The impact of wars and conflicts on mental health of Arab population. *Int. J. Humanit. Soc. Sci.* 4, 237–242.

Alpak, G., Unal, A., Bulbul, F., Sagaltici, E., Bez, Y., Altindag, A., et al. (2015). Post-traumatic stress disorder among Syrian refugees in Turkey: a cross-sectional study. *Int. J. Psychiatry Clin. Pract.* 19, 45–50. doi: 10.3109/13651501.2014.961930

Aragona, M., Pucci, D., Mazzetti, M., Maisano, B., and Geraci, S. (2013). Traumatic events, post-migration living difficulties and post-traumatic symptoms in first generation immigrants: a primary care study. *Ann. Ist. Super. Sanita* 49, 169–175. doi: 10.4415/ANN_13_02_08

Atwoli, L., Stein, D. J., Koenen, K. C., and McLaughlin, K. A. (2015). Epidemiology of posttraumatic stress disorder. *Curr. Opin. Psychiatry* 28, 307–311. doi: 10.1097/YCO.0000000000000167

Ayazi, T., Lien, L., Eide, A., Swartz, L., and Hauff, E. (2014). Association between exposure to traumatic events and anxiety disorders in a post-conflict setting: a cross-sectional community study in South Sudan. *BMC Psychiatry* 14:6. doi: 10.1186/1471-244X-14-6

Badri, A., Crutzen, R., and den Borne, H. W. (2012). Exposures to war-related traumatic events and post-traumatic stress disorder symptoms among displaced Darfuri female university students: an exploratory study. *BMC Public Health* 12:603. doi: 10.1186/1471-2458-12-603

Bland, J. M., and Altman, D. G. (1995). Multiple significance tests: the Bonferroni method. *BMJ* 310:170. doi: 10.1136/bmj.310.6973.170

Bogic, M., Ajdukovic, D., Bremner, S., Franciskovic, T., Galeazzi, G. M., Kucukalic, A., et al. (2012). Factors associated with mental disorders in long-settled war refugees: refugees from the former Yugoslavia in Germany, Italy and the UK. *Br. J. Psychiatry* 200, 216–223. doi: 10.1192/bjp.bp.110.084764

Bogic, M., Njoku, A., Priebe, S., Fazel, M., Wheeler, J., Danesh, J., et al. (2015). Long-term mental health of war-refugees: a systematic literature review. *BMC Int. Health Hum. Rights* 15, 29. doi: 10.1186/s12914-015-0064-9

Bolton, P., Michalopoulos, L., Ahmed, A. M. A., Murray, L. K., and Bass, J. (2013). The mental health and psychosocial problems of survivors of torture and genocide in Kurdistan, Northern Iraq: a brief qualitative study. *Torture* 23, 1–14.

Elbedour, S., Onwuegbuzie, A. J., Ghannam, J., Whitcome, J. A., and Hein, F. A. (2007). Post-traumatic stress disorder, depression, and anxiety among Gaza Strip adolescents in the wake of the second Uprising (Intifada). *Child Abuse Negl.* 31, 719–729. doi: 10.1016/j.chiabu.2005.09.006

Elklit, A., Kjær, K. Ø, Lasgaard, M., and Palic, S. (2012). Social support, coping and posttraumatic stress symptoms in young refugees. *Torture* 22, 11–23.

Elsass, P. (1997). *Treating Victims of Torture and Violence: Theoretical, Cross-Cultural, and Clinical Implications* (J. Andersen and H. Fuglsang, trans.). New York, NY: New York University Press.

Farhood, L., Dimassi, H., and Strauss, N. L. (2013). Understanding post-conflict mental health: assessment of PTSD, depression, general health and life events in civilian population one year after the 2006 War in South Lebanon. *J. Trauma. Stress Disord. Treat.* 2, 1–8.

Fasfous, A. F., Peralta-Ramírez, I., and Pérez-García, M. (2013). Symptoms of PTSD among children living in War zones in same cultural context and different situations. *J. Muslim Ment. Health* 7, 47–61. doi: 10.3998/jmmh.10381607.0007.203

Fazel, M., Wheeler, J., and Danesh, J. (2005). Prevalence of serious mental disorder in 7000 refugees resettled in western countries: a systematic review. *Lancet* 365, 1309–1314. doi: 10.1016/S0140-6736(05)61027-6

Ghasemi, A., and Zahediasl, S. (2012). Normality tests for statistical analysis: a guide for non-statisticians. *Int. J. Endocrinol. Metab.* 10, 486–489. doi: 10.5812/ijem.3505

Gorman, W. (2001). Refugee survivors of torture: trauma and treatment. *Prof. Psychol. Res. Pract.* 32, 443–451. doi: 10.1037/0735-7028.32.5.443

Gorst-Unsworth, C., and Goldenberg, E. (1998). Psychological sequelae of torture and organised violence suffered by refugees from Iraq. Trauma-related factors compared with social factors in exile. *Br. J. Psychiatry* 172, 90–94. doi: 10.1192/bjp.172.1.90

Green, D., Rasmussen, A., and Rosenfeld, B. (2010). Defining torture: a review of 40 years of health science research. *J. Trauma. Stress* 23, 215–222. doi: 10.1002/jts

Heeren, M., Mueller, J., Ehlert, U., Schnyder, U., Copiery, N., and Maier, T. (2012). Mental health of asylum seekers: a cross-sectional study of psychiatric disorders. *BMC Psychiatry* 12:114. doi: 10.1186/1471-244X-12-114

Herbert, J. D., and Forman, E. M. (2010). "Cross – cultural perspectives on posttraumatic stress," in *Clinician's Guide to Posttraumatic Stress Disorder*, 1st Edn, eds B. C. Rosen and G. M. Frueh (Hoboken, NJ: John Wiley & Sons), 235–261.

Human Rights Watch (1996). *Syria the Silenced Kurds*, Vol. 8. Available at: https://www.hrw.org/sites/default/files/reports/SYRIA96.pdf

Johnson, H., and Thompson, A. (2008). The development and maintenance of post-traumatic stress disorder (PTSD) in civilian adult survivors of war trauma and torture: a review. *Clin. Psychol. Rev.* 28, 36–47. doi: 10.1016/j.cpr.2007.01.017

Karunakara, U. K., Neuner, F., Schauer, M., Singh, K., Hill, K., Elbert, T., et al. (2004). Traumatic events and symptoms of post-traumatic stress disorder amongst Sudanese nationals, refugees and Ugandans in the West Nile. *Afr. Health Sci.* 4, 83–93.

Kastrup, M., Lunde, I., Ortmann, J., and Genefke, I. K. (1986). MENTAL CONSEQUENCES OF TORTURE: the method of rehabilitation at a rehabilitation centre at Copenhagen. *Indian J. Psychiatry* 28, 225–229.

Kazour, F., Zahreddine, N. R., Maragel, M. G., Almustafa, M. A., Haddad, R., Soufia, M., et al. (2016). Post-traumatic stress disorder in a sample of Syrian refugees in Lebanon. *Compr. Psychiatry* 72, 41–47. doi: 10.1016/j.comppsych.2016.09.007

Keane, T. M., and Kaloupek, D. G. (2002). "Diagnosis, assessment, and monitoring outcomes in PTSD," in *Treating Trauma Survivors with PTSD*, 1st Edn, ed. R. Yehuda (Washington, DC: American Psychiatric Publishing), 21–42.

Keller, A., Lhewa, D., Rosenfeld, B., Sachs, E., Aladjem, A., Cohen, I., et al. (2006). Traumatic experiences and psychological distress in an urban refugee population seeking treatment services. *J. Nerv. Ment. Dis.* 194, 188–194. doi: 10.1097/01.nmd.0000202494.75723.83

Khamis, V. (2005). Post-traumatic stress disorder among school age Palestinian children. *Child Abuse Negl.* 29, 81–95. doi: 10.1016/j.chiabu.2004.06.013

Kimerling, R., Ouimette, P., and Weitlauf, J. C. (2007). "Gender Issues in PTSD," in *Handbook of PTSD: Science and Practice*, 1st Edn, eds M. J. Friedman, T. M. Keane, and P. A. Resick (New York, NY: The Guilford Press), 207–228.

Masmas, T., Student, E., and Buhmann, C. (2008). Asylum seekers in Denmark. *Torture* 18, 77–86.

Naja, W. J., Aoun, M. P., El Khoury, E. L., Abdallah, F. J. B., and Haddad, R. S. (2016). Prevalence of depression in Syrian refugees and the influence of religiosity. *Compr. Psychiatry* 68, 78–85. doi: 10.1016/j.comppsych.2016.04.002

Onyut, L. P., Neuner, F., Ertl, V., Schauer, E., Odenwald, M., and Elbert, T. (2009). Trauma, poverty and mental health among Somali and Rwandese refugees living in an African refugee settlement – an epidemiological study. *Confl. Health* 3:6. doi: 10.1186/1752-1505-3-6

Piwowarczyk, L. (2007). Asylum seekers seeking mental health services in the United States: clinical and legal implications. *J. Nerv. Ment. Dis.* 195, 715–722. doi: 10.1097/NMD.0b013e318142ca0b

Priebe, S., Bogic, M., Ajdukovic, D., Franciskovic, T., Galeazzi, G. M., Kucukalic, A., et al. (2010). Mental disorders following war in the Balkans a study in 5 countries. *Arch. Gen. Psychiatry* 67, 518–528. doi: 10.1001/archgenpsychiatry.2010.37

Qouta, S., and El Sarraj, E. (2004). Prevalence of PTSD among Palestinian children in Gaza Strip. *Arab Psynet J.* 2:6.

Salman, M. (2012). *Assessment of the Situation of the Syrian Refugees in Kurdistan Region Iraq. MPC Research Report.* Available at: http://hdl.handle.net/1814/24837

Schweitzer, R., Melville, F., Steel, Z., and Lacherez, P. (2006). Trauma, post-migration living difficulties, and social support as predictors of psychological adjustment in resettled Sudanese refugees. *Aust. N. Z. J. Psychiatry* 40, 179–187. doi: 10.1111/j.1440-1614.2006.01766.x

Shaar, K. H. (2013). Post-traumatic stress disorder in adolescents in Lebanon as wars gained in ferocity: a systematic review. *J. Public Health Res.* 2, 17–99. doi: 10.4081/jphr.2013.e17

Shoeb, M., Weinstein, H., and Mollica, R. (2007). The harvard trauma questionnaire: adapting a cross-cultural instrument for measuring torture, trauma and posttraumatic stress disorder in Iraqi refugees. *Int. J. Soc. Psychiatry* 53, 447–463. doi: 10.1177/0020764007078362

Shrestha, N. M., Sharma, B., Van Ommeren, M., Regmi, S., Makaju, R., Komproe, I., et al. (1998). Impact of torture on refugees displaced within the developing world: symptomatology among Bhutanese refugees in Nepal. *JAMA* 280, 443–448. doi: 10.1001/jama.280.5.443

Silove, D., Sinnerbrink, I., Field, A., Manicavasagar, V., and Steel, Z. (1997). Anxiety, depression and PTSD in asylum-seekers: assocations with pre-migration trauma and post-migration stressors. *Br. J. Psychiatry* 170, 351–357. doi: 10.1192/bjp.170.4.351

Sleijpen, M., Haagen, J., Mooren, T., and Kleber, R. J. (2016). Growing from experience: an exploratory study of posttraumatic growth in adolescent refugees. *Eur. J. Psychotraumatol.* 7:28698. doi: 10.3402/ejpt.v7.28698

Tolin, D. F., and Foa, E. B. (2006). Sex differences in trauma and posttraumatic stress disorder: a quantitative review of 25 years of research. *Psychol. Bull.* 132, 959–992. doi: 10.1037/0033-2909.132.6.959

Tufan, A. E., Alkin, M., and Bosgelmez, S. (2013). Post-traumatic stress disorder among asylum seekers and refugees in Istanbul may be predicted by torture and loss due to violence. *Nord. J. Psychiatry* 67, 219–224. doi: 10.3109/08039488.2012.732113

UNHCR and REACH Initiative (2015). *Intentions Assessment of Syrian Refugees in Camps.* Kurdistan Region of Iraq Assessment Report. Available at: http://www.reachresourcecentre.info/system/files/resource-documents/reach_irq_report_comparativeintentionssyrianrefugeesincamps_march2015_2.pdf

Van Ommeren, M., de Jong, J. T. V. M., Sharma, B., Komproe, I., Thapa, S. B., and Cardeña, E. M. V. O. (2001). Psychiatric disorders among tortured Bhutanese refugees in Nepal. *Arch. Gen. Psychiatry* 58, 475–482. doi: 10.1001/archpsyc.58.5.475

Van Ommeren, M., Sharma, B., Sharma, G. K., Komproe, I., Cardeña, E., and De Jong, J. T. V. M. (2002). The relationship between somatic and PTSD symptoms among Bhutanese refugee torture survivors: examination of comorbidity with anxiety and depression. *J. Trauma. Stress* 15, 415–421. doi: 10.1023/A:1020141510005

Veronese, G., and Pepe, A. (2015). Sense of coherence as a determinant of psychological well-being across professional groups of aid workers exposed to war trauma. *J. Interpers. Violence* doi: 10.1177/0886260515590125 [Epub ahead of print].

von Peter, S. (2008). The experience of "mental trauma" and its transcultural application. *Transcult. Psychiatry* 45, 639–651. doi: 10.1177/1363461508100786

Wendland, L. (2002). *A Handbook on State Obligations under the UN Convention against Torture.* Geneva: Association for the Prevention of Torture.

Widmann, M., Warsame, A. H., Mikulica, J., von Beust, J., Isse, M. M., Ndetei, D., et al. (2014). Khat use, PTSD and psychotic symptoms among Somali refugees in Nairobi – A pilot study. *Front. Public Health* 2:71. doi: 10.3389/fpubh.2014.00071

Wittchen, H.-U., Gloster, A., Beesdo, K., Schönfeld, S., and Perkonigg, A. (2009). Posttraumatic stress disorder: diagnostic and epidemiological perspectives. *CNS Spectr.* 14(1 Suppl. 1), 5–12.

World Medical Association (1975). "WMA declaration of Tokyo – Guidelines for physicians concerning torture and other cruel, inhuman or degrading treatment or punishment in relation to detention and imprisonment," in *Proceedings of the 29th World Medical Assembly* (Tokyo: World Medical Association).

16

Feasibility and Efficacy of Prolonged Exposure for PTSD among Individuals with a Psychotic Spectrum Disorder

Anouk L. Grubaugh[1,2], Kimberly Veronee[1,2], Charles Ellis[3], Wilson Brown[1,2] and Rebecca G. Knapp[4]*

[1] Ralph H. Johnson Veterans Affairs Medical Center, Charleston, SC, United States, [2] Department of Psychiatry and Behavioral Sciences, Medical University of South Carolina, Charleston, SC, United States, [3] Department of Communication Sciences and Disorders, East Carolina University, Greenville, NC, United States, [4] Department of Public Health Sciences, Medical University of South Carolina, Charleston, SC, United States

Edited by:
Kim T. Mueser,
Boston University, United States

Reviewed by:
Andres Ricardo Schneeberger,
Psychiatrische Dienste Graubuenden,
Switzerland
Pallavi Mishra Nishith,
Places For People, United States

***Correspondence:**
Anouk L. Grubaugh
grubaugh@musc.edu

Objective: Few empirical studies have examined the feasibility of trauma-focused treatment among individuals with schizophrenia. This lack of research is important given the substantial overlap of trauma exposure and subsequent PTSD with psychotic spectrum disorders, and the potential for PTSD to complicate the course and prognosis of schizophrenia and other variants of severe mental illness.

Method: As part of a larger study, 14 veterans with a psychotic spectrum disorder were enrolled to receive prolonged exposure (PE) for PTSD within a single arm open trial study design. Patient reactions and responses to PE were examined using feasibility indices such as attrition, survey reactions, and treatment expectancy; pre and post-changes in PTSD severity and diagnostic status; and thematic interviews conducted post-intervention.

Results: Quantitative and qualitative data indicate that implementation of PE is feasible, subjectively well-tolerated, and may result in clinically significant reductions in PTSD symptoms in patients with psychotic spectrum disorders.

Conclusion: Consistent with treatment outcome data in clinical populations with a broader range of severe mental illnesses, the current results support the use of PTSD exposure-based interventions, such as PE, for individuals with psychotic spectrum disorders.

Keywords: severe mental illness (SMI), trauma, exposure therapy, psychotic disorder, schizophrenia

INTRODUCTION

It is well documented that individuals with severe and persistent forms of mental illness (SMI) are at increased risk for the experience of a traumatic event and subsequent development of post-traumatic stress disorder (PTSD; see Grubaugh et al., 2011 for review). Specifically, current and lifetime prevalence rates of PTSD in this population range between 46 and 53% (Grubaugh et al., 2011). Additionally, a comorbid diagnosis of PTSD among individuals with SMI is highly correlated with decreased psychosocial functioning, worse quality of life, and substance use (e.g.,

Mueser et al., 2004a,b; Ford and Fournier, 2007; Fan et al., 2008; Grubaugh et al., 2011); as well as a range of other prognostic indicators such as homelessness, disability ratings, suicidal ideation (e.g., Sautter et al., 1999; Mueser et al., 2004b; Strauss et al., 2006; Newman et al., 2010), and exacerbations in the core symptoms of SMI diagnoses (e.g., Kilcommons and Morrison, 2005; Lysaker et al., 2005; Schenkel et al., 2005; Üçok and Bikmaz, 2007; Lysaker and Larocco, 2008; Meade et al., 2009).

Despite elevated risk of PTSD and the associated impairment among individuals with SMI, the literature regarding the implementation of trauma- and PTSD-focused psychotherapy in this clinical population remains underdeveloped. This gap in data is due in part to the historical exclusion of patients with current psychotic symptoms, recent histories of suicidal or unstable behavior, and/or severe illness burden from participation in PTSD clinical trials (Spinazzola et al., 2005); as well as concerns by some clinicians that intense trauma focused interventions may be 'over-stimulating' for individuals with SMI (Braiterman, 2004; Fowler, 2004; Frueh et al., 2006a). Published studies include a handful of small open trials (Rosenberg et al., 2004; Mueser et al., 2007; Lu et al., 2009) and one randomized controlled trial (RCT), each of which used a similar cognitive restructuring intervention in samples of community mental health center (CMHC) patients (Mueser et al., 2008). Two additional open trials examined the efficacy of an exposure-based intervention for PTSD among individuals with SMI, one in a CMHC and the other in a VA Medical Center (Frueh et al., 2009; Grubaugh et al., 2016, respectively). Finally, one small RCT and two larger RCTs conducted in the Netherlands with community outpatients reported on the efficacy of two common types of exposure therapy (de Bont et al., 2013, 2016; van den Berg et al., 2015). Collectively, results from these trials suggest that specialized PTSD interventions are effective among patients with SMI (both civilian and veteran) and result in statistically significant reductions in PTSD symptoms across treatment (Frueh et al., 2009; Grubaugh et al., 2016) or between active and control group conditions (Mueser et al., 2008).

Although preliminary PTSD treatment outcome data for individuals with SMI are promising, there is significant room for an increased understanding of how this subset of trauma survivors respond to targeted PTSD intervention—particularly individuals with a psychotic spectrum disorder, given diathesis stress models of psychosis (Grubaugh et al., 2011). As such, the current manuscript used mixed qualitative/quantitative methods to better understand how a sample of 14 patients with a psychotic spectrum disorder (i.e., schizophrenia, schizoaffective, and psychotic disorder NOS) responded to Prolonged Exposure (PE) for PTSD (Foa and Rothbaum, 1998) using a range of feasibility indices, post-treatment thematic interview data, and symptom severity measures.

MATERIALS AND METHODS

Overview of Study

The current study was part of a larger open trial of PE for PTSD among veterans with a psychotic spectrum disorder (Grubaugh et al., 2016). The active intervention phase (i.e., treatment phase) consisted of approximately 10–15 weekly individual sessions of PE, a widely disseminated manualized exposure-based intervention for trauma and PTSD (Foa and Rothbaum, 1998). Participants completed an initial (baseline) assessment prior to the initiation of treatment, an assessment immediately following the conclusion of treatment, and a final follow-up assessment 6 months after treatment completion. Follow-up assessment data reported in the current study reflects immediate post-treatment data due to low frequency of 6-month follow-up data.

Participants

Fourteen (14) veterans with a psychotic spectrum disorder were enrolled in the current study and included in the current analysis plan. These veterans were part of a larger clinical trial for PTSD that included a broader case-mix of SMI diagnoses (Grubaugh et al., 2016). The 14 veterans in the current study consist of the subset of patients from the larger trial that had a diagnosis of a psychotic disorder. Procedures for the current study were identical to that of the larger trial. All veterans had a history of psychiatric hospitalization and impaired psychosocial functioning and generally required assistance with independent living and symptom/medication management as documented within individual patient clinical records and by their disability status. Medication titration was not part of the study, and veterans remained on their current medications and dosing pre- to post-intervention. Diagnoses of a psychotic disorder and PTSD were verified via clinician-administered semi-structured diagnostic interviews (detailed below). Exclusion criteria for study consisted of current substance dependence, current psychiatric hospitalization, or a recent suicide attempt within 2 months of enrollment in the study.

Assessment Measures

Eligibility for the intervention trial was determined using the following measures:

The Trauma Assessment for Adults (TAA; Resnick, 1996) was used to identify an index trauma for treatment at baseline (i.e., to confirm PTSD criterion A; American Psychiatric Association [APA], 2000). The index trauma was limited to one "type" of traumatic event (i.e., combat or sexual assault) but could include both discrete and/or chronic types of trauma (i.e., single sexual assault, child sexual abuse). In cases where there were multiple events related to the same trauma (i.e., child sexual abuse) a 'worst' event was selected if possible and the PTSD assessment was anchored that that 'worst' event.

The Clinician-Administered PTSD Scale (CAPS; Blake et al., 2005) assessed the frequency and intensity of current PTSD symptoms using DSM-IV criteria. The CAPS is a well-established measure for determining PTSD diagnoses and possesses strong psychometric properties and diagnostic application (Weathers et al., 2001), and it has been previously utilized to reliably diagnose PTSD in SMI populations (Grubaugh et al., 2011). PTSD diagnoses were confirmed during the baseline assessment with the CAPS using the F1/I2 scoring algorithm (Weathers et al., 1999). Likewise, the CAPS was used as the primary clinical outcome at follow-up.

The Mini-International Neuropsychiatric Interview for DSM-IV (MINI for DSM-IV; Sheehan et al., 1998) is a clinician-administered, semi-structured diagnostic interview that was used to confirm the presence of a psychotic disorder at baseline. Comorbid psychiatric conditions were also identified using the MINI. Veterans who endorsed current alcohol/substance dependence during the MINI were excluded from the intervention trial. The MINI is a well regarded diagnostic tool that demonstrates sufficient diagnostic sensitivity and specificity in comparison to more extensive clinician-administered diagnostic interviews (e.g., SCID; Sheehan et al., 1998).

The PTSD Checklist (PCL; Weathers et al., 1993) is a brief self-report measure of PTSD symptoms based on DSM-IV diagnostic criteria. In the current study, the PCL was administered at each assessment time point and during each treatment session. The PCL has 17 items, and individual item scores are summed to yield a total score ranging from 17 to 85. The PCL demonstrates a high correlation with the CAPS ($r = 0.93$) and sufficient diagnostic efficiency of PTSD (>0.70) within multiple trauma populations (Weathers et al., 1993; Blanchard et al., 1996).

A Reactions to PTSD Research Survey, developed by the study team in previous research, was used at the post-assessment to obtain quantitative ratings of veterans' reactions to the intervention. The survey used a 10-point Likert scale that assessed six domains: (1) distress, (2) difficulty, and (3) confusion associated with study research procedures; (4) participation satisfaction; (5) perceived value of the research experience; and (6) willingness to participate in comparable research in the future.

A modified Treatment Expectancy (Borkovec and Nau, 1972) form was administered after the third treatment session to assess the subjective treatment outcome expectancies and perceptions of treatment credibility of study participants. Four questions on this measure were selected for use in the current study: (1) patient perception of the treatment rationale; (2) patient confidence in the treatment addressing PTSD; (3) patient willingness to recommend the treatment to others; and (4) patient expectation for treatment success.

Procedure

Participants were recruited through direct referrals from VA service providers in a specialized mental health clinic, the PTSD Clinical Team (PCT), of a Southeastern VAMC. That is, veterans initially presenting for treatment to this clinic were referred to study personnel if they had a diagnosis of a psychotic disorder in their electronic medical records. Veterans who expressed an interest in receiving treatment through the study were then contacted by study staff to schedule a baseline assessment and determine eligibility. At the time of enrollment, veterans had VA case managers and were on psychotropic medications at the time of enrollment but were not receiving any other psychotherapy at the time. The baseline assessment was conducted by the study team and included a thorough review of the study rationale and procedures followed by informed consent and a battery of instruments. Eligibility was determined by a positive diagnosis of PTSD on the CAPS and a positive diagnosis of a psychotic disorder on the MINI. The study was conducted with full approval from the associated institutional review boards and data collection occurred between January 2008 and December 2012.

Intervention

Prolonged Exposure was administered, consistent with the PE manual, in 10–15 weekly individual sessions (Foa and Rothbaum, 1998). While PE is implemented in 10 sessions as standardized by the protocol, up to five additional sessions were allowed if clinically warranted, given the novelty of the patient population[1]. Sessions 1 and 2 included psychoeducation, discussion of expectations for therapy, and instruction in diaphragmatic breathing and progressive muscle relaxation. Subsequent sessions consisted of imaginal exposure of the trauma narrative based on the identified index event and *in vivo* exposure exercises based upon a constructed hierarchy of fear provoking stimuli or situations. For patients with multiple traumas of the same theme (i.e., those with multiple combat experiences or child sexual abuse), exposure exercises focused on the 'worst' event first and then proceeded to other events as warranted based on habituation to this 'worst' event. Treatment sessions lasted approximately 60–90 min and generally included at least 45 min of imaginal exposure.

Quantitative Statistical Analyses

Descriptive Analyses

Statistical assumptions for planned data analyses were evaluated via calculations of demographic and baseline clinical variables descriptive statistics (i.e., measures of central tendency, variability, and frequency distributions). Baseline characteristics for those who completed eight or more sessions of the intervention were compared to the remainder of the sample using Chi-square or Fisher's Exact Test for dichotomous variables and t-tests for continuous variables. Similar comparisons were made between those who attended four or more sessions of the intervention to the remainder of the sample.

Feasibility Analyses

The feasibility analyses used the full sample size of 14 veterans with a psychotic spectrum disorder enrolled to receive PE for PTSD. Feasibility outcomes included patients enrolled in the intervention who did not attend any sessions, those who completed only one session, those who completed less than four sessions, those who completed less than eight sessions, and those who completed 11–15 sessions. Assessment items related to treatment expectations and study participation reactions were evaluated with mean/standard deviation calculations.

Clinical Outcome Analyses

Clinician-Administered PTSD Scale PTSD analyses consisted of participants who completed at least four treatment sessions ($n = 10$; i.e., received at least two sessions of imaginal exposure). Post-scores were missing for one of the ten subjects who attended at least four sessions, yielding a completer sample

[1]Veterans were offered additional sessions by their therapist if they reported significant symptoms on the PTSD Symptom Checklist (PCL) toward the end of the standard course of treatment (i.e., by session 7 or 8). Only one Veteran in the current sample was offered and received additional sessions.

of nine participants for CAPS outcome analyses pre- to post-intervention. The full sample size ($n = 14$) was not used because the assumption of missing at random (MAR) was questionable for methods such as multiple imputation, and the sample size was prohibitively small for complex methods for data not missing at random.

The secondary efficacy outcome measure was the PCL evaluated prior to participation in therapy (baseline), after each therapy session during the active intervention phase, and at post-intervention. 95% confidence intervals and the paired *t*-test were used to estimate the magnitude and test statistical significance of change from baseline to post-treatment for CAPS total score and PCL. In a second approach for the PCL, mixed effects modeling (MEM) was used to estimate the slope of scores across the study time period. The trajectory for sessions 1–10 was used for these analyses as this was the standard course of treatment recommended for all patients by the PE manual. Because of the single arm design, analyses of symptom improvement (i.e., efficacy) are considered descriptive and hypothesis generating rather than hypothesis testing.

Qualitative Data Collection and Analysis

Thematic Interview

All participants completed a clinician administered thematic interview at the end of treatment (or when patient was willing, at drop-out) to learn more about their reactions, perceptions, beliefs, preferences, and suggestions for PE. A flexible interview approach was used, providing the patient with topics and subject areas of inquiry but allowing for additional commentary or queries as indicated. Discussions lasted about 30 min and were audiotaped for later transcription and analysis.

Data Management/Analysis

Data was coded using a constructivist grounded theory approach (e.g., Charmaz, 2006). First, multiple thorough readings of interview transcriptions by three independent coders was conducted for content analysis. Each independent coder then generated an independent list of thematic categories and subcategories. After the primary coder further developed and ordered the data, the themes were reviewed, refined, and finalized by the group. This analytic approach has been used successfully by the authors with a range of patient and provider samples (e.g., Robins et al., 2005; Frueh et al., 2006a,b, 2012).

TABLE 1 | Demographics and baseline symptom severity.

	Full sample $n = 14$	Completer sample $n = 10$
Age	$M = 46.8$ $SD = 12.9$	$M = 52.88$ $SD = 11.75$
Employment		
Full-time	7% ($n = 1$)	10% ($n = 1$)
Part-time	7% ($n = 1$)	0%
Unemployed	86% ($n = 12$)	90% ($n = 13$)
Race		
African American	50% ($n = 7$)	
Caucasian	50% ($n = 7$)	
Relationship status		
Married/cohabitating	57% ($n = 8$)	70% ($n = 10$)
Not married/cohabitating	43% ($n = 6$)	30% ($n = 4$)
Gender		
Male	93% ($n = 13$)	100%
Disability Connection PTSD		
Yes		42.9% ($n = 6$)
Service Era		
Vietnam	43% ($n = 6$)	
Post-Vietnam	14% ($n = 2$)	
Persian Gulf	14% ($n = 2$)	
OEF/OIF	29% ($n = 4$)	
Index trauma		
Combat	62.5% ($n = 8$)	
Physical assault	12.5% ($n = 2$)	
Adult sexual assault	12.5% ($n = 2$)	
Serious accident	12.5% ($n = 2$)	
CAPS	$M = 75.64$ $SD = 19.91$	$M = 68.00$ $SD = 18.04$
PCL	$M = 64.14$ $SD = 8.31$	$M = 62.00$ $SD = 8.99$

Completers attended four or more sessions and had available CAPS post-data ($n = 9$). Non-completers attended fewer than four session ($n = 4$) or were missing post-data ($n = 1$), yielding a total of $n = 5$ participants.

RESULTS

Descriptive Analyses

See **Table 1** for demographics and baseline severity data on the full sample ($n = 14$) and those included in the completer efficacy analyses ($n = 10$). Comparisons were made between veterans who completed a minimum of eight sessions (i.e., standard course of therapy; $n = 8$) relative to the remainder of the sample ($n = 6$) by age, service era, baseline CAPS total scores, race/ethnicity, marital status, and index trauma. Race/ethnicity, marital status, or index trauma were not statistically different across groups. However, statistically significant group differences emerged by age, service era, and baseline CAPS total scores. More specifically, veterans completing less than eight sessions tended to be younger, *M(SD)* = 38.67(12.50) versus 52.88(11.08), $t = -2.38, p = 0.04$; and 50% of those who received less than eight sessions were Operation Enduring Freedom/Operation Iraqi Freedom (OEF/OIF) $[\chi^2(3, n = 14) = 8.90, p = 0.03]$. Veterans completing less than eight sessions also had higher baseline CAPS total severity scores relative to the remainder of the sample, *M(SD)* = 87.17(20.12) versus 67.00(15.75), respectively, $t = 2.11$, $p = 0.05$.

Similar comparisons between veterans completing four or more sessions (minimum course of therapy; $n = 10$) relative to the remainder of the sample ($n = 4$), yielded more pronounced differences by CAPS pre-treatment severity scores, *M(SD)* = 94.75(7.80) for those completing less than four sessions versus *M(SD)* = 68.00(18.04) those completing four or more sessions, $t = 2.81$, $p = 0.01$. Age and service era differences became non-significant but demonstrated similar trends, and employment status, race/ethnicity, marital status, and index trauma remained non-significant.

Feasibility Data

Of the 14 veterans enrolled with a psychotic spectrum disorder, 9 completed a post-treatment assessment/thematic interview (i.e., had complete data). Of the five who did not complete the assessment immediately following the completion of therapy, three dropped out of treatment prior to session three and were not invited for a post-assessment given the recent timing of their initial assessment; the other two declined follow-up. With regard to treatment, 2 veterans attended one session of PE, 10 attended four or more sessions of PE, and 8 attended eight or more sessions of PE, including one (1) veteran who received fifteen sessions (i.e., more than the standard course of treatment)[2].

Treatment Expectancy

Treatment expectancy variables collected *at the end of session 3* suggested that veterans generally found the intervention to be logical, $M(SD) = 8.14(1.57)$. Ratings regarding how confident veterans were in a) the treatment addressing PTSD symptoms [$M(SD) = 5.71(2.56)$]; b) likelihood of recommending PE to others [$M(SD) = 6.43(3.21)$]; and c) the intervention successfully decreasing another fear [$M(SD) = 6.25(3.01)$] were all in the moderate to high end.

Survey Based Reactions to the Intervention

Reactions to the intervention variables were in the low to moderate range with regard to how (a) distressing [$M(SD) = 5.33(3.04)$]; (b) difficult [$M(SD) = 2.67(2.40)$]; and (c) confusing veterans found the research procedures and intervention [$M(SD) = 5.22(3.42)$]; and in the moderate to high range with regard to how (a) satisfied they were with their participation [$M(SD) = 8.00(1.50)$]; (b) worthwhile they perceived their research participation to be [$M(SD) = 8.11(1.36)$]; and (c) willing they would be to participate in a similar study in the future [$M(SD) = 7.78(2.73)$].

Clinical Outcomes

Completer clinical outcome analyses ($n = 9$) yielded significant pre- to post-changes in CAPS severity scores, −24.8 (95% CI: −44.5, −5.0), $p = 0.02$; as well as significant pre- to post-changes in PCL scores, −14.1(95% CI: −20.0, −8.1), $p = 0.001$. See **Figures 1, 2** for trajectories of CAPS and PCL scores from baseline to post-intervention. With regard to total % change in CAPS scores pre- to post-intervention, 78% of veterans had at least a 10% decrease from baseline to post-intervention, and 55.6% ($n = 9$) had at least a 50% decrease baseline to post-intervention (i.e., responder proportion). Additional analyses examining the trajectory of PCL scores across treatment sessions using MEM provided supportive evidence of a significant decline in PCL means over the treatment trajectory (Estimated slope from MEM: −1.3 (SE = 0.3), $p = 0.002$) (**Figure 3**).

Of the veterans who attended at least eight treatment sessions, six of eight experienced remission of PTSD diagnosis at post-intervention. Additionally, one (1) of the veterans who attended five sessions no longer met criteria for PTSD at post-intervention, yielding a total of seven of nine treatment responders among those who received at least four sessions of the intervention (National Center for PTSD, 2006).

Two veterans remained symptomatic at post-despite receiving at least 10 sessions and another veteran remained symptomatic at post-after completing 8 sessions and dropping out of treatment prematurely. As noted previously, three veterans dropped out of treatment prior to session three, one prior to session four, and another prior to session 6.

Thematic Interviews

Thematic interviews were designed to learn more about veterans' reactions, beliefs, preferences, and suggestions for PE. Of the nine thematic interviews available for analysis, six were with veterans who were considered treatment responders (i.e., no longer had PTSD at follow-up and/or experienced a statistically significant decrease in CAPS severity pre- to post-intervention). The other 3 interviews were with veterans who remained symptomatic post-treatment [2 who completed 10 sessions (i.e., the standard course of treatment) and 1 who dropped out of treatment after 8 sessions].

With regard to the content of thematic interviews, five higher order categories were derived based on relative frequency of occurrence in the thematic interview transcriptions:

Veterans reported long histories of untreated trauma-related symptoms. Most veterans reported suffering from PTSD for several years, with some index traumas occurring more than 20 years prior to the baseline assessment. Despite this, none of the veterans interviewed reported having received specialized therapy for PTSD in the past. One veteran stated, "*Nobody said anything about PTSD even though I had this problem for a long time, and this is what I kept telling them over and over again, you know.*" Yet another veteran noted, "*Well I'm 52 now and this happened when I was 14 years old and I have never spoken to anyone about it. Till, you know, I did it here...When people used to ask me about it, I would just brush it off, or say I don't want to talk about it, or that's the past, I don't really want to visit it.*"

Veterans reported being apprehensive at the start of treatment regarding their ability to deal with the difficult emotions and memories that they believed the intervention would solicit. Veterans, similar to other patient populations enrolled in PE or trauma intensive services, expressed concerns about their ability to manage imaginal exposure sessions (i.e., talking about their trauma in detail) and about the potential adverse consequences of bringing up upsetting/distressing memories. Among those who responded to the intervention, these fears seemed to decrease as treatment progressed. For example, one treatment responder stated, "*Like at first when we started, like it was really difficult to tell the story. It made me upset and made me feel as if I was reliving it as I told it...*

[2]Of the 6 veterans who did not complete the standard course of treatment (i.e., 8 or more sessions), 2 cited transportation problems as their reason for drop-out; 2 did not respond to follow-up attempts, 1 was a treatment responder who no longer wanted treatment due to symptom amelioration; and 1 stated he was no longer interested in participating in the study.

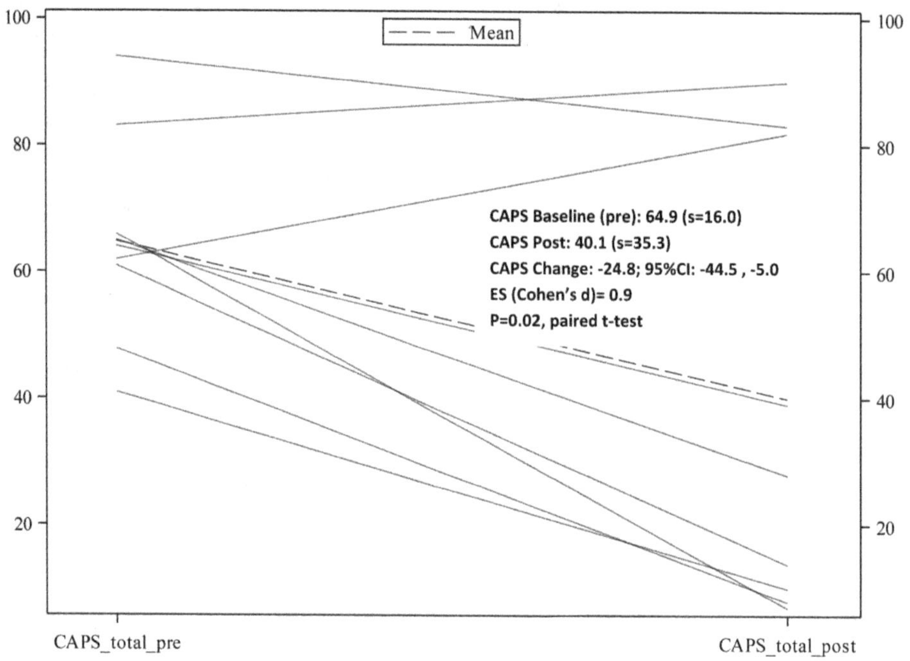

FIGURE 1 | Trajectories of CAPS total scores from baseline to immediate post-treatment.

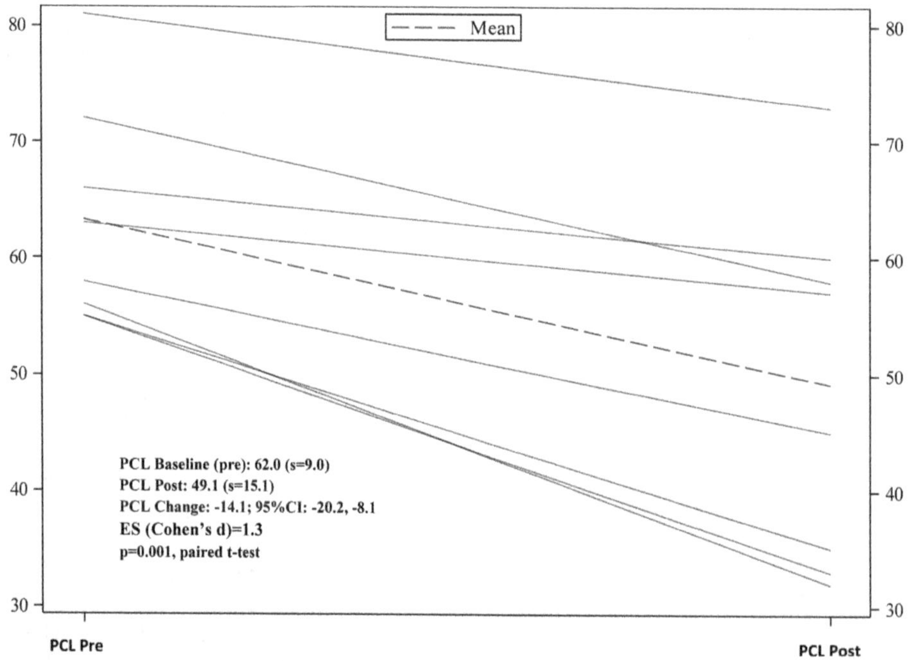

FIGURE 2 | Trajectories of PCL scores from baseline to immediate post-treatment.

and as I got to the end, it was almost boring." Other treatment responders stated, *"I was a little scared of what it would stir up but I'm happy with the outcome"*; and *"It's still upsetting, but not like just the whole thing before, it would upset me for like a long time too—you know, for like a couple of hours I would just be in a bad mood, and now not so much, so I think it's really helped."* For the three veterans who did not respond to treatment or dropped out prematurely this distress/anxiety seemed to persist.

Veterans tended to view the treatment and/or treatment team as credible, and this seemed to encourage veterans to "stick with the treatment" despite their anxiety. One veteran

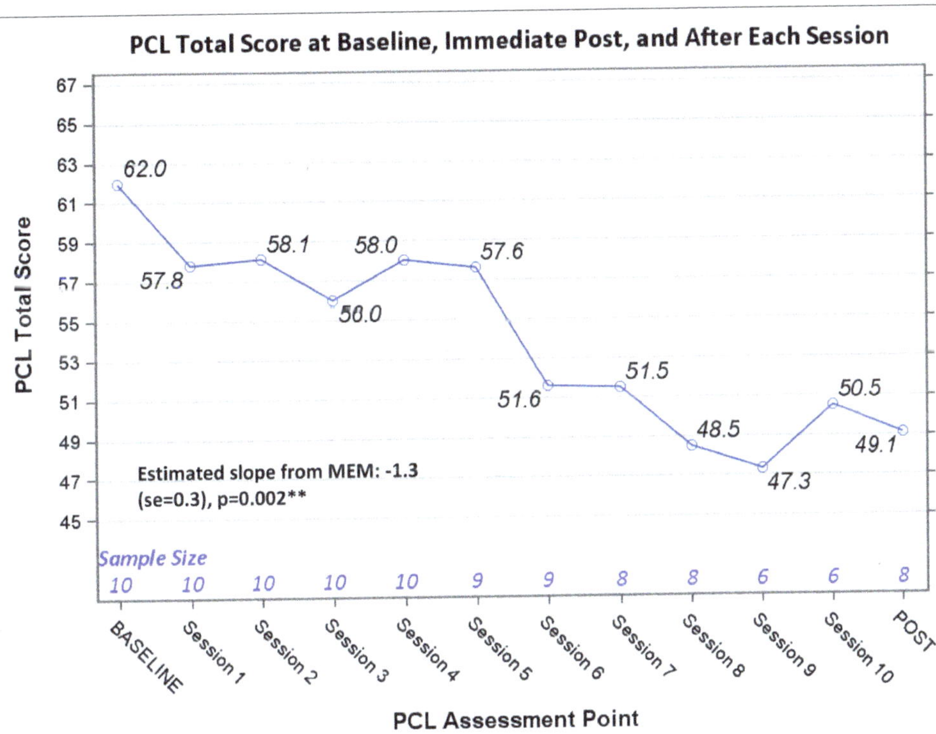

FIGURE 3 | PTSD checklist total score at baseline, immediate post, and after each session.

[treatment responder] who reported having a lot of anxiety in the beginning of treatment was asked by the interviewer how he managed his anxiety, and he stated, *"I guess I took a chance and trusted that you guys would help me through it, and that my wife would help me through it."* Another treatment responder who was not initially confident noted, *"Well at first I thought it's not going to work. Just the way I can't really open up that much. But it happened though, something happened and you now, once I got to talking about it and the way I felt afterward, I felt you know real shaky and stuff like that but funny thing about it is, I feel good."*

Even the three veterans who did not respond to treatment or dropped out prematurely viewed the treatment as logical. One of these veterans stated, *"When I first started right, I felt that the treatment was helping and um I was confident -you know—that I could be helped. Then, as I got deeper into the sessions, I felt that it was bringing things out of me that I didn't want to deal with. But as far as the treatment, it makes sense. The things that Ms. **** was showing me made sense and I feel that I, my part of the bargain, you know, I failed because I couldn't handle it."*

Both treatment responders and non-responders reported a number of benefits of the intervention. Treatment responders tended to report an improved ability to manage thoughts related to the trauma and a greater awareness of how their symptoms were affecting their daily lives. For example, one veteran stated *"It's okay for me to deal with it now. I realize you know, that it was over there, you know, and it's not going to happen over here"*; and another reported *"I could think about what happened and not fall to pieces anymore and not have to go to the hospital and stick my head in the sand."*

Treatment non-responders tended to report being better able to talk about the trauma, a decrease in overall severity of distress [albeit not an elimination of symptoms], and/or having a better ability to manage their trauma-related distress. For example, one veteran stated *"I can talk about it now and before I didn't want to"*; and yet another veteran who was a treatment non-responder stated, *"On command now I can say stop and gather my thoughts when I'm getting to that point. That helps me you know. The things that I learned I got pretty well embedded in me. So I can always say, well okay, I don't have to be in control."*

Although there was little evidence of relapse or exacerbations in symptoms, some difficulties with the intervention were noted. Generally speaking, veterans did not report experiencing a worsening of symptoms -either with regard to PTSD or their primary SMI symptoms. Consistent with this, when asked directly whether his symptoms were worse, better, or the same since his enrollment in the study, one veteran [a treatment non-responder] stated, *"They're about the same. Most days, as long as I don't think about it, I can live a normal life."*

Difficulties and/or challenges associated with the intervention generally consisted of initial fears regarding the intensity of the intervention (as noted above) and difficulty managing negative affect outside of sessions. With regard to the latter, one veteran [a treatment non-responder] stated, *"It's like I said, once I'm here, I can be in here, and talk with her (therapist). She will speak to me and I can go home that day and feel less symptoms, but then another day I'm not seeing her, or something, and I'm back in this rut or whatever, and start not feeling so good, and start thinking about these things, and start hearing things, and seeing things I guess. But I hear them a lot of times too.... It just didn't stick, you know. Just not how I would like it to be."*

DISCUSSION

Results of the current study suggest that an exposure-based intervention for PTSD is generally well tolerated and can be therapeutically beneficial among patients with a psychotic spectrum disorder. Quantitative data indicate that seven out of nine veterans experienced remission of PTSD diagnosis at follow-up, and the trajectory of PTSD symptoms over the course of treatment was comparable to general population samples (e.g., Bradley et al., 2005; Cloitre, 2009). Additional data suggest that PE was generally perceived as feasible, logical, and not overly distressing; and veterans typically held favorable expectations with regard to treatment. Qualitative data further suggest that individuals with a psychotic spectrum disorder tend to have similar reactions to PE as other PTSD clinical populations (Foa and Rothbaum, 1998). That is, they have concerns about their ability to manage their distress at the onset of treatment, but this distress typically decreases as they progress through treatment and make gains. Additionally, even treatment non-responders/drop-outs noted some benefits of the intervention, and no veteran experienced a significant exacerbation in PTSD symptoms [or other symptoms] as a result of treatment. Despite misassumptions that trauma-focused therapy may exacerbate symptoms of SMI, no study-related adverse events occurred during the course of the intervention trial. Collectively, these data suggest that individuals with psychotic spectrum disorders do not respond to targeted PTSD intervention in a dramatically different manner than individuals without an SMI.

Notwithstanding a number of positive findings with regard to treatment completers, there were some meaningful differences between those who failed to complete at least four or eight sessions of the intervention and the remainder of the sample. Younger veterans and OEF/OIF veterans were at increased risk to prematurely drop out of the intervention relative to older veterans and other service era cohorts. Given the overlap between age and service era, it is difficult to reach a conclusion regarding the variable dropout of younger veterans and/or OEF/OIF veterans. This result should also be interpreted cautiously, as the non-completer group was small ($n = 6$). Future studies should seek to further understand attrition among OEF/OIF veterans relative to other veteran service era cohorts.

Interestingly, differences in baseline PTSD severity suggested that veterans with the highest levels of PTSD symptoms were at greatest risk for premature treatment dropout in the current analysis. High levels of distress may interfere with treatment adherence. As such, veterans in 'high' distress may have benefited from a stronger "buy-in" at the onset of treatment; a shorter time frame between the start of treatment and receipt of imaginal and *in vivo* exposure (i.e., the active elements of PE); motivational interviewing strategies to address ambivalence about treatment; and/or behavioral activation or distress tolerance strategies to manage intense emotions and reduce overall distress. Worth noting again, most veterans dropped out of treatment prior to the start of imaginal exposure, as these patients may not have experienced symptom relief quickly enough to maintain treatment engagement. With regard to treatment non-responders, qualitative data suggest that these individuals continued to have fears about their ability to manage the distress associated with their treatment participation.

Given documented rates of attrition, treatment retention in trauma-focused and/or exposure-based therapies can still be significantly improved. Worth noting, however, the rate of attrition, retention, and treatment completion in the current study is comparable to prior PTSD treatment outcome studies of veterans with combat-related PTSD (Bradley et al., 2005; Cloitre, 2009) and SMI or psychotic spectrum disorders (Rosenberg et al., 2004; Mueser et al., 2007, 2008; Frueh et al., 2009). Additionally, there are no clear guidelines with regard to standard cutoffs for a minimum threshold of dosing for PE. If 3, rather than four sessions, had been used as the cut-off in the current study, our study results would be comparable to a recent study using exposure-based interventions among individuals with a psychotic disorder (van den Berg et al., 2015). With regard to therapeutic dosing, it appears that most veterans responded to a standard course of treatment—and those who remained in treatment tended to get better with some exceptions.

There were some limitations to the current study that require discussion. First and foremost, the sample is small and study data are based on a single arm study design, thus limiting firm conclusions that can be made. Due to the single arm design of our study, inferential analyses of symptom improvement (i.e., efficacy) are considered descriptive and can only provide indications (based on statistically significant p-values) that the observed improvement in symptom severity is unlikely the result of chance. That is, the results cannot firmly establish that the treatment produced the changes because unknown intervening events cannot be eliminated as causal factors in the observed improvements in outcomes. Those included in the clinical outcome analyses were significantly older, had less severe PTSD symptoms at baseline, and were predominantly Vietnam era veterans compared to those not included in the analysis sample. Generalization of efficacy results, therefore, is restricted to the population of veterans with SMI having characteristics similar to that of the analysis sample (older veterans with less severe PTSD symptoms). A final limitation concerns the assessment of possible variables that influence successful treatment outcomes. The current study did not include a measure of primary symptoms of psychosis or other well-established predictors of treatment success (i.e., therapist adherence to protocol, rapport, etc.). Addressing such limitations in future studies may provide information regarding how to maximize treatment response and possible additional benefits associated with PTSD treatment in individuals with psychotic spectrum disorders.

The current study addresses important knowledge gaps in the PTSD treatment outcome literature. First, the current study used a mixed methods approach to develop a more comprehensive picture of how individuals with a psychotic spectrum disorder respond to targeted PTSD intervention. Second, the current study represents one of a few examinations of PE, a widely used, researched, and disseminated exposure-based intervention for PTSD, in a patient population with a psychotic spectrum disorder. In this regard the current study findings can be examined within the context of the broader PTSD treatment outcome literature. Finally, study participants reflected a diverse patient population with regards to ethnic/racial identification [i.e., the majority of the sample ($n = 7$; 50%) identified as minority].

Altogether, the current study findings are promising and serve to mitigate both provider and patient beliefs that individuals with psychotic spectrum disorders such as schizophrenia cannot benefit from intense trauma focused treatment. Additional data along this theme would further disseminate the use of empirically supported PTSD interventions in this patient population. Such efforts would undoubtedly facilitate the establishment of an evidence-based standard of care and the incorporation of trauma-focused interventions into the psychosocial rehabilitation conceptualization for this patient population.

ETHICS STATEMENT

Medical University of SC Institutional Review Board and Ralph H. Johnson VAMC Research and Development Office Participants were recruited via direct referrals from VA providers to a PTSD Clinical Team (PCT) of a Southeastern VAMC. All interested individuals were given a description of the study over the phone by project staff (or in-person if a patient stopped by without an appointment); and if willing, were scheduled for a formal baseline assessment. The baseline assessment included a detailed explanation of the study and informed consent. The study was conducted between January of 2008 and December of 2012 with full approval from appropriate institutional review boards. All participants completed a brief multiple choice quiz to ensure their understanding of the study procedures.

AUTHOR CONTRIBUTIONS

AG oversaw manuscript development, participated in the analysis and interpretation of data, and took the lead in drafting the majority of the manuscript. CE, RK, WB, and KV contributed to the analysis and interpretation of the data; RK drafted portions of the quantitative analysis section; WB, KV, and CE contributed to the write-up of the qualitative analysis section. All authors contributed feedback for the Discussion section.

REFERENCES

American Psychiatric Association [APA] (2000). *Diagnostic and Statistical Manual of Mental Disorders*, 4th Edn, Text Rev. Washington, DC: American Psychiatric Association.

Blake, D., Weathers, F., Nagy, L. M., Kaloupek, D. G., Gusman, F. D., Charney, D. S., et al. (2005). The development of a Clinician-Administered PTSD Scale. *J. Trauma. Stress* 8, 75–90. doi: 10.1002/jts.2490080106

Blanchard, E. B., Jones-Alexander, J., Beckley, T. C., and Forneris, C. A. (1996). Psychometric properties of the PTSD Checklist (PCL). *Behav. Res. Ther.* 34, 669–673. doi: 10.1016/0005-7967(96)00033-2

Borkovec, T., and Nau, S. (1972). Credibility of analogue therapy rationales. *J. Behav. Ther. Exp. Psychiatry* 3, 257–260. doi: 10.1016/0005-7916(72)90045-6

Bradley, R., Greene, J., Russ, E., Dutra, L., and Westin, D. (2005). A multidimensional meta-analysis of psychotherapy for PTSD. *Am. J. Psychiatry* 162, 214–227. doi: 10.1176/appi.ajp.162.2.214

Braiterman, K. (2004). Commentary. *Am. J. Psychiatr. Rehabil.* 7, 187–191. doi: 10.1080/15487760490476219

Charmaz, K. (2006). Measuring pursuits, marking self: meaning construction in chronic illness. *Int. J. Qual. Stud. Health Well-being* 1, 27–37. doi: 10.1080/17482620500534488

Cluitre, M. (2009). Effective psychotherapies for PTSD: a review and critique. *CNS Spectr.* 13, 32–43.

de Bont, P. A., van Minnen, A., and de Jongh, A. (2013). Treating PTSD in patients with psychosis: a within group controlled feasibility study examining the efficacy and safety of evidence based PE and EMDR protocols. *Behav. Ther.* 44, 717–730. doi: 10.1016/j.beth.2013.07.002

de Bont, P. A. J. M., van den Berg, D. P. G., van der Vleugel, B. M., de Roos, C., de Jongh, A., van der Gaag, M., et al. (2016). Prolonged exposure and EMDR for PTSD v. a PTSD waiting-list condition: effects on symptoms and psychosis, depression, and social functioning in patients with chronic psychotic disorders. *Psychol. Med.* 46, 2411–2421. doi: 10.1017/S0033291716001094

Fan, X., Henderson, D. C., Nguyen, D. D., Cather, C., Freudenreich, O., Evins, A. E., et al. (2008). Posttraumatic stress disorder, cognitive function and quality of life in patients with schizophrenia. *Psychiatry Res.* 159, 140–146. doi: 10.1016/j.psychres.2007.10.012

Foa, E. B., and Rothbaum, B. O. (1998). *Treating the Trauma of Rape: Cognitive Behavioral Therapy for Rape*. New York, NY: Guilford Press.

Ford, J. D., and Fournier, D. (2007). Psychological trauma and posttraumatic stress disorder among women in community mental health aftercare following psychiatric intensive care. *J. Psychiatr. Intensive Care* 3, 27–34. doi: 10.1017/S1742646407001094

Fowler, D. (2004). The case for treating trauma in severe mental illness: a commentary. *Am. J. Psychiatr. Rehabil.* 7, 205–212. doi: 10.1080/15487760490476246

Frueh, B. C., Cusack, K. J., Grubaugh, A. L., Sauvageot, J. A., and Wells, C. (2006a). Clinicians' perspectives on cognitive-behavioral treatment for PTSD among persons with severe mental illness. *Psychiatr. Serv.* 57, 1027–1031.

Frueh, B. C., Grubaugh, A. L., Cusack, K. J., Kimble, M. O., Elhai, J. D., and Knapp, R. G. (2009). Exposure-based CBT of PTSD in adults with schizophrenia or schizoaffective disorder: a pilot study. *J. Anxiety Disord.* 23, 665–675. doi: 10.1016/j.janxdis.2009.02.005

Frueh, B. C., Grubaugh, A. L., Lo Sasso, A., Jones, W., Oldham, J. M., and Lindrooth, R. G. (2012). Key stakeholders perceptions regarding acute care psychiatry in distressed publicly funded mental health care markets. *Bull. Menninger Clin.* 76, 1–20. doi: 10.1521/bumc.2012.76.1.1

Frueh, B. C., Sauvageot, J. A., and Grubaugh, A. L. (2006b). Perceptions of elderly former prisoners of war regarding care and benefits provided by the Veterans Affairs System: a qualitative study. *J. Trauma Pract.* 5, 1–11. doi: 10.1300/J189v05n03_01

Grubaugh, A. L., Clapp, J., Frueh, B. C., Tuerk, P. W., Knapp, R. G., and Egede, L. F (2016). Open trial of exposure therapy for PTSD among patients with persistent mental illness. *Behav. Res. Ther.* 78, 1–12. doi: 10.1016/j.brat.2015.12.006

Grubaugh, A. L., Zinzow, H. M., Paul, L., Egede, L. E., and Frueh, B. C. (2011). Trauma exposure and PTSD in adults with severe mental illness: a critical review. *Clin. Psychol. Rev.* 31, 883–899. doi: 10.1016/j.cpr.2011.04.003

Kilcommons, A. M., and Morrison, A. P. (2005). Relationship between trauma and psychosis: an exploration of cognitive and dissociative factors. *Acta Psychiatr. Scand.* 112, 351–359. doi: 10.1111/j.1600-0447.2005.00623.x

Lu, W., Fite, R., Kim, E., Hyer, L., Yanos, P. T., Mueser, K. T., et al. (2009). Cognitive-behavioral treatment of PTSD in severe mental illness: pilot study replication in an ethnically diverse population. *Am. J. Psychiatr. Rehabil.* 12, 73–91. doi: 10.1080/15487760802615863

Lysaker, P. H., Beattie, N. L., Strasburger, A. M., and Davis, L. W. (2005). Reported history of child sexual abuse in schizophrenia: associations with heightened symptom levels and poorer participation over four month in vocational rehabilitation. *J. Nerv. Ment. Dis.* 193, 790–795. doi: 10.1097/01.nmd.0000188970.11916.76

Lysaker, P. H., and Larocco, V. A. (2008). The prevalence and correlates of trauma-related symptoms in schizophrenia spectrum disorder. *Compr. Psychiatry* 49, 330–334. doi: 10.1016/j.comppsych.2007.12.003

Meade, C. S., McDonald, L. J., Graff, F. S., Fitzmaurice, G. M., Griffin, M. L., and Weiss, R. D. (2009). A prospective study examining the effects of gender and sexual/physical abuse on mood outcomes in patients with co-occurring bipolar I and substance use disorders. *Bipolar Disord.* 11, 425–433. doi: 10.1111/j.1399-5618.2009.00682.x

Mueser, K. T., Bolton, E., Carty, P. C., Bradley, M. J., Ahlgren, K. F., DiStaso, D. R., et al. (2007). The trauma recovery group: a cognitive-behavioral program for posttraumatic stress disorder in persons with severe mental illness. *Community Ment. Health J.* 43, 281–304. doi: 10.1007/s10597-006-9075-2

Mueser, K. T., Essock, S. M., Haines, M., Wolfe, R., and Xie, H. (2004a). Posttraumatic stress disorder, supported employment, and outcomes in people with severe mental illness. *CNS Spectr.* 9, 913–925.

Mueser, K. T., Rosenberg, S. D., Xie, H., Jankowski, M. K., Bolton, E. E., Lu, W., et al. (2008). A randomized controlled trial of cognitive-behavioral treatment for posttraumatic stress disorder in severe mental illness. *J. Consult. Clin. Psychol.* 76, 259–271. doi: 10.1037/0022-006X.76.2.259

Mueser, K. T., Salyers, M. P., Rosenberg, S. D., Goodman, L. A., Essock, S. M., Osher, F. C., et al. (2004b). Interpersonal trauma and posttraumatic stress disorder in patients with severe mental illness: demographic, clinical, and health correlates. *Schizophr. Bull.* 30, 45–57.

National Center for PTSD (2006). *Dissemination and Education within the VA.* Available at: http://www.ptsd.va.gov/about/majorinitiatives/education/dissemination_education_within_the_va.asp

Newman, J. M., Turnbull, A., Berman, B. A., Rodrigues, S., and Serper, M. R. (2010). Impact of traumatic and violent victimization experiences in individuals with schizophrenia and schizooaffective disorder. *J. Nerv. Ment. Dis.* 198, 708–714. doi: 10.1097/NMD.0b013e3181f49bf1

Resnick, H. (1996). "Psychometric review of trauma assessment for adults (TAA)," in *Measurement of Stress, Trauma and Adaptation*, ed. B. H. Stamm (Lutherville, MD: Sidran Press).

Robins, C. S., Sauvageot, J. A., Cusack, K. J., Suffoletta-Maierle, S., and Frueh, B. C. (2005). Consumers' perceptions of negative experiences and 'Sanctuary Harm' in psychiatric settings. *Psychiatr. Serv.* 56, 1134–1138. doi: 10.1176/appi.ps.56.9.1134

Rosenberg, S. D., Mueser, K. T., Jankowski, M. K., Salyers, M. P., and Acher, K. (2004). Cognitive-behavioral treatment of PTSD in severe mental illness: results of a pilot study. *Am. J. Psychiatr. Rehabil.* 7, 171–186. doi: 10.1080/15487760490476200

Sautter, F. J., Brailey, K., Uddo, M. M., Hamilton, M. F., Beard, M. G., and Borges, A. H. (1999). PTSD and comorbid psychotic disorder: comparison with veterans diagnosed with PTSD or psychotic disorder. *J. Trauma. Stress* 12, 73–88. doi: 10.1023/A:1024794232175

Schenkel, L. S., Spaulding, W. D., DiLillo, D., and Silverstein, S. M. (2005). Histories of childhood maltreatment in schizophrenia: relationships with premorbid functioning, symptomatology, and cognitive deficits. *Schizophr. Res.* 76, 273–286. doi: 10.1016/j.schres.2005.03.003

Sheehan, D. V., Lecrubier, Y., Sheehan, K. H., Amorim, P., Janavs, J., Weiller, E., et al. (1998). The Mini-International Neuropsychiatric Interview (M.I.N.I.): the development and validation of a structured diagnostic psychiatric interview for DSM-IV and ICD-10. *J. Clin. Psychiatry* 59(Suppl. 20), 22–33.

Spinazzola, J., Blaustein, M., and van der Kolk, B. A. (2005). PTSD treatment outcome research: the study of unrepresentative samples. *J. Trauma. Stress* 18, 425–436. doi: 10.1002/jts.20050

Strauss, J. L., Calhoun, P. S., Marx, C. E., Stechuchak, K. M., Oddone, E. Z., Swartz, M. S., et al. (2006). Comorbid posttraumatic stress disorder is associated with suicidality in male veterans with schizophrenia or schizoaffective disorder. *Schizophr. Res.* 84, 165–169. doi: 10.1016/j.schres.2006.02.010

Üçok, A., and Bikmaz, S. (2007). The effects of childhood trauma in patients with first-episode schizophrenia. *Acta Psychiatr. Scand.* 116, 371–377. doi: 10.1111/j.1600-0447.2007.01079.x

van den Berg, D. P. G., de Bont, P. A. J. M., van der Vleugel, B. M., de Roos, C., de Jongh, A., Van Minnen, A., et al. (2015). Prolonged exposure vs eye movement desensitization and reprocessing vs waiting list for PTSD in patients with a psychotic disorder: a randomized clinical trial. *JAMA Psychiatry* 72, 259–267. doi: 10.1001/jamapsychiatry.2014.2637

Weathers, F., Litz, B., Herman, D., Huska, J., and Keane, T. (1993). The PTSD checklist (PCL): reliability, validity, and diagnostic utility. *Paper Presented at the Annual Convention of the International Society for Traumatic Stress Studies*, San Antonio, TX.

Weathers, F. W., Keane, T. M., and Davidson, J. R. (2001). Clinician-Administered PTSD Scale: a review of the first ten years of research. *Depress. Anxiety* 13, 132–156. doi: 10.1002/da.1029

Weathers, F. W., Ruscio, A. M., and Keane, T. M. (1999). Psychometric properties of nine scoring rules for the Clinician-Administered Posttraumatic Stress Disorder Scale. *Psychol. Assess.* 11, 124–133. doi: 10.1037/1040-3590.11.2.124

17

Cognitive Attachment Model of Voices: Evidence Base and Future Implications

Katherine Berry, Filippo Varese and Sandra Bucci*

Division of Psychology and Mental Health, School of Health Sciences, Manchester Academic Health Science Centre, The University of Manchester, Manchester, United Kingdom

Edited by:
Kate Hardy,
Stanford University, United States

Reviewed by:
Tiril Østefjells,
Oslo University Hospital, University of Oslo and Akershus University Hospital, Norway
Louise Isham,
Oxford Health NHS Foundation Trust, United Kingdom

***Correspondence:**
Katherine Berry
katherine.berry@manchester.ac.uk

There is a robust association between hearing voices and exposure to traumatic events. Identifying mediating mechanisms for this relationship is key to theories of voice hearing and the development of therapies for distressing voices. This paper outlines the Cognitive Attachment model of Voices (CAV), a theoretical model to understand the relationship between earlier interpersonal trauma and distressing voice hearing. The model builds on attachment theory and well-established cognitive models of voices and argues that attachment and dissociative processes are key psychological mechanisms that explain how trauma influences voice hearing. Following the presentation of the model, the paper will review the current state of evidence regarding the proposed mechanisms of vulnerability to voice hearing and maintenance of voice-related distress. This review will include evidence from studies supporting associations between dissociation and voices, followed by details of our own research supporting the role of dissociation in mediating the relationship between trauma and voices and evidence supporting the role of adult attachment in influencing beliefs and relationships that voice hearers can develop with voices. The paper concludes by outlining the key questions that future research needs to address to fully test the model and the clinical implications that arise from the work.

Keywords: voice hearing, attachment, dissociation, trauma, psychosis, auditory hallucinations

INTRODUCTION

Voice hearing (auditory verbal hallucinations) is present in many mental health problems and psychosis in particular (1). Although not necessarily pathological, voices are often associated with distress (2). Over the past three decades, theoretical models have attempted to clarify the underpinnings of these unusual perceptual experiences and inform the development of psychological interventions for distressing voices. Broadly speaking, existing psychological models of voice hearing can be divided into two separate "families" ("vulnerability" models and "distress maintenance" models), depending on the scope and specific aspects of voice-hearing experiences they attempt to examine and explain. Several "vulnerability" models informed by cognitive theory have attempted to identify the psychological/cognitive factors responsible for the formation of hallucinatory experiences. These models include accounts pointing to the importance of a number of putative mechanisms assumed to underpin auditory verbal hallucinations, such as self-monitoring abnormalities (3, 4), source monitoring difficulties (5, 6), and dissociative processes (7). Despite many of these accounts undergoing considerable empirical scrutiny, the "causes" of voice hearing are still largely unknown and there is increasing consensus that a complex interaction between multiple factors rather than single deficits can best account for the vulnerability toward these unusual experiences (8, 9).

In parallel with vulnerability accounts, other psychological models have been proposed to explain why voices are associated with distress and impairment in some individuals but not others [e.g., Ref. (10)]. Arguably the most well-established "distress maintenance" model of voice hearing is the cognitive model of voices, which proposes that the way individuals think about their voice(s) influences their reactions to these experiences (11–14). Consistent with this model, a review of 26 studies found that several types of cognitive appraisals were linked to more distress in voice hearers, including voices appraised as malevolent, powerful, having personal relationship with the individual, and disapproval and rejection toward voices (15).

Vulnerability models are not clear about the factors that differentiate "benign voices" from voices that require intervention. Similarly, psychological distress maintenance models of voice hearing do not offer a suitable explanation of the etiology of these distressing experiences. Another area of inquiry not well delineated by previous models is the extent to which life experiences, and in particular potentially traumatic events (such as experiences of victimization, abuse, and physical and emotional neglect) influence the processes of symptom formation and distress maintenance. The robust association observed between exposure to traumatic life experiences and psychosis more generally (16), and hearing voices more specifically [e.g., Ref. (17, 18)], suggests that trauma represents an important risk factor for voice hearing. Although the specific psychological mechanisms responsible for vulnerability to voice hearing remain unclear, several researchers have proposed, for example, that auditory hallucinations may be conceptualized as trauma-related intrusions [e.g., Ref. (19)] and that several peri- and posttraumatic processes may contribute the formation of hallucinatory experiences, including peritraumatic dissociation and several symptoms of posttraumatic stress [e.g., Ref. (20, 21)].

There is also evidence that trauma exposure may aggravate the psychological processes responsible for voice-related distress and impairment. The cognitive model proposes that beliefs about voices are influenced by the individuals' life experiences, including trauma and relationships with significant others. For example, Andrew et al. (22) report associations between traumatic life events, including childhood sexual abuse, and negative beliefs about voices (22). Birchwood et al. (23) also present data suggesting that an individual's perception of being powerless and controlled by others within external social relationships is reflected in the voice/voice-hearer relationship.

In the present article, we outline a recent model of voice hearing informed by both cognitive models of voice hearing and attachment theory (24): the Cognitive Attachment model of Voices [CAV (25)]. The CAV draws on attachment theory to integrate previous vulnerability accounts of voice hearing (trauma-related dissociation and source monitoring accounts) with cognitive and relational models of distress exacerbation and maintenance. In doing so, it aims to (1) explain the complex interplay between contextual and psychological factors that may increase vulnerability to voice-hearing experiences in people who are exposed to adverse life experiences (in particular interpersonal trauma) and (2) understand the psychological processes responsible for variations in how people appraise, respond to, and relate to their voices in ways that may exacerbate and maintain voice-related distress. After presenting a summary of the model, we will elaborate on the theoretical and empirical base regarding the core psychological constructs and processes included in the model and examine the available evidence in support of each hypothesized pathway within the CAV. While we do not present any new data in this paper, we attempt to review existing evidence to test the validity of the model and to highlight opportunities for further research that will help to test the model empirically and progress an evidence-based understanding of the role of putative psychological processes in voice hearing. Finally, we describe clinical implications to illustrate how the CAV model can be used to guide therapeutic work with distressing voices.

DESCRIPTIONS OF KEY CONCEPTS

Prior to presenting the model, we will define key concepts, including attachment, dissociation, and source monitoring, for readers not familiar with the respective literatures.

Attachment

Bowlby's (24) attachment theory is one of the most well-established theories of interpersonal relationships. Attachment is an affectional bond, which the individual forms with a significant other, who is approached in response to distress. The theory argues that as a result of their interactions with caregivers during infancy and childhood, individuals develop mental representations of the self in relation to significant others and expectations about how others behave in relationships (26). These "internal working models" guide attention, interpretation, memory, and predictions about future interpersonal interactions. The Strange Situation procedure for assessing attachment behaviors in infancy was crucial in providing empirical support for Bowlby's theory and measuring individual differences in the quality of attachment relationships to different caregivers. It involves a laboratory-based observation of the infant's response to two brief separations from, and reunions with his or her caregiver (27).

Although early empirical support for attachment theory came from observations of infants and caregivers, attachment theory is a lifespan developmental theory. In this respect attachment relationships with significant others (most commonly romantic partners) continue to serve an important function in adult lives and attachment working models established in earlier caregiver relationships influence how the individual relates to later attachment figures and regulates negative affect (28). There is evidence of individual differences with respect to adult attachment and some evidence that attachment patterns are stable over time. However, changes in patterns can occur particularly if the individual experiences relationships that are different to their experience of earlier relationships (29).

Unlike attachment in childhood, attachment behaviors in adulthood are most commonly conceptualized in general terms, whereby one has a general attachment style or pattern across relationships, as opposed to an attachment in a relationship with a specific person. However, it is recognized in the literature that people can have different attachment patterns with different people as in childhood (30). Attachment patterns in adulthood are also most commonly assessed using self-report questionnaires or interviews where trained raters ask the person about their experiences of attachment relationships and code attachment patterns based factors such as the coherence of the person's narrative in describing their experiences (31). In terms of different attachment styles in adulthood, secure attachment is characterized by positive beliefs about the self and others, capacity to regulate affect and form relationships with other people. Conversely, there are insecure attachment patterns, including avoidant and anxious/ambivalent attachment that result from suboptimal experiences of caregiving and are associated with less adaptive interpersonal functioning and affect regulation in adulthood (28). For example, anxious attachment is characterized by negative beliefs about self and sensitivity to rejection from others whereas avoidant attachment is characterized by negative beliefs about others, mistrust of others, and withdrawal from social relationships (28). Individuals who score highly on measures of both anxious and avoidant attachment are conceptualized as having a disorganized pattern of attachment, involving vacillation between approach and avoidance behaviors in relationships, wanting intimacy with others, but fearing rejection and closeness (32).

Dissociation

The term dissociation refers to a range of clinical and non-clinical psychological phenomena that are relatively common in both the general population as well as individuals with clinically significant mental health difficulties [e.g., Ref. (33)]. Often defined as the "lack of normal integration of thoughts, feelings and experiences into the stream of consciousness and memory" [(34), p. 727], dissociation represents the core component of several DSM-5 several (35), most notably dissociative disorders (e.g., dissociative identity disorder, dissociative amnesia, and depersonalization/derealization disorder), but also specific trauma and stress-related presentations (in particular the dissociative subtype of posttraumatic stress disorder (PTSD) introduced in the latest revision of the DSM). A widely accepted unitary conceptualization of dissociation assumes that different dissociative experiences lie on a single continuum of severity ranging from the relatively benign forms of absorption and other fleeting dissociative states frequently experienced in non-clinical populations, to more pervasive experiences of depersonalization, derealization, and identity alteration that can sometimes cause severe distress or discomfort. More recently, several authors (36, 37) have proposed that the different experiences traditionally described with the term dissociation may reflect two qualitatively distinct classes of phenomena, namely, detachment (which encompasses derealization, depersonalization, and similar experiences characterized by a sense of separation or detachment from aspects of everyday experience) and compartmentalization phenomena (such as dissociative amnesia and other symptoms that allegedly result from reversible disruptions in normal processes for the monitoring and control of mental experiences, resulting in the functional or perceived "separation" of certain elements of one's current experience and mental functioning). Due to the current lack of convincing research clarifying whether voice hearing is more robustly related to specific dissociative experiences, in the context of the current paper, we use the term dissociation broadly to describe the altered states of consciousness captured by multifactorial measures that are used widely in both research and clinical settings [e.g., the Dissociative Experiences Scale (DES)].

Although it can be experienced in the absence of a history of trauma, dissociation is frequently observed in the immediate aftermath of traumatic events, and trauma survivors can sometimes experience a heightened predisposition to dissociative many years after the original traumatic event [e.g., Ref. (38)]. The alleged link between trauma and dissociation has been the subject of extensive theoretical debate and empirical scrutiny, with some regarding this association as spurious or artifactual, and others as consistent with the alleged action of an in-built "defense mechanisms" that allows people to reduce the overwhelming emotional and cognitive consequences of traumatic experiences [for a critical appraisal of these theoretical debates and associated empirical research, see Ref. (38)].

Source Monitoring

The cognitive processes that might ultimately account for the genesis of hearing voices and other hallucinatory experiences are still unclear. However, there is some agreement that they are the result of the misattribution of internally generated cognitive events (e.g., inner speech) to sources that are alien or external to the self [e.g., Ref. (5, 39–41)]. Several cognitive accounts have assumed that specific anomalous cognitive processes may underlie this misattribution. Bentall (5) proposed that the origin of hallucinatory experiences can be explained in terms of source monitoring (also described in some papers with the term "reality discrimination"), a metacognitive process used to discriminate between internal and external perceptions and make attributions about the origin of mental experiences. This account argues that hallucination-prone individuals are less able to discriminate between internally and externally generated cognitive events and have a bias toward misattributing internal cognitive events to external sources. A wealth of studies using various experimental procedures, including signal detection [e.g., Ref. (42)], self-monitoring [e.g., Ref. (43)], and source memory [e.g., Ref. (44)] paradigms, has provided strong empirical support for the proposal that source monitoring biases might underpin a vulnerability toward hallucinatory experiences. In a meta-analysis of this literature, Brookwell et al. (6) found that these source monitoring biases are evident both clinical and non-clinical hallucination-prone individuals (i.e., hallucinating patients or non-clinical participants with high scores on hallucination-proneness measures) when compared to non-prone sample samples. The exact etiology of such biases, however, and the extent to which they might be influenced by environmental risk factors for hallucinations and other psychotic experiences (e.g., trauma exposure), remains to be clarified.

THE CAV

The CAV model draws on cognitive, attachment, and dissociative processes to explain the development and maintenance of distressing voice hearing (**Figure 1**). Further to the original publication

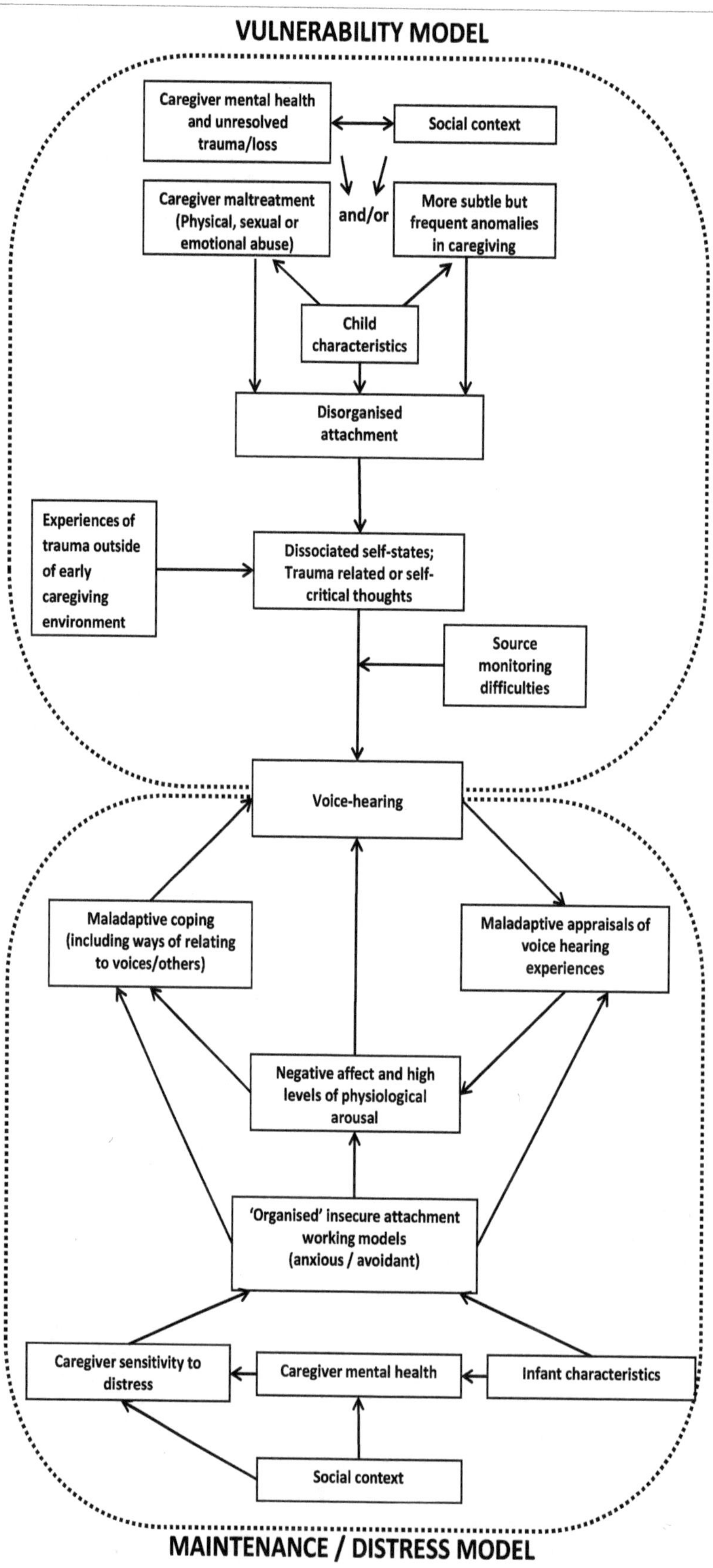

FIGURE 1 | Graphical representation of the cognitive attachment voice-hearing model [adapted from Ref. (25)].

of the CAV model (25), in this paper, we more clearly delineate the vulnerability and distress maintenance aspects of the CAV model, which we will now describe in more detail. Essentially, in line with cognitive and relational models of psychosis, the CAV proposes that disorganized attachment, coupled with dissociative and cognitive processes, can help explain the link between trauma and voice hearing. Insecure internal working models, combined with appraisals, influence affective emotional and behavioral reactions to voice-hearing experiences. As a caveat, readers should note that the CAV proposes one route to the development of voice hearing and the maintenance of voice-related distress; we are not purporting to explain all voice experiences.

Vulnerability Components of the CAV Model

In line with previous accounts of voice hearing, the CAV proposes that voices can be understood as dissociated components of the self or "compartmentalized" trauma-related intrusive memories [e.g., Ref. (7, 19, 45)] (see top circle, **Figure 1**). In some predisposed individuals, these internal states and cognitive events are experienced and/or interpreted as external and current rather than internal and memory based, possibly as a result of biased source monitoring processes that have been shown to underpin hallucination proneness in numerous clinical and non-clinical studies [e.g., Ref. (6, 46)]. A central tenet of the CAV model is that the propensity to experience dissociative states is driven or exacerbated by a specific type of attachment pattern, namely, disorganized attachment. This attachment pattern was originally observed in the context of infant research where some infants were found to display disorganized and disoriented responses to separation and reunion from caregivers that appeared contradictory and inconsistent with the "organized" attachment patterns such as avoidant or anxious/ambivalent attachment previously identified [e.g., Ref. (47)]. Disorganization is the outcome of interactions in which the infant experiences the attachment figure as frightening, frightened, or dissociated in times of stress. The caregiver might act in ways that are confusing and unpredictable for the infant, rendering it difficult for them to develop an "organized" pattern of self-protection. According to Liotti (48), the infant experiences "fright without solution" at being confronted with the biological paradox that the attachment figure, the primary source of safety and protection, is also the source of the infant distress. There is evidence of associations between attachment disorganization and parental maltreatment (49), but the development of a disorganized attachment pattern could also be influenced by more subtle (but frequent or pervasive) disruptions in parental attunement, possibly caused by a range of adverse conditions and circumstances [e.g., parental poor mental health, trauma, and experiences of loss (49–54)]. Critically, disorganized attachment has been identified as a developmental antecedent of dissociation in response to later trauma (48, 55–57), a factor believed to contribute to one's predisposition to experience hallucinations [e.g., Ref. (46, 58)].

Distress and Maintenance Component of the Model

In addition to implicating disorganized attachment in the processes leading to the formation of hallucinatory experiences, the CAV model proposes a distress maintenance cycle, whereby "organized" but insecure attachment working models influence the appraisals and cognitive-behavioral responses that could exacerbate voice-related distress and contribute to the maintenance of distressing voice-hearing experiences (see bottom circle, **Figure 1**). In terms of the distress maintenance cycle of distressing voice hearing, we suggest that, once voices develop, insecure attachment styles (which are influenced by early relational caregiver experiences) could also influence how voices are appraised, the way in which different voice hearers relate to their voices, and the subsequent cognitive-behavioral strategies that different voice hearers employ to control these experiences. While for the purpose of the model it appears that attachment patterns are categorically assigned to individuals, we recognize that there can be considerable overlap in attachment patterns and that allocating people into a specific attachment "category" is somewhat artificial; individuals can display characteristics associated with various attachment patterns (59).

Drawing from attachment and cognitive theories, the CAV predicts that high levels of anxious attachment in voice hearers' relationship with their voices, or a general anxious attachment style (i.e., an attachment style characterized by beliefs that they need to rely on other people, negative beliefs about the self and an expectation that other people will let them down), will result in beliefs that voices are powerful, but also fluctuating beliefs about voice benevolence and malevolence. The voice-hearer relationship is likely to be characterized by hearer dependence and voice dominance, and the individual is likely to be hypervigilant and sensitive to the voices reaction to them. For example, in the context of command hallucinations, the hearer may follow through with the voice(s) command to please or appease the voice, but at the point that commands become more unreasonable or in conflict to a high degree with the hearer's core values, s/he may fear rejection and even punishment. Those with anxious attachment styles and access to alternate attachment figures in the external social world will also increase proximity to, and dependence on, these individuals in response to voice hearing-related distress. Furthermore, an anxious attachment style would be associated with negative beliefs about the individual's capacity to cope with the voice. In contrast, individuals with high levels of avoidant attachment in their relationships with their voices or relationships more broadly may hold malevolent beliefs about voices and may suppress and/or resist the voice, with this avoidant response ultimately maintaining negative beliefs and voices over time. For example, a hearer with avoidant attachment may believe that voices cannot be trusted and either attempt to distract themselves from the experience or fight back by being hostile and aggressive in response. A general avoidant attachment may serve to maintain voice-related distress by reducing the probability that individuals will develop new attachments or utilize social supports to help cope with distress.

In summary, attachment style influences the maintenance of voices *via* two routes: an engagement route (anxiously attached voice hearers may tend to "actively seek" the voices) and a suppression route (people employing different suppression strategies that ultimately fail *via* rebound effects). Within the model, disorganized attachment is conceptualized as a *precursor* to voice hearing. However, as the concept of disorganized attachment has been conceptualized in terms of high levels of anxious and avoidant attachment, it could be hypothesized that some individuals oscillate between an anxious and avoidant pattern of relating to voices.

EVIDENCE TO SUPPORT THE MODEL

Early Relational Trauma and Attachment

Attachment theory argues that insecure attachment styles arise from adverse childhood experience. Suboptimal caregiving, including both subtle but frequent disruptions in caregiving and more extreme experiences of neglect and abuse, has all been identified as predictors of attachment difficulties (60, 61). In terms of associations between specific types of experience and different attachment patterns, anxious attachment (or ambivalent attachment in infancy) has been associated with inconsistent parenting, typified by over intrusiveness and overt expressions of devotion followed by neglect (62). As the attachment figure's responses are inconsistent, as opposed to completely rejecting, the preoccupied individual is hypothesized to develop a strategy of increasing negative affect in an attempt to elicit attention (28). Avoidant attachment has been associated with more consistent levels of neglect or uncaring and critical behavior from caregivers (63). As indicated above, there is evidence of associations between attachment disorganization and parental maltreatment (49), but the development of a disorganized attachment pattern could also be influenced by more subtle (but frequent or pervasive) disruptions in parental attunement, possibly caused by a range of adverse conditions and circumstances [e.g., parental poor mental health, trauma, and experiences of loss (49–54)].

These relationships have not been tested through longitudinal research in voice hearers, but a number of cross-sectional studies in psychosis report associations between earlier caregiving and insecure attachment (64–66). For example, in a sample of 80 people, Berry et al. (64) found a negative relationship association between participant reports of neglectful parental care and insecure avoidant attachment. The authors also compared levels of attachment across four different groups: 26 participants reporting trauma with significant others in childhood; 12 participants reporting trauma with significant others in adulthood only; 28 participants reporting traumatic interpersonal events involving non-significant others; and 14 participants reporting no traumatic interpersonal events. The groups differed in terms of attachment anxiety and there were higher levels of anxious attachment in people who experienced trauma with significant others in childhood. Unexpectedly, there were no group differences for attachment avoidance. Avoidant attachment has been characterized by a tendency to underreport distress (67), thus making it difficult to detect possible associations between interpersonal trauma and avoidant attachment. As discussed below, these associations between trauma and anxious attachment have been replicated in a recent study with voice hearers that also attempted to test a mediation model whereby insecure attachment mediates associations between earlier trauma and dimensions of voice hearing (68). Finally, in the largest study examining attachment profiles in psychosis to date, data from 588 participants who met criteria for non-affective psychosis showed that a disorganized attachment pattern was associated with a higher proportion of sexual and physical abuse and more severe positive symptoms compared to other attachment patterns (69), suggesting that disorganized attachment is a more putative attachment style compared to other types of attachment for positive symptoms. However, despite relatively robust evidence of associations between earlier relational trauma and attachment, it is important to note that not all people who have experienced trauma develop problematic attachment patterns [e.g., Ref. (54)], suggesting that other biological, psychological, or social resilience factors may be important in predicting later outcomes including the development of psychopathology and distressing voices.

Trauma and Dissociation

Despite the popularity of proposals arguing that the apparent link between dissociation and adverse life experiences may be artifactual, and accounted for by the high levels of fantasy proneness and other cognitive distortions observed in individuals with dissociative experiences [e.g., Ref. (70)], there is considerable evidence suggesting that dissociation is a pervasive psychological sequela of traumatic life experiences (38). For example, the findings of cross-sectional studies suggesting a robust association between histories of childhood abuse and adult dissociation [e.g., Ref. (71)] have been corroborated by a growing number of prospective investigations and studies that sought objective confirmation of self-reported trauma histories [for a review, see Ref. (38)]. Although heightened dissociation has been linked to a wide range of traumatic life experiences, empirical studies indicate that the risk of experiencing pervasive dissociative symptoms is particularly elevated in individuals exposed to severe interpersonal traumas, such as acts of abuse, maltreatment, or victimization perpetrated by close family members or significant others. For example, the findings of studies conducted in the context of Betrayal Trauma Theory, a theoretical model that views dissociation as an adaptive response that minimizes the distress and conflict faced when perpetrators are also the very same persons and/or institutions on which the victim depends for his/her survival or well-being (72), suggests that associations between dissociative phenomena and interpersonal traumatic experiences characterized by high interpersonal closeness is particularly robust relatively to those between dissociation and other types of traumas [e.g., Ref. (73, 74)]. In the light of this evidence, traumatic events that occur in the context of salient attachment relationships can be regarded as particularly influential to the development of dissociation and related phenomena, including hallucinatory experiences, as explained in subsequent sections.

Recent meta-analytic studies indicate that dissociative experiences are common among people experiencing psychosis (75), a finding that is not surprising in the light of the plethora of evidence reflecting high prevalence of interpersonal traumatic life experiences in this clinical population [e.g., Ref. (46)]. Several empirical studies suggest that the heightened levels of dissociation reported by people with psychosis relative to non-psychiatric controls are explained by trauma exposure [e.g., Ref. (46, 76, 77)], and therefore are unlikely to simply be a byproduct of psychotic symptoms presence. Similar findings were obtained in studies that specifically considered samples of clinical and non-clinical voice hearers [e.g., Ref. (46, 78–80)], with some notable non-replications (81, 82) that are possibly explained by a number of methodological drawbacks in these studies [insufficient statistical power and/or variance in trauma exposure; use of crude measures of trauma exposure; see Ref. (58)].

Attachment and Dissociation

Liotti (83) suggested that if infants experience interactions with parents exhibiting frightened/frightening behaviors as a result of their own unresolved loss or trauma this can create long-term vulnerabilities to dissociative disorders. Liotti (48) proposes that disorganized attachment in infancy reflects incoherent and confusing emotional and behavioral coping strategies in which the person is unable to resolve the conflict between simultaneously seeking safety from their attachment figure and avoiding distress from them. Liotti (48) suggests that in adulthood, when faced with a stressor, these incoherent coping strategies are activated causing reactions that mirror dissociative experiences in which an individual is unable to coherently integrate memories, consciousness, and self-identity. Although a detailed discussion of the neurobiology of attachment and the neurological effects of trauma is beyond the scope of this paper, it is possible that repeated exposure to relational traumas in childhood results in oversensitivity to threat in the context of later stressors, as smaller hippocampal and frontal volume lead to a predominance of amygdala-driven processing rather than hippocampal or frontal cortex-driven processes (84).

There is evidence of associations between reports of parental loss and later dissociation/absorption in offspring (83, 85). Prospective, longitudinal studies have found similar results in terms of developmental pathways to dissociation [e.g., Ref. (56, 57, 86, 87)]. For example, Ogawa et al. (57) examined dissociative behaviors and their relation to self-organization in 168 young adults at high risk of poor developmental outcomes due to poverty using a longitudinal design, which assessed traumatic life events, attachment quality, adaptational functioning, and dissociative symptomatology at five time points from birth to 19 years. In addition to age of onset, severity, and chronicity of trauma, disorganized and avoidant attachment to parents was a significant predictor for scores on all the measures of dissociative phenomena. Surprisingly, few studies have investigated associations between adult attachment and dissociation. One study investigating PTSD and dissociation in victimized female college students with and without a history of childhood abuse found that self-reported secure attachment style was negatively related to dissociation as measured by the DES [the most widely used questionnaire measure of dissociative experiences (34)], and self-reported preoccupied and fearful attachment were positively associated with dissociation (88). When victimization/abuse and the four attachment scores were entered into the same model, only fearful attachment uniquely contribution to dissociation. Dismissing-avoidant attachment was not significantly related to dissociation. The authors propose that their findings are consistent with Liotti's (83) view that dissociation is better understood as a form of fear-based disorganization rather than emotional detachment. Although the study did not directly measure disorganized attachment, it has previously been argued that fearful attachment as assessed on self-report adult attachment questions has conceptual overlap with the concept of disorganized attachment in infancy and unresolved attachment on the Adult Attachment Interview (AAI) (32).

Dissociation, Source Monitoring, and Voices

There have been several proposals arguing that dissociation could represent a candidate process to explain the well-replicated association between trauma and the predisposition to experience psychotic symptoms, in particular hearing voices [e.g., Ref. (45, 89, 90)]. In recent years, a growing body of cross-sectional studies has examined the association between dissociative states and voice-hearing experiences across several clinical and non-clinical populations. Our recent systematic review and meta-analysis of this literature found robust associations between voice hearing and dissociation, which were observed not only in research with individuals with a diagnosis of schizophrenia and related psychoses but also in PTSD, DID, and non-clinical studies (58). There is also growing empirical evidence suggesting that dissociation mediates the relationship between childhood trauma and the proneness to hearing voices, a finding that has been already been independently replicated in both clinical (46, 79, 91) and non-clinical samples [e.g., Ref. (91, 92)]. In a recent prospective study, Geddes et al. (93) found that peritraumatic dissociation (meaning, the extent to which the victim dissociated during the traumatic event), in conjunction with other peritraumatic and trauma-related psychological variables, predicted the onset of hallucinatory experiences in survivors of interpersonal assaults. The exact processes through which dissociation might lead to the formation of hallucinatory experiences, and the extent to which the cognitive underpinnings of dissociation interact or overlap with those that promote hallucinatory experiences, remain a matter of theoretical debate as very few empirical investigations have attempted to tackle these research questions. In a rare study of this kind, Varese et al. (46) tested service users with psychosis on self-report measures of dissociation and experimental measures of reality discrimination (source monitoring). In this study, hallucinating individuals reported significantly higher levels of dissociation compared to both service users who were currently hallucination-free but had suffered from hallucinations in the past (in other word, individuals whose hallucinations were in remission), and service users with diagnoses in the schizophrenia spectrum who had *never* experienced hallucinations at any point of their lives. In contrast, the analyses of reality discrimination data indicated that the performance of hallucinating individuals and remitted hallucinators was significantly (and equally) more biased relative to service users who never experienced hallucinated perceptions. These findings suggest that heightened dissociation only characterized participants who were currently suffering from hallucinations rather than representing an enduring trait, whereas reality discrimination difficulties could be regarded as a trait-like vulnerability present in both current and remitted hallucinating individuals. Additional analyses of these data indicated that dissociation was unlikely to be directly responsible for the reality discrimination difficulties assessed in the context of this study;

the reality discrimination scores of service users who presented with "pathological" levels of dissociative symptoms (94) were in fact no different than those of "non-dissociative" service users. Varese et al. (46) argue that this may reflect a possible "two-hit" model, in which dissociation triggers voices in those vulnerable to reality discrimination (or source monitoring) difficulties. In the lack of better evidence, the current representation of the CAV model reflects and incorporates the findings of this study, but we recognize that further investigations in this area are required to corroborate or clarify the interplay between dissociation and the cognitive underpinnings of hallucinatory experiences.

Attachment and Voices

There is substantial evidence that insecure attachment increases vulnerability to the development of mental health problems (28). For example, there is evidence from prospective research that insecure attachment increases vulnerability to PTSD (95) and mediates associations between childhood maltreatment and later anxiety and depression (96).

More specifically in the context of psychosis, Ponizovsky et al. (97) and Berry et al. (98) investigated adult attachment and symptoms in participants diagnosed with schizophrenia or related psychoses. Both research groups found associations between attachment anxiety and voices, but Ponizovsky and colleagues (97) also found relationships between attachment avoidance and voices. Bentall et al. (99) explored the issue of symptom specificity by examining relationships between childhood adversities and both paranoia and hallucinations with data from Adult Psychiatric Morbidity Survey. Using analyses that controlled for the covariation between paranoia and hallucinations, the authors found that childhood rape was specifically associated with hallucinations whereas being brought up in institutional care was associated with paranoia, but not with hallucinations. The authors argue that severe trauma increases vulnerability to voice hearing, whereas attachment disturbance increases susceptibility to paranoia. Wickham et al. (100) explored associations between attachment, paranoia, and hallucinations in people diagnosed with a schizophrenia-spectrum disorder and non-clinical controls. Similar to the findings of Bentall et al. (99), attachment was not correlated with hallucinations when controlling for paranoia.

However, research to date has focused on insecure attachment patterns and their association with psychotic symptoms as a disorganized attachment pattern has been difficult to measure using self-report measurement tools. However, researchers have long made conceptual links between disorganized attachment and voice-related distress, suggesting that high scores on the two organized attachment dimensions likely reflect a disorganized attachment pattern. Yet, specific correlates of disorganized attachment more specifically have only very recently been investigated. To the best of our knowledge, there are two studies that have attempted to explore disorganized attachment and voice-hearing correlates.

Using a covariance modeling approach to explore associations between attachment and non-clinical psychotic phenomena, MacBeth et al. (101) found that paranoia was predicted by an "organized" model consisting of attachment anxiety, avoidance, and interpersonal distancing strategies, whereas hallucinations were predicted by a more complex model represented by a combination of attachment anxiety and interpersonal affiliating strategies with attachment avoidance and interpersonal distancing strategies. The authors argue that the hallucinations model characterizes the contradictory and competing interpersonal strategies of a disorganized attachment pattern.

Bucci and colleagues (69) combined observations of 588 psychosis patients on the Psychosis Attachment Measure (98), the most frequently used self-report attachment measure in psychosis research, to examine associations between attachment patterns and positive psychotic symptoms (hallucinations and delusions). In line with CAV predictions, Bucci et al. (69) found that those with more frequent reports of trauma history, in particular sexual and physical abuse, and more frequent positive psychotic symptoms, were assigned to a disorganized attachment class using latent profile analysis.

Attachment, Beliefs about/Ways of Relating to Voices, and Voice-Related Distress

Berry et al. (102) explored associations between attachment and the nature of the person's relationship with voices. The authors found evidence of associations between avoidance in attachment relationships and themes of rejection, criticism, and threat in relationships with voices. This study was novel in investigating attachment and voice hearing but was limited by the fact that themes from symptom assessments were used to derive the content of voices; participants were not specifically asked about the nature of their relationships with voices.

In a sample of 44 voice hearers, Robson and Mason (103) found that avoidant attachment was associated with voice intrusiveness (voice perceived by hearer as intrusive) and hearer distance (hearer relates to their voice from a position of distance), and anxious attachment was related to voice intrusiveness and hearer dependence (hearer relates to their voice from a dependent position). Furthermore, the relationship between insecure attachment and voice-related distress was mediated by voice malevolence and omnipotence. In a similar study involving 55 voice hearers, Pilton et al. (68) found that anxious attachment was associated with voice-related severity and distress and further dimensions of voice hearing including: voice omnipotence, voice dominance, voice intrusiveness, and hearer dependence, but there were no associations between avoidant attachment and voices. Pilton et al.'s (68) mediation analyses showed that anxious attachment mediated the relationship between childhood trauma and voice dimensions including voice-related severity, voice distress, voice malevolence, voice omnipotence, voice resistance, and hearer dependence. Consistent with Robson and Mason's (103) research, further mediation analyses also found that the relationship between anxious attachment and voice-related distress was mediated by beliefs about voices including voice malevolence, voice omnipotence, and voice resistance. These findings suggest that anxious attachment may have a direct effect on voice-related distress but also influence voice-related distress *via* negative beliefs about voices and maladaptive ways of responding to voices.

The idea that people form specific attachments with voices also raises the question whether or not relationships with voices can be conceptualized as attachment relationships. There is evidence that, for some people, voices do provide a source of comfort from distress as well as companionship and that people anticipate and experience a sense of loss following reductions in voice hearing and when their voices are not present (104, 105). Speculatively, it may be particularly likely that voices take on an attachment quality if other social relationships diminish following the onset of psychosis.

THE ADDED VALUE OF THE MODEL

We recognize that there may be multiple routes to voices, but our model aims to clarify the nature of one of these possible pathways. The unique aspect of the CAV is the concept of attachment, and specifically the role of disorganized attachment and dissociative processes, in helping to explain the association between trauma and voice hearing. Although previous theories have highlighted the importance of trauma-related dissociation in voice hearing, one of the strengths of attachment theory is that it not only highlights the role of overtly abusive events but also emphasizes the role of more subtle childhood experiences in influencing the way individuals manage distressing emotions and relate to other people (106), which in turn may also influence susceptibility to voices.

A further advantage of the CAV is that it integrates vulnerability and maintenance distress models of voice hearing. Within the model disorganized attachment patterns increase vulnerability to hear voices, but secondary attachment strategies including insecure avoidant and anxious styles attachment styles influence belief appraisal processes, affect emotional regulation strategies and interpersonal relationships with both others in the social world and voices, once voices develop. Relatedly and perhaps less well articulated in the literature is the notion of secure attachment. Our own data suggest that a substantial proportion of people with psychosis have secure attachment styles (69), and our model predicts that such individuals would develop more psychologically healthy ways of thinking about and relating to their voices and seeking support from others in their social world, including mental health services. The CAV therefore has the potential to predict resilience to distressing voices as well as vulnerability and maintenance.

LIMITATIONS AND FURTHER RESEARCH

Further research is needed to investigate associations between specific childhood adversities and attachment, including disorganized attachment, which is not well captured by self-report measures of attachment styles. Bucci et al. (69) describe using a simple self-report measure of attachment to derive a measure of disorganized attachment using latent class analysis, but arguably we need processes for measuring disorganized attachment that more directly assess the concept and are more feasible to use in the context of large research studies than the AAI (107).

A more nuanced understanding of dissociation is also needed in the psychosis literature. Current definitions of dissociation are rather global and general whereby dissociation has traditionally been conceptualized as a unitary phenomenon (37). For example, the broad use of the term dissociation is often used to describe experiences ranging from relatively benign forms of psychological disengagement (e.g., absorption) to more pervasive dissociative experiences such as derealization, depersonalization and identity alteration. However, the concept of a dissociative continuum has been criticized for being overly generic (37). For example, Holmes et al. (36) argue that there are two different kinds of dissociation: detachment and compartmentalization. Detachment is defined as a state of consciousness that is removed from everyday experience and caused by a neurobiological response to threat (108). Compartmentalization is defined as an inability to deliberately control cognitive processes or behaviors that would normally be controllable and is caused by disturbances in processes underlying consciousness and mental control (109, 110). It is as yet unclear if disorganized attachment predisposes individuals to develop specific dissociative phenomena. Similarly, it is unclear which aspects of dissociation are important in determining the development of voice hearing. Whereas existing measures, such as the DES (34), might be regarded as well suited for the assessment of prototypical examples of dissociative detachment (e.g., experiences of depersonalization and derealization), no comprehensive measure of dissociative compartmentalization has been developed yet. This line of research will require the development of novel, purposely designed and psychometrically robust measures to assess dissociative detachment and compartmentalization. Furthermore, existing research has predominantly conceptualized AVHs as a unitary construct, despite indications that they may be phenomenologically heterogeneous experiences. Like in the case of dissociative experiences, researchers have proposed the existence of phenomenologically distinct subtypes of hearing voices, which are possibly characterized by different psychological underpinnings and might require different treatment approaches [e.g., Ref. (111–115)]. Research carried out to identify these phenomenologically distinct subtypes is, however, in its infancy. As this line of research develops, it will be possible to clarify whether the psychological processes outlined in the CAV model are applicable across different types of voices, or may be particularly implicated in certain subtypes (e.g., dialogical voices characterized by a specific identity, as voice hearers may be particularly prone to respond to these voices according to their attachment styles).

Finally, there is a growing call to examine resilience factors within the context of trauma and voice hearing. Secure attachment, which is shaped by biological, psychological, and social influences, may be an important resilience factor that both influences the likelihood of experiencing dissociation in response to trauma and/or how adaptively people respond to the voice hearing once it develops. Indeed, evidence that secure attachment is a potentially important resilience factor in preventing the development of PTSD following exposure to trauma (95), suggests it would be important to examine if these findings generalize to other trauma-related symptoms, such as dissociation and psychotic symptoms.

CLINICAL IMPLICATIONS

The model presented here has a number of clinical implications. First, the proposed model highlights the importance of asking voice hearers about their histories of relational trauma and experiences in attachment relationships (116, 117). Staff are likely to need further training and supervision in how to sensitively ask about, and response to, distressing disclosures of abuse and neglect in a psychologically informed way (117, 118). The CAV also emphasizes the overlap between relationships with voices and broader social relationships. This has the advantage of normalizing voice hearing and suggests that therapeutic strategies that have been shown to improve relationships in the social world might also be beneficial in voice hearing (119). In addition, Bowlby (120) conceptualized the therapeutic relationship as an attachment relationship and argued that effective psychotherapeutic intervention can provide an alternative interpersonal experience termed "corrective emotional experience," affording individuals the opportunity to develop a broader range of interpersonal behaviors. Therapist sensitivity, responsiveness, reliability, and consistency are key to the development of a secure therapeutic base. In the context of voice hearing, once a "secure base" has been established and the person is willing, individuals may feel more comfortable to explore and process the links between previous relationships and relationships with voices. Perhaps most fundamentally, the possible role of attachment in voice hearing highlights the likely benefits of interventions that help children foster secure attachments and therefore stronger resilience to voice hearing in the first place. Indeed, randomized control trials demonstrate the effectiveness of attachment-based interventions for maltreating families (121). If disorganized attachment is critical in the developmental pathway of voice hearing, early identification of this vulnerability is crucial as working with a disorganized attachment patterns takes time, consistency, and persistence. Reliable and consistent boundaries are essential; consistent and predictable staff members and service response to incidents over time are needed to make it possible to develop a corrective attachment experience for individuals (122).

Given the finding that a significant proportion of voice hearers do have secure attachment styles [e.g., Ref. (69)], identifying resilience factors and adopting a strengths-based approach may also be important in clinical work and intervention development.

While it could be argued that some of the above implications are also indicated by the existing cognitive model of voice hearing, such as the importance of asking about trauma and exploring how the meaning from these experiences influences relating to voices, in line with the previous section, we argue that an attachment perspective provides added value both clinically and theoretically. Most notably, the fact that attachment theory is a universal theory of relationships, which applies to both voice hearers and mental health workers alike and emphasizes the functional nature of insecure attachment styles in the context of earlier relationships means that it has the potential to be less pathologizing than other models. Relatedly, attachment theory also provides a framework for conceptualizing the role of the mental health workers' own relational histories and attachment styles within the therapeutic processes, including how these interact with those experiences and attachment patterns of voice hearers (122, 123).

CONCLUSION

It is important to understand the psychological mechanisms underlying voices so this can inform the development of psychological therapies for distressing voices (124). Here, we argue that the CAV model identifies the way in which the psychological mechanisms of attachment and dissociation might develop cognitive theories of voices. Other researchers have developed theories about the role earlier experiences in voice hearing without drawing on attachment theory, and other models have noted the importance of voices being understood as an interpersonal relationship, but this is the first attempt at integrating attachment theory within cognitive and dissociative frameworks for understanding voices.

Attachment theory does not, in itself, explain all instances of voice hearing- or voice-related distress. Nevertheless, we hope that we have argued that attachment theory, a key theory of emotional regulation and interpersonal relationships, should not be ignored when developing an understanding of how individuals cope with voice-related distress and relate to the voice-hearing experience.

AUTHOR CONTRIBUTIONS

All authors—development of ideas and writing paper.

REFERENCES

1. Waters F, Fernyhough C. Hallucinations: a systematic review of points of similarity and difference across diagnostic classes. *Schizophr Bull* (2017) 43(1):32–43. doi:10.1093/schbul/sbw132
2. Woods A, Jones N, Alderson-Day B, Callard F, Fernyhough C. Experiences of hearing voices: analysis of a novel. *Lancet Psychiatry* (2015) 2:323–31. doi:10.1016/S2215-0366(15)00006-1
3. Feinberg I. Efference copy and corollary discharge: implications for thinking and its disorders. *Schizophr Bull* (1978) 4:636–40. doi:10.1093/schbul/4.4.636
4. Waters F, Allen P, Aleman A, Fernyhough C, Woodward TS, Badcock JC, et al. Auditory hallucinations in schizophrenia and nonschizophrenia populations: a review and integrated model of cognitive mechanisms. *Schizophr Bull* (2012) 38(4):683–93. doi:10.1093/schbul/sbs045
5. Bentall RP. The illusion of reality: a review and integration of psychological research on hallucinations. *Psychol Bull* (1990) 107(1):82–95. doi:10.1037/0033-2909.107.1.82
6. Brookwell ML, Bentall RP, Varese F. Externalizing biases and hallucinations in source monitoring, self-monitoring and signal detection studies: a meta-analytic review. *Psychol Med* (2013) 43(12):2465–75. doi:10.1017/S0033291712002760
7. Longden E, Madill A, Waterman MG. Dissociation, trauma, and the role of lived experience: toward a new conceptualization of voice hearing. *Psychol Bull* (2012) 138(1):28–76. doi:10.1037/a0025995
8. Waters F, Woodward T, Allen P, Aleman A, Sommer I. Self-recognition deficits in schizophrenia patients with auditory hallucinations: a meta-analysis of the literature. *Schizophr Bull* (2012) 38(4):741–50. doi:10.1093/schbul/sbq144
9. Upthegrove R, Broome MR, Caldwell K, Ives J, Oyebode F, Wood SJ. Understanding auditory verbal hallucinations: a systematic review of current evidence. *Acta Psychiatr Scand* (2016) 133(5):352–67. doi:10.1111/acps.12531

10. Daalman K, Boks MP, Diederen KM, de Weijer AD, Blom JD, Kahn RS, et al. The same or different? A phenomenological comparison of auditory verbal hallucinations in healthy and psychotic individuals. *J Clin Psychiatry* (2011) 72(3):320–5. doi:10.4088/JCP.09m05797yel
11. Chadwick P, Birchwood M. The omnipotence of voices. A cognitive approach to auditory hallucinations. *Br J Psychiatry* (1994) 164(2):190–201. doi:10.1192/bjp.164.2.190
12. Chadwick P, Birchwood M. Cognitive therapy for voices. In: Haddock G, Slade PD, editors. *Cognitive Behavioural Interventions for Psychotic Disorders*. London: Routledge (1996). p. 71–85.
13. Morrison AP. A cognitive analysis of the maintenance of auditory hallucinations: are voices to schizophrenia what bodily sensations are to panic? *Behav Cogn Psychother* (1998) 26(04):289–302.
14. Morrison AP. The interpretation of intrusions in psychosis: an integrative cognitive approach to hallucinations and delusions. *Behav Cogn Psychother* (2001) 29(3):257–76. doi:10.1017/S1352465801003010
15. Mawson A, Cohen K, Berry K. Reviewing evidence for the cognitive model of auditory hallucinations: the relationship between cognitive voice appraisals and distress during psychosis. *Clin Psychol Rev* (2010) 30(2):248–58. doi:10.1016/j.cpr.2009.11.006
16. Varese F, Barkus E, Bentall RP. Dissociation mediates the relationship between childhood trauma and hallucination-proneness. *Psychol Med* (2012) 42(05):1025–36. doi:10.1017/S0033291711001826
17. Shevlin M, Murphy J, Read J, Mallett J, Adamson G, Houston JE. Childhood adversity and hallucinations: a community-based study using the National Comorbidity Survey Replication. *Soc Psychiatry Psychiatr Epidemiol* (2011) 46(12):1203–10. doi:10.1007/s00127-010-0296-x
18. Varese F, Barkus E, Bentall RP. Dissociative and metacognitive factors in hallucination-proneness when controlling for comorbid symptoms. *Cogn Neuropsychiatry* (2011) 16(3):193–217. doi:10.1080/13546805.2010.495244
19. Bentall RP, Fernyhough C. Social predictors of psychotic experiences: specificity and psychological mechanisms. *Schizophr Bull* (2008) 34(6):1012–20. doi:10.1093/schbul/sbn103
20. Steel C. Hallucinations as a trauma-based memory: implications for psychological interventions. *Front Psychol* (2015) 6:1262. doi:10.3389/fpsyg.2015.01262
21. Hardy A, Emsley R, Freeman D, Bebbington P, Garety PA, Kuipers EE, et al. Psychological mechanisms mediating effects between trauma and psychotic symptoms: the role of affect regulation, intrusive trauma memory, beliefs, and depression. *Schizophr Bull* (2016) 42(1):34–43. doi:10.1093/schbul/sbv175
22. Andrew E, Gray N, Snowden R. The relationship between trauma and beliefs about hearing voices: a study of psychiatric and non-psychiatric voice hearers. *Psychol Med* (2008) 38(10):1409–17. doi:10.1017/S003329170700253X
23. Birchwood M, Gilbert P, Gilbert J, Trower P, Meaden A, Hay J, et al. Interpersonal and role-related schema influence the relationship with the dominant 'voice' in schizophrenia: a comparison of three models. *Psychol Med* (2004) 34(08):1571–80. doi:10.1017/S0033291704002636
24. Bowlby J. *Attachment and Loss*. (Vol. I). London: Hogarth (1969).
25. Berry K, Bucci S. What does attachment theory tell us about working with distressing voices? *Psychosis* (2016) 8:60–71. doi:10.1080/17522439.2015.1070370
26. Bowlby J. Attachment and loss: retrospect and prospect. *Am J Orthopsychiatry* (1982) 52(4):664–78. doi:10.1111/j.1939-0025.1982.tb01456.x
27. Ainsworth MDS, Blehar MC, Waters E, Wall S. *Patterns of attachment: A psychological study of the strange situation*. Hillsdale, NJ: Erlbaum (1978).
28. Mikulincer M, Shaver PR. Attachment theory and emotions in close relationships: exploring the attachment-related dynamics of emotional reactions to relational events. *Pers Relatsh* (2005) 12(2):149–68. doi:10.1111/j.1350-4126.2005.00108.x
29. McConnell M, Moss E. Attachment across the life span: factors that contribute to stability and change. *Aust J Educ Dev Psychol* (2011) 11:60–77.
30. Berry K, Wearden A, Barrowclough C. Adult attachment styles and psychosis: an investigation of associations between general attachment styles and attachment relationships with specific others. *Soc Psychiatry Psychiatr Epidemiol* (2007) 42(12):972–6. doi:10.1007/s00127-007-0261-5
31. Crowell JA, Fraley RC, Shaver PR. Measurement of individual differences in adolescent and adult attachment. *Handb Attach Theory Res Clin Appl* (1999) 2:635.
32. Bartholomew K. Assessment of individual differences in adult attachment. *Psychol Inq* (1994) 5(1):23–67. doi:10.1207/s15327965pli0501_2
33. Waller NG, Ross CA. The prevalence and biometric structure of pathological dissociation in the general population: taxometric and behavior genetic findings. *J Abnorm Psychol* (1997) 106(4):499. doi:10.1037/0021-843X.106.4.499
34. Bernstein EM, Putnam FW. Development, reliability, and validity of a dissociation scale. *J Nerv Ment Dis* (1986) 174(12):727–35. doi:10.1097/00005053-198612000-00004
35. American Psychiatric Association (APA). *Diagnostic and Statistical Manual of Mental Disorders*. 5th ed. Washington, DC: American Psychiatric Association (2013).
36. Holmes EA, Brown RJ, Mansell W, Fearon RP, Hunter EC, Frasquilho F, et al. Are there two qualitatively distinct forms of dissociation? A review and some clinical implications. *Clin Psychol Rev* (2005) 25(1):1–23. doi:10.1016/j.cpr.2004.08.006
37. Brown RJ. Different types of "dissociation" have different psychological mechanisms. *J Trauma Dissociation* (2006) 7(4):7–28. doi:10.1300/J229v07n04_02
38. Dalenberg CJ, Brand BL, Gleaves DH, Dorahy MJ, Loewenstein RJ, Cardena E, et al. Evaluation of the evidence for the trauma and fantasy models of dissociation. *Psychol Bull* (2012) 138(3):550–88. doi:10.1037/a0027447
39. Frith C. *The Cognitive Neuropsychology of Schizophrenia*. London: Lawrence Erlbaum Associates (1992).
40. Larøi F and Woodward TS. Hallucinations from a cognitive perspective. *Harv Rev Psychiatry* (2007) 15:109–17.
41. Waters FA, Badcock JC, Michie PT, Maybery MT. Auditory hallucinations in schizophrenia: intrusive thoughts and forgotten memories. *Cogn Neuropsychiatry* (2006) 11:65–83. doi:10.1080/13546800444000191
42. Bentall RP, Slade PD. Reality testing and auditory hallucinations: a signal detection analysis. *Br J Clin Psychol* (1985) 24(Pt 3):159–69.
43. Johns LC, Rossell S, Frith C, Ahmad F, Hemsley D, Kuipers E, et al. Verbal self-monitoring and auditory verbal hallucinations in patients with schizophrenia. *Psychol Med* (2001) 31(4):705–15.
44. Bentall RP, Baker GA. Havers S. Reality monitoring and psychotic hallucinations. *Br J Clin Psychol* (1991) 30:213–22.
45. Moskowitz A, Corstens D. Auditory hallucinations: psychotic symptom or dissociative experience? *J Psychol Trauma* (2008) 6(2–3):35–63. doi:10.1300/J513v06n02_04
46. Varese F, Smeets F, Drukker M, Lieverse R, Lataster T, Viechtbauer W, et al. Childhood adversities increase the risk of psychosis: a meta-analysis of patient-control, prospective-and cross-sectional cohort studies. *Schizophr Bull* (2012) 8(4):661–71. doi:10.1093/schbul/sbs050
47. Main M, Solomon J. Discovery of an insecure-disorganized/disoriented attachment pattern. In: Brazelton TB, Yogman MW, editors. *Affective Development in Infancy*. Westport, CT: Ablex Publishing (1986). p. 95–124.
48. Liotti G. Trauma, dissociation, and disorganized attachment: three strands of a single braid. *Psychother Theory Res Pract Train* (2004) 41(4):472. doi:10.1037/0033-3204.41.4.472
49. Lyons-Ruth K, Jacobvitz D. Attachment disorganisation. In: Shaver JCPR, editor. *Handbook of Attachment. Theory, Research and Clinical Implications*. London: Guilford Press (1999). p. 520–54.
50. Cyr C, Euser EM, Bakermans-Kranenburg MJ, Van Ijzendoorn MH. Attachment security and disorganization in maltreating and high-risk families: a series of meta-analyses. *Dev Psychopathol* (2010) 22(01):87–108. doi:10.1017/S0954579409990289
51. Hesse E, Main M. Frightened, threatening, and dissociative parental behavior in low-risk samples: description, discussion, and interpretations. *Dev Psychopathol* (2006) 18(02):309–43. doi:10.1017/S0954579406060172
52. Lyons-Ruth K, Yellin C, Melnick S, Atwood G. Expanding the concept of unresolved mental states: hostile/helpless states of mind on the Adult Attachment Interview are associated with disrupted mother-infant communication and infant disorganization. *Dev Psychopathol* (2005) 17(1):1–23. doi:10.1017/S0954579405050017
53. Van Ijzendoorn MH. Adult attachment representations, parental responsiveness and infant attachment: a meta-analysis on the predictive validity of the Adult Attachment Interview. *Psychol Bull* (1995) 117:387–403. doi:10.1037/0033-2909.117.3.387
54. Van Ijzendoorn MH, Schuengel C, Bakerman-Kranenburg MJ. Disorganized attachment in early childhood: meta-analysis of precursors, concomitants,

and sequelae. *Dev Psychopathol* (1999) 11(2):225–50. doi:10.1017/S0954579499002035

55. Carlson EA. A prospective longitudinal study of attachment disorganization/disorientation. *Child Dev* (1998) 69(4):1107–28. doi:10.2307/1132365
56. Dutra L, Bureau JF, Holmes B, Lyubchik A, Lyons-Ruth K. Quality of early care and childhood trauma: a prospective study of developmental pathways to dissociation. *J Nerv Ment Dis* (2009) 197(6):383–90. doi:10.1097/NMD.0b013e3181a653b7
57. Ogawa JR, Sroufe LA, Weinfield NS, Carlson EA, Egeland B. Development and the fragmented self: longitudinal study of dissociative symptomatology in a nonclinical sample. *Dev Psychopathol* (1997) 9(04):855–79. doi:10.1017/S0954579497001478
58. Pilton M, Varese F, Berry K, Bucci S. The relationship between dissociation and voices: a systematic literature review and meta-analysis. *Clin Psychol Rev* (2015) 40:138–55. doi:10.1016/j.cpr.2015.06.004
59. Fraley RC, Waller NG. Adult attachment patterns: a test of the typological model. In: Simpson JA, Rholes WS, editors. *Attachment Theory and Close Relationships*. New York, NY: Guilford Press (1998). p. 77–114.
60. Bifulco A, Moran PM, Ball C, Lillie A. Adult attachment style. II: its relationship to psychosocial depressive-vulnerability. *Soc Psychiatry Psychiatr Epidemiol* (2002) 37(2):60–7. doi:10.1007/s127-002-8215-0
61. Whiffen VE, Judd ME, Aube JA. Intimate relationships moderate the association between childhood sexual abuse and depression. *J Interpers Violence* (1999) 14(9):940–54. doi:10.1177/088626099014009002
62. Kobak RR, Cole HE, Ferenz-Gillies R, Fleming WS, Gamble W. Attachment and emotion regulation during mother-teen problem-solving: a control theory analysis. *Child Dev* (1993) 64:231–45.
63. Larose S, Bernier A, Tarabulsy GM. Attachment state of mind, learning dispositions, and academic performance during the college transition. *Dev Psychol* (2005) 41(1):281–89. doi:10.1037/0012-1649.41.1.281
64. Berry K, Barrowclough C, Wearden A. Adult attachment, perceived earlier experiences of care giving and trauma in people with psychosis. *J Ment Health* (2009) 18(4):280–7. doi:10.1080/09638230701879185
65. Mulligan A, Lavender T. An investigation into the relationship between attachment, gender and recovery from psychosis in a stable community-based sample. *Clin Psychol Psychother* (2010) 17(4):269–84. doi:10.1002/cpp.655
66. Tait L, Birchwood M, Trower P. Adapting to the challenge of psychosis: personal resilience and the use of sealing-over (avoidant) coping strategies. *Br J Psychiatry* (2004) 185:410–5. doi:10.1192/bjp.185.5.410
67. Dozier M, Lee SW. Discrepancies between self-and other-report of psychiatric symptomatology: effects of dismissing attachment strategies. *Dev Psychopathol* (1995) 7(1):217–26. doi:10.1017/S095457940000643X
68. Pilton M, Bucci S, McManus J, Hayward M, Emsley R, Berry K. Does insecure attachment mediate the relationship between trauma and voice-hearing in psychosis? *Psychiatry Res* (2016) 246:776–82. doi:10.1016/j.psychres.2016.10.050
69. Bucci S, Emsley R, Berry K. Attachment in psychosis: a latent profile analysis of attachment styles and association with symptoms in a large psychosis cohort. *Psychiatry Res* (2017) 247:243–9. doi:10.1016/j.psychres.2016.11.036
70. Merckelbach H, Muris P. The causal link between self-reported trauma and dissociation: a critical review. *Behav Res Ther* (2001) 39(3):245–54. doi:10.1016/S0005-7967(99)00181-3
71. Van Ijzendoorn MH, Schuengel C. The measurement of dissociation in normal and clinical populations: meta-analytic validation of the Dissociative Experiences Scale (DES). *Clin Psychol Rev* (1996) 16(5):365–82. doi:10.1016/0272-7358(96)00006-2
72. Freyd JJ. What juries don't know: dissemination of research on victim response is essential for justice. *Trauma Psychol Newsl* (2008) 3:15–8.
73. Hulette AC, Kaehler LA, Freyd JJ. Intergenerational associations between trauma and dissociation. *J Fam Violence* (2011) 26(3):217–25. doi:10.1007/s10896-011-9357-5
74. Gómez JM, Kaehler LA, Freyd JJ. Are hallucinations related to betrayal trauma exposure? A three-study exploration. *Psychol Trauma Theory Res Pract Policy* (2014) 6(6):675. doi:10.1037/a0037084
75. O'Driscoll C, Laing J, Mason O. Cognitive emotion regulation strategies, alexithymia and dissociation in schizophrenia, a review and meta-analysis. *Clin Psychol Rev* (2014) 34(6):482–95. doi:10.1016/j.cpr.2014.07.002
76. Schäfer I, Harfst T, Aderhold V, Briken P, Lehmann M, Moritz S, et al. Childhood trauma and dissociation in female patients with schizophrenia spectrum disorders: an exploratory study. *J Nerv Ment Dis* (2006) 194(2):135–8. doi:10.1097/01.nmd.0000198199.57512.84
77. Schäfer I, Fisher HL, Aderhold V, Huber B, Hoffmann-Langer L, Golks D, et al. Dissociative symptoms in patients with schizophrenia: relationships with childhood trauma and psychotic symptoms. *Compr Psychiatry* (2012) 53:364–71. doi:10.1016/j.comppsych.2011.05.010
78. Goff DC, Brotman AW, Kindlon D, Waites M, Amico E. Self-reports of childhood abuse in chronically psychotic patients. *Psychiatry Res* (1991) 37(1):73–80. doi:10.1016/0165-1781(91)90107-Z
79. Perona-Garcelán S, Carrascoso-López F, García-Montes JM, Ductor-Recuerda MJ, López Jiménez AM, Vallina-Fernández O, et al. Dissociative experiences as mediators between childhood trauma and auditory hallucinations. *J Trauma Stress* (2012) 25(3):323–9. doi:10.1002/jts.21693
80. Perona-Garcelán S, García-Montes JM, Rodríguez-Testal JF, López-Jiménez AM, Ruiz-Veguilla M, Ductor-Recuerda MJ, et al. Relationship between childhood trauma, mindfulness, and dissociation in subjects with and without hallucination proneness. *J Trauma Dissociation* (2014) 15(1):35–51. doi:10.1080/15299732.2013.821433
81. Honig A, Romme M, Ensink B, Escher S, Pennings M, DeVries M. Auditory hallucinations: a comparison between patients and nonpatients. *J Nerv Ment Dis* (1998) 186(10):646–51. doi:10.1097/00005053-199810000-00009
82. Laddis A, Dell PF. Dissociation and psychosis in dissociative identity disorder and schizophrenia. *J Trauma Dissociation* (2012) 13(4):397–413. doi:10.1080/15299732.2012.664967
83. Liotti G. Disorganized/disoriented attachment in the etiology of the dissociative disorders. *Dissociation Prog Dissociat Disord* (1992) 5:196–204.
84. Read J, Fosse R, Moskowitz A, Perry B. The traumagenic neurodevelopmental model of psychosis revisited. *Neuropsychiatry* (2014) 4(1):65–79. doi:10.2217/npy.13.89
85. Hesse E, Van IJzendoorn MH. Parental loss of close family members and propensities towards absorption in offspring. *Dev Sci* (1998) 1(2):299–305. doi:10.1111/1467-7687.00045
86. Lyons-Ruth K, Dutra L, Schuder MR, Bianchi I. From infant attachment disorganization to adult dissociation: relational adaptations or traumatic experiences? *Psychiatr Clin North Am* (2006) 29(1):63. doi:10.1016/j.psc.2005.10.011
87. Sroufe LA. Attachment and development: a prospective, longitudinal study from birth to adulthood. *Attach Hum Dev* (2005) 7(4):349–67. doi:10.1080/14616730500365928
88. Sandberg DA. Adult attachment as a predictor of posttraumatic stress and dissociation. *J Trauma Dissociation* (2010) 11(3):293–307. doi:10.1080/15299731003780937
89. Altman H, Collins M, Mundy P. Subclinical hallucinations and delusions in nonpsychotic adolescents. *J Child Psychol Psychiatry* (1997) 38(4):413–20. doi:10.1111/j.1469-7610.1997.tb01526.x
90. Anketell C, Dorahy MJ, Shannon M, Elder R, Hamilton G, Corry M, et al. An exploratory analysis of voice hearing in chronic PTSD: potential associated mechanisms. *J Trauma Dissociation* (2010) 11(1):93–107. doi:10.1080/15299730903143600
91. Perona-Garcelán S, García-Montes JM, Ductor-Recuerda MJ, Vallina-Fernández O, Cuevas-Yust C, Pérez-Álvarez M, et al. Relationship of metacognition, absorption, and depersonalization in patients with auditory hallucinations. *Br J Clin Psychol* (2012) 51(1):100–18. doi:10.1111/j.2044-8260.2011.02015.x
92. Cole CL, Newman-Taylor K, Kennedy F. Dissociation mediates the relationship between childhood maltreatment and subclinical psychosis. *J Trauma Dissociation* (2016) 17(5):577–92. doi:10.1080/15299732.2016.1172537
93. Geddes G, Ehlers A, Freeman D. Hallucinations in the months after a trauma: an investigation of the role of cognitive processing of a physical assault in the occurrence of hallucinatory experiences. *Psychiatry Res* (2016) 246:601–5. doi:10.1016/j.psychres.2016.10.081
94. Waller N, Putnam FW, Carlson EB. Types of dissociation and dissociative types: a taxometric analysis of dissociative experiences. *Psychol Methods* (1996) 1(3):300. doi:10.1037/1082-989X.1.3.300
95. Woodhouse S, Ayers S, Field AP. The relationship between adult attachment style and post-traumatic stress symptoms: a meta-analysis. *J Anxiety Disord* (2015) 35:103–17. doi:10.1016/j.janxdis.2015.07.002

96. Bifulco A, Kwon J, Jacobs C, Moran PM, Bunn A, Beer N. Adult attachment style as mediator between childhood neglect/abuse and adult depression and anxiety. *Soc Psychiatry Psychiatr Epidemiol* (2006) 41(10):796–805. doi:10.1007/s00127-006-0101-z
97. Ponizovsky AM, Vitenberg E, Baumgarten-Katz I, Grinshpoon A. Attachment styles and affect regulation among outpatients with schizophrenia: relationships to symptomatology and emotional distress. *Psychol Psychother* (2013) 86(2):164–82. doi:10.1111/j.2044-8341.2011.02054.x
98. Berry K, Barrowclough C, Wearden A. Attachment theory: a framework for understanding symptoms and interpersonal relationships in psychosis. *Behav Res Ther* (2008) 46(12):1275–82. doi:10.1016/j.brat.2008.08.009
99. Bentall RP, Wickham S, Shevlin M, Varese F. Do specific early-life adversities lead to specific symptoms of psychosis? A study from the 2007 the adult psychiatric morbidity survey. *Schizophr Bull* (2012) 38(4):734–40. doi:10.1093/schbul/sbs049
100. Wickham S, Sitko K, Bentall RP. Insecure attachment is associated with paranoia but not hallucinations in psychotic patients: the mediating role of negative self-esteem. *Psychol Med* (2015) 45(07):1495–507. doi:10.1017/S0033291714002633
101. MacBeth A, Gumley A, Schwannauer M, Fisher R. Attachment states of mind, mentalization, and their correlates in a first-episode psychosis sample. *Psychol Psychother Theory Res Pract* (2011) 84(1):42–57. doi:10.1348/147608310X530246
102. Berry K, Wearden A, Barrowclough C, Oakland L, Bradley J. An investigation of adult attachment and the nature of relationships with voices. *Br J Clin Psychol* (2012) 51(3):280–91. doi:10.1111/j.2044-8260.2011.02027.x
103. Robson G, Mason O. Interpersonal processes and attachment in voice hearers. *Behav Cogn Psychother* (2015) 43(6):655–68. doi:10.1017/S1352465814000125
104. Chin JT, Hayward M, Drinnan A. Relating to voices: exploring the relevance of this concept to people who hear voices. *Psychol Psychother* (2009) 82(1):1–17. doi:10.1348/147608308X320116
105. Moritz S, Favrod J, Andreou C, Morrison AP, Bohn F, Veckenstedt R, et al. Beyond the usual suspects: positive attitudes towards positive symptoms is associated with medication noncompliance in psychosis. *Schizophr Bull* (2013) 39(4):917–22. doi:10.1093/schbul/sbs005
106. Read J, Gumley A. Can attachment theory help explain the relationship between childhood adversity and psychosis? *Attach New Dir Psychother Relation Psychoanal* (2008) 2(1):1–35.
107. George C, Kaplan N, Main M. *The Adult Attachment Interview*. Berkeley, CA: University of California (1985).
108. Sierra M, Berrios GE. Depersonalization: neurobiological perspectives. *Biol Psychiatry* (1998) 44(9):898–908. doi:10.1016/S0006-3223(98)00015-8
109. Brown RJ. Psychological mechanisms of medically unexplained symptoms: an integrative conceptual model. *Psychol Bull* (2004) 130(5):793. doi:10.1037/0033-2909.130.5.793
110. Brown RJ. Dissociation and somatoform disorders. In: Kennedy F, Kennerley H, Pearson D, editors. *Cognitive Behavioural Approaches to the Understanding and Treatment of Dissociation*. London: Routledge (2013). p. 133–147.
111. Jones SR. Do we need multiple models of auditory verbal hallucinations? Examining the phenomenological fit of cognitive and neurological models. *Schizophr Bull* (2010) 36(3):566–75. doi:10.1093/schbul/sbn129
112. Dodgson G, Gordon S. Avoiding false negatives: are some auditory hallucinations an evolved design flaw? *Behav Cogn Psychother* (2009) 37(03):325–34. doi:10.1017/S1352465809005244
113. Garwood L, Dodgson G, Bruce V, McCarthy-Jones S. A preliminary investigation into the existence of a hypervigilance subtype of auditory hallucination in people with psychosis. *Behav Cogn Psychother* (2015) 43(01):52–62. doi:10.1017/S1352465813000714
114. McCarthy-Jones S, Trauer T, Mackinnon A, Sims E, Thomas N, Copolov DL. A new phenomenological survey of auditory hallucinations: evidence for subtypes and implications for theory and practice. *Schizophr Bull* (2014) 40(1):231–5. doi:10.1093/schbul/sbs156
115. McCarthy-Jones S, Thomas N, Strauss C, Dodgson G, Jones N, Woods A, et al. Better than mermaids and stray dogs? Subtyping auditory verbal hallucinations and its implications for research and practice. *Schizophr Bull* (2014) 40(4):S275–84. doi:10.1093/schbul/sbu018
116. Corstens D, Longden E, May R. Talking with voices: exploring what is expressed by the voices people hear. *Psychosis* (2012) 4(2):95–104. doi:10.1080/17522439.2011.571705
117. Read J, Hammersley P, Rudegeair T. Why, when and how to ask about childhood abuse. *Adv Psychiatr Treat* (2007) 13(2):101–10. doi:10.1192/apt.bp.106.002840
118. Toner J, Daiches A, Larkin W. Asking about trauma: the experiences of psychological therapists in early intervention services. *Psychosis* (2013) 5(2):175–86. doi:10.1080/17522439.2012.697484
119. Meaden A, Keen N, Aston R, Barton K, Bucci S. *Cognitive Therapy for Command Hallucinations: An Advanced Practical Companion*. London: Routledge (2012).
120. Bowlby J. *A Secure Base: Clinical Applications of Attachment Theory*. London: Routledge (1988).
121. Cicchetti D, Rogosch FA, Toth SL. Fostering secure attachment in infants in maltreating families through preventive interventions. *Dev Psychopathol* (2006) 18(03):623–49. doi:10.1017/S0954579406060329
122. Bucci S, Roberts NH, Danquah AN, Berry K. Using attachment theory to inform the design and delivery of mental health services: a systematic review of the literature. *Psychol Psychother* (2015) 88(1):1–20. doi:10.1111/papt.12029
123. Degnan A, Seymour-Hyde A, Harris A, Berry K. The role of therapist attachment in alliance and outcome: a systematic literature review. *Clin Psychol Psychother* (2016) 23(1):47–65. doi:10.1002/cpp.1937
124. Thomas N, Hayward M, Peters E, van der Gaag M, Bentall RP, Jenner J, et al. Psychological therapies for auditory hallucinations (voices): current status and key directions for future research. *Schizophr Bull* (2014) 40(4):S202–12. doi:10.1093/schbul/sbu037

18

Posttraumatic Reactions to Psychosis

Weili Lu[1], Kim T. Mueser[2], Stanley D. Rosenberg[3,4], Philip T. Yanos[5] and Neisrein Mahmoud[1]*

[1] Department of Psychiatric Rehabilitation and Counseling Professions, Rutgers University, Scotch Plains, NJ, United States, [2]Center for Psychiatric Rehabilitation, Sargent College of Health and Rehabilitation Sciences, Boston University, Boston, MA, United States, [3] Department of Psychiatry, Dartmouth Medical School, Hanover, NH, United States, [4] Dartmouth Trauma Intervention Research Center, Lebanon, NH, United States, [5]Department of Psychology, John Jay College of Criminal Justice, CUNY, New York, NY, United States

Edited by:
Gretchen Hermes,
Yale University, United States

Reviewed by:
Bernhard J. Mitterauer,
Volitronics-Institute for Basic Research Psychopathology and Brain Philosophy, Austria
Wissam El-Hage,
François Rabelais University, France

***Correspondence:**
Weili Lu
luwe1@shp.rutgers.edu

The current study aimed to evaluate the potentially traumatic aspects of psychotic symptoms and psychiatric treatment of psychosis using qualitative methods. Participants included 63 people with first episode psychosis or multiple psychotic episodes recruited from an inpatient psychiatric unit and an urban state psychiatric hospital in the North East region of the United States. Quasi-structured interviews were used to explore those aspects of symptoms and treatment that were perceived as traumatic Emotional reactions to the most traumatic aspect of symptoms and treatment, during and after the event, were also examined. Participants described a number of traumatogenic aspects of psychotic symptoms, including frightening hallucinations; suicidal thought/attempts, thoughts/attempts to hurt others; paranoia/delusions and bizarre/disorganized behavior or catatonia. Traumatic aspects of psychosis elicited emotions including anger, sadness and confusion, anxiety, and numbness at the time of event. Furthermore, many participants found aspects of treatment to be traumatic, including: being forced to stay in the hospital for a long time; experiencing upsetting side-effects; coercive treatments, including involuntary hospitalization, use of restraints, and forced medication; being exposed to aggressive patients; and mistreatment by professionals. These experiences elicited emotions of anger, sadness, distrust, and a sense of helplessness. Study findings suggest that the experiences both of psychotic symptoms and psychiatric treatment, potentially traumatic, can be a powerful barrier to engaging people in mental health services and facilitating recovery. Clinical implications were discussed.

Keywords: trauma, psychosis, posttraumatic stress disorder, treatment, qualitative analysis

INTRODUCTION

The emergence of a psychotic disorder can be a devastating event for an individual, with major impact on perception of self, self-esteem, and ability to function adequately (1). Psychotic symptoms and treatment experiences can lead to posttraumatic stress disorder (PTSD) symptoms similar to those observed in individuals who have experienced traumatic events such as disasters and rape (2–4). Psychotic symptoms such as command hallucinations to hurt self or others, persecutory delusions, or disorganized behavior can be frightening (2, 4–6). Coercive interventions, such as involuntary hospitalization, seclusion/restraint, and being forced to take medication can be further traumatizing (7–10). These aspects of psychotic episodes are often perceived as threatening and can lead to feelings of fear, helplessness, or horror (4, 11).

The literature regarding psychological reactions to psychosis and its treatment has emphasized both post-psychotic depression and post-psychotic, PTSD symptoms (2, 12, 13). In fact, PTSD is now considered by some as a secondary psychiatric morbidity following psychosis (2). Over 20 years ago, Shaner and Eth (14) reported a case study of a person who developed symptoms, following a schizophrenic episode, that were consistent with PTSD. These symptoms included re-experiencing the traumatic event(s), avoidance of trauma-related stimuli, and over-arousal. Since then, over 17 studies have reported high rates of post-psychotic PTSD symptoms related to these experiences. These 17 studies have included 760 participants, primarily composed of non-affective psychotic disorders (2, 6, 10, 11, 15–27). Using a variety of assessment methods among inpatients and outpatients with psychosis, participants have been asked to respond to the questions based on their reactions toward potentially frightening psychotic symptoms and/or treatment experiences (i.e., negative aspects of treatment). When excluding consideration of whether psychotic or treatment experiences met criterion A for PTSD as defined by DSM-IV, symptoms consistent with a diagnosis of PTSD have been found in 11–67% of the samples, with an average rate of 46%. In addition to traumatic reactions similar to PTSD, depression, suicidality, and low self-esteem are common negative emotional reactions after a psychotic episode.

Post-psychotic depression has been well documented in studies conducted in England (12, 22, 28, 29). It has been found that 36% of patients develop depression following a psychotic episode (12). Depression is common in patients with a first episode psychosis (FEP). Reported prevalence rates varied from 17 to 83% in the different studies (30–33, 34). Relevant studies have generally found that, as treatment progressed, rates of depression decreased. For example, in a sample of 198 Norwegian clients with FEP, 50% of the participants were depressed at the start of treatment, while 35% exhibited depression at one year follow-up after treatment (34). Upon becoming depressed, patients with post-psychotic depression developed lower self-esteem and a worsening of their appraisals of psychosis (35). Additionally, the lifetime risk of suicide in psychotic illness remains high at approximately 7% (29, 36). Suicide risk is highest in the early phases of psychosis (31, 36–39). Upthegrove et al. (36) conducted a study among persons with a first episode of psychosis and found frequent suicidal acts such as overdosing and attempted hanging in this group. Reactions toward psychosis and its treatment are further compounded by the effects of being labeled with a mental illness, rejection and the internalization, acceptance, and resignation to societal stigma toward mental illness (40, 41). Individuals early in the course of psychosis frequently avoid professional help because of concerns about stigma (42), and the negative effects of the internalization of stigma on functioning and well-being have been well-documented [e.g., Ref. (43)].

In the study of psychosis and trauma, there has been significant evidence documenting increased trauma exposure in psychosis and schizophrenia (44–46). Trauma exposure is common among patients with psychosis ranging from 49 to 100% [see, Ref. (46) for a review]: childhood sexual abuse reported by 13 to 64%, childhood physical abuse by 22 to 66%, adulthood sexual assault by 13 to 79%, and adulthood physical assault by 30 to 87% of persons with serious mental illness. Multiple traumatization is common with 75 to 98% of participants report multiple trauma [see, Ref. (46) for a review]. Among 962 participants with psychosis, 17.9% of their sample reported criminal victimization in the past year (47). PTSD is common as a result of trauma exposure among people with psychosis. The current rate of PTSD has been reported as between 25 and 48% in this population in various studies [see, Ref. (46) for a review], nearly ten times higher than that of the general population (48). These traumatic life events, along with the traumatic experience of psychotic episodes and psychiatric treatment, have drawn attention to the need for treatments to reduce the consequences of trauma in this population (49).

Although quantitative literature has documented psychological reactions toward psychosis and its treatment, research is less clear about how psychotic symptoms or coercive treatment experiences are perceived by persons with psychosis. Qualitative research methods are a promising strategy for understanding subjective experience and offering suggestions for potentially useful treatment approaches (42, 50, 51). However, few qualitative inquiries have investigated the subjective experiences of reactions toward psychosis and its treatment.

The current study aimed to evaluate subjective experiences related to psychotic symptoms and treatment in clients with multiple psychotic episodes using qualitative methods. Aspects of symptoms and treatment that were perceived as traumatic, as well as emotional reactions to the most traumatic aspect of symptoms and treatment, were explored.

MATERIALS AND METHODS

The current investigation is part of a study evaluating prevalence of PTSD symptoms in FEP or multi-episode participants with psychosis (6, 10). The study was conducted at an inpatient psychiatric unit at a general hospital affiliated with a medical school in North East region as well as an urban state hospital which included both acute inpatient care, as well as intermediate and longer-term treatment. Treatment team members (attending psychiatrists, psychologists, and nurses) were informed about the study and eligibility criteria and then identified potentially eligible participants and referred them to the study team. An important question addressed in the study was the importance of the A1/A2 criteria for traumatic event in diagnosing PTSD related to a psychotic episode. For this reason, we chose to assess participants as soon as possible after the symptoms of their episode had been stabilized to enhance the accuracy of their perceptions and emotional reactions during the index events. Participants were referred to the study after they were judged to be symptomatically stable by their treatment team, and able to provide consent. All of the study procedures were approved of by the appropriate university and hospital Institutional Review Boards.

Participants

Inclusion criteria for participation in the study were:

(a) age 18 and above;
(b) chart or clinician diagnosis of schizophrenia, schizoaffective disorder, schizophreniform disorder, bipolar disorder with psychotic features, major depression with psychotic features, brief reactive psychosis, or unspecified psychosis;
(c) presentation for treatment of a psychotic episode within the past 6 weeks;
(d) psychotic symptoms of moderate severity or greater on any item on the Brief Psychiatric Rating Scale (52) thought disturbance subscale which includes hallucinatory behavior, unusual thought content, grandiosity, and suspiciousness persisting for at least 2 days in the absence of substance use (53).
(e) history of treatment for at least one psychotic episode including the current episode. A psychotic episode was defined as an episode in which there was the presence of one (or more) of the following symptoms: delusions, hallucinations, disorganized speech, or grossly disorganized or catatonic behavior for at least one week; and
(f) voluntary signed informed consent to participate in the study.

A total of 63 individuals met eligibility criteria and agreed to participate in the study. The characteristics of the study sample are summarized in **Table 1**. Participants tended to be in their 30s, with an average of over eight past hospitalizations, with 54% of participants were diagnosed with schizophrenia or schizoaffective disorders. A large proportion of the participants in this study were never married (76.9%), and the majority of the participants were African–American or Latino/a.

TABLE 1 | Demographic and diagnostic characteristics, and trauma history of study sample (*N* = 63).

	N	%
Gender		
Male	36	57.1
Female	27	41.9
Race/ethnicity		
White	24	38.1
African American	20	31.7
Hispanic	16	25.4
Other	3	4.8
Marital status		
Never married	50	79.4
Married	6	9.5
Separated/divorced	7	11.1
Work status before hospitalization		
Not employed	46	73.0
Employed	16	25.4
Missing	1	1.6
Diagnosis		
Bipolar disorder	17	27.0
Psychotic or delusional disorder	10	15.6
Schizoaffective disorder	12	19.0
Schizophrenia	22	34.9
Other mood disorders	2	3.2
Traumatic event (yes)		
Serious accident	28	44.4
Natural disaster	13	20.6
Physical assault by family	37	58.7
Physical assault by stranger	30	47.6
Sexual assault by family	23	36.5
Sexual assault by stranger	21	33.3
Military combat/war zone	1	1.6
Sexual contact younger than 18	27	42.9
Imprisonment	16	25.4
Torture	16	25.4
Life-threatening illness	3	4.8
Other traumatic event	27	42.9
	Mean	**SD**
Age	34.43	11.74
Highest grade completed	11.92	2.66
Total # of hospitalization	8.54	7.03
Total # of psychotic episodes	8.49	7.14

Measures

Trauma and PTSD Symptoms

Lifetime exposure to trauma (e.g., sexual assault, serious accident) was evaluated with an abbreviated version of the Traumatic Life Events Questionnaire (54) that included 12 items, each rated on a no/yes basis. After completion of the questionnaire, the participant was oriented to the assessment of psychologically traumatic events related to psychotic symptoms or treatment experiences with the following statement: "I would now like to spend a few minutes finding out about your experiences with psychiatric symptoms." Interviewers were instructed to adopt the participant's language when referring to psychiatric symptoms and psychiatric illnesses, such as using terms like "nervous breakdown," "mental illness," "stress reaction," or "emotional upset." A modified version of the PTSD Assessment Tool for Schizophrenia (PATS), a semi-structured interview designed to elicit posttraumatic reactions to psychosis and treatment experiences (55), was used to guide the discussion. The modified PATS was divided into two sections: reactions to psychotic symptoms; and reactions to treatment experiences. For the first section, reactions to psychotic symptoms were assessed by initially asking a series of 15 questions (e.g., "Have the symptoms of your psychiatric illness ever caused you to feel extremely anxious or terrified?" "Did you believe that groups of people wanted to hurt you?"). An affirmative response to any item was followed up by probes to elicit specific examples. After these questions, participants were asked to identify which experience across all their episodes was most distressing when they looked back on it. Additional questions were then directed at eliciting further details of the event (e.g., when and where it happened, other people who were involved) and how the person reacted to it at the time. Respondents were asked directly: "How did you respond emotionally," and "What was that like?" Participants were also asked about their immediate and subsequent emotional reactions after the event by inquiring: "What about after the event, how did you respond emotionally?"

Reactions to treatment experiences were assessed in a similar fashion, by initially asking a series of questions (nine in total; e.g., "Have you ever been given a treatment that frightened you?" "Have you ever been forcibly taken to the hospital or to jail?"). Any affirmative response was followed up by questions to elicit

TABLE 2 | Themes and illustrative quotations from personal narratives of psychotic symptoms.

Frightening hallucinations

- "Voices telling me something bad is going to happen to you."
- "Hearing voices that say 'you are gay'."

Thoughts/attempts to hurt self

- "I wanted to die no girl-friend, took a lot of pills that could kill 20 people."
- "I heard things, I heard devil telling me to do it I did it before when I was sad, he begged me that I could not do it and survive it and I did it again."
- "I tried to hang myself."

Thoughts/attempts to hurt others

- "I was obsessed with killing people."
- "I wanted to kill everyone who give me harm, like my abusive grandmother."

Paranoid/Delusions/grandiose delusions (i.e., feeling like God)

- "I had a suspicion that my aunt who is a psychologist want to hurt me. She knows black magic."
- "Going to jail, [there I was feeling that] people trying to poison me."

Bizarre behavior/disorganized behavior or catatonia

- "One afternoon, i took my clothes off, I was crazy, ran in the street for 2 miles, people were laughing at me, police took me to hospital."
- "I was catatonic, I could not walk or talk, that was traumatic."

specific examples. After these questions, participants were asked to identify the most distressing treatment experience, followed by asking questions aimed at understanding what happened and the person's reactions to the event both at the time of the event and after the event.

Following the end of the qualitative-portion of the interview, standardized assessments were completed to evaluate PTSD and other symptoms, which have been previously reported (6). The qualitative portion of the interview ranged in length from 15 to 35 min. Field notes by the interviews were used to maintain a record of responses.

Procedures

Study participants were identified by the clinical treatment team. When potentially eligible patients were identified and were symptomatically stable, permission was obtained from the client for a research team member to discuss the study with them. If permission was granted, a meeting was set up between a research team member and the client, the study was explained, and if the client was interested he or she provided signed informed consent. An interview was then arranged to conduct the assessment, and a chart review was performed. Patients were paid for their participation in the study.

Analysis

The data analysis for this study was informed by grounded theory, which seeks to generate theory from a data set and is utilized to generate hypotheses (56, 57). The data analysis process in this investigation consisted of an initial open coding of the participant's responses from the field notes into initial categories by two graduate students. Three raters reviewed the data and the initial categories. They performed axial coding and deleted or combined several of the original codes. After several iterations, a final selective coding process among reviewers which determined the core themes and concepts was implemented (56, 57). Two raters rated the responses independently using the coding theme. The differences and discrepancies were discussed and reconciled after clarifying the original coding scheme.

RESULTS

Themes specifically regarding one's perception and emotional reactions toward psychosis and one's encounters with the mental health system are presented here. Participants described a number of traumatogenic aspects of psychotic symptoms. Five themes concerning traumatogenic aspects of psychosis emerged (see **Table 2**): (1) frightening hallucinations, reported by 23.8% of the participants; (2) paranoia/delusions, reported by 20.6% of the participants; (3) suicidal thoughts/attempts, reported by 15.9% of the participants; (4) thoughts/attempts to hurt others, reported by 9.5% of the participants; (5) bizarre/disorganized behavior or catatonia; reported by 7.9% of the participants. Other categories included various themes such as flashbacks of past abuse, panic attacks, mania, loss of child custody, etc., were reported by 22.2% of the participants. The most commonly reported theme of traumatogenic aspects of psychosis was that of frightening hallucinations including command hallucinations or persistent hallucinations that last for years, followed by thought/attempts to hurt self, and next by thought/attempts to hurt others. A patient reporting a frightening hallucination (the most commonly identified trauma) is quoted below:

> [The most traumatic part is] hearing voices telling me where to move. Three years ago I started to hear voices on TV and radio, telling me to move. I moved non-stop in the past two years, not finding a place to live. People on radio and TV suggest places for me to go.

Another participant described how hearing critical voices led to thoughts which led to self-harm:

> I was just feeling very guilty about not being a good mother and a good wife. I just felt very bad, and did not think I should be allowed to live, so that's when I decided that I should hurt myself.

In terms of having experienced thoughts/attempts to hurt self as the most traumatic aspect of symptoms, one participant reported, "I don't think about killing myself but killing comes to me." Another reported, "I tried to hang myself." Another reported, "During [my] first breakdown, when I thought of running into traffic, [that was most traumatic.]" In terms of having experienced thoughts/attempts to hurt others as the most traumatic aspect of symptoms, one participant reported: "I was obsessed with idea of killing people." One participant reported experiencing homicidal ideas toward her mother and found it traumatic. Participants also found paranoia/delusions the most disturbing. One reported having experienced people spying on him: "[I felt] people spying on me. It happened gradually, everybody saw signs except me." Another reported, "I feel like I was going to die. Because my other friends will do anything for money there is a possible thing that I may die. People may set things up to get me before my birthday." A few participants found their bizarre/disorganized behavior most traumatic. One reported great humiliation at having run through the streets naked. He stated, "One afternoon, I took my clothes off, and ran in the street for two miles. People were laughing at me. The police took me to hospital." Another reported, "I was catatonic, I could not walk or talk, that was traumatic."

Emotions Associated With Traumatic Aspects of Psychosis

Emotions associated with traumatic aspects of psychosis involved anger; sadness; mixed feelings such as confusion, sadness, and anger; numbness; sense of shock and anxiety (**Table 3**). The most commonly experienced emotion in relation to symptoms was anger (reported by 22.0% of participants), followed by shock/anxiety (reported by 18.6% of participants); mixture of the above feelings, or a mixture of sadness and anger (reported by 16.9%); sadness (reported by 15.3%); and numbness (reported by 11.9%). Other categories were reported by 15.3% of the participants. With regard to anger, one participant reported, "I felt angry, clumsy, and confused. I can't break the spell." One reported confusion, "I could not understand why I was doing that." A few participants reported feeling shocked/nervous about their psychotic symptoms. One stated being horrified. Another reported feeling nervous and out of control. One participant specifically reported feeling sad at hearing voices, stating "[After hearing the voices], I was falling apart, crying, always sleeping, never wanted to go out of the house." Not all participants reported experiencing emotions, but rather reported feeling numb toward what happened during psychosis. One stated, "I felt emotionless" after slashing wrists. Two participants reported they did not know how they felt.

Descriptions of emotion looking back after the episode of psychosis involved a wider range of reactions. These involved sadness (14.5%); relief that symptoms went away (14.5% of participants reported); anxiety (12.9%); neutral feelings (11.2%); mixed emotions such as relief mixed with anxiety (9.7%); anger (9.7%); numbness (9.7%); shame (8.1%) and distrust/helplessness (8.1%). Looking back at the most traumatic aspect of psychosis, participants most commonly expressed experiencing sadness about what had happened. It was interesting that equal number of people reported feeling relieved that symptoms were lessened compared to the number of people who expressed sadness about what had happened. Some participants reported feeling neutral about what happened when looking back. Anxiety, mixed emotions, anger, numbness, shame, distrust, and helplessness were also reported by approximately 8–13% of people for each category.

Traumatogenic Aspects of Psychiatric Treatment

Participants described a number of traumatogenic aspects of psychiatric treatment (**Table 4**). Amongst the participants who experienced at least one episode of psychosis, five major themes concerning traumatogenic aspects of treatment emerged: (1) long stay in the hospital; (2) medication side effects; (3)coercive treatments, including involuntary hospitalization, use of restraints, and forced medication, and (4) being with other patients; and (5) mistreatment by professionals, not including the use of coercive treatments. The mostly commonly reported theme of traumatogenic aspects of psychiatric treatment was long stay in the hospital, reported by 25 participants (25.8%). One participant in his early 20s was in the hospital for more than 1 year for his first psychotic episode. Another reported, "Staying here for 9 months; I don't have

TABLE 3 | Themes and illustrative quotations of emotional reaction to symptoms at the time of psychosis.

Anger
- "Very angry, I wanted to hurt her."
- "Upset, should not happen to me."

Sadness
- "I cried a lot, depressed."
- "[I felt] sad, confused, inconsolable."

Mixed feelings such as confusion, sadness and anger
- "I felt sad and angry."
- "It feels a little down, angry."
- "I felt angry, clumsy, and confused. I can't break the spell."

Numbness
- "I felt emotionless."
- "I felt no emotions."
- "I don't know [how I felt]."

Nervousness/fear/anxiety
- "Nervous, out of control, felt pressured."
- "I knew I was in serious trouble police were almost ready to shoot me."
- "I was horrified."
- "I felt shocked and betrayed."

TABLE 4 | Themes and illustrative quotations for the most traumatic aspect of treatment.

Long stay in hospital
- "Being in the hospital for 1 year and 3 months is the most traumatic; the cops thought I was living in my car. I was driving from VA to NJ to be with aunt and uncle. Had a lot of stuff in the car. Got arrested for making a call. The cops took me to hospital and I have been here since."
- "Since 2001 only released for 4 months and in the hospital for over 6 years."

Coercive treatment
- "The fact that my friend and cops should have been more civil to me rather than forcing me to come to the hospital." (Involuntary hospitalization)
- "The fact that I was restrained, three guys restrained me [and] gave me a med." (Restraints)
- "Several times, I was physically restrained to take meds; I was held down to take injection." (Forced medication)

Medications side effects
- "I had prolixin injection, could not sit or stand still after injection."
- "Medicines make me fat and destroyed my beauty."

Mistreatment by professionals
- "Staff was taking clothes off for me when I took shower."
- "Last hospitalization, I felt harassed by pts' and staff."

Being with other psychiatric patients
- "Being exposed to a whole bunch of very sick people for 2 months."
- "Seeing a patient pulling her hair and throwing up was the most traumatic."

TABLE 5 | Themes and illustrative quotations of emotional reaction to treatment at the time of event.

Anger
- "I felt angry and hurt."
- "Get very angry. Personally [I felt] being violated."

Sadness
- "Crying, sad, miserable, wished I would die."

Mixed feeling
- "I got upset."
- "[I was] mad and depressed."

Shock/frustration/helplessness
- "[I felt] helpless."
- "[I was] shocked."

Fear/anxiety
- "Scared, loss of dignity."
- "[I was] terrified."

Paranoia/distrust
- "I could have reacted worse. I wanted to contact attorney."
- "I feel paranoid, feel like things are not going to happen in my way."
- "I feel threatened."

Numbness
- "I don't know. Nothing upsets me anymore."

an apartment, my mom and I don't get along; [I don't have a place to go], it feels ridiculous." Participants also indicated feeling confused about a long stay in the hospital. One person said, "I don't understand why I am here; they say I should be here for at least 21 days, but I've been here for 12 years; the psychologists say I'll be here permanently." Another reported, "Since 2001, [I was] only released for 4 months and [I have been] in the hospital for over 6 years."

The next most commonly reported traumatic event related to treatment was coercive treatments, reported by 14 patients (22.6%), including involuntary hospitalization, use of restraints, and forced medication. In the category of restraints, one reported, "The fact that I was restrained by three guys was the most traumatic." In the category of involuntary hospitalization, one reported, "The fact that my friend and cops should have been more civil to me rather than forcing me. My friend called cops who hand-cuffed me, and brought me to the ER. Then they shifted me to psych ward." In the category of forced medication, participants reported that being forced to take medication could be traumatogenic. One reported, "Having them give me Risperdal every two weeks; When I was in the quiet room, they told me if I don't take it, then they will force me to take it—restrain me to the bed."

Side effects of psychotropic medication were the third most commonly reported traumatic aspect of treatment (reported by 12 participants; 19.3%). One participant said, "I had Prolixin injections, [and] could not sit or stand still after injection." Another said she passed out after taking medication. One stated, "Taking bad medications with side effects [was really traumatic]. The psychiatrist gave me a lot of milligrams of medications. After taking them, I could not walk. I felt like I was drunk. It felt like I was being poisoned by the medications." Others reported medication side effects of weight gain, sleepiness, and fatigue as the most disturbing aspect of treatment.

Mistreatment by professionals, not including the use of coercive treatments, was reported by 14.5% of participants. One stated, "Verbal abuse by staff [was the most traumatic aspect of treatment]. They make fun of our feelings, make me behave the way I don't want to. If I don't keep staff happy they will drop my level like a punishment."

Last, participants also found being exposed to other patients in the hospital, particularly aggressive patients, was traumatic. This was reported by seven participants (11.2%). One reported, "Seeing a patient pulling her hair and throwing up [was the most traumatic aspect of treatment]." Another reported, "I miss my family, I was physically assaulted by two patients, one punched me and the other squeezed my breast." One reported, "Being exposed to a whole bunch of very sick people for two months was traumatic. At admission, they would scream, cry really loud, there were fights among the patients."

Emotions Associated With Traumatic Aspects of Psychiatric Treatment

Participants described a wide range of emotions related to traumatic treatment experiences (**Table 5**). Participants frequently expressed feeling angry about their psychiatric treatment (reported by 19.0% of participants). One reported, "I got angry. [I felt] violated." Some participants reported a mixture of feelings such as feeling upset, sad, and angry at the same time: "I got upset," or "[I was] mad and depressed." This was reported by 14.3% of participants. Participants commonly dealt with feelings of sadness related to psychiatric treatment (11.1% reported so). One reported, "I felt frustrated, sad, depressed." Themes of shock, frustration, and helplessness were described by 14.3% of participants. Fear and anxiety were also experienced by 7.9% of participants. One reported, "I was scared." Another reported, "[I was] terrified." Feelings of distrust were reported by 6.3% of participants: "I feel paranoid, feel like things are not going to happen in my way." Lastly, a sense of numbness was reported by 6.3% of participants.

When asked to how they responded emotionally subsequently to the most traumatic aspect of the treatment, participants described a wider range of emotions related to traumatic treatment experiences. 10% of participants reported feeling neutral about the most traumatic aspect of treatment, when looking back; 8% reported developing a distrust of the system, while another 8% reported numbness or having no emotions after the event. 8% of participants reported feeling relieved that the worst part of treatment was over, while 7% remained sad at what happened. Another 7% of people reported feeling angry or frustrated with the treatment, while 6% of participants reported helplessness or feeling threatened. Mixed emotions or other emotions were reported by four percent of the participants. In total, approximately one-third of the participants continued to experience negative emotions such as sadness, hurt, anger, feeling violated, distrust, dislike, helplessness, or anxiety regarding treatment received.

DISCUSSION

This study examined traumatic reactions to the experience of psychosis and associated treatment for people with FEP or multiple episodes of psychosis. It supports the conclusion of previous studies that psychosis itself, and related treatment, can both be traumatic for many people. Most of the participants reported traumatic responses related to both their psychotic symptoms and their treatment experiences, consistent with previous reports [i.e., Ref. (11, 18, 20, 21)]. Participants described a number of traumatogenic aspects of psychotic symptoms, corresponding to five themes: (1) frightening hallucinations, (2) suicidal thought/attempts, (3) thoughts/attempts to hurt others, (4) paranoia/delusions, and (5) bizarre/disorganized behavior or catatonia. Traumatic aspects of psychosis elicited emotions including anger, sadness and confusion, anxiety, and numbness. Furthermore, many participants found aspects of treatment to be traumatic, including being forced to stay in the hospital for a long time, experiencing upsetting side-effects, coercive treatments, including involuntary hospitalization, use of restraints, and forced medication, being exposed to aggressive patients, and mistreatment by professionals, and that these experiences elicited emotions such as anger, sadness, distrust, and a sense of helplessness. These findings suggest that the experiences of both symptoms and treatment as traumatic can be a powerful barrier to engaging people in mental health services and facilitating recovery.

Results document the need to address the issues related to posttraumatic reactions to psychosis in people with multiple psychotic episodes. Our findings can inform the development of treatment that is sensitive to these issues. Specifically, findings suggest the need to validate the intense and negative emotional reactions people frequently experience during a psychotic episode and during treatment episodes. Reactions following the acute psychotic episode were more varied, with a small percentage of people reported relief that the worst part was over, while others remained traumatized about what happened. Psychotherapy can be offered to clients who show evidence of posttraumatic reactions and should address these reactions through validation to alleviate traumatic reactions to psychosis. Findings on aspects of symptoms that can cause traumatogenic reactions among clients could also inform the development of treatment protocols so that patients can know what to expect when going to a psychotic episode. Clients commonly reported negative, often traumatizing treatment experiences. The damaging effects of such experiences on client's trust of mental health professionals were evident in client interviews. Effective treatment of posttraumatic reactions to psychosis can potentially improve clients' ability to form more collaborative relationships with treatment providers and to play a more active role in the management of their psychiatric disorder (8, 58). Emerging research addressing post-psychotic depression indicates promising results for cognitive behavior therapy (CBT) as a treatment for traumatic reactions toward psychosis (59). Jackson et al. (59) evaluated a form of CBT in reducing trauma, depression, and low self esteem following a first episode of psychosis, in a randomized controlled trial among 66 patients who had recently experienced a first episode of psychosis. CBT has also been found to be effective in reducing hopelessness, when compared to treatment as usual, among a total of 66 participants recovering from FEP (28). In a third study (60), among 22 people recovering from psychosis, those who wrote about the most stressful aspects of their illness showed fewer traumatic symptoms than those who wrote about emotionally neutral topics. Findings suggest that narrative statements disclosing the most stressful aspects of psychosis may lessen the traumatic impact of psychosis (60). Future research on focused intervention for posttraumatic reactions toward psychosis is needed.

Findings from this study underline some of the complicated issues facing the mental health service system. On one hand, participants reported being traumatized by symptoms of mental illness such as distressing auditory hallucinations, bizarre behavior, and persecutory delusions. Simultaneously participants reported being traumatized by interventions (such as involuntary hospitalization, restraints, and forced medication) designed to alleviate these symptoms. However, in many cases, participants experienced these interventions as humiliating or violations of self. Trauma informed care (61) may offer alternatives to restraints and seclusion. Newer models of treatment that place an emphasis on "shared-decision making," such as the Open Dialog Model (62), have been recommended for people experiencing a first psychotic episode, but our findings suggest that these approaches may need to be offered for persons experiencing multiple psychotic episodes as well. Shared-decision making in medication management, which emphasizes "partnership between two experts: the client and the practitioner," provides a model for the client to "assess a treatment's advantages and disadvantages" in medication management [Ref. (63), p. 1636]. Commonground, a web-based application of shared decision making model, encourages the use of resilient self-care strategy in addition to the use of psychotropic medication. It has been found that when CommonGround is implemented, the use of self-management strategies among clients correlated with less concerns about medication side effect, increased perception that medicines were helping, and improved recovery (64). CommonGround has been implemented successfully in community mental health centers (65) while its implementation in psychiatric hospitals has not been reported in the literature. The adoption of shared decision model may reduce traumatic reactions during treatment and foster better trust between providers and clients.

The limitations of this study include sampling issues and the retrospective nature of the data collected. The inpatient participants in the present study were significantly younger (mean age was 33.78) than studies of multi-episode patients with severe mental illness [e.g., Ref. (44, 66–68)]. The participants also had a higher number of hospitalizations (8.55) upon the time of assessments compared to the participants in other studies of persons with severe mental illness. Participants also were more likely to be diagnosed with schizophrenia or schizoaffective disorders (54%), and to be non-white compared to other studies of persons with severe mental illness. These divergences with previous studies suggest that our findings may not be generalizable to a wider range of persons with psychotic disorders. Additionally, experiences of psychosis and contact with psychiatric services were reported retrospectively, recall bias may have affected the accuracy of people's recollections about their reactions to psychotic experiences and treatment. Finally, during a psychotic episode such as during the height of hallucinations or delusions, the patient may be unable to distinguish reality from non-reality, or even self from other. Therefore, technically, the experience of delusions or hallucinations may not be considered as a traumatic life event, to the same extent as events such as criminal victimization. For some patients with chronic schizophrenia, there is a possibility that these patients never experienced traumatic life events such as abuse or criminal victimization. While we would caution the distinction between a traumatic life event and a traumatic experience of psychosis, treatment however could be similar. Clinical experience has indicated that PTSD-like symptoms induced by delusions can be similarly treated using CBT. For example, a client experienced the delusion of police "shooting" and "killing" his best friend who "stalked" him. Client held onto this fixed delusion and blamed himself for causing the "death" of his best friend. He in turn suffered PTSD-like symptoms including avoidance, hypervigilance, and re-experiencing symptoms. He was successfully treated with CBT by treating his delusion as though the event was real. Once his beliefs in causing the "death" of his best friend were challenged, his PTSD-like symptoms went away. The fixed delusion no longer significantly impacted his life as his guilt for causing his friend's "death" went away (Lu, unpublished manuscript). Further research is needed in this regard for trauma informed care for persons with psychosis.

In summary, this qualitative study describes the experiences of people during the episodes of psychosis. We found multiple factors contributing to traumatic dimensions of the experience, including actual or perceived coercive aspects of psychiatric treatment. Further research is needed to determine how mental health services can be improved to reduce illness related trauma and facilitate recovery.

ETHICS STATEMENT

This study was carried out in accordance with the recommendations of Rutgers RBHS Institutional Review Board (previously UMDNJ-Newark IRB) and Dartmouth College Institutional Review Board with written informed consent from all subjects. All subjects gave written informed consent in accordance with the Declaration of Helsinki. The protocol was approved by the Rutgers RBHS Institutional Review Board (previously UMDNJ-Newark IRB) and Dartmouth College Institutional Review Board.

AUTHOR CONTRIBUTIONS

WL was the site PI for this project. She supervised the operation the project, collected some of the data herself, supervised the data entry and data analysis. She contributed to the conception and the writing of the manuscript. KM obtained the grant. Was the PI of the grant. He supervised WL in the conduction of the research activities in this grant. He provided the research instruments, research ideas, and supervision for the original project. He also contributed to the writing of the manuscript. SR was the co-PI of the project. He provided the research instruments, research ideas, and supervision for the original project. He also contributed to the writing of the manuscript. PY contributed to the writing of the manuscript. NM contributed to the data analysis of the manuscript, composition of the tables, and the editorial assistance of the manuscript.

REFERENCES

1. Davidson L. *Living Outside Mental Illness: Qualitative Studies of Recovery in Schizophrenia*. New York, NY: New York University Press (2003).
2. Shaw K, McFarlane A, Bookless C. The phenomenology of traumatic reactions to psychotic illness. *J Nerv Ment Dis* (1997) 185(7):434–41. doi:10.1097/00005053-199707000-00003
3. Birchwood M. Pathways to emotional dysfunction in first-episode psychosis. *Br J Psychiatry* (2003) 182(5):373–5. doi:10.1192/bjp.02.153
4. Boevink WA. From being a disorder to dealing with life: an experiential exploration of the association between trauma and psychosis. *Schizophr Bull* (2006) 32(1):17–9. doi:10.1093/schbul/sbi068
5. Cohen LJ. Psychiatric hospitalization as an experience of trauma. *Arch Psychiatr Nurs* (1994) 8(2):78–81. doi:10.1016/0883-9417(94)90037-X
6. Lu W, Mueser KT, Shami A, Siglag M, Petrides G, Schoepp E, et al. Post-traumatic reactions to psychosis in people with multiple psychotic episodes. *Schizophr Res* (2011) 127(1):66–75. doi:10.1016/j.schres.2011.01.006
7. Frueh BC, Knapp RG, Cusack KJ, Grubaugh AL, Sauvageot JA, Cousins VC, et al. Patients' reports of traumatic or harmful experiences within the psychiatric setting. *Psychiatr Serv* (2005) 56(9):1123–33. doi:10.1176/appi.ps.56.9.1123
8. Gallop R, McCay E, Guha M, Khan P. The experience of hospitalization and restraint of women who have a history of childhood sexual abuse. *Health Care Women Int* (1999) 20(4):401–16. doi:10.1080/073993399245683
9. Ray NK, Myers KJ, Rappaport ME. Patient perspectives on restraint and seclusion experiences: a survey of former patients of New York State psychiatric facilities. *Psychiatr Rehabil J* (1996) 20(1):11–8. doi:10.1037/h0095407
10. Mueser KT, Lu W, Rosenberg SD, Wolfe R. The trauma of psychosis: posttraumatic stress disorder and recent onset psychosis. *Schizophr Res* (2010) 116(2):217–27. doi:10.1016/j.schres.2009.10.025
11. Chisholm B, Freeman D, Cooke A. Identifying potential predictors of traumatic reactions to psychotic episodes. *Br J Clin Psychol* (2006) 45(4): 545–59. doi:10.1348/014466505X90136
12. Birchwood M, Iqbal Z, Chadwick P, Trower P. Cognitive approach to depression and suicidal thinking in psychosis. *Br J Psychiatry* (2000) 177(6):516–28. doi:10.1192/bjp.177.6.516
13. Barrett LF, Mesquita B, Gendron M. Context in emotion perception. *Curr Direct Psychol Sci* (2011) 20(5):286–90. doi:10.1177/0963721411422522
14. Shaner A, Eth S. Can schizophrenia cause posttraumatic stress disorder. *Am J Psychother* (1989) 4:588–97.
15. McGorry PD, Chanen A, McCarthy E, Van Riel R, McKenzie D, Singh BS. Posttraumatic stress disorder following recent-onset psychosis an unrecognized postpsychotic syndrome. *J Nerv Ment Dis* (1991) 179(5):253–8. doi:10.1097/00005053-199105000-00002
16. Priebe S, Bröker M, Gunkel S. Involuntary admission and posttraumatic stress disorder symptoms in schizophrenia patients. *Compr Psychiatry* (1998) 39(4):220–4. doi:10.1016/S0010-440X(98)90064-5
17. Meyer H, Taiminen T, Vuori T, Äijälä A, Helenius H. Posttraumatic stress disorder symptoms related to psychosis and acute involuntary hospitalization in schizophrenic and delusional patients. *J Nerv Ment Dis* (1999) 187(6): 343–52. doi:10.1097/00005053-199906000-00003

18. Morrison AP, Bowe S, Larkin W, Nothard S. The psychological impact of psychiatric admission: some preliminary findings. *J Nerv Ment Dis* (1999) 187(4):250–3. doi:10.1097/00005053-199904000-00011
19. Frame L, Morrison AP. Causes of posttraumatic stress disorder in psychotic patients. *Arch Gen Psychiatry* (2001) 58(3):305–6. doi:10.1001/archpsyc.58.3.305
20. Shaw K, McFarlane AC, Bookless C, Air T. The aetiology of postpsychotic posttraumatic stress disorder following a psychotic episode. *J Trauma Stress* (2002) 15(1):39–47. doi:10.1023/A:1014331211311
21. Jackson C, Knott C, Skeate A, Birchwood M. The trauma of first episode psychosis: the role of cognitive mediation. *Aust N Z J Psychiatry* (2004) 38(5):327–33. doi:10.1080/j.1440-1614.2004.01359.x
22. Tarrier N, Khan S, Cater J, Picken A. The subjective consequences of suffering a first episode psychosis: trauma and suicide behaviour. *Soc Psychiatry Psychiatr Epidemiol* (2007) 42(1):29–35. doi:10.1007/s00127-006-0127-2
23. White RG, Gumley AI. Postpsychotic posttraumatic stress disorder: associations with fear of recurrence and intolerance of uncertainty. *J Nerv Ment Dis* (2009) 197(11):841–9. doi:10.1097/NMD.0b013e3181bea625
24. Beattie N, Shannon C, Kavanagh M, Mulholland C. Predictors of PTSD symptoms in response to psychosis and psychiatric admission. *J Nerv Ment Dis* (2009) 197(1):56–60. doi:10.1097/NMD.0b013e31819273a8
25. Sin GL, Abdin E, Lee J, Poon L-Y, Verma S, Chong S-A. Prevalence of post-traumatic stress disorder in first-episode psychosis. *Early Interv Psychiatry* (2010) 4:299–304. doi:10.1111/j.1751-7893.2010.00199.x
26. van den Berg DP, van der Gaag M. Treating trauma in psychosis with EMDR: a pilot study. *J Behav Ther Exp Psychiatry* (2012) 43(1):664–71. doi:10.1016/j.jbtep.2011.09.011
27. Bendall S, Alvarez-Jimenez M, Hulbert CA, McGorry PD, Jackson HJ. Childhood trauma increases the risk of post-traumatic stress disorder in response to first-episode psychosis. *Aust N Z J Psychiatry* (2012) 46(1):35–9. doi:10.1177/0004867411430877
28. Power PJR, Bell RJ, Mills R, Herrman-Doig T, Davern M, Henry L, et al. Suicide prevention in first episode psychosis: the development of a randomized controlled trial of cognitive therapy for acutely suicidal patients with early psychosis. *Aust N Z J Psychiatry* (2003) 37(4):414–20. doi:10.1046/j.1440-1614.2003.01209.x
29. Pompili M, Serafini G, Innamorati M, Lester D, Shrivastava A, Girardi P, et al. Suicide risk in first episode psychosis: a selective review of the current literature. *Schizophr Res* (2011) 129(1):1–11. doi:10.1016/j.schres.2011.03.008
30. Sim K, Mahendran R, Siris SG, Heckers S, Chong SA. Subjective quality of life in first episode schizophrenia spectrum disorders with comorbid depression. *Psychiatry Res* (2004) 129(2):141–7. doi:10.1016/j.psychres.2004.07.007
31. Addington D, Addington J, Patten S. Depression in people with first-episode schizophrenia. *Br J Psychiatry* (1998) 172(33):90–2.
32. Bottlender R, Strauss A, Möller HJ. Prevalence and background factors of depression in first admitted schizophrenic patients. *Acta Psychiatr Scand* (2000) 101(2):153–60. doi:10.1034/j.1600-0447.2000.90063.x
33. Romm KL, Rossberg JI, Berg AO, Barrett EA, Faerden A, Agartz I, et al. Depression and depressive symptoms in first episode psychosis. *J Nerv Ment Dis* (2010) 198(1):67–71. doi:10.1097/NMD.0b013e3181c81fc0
34. Sönmez N, Romm KL, Andreasssen OA, Melle I, Røssberg JI. Depressive symptoms in first episode psychosis: a one-year follow-up study. *BMC Psychiatry* (2013) 13:106. doi:10.1186/1471-244X-13-106
35. Iqbal Z, Birchwood M, Chadwick P, Trower P. Cognitive approach to depression and suicidal thinking in psychosis. 2. Testing the validity of a social ranking model. *Br J Psychiatry* (2000) 177:522–8. doi:10.1192/bjp.177.6.522
36. Upthegrove R, Birchwood M, Ross K, Brunett K, McCollum R, Jones L. The evolution of depression and suicidality in first episode psychosis. *Acta Psychiatr Scand* (2010) 122(3):211–8. doi:10.1111/j.1600-0447.2009.01506.x
37. González-Pinto A, Aldama A, González C, Mosquera F, Arrasate M, Vieta E. Predictors of suicide in first-episode affective and nonaffective psychotic inpatients: five-year follow-up of patients from a catchment area in Vitoria, Spain. *J Clin Psychiatry* (2007) 68(2):242–7. doi:10.4088/JCP.v68n0209
38. Mortensen PB, Juel K. Mortality and causes of death in first admitted schizophrenic patients. *Br J Psychiatry* (1993) 163(2):183–9. doi:10.1192/bjp.163.2.183
39. Verdoux H, Liraud F, Gonzales B, Assens F, Abalan F, Van Os J. Predictors and outcome characteristics associated with suicidal behaviour in early psychosis: a two-year follow-up of first-admitted subjects. *Acta Psychiatr Scand* (2001) 103(5):347–54. doi:10.1034/j.1600-0447.2001.00202.x
40. Deegan PE. Recovering our sense of value after being labeled: mentally Ill. *J Psychosoc Nurs Ment Health Serv* (1993) 31(4):7–9.
41. Estroff SE. *Making It Crazy: An Ethnography of Psychiatric Clients in an American Community*. Berkeley, CA: University of California Press (1985).
42. Judge AM, Estroff SE, Perkins DO, Penn DL. Recognizing and responding to early psychosis: a qualitative analysis of individual narratives. *Psychiatr Serv* (2008) 59(1):96–9. doi:10.1176/appi.ps.59.1.96
43. Yanos PT, Roe D, Markus K, Lysaker PH. Pathways between internalized stigma and outcomes related to recovery in schizophrenia-spectrum disorders. *Psychiatr Serv* (2008) 59:1437–42. doi:10.1176/ps.2008.59.12.1437
44. Mueser KT, Goodman LA, Trumbetta SL, Rosenberg SD, Osher FC, Vidaver R, et al. Trauma and posttraumatic stress disorder in severe mental illness. *J Consult Clin Psychol* (1998) 66:493–9. doi:10.1037/0022-006X.66.3.493
45. Neria Y, Bromet EJ, Sievers S, Lavelle J, Fochtmann LJ. Trauma exposure and posttraumatic stress disorder in psychosis: findings from a first-admission cohort. *J Consult Clin Psychol* (2002) 70:246–51. doi:10.1037/0022-006X.70.1.246
46. Grubaugh AL, Zinzow HM, Paul L, Egede LE, Frueh BC. Trauma exposure and posttraumatic stress disorder in adults with severe mental illness: a critical review. *Clin Psychol Rev* (2011) 31:883–99. doi:10.1016/j.cpr.2011.04.003
47. Chapple B, Chant D, Nolan P, Cardy S, Whiteford H, McGrath J. Correlates of victimisation amongst people with psychosis. *Soc Psychiatry Psychiatr Epidemiol* (2004) 39:836–40. doi:10.1007/s00127-004-0819-4
48. Kessler RC, Bergland P, Demler O, Jin R, Merikangas KR, Walters EE. Lifetime prevalence and age-of-onset distributions of DSM-IV disorders in the National Comorbidity Survey Replication. *Arch Gen Psychiatry* (2005) 62:593–602. doi:10.1001/archpsyc.62.6.617
49. Mueser KT, Gottlieb JD, Xie H, Lu W, Yanos PT, Rosenberg SD, et al. Evaluation of cognitive restructuring for post-traumatic stress disorder in people with severe mental illness. *Br J Psychiatry* (2015) 201(6):501–8. doi:10.1192/bjp.bp.114.147926
50. Davidson L, Ridgway P, Kidd S, Topor A, Borg M. Using qualitative research to inform mental health policy. *Can J Psychiatry* (2008) 53(3):137–44. doi:10.1177/070674370805300303
51. Tanskanen S, Morant N, Hinton M, Lloyd-Evans B, Crosby M, Killaspy H, et al. Service user and carer experiences of seeking help for a first episode of psychosis: a UK qualitative study. *BMC Psychiatry* (2011) 11(1):157. doi:10.1186/1471-244X-11-157
52. Lukoff D, Nuechterlein KH, Ventura J. Manual for the expanded Brief Psychiatric Rating Scale (BPRS). *Schizophr Bull* (1986) 12:594–602.
53. Mueser KT, Curran PJ, McHugo GJ. Factor structure of the Brief Psychiatric Rating Scale in schizophrenia. *Psychol Assess* (1997) 9:196–204. doi:10.1037/1040-3590.9.3.196
54. Kubany E, Haynes S, Leisen M, Owens J, Kaplan A, Watson S, et al. Development and preliminary validation of a brief broad-spectrum measure of trauma exposure: the Traumatic Life Events Questionnaire. *Psychol Assess* (2000) 12(2):210–24. doi:10.1037/1040-3590.12.2.210
55. Williams-Keeler, L. (1999). PTSD assessment tool for schizophrenia. *Unpublished Scale.*
56. Creswell JW. *Qualitative Inquiry and Research Design: Choosing among Five Approaches*. Thousand Oaks, CA: SAGE (2013).
57. Krathwohl DR. *Methods of Educational and Social Science Research: An Integrated Approach*. New York, NY: Longman/Addison Wesley Longman (1993).
58. Hughes R, Hayward M, Finlay WML. Patients' perceptions of the impact of involuntary inpatient care on self, relationships and recovery. *J Ment Health* (2009) 18(2):152–60. doi:10.1080/09638230802053326
59. Jackson C, Trower P, Reid I, Smith J, Hall M, Townend M, et al. Improving psychological adjustment following a first episode of psychosis: a randomized controlled trial of cognitive therapy to reduce post psychotic trauma symptoms. *Behav Res Ther* (2009) 47(6):454–62. doi:10.1016/j.brat.2009.02.009
60. Bernard M, Jackson C, Jones C. Written emotional disclosure following first-episode psychosis: effects on symptoms of post-traumatic stress disorder. *Br J Clin Psychol* (2006) 45:403–15. doi:10.1348/014466505X68933

61. Fallot RD, Harris M. Trauma-informed services. In: Reyes G, Elhai JD, Ford JD, editors. *The Encyclopedia of Psychological Trauma*. Hoboken, NJ: John Wiley (2008). p. 660–2.
62. Seikkula J, Alakare B. Open dialogues with patients with psychosis and their families. In: Romme M, Escher S, editors. *Psychosis as a Personal Crisis: An Experience-Based Approach*. New York: Routledge (2012). p. 116–28.
63. Deegan PE, Drake RE. Shared decision making and medication management in the recovery process. *Psychiatr Serv* (2006) 57(11):1636–9. doi:10.1176/ps.2006.57.11.1636
64. MacDonald-Wilson KL, Deegan PE, Hutchison SL, Parrotta N, Schuster JM. Integrating personal medicine into service delivery: empowering people in recovery. *Psychiatr Rehabil J* (2013) 36(4):258–63. doi:10.1037/prj0000027
65. MacDonald-Wilson KL, Hutchison SL, Karpov I, Wittman P, Deegan PE. A successful implementation strategy to support adoption of decision making in mental health services. *Community Ment Health J* (2017) 53(3):251–6. doi:10.1007/s10597-016-0027-1
66. Rosenberg SD, Goodman LA, Osher FC, Swartz M, Essock SM, Butterfield MI, et al. Prevalence of HIV, hepatitis B and hepatitis C in people with severe mental illness. *Am J Public Health* (2001) 91:31–7. doi:10.2105/AJPH.91.1.31
67. Lommen MJ, Restifo K. Trauma and posttraumatic stress disorder (PTSD) in patients with schizophrenia or schizoaffective disorder. *Community Ment Health J* (2009) 45:485–96. doi:10.1007/s10597-009-9248-x
68. Resnick SG, Bond GR, Mueser KT. Trauma and posttraumatic stress disorder in people with schizophrenia. *J Abnorm Psychol* (2003) 112:415–23. doi:10.1037/0021-843X.112.3.415

19

The Role of Trauma and Stressful Life Events among Individuals at Clinical High Risk for Psychosis

Danessa Mayo[1], Sarah Corey[2], Leah H. Kelly[2], Seghel Yohannes[2], Alyssa L. Youngquist[2], Barbara K. Stuart[2], Tara A. Niendam[1] and Rachel L. Loewy[2]*

[1] Imaging Research Center, Department of Psychiatry and Behavioral Sciences, University of California Davis, Sacramento, CA, USA, [2] Department of Psychiatry, University of California San Francisco, San Francisco, CA, USA

Edited by:
Kim T. Mueser,
Boston University, USA

Reviewed by:
Lauren Gibson,
Temple University, USA
Craig Steel,
University of Reading, UK

***Correspondence:**
Danessa Mayo
dmayo@ucdavis.edu

The experience of childhood trauma (CT) and stressful life events (SLEs) is associated with subsequent development of a variety of mental health conditions, including psychotic illness. Recent research identifying adolescents and young adults at clinical high risk (CHR) for psychosis allows for prospective evaluation of the impact of trauma and adverse life events on psychosis onset and other outcomes, addressing etiological questions that cannot be answered in studies of fully psychotic or non-clinical populations. This article provides a comprehensive review of the current emerging literature on trauma and adverse life events in the CHR population. Up to 80% of CHR youth endorse a lifetime history of childhood traumatic events and victimization (e.g., bullying). Several studies have shown that the experience of CT predicts psychosis onset among CHR individuals, while the literature on the influence of recent SLEs (e.g., death of a loved one) remains inconclusive. Multiple models have been proposed to explain the link between trauma and psychosis, including the stress-vulnerability and stress-sensitivity hypotheses, with emphases on both cognitive processes and neurobiological mechanisms (e.g., the hypothalamic–pituitary–adrenal axis). Despite the preponderance of CHR individuals who endorse either CT or SLEs, no clinical trials have been conducted evaluating interventions for trauma in CHR youth to date. Furthermore, the current process of formal identification and assessment of trauma, SLEs, and their impact on CHR youth is inconsistent in research and clinical practice. Recommendations for improving trauma assessment, treatment, and future research directions in the CHR field are provided.

Keywords: clinical high risk, trauma, early psychosis, stressful life events, ultra-high risk, schizophrenia

INTRODUCTION

While a wealth of data has demonstrated indirect associations between childhood trauma (CT) and psychosis in adulthood, the role of CT in the etiology of psychosis and its potential underlying mechanisms are not yet well-understood (1–4). CT is the experience of a highly distressing event or situation during youth that is beyond one's capacity for coping and/or control (5, 6). Prospective studies of individuals who later develop psychosis provide a unique opportunity to examine potential risk factors, resilience factors, and mechanisms that may link CT and psychosis. Over the past decade, the "clinical high risk" (CHR) paradigm has been used to identify adolescents and young adults at increased imminent risk for developing psychotic disorders. Thus, CHR research makes an important contribution to understanding the potential etiologic role of CT in the development of psychosis. In this paper, we review the emerging literature on trauma and stressful life events (SLEs) in CHR individuals, with a focus on both behavioral and neurobiological studies. This paper also provides a risk model that explains the trauma and psychosis relationship. Further, current and important future directions for assessment, research, and clinical care are highlighted.

The CHR Syndrome

The CHR syndrome, also termed "ultra high risk" by some research groups, is typically diagnosed using one of two semi-structured interviews—the Structured Interview for Psychosis Risk Syndromes (SIPS) or the Comprehensive Assessment of At-Risk Mental States (CAARMS) (7, 8). The interviews assess a variety of subthreshold psychotic-like experiences (i.e., positive, negative, and disorganized symptoms), general psychopathology (e.g., depression, anxiety), functioning, and family history. Despite slight differences in diagnostic criteria and terminology, both instruments diagnose three possible risk syndromes and have shown high agreement ratings (86%) (9). Other instruments are also used to diagnose individuals at elevated risk for psychosis based on subjective cognitive changes (10, 11). As such, these selected standardized measures have been utilized in international early psychosis (EP) clinics and research programs in an effort to reach diagnostic consensus and validity across sites.

Psychosis Risk and Outcomes

Outcomes for CHR individuals are heterogeneous: proportion estimates of individuals who transition to full psychosis range from 10–70% due to ascertainment strategy, diagnostic instrument, and follow-up period used (12). The largest individual study using the SIPS demonstrated a conversion rate of 35% to full psychosis by 2.5 years (12, 13). The CHR syndrome confers higher and more immediate risk than heritability estimates of 10% risk among first-degree family members (i.e., parent-offspring; full siblings), although not as high as the 50% rate of psychosis among identical twins (14, 15). Several factors appear to increase the risk for developing psychotic disorders among those with CHR syndromes: poor premorbid functioning, severe positive symptoms (i.e., elevated unusual thought content, increased suspiciousness), increased anhedonia, poor cognition (i.e., impaired verbal learning, decision-making, memory), decline in social and role functioning, substance abuse history, and family history of psychosis (16–19).

It is important to note that approximately 65% of CHR individuals do *not* develop psychosis within the first 3 years after diagnosis of the syndrome. A significant proportion (46%) of non-converters experience remission of their attenuated psychosis (20). Yet, many of those who do not develop psychosis continue to experience psychiatric problems such as mood, anxiety, and substance use disorders (21, 22). By targeting individuals presenting with attenuated psychotic symptoms or other markers indicative of increased psychosis risk, CHR programs seek to identify factors that could be addressed in order to mitigate a variety of negative outcomes and support resilience. To date, a number of potential factors related to outcomes in CHR populations have been identified, including the role of trauma and stress.

TRAUMA EXPERIENCES IN THE CHR POPULATION

The experience of CT leads to a cascade of negative effects on typical child and adult development (6, 23). A strong body of literature on the general population of adolescents and young adults (*via* school-wide samples, research and clinical settings, and longitudinal population studies) suggests that CT contributes to poor cognitive, social, medical, and developmental functioning; moreover, CT is a significant risk factor for later development of serious mental illness (SMI), including schizophrenia (24–34). The lifetime prevalence rate of trauma exposure is high among both men (60.7%) and women (51.2%) (35). Individuals ages 14–24 reported exposure to one or more traumatic experiences, such as physical abuse (50%), child abuse, or neglect (13%) (36); approximately 68% of youth by age 16 endorsed at least one trauma experience (37). CT is linked with a variety of adult psychopathology outcomes. Compared to adult participants with no history of CT, those with exposure to four or more traumas were at substantial risk (4- to 12-fold) for developing substance use, depression, and suicidality (38). Thus, several studies on stress and trauma posit that the experience of CT and prolonged early stressors may contribute to the increased risk of future SMI (24–34, 39–41).

To date, only 24 studies, representing 14 distinct samples, report on CT in CHR populations; of these, 11 followed the participants longitudinally to examine CT as a risk factor for developing psychosis (2, 34, 40, 42–62). Sixteen of these studies were included in a recent review and meta-analysis (5), which summarized the existing studies in a series of tables. We refer the reader to this paper by Kraan and colleagues (5) and have summarized more recent publications (8, 34, 45, 49, 51, 52, 55, 59) in a parallel table below (see **Table 1**).

The meta-analysis concluded that CT is a largely prevalent experience among the CHR population (86.8%) compared to healthy controls (HC) (5). Such alarmingly high rates of CT endorsed by the CHR population is comparable to the prevalence rate among individuals with schizophrenia (85%) (5). We expand upon the meta-analysis by reviewing different types of trauma in the CHR syndrome based on all current available information below.

Associated Findings on Trauma in the CHR Population

Clinical high risk individuals may be at risk for experiencing various forms of traumatic experiences that are common within the general population. The meta-analysis by Kraan and colleagues (5) reported a mean prevalence rate of 86.8% CT in CHR studies (2, 40, 42, 51, 56). The range of rates (35.9–70%) may be partially explained by the type of trauma being examined and the gender sample distribution (e.g., sexual abuse) (40, 53) and type of

TABLE 1 | Studies on clinical high risk (CHR) individuals with trauma history and/or stressful life events.

Reference	Study	Outcome measure	Trauma instrument	CHR instrument	Study design	Participants	Gender (male)	Mean age (range)	Conclusion
Russo et al. (49)	CAMEO United Kingdom; NIHR, United Kingdom	Examine trauma characteristics associated with CHR	THS	CAARMS	2-year follow along	*N* = 60 CHR; *N* = 60 HC	51.7; 43.3%	19.89 (16.41–30.21) 22.6 (16.18–35.57)	Age at study entry, number of traumas, and age at trauma exposure were predictors of CHR group association
Thompson et al. (55)	PACE, Australia	Examine relationship between trauma (specifically sexual trauma) and conversion to psychosis	CTQ	CAARMS	Follow along, length not specified	*N* = 416 CHR [similar sample as Thompson et al. (52)]	Unspecified	Unspecified age and range	Positive correlation between childhood sexual abuse and conversion to psychosis. Relationship unique to sexual trauma.
Kraan et al. (34)	Dutch Prediction of Psychosis Study, Netherlands	Determine the relationship between childhood trauma (CT) and functional/clinical outcome overtime	TADS	SIPS	24-month follow along; follow-up at 9-month, 18-month, and 24-month	*N* = 125 CHR	68.00%	17.7 (unspecified)	Trauma not related to conversion, differential symptom, or functioning overtime. Positive correlations between level of trauma and attenuated positive symptoms, general symptoms, and depression. Trauma negatively correlated with functioning at baseline and follow-up
Üçok et al. (59)	Psychotic Disorders Research Program, Istanbul	Investigate association between CT and CHR cognitive functioning	CTQ	BPRS	Cross-sectional	*N* = 53 CHR	73.60%	21.1 (unspecified)	CHR participants with trauma history had worse attention and working memory. Cognitive flexibility and interference inhibition scores lower than those without a history of CT. No association between trauma and verbal learning/memory. Suggests CT and cognitive deficits may be associated with types of trauma
Yung et al. (61)	PACE, Australia	Examine clinical predictors for poor functional outcomes in CHR patients. Examine a relationship between poor functioning and conversion to psychosis	CTQ	CAARMS	14-year follow along	*N* = 268 CHR	43.20%	Unspecified (15–30)	Childhood maltreatment and psychosis significantly predicted poor functional outcome. No association between positive symptoms and follow-up functioning. Cross-sectional relationship found between long-term poor functioning and negative symptoms at follow-up in both converters and non-converters
Kline et al. (45)	Strive for Wellness, Maryland	Examine relationship between trauma and early psychosis and psychosis risk symptoms in youth	KSADS-PL	SIPS	Cross-sectional	*N* = 60 CHR/EP; *N* = 65 LR	49.00%	15.88 (unspecified)	Trauma history related to positive symptoms in both groups. LR group reported heightened suspiciousness with a history of exposure to violence. CHR/EP group reported heightened levels of suspiciousness regardless of type of violence exposure

(Continued)

TABLE 1 | Continued

Reference	Study	Outcome measure	Trauma instrument	CHR instrument	Study design	Participants	Gender (male)	Mean age (range)	Conclusion
Stowkowy et al. (51)	NAPLS-2, North America	Determine whether trauma and discrimination are predictors of conversion to psychosis	Childhood Trauma and Abuse Scale; Adapted self-report measure used for perceived discrimination	SIPS	Cross-sectional	*N* = 764 CHR; *N* = 280 HC	55.30%	18.5 (unspecified) 19.7 (unspecified)	CHR group reported higher levels of trauma, perceived discrimination, and bullying than HC. Discrimination was a significant predictor of conversion. Discrimination correlated with ethnic minority groups
Thompson et al. (52)	PACE, Australia	Examine if certain factors mediate the relationship between sexual trauma and psychosis	CTQ	CAARMS	Follow along, 2.4–14.9 years later	*N* = 416 CHR	Unspecified	Unspecified (15–30)	Anxiety, dissociation, mood instability and mania symptoms did not mediate the relationship between sexual trauma and psychosis

Trauma measures: THS, Trauma History Screen; TADS, Trauma and Distress Scale; CTQ, Childhood Trauma Questionnaire; PACE, Personal Assessment and Crisis Evaluation.
Psychiatric assessments: MINI, Mini International Neuropsychiatric Interview Version 6.0.0; PANSS, Positive and Negative Symptom Scale; SIPS, Structured Interview for Psychosis Risk Syndromes; KSADS-PL, Kiddie Schedule for Affective Disorders and Schizophrenia-Present and Lifetime; BPRS, Brief Psychiatric Rating Scale-expanded; SANS, Scale for the Assessment of Negative Symptoms; SAPS, Scale for the Assessment of Positive Symptoms; CAARMS, Comprehensive Assessment of At-Risk Mental State.
Studies: NAPLS-2, North American Prodrome Longitudinal Study-2; NIHR, National Institute for Health Research Mental States; CHR, clinical high risk; EP, early psychosis; LR, low risk; HC, healthy control.

assessment used (e.g., medical records review, semi-structured interview, self-report), with self-report measures associated with higher rates of trauma disclosure [e.g., Childhood Trauma Questionnaire (CTQ), Early Trauma Inventory] (40–91%) (40, 42, 44, 55, 59). Some measures assess narrowly defined trauma, while others are more broad, including major life events. Eight of the studies were based on small samples of less than 100 participants, with some as small as 25 subjects (40, 44, 46, 50, 53, 56, 58, 62). Smaller samples are more easily biased by sampling differences and thus contribute to heterogeneity of results and lack of reproducibility (63). The largest sample reported 46.2% of CHR individuals with CT (n = 764), a majority of those who endorsed severe to extreme rates of trauma on the brief CTQ (51, 52, 55). As a whole, these studies highlight the preponderance of CT experiences among the CHR population and the importance of such information for clinical consideration.

Four studies formally compared CT rates in CHR samples with HC populations matched on demographic variables (i.e., age, gender, socioeconomic status) and found higher rates of abuse among CHR groups (2, 50, 58). Research suggests that CHR individuals may be at greater risk for physical trauma than the general population (17%) (64). In a small study of 30 CHR participants, 83% reported a physical abuse history (56). A study on a CHR sample reported more violent (71.7%) and non-violent events (53.3%) than the low-risk group (48.4% violent; 33.9% non-violent events) (45). Physical trauma is also associated with poorer cognitive functioning, which is a significant concern for CHR individuals, as poor premorbid cognitive functioning may add to their psychopathology risk (59, 61).

Individuals with a sexual abuse history are at higher risk for developing mood and anxiety disorders, substance abuse, posttraumatic stress disorder (PTSD), eating disorders, suicidal behaviors, and psychosis (65–69). Across studies, approximately 22–31.1% of CHR individuals endorsed a sexual trauma history (34, 40, 44, 49, 52, 53, 56) compared to the lifetime prevalence rate in the general population (15–25%) (70). Similarly, a study of 92 CHR individuals with a sexual abuse history endorsed higher rates of positive symptoms of a sexual nature (e.g., feelings of being watched while bathing, hearing voices say sexual statements) than HC (53). This may indicate that previous experiences of sexual trauma contribute in part to the nature of CHR individuals' emerging positive psychotic symptoms. CHR youth showed even higher rates of emotional abuse (41.5–75%) and emotional neglect (59–100%) (56, 58, 59) compared to HC (33%) (58). Furthermore, emotional abuse and neglect among CHR individuals have also been associated with greater Schneiderian first-rank symptoms, more elevated Schneiderian total score, and depression severity level (2).

Bullying victimization is becoming increasingly recognized as an important form of adverse childhood experience (24). Bullying has been associated with a variety of poor outcomes, ranging from poor self-esteem, depression, suicidality, aggression, and psychosis being the most serious (71). CHR youth endorsed a lifetime history of physical and psychological bullying (30 and 60%, respectively) that was much higher than HC (14 and 36%, respectively) (42). Bullying history among CHR youth was significantly associated with poorer social functioning (42) and was more likely to persist into adult psychiatric disorders (71). As such, it is imperative that more research is conducted to examine the relationship between childhood bullying and psychosis symptoms.

Trauma is often experienced as a result of developing psychosis, due to the experience of frightening psychotic symptoms or hospitalizations, especially involuntary treatment. Prevalence of psychosis-associated trauma symptoms among individuals with full psychotic disorders varies from 11–67% (72, 73). They may be associated with factors such as trauma history prior to inpatient hospitalization (e.g., physical or sexual abuse) and other psychological factors (e.g., negative event appraisals, poor coping skills) (74, 75). However, some studies did not find any associations with psychosis-related trauma symptoms and the number of negative experiences from inpatient psychiatric hospitalizations (73, 76). It may be important to ascertain whether other patient-level factors, such as the level of distress attributed to the inpatient hospitalization, legal status, and involuntary hospitalization may be associated with psychosis-related trauma symptoms (73, 75, 76). To date, there are no specific studies that focus on trauma symptoms associated with psychiatric hospitalization among CHR individuals. This is an important research area in need of further exploration and highlights the usefulness of examining the impact of CT in the CHR population, prior to the potentially traumatizing effects of involuntary hospitalization that can accompany the onset of a full psychotic disorder.

Only a few published studies have explored the demographic characteristics of trauma in CHR individuals. A study on gender differences showed that stress-sensitivity scores among CHR females (but not males) mediated the association between trauma and attenuated positive psychotic symptoms, which suggests that females cope with trauma differently and tend to internalize their experiences (77). While ethnic sample variability (i.e., majority Caucasian women) was a possible research limitation, this is consistent with the common finding that females with psychosis are more likely to endorse a trauma history (e.g., sexual abuse) than males (42, 53) and are more likely to have an affective disorder associated with their diagnosis (78). Similarly, limited studies regarding ethnicity (e.g., perceived discrimination, social adversity) and its relationship with trauma in CHR groups currently exist (51). The current collective studies on CHR groups with trauma experiences suggest the importance of continued research into its associated influence on psychosis risk.

Trauma and CHR Conversion to Psychosis

Trauma has been repeatedly found to predict transition to psychosis in CHR samples. Sexual abuse is the most common form of CT associated with later psychosis conversion, followed by physical abuse (3, 40, 53, 55, 60). Moreover, emotional abuse and physical neglect have been identified as potential risk factors for psychosis conversion (58). Similar to findings on sexual abuse history, the increased severity and duration of individuals' bullying history has been linked to the emergence of psychosis symptoms (71). While elevated rates of trauma history were found among CHR individuals in the NAPLS sample and trauma history was a significant predictor of psychosis conversion in the univariate and multivariate analyses, it was not a statistically significant predictor after controlling for prodromal symptom severity, social functioning decline, verbal learning, and memory (16). Thus, the power of trauma to predict conversion must be examined in the context of other predictors in order to determine its relative impact and possible relationship to other predictive factors.

SLEs IN THE CHR POPULATION

It is not yet clear whether the impact of trauma on individuals with CHR is specific to narrowly defined traumatic events or also includes the cumulative effects of adverse or SLEs that have also been linked with adult psychopathology, including psychosis risk (79, 80). In fact, many studies that purport to measure traumatic events include less severe SLEs, which consist of dangerous or life-changing experiences that have occurred for an individual (5) and may cause disruption in the typical developmental trajectory of youth through adulthood. Exposure to SLEs are associated with increased risk for depressed mood, anxiety, eating disorders, suicidality, substance use, and psychosis symptoms in later adolescence (29, 81–85). Current findings on the SLE–psychosis risk relationship are inconclusive; some cited a positive relationship (39, 51, 86, 87) while others did not (43, 47, 48, 57). Kraan and colleagues (5) indicated that recent SLEs were less commonly endorsed by CHR youth than HC, which may be due to increasing negative symptoms of psychosis (e.g., increased avolition, social withdrawal) that limit activities. Increased research efforts are underway to improve current understanding of the relationship between SLEs and psychosis.

COMORBID DISORDERS AND DIFFERENTIAL DIAGNOSIS IN THE CHR POPULATION

The specificity of the relationship between trauma and CHR symptoms is muddied by the high level of comorbidity in this population (88–90). Around 73% of CHR individuals have at least one other Axis I disorder (89). Long-term studies show persistence of comorbid disorders such as mood (15–38%), anxiety (5–16%), substance use (11%), personality disorders (2.7%), and other diagnoses (43–52%) (91, 92). At a 6-year follow-up, approximately 56.8% of CHR patients endorsed at least one comorbid disorder and 61.5% of them reported continued comorbidity from baseline (91). Only a small group of CHR individuals (7–16%) reported no comorbid diagnoses at baseline or follow-up (91, 92). Clearly, comorbidity is the rule and not the exception when dealing with EP symptomatology. Since up to 65% of CHR individuals do *not* go on to develop psychotic disorders within 3 years after initial CHR diagnosis, such subthreshold psychotic symptoms experienced may have responded to treatment, resolved over time, or may be better explained by another psychiatric diagnosis. In a strict sense, these non-converters may be considered "false positive" diagnoses regarding a pre-psychotic phase of illness. Thus, the CHR syndrome may best be understood as a mixture of individuals identified prior to the onset of psychosis, along with adolescents/young adults who experience subthreshold positive symptoms in the context of a primary mood, anxiety or PTSD. Any relationships to trauma must be understood in this context, given the extensive literature that links trauma to later mood and anxiety disorders. In this section, we examine the various comorbid disorders within the CHR and other psychotic disorders and their symptom interaction with CT.

Mood/Anxiety Disorders

Clinical high risk individuals with CT showed high comorbid mood (40–45%) and anxiety disorders (15.3%) (5, 42, 93), as did CHR individuals with SLEs [i.e., major depressive disorder (13%), bipolar disorder (8.7%), dysthymic disorder (4.3%), social phobia (17.4%), generalized anxiety disorder (8.7%), panic disorder (4.3%)] (57). However, a study on CHR samples was unable to show a relationship between CT and mood/anxiety disorders, possibly due to low sample size ($n = 30$) (56). Available studies on CHR and first-episode psychosis (FEP) individuals with CT show that both groups had higher rates of suicidal attempts, elevated rates of psychiatric hospitalization, and poorer clinical functioning (3, 59). Studies on individuals with schizophrenia suggest that CT is associated with increased severity of depression and anxiety disorders (94, 95). The small number of current findings related to comorbid mood and anxiety disorders among CHR groups with CT warrants additional research in this area to untangle whether trauma is specifically related to positive psychotic symptoms.

Substance Use

Despite high rates of comorbid substance use in CHR populations, particularly tobacco (34.4%), alcohol (17–44%), and cannabis (3–54%) (96), there is currently limited research specifically focused on CHR individuals with trauma and substance use. However, there are well-documented links between trauma and substance use in the general population (97) and the role of substance use in triggering psychotic episodes (98, 99). While there is minimal support as of yet for the direct relationship between substance use and conversion to psychosis in the CHR group, there is stronger evidence for the relationship between substance use and increased severity of subthreshold psychosis symptoms among CHR individuals (96). School-aged youth showed an interaction effect between CT and cannabis use that accounted for 83% of their reported psychosis symptoms (100). Better understanding potential interactions between trauma and substance use as risk factors for psychosis is a critical need in the literature, as well as highly relevant to designing interventions for this population.

Posttraumatic Stress Disorder

Most critical to comorbidity issues in our review of trauma and the CHR syndrome is the presence of PTSD in this population. A multisite CHR study reported a significantly higher prevalence rate of current (2.6%) and lifetime (4.1%) formal PTSD diagnosis than in HCs (101). Specifically, CHR youth with a CT history demonstrates PTSD rates of 15.2% (3). Similar to mood and other anxiety disorders, comorbid PTSD diagnoses with FEP individuals who have a trauma history are associated with longer treatment duration and more intensive treatment to address all presenting symptoms (3). A meta-analysis indicated that individuals who suffer from comorbid psychosis and PTSD endorse symptoms of faulty cognitive appraisals, feelings of helplessness, and lack of control (75). These are, of course, important targets for treatment with individuals who have comorbid PTSD and psychosis, and may be relevant for CHR treatment.

Differential Diagnosis of PTSD and CHR Status

A common referral question posed by clinicians seeking evaluation for a consumer asks— "Is it trauma or EP?" Indeed, the symptoms associated with PTSD can create diagnostic uncertainty. There are a number of similarities between the symptoms of PTSD and psychosis (102). Hallucinations in psychosis are analogous to the experience of flashbacks and intrusive images and bodily sensations associated with PTSD as they both present in visual, auditory, or tactile modalities and are usually experienced as distressing and unbidden. Suspiciousness in psychosis resembles the hypervigilance in PTSD and avoidance behaviors, which are a hallmark of PTSD and can be similar to safety-seeking behaviors or negative symptoms in psychosis. Hallucinations in an adolescent sample were found to be highly prevalent in both PTSD and psychotic disorders, and the hallucinations of psychosis and PTSD could not be differentiated in terms of content, modality, location, or form (103, 104).

It may also pose additional difficulties when evaluating individuals with more severe symptoms. Data from the U.S. National Comorbidity Survey Part II indicated that all of the positive psychotic symptoms examined in the sample were more likely to be endorsed by respondents who met diagnostic criteria for PTSD than those without PTSD (105). A dose–response relationship was also found, such that with more PTSD symptoms endorsed, the higher likelihood for experiencing both symptoms of paranoia and hallucinations. Among the psychotic symptoms, auditory hallucinations had the greatest odds ratios with lifetime PTSD diagnosis. Several studies on non-clinical, community samples suggest that CT is a strong risk factor for visual, auditory, and tactile hallucinations (106, 107). Data from the National Comorbidity Survey indicated that a history of childhood rape was significantly associated with auditory hallucinations in a non-clinical adult (Age $M = 32$ years, $SD = 10.59$) sample (107).

Despite the substantial similarities, one study of adolescents suggests that command hallucinations and derogatory themes were more common in PTSD and were associated with higher emotional distress, self-injury, and suicidal ideation, compared to hallucinations in schizophrenia (103). Furthermore, the presence of PTSD in children and adolescents has been noted to confer a substantial likelihood of disturbances of reality testing. Maltreated and traumatized children with a PTSD diagnosis are more likely than children with a history of trauma with no PTSD diagnosis to also meet criteria for a brief psychotic episode or unspecified psychotic disorder with symptoms analogous to the CHR syndrome (108). However, children with PTSD rarely exhibited full-blown delusions or illogicality. Thus, perceptual disturbances and suspiciousness may be present both in the CHR syndrome and in PTSD while other types of delusional thinking, cognitive disorganization, and negative symptoms (differentiated from mood disturbance or avoidant behaviors) may be more specific to psychotic disorders.

MECHANISMS OF TRAUMA AND STRESS IN THE CHR POPULATION

Multiple models have been cited to explain the link between trauma and later psychosis, including the stress-vulnerability and stress-sensitivity hypotheses, with emphases on both cognitive processes and neurobiological mechanisms (e.g., the hypothalamic–pituitary–adrenal axis). Consistent with a gene–environment interaction model, trauma history appears to contribute to psychosis in adulthood somewhat independent of genetics (109). A recent gene–environment interaction study supports the idea that genes associated with schizophrenia lead to changes in not only dopamine but also serotonin signaling pathways in the brain, thus suggesting an "affective pathway" to psychosis (110). Below, we address models that have been referenced in previous works to explain the potential interplay between trauma, stress, and psychosis. Following the discussion of currently identified relationship models of trauma and psychosis, we propose our own comprehensive model that conceptualizes a cyclical relationship between trauma and psychosis risk.

Stress-Vulnerability Model

In an effort to understand the mechanism through which trauma and stress may lead to psychosis, Zubin and Spring (111) proposed the stress-vulnerability model. This model posits that individuals possess a genetic or biological vulnerability to psychosis that can withstand a certain amount of stressors due to genes and other biological risk factors. However, once the stress threshold is surpassed, psychosis may be at higher risk of development (see **Figure 1**) (111). From this perspective, the experience of trauma increases one's experienced stress and, therefore, leaves them at greater susceptibility to experiencing psychopathology. One way this has been examined biologically is through research on the functioning of the hypothalamic–pituitary–adrenocortical (HPA) axis (see **Figure 2**), one of the primary stress response systems in the human body.

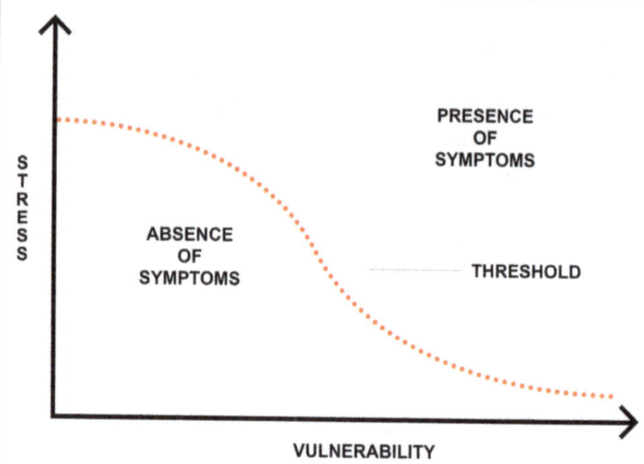

FIGURE 1 | Stress-vulnerability model (111).

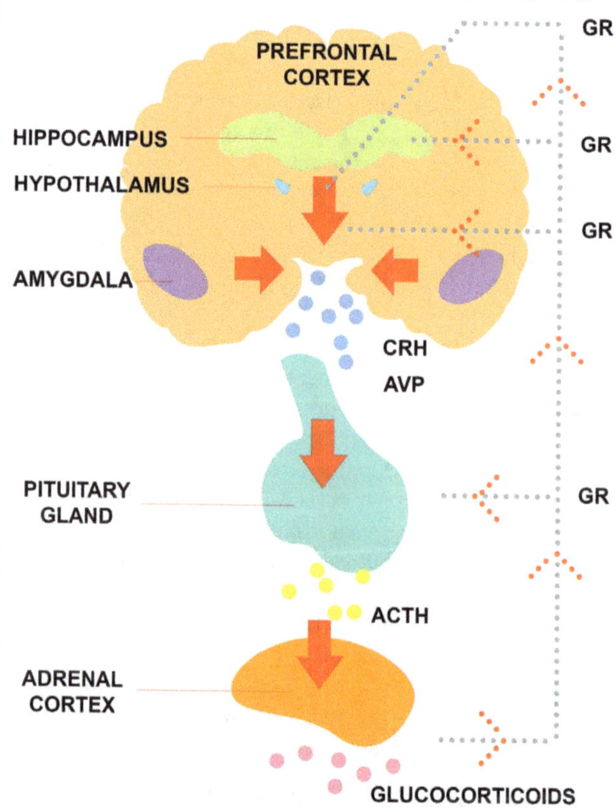

FIGURE 2 | Functioning of the hypothalamic–pituitary–adrenal axis. Abbreviations: GR, glucocorticoid receptor; ACTH, adrenocorticotropic hormone; CRH, corticotropin-releasing hormone; AVP, arginine vasopressin.

Stress-Sensitization Model

The impact of stress on psychopathology has also been discussed in the context of stress sensitization (112). The origins of this concept come from animal models that indicated individual differences in stress-sensitivity and -reactivity due to interactions between genes and environments. Similar to the stress-vulnerability model, the stress-sensitization theory hypothesizes that for a person to experience their first psychiatric illness, they may have a biological vulnerability, and then need to experience a major stressor. After the initial emergence of psychopathology, vulnerability increases, requiring less stress for the person to develop recurrent or more severe psychiatric issues (113). Thus, experience of CT may render an individual more susceptible to psychosis triggered by later stressors. Walker and Diforio (114) describe the connection of behavioral and biological stressors in psychosis and how dysregulation of stress response in both of these capacities overtime can create even greater disturbances in the HPA axis, thereby creating even more damaging effects on one's functioning. Support for the concept of a dysregulated response to stress following trauma can be seen in other mental health conditions. In a study of 18,713 individuals without a psychiatric diagnosis prior to the September 11 attack in the US, those who reported a CT history and were either directly or indirectly affected by the attack were at significantly greater risk of experiencing an internalizing disorder and were more vulnerable to elevated stress in comparison to those that did not report CT (115). Within the CHR population, the stress-sensitization model has never been formally tested; that is, no study has examined the possibility of an interaction between CT or SLEs and raising the risk for psychosis onset. A very large sample would be required to test an interaction model to predict conversion to psychosis, which one would only expect for up to a third of CHR individuals. However, partial behavioral evidence for stress sensitization was reported from the NAPLS study, in which CHR individuals who converted to psychosis not only reported more SLEs but also experienced higher levels of self-reported stress than CHR participants whose symptoms remitted. Additionally, those who rated more SLE also indicated higher stress from daily hassles (116). However, they did not examine any relationship of CT to SLE response. We have begun to investigate this possible interaction in our own work as described below.

Dysregulated Stress Response

Cortisol is a biological stress marker, the final product of activation of the HPA axis in response to stress and can be obtained through plasma, saliva, and urine (117). Cortisol has a standard diurnal rhythm that can be assessed when samples are collected throughout the day (118). In addition to quantifying its daily cycle, stress reactivity can be measured when cortisol is measured in saliva samples that have been collected when a person is undergoing a stressful task (119). Therefore, dysregulation of the HPA axis can be evaluated globally to address the underlying vulnerability to stress, and locally, sensitivity can be evaluated in response to a specific stress task. Findings within the schizophrenia population indicate elevated cortisol (a physiologic measure of stress responsivity) in many individuals with psychosis (120, 121), with some variable results indicating both hyper- and hypo-function of the HPA axis (122). Some of the heterogeneity in results could be due to the presence of antipsychotic medication, which has shown to decrease cortisol levels (122, 123) or potentially to the experience of trauma.

Trauma and the HPA Axis

There is currently some evidence for the impact of trauma on the development of altered stress responses and psychopathology. Indeed, research has shown blunted cortisol secretion in patients with PTSD (124), and in women with a history of sexual trauma (125), as well as for patients with schizophrenia who reported CT. In a study of 14 individuals who met diagnostic criteria for DSM-IV schizophrenia, those who reported moderate to severe CT experiences had lower diurnal cortisol secretion, especially within the first hour of the waking, whereas those without the experience of CT exhibited higher levels of cortisol throughout the day (126). Following the same pattern, Phassouliotis and colleagues (127) found lower basal cortisol levels, in a sample of first-episode patients who reported significantly higher rates of CT than HC. However, due to the small sample size, within-group comparisons of first-episode patients with and without CT could not be explored. Within the CHR population, this theory has had a lack of attention, but one study has supported the idea. Although trauma was not explicitly assessed, decreased cortisol secretion as a response to Trier Social Stress Test administration was found in a small sample of CHR individuals who also reported higher levels of chronic stress compared to HCs (119). Further research evaluating CT history explicitly within the CHR population is necessary to understand its impact on cortisol secretion.

Evidence suggests that psychosocial stress activates the HPA axis and, in turn, the dopamine and serotonin systems, where exaggerated effects have been observed in individuals who experienced childhood adversity (110, 128). Neuroimaging studies (i.e., magnetic resonance imaging; functional magnetic resonance imaging; positron emission tomography; diffusion tensor imaging; multimodal) have revealed that in those CHR individuals who converted to psychosis, functional changes in striatal dopamine synthesis and release were observed (129–131). In addition, Oswald and colleagues (132) found that perceived stress partially mediated the association between childhood adversity and ventral striatal dopamine responses. A full exploration of the potential neurobiological mechanisms linking trauma and psychosis are beyond the scope of this paper, but we provide these examples of one possible relationship and highlight the need for further research in this area.

Overall, a majority of studies has demonstrated abnormalities in cortisol secretion in CHR samples compared to HC (133). In a large sample of 256 CHR patients and 141 HC, the CHR group exhibited significantly higher mean diurnal salivary cortisol levels (134). Participants who converted to full psychosis in the CHR group had higher mean daily cortisol levels than those who remitted. However, the specificity of this result to psychosis is unclear, as well as whether it is a cause or consequence of attenuated psychosis. It may be related to the high rates of mood and anxiety disorders in this group rather than be central to psychosis, specifically. Its relative contribution to psychotic transition in the context of other significant risk factors is also not yet fully understood. Additional research that follows HPA axis functioning overtime and relates it to symptom expression and other biomarkers, such as genetics and neuroimaging, are critical to understanding the role it may (or may not) play in psychosis risk. A dysregulated stress response with altered cortisol secretion may be evidence of a subgroup of CHR individuals who experience an affective/stress pathway to psychosis, and thus moderating the stress response at a biological or behavioral level could be an important target for intervention in those with a demonstrated dysregulated response.

Cognitive Mechanisms

Several cognitive mechanisms may explain the associated link between trauma and psychotic disorders. For instance, it has been suggested that early adversity may lead to the formation of negative schemas of the self, others, and the surrounding environment (135). Such negative views may eventually contribute to greater external locus of control (54) and increased symptoms of suspicious or paranoia (136). CT may be associated with faulty responses to environmental stimuli, such as informational processing bias for negative or irrelevant stimuli (137, 138). Such focus on irrelevant or what may appear to be threatening stimuli has been thought to lead to reasoning bias (e.g., jumping into conclusions) (136, 139) and paranoid thinking (140). For a more detailed overview of cognitive and neurobiological mechanisms involving trauma and psychosis, we refer the reader to a recent review by Gibson and colleagues (141).

The Cycle of Trauma, Psychosis, and Future Risk of Trauma

To comprehend the impact of CT and SLE on the development of psychosis, the synthesized findings point to the cyclical nature of trauma, psychosis risk, and increased vulnerability for future traumatic experiences. However, given the current weak findings associating SLE with CHR transition to psychosis, our conceptualized model focuses primarily on CT. Individuals exposed to CT are at elevated risk for abnormal childhood development in terms of neurocognitive, social, and emotional functioning. Depending on the form and severity of CT, some may have a more negative impact on learning and development. For instance, exposure to physical abuse or witness of domestic violence can create globally negative views of the self, others, and the world (142). Maladaptive behaviors (e.g., non-suicidal self-injury, suicidal behaviors, aggression), poor coping skills, and impaired emotional regulation may also arise out of CT experiences, increasing one's risk for developing mood and anxiety disorders (143). These same behaviors can result in poorer role and social functioning overtime (e.g., bullying, increased peer isolation), thus decreasing protective factors, such as social support and adaptive problem-solving skills. Several studies have also highlighted that the sole experience of trauma does not predict poor clinical functioning and CHR status (34, 52). Instead, as explained by the stress-sensitivity model, one's trauma history creates an initial level of elevated vulnerability for later psychopathology, such as SMI. Other risk factors (e.g., genetic, environmental) may add or interact with trauma to confer increased risk for psychosis. While the current evidence does not support SLE as a trigger for psychosis onset, they do lead to increased levels of depression in both episodes and severity (143). Severe mood disorders that are characterized with psychotic features are often more difficult to treat (144, 145). Thus, the dose–response relationship suggests that with increased CT experiences, the risk for later psychosis becomes greater.

Unfortunately, the negative impact of CT does not end at the onset of psychotic illness. For CHR individuals who endorsed CT, the emergence of psychosis creates a string of increased vulnerability for future traumatic experiences. CHR individuals with CT who go on to full psychosis conversion tend to have poor long-term functioning outcomes (61). In general, increased psychosis risk is associated with a decline in global functioning (e.g., social, role), emergence of comorbid disorders (e.g., depressed mood and anxiety disorders, PTSD, substance use), poor treatment engagement, and increased maladaptive coping skills and behaviors (16–19). The influence of CT further adds to the complexity of their symptom presentation and severity. As a result, the cascade of abnormal development and increased psychopathology leads to the resurgence of future vulnerability to other trauma.

The trauma–psychosis risk relationship postulates that following an initial traumatic experience, an individual experiences an abrupt change in their normal developmental course, is weakened in various areas of functioning, and therefore, is made more vulnerable moving forward in development. Based on the interaction between an individual's genetic foundation and their interaction with environmental stressors, including increased stress sensitization, the risk of psychosis conversion escalates. With the onset of full psychosis, individuals are further weakened in their ability to adaptively respond to stressful situations and adverse events moving forward, leading to increased risk of experiencing additional future trauma/SLEs. Nevertheless, the findings which highlight no associations between trauma and transition to full psychosis offer hope that there may be strong protective factors that can be bolstered during treatment of early subthreshold psychotic symptoms or that there may be additional risk factors that can help identify a subgroup of CHR individuals at particular risk for worsening psychosis related to CT.

TRAUMA ASSESSMENT IN THE CHR SYNDROME

To better understand the role of trauma in the CHR syndrome, current methods of trauma assessment must be harmonized. Although they are used regularly with individuals with psychosis or the CHR syndrome, no existing trauma or SLE measures have been developed or validated specifically with these populations. The National Child Trauma Stress Network (146) and the American Academy of Child and Adolescent Psychiatry (147) provide guidelines on the appropriate assessment and treatment of children and adolescent who may have experienced trauma. These guidelines stress the need to briefly screen all children in a given setting for the experience of traumatic events and, in the presence of a positive screen, to follow up with a more detailed assessment in order to appropriately guide treatment planning.

Trauma experiences and associated clinical consequences can be identified through a variety of methods. Brief self-report screening questionnaires retrospectively assess for the occurrence and reaction to a variety of traumatic events. Brief screening measures for assessing only exposure to traumatic events include the Brief Trauma Questionnaire (148) and the CTQ (149). Measures examining both the experience of trauma *and* its psychological impact (e.g., assesses symptoms and distress) include the Trauma Symptom Checklist for Children (150) and the Child Posttraumatic Symptom Scale (151). The UCLA PTSD Reaction Index for DSM-IV (152) is an example of a combined measure that starts with a brief questionnaire to assess for a history of traumatic events, which is then followed by a semi-structured interview to determine distress and impact of those events to support a diagnosis of PTSD. Some measures also include a collateral informant report, such as the Trauma Symptom Checklist for Young Children (153). Finally, semi-structured diagnostic interviews such as the Structured Clinical Interview for DSM-IV Axis-I Disorders (SCID-I) (154) and the Kiddie Schedule for

Affective Disorders and Schizophrenia (155) include sections to assess for a history of traumatic events and their clinical sequelae. Measures most commonly used in CHR research studies are the CTQ, Trauma History Screen, and the CT and Abuse Scale. For a comprehensive list of trauma experience and symptom measures, please refer to the National Child Traumatic Stress Network and the American Academy of Child and Adolescent Psychiatry resources (146, 147).

While various measures of traumatic experiences and SLEs are available, there may be concerns about using them with CHR individuals. For instance, if there are concerns about early trauma experiences being distorted by the delusional thinking (e.g., suspiciousness), collateral reports from family, previous treatment providers, and school staff can clarify the validity of the individual's reported experience. Conversely, it may be difficult to determine if certain attenuated symptoms (e.g., suspiciousness) are associated with reality-based experiences of victimization and better accounted for by a trauma reaction than a psychotic-spectrum symptom. However, a previous study that has examined the reliability of reported CT experiences by individuals with psychotic disorders found that they were retrospectively accurate and stable over time irrespective of current psychopathology (156). Patients may tend to underreport CT while in treatment for psychosis and could be more forthcoming when experiencing more severe psychotic symptoms. Nevertheless, studies have tackled this issue by enforcing other measures for additional precaution. A UK study on a national sample of (n = 2,172) 12-year-old twin children showed that research protocol can easily be structured to determine credibility of children's reporting in clinical interviews, such as enforcing a rating system that codes from 0 (i.e., not a symptom), 1 (i.e., a likely symptom), to 2 (i.e., definite symptom); and enlisting the clinical judgment of various professionals who are familiar with the CHR group/symptoms within the psychosis spectrum or whose area of specialization is with youth (41). Additionally, clinicians may worry that discussing trauma as part of an evaluation can trigger worsening of psychotic symptoms, which may lead to avoidance of appropriate assessment. Contrary to this belief, research suggests that appropriate and sensitive evaluation of trauma does not increase subjective distress (157, 158).

One significant challenge of concordant trauma and SLE assessment in this population is that the age of individuals often ranges from 12–30, and instruments are often designed for either children, adolescents, or adults. The types of trauma and SLEs experienced by these different age groups vary considerably, with school and family-related stressors (e.g., divorce of parents) relevant for children and work and romantic relationship-related stressors (e.g., one's own divorce) more relevant for young adults. The measurement of trauma and stressors overtime in the same individual creates challenges in the consistent use of instruments. While a variety of appropriate measures exists to aide in the identification of trauma, there is currently no standardized trauma evaluation protocol for CHR groups as part of research or clinical practice. This lack of detailed information related to trauma or SLE that can be compared across clinics and research precludes our ability to effectively target treatment or elucidate relationships in research.

CHR and Trauma Interventions

Given the high prevalence and relevance of trauma in the CHR syndrome, which we have outlined above, the next step is translating this knowledge to improve interventions for this population. Trauma and psychosis are two of the most difficult clinical symptoms to target and manage in psychiatric treatment; combined, they are considered by most mental health providers to be one of the most complex forms of mental illness, usually requiring a greater level of care. Typically, when individuals present to clinical treatment settings for either symptoms of trauma or psychosis, they are often referred to clinics with an expertise in one of the two areas of concern because few programs provide integrated care for both issues (159). Consequently, there is a growing need for treatment settings that provide clinical expertise on both trauma and psychosis. Given the complex interplay of symptoms, the current model of the trauma-psychosis cycle (see **Figure 3**) suggests that CHR individuals who present with trauma history do not share the same expected course of treatment and recovery as those without a history of trauma. As shown by Cragin and colleagues (159), there is a growing need to address trauma in EP care. Recent research on trauma treatment in psychosis has shown the impact of prolonged exposure, an evidence-based trauma treatment, on reducing trauma symptoms and psychosis in individuals with chronic schizophrenia and comorbid trauma (160). However, many clinicians are concerned that addressing trauma in treatment may trigger worsening of psychosis (161). Given the lack of attention to trauma-focused treatments in psychosis, it is no surprise that even less has been developed in EP, despite the preponderance of first episode and CHR individuals who endorse CT. To date, no clinical trials have been published evaluating interventions for trauma in CHR youth. Currently, many CHR clinics utilize treatment based on cognitive–behavioral therapy (CBT) methods for individual treatment and family-based treatments [e.g., multi-family group (MFG) or functional family therapy (FFT)] to address social stress and support. The addition of components from Trauma-Focused Cognitive Behavioral Therapy (TF-CBT) represent a potential approach to providing trauma-informed care for CHR individuals that is consistent with prominent treatment models for this population. Both CBTp and TF-CBT start with providing psychoeducation and enhancing coping skills, then introduce methods of cognitive coping, before providing opportunities to address psychotic symptoms, or trauma symptoms *via* exposure. Similar to MFG and FFT, TF-CBT also integrates family members to maintain support for the individual and ensure generalization outside of the therapeutic context. While TF-CBT is a promising approach for the CHR population, it has not yet been fully developed nor evaluated. This is a critical area of future research.

IMPLICATIONS AND FUTURE DIRECTIONS

Overall, recent findings continue to provide supporting evidence for higher rates of trauma among CHR individuals compared to HC, consistent with Kraan and colleagues (5). Emerging studies

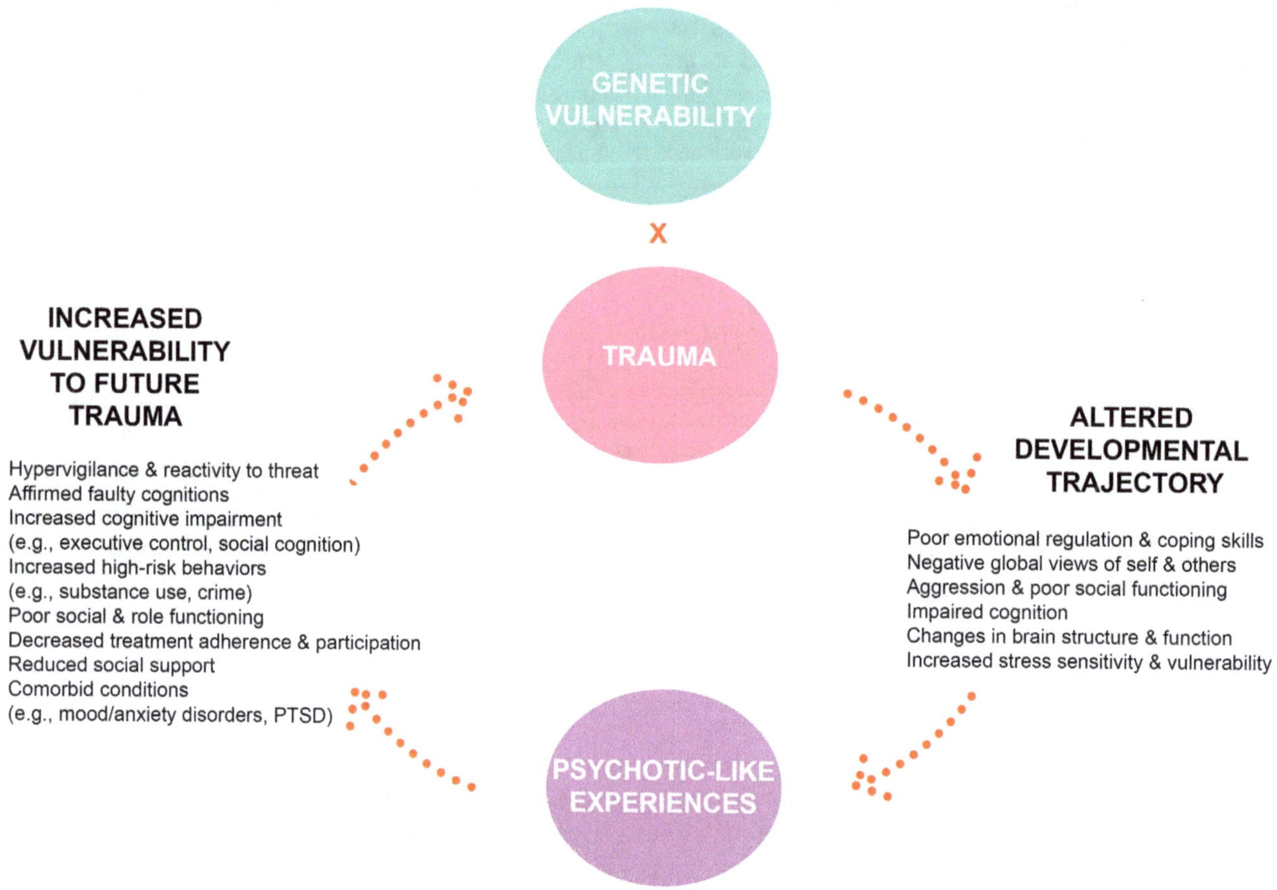

FIGURE 3 | **The cycle of trauma, psychotic-like experiences, and vulnerability.**

continue to show a strong relationship between CT and severity of psychosis symptoms in the CHR population (34, 45, 51). Studies of CHR individuals with CT also repeatedly demonstrate a negative relationship with cognitive, clinical, and social functioning outcomes overtime (34, 59). Trauma appears to predict conversion to psychosis, but may not function independently of other known risk factors such as more severe positive symptoms, cognition, and functioning (16). While CHR individuals may demonstrate heightened stress reactivity at the clinical and biological levels (119, 134), the role of SLEs in triggering transition to psychosis has not been clearly substantiated. As a result, the current proposed model of the trauma-psychosis cycle (**Figure 3**) focuses solely on CT and not SLE. However, SLE may be an important area to consider when refining the proposed trauma–psychosis model when additional studies provide a richer understanding of its influence on psychosis risk. Finally, the mechanisms underlying the relationship of trauma to psychosis onset in CHR individuals are not fully understood, although there is some evidence for both cognitive and biological (HPA axis, gene–environment interaction) models (111, 141). Most importantly, no appropriate interventions have been developed and validated specifically for trauma in CHR individuals, despite an enormous need for such an approach. The overall findings suggest that the study of trauma, stress, and psychosis risk is still in its early stages and requires continued work. Several suggestions are provided to further research and clinical interventions in addressing the role of trauma and SLEs in psychosis among CHR individuals.

Recommendations for Future Research

First, larger sample sizes in CHR trauma studies would support stronger inferences in research findings *via* increased statistical power that allows for testing of interaction models, mechanistic mediation models, and simultaneous testing of multiple predictors of outcomes. Adequate representation of minority groups and more international research would help to evaluate potential demographic differences. Second, inclusion of a psychiatric control group (e.g., mood and anxiety disorders without psychotic-like experiences) would prove useful in delineating what is unique to CHR individuals and what is shared with other symptom domains. Third, a standardized measure, validated for the adolescent/young adult population would help to compare across studies and assess cohorts longitudinally. The measure should assess both the number and age of occurrence of traumatic events in order to investigate whether there is a "critical period" for CT and to test stress-sensitization models.

Moving forward, the research definitions for trauma types and SLEs should be consistent and specific in order to facilitate comparison of research results across studies. For instance, some measures assess narrow definitions of trauma while other "trauma" measures also include events that are less severe and are better categorized as SLE. As another example, there is great disparity between individuals and families concerning the definition of childhood physical abuse. Researchers would benefit by providing participants with an operational definition of childhood physical abuse to help increase their responses' internal validity. Similarly, differences in the definitions of abuse across cultures should also be investigated to clarify the constructs that are measures as part of a study. In addition, the current studies examined suggest that sexual abuse history is a prominent area that demands greater focus and consideration in CHR population research, given the psychological cost of illness that may follow. Based on the current review's proposed conceptualization of trauma and psychosis risk occurring in a cyclical and repeated pattern, it is suggested that future studies on CHR individuals should consider examining the influence of complex trauma (i.e., multiple types of trauma) on psychosis risk. Additional variables to consider would be the severity and duration of trauma experiences as well as differentiating between a single traumatic event and chronic abuse, with the latter potentially conferring greater risk. Furthermore, research should delve deeper into gender differences among CHR individuals with trauma, given evidence of differential rates and effects in psychosis (42, 53).

Recommendations for Treatment and Interventions

For clinical recommendations and improved delivery of service, it would be important for clinicians to determine a treatment plan that considers both trauma and psychosis symptoms. A decision-tree process that decides primary areas to initially target would be helpful and should be a focus of future clinical research (90). Clinicians should be able to determine whether trauma is a significant centerpiece of the presenting problem or a complicating factor that aggravates the individual's psychosis symptoms. Case conceptualizations should also consider modifications of standard treatment when necessary in order to better address the client's needs. During intake and clinical evaluations, it may be useful to create a timeline of CHR individual's trauma and SLEs in relation to their other clinical symptoms and associated functional decline. This documented information may prove imperative use for case conceptualization and treatment planning. In reference to the trauma psychosis cycle (**Figure 3**), the timeline of events in a CHR individual's life may give helpful information into the nature of their trauma history, its severity, and the level of treatment required.

The accumulated knowledge on trauma and psychosis thus far highlights that children and youth who experience CT and/or SLEs should be referred for immediate clinical evaluation and intervention. In particular, youth who report early bullying experiences should be taken seriously, as it can be one of the earliest forms of social stress that persists and influences various domains of functioning and well-being. Individuals experiencing psychotic-like symptoms should be encouraged to seek treatment to boost their cognitive and behavioral coping skills in order to help them combat increased vulnerability to future trauma. Families and parents have a pivotal role in increasing the effectiveness of any treatment intervention. As demonstrated by the trauma-psychosis cycle (**Figure 3**), the experience of trauma can be pervasive and persistent. Clinicians are strongly urged to involve parents, family members, or other significant people in treatment with CHR youth dealing with trauma and psychosis to enhance their social support system and buffer them against additional stressors.

A particular challenge is that many clinicians working with adolescents have not received sufficient training regarding psychotic-spectrum conditions, and specialists in EP may not have sufficient training in trauma treatment (159). Broad availability of training across clinical degree programs in the US regarding assessment and treatment of psychosis would help to improve community providers' accurate detection of potential CHR syndromes in traumatized youth. Further, training for coordinated specialty care programs that treat EP should include training modules on the appropriate assessment and treatment of trauma.

As advocated by previous research (61, 142), a standard protocol for CT or SLE assessment during all initial patient evaluations should be used in pediatric and behavioral health settings. Due to the sensitive nature of the assessment questions, clinicians and other medical providers should recognize the appropriate format of assessing trauma history in youth (i.e., separately or with their parents/caregivers in the room). Akin to training on suicide risk screening, clinical staff should be knowledgeable on how to identify and assess for trauma when working with CHR youth.

Most importantly, based on the current collective knowledge on trauma and stress in EP, we conclude that evidence-based treatments addressing trauma symptomology in the CHR population is desperately needed. Without a targeted and evidence-based treatment for a large number of CHR youth with trauma history and/or SLE, current interventions may not always be successful in impacting their illness trajectory. Yet, the preliminary outcomes from current studies show promising evidence; with improved understanding of the mechanisms that perpetuate the cycle of trauma among CHR individuals, we can promote resilience and mitigate the vulnerability of CHR individuals to developing a psychotic disorder and improve their chances of recovery from the CHR syndrome.

AUTHOR CONTRIBUTIONS

All the authors participated in the writing of the manuscript. DM was the lead author and primary writer. SC and AY contributed in the writing of Section "Mechanisms of Trauma and Stress in the CHR Population." LK conducted a wide literature review of CHR studies and contributed in the writing of Section "Trauma Experiences in the CHR Population." SY coauthored Section "Trauma Experiences in the CHR Population" and

Section "Recommendations for Future Research." BS coauthored the "Differential Diagnosis of PTSD and CHR Status" subsection. TN coauthored Sections "Trauma Assessment in the CHR Syndrome" and "Implications and Future Directions" and provided overall feedback on the manuscript. RL was the senior author of the manuscript and provided overall guidance and feedback on topic of trauma, stress, and psychosis risk in CHR group. All authors approved the final version of the manuscript.

REFERENCES

1. Aakre JM, Brown CH, Benson KM, Drapalski AL, Gearon JS. Trauma exposure and PTSD in women with schizophrenia and coexisting substance use disorders: comparisons to women with severe depression and substance use disorders. *Psychiatry Res* (2014) 220(3):840–5. doi:10.1016/j.psychres.2014.10.004
2. Sahin S, Yuksel C, Guler J, Karadayi G, Akturan E, Gode E, et al. The history of childhood trauma among individuals with ultra high risk for psychosis is as common as among patients with first-episode schizophrenia. *Early Interv Psychiatry* (2013) 7(4):414–20. doi:10.1111/eip.12022
3. Conus P, Cotton S, Schimmelmann BG, McGorry PD, Lambert M. Pretreatment and outcome correlates of sexual and physical trauma in an epidemiological cohort of first-episode psychosis patients. *Schizophr Bull* (2010) 36(6):1105–14. doi:10.1093/schbul/sbp009
4. Kilcommons AM, Morrison AP. Relationships between trauma and psychosis: an exploration of cognitive and dissociative factors. *Acta Psychiatr Scand* (2005) 112(5):351–9. doi:10.1111/j.1600-0447.2005.00623.x
5. Kraan T, Velthorst E, Smit F, de Haan L, van der Gaag M. Trauma and recent life events in individuals at ultra high risk for psychosis: review and meta-analysis. *Schizophr Res* (2015) 161(2–3):143–9. doi:10.1016/j.schres.2014.11.026
6. Gerrity E, Folcarelli C. *Child Traumatic Stress: What Every Policymaker Should Know*. Los Angeles, CA; Durham, NC: National Center for Child Traumatic Stress (2008).
7. Miller TJ, McGlashan TH, Woods SW, Stein K, Driesen N, Corcoran CM, et al. Symptom assessment in schizophrenic prodromal states. *Psychiatr Q* (1999) 70(4):273–87. doi:10.1023/A:1022034115078
8. Yung AR, Yuen HP, McGorry PD, Phillips LJ, Kelly D, Dell'Olio M, et al. Mapping the onset of psychosis: the comprehensive assessment of at-risk mental states. *Aust N Z J Psychiatry* (2005) 39(11–12):964–71. doi:10.1080/j.1440-1614.2005.01714.x
9. Fusar-Poli P, Cappucciati M, Rutigliano G, Lee T, Beverly Q, Bonoldi I, et al. Towards a standard psychometric diagnostic interview for subjects at ultra high risk of psychosis: CAARMS versus SIPS. *Psychiatry J* (2016) 2016:7146341. doi:10.1155/2016/7146341
10. Gross G, Huber G, Klosterkötter J, Linz M. *Bonner Skala für die Beurteilung von Basissymptomen Bonn Scale for the Assessment of Basic Symptoms Manual, Kommentar, Dokumentationsbogen*. New York: Springer-Verlag (1987).
11. Klosterkotter J, Hellmich M, Steinmeyer EM, Schultze-Lutter F. Diagnosing schizophrenia in the initial prodromal phase. *Arch Gen Psychiatry* (2001) 58(2):158–64. doi:10.1001/archpsyc.58.2.158
12. Fusar-Poli P, Bonoldi I, Yung AR, Borgwardt S, Kempton MJ, Valmaggia L, et al. Predicting psychosis meta-analysis of transition outcomes in individuals at high clinical risk. *Arch Gen Psychiatry* (2012) 69(3):220–9. doi:10.1001/archgenpsychiatry.2011.1472
13. Cannon TD, Cadenhead K, Cornblatt B, Woods SW, Addington J, Walker E, et al. Prediction of psychosis in youth at high clinical risk: a multisite longitudinal study in North America. *Arch Gen Psychiatry* (2008) 65(1):28–37. doi:10.1001/archgenpsychiatry.2007.3
14. Lichtenstein P, Yip BH, Bjork C, Pawitan Y, Cannon TD, Sullivan PF, et al. Common genetic determinants of schizophrenia and bipolar disorder in Swedish families: a population-based study. *Lancet* (2009) 373(9659):234–9. doi:10.1016/S0140-6736(09)60072-6
15. Kendler KS, Diehl SR. The genetics of schizophrenia: a current, genetic-epidemiologic perspective. *Schizophr Bull* (1993) 19(2):261–85. doi:10.1093/schbul/19.2.261
16. Cannon TD, Yu C, Addington J, Bearden CE, Cadenhead KS, Cornblatt BA, et al. An individualized risk calculator for research in prodromal psychosis. *Am J Psychiatry* (2016) 173(10):980–8. doi:10.1176/appi.ajp.2016.15070890
17. Fusar-Poli P, Borgwardt S, Bechdolf A, Addington J, Riecher-Rossler A, Schultze-Lutter F, et al. The psychosis high-risk state: a comprehensive state-of-the-art review. *JAMA Psychiatry* (2013) 70(1):107–20. doi:10.1001/jamapsychiatry.2013.269
18. Marshall C, Deighton S, Cadenhead KS, Cannon TD, Cornblatt BA, McGlashan TH, et al. The violent content in attenuated psychotic symptoms. *Psychiatry Res* (2016) 242:61–6. doi:10.1016/j.psychres.2016.05.005
19. Schmidt A, Cappucciati M, Radua J, Rutigliano G, Rocchetti M, Dell'Osso L, et al. Improving prognostic accuracy in subjects at clinical high risk for psychosis: systematic review of predictive models and meta-analytical sequential testing simulation. *Schizophr Bull* (2017) 43(2):375–88. doi:10.1093/schbul/sbw098
20. Simon AE, Borgwardt S, Riecher-Rossler A, Velthorst E, de Haan L, Fusar-Poli P. Moving beyond transition outcomes: meta-analysis of remission rates in individuals at high clinical risk for psychosis. *Psychiatry Res* (2013) 209(3):266–72. doi:10.1016/j.psychres.2013.03.004
21. Nelson B, Yuen HP, Wood SJ, Lin A, Spiliotacopoulos D, Bruxner A, et al. Long-term follow-up of a group at ultra high risk ("prodromal") for psychosis: the PACE 400 study. *Jama Psychiatry* (2013) 70(8):793–802. doi:10.1001/jamapsychiatry.2013.1270
22. Addington J, Cornblatt BA, Cadenhead KS, Cannon TD, McGlashan TH, Perkins DO, et al. At clinical high risk for psychosis: outcome for nonconverters. *Am J Psychiatry* (2011) 168(8):800–5. doi:10.1176/appi.ajp.2011.10081191
23. Putnam FW. The impact of trauma on child development. *Juv Fam Court J* (2006) 57(1):1–11. doi:10.1111/j.1755-6988.2006.tb00110.x
24. Tunnard C, Rane LJ, Wooderson SC, Markopoulou K, Poon L, Fekadu A, et al. The impact of childhood adversity on suicidality and clinical course in treatment-resistant depression. *J Affect Disord* (2014) 15(2–154):122–30. doi:10.1016/j.jad.2013.06.037
25. Ashford CD, Ashcroft K, Maguire N. Emotions, traits and negative beliefs as possible mediators in the relationship between childhood experiences of being bullied and paranoid thinking in a non-clinical sample. *J Exp Psychopathol* (2012) 3(4):624–38. doi:10.5127/jep.020611
26. Bentall RP, Wickham S, Shevlin M, Varese F. Do specific early-life adversities lead to specific symptoms of psychosis? A study from the 2007 the adult psychiatric morbidity survey. *Schizophr Bull* (2012) 38(4):734–40. doi:10.1093/schbul/sbs049
27. De Loore E, Drukker M, Gunther N, Feron F, Deboutte D, Sabbe B, et al. Childhood negative experiences and subclinical psychosis in adolescence: a longitudinal general population study. *Early Interv Psychiatry* (2007) 1(2):201–7. doi:10.1111/j.1751-7893.2007.00027.x
28. Heiervang E, Goodman R. Advantages and limitations of web-based surveys: evidence from a child mental health survey. *Soc Psychiatry Psychiatr Epidemiol* (2011) 46(1):69–76. doi:10.1007/s00127-009-0171-9
29. Kelleher I, Harley M, Lynch F, Arseneault L, Fitzpatrick C, Cannon M. Associations between childhood trauma, bullying and psychotic symptoms among a school-based adolescent sample. *Br J Psychiatry* (2008) 193(5):378–82. doi:10.1192/bjp.bp.108.049536
30. Kelleher I, Keeley H, Corcoran P, Ramsay H, Wasserman C, Carli V, et al. Childhood trauma and psychosis in a prospective cohort study: cause, effect, and directionality. *Am J Psychiatry* (2013) 170(7):734–41. doi:10.1176/appi.ajp.2012.12091169
31. Lataster T, van Os J, Drukker M, Henquet C, Feron F, Gunther N, et al. Childhood victimisation and developmental expression of non-clinical delusional ideation and hallucinatory experiences: victimisation and non-clinical psychotic experiences. *Soc Psychiatry Psychiatr Epidemiol* (2006) 41(6):423–8. doi:10.1007/s00127-006-0060-4

32. Campbell ML, Morrison AP. The relationship between bullying, psychotic-like experiences and appraisals in 14-16-year olds. *Behav Res Ther* (2007) 45(7):1579–91. doi:10.1016/j.brat.2006.11.009
33. Read J, van Os J, Morrison AP, Ross CA. Childhood trauma, psychosis and schizophrenia: a literature review with theoretical and clinical implications. *Acta Psychiatr Scand* (2005) 112(5):330–50. doi:10.1111/j.1600-0447.2005.00634.x
34. Kraan T, van Dam DS, Velthorst E, de Ruigh EL, Nieman DH, Durston S, et al. Childhood trauma and clinical outcome in patients at ultra-high risk of transition to psychosis. *Schizophr Res* (2015) 169(1–3):193–8. doi:10.1016/j.schres.2015.10.030
35. Kessler RC, Sonnega A, Bromet E, Hughes M, Nelson CB. Posttraumatic stress disorder in the National Comorbidity Survey. *Arch Gen Psychiatry* (1995) 52(12):1048–60. doi:10.1001/archpsyc.1995.03950240066012
36. Finkelhor D, Ormrod R, Turner H, Hamby SL. The victimization of children and youth: a comprehensive, national survey. *Child Maltreat* (2005) 10(1):5–25. doi:10.1177/1077559504271287
37. Copeland WE, Keeler G, Angold A, Costello EJ. Traumatic events and posttraumatic stress in childhood. *Arch Gen Psychiatry* (2007) 64(5):577–84. doi:10.1001/archpsyc.64.5.577
38. Felitti VJ, Anda RF, Nordenberg D, Williamson DF, Spitz AM, Edwards V, et al. Relationship of childhood abuse and household dysfunction to many of the leading causes of death in adults. The Adverse Childhood Experiences (ACE) Study. *Am J Prev Med* (1998) 14(4):245–58.
39. Muenzenmaier KH, Seixas AA, Schneeberger AR, Castille DM, Battaglia J, Link BG. Cumulative effects of stressful childhood experiences on delusions and hallucinations. *J Trauma Dissociation* (2015) 16(4):442–62. doi:10.1080/15299732.2015.1018475
40. Bechdolf A, Thompson A, Nelson B, Cotton S, Simmons MB, Amminger GP, et al. Experience of trauma and conversion to psychosis in an ultra-high-risk (prodromal) group. *Acta Psychiatr Scand* (2010) 121(5):377–84. doi:10.1111/j.1600-0447.2010.01542.x
41. Arseneault L, Cannon M, Fisher HL, Polanczyk G, Moffitt TE, Caspi A. Childhood trauma and children's emerging psychotic symptoms: a genetically sensitive longitudinal cohort study. *Am J Psychiatry* (2011) 168(1):65–72. doi:10.1176/appi.ajp.2010.10040567
42. Addington J, Stowkowy J, Cadenhead KS, Cornblatt BA, McGlashan TH, Perkins DO, et al. Early traumatic experiences in those at clinical high risk for psychosis. *Early Interv Psychiatry* (2013) 7(3):300–5. doi:10.1111/eip.12020
43. Devylder JE, Ben-David S, Schobel SA, Kimhy D, Malaspina D, Corcoran CM. Temporal association of stress sensitivity and symptoms in individuals at clinical high risk for psychosis. *Psychol Med* (2013) 43(2):259–68. doi:10.1017/S0033291712001262
44. Falukozi E, Addington J. Impact of trauma on attenuated psychotic symptoms. *Psychosis* (2012) 4(3):203–12. doi:10.1080/17522439.2011.62686712
45. Kline E, Millman ZB, Denenny D, Wilson C, Thompson E, Demro C, et al. Trauma and psychosis symptoms in a sample of help-seeking youth. *Schizophr Res* (2016) 175(1–3):174–9. doi:10.1016/j.schres.2016.04.006
46. Magaud E, Nyman K, Addington J. Cyberbullying in those at clinical high risk for psychosis. *Early Interv Psychiatry* (2013) 7(4):427–30. doi:10.1111/eip.12013
47. Mason O, Startup M, Halpin S, Schall U, Conrad A, Carr V. Risk factors for transition to first episode psychosis among individuals with 'at-risk mental states'. *Schizophr Res* (2004) 71(2–3):227–37. doi:10.1016/j.schres.2004.04.006
48. Phillips LJ, Edwards J, McMurray N, Francey S. Comparison of experiences of stress and coping between young people at risk of psychosis and a non-clinical cohort. *Behav Cogn Psychother* (2012) 40(1):69–88. doi:10.1017/S1352465811000397
49. Russo DA, Stochl J, Painter M, Dobler V, Jackson E, Jones PB, et al. Trauma history characteristics associated with mental states at clinical high risk for psychosis. *Psychiatry Res* (2014) 220(1–2):237–44. doi:10.1016/j.psychres.2014.08.028
50. Stowkowy J, Addington J. Predictors of a clinical high risk status among individuals with a family history of psychosis. *Schizophr Res* (2013) 147(2–3):281–6. doi:10.1016/j.schres.2013.03.030
51. Stowkowy J, Liu L, Cadenhead KS, Cannon TD, Cornblatt BA, McGlashan TH, et al. Early traumatic experiences, perceived discrimination and conversion to psychosis in those at clinical high risk for psychosis. *Soc Psychiatry Psychiatr Epidemiol* (2016) 51(4):497–503. doi:10.1007/s00127-016-1182-y
52. Thompson A, Marwaha S, Nelson B, Wood SJ, McGorry PD, Yung AR, et al. Do affective or dissociative symptoms mediate the association between childhood sexual trauma and transition to psychosis in an ultra-high risk cohort? *Psychiatry Res* (2016) 236:182–5. doi:10.1016/j.psychres.2016.01.017
53. Thompson A, Nelson B, McNab C, Simmons M, Leicester S, McGorry PD, et al. Psychotic symptoms with sexual content in the "ultra high risk" for psychosis population: frequency and association with sexual trauma. *Psychiatry Res* (2010) 177(1–2):84–91. doi:10.1016/j.psychres.2010.02.011
54. Thompson A, Papas A, Bartholomeusz C, Nelson B, Yung A. Externalized attributional bias in the ultra high risk (UHR) for psychosis population. *Psychiatry Res* (2013) 206(2–3):200–5. doi:10.1016/j.psychres.2012.10.017
55. Thompson AD, Nelson B, Yuen HP, Lin A, Amminger GP, McGorry PD, et al. Sexual trauma increases the risk of developing psychosis in an ultra high-risk "prodromal" population. *Schizophr Bull* (2014) 40(3):697–706. doi:10.1093/schbul/sbt032
56. Thompson JL, Kelly M, Kimhy D, Harkavy-Friedman JM, Khan S, Messinger JW, et al. Childhood trauma and prodromal symptoms among individuals at clinical high risk for psychosis. *Schizophr Res* (2009) 108(1–3):176–81. doi:10.1016/j.schres.2008.12.005
57. Thompson KN, Phillips LJ, Komesaroff P, Yuen HP, Wood SJ, Pantelis C, et al. Stress and HPA-axis functioning in young people at ultra high risk for psychosis. *J Psychiatr Res* (2007) 41(7):561–9. doi:10.1016/j.jpsychires.2006.05.010
58. Tikka M, Luutonen S, Ilonen T, Tuominen L, Kotimaki M, Hankala J, et al. Childhood trauma and premorbid adjustment among individuals at clinical high risk for psychosis and normal control subjects. *Early Interv Psychiatry* (2013) 7(1):51–7. doi:10.1111/j.1751-7893.2012.00391.x
59. Üçok A, Kaya H, Ugurpala C, Cikrikcili U, Ergul C, Yokusoglu C, et al. History of childhood physical trauma is related to cognitive decline in individuals with ultra-high risk for psychosis. *Schizophr Res* (2015) 169(1–3):199–203. doi:10.1016/j.schres.2015.08.038
60. Velthorst E, Nelson B, O'Connor K, Mossaheb N, de Haan L, Bruxner A, et al. History of trauma and the association with baseline symptoms in an ultra-high risk for psychosis cohort. *Psychiatry Res* (2013) 210(1):75–81. doi:10.1016/j.psychres.2013.06.007
61. Yung AR, Cotter J, Wood SJ, McGorry P, Thompson AD, Nelson B, et al. Childhood maltreatment and transition to psychotic disorder independently predict long-term functioning in young people at ultra-high risk for psychosis. *Psychol Med* (2015) 45(16):3453–65. doi:10.1017/S003329171500135X
62. Zimbron J, Ruiz de Azua S, Khandaker GM, Gandamaneni PK, Crane CM, Gonzalez-Pinto A, et al. Clinical and sociodemographic comparison of people at high-risk for psychosis and with first-episode psychosis. *Acta Psychiatr Scand* (2013) 127(3):210–6. doi:10.1111/acps.12000
63. Asendorpf JB, Conner M, De Fruyt F, De Houwer J, Denissen JJ, Fiedler K, et al. Recommendations for increasing replicability in psychology. *Eur J Pers* (2013) 27(2):108–19. doi:10.1002/per.1919
64. U.S. Department of Health and Human Services, Administration for Children and Families, Administration on Children Youth and Families, Children's Bureau. *Child Maltreatment 2014*. (2016). Available from http://www.acf.hhs.gov/programs/cb/research-data-technology/statistics-research/child-maltreatment
65. Dube SR, Anda RF, Whitfield CL, Brown DW, Felitti VJ, Dong M, et al. Long-term consequences of childhood sexual abuse by gender of victim. *Am J Prev Med* (2005) 28(5):430–8. doi:10.1016/j.amepre.2005.01.015
66. Al Mamun A, Alati R, O'Callaghan M, Hayatbakhsh MR, O'Callaghan FV, Najman JM, et al. Does childhood sexual abuse have an effect on young adults' nicotine disorder (dependence or withdrawal)? Evidence from a birth cohort study. *Addiction* (2007) 102(4):647–54. doi:10.1111/j.1360-0443.2006.01732.x/abstract
67. Kendler KS, Bulik CM, Silberg J, Hettema JM, Myers J, Prescott CA. Childhood sexual abuse and adult psychiatric and substance use disorders in women: an epidemiological and Cotwin control analysis. *Arch Gen Psychiatry* (2000) 57(10):953–9. doi:10.1001/archpsyc.57.10.953
68. Young MS, Harford K-L, Kinder B, Savell JK. The relationship between childhood sexual abuse and adult mental health among undergraduates: victim gender doesn't matter. *J Interpers Violence* (2007) 22(10):1315–31. doi:10.1177/0886260507304552

69. Leserman J. Sexual abuse history: prevalence, health effects, mediators, and psychological treatment. *Psychosom Med* (2005) 67(6):906–15. doi:10.1097/01.psy.0000188405.54425.20
70. Child Welfare Information Gateway. *Definitions of Child Abuse and Neglect*. Washington, DC: U.S. Department of Health and Human Services Children's Bureau (2016).
71. Arseneault L, Bowes L, Shakoor S. Bullying victimization in youths and mental health problems: 'much ado about nothing'? *Psychol Med* (2010) 40(5):717–29. doi:10.1017/S0033291709991383
72. Frame L, Morrison AP. Causes of posttraumatic stress disorder in psychotic patients. *Arch Gen Psychiatry* (2001) 58(3):305–6. doi:10.1001/archpsyc.58.3.305
73. Meyer H, Taiminen T, Vuori T, Aijala A, Helenius H. Posttraumatic stress disorder symptoms related to psychosis and acute involuntary hospitalization in schizophrenic and delusional patients. *J Nerv Ment Dis* (1999) 187(6):343–52. doi:10.1097/00005053-199906000-00003
74. Reddy LF, Spaulding WD. Understanding adverse experiences in the psychiatric institution: the importance of child abuse histories in iatrogenic trauma. *Psychol Serv* (2010) 7(4):242–53. doi:10.1037/a0020316
75. Berry K, Ford S, Jellicoe-Jones L, Haddock G. PTSD symptoms associated with the experiences of psychosis and hospitalisation: a review of the literature. *Clin Psychol Rev* (2013) 33(4):526–38. doi:10.1016/j.cpr.2013.01.011
76. Centofanti AT, Smith DI, Altieri T. Posttraumatic stress disorder as a reaction to the experience of psychosis and its sequelae. *Clin Psychol* (2005) 9(1):15–23. doi:10.1080/13284200500116963
77. Gibson LE, Anglin DM, Klugman JT, Reeves LE, Fineberg AM, Maxwell SD, et al. Stress sensitivity mediates the relationship between traumatic life events and attenuated positive psychotic symptoms differentially by gender in a college population sample. *J Psychiatr Res* (2014) 53:111–8. doi:10.1016/j.jpsychires.2014.02.020
78. Garcia M, Montalvo I, Creus M, Cabezas A, Sole M, Algora MJ, et al. Sex differences in the effect of childhood trauma on the clinical expression of early psychosis. *Compr Psychiatry* (2016) 68:86–96. doi:10.1016/j.comppsych.2016.04.004
79. Chapman DP, Whitfield CL, Felitti VJ, Dube SR, Edwards VJ, Anda RF. Adverse childhood experiences and the risk of depressive disorders in adulthood. *J Affect Disord* (2004) 82(2):217–25. doi:10.1016/j.jad.2003.12.013
80. Whitfield CL, Dube SR, Felitti VJ, Anda RF. Adverse childhood experiences and hallucinations. *Child Abuse Negl* (2005) 29(7):797–810. doi:10.1016/j.chiabu.2005.01.004
81. Wolke D, Lereya ST, Fisher HL, Lewis G, Zammit S. Bullying in elementary school and psychotic experiences at 18 years: a longitudinal, population-based cohort study. *Psychol Med* (2014) 44(10):2199–211. doi:10.1017/S0033291713002912
82. Trotta A, Di Forti M, Mondelli V, Dazzan P, Pariante C, David A, et al. Prevalence of bullying victimisation amongst first-episode psychosis patients and unaffected controls. *Schizophr Res* (2013) 150(1):169–75. doi:10.1016/j.schres.2013.07.001
83. Shakoor S, McGuire P, Cardno AG, Freeman D, Plomin R, Ronald A. A shared genetic propensity underlies experiences of bullying victimization in late childhood and self-rated paranoid thinking in adolescence. *Schizophr Bull* (2015) 41(3):754–63. doi:10.1093/schbul/sbu142
84. Schreier A, Wolke D, Thomas K, Horwood J, Hollis C, Gunnell D, et al. Prospective study of peer victimization in childhood and psychotic symptoms in a nonclinical population at age 12 years. *Arch Gen Psychiatry* (2009) 66(5):527–36. doi:10.1001/archgenpsychiatry.2009.23
85. Bond L, Carlin JB, Thomas L, Rubin K, Patton G. Does bullying cause emotional problems? A prospective study of young teenagers. *BMJ* (2001) 323(7311):480–4. doi:10.1136/bmj.323.7311.480
86. Walker E. Independent and joint predictive power of life events, daily stress, and cortisol in relation to conversion to psychosis. *Psychoneuroendocrinology* (2016) 71:9. doi:10.1016/j.psyneuen.2016.07.032
87. Beards S, Gayer-Anderson C, Borges S, Dewey ME, Fisher HL, Morgan C. Life events and psychosis: a review and meta-analysis. *Schizophr Bull* (2013) 39(4):740–7. doi:10.1093/schbul/sbt065
88. Niendam TA, Berzak J, Cannon TD, Bearden CE. Obsessive compulsive symptoms in the psychosis prodrome: correlates of clinical and functional outcome. *Schizophr Res* (2009) 108(1–3):170–5. doi:10.1016/j.schres.2008.11.023
89. Fusar-Poli P, Nelson B, Valmaggia L, Yung AR, McGuire PK. Comorbid depressive and anxiety disorders in 509 individuals with an at-risk mental state: impact on psychopathology and transition to psychosis. *Schizophr Bull* (2014) 40(1):120–31. doi:10.1093/schbul/sbs136
90. Salokangas RK, Ruhrmann S, von Reventlow HG, Heinimaa M, Svirskis T, From T, et al. Axis I diagnoses and transition to psychosis in clinical high-risk patients EPOS project: prospective follow-up of 245 clinical high-risk outpatients in four countries. *Schizophr Res* (2012) 138(2–3):192–7. doi:10.1016/j.schres.2012.03.008
91. Rutigliano G, Valmaggia L, Landi P, Frascarelli M, Cappucciati M, Sear V, et al. Persistence or recurrence of non-psychotic comorbid mental disorders associated with 6-year poor functional outcomes in patients at ultra high risk for psychosis. *J Affect Disord* (2016) 203:101–10. doi:10.1016/j.jad.2016.05.053
92. Lin A, Wood SJ, Nelson B, Beavan A, McGorry P, Yung AR. Outcomes of nontransitioned cases in a sample at ultra-high risk for psychosis. *Am J Psychiatry* (2015) 172(3):249–58. doi:10.1176/appi.ajp.2014.13030418
93. Fairbank JA, Putnam FW, Harris WW. The prevalence and impact of child traumatic stress. In: Friedman MJ, Keane TM, Resick PA, editors. *Handbook of PTSD: Science and Practice*. New York, NY: The Guilford Press (2007). p. 229–51.
94. Spence W, Mulholland C, Lynch G, McHugh S, Dempster M, Shannon C. Rates of childhood trauma in a sample of patients with schizophrenia as compared with a sample of patients with non-psychotic psychiatric diagnoses. *J Trauma Dissociation* (2006) 7(3):7–22. doi:10.1300/J229v07n03_02
95. Lysaker PH, Davis LW, Gatton MJ, Herman SM. Associations of anxiety-related symptoms with reported history of childhood sexual abuse in schizophrenia spectrum disorders. *J Clin Psychiatry* (2005) 66(10):1279–84. doi:10.4088/JCP.v66n1010
96. Addington J, Case N, Saleem MM, Auther AM, Cornblatt BA, Cadenhead KS. Substance use in clinical high risk for psychosis: a review of the literature. *Early Interv Psychiatry* (2014) 8(2):104–12. doi:10.1111/eip.12100
97. Simpson TL, Miller WR. Concomitance between childhood sexual and physical abuse and substance use problems: a review. *Clin Psychol Rev* (2002) 22(1):27–77. doi:10.1016/S0272-7358(00)00088-X
98. Buchy L, Cadenhead KS, Cannon TD, Cornblatt BA, McGlashan TH, Perkins DO, et al. Substance use in individuals at clinical high risk of psychosis. *Psychol Med* (2015) 45(11):2275–84. doi:10.1017/S0033291715000227
99. Paparelli A, Di Forti M, Morrison PD, Murray RM. Drug-induced psychosis: how to avoid star gazing in schizophrenia research by looking at more obvious sources of light. *Front Behav Neurosci* (2011) 5:1. doi:10.3389/fnbeh.2011.00001
100. Harley M, Kelleher I, Clarke M, Lynch F, Arseneault L, Connor D, et al. Cannabis use and childhood trauma interact additively to increase the risk of psychotic symptoms in adolescence. *Psychol Med* (2010) 40(10):1627–34. doi:10.1017/S0033291709991966
101. Addington J, Cadenhead KS, Cornblatt BA, Mathalon DH, McGlashan TH, Perkins DO, et al. North American prodrome longitudinal study (NAPLS 2): overview and recruitment. *Schizophr Res* (2012) 142(1):77–82. doi:10.1016/j.schres.2012.09.012
102. Morrison AP, Frame L, Larkin W. Relationships between trauma and psychosis: a review and integration. *Br J Clin Psychol* (2003) 42(4):331–53. doi:10.1348/014466503322528892
103. Graham Scott J, Nurcombe B, Sheridan J, McFarland M. Hallucinations in adolescents with post-traumatic stress disorder and psychotic disorder. *Australas Psychiatry* (2007) 15(1):44–8. doi:10.1080/10398560601083084
104. Jessop M, Scott J, Nurcombe B. Hallucinations in adolescent inpatients with post-traumatic stress disorder and schizophrenia: similarities and differences. *Australas Psychiatry* (2008) 16(4):268–72. doi:10.1080/10398560801982580
105. Sareen J, Cox BJ, Goodwin RD, JG Asmundson G. Co-occurrence of post-traumatic stress disorder with positive psychotic symptoms in a nationally representative sample. *J Trauma Stress* (2005) 18(4):313–22. doi:10.1002/jts.20040
106. Alsawy S, Wood L, Taylor P, Morrison A. Psychotic experiences and PTSD: exploring associations in a population survey. *Psychol Med* (2015) 45(13):2849–59. doi:10.1017/S003329171500080X
107. Shevlin M, Dorahy M, Adamson G. Childhood traumas and hallucinations: an analysis of the national comorbidity survey. *J Psychiatr Res* (2007) 41(3):222–8. doi:10.1016/j.jpsychires.2006.03.004

108. Famularo R, Fenton T, Kinscherff R, Augustyn M. Psychiatric comorbidity in childhood post traumatic stress disorder. *Child Abuse Negl* (1996) 20(10):953–61. doi:10.1016/0145-2134(96)00084-1
109. Husted JA, Ahmed R, Chow EW, Brzustowicz LM, Bassett AS. Childhood trauma and genetic factors in familial schizophrenia associated with the NOS1AP gene. *Schizophr Res* (2010) 121(1):187–92. doi:10.1016/j.schres.2010.05.021
110. Bernardo M, Bioque M, Cabrera B, Lobo A, Gonzalez-Pinto A, Pina L, et al. Modelling gene-environment interaction in first episodes of psychosis. *Schizophr Res* (2017). doi:10.1016/j.schres.2017.01.058
111. Zubin J, Spring B. Vulnerability: a new view of schizophrenia. *J Abnorm Psychol* (1977) 86(2):103–26. doi:10.1037/0021-843X.86.2.103
112. Harkness KL, Hayden EP, Lopez-Duran NL. Stress sensitivity and stress sensitization in psychopathology: an introduction to the special section. *J Abnorm Psychol* (2015) 124(1):1–3. doi:10.1037/abn0000041
113. Monroe SM, Harkness KL. Life stress, the "Kindling" hypothesis, and the recurrence of depression: considerations from a life stress perspective. *Psychol Rev* (2005) 112(2):417–45. doi:10.1037/0033-295x.112.2.417
114. Walker E, Diforio D. Schizophrenia: a neural diathesis-stress model. *Psychol Rev* (1997) 104(4):667–85. doi:10.1037/0033-295X.104.4.667
115. Meyers JL, Lowe SR, Eaton NR, Krueger R, Grant BF, Hasin D. Childhood maltreatment, 9/11 exposure, and latent dimensions of psychopathology: a test of stress sensitization. *J Psychiatr Res* (2015) 68:337–45. doi:10.1016/j.jpsychires.2015.05.005
116. Trotman HD, Holtzman CW, Walker EF, Addington JM, Bearden CE, Cadenhead KS, et al. Stress exposure and sensitivity in the clinical high-risk syndrome: initial findings from the North American Prodrome Longitudinal Study (NAPLS). *Schizophr Res* (2014) 160(1–3):104–9. doi:10.1016/j.schres.2014.09.017
117. Kahn JP, Rubinow DR, Davis CL, Kling M, Post RM. Salivary cortisol: a practical method for evaluation of adrenal function. *Biol Psychiatry* (1988) 23(4):335–49. doi:10.1016/0006-3223(88)90284-3
118. Day FL, Valmaggia LR, Mondelli V, Papadopoulos A, Papadopoulos I, Pariante CM, et al. Blunted cortisol awakening response in people at ultra high risk of developing psychosis. *Schizophr Res* (2014) 158(1–3):25–31. doi:10.1016/j.schres.2014.06.041
119. Pruessner M, Bechard-Evans L, Boekestyn L, Iyer SN, Pruessner JC, Malla AK. Attenuated cortisol response to acute psychosocial stress in individuals at ultra-high risk for psychosis. *Schizophr Res* (2013) 146(1–3):79–86. doi:10.1016/j.schres.2013.02.019
120. Walker E, Mittal V, Tessner K. Stress and the hypothalamic pituitary adrenal axis in the developmental course of schizophrenia. *Annu Rev Clin Psychol* (2008) 4:189–216. doi:10.1146/annurev.clinpsy.4.022007.141248
121. Girshkin L, Matheson SL, Shepherd AM, Green MJ. Morning cortisol levels in schizophrenia and bipolar disorder: a meta-analysis. *Psychoneuroendocrinology* (2014) 49:187–206. doi:10.1016/j.psyneuen.2014.07.013
122. Bradley AJ, Dinan TG. A systematic review of hypothalamic-pituitary-adrenal axis function in schizophrenia: implications for mortality. *J Psychopharmacol* (2010) 24(4 Suppl):91–118. doi:10.1177/1359786810385491
123. Sugranyes G, Thompson JL, Corcoran CM. HPA-axis function, symptoms, and medication exposure in youths at clinical high risk for psychosis. *J Psychiatr Res* (2012) 46(11):1389–93. doi:10.1016/j.jpsychires.2012.07.011
124. Van Voorhees E, Scarpa A. The effects of child maltreatment on the hypothalamic-pituitary-adrenal axis. *Trauma Violence Abuse* (2004) 5(4):333–52. doi:10.1177/1524838004269486
125. Martinson A, Craner J, Sigmon S. Differences in HPA axis reactivity to intimacy in women with and without histories of sexual trauma. *Psychoneuroendocrinology* (2016) 65:118–26. doi:10.1016/j.psyneuen.2015.12.025
126. Braehler C, Holowka D, Brunet A, Beaulieu S, Baptista T, Debruille JB, et al. Diurnal cortisol in schizophrenia patients with childhood trauma. *Schizophr Res* (2005) 79(2):353–4. doi:10.1016/j.schres.2004.07.007
127. Phassouliotis C, Garner BA, Phillips LJ, Bendall S, Yun Y, Markulev C, et al. Enhanced cortisol suppression following administration of low-dose dexamethasone in first-episode psychosis patients. *Aust N Z J Psychiatry* (2013) 47(4):363–70. doi:10.1177/0004867412465125
128. Pruessner JC, Champagne F, Meaney MJ, Dagher A. Dopamine release in response to a psychological stress in humans and its relationship to early life maternal care: a positron emission tomography study using [11C]raclopride. *J Neurosci* (2004) 24(11):2825–31. doi:10.1523/JNEUROSCI.3422-03.2004
129. Bois C, Whalley H, McIntosh A, Lawrie S. Structural magnetic resonance imaging markers of susceptibility and transition to schizophrenia: a review of familial and clinical high risk population studies. *J Psychopharmacol* (2015) 29(2):144–54. doi:10.1177/0269881114541015
130. Howes OD, McCutcheon R, Owen MJ, Murray RM. The role of genes, stress, and dopamine in the development of schizophrenia. *Biol Psychiatry* (2017) 81(1):9–20. doi:10.1016/j.biopsych.2016.07.014
131. Howes OD, Bose SK, Turkheimer F, Valli I, Egerton A, Valmaggia LR, et al. Dopamine synthesis capacity before onset of psychosis: a prospective [18F]-DOPA PET imaging study. *Am J Psychiatry* (2011) 168(12):1311–7. doi:10.1176/appi.ajp.2011.11010160
132. Oswald LM, Wand GS, Kuwabara H, Wong DF, Zhu S, Brasic JR. History of childhood adversity is positively associated with ventral striatal dopamine responses to amphetamine. *Psychopharmacology* (2014) 231(12):2417–33. doi:10.1007/s00213-013-3407-z
133. Chaumette B, Kebir O, Mam-Lam-Fook C, Morvan Y, Bourgin J, Godsil BP, et al. Salivary cortisol in early psychosis: new findings and meta-analysis. *Psychoneuroendocrinology* (2016) 63:262–70. doi:10.1016/j.psyneuen.2015.10.007
134. Walker EF, Trotman HD, Pearce BD, Addington J, Cadenhead KS, Cornblatt BA, et al. Cortisol levels and risk for psychosis: initial findings from the North American prodrome longitudinal study. *Biol Psychiatry* (2013) 74(6):410–7. doi:10.1016/j.biopsych.2013.02.016
135. Addington J, Tran L. Using the brief core schema scales with individuals at clinical high risk of psychosis. *Behav Cogn Psychother* (2009) 37(2):227–31. doi:10.1017/S1352465809005116
136. van Os J, Krabbendam L, Myin-Germeys I, Delespaul P. The schizophrenia envirome. *Curr Opin Psychiatry* (2005) 18(2):141–5. doi:10.1097/00001504-200503000-00006
137. Nieman DH, Ruhrmann S, Dragt S, Soen F, van Tricht MJ, Koelman JH, et al. Psychosis prediction: stratification of risk estimation with information-processing and premorbid functioning variables. *Schizophr Bull* (2014) 40(6):1482–90. doi:10.1093/schbul/sbt145
138. Roiser JP, Howes OD, Chaddock CA, Joyce EM, McGuire P. Neural and behavioral correlates of aberrant salience in individuals at risk for psychosis. *Schizophr Bull* (2013) 39(6):1328–36. doi:10.1093/schbul/sbs147
139. van Os J, Reininghaus U. Psychosis as a transdiagnostic and extended phenotype in the general population. *World Psychiatry* (2016) 15(2):118–24. doi:10.1002/wps.20310
140. Sherrer MV. The role of cognitive appraisal in adaptation to traumatic stress in adults with serious mental illness: a critical review. *Trauma Violence Abuse* (2011) 12(3):151–67. doi:10.1177/1524838011404254
141. Gibson LE, Alloy LB, Ellman LM. Trauma and the psychosis spectrum: a review of symptom specificity and explanatory mechanisms. *Clin Psychol Rev* (2016) 49:92–105. doi:10.1016/j.cpr.2016.08.003
142. Evans GJ, Reid G, Preston P, Palmier-Claus J, Sellwood W. Trauma and psychosis: the mediating role of self-concept clarity and dissociation. *Psychiatry Res* (2015) 228(3):626–32. doi:10.1016/j.psychres.2015.04.053
143. Palmier-Claus J, Berry K, Darrell-Berry H, Emsley R, Parker S, Drake R, et al. Childhood adversity and social functioning in psychosis: exploring clinical and cognitive mediators. *Psychiatry Res* (2016) 238:25–32. doi:10.1016/j.psychres.2016.02.004
144. Coryell W, Leon A, Winokur G, Endicott J, Keller M, Akiskal H, et al. Importance of psychotic features to long-term course in major depressive disorder. *Am J Psychiatry* (1996) 153(4):483. doi:10.1176/ajp.153.4.483
145. Keck PE Jr, McElroy SL, Havens JR, Altshuler LL, Nolen WA, Frye MA, et al. Psychosis in bipolar disorder: phenomenology and impact on morbidity and course of illness. *Compr Psychiatry* (2003) 44(4):263–9. doi:10.1016/S0010-440X(03)00089-0
146. The National Child Traumatic Stress Network. *Trauma-Informed Screening & Assessment*. (n.d.) (2015). Available from: http://www.nctsn.org/resources/topics/trauma-informed-screening-assessment/trauma-screening
147. Cohen JA, Bukstein O, Walter H, Benson SR, Chrisman A, Farchione TR, et al. Practice parameter for the assessment and treatment of children and adolescents with posttraumatic stress disorder. *J Am Acad Child Adolesc Psychiatry* (2010) 49(4):414–30. doi:10.1016/j.jaac.2009.12.020

148. Schnurr P, Vielhauer M, Weathers F, Findler M. *The Brief Trauma Questionnaire*. White River Junction, VT: National Center for PTSD (1999).
149. Bernstein DP, Stein JA, Newcomb MD, Walker E, Pogge D, Ahluvalia T, et al. Development and validation of a brief screening version of the childhood trauma questionnaire. *Child Abuse Negl* (2003) 27(2):169–90. doi:10.1016/S0145-2134(02)00541-0
150. Briere J. *Trauma Symptom Checklist for Children (TSCC): Professional Manual*. Odessa, FL: Psychological Assessment Resources (1996).
151. Foa EB, Johnson KM, Feeny NC, Treadwell KRH. The child PTSD symptom scale: a preliminary examination of its psychometric properties. *J Clin Child Psychol* (2001) 30(3):376–84. doi:10.1207/S15374424JCCP3003_9
152. Rodriguez N, Steinberg A, Pynoos R. *UCLA Posttraumatic Stress Disorder Reaction Index for DSM-IV: Child, Adolescent, and Parent versions*. Los Angeles, CA: University of California at Los Angeles (1998).
153. Briere J. *Trauma Symptom Checklist for Young Children*. Odessa, FL: Psychological Assessment Resources, Inc (2005).
154. First M, Spitzer RL, Gibbon M, Williams B, Williams JBW. *Structured Clinical Interview for DSM-IV Axis I Disorders, Patient Edition*. New York: Biometrics Research Department, New York State Psychiatric Institute (1995).
155. Puig-Antich J, Ryan N. *Kiddie Schedule for Affective Disorders and Schizophrenia*. Pittsburgh, PA: Western Psychiatric Institute (1986).
156. Fisher HL, Craig TK, Fearon P, Morgan K, Dazzan P, Lappin J, et al. Reliability and comparability of psychosis patients' retrospective reports of childhood abuse. *Schizophr Bull* (2011) 37(3):546–53. doi:10.1093/schbul/sbp103
157. Kassam-Adams N, Newman E. Child and parent reactions to participation in clinical research. *Gen Hosp Psychiatry* (2005) 27(1):29–35. doi:10.1016/j.genhosppsych.2004.08.007
158. Legerski JP, Bunnell SL. The risks, benefits, and ethics of trauma-focused research participation. *Ethics Behav* (2010) 20(6):429–42. doi:10.1080/10508422.2010.521443
159. Cragin CA, Straus MB, Blacker D, Tully LM, Niendam TA. Early psychosis and trauma-related disorders: clinical practice guidelines and future directions. *Front Psychiatry* (2017) 8:33. doi:10.3389/fpsyt.2017.00033
160. de Bont P, van den Berg D, van der Vleugel B, de Roos C, de Jongh A, van der Gaag M, et al. Prolonged exposure and EMDR for PTSD v. a PTSD waiting-list condition: effects on symptoms of psychosis, depression and social functioning in patients with chronic psychotic disorders. *Psychol Med* (2016) 46(11):2411. doi:10.1017/S0033291716001094
161. van den Berg DP, van der Vleugel BM, de Bont PA, Thijssen G, de Roos C, de Kleine R, et al. Exposing therapists to trauma-focused treatment in psychosis: effects on credibility, expected burden, and harm expectancies. *Eur J Psychotraumatol* (2016) 7:31712. doi:10.3402/ejpt.v7.31712

20

Psychological Interventions for Working with Trauma and Distressing Voices: The Future is in the Past

Craig Steel *

School of Psychology and Clinical Language Sciences, University of Reading, Reading, UK

Keywords: voices, posttraumatic stress disorder, schizophrenia, dialogue, cognitive therapy

Edited by:
Kate Hardy,
Stanford University, USA

Reviewed by:
Mahesh Menon,
University of British Columbia, Canada

Correspondence:
Craig Steel
c.steel@reading.ac.uk

The relationship between stressful or traumatic life events and the content of experiences associated with a diagnosis of schizophrenia is clinically intriguing but lacks developed theoretical understanding. The high prevalence of traumatic events in this group indicates the need to develop psychosocial interventions. However, antipsychotic medication remains the frontline treatment within most mental health services, frequently prescribed by a doctor implicitly (or explicitly) imposing a simplistic disease model, along with the associated lack of hope for those who do not respond well. The essence of this model being that the distressing experiences associated with the diagnosis, typically paranoia and/or hearing voices, are abnormal and symptoms of a disease. Staying within a diagnostic approach, it is worth noting that recent studies suggest that ~15% of people diagnosed with schizophrenia will also present with experiences consistent with a diagnosis of posttraumatic stress disorder (PTSD; Achim et al., 2011). To date the clinical trials aimed at treating PTSD within this group suggest that exposure and eye movement desensitization and reprocessing (EMDR) are effective (Van den Berg et al., 2015) whilst cognitive restructuring alone may not be (Steel et al., 2017). It is likely that psychological interventions for this group will evolve alongside developments in evidence-based interventions for PTSD.

Whilst 85% of people diagnosed with schizophrenia do not fulfill the diagnostic criteria for PTSD, the majority have suffered stressful and traumatic life events (Grubaugh et al., 2011). For many of these people, there appears to be a relationship between their life events and the content of their "psychotic" experiences. For example, Hardy et al. (2005) showed that whilst 12.5% of a sample heard distressing voices which were a direct repetition of a past traumatic event, 45% reported a broader emotional link, e.g., hearing a voice content which made them feel humiliated, replicating the emotional state they experienced during the trauma. There is a need to develop trauma informed approaches for this group, especially when considering the negative relationship between adverse life events and antipsychotic treatment outcome (Hassan and De Luca, 2015).

THE COGNITIVE MODEL AND WORKING WITH VOICES

The current dominant approach underlying evidence-based psychological interventions is the cognitive model. One strength of this approach is that it is based on some basic premises which can be shared with recipients, thus promoting collaboration. Key premises are that adverse childhood events shape the development of core beliefs about oneself and the world, that thoughts determine emotions, and that behavior maintains beliefs (Beck, 1979). These premises underlie the development of all cognitive behavioral interventions, including cognitive behavioral therapy for psychosis (CBTp). Whilst clinical trials have produced impressive results within CBT for anxiety disorders such as panic and social phobia, the outcomes of CBTp trials have been modest with an effect size typically in the region of 0.4 (Wykes et al., 2008). One area of CBTp promising to move beyond this modest effect is within interventions for the socially disabling experience of paranoia (see Freeman and Garety, 2014). This work sits comfortably within the cognitive model, whereby paranoid beliefs can be formulated as threat beliefs which arise within the context of adverse and traumatic life events.

A recent meta-analysis suggests that the effect size of CBT for distressing voices is small to moderate, and much the same as the outcomes of CBTp for general psychotic symptoms. A key premise in this work is that the interpretation of a voice hearing experience determines the emotional reaction. Making sense of a voice as malevolent, omniscient and powerful is associated with distress. This approach has been evaluated within the recent COMMAND trial (Birchwood et al., 2014), which produced an effect size of 0.57 for the main outcome of "compliance with the voice." Whilst CBTp for voices is capable of producing significant change, it is not clear what opportunity there is for further significant clinical development within interventions based on the cognitive model.

There are promising developments which attend to the relational aspect of voice hearing (e.g., Hayward et al., 2014). However, it can—and should—be debated whether the underlying premise of these approaches is consistent with the cognitive model. This is not just an academic debate. It is important to clarify what is, and what is not CBTp, to avoid the term becoming so broad and theoretically detached that it has lost all meaning. Defining what constitutes CBTp is particularly important when considering dissemination. It would seem reasonable to suggest that CBTp interventions are ones that are primarily based on the theoretical premises underlying the approach.

Although lacking an established theoretical basis, the relationship between traumatic life events, voice hearing and dissociation is often cited (Pilton et al., 2015). A state of dissociation includes derealization and detachment and can be described as a separation of mental processes which normally work together, but have moved toward independent functioning. Several models of PTSD refer to people entering a dissociative state during a traumatic event. This is argued to be functional and protective at the time of a trauma, but is also the source of information processing changes which underlie the development of trauma-related intrusions, or "flashbacks." High levels of dissociation have been observed within individuals diagnosed with schizophrenia (Ross and Keyes, 2004), with some clinical researchers proposing a "dissociative trauma" subtype of schizophrenia and associated treatment implications. It has also been argued that dissociation mediates the relationship between traumatic life events and hearing voices (Varese et al., 2012). However, in part due to the lack of theoretical development of the concept of dissociation itself, we are some way short of a theory which is of any clinical utility when working with the content of distressing voices. However, a voice can be conceptualized as representing a dissociated "part of the self" (Corstens et al., 2012), which would suggest that engagement with the content of the voice may be of therapeutic value.

TALKING WITH THE "ENEMY"

As noted above, the contents of voice-hearing experiences are rarely repetitive memories of a traumatic event. They often seem to be linked to past experiences within a context that does not sit easily within the cognitive model. Clinicians often refer to a voice being linked to a life event, but that the content and communication has "evolved" beyond the specific event which is considered to be the trigger. The premise that voices "arrive" in peoples' lives as part of a meaningful reaction to traumatic life events, and that voice content is relevant and should be engaged with (including active "Voice Dialogue"), underlies an approach put forward by Romme and Escher (2000) often called the "Maastricht approach." The approach has become established within the hearing voices movement but has largely remained outside academic investigation and mainstream clinical services. Another important premise within the Maastricht approach is that a voice is serving a function. Therefore, active engagement with the voice may reduce conflict between "parts of the self." This form of voice dialogue work invites the voice to communicate directly with the therapist, often with the voice-hearer sitting in a different chair when communicating as "the voice." The therapist is respectful to the voice, whatever the voice may be believed to represent, and can maintain a dialogue over a number of sessions with the aim of exploring the voice's function. Once the function is understood the clinical work can move toward the wider issues within the voice hearers' life, with reduced direct communication with the voice. For example, during dialogue, a voice may state that it shouts and is aggressive because it has become tired of being ignored. A voice may reveal that it became "active" during a period of abuse in someone's life, and that at the time it was trying to help. However, the voice goes on to say that the reason it currently sounds critical of the voice-hearer is because it wants them to stand up for themself, and to "kill" the part of them that behaves like a victim.

As noted in the literature, it is not uncommon for a voice hearer to hear the voice in the form of a past abuser or torturer. In this circumstance, therapists are often anxious that dialogue with the voice may retraumatize the voice hearer. However, through voice dialogue, the voice hearer is likely to realize that the voice represents a view about the abuse and is not actually the abuser talking to them. It is worth drawing a parallel with psychological therapy for depression. The negative internal thoughts associated with depression are (usually) considered to have developed through adverse life events and a direct confrontational approach to the content of these thoughts is typically considered to be cognitive therapy done badly. If a voice is part of an individual, and the content also linked to past events, then it would seem that direct confrontation is also ill-advised in this context. Further, it can be argued that to avoid voice dialogue work is to collude with the voice hearer, that the voice is powerful and to be feared.

As argued above, it is important to acknowledge the premises upon which interventions are based. There are clear differences between the underlying premises of CBT for voices and the Maastricht approach. A misplaced absorption of the latter within the former is likely to impede the development of the Maastricht approach. Further, the two approaches would advocate fundamentally different positions when working with some voice hearers. It is not uncommon for a voice hearer to report a voice which undermines and criticizes the voice hearer.

Although there is no single approach to this scenario within CBT for voices, common strategies include distracting oneself from the experience, and tackling the negative voice content by talking back to it with assertive statements. These strategies would seem diametrically opposite to opening a meaningful dialogue, in order to understand the function behind the voice and to reduce conflict. Within the Maastricht approach, the process adopted within some forms of CBT for voices would be considered likely to increase internal conflict and the associated distress. There is, therefore, an opportunity to empirically test these predictions. To date, voice dialogue and the Maastricht approach have been reported in the context of single cases (Corstens et al., 2012) and an ongoing case series (ISRCTN54370851).

Research aimed at the development of the Maastricht approach would best start with a focused assessment of voice dialogue. As within clinical trials of medication, there is the need for the close monitoring of adverse events when evaluating psychological interventions. Pre–post dialogue assessment and feedback from voice hearers are also required. However, ahead of larger scale clinical trials, there is the need to develop two important aspects of wider research into voice hearing. One is the need for measures that better reflect the priorities of voice hearers. Second, is the need for criteria to define meaningful subgroups of voice hearers so as to inform appropriate intervention. The Maastricht approach is most likely to be appropriate for the frequently mentioned "trauma dissociative" subgroup which requires further distinction.

In summary, there is increased awareness that voice hearing is linked to life events, but a lack of theoretical development has restricted clinical development. The role of appraisal which is embedded within the cognitive model has proved to be clinically useful, but we seem to have reached the limit of what can be offered from this approach. We should resist the temptation to categorize an increasing range of interventions under a broad definition of CBT. Distinct interventions should be recognized as such and evaluated independently. Although voice dialogue does not sit within an established theoretical framework, it does offer a distinct approach to working with voice content which warrants systematic evaluation. It is worth noting the current widely held perception of voice hearing as part of normal human experience was held back by the mainstream mental health professions during the twentieth century. It is hoped that the same assumptions do not inhibit the widespread acceptability of voice dialogue.

AUTHOR CONTRIBUTIONS

The author confirms being the sole contributor of this work and approved it for publication.

ACKNOWLEDGMENTS

The opinion expressed here is produced within the context of collaborative work with Dirk Corstens, Joachim Schnackenberg, and Eleanor Longden.

REFERENCES

Achim, A. M., Maziade, M., Raymond, E., Olivier, D., Mérette, C., and Roy, M. (2011). How prevalent are anxiety disorders in schizophrenia? A meta-analysis and critical review on a significant association. *Schizophr. Bull.* 37, 811–821. doi: 10.1093/schbul/sbp148

Beck, A. T. (1979). *Cognitive Therapy for Depression.* New York, NY: Guildford Press.

Birchwood, M., Michail, M., Meaden, A., Tarrier, N., Lewis, S., Wykes, T., et al. (2014). Cognitive behaviour therapy to prevent harmful compliance with command hallucinations (COMMAND): a randomised controlled trial. *Lancet* 1, 23–33. doi: 10.1016/s2215-0366(14)70247-0

Corstens, D., Longden, E., and May, R. (2012). Talking with voices: exploring what is expressed by the voices people hear. *Psychosis* 4, 95–101. doi: 10.1080/17522439.2011.571705

Freeman, D., and Garety, P. (2014). Advances in understanding and treating persecutory delusions: a review. *Soc. Psychiatry Psychiatr. Epidemiol.* 49, 1179–1189. doi: 10.1007/s00127-014-0928-7

Grubaugh, A. L., Zinzow, H. M., Paul, L., Egede, L. E., and Frueh, B. C. (2011). Trauma exposure and posttraumatic stress disorder in adults with severe mental illness: a critical review. *Clin. Psychol. Rev.* 31, 883–899. doi: 10.1016/j.cpr.2011.04.003

Hardy, A., Fowler, D., Freeman, D., Smith, B., Steel, C., Evans, J., et al. (2005) Trauma and hallucinatory experience in psychosis. *J. Nerv. Ment. Dis.* 193, 501–507. doi: 10.1097/01.nmd.0000172480.56308.21

Hassan, A. N., and De Luca, V. (2015). The effect of lifetime adversities on resistance to antipsychotic treatment in schizophrenia patients. *Schizophr. Res.* 161, 496–500. doi: 10.1016/j.schres.2014.10.048

Hayward, M., Berry, K., McCarthy-Jones, S., Strauss, C., and Thomas, N. (2014). Beyond the omnipotence of voices: further developing a relational approach to auditory hallucinations. *Psychosis* 6, 242–252. doi: 10.1080/17522439.2013.839735

Pilton, M., Varese, F., Berry, K., and Bucci, B. (2015). The relationship between dissociation and voices: a systematic literature review and meta-analysis. *Clin. Psychol. Rev.* 40, 138–155. doi: 10.1016/j.cpr.2015.06.004

Romme, M., and Escher, S. (2000). *Making Sense of Voices.* London: Mind Publications.

Ross, C. A., and Keyes, B. (2004). Dissociation and Schizophrenia. *J. Trauma Dissoc.* 5, 69–83. doi: 10.1300/J229v05n03_05

Steel, C., Hardy, A., Smith, B., Wykes, T., Rose, S., Enright, S., et al. (2017). Cognitive-behaviour therapy for post-traumatic stress in schizophrenia. A randomised controlled trial. *Psych. Med.* 47, 43–51. doi: 10.1017/S0033291716002117

Van den Berg, D., de Bont, P., van der Vleugel, B. M., de Roos, C., de Jongh, A., van Minnen, A., et al. (2015). Prolonged exposure vs eye movement desensitization and reprocessing vs waiting list for posttraumatic stress disorder in patients with a psychotic disorder: a randomized clinical trial. *Schizophr. Bull.* 72, 259–267. doi: 10.1001/jamapsychiatry.2014.2637

Varese, F., Barkus, E., and Bentall, R. P. (2012). Dissociation mediates the relationship between childhood trauma and psychosis-proneness. *Psychol. Med.* 42, 1025–1036. doi: 10.1017/S0033291711001826

Wykes, T., Steel, C., Everitt, B., and Tarrier, N. (2008). Cognitive behavior therapy for schizophrenia: effect sizes, clinical models, and methodological rigor. *Schizophr. Bull.* 34, 523–537. doi: 10.1093/schbul/sbm114

21

Acute and Post-traumatic Stress Disorder Symptoms in Mothers and Fathers Following Childbirth

*Elisabeth Schobinger [1], Suzannah Stuijfzand [1] and Antje Horsch [1,2]**

[1] Institute of higher Education and Research in Healthcare in French, University of Lausanne, Lausanne, Switzerland,
[2] Department Woman-Mother-Child, Lausanne University Hospital, Lausanne, Switzerland

Edited by:
Suraj Bahadur Thapa,
University of Oslo, Norway

Reviewed by:
Rafael Caparros-Gonzalez,
University of Granada, Spain
Zoe Josephine Darwin,
University of Huddersfield,
United Kingdom

***Correspondence:**
Antje Horsch
antje.horsch@chuv.ch
orcid.org/0000-0002-9950-9661

Introduction: Up to 30% of women view their childbirth as traumatic. This experience can lead to acute stress disorder or post-traumatic stress disorder. The negative impact of maternal post-traumatic stress disorder following childbirth reaches beyond the mother, potentially affecting her child's development and the couple's relationship. Research on *paternal* post-traumatic stress disorder following childbirth is scarce. Acute stress disorder is suggested to be an important predictor of post-traumatic stress disorder in mothers, but little is known about *paternal* acute stress disorder following childbirth. Furthermore, there is limited information about the comparison or relation of acute stress disorder and post-traumatic stress disorder following childbirth between parents.

Aim: [1] To compare the prevalence rates and severity of acute stress disorder and post-traumatic stress disorder symptoms between parents following childbirth by taking anxiety and depression symptoms, as well as obstetric variables and previous traumatic events into account and [2] To determine if acute stress disorder is a predictor of post-traumatic stress disorder.

Method: A prospective population-based design was used. $N = 647$ participants were recruited from future parents who attended appointments at the Obstetrics and Gynecology unit at a Swiss university hospital. Self-report questionnaires were used: Post-traumatic Diagnostic Scale in the third trimester of pregnancy (T1) and 1 month post-partum (T3), Acute Stress Disorder Scale at 1 week post-partum (T2), and Hospital Anxiety and Depression Scale at all time points. Obstetric and neonatal variables were retrieved from hospital records.

Results: At T2, 63.9% of mothers and 51.7% of fathers presented symptoms of acute stress disorder. At T3, 20.7% of mothers and 7.2% of fathers had symptoms of post-traumatic stress disorder. Acute stress disorder was a predictor of post-partum post-traumatic stress disorder (Odds ratio: 8.6, IC 95% [1.85; 40.42]). Depression symptoms was a significant confounder in the prediction of post-traumatic stress disorder following childbirth, but not anxiety or previous perinatal loss.

Conclusion: Little is known about parental differences in acute stress disorder and post-traumatic stress disorder symptoms following childbirth. Results indicate that *both* parents may suffer from acute stress disorder and post-traumatic stress disorder symptoms after childbirth and that acute stress disorder is a predictor of post-traumatic stress disorder after childbirth for both parents. Sensitization of maternity staff to these results may assist in earlier identification of and appropriate treatment for at-risk parents.

Keywords: acute stress (disorder), PTSD-post-traumatic stress disorder, parents, mothers, fathers, nurses and midwives, childbirth

INTRODUCTION

Childbirth is often experienced as a happy event, but up to one third of women view their childbirth as traumatic, which can lead to different psychological problems like depression, acute stress disorder (ASD) or post-traumatic stress disorder (PTSD) (1). ASD and PTSD are both trauma- and stressor-related disorders (2). ASD may appear after 3 days and lasts up to 1 month; if symptoms persist, then a diagnosis of PTSD becomes likely. ASD is thought to be a predictor of PTSD (3, 4). Both share the following symptom clusters: re-experiencing, avoidance, negative cognitions and mood, but ASD has one more cluster: dissociation (2).

For trauma-related symptoms occurring up to 1 month following traumatic childbirth, the diagnosis of ASD is given. ASD corresponds to PTSD in terms of symptoms, with some variations. ASD requires at least nine symptoms of any clusters cited above. If the symptoms last beyond 1 month, then a diagnosis of PTSD is relevant (2). PTSD following childbirth (PTSD-CB) is highly comorbid with depression (5–7). Furthermore, of those with PTSD-CB, 24% of mothers present symptoms of anxiety during pregnancy, whereas the fathers' rate tends to be lower (7–9).

PTSD according to DSM-5 (2) occurs after experiencing or witnessing an event that induced a threat of death or death, a severe injury, or physical threat. During childbirth, some women may experience an actual or perceived threat to their physical integrity, to their life and/or the child's (1). Symptoms of PTSD are grouped in four clusters: re-experiencing, avoidance, negative cognitions and mood, and hyperarousal. All of these symptoms must be present for at least 1 month and impede both social and professional life (2).

PTSD-CB has been widely studied in mothers after childbirth. Its prevalence is between three and six percent in community samples (without any complications/interventions) and increases to 18.5% in high risk samples (e.g., cesarean section) (5, 10, 11). ASD following childbirth (ASD-CB) has been less studied and prevalence rates of around 5.6% have been found (12).

PTSD-CB can impact negatively not only on the mother but also on the baby and the couple (10, 13, 14). Mothers can have negative feelings toward themselves (15, 16) and they may alter their family planning (17). Maternal PTSD-CB has also been associated with difficulties in establishing the mother-baby bond (18, 19), may impact breastfeeding initiation and continuation (20, 21) and negatively impact the child's sleep and development (13, 22). Perinatal mental health problems like post-partum PTSD have important economic costs, representing £8.1 billion in 2014 in the United Kingdom. The majority of those costs are related to the child, clearly showing the negative impact on the future generation (23).

Since the 1960's, fathers tend to be more present during labor and delivery, thus potentially increasing their risk of PTSD-CB (24, 25). Research on paternal PTSD-CB, however, is scarce. Paternal PTSD-CB incidence is between 0 and 5% (25–31). These estimates are based on the results of four studies using small samples size and cross-sectional designs at different times of measurement. Fathers' PTSD-CB has been studied in other contexts, like the Neonatal Intensive Care Unit (NICU), where the prevalence tends to be higher: from eight to 66% (4, 32–37). To our knowledge, ASD-CB has never been studied in fathers after childbirth. Given the multiple negative consequences of ASD-CB and PTSD-CB on the whole family, it is primordial that healthcare professionals be sensitive to this topic.

Fathers' ASD, to our knowledge, has not been studied after childbirth in the general population. Following the admission of their child to the NICU, fathers' ASD prevalence is between 20 and 28% (35, 38, 39). Studies on both parents' ASD in the pediatric intensive care unit (PICU) and NICU (35, 40) have found that ASD is a predictor of PTSD. Results show that 70% of parents suffering from ASD will suffer from PTSD (41), whereas 90% of parents who have no ASD will not develop PTSD (36, 42). Other studies in the general population have found that ASD is not specific enough to predict PTSD (43–45) and that ASD is a greater predictor of PTSD in women than men (46).

The lifetime risk for women to develop ASD and PTSD is two or three times higher than men (47). This is also supported by studies in the NICU comparing rates of parental ASD (35, 38, 48). ASD and PTSD also seem to present themselves differently according to gender. Mothers have been shown to have a higher severity score of ASD or PTSD than fathers (38, 49). Some studies have found that mothers have more intrusion, avoidance and hypervigilance symptoms than fathers (33, 50), although others found no symptom difference between parents (26, 48).

Although fathers seem to have less risk and symptoms, they remain important to the study of PTSD-CB. Fathers are the main support of their spouse after birth (27). They often put their spouse's needs first and tend to underreport difficulties (35, 51). It is also likely that a correlation between both parents' mental health status exists and that the immediate emotional state of the father in the post-partum might affect the mother's (26, 52, 53).

The aim of the study was firstly to compare the prevalence rates and severity of ASD-CB and PTSD-CB symptoms between parents following childbirth by taking anxiety and depression symptoms, as well as obstetric variables and previous traumatic events into account and secondly to determine if ASD-CB is a predictor of PTSD-CB.

The choice of study variables (and confounding variables in particular) is based on the diathesis-stress model of the etiology of PTSD-CB (54). The model of the etiology of PTSD-CB highlights the vulnerability and risks factors that can be divided into three categories: prepartum, peri-partum, and post-partum (54). Prepartum risk factors found to be significant are, previous traumatic birth or previous perinatal loss and previous mental health factors (54, 55). Some studies have found inconsistent results regarding sociodemographic factors, such as age or socio-economic status (55). Prepartum factors relevant for this study were: age, education, previous perinatal loss or traumatic birth, and psychological problems during pregnancy, such as depression and anxiety. A peripartum risk factor relevant here is operative birth (OB) (18, 56). Post-partum risk factors retained in our study are depression and anxiety symptoms.

The study set out to answer the following questions and associated hypotheses:

1. Is there a difference between maternal and paternal probable ASD/ PTSD in terms of prevalence and symptoms (clusters, severity, frequency)? We hypothesized that the ASD/ PTSD prevalence would be higher in mothers than fathers, that ASD/ PTSD symptoms would be higher in mothers, and that mothers would suffer more from arousal, avoidance, and intrusions.
2. Is ASD a predictor of PTSD after childbirth? We hypothesized that ASD would be a significant predictor of PTSD in mothers and fathers after controlling for confounders such as anxiety/depression, previous traumatic birth and the perinatal loss of a previous child (e.g., miscarriage, stillbirth). We also hypothesized that the predictive aspect of ASD would be stronger for mothers than fathers.
3. Is there a difference between maternal and paternal ASD, PTSD according to the type of birth: vaginal birth (VB), planned cesarean section (PCS) vs. unplanned operative birth (UOB) (e.g., forceps, ventouse and emergency cesarean section)? Our hypothesis was that ASD and PTSD prevalence would be higher for those who had an UOB compared to those who had a VB or a PCS, for both fathers and mothers, respectively.

MATERIALS AND METHODS

Design

This study is part of a larger ongoing prospective population-based cohort (Lausanne Well-being Cohort), where data is collected during the third trimester of pregnancy up to 6 months post-partum.

Participant Recruitment

Women in their third trimester of pregnancy and their partner were recruited at the Department of Obstetrics and Gynecology at a Swiss University Hospital. This study concerns those recruited between January 2013 to February 2019.

This study used a convenience sampling method. Inclusion criteria were: pregnant women in the second or third trimester and their partner (both $\geq$ 18 years of age) intending to attend the birth. Participants were excluded if: they had an insufficient knowledge of French to complete the questionnaires or if they had an acute psychosis or a suicidal risk. Following childbirth, parents whose child had serious complications, parents who had a stillborn child or experienced the death of their child shortly after birth, or partners who had not attended the birth were excluded. Partners' presence at the birth was indicated by their or their partner's response to a question about who was present at the birth (note that this question was only introduced into the cohort study later) or completed the Peritraumatic Dissociation Questionnaire [French Version; PDQ-FR; (57)], completed at 1 week. The rationale here was that the partner would not be able to complete this questionnaire if they had not been present at the birth.

A power analysis was conducted on the basis of a power of 0.80 and a 0.05 alpha to detect differences in means of ASD and PTSD symptoms, with effect sizes drawn from previous studies using the same instruments for ASD and PTSD (30, 36). This analysis estimated a sample size of 143 participants in each group, then 15% was added to account for attrition. The total expected sample size was therefore 330: 165 mothers and 165 fathers.

Data Collection

Fathers and mothers separately completed online questionnaires at all time points. This prospective study used self-report questionnaires from three time points of the Cohort: during the third trimester of pregnancy (T1), 1 week post-partum (T2), and 1 month post-partum (T3). Hospital record data (obstetric and neonatal data) was extracted shortly after birth.

Instruments

ASDS-F

ASD symptoms were assessed at 1 week post-partum using the 14-item validated instrument Acute Stress Disorder Scale (ASDS), (58, 59). Participants rated symptom items on a Likert scale from 1 (not at all) to 5 (a lot). Individual item scores are summed up and a score above 17 corresponds to probable ASD (3). For this study, the Cronbach $\alpha = 0.83$.

PDS-F

PTSD was assessed 1 month post-partum using the validated 17 item self-report questionnaire Post-traumatic Diagnostic Scale-French version (PDS-F) (60). Participants were asked to complete the questionnaire in relation to a previous traumatic event that they were asked to identify at T1 and in relation to their childbirth at T3. Items are rated on a Likert scale from 0 (not at all) to 3 (more than five times a week); if an item has a response of 1 or higher, the symptom is considered as present. If responses corresponded to at least one re-experiencing symptom, three avoidance symptoms, and two arousal symptoms, participants were considered probable PTSD (61). Items were summed to create a total score, reflecting the severity of PTSD symptoms. For this study, the Cronbach $\alpha = 0.88$.

HADS-F

The 14-item Hospital Anxiety and Depression Scale (HADS) was completed as a validated instrument of general psychological distress of parents at all time points: Seven items assess anxiety and seven items assess depression symptoms (62, 63). Items are rated on a Likert scale from 0 (no, not at all) to 3 (yes, definitely). Total scores were calculated by summing all items, the items of the two subscales were summed to create separate anxiety and depression scores. A higher score indicates greater severity of psychological distress, anxiety or depression. The cutoff used was as follows: above 14 was considered to have probable anxiety/depression (62). For this study, the Cronbach α for the HADS total and subscales was acceptable [$HADS_{anxiety}$: $\alpha = 0.72$ (T1)–$\alpha = 0.79$ (T2); $HADS_{depression}$: $\alpha = 0.66$ (T1)–$\alpha = 0.79$ (T2); $HADS_{total}$ $\alpha = 0.76$ (T1)–$\alpha = 0.86$ (T2)].

Data Analyses

Analyses were carried out using STATA version 13. Prevalence for ASD and PTSD diagnosis was first established for the entire sample according to gender, then by gender and birth mode. Regarding hypothesis 2 and 3, we conducted regression models, where potential confounders identified from the literature that showed a significant correlation with the dependent variable were included.

Test of proportions or chi-squared tests were used to investigate gender differences in the prevalence of ASD and PTSD diagnosis, and if there was a difference between genders in each birth group. To further investigate this question, we conducted a logistic regression for mothers and fathers to see if there was a relation between the mode of birth and ASD prevalence. Symptoms of ASD and PTSD were compared according to gender, using a Mann Whitney U-test, independently of the birth mode. Following hypothesis 1, unilateral tests were performed.

Second, to determine if PTSD diagnosis was associated with ASD diagnosis after birth according to gender, a logistic regression was conducted, with PTSD at 1 month post-partum as the dependent variable. We also conducted a linear regression to determine if PTSD severity was associated with ASD severity. According to the model of the etiology of PTSD-CB, we tested the correlations between cited confounders and ASD and PTSD. In both models, ASD and gender were included as independent variables with anxiety/depression at 1 week post-partum and previous perinatal loss as covariates if significantly correlated.

Ethical Considerations

This study was approved by the ethics committee of the Canton Vaud, Switzerland (approval number: 480/2012). Written informed consent was obtained from participants. They all had the possibility to ask questions or to withdraw from the study at any time and without explanation. All participant data was coded.

RESULTS

Participant Characteristics

The final sample was composed of 647 participants (419 birthing mothers, 228 fathers). At T1, 385 mothers and 209 fathers completed the questionnaires, 81.8% of mothers and 73.2% of fathers returned the questionnaires at T2, and 76.6% of mothers and 64.8% of fathers at T3. In total, 178 couples are represented in the study.

During pregnancy, mean maternal age was 32.8 ± 4.5, range 18 to 45 years and mean paternal age was 34.2 ± 5.25, range 18 to 53 years. Most of the participants (73%) were cohabiting or married, and 65% had an education level beyond high school (see **Table 1**). 63% of participants were expecting their first child. 56% of mothers had a VB and 27% had an UOB, of which 17% were unplanned C-sections.

There were no sociodemographic differences between mothers and fathers, except in age ($z = -3.01$; $p = 0.0026$; $d = 0.296$), where mothers were younger than fathers. Participants who did not complete the ASDS at T2 had the same characteristics as those who responded at T1 (data not shown). For PTSD symptoms at T3, the participants who did not answer the questionnaire did not differ from T1, except for the proportion of individuals of European origin ($z = -2.31$; $p = 0.0211$, $h = 0.203$) and those having an education level below secondary/high school (primary school: $z = 1.97$; $p = 0.049$; $h = 0.651$, secondary school: $z = 2.59$; $p = 0.0097$; $h = 0.912$).

Mental Health of Participants During the Third Trimester of Pregnancy

Prevalence rates for probable PTSD diagnosis in the third trimester was 24.3% for mothers and 20.3% for fathers. The mean score for maternal PTSD symptoms was 7.37 ± 8.01 and for paternal PTSD symptoms was 6.54 ± 7.08. Neither rates nor means differed significantly (p = ns). 1/3 of mothers and fathers had experienced a previous traumatic event (e.g., car accident, sexual abuse). More mothers (16.2%) than fathers (9%) had experienced a previous traumatic childbirth ($z = 2.29$; $p = 0.0220$; $h = 0.213$). 23.5% of mothers and 18.6% of fathers had experienced a previous perinatal loss but this difference was non-significant (p = ns).

Anxiety and Depression Symptoms of Parents During the Study

Mothers had a higher prevalence of psychological distress and higher means of anxiety and depression symptoms than fathers, at all time points (see **Table 2**).

Prevalence and Symptoms Severity of ASD Symptoms Following Childbirth

At 1 week post-partum (T2), 63.9% of mothers and 51.7% of fathers showed symptoms of probable ASD, regardless of the delivery mode. The difference in prevalence found between mothers and fathers regardless of the delivery mode was significant ($z = 1.90$; $p = 0.0287$; $h = 0.243$), and in accordance with hypothesis 1, i.e., mothers had a higher prevalence of probable ASD diagnosis than fathers. 57.5% of mothers with a

TABLE 1 | Sociodemographic characteristics at T1 for mothers, fathers, obstetric and neonatal variables.

	Frequency (%)	Mean (SD)
Maternal sociodemographic variables		
Age (years; mean, SD)		32.8 (4.5)
Nationality (*n*, %)		
Swiss	13 (3.6%)	
Other European	224 (61.2%)	
Non-European	129 (35.3%)	
Migration status (*n*, %)		
Migrant	89 (37.6%)	
Non-migrant	148 (62.5%)	
Marital status (*n*, %)		
Single	96 (22.9%)	
Co-habiting/Married	312 (74.6%)	
Divorced	6 (1.4%)	
Education (n, %)		
Middle school	17 (4.2%)	
Secondary/high school	28 (7%)	
Apprenticeship	80 (19.9%)	
University	256 (63.5%)	
Largo score (mean, SD)†		7.68 (1.22)
Obstetric variables		
Parity (mean, SD)		0.49 (0.69)
Gestity (mean, SD)		1.80 (0.96)
Arterial cord blood pH (mean, SD)		7.24 (0.08)
Venous cord blood pH (mean, SD)		7.31 (0.07)
Delivery mode		
Vaginal birth	285 (56.2%)	
Planned cesarean section (PCS)	82 (16.2%)	
Unplanned operative birth (UOB)	140 (27.6%)	
Ventouse, forceps	54 (10.6%)	
Unplanned C-section	86 (17%)	
Paternal sociodemographic variables		
Age (years; mean, SD)		34.25 (5.25)
Nationality (*n*, %)		
Swiss	8 (3.8%)	
Other European	129 (61.4%)	
Non-European	73 (34.8%)	
Migration status (n, %)		
Migrant	50 (37%)	
Non-migrant	85 (63%)	
Marital status (*n*, %)		
Single	56 (24.7%)	
Co-habiting/Married	164 (72.3%)	
Divorced	6 (2.6%)	
Education (*n*, %)		
Middle school	9 (4.1%)	
Secondary/high school	6 (2.8%)	
Apprenticeship	40 (18.4%)	
University	152 (69.7%)	
Largo score (mean, SD)†		7.68 (0.094)

†*Largo score: parental socioeconomic status was obtained by adding the education level of the mother and the professional activity of the father (64).*

TABLE 2 | Parental psychological distress during the study.

	T1	T2	T3
General psychological distress (%)			
Mothers	20.2%*	30.86%*	24.12%*
Fathers	10.9%*	12.09%*	12.36%*
All	16.82%	24.11%	19.83%
HADS severity [mean; (SD)]			
Mothers	10.91 (5.20)*	11.66 (6.82)*	11.04 (5.94)*
Fathers	8.70 (4.56)*	7.86 (6.20)*	7.8 (5.21)*
All	10.10 (5.07)	10.29 (6.82)	9.86 (5.88)
Anxiety (mean; SD)			
Mothers	6.88 (3.18)*	6.50 (3.77)*	6.40 (3.56)*
Fathers	6.07 (3.09)*	5.01 (3.18)*	4.64 (2.89)*
All	6.60 (3.17)	6.02 (3.65)	5.83 (3.46)
Depression (mean; SD)			
Mothers	3.35 (2.57)*	4.32 (4.13)*	3.71 (3.21)*
Fathers	3.71 (2.92)*	4.56 (3.57)*	4.44 (3.29)*
All	3.55 (2.77)	4.46 (3.80)	4.15 (3.27)

$^*p < 0.050$.

VB reported ASD symptoms compared to 67.9 and 78.1% of those who, respectively had a PCS and an UOB. Fifty percent of fathers attending a VB had probable ASD compared to 43.7 and 55% of those who, respectively attended a PCS and an UOB. Regarding the delivery mode, the difference was found to be non-significant for mothers and fathers (p = ns). Thus informing hypothesis 3. However, in the logistic regression [$\chi^2_{(4,N=128)} = 12.9$; $p = 0.0118$] where we included significant psychological and sociodemographic covariates (e.g., age, anxiety/depression, previous perinatal loss) (see **Table 3**), mothers who had an UOB had a higher risk (OR = 3.1) to develop ASD (see **Table 4**). For fathers, according to the logistic regression [$\chi^2_{(3,N=80)} = 3.52$; $p = 0.318$], PCS seems to be a protective factor regarding the development of ASD, however, it did not show as a significant predictor of ASD (see **Table 5**).

For ASD symptoms, the mean severity score for mothers was 21.58 (SD = 7.21) and 18.83 (SD = 4.42) for fathers. The difference in the ASD symptom severity was significant (z = 2.76; $p = 0.0058$; $d = 0.433$) and in line with hypothesis 1. The four symptom clusters of ASD were also higher for mothers than fathers, as hypothesized (see **Table 6**).

Prevalence and Symptoms Severity of PTSD Symptoms Following Childbirth

At 1 month post-partum (T3), 20.7% of mothers and 7.2% of fathers had probable PTSD, regardless of delivery mode. This difference was significant [$\chi^2_{(1,N=424)} = 12.51$; $p < 0.0001$; $h = 0.391$] and in accordance with hypothesis 1. Some mothers (18.8%) with a VB presented PTSD symptoms compared to 21.6 and 27.3% of those who respectively had a PCS and an UOB. Fathers attending a VB were 6.6% to report PTSD symptoms compared to 9.5 and 10% of those who, respectively attended a PCS and an UOB. However, none of these differences was

TABLE 3 | Bivariate Pearson correlations with probable ASD and PTSD diagnosis and with PTSD severity at 1 month post-partum.

	ASD probable diagnosis (mothers; fathers)	PTSD probable diagnosis (mothers; fathers; both parents[a])		PTSD severity
Gender			**−0.17***[a]	**−0.24***[b]
Age	−0.05; **−0.29***	0.00; −0.00	−0.02[a]	−0.03[b]
Socio-economic status (Largo)	−0.16: 0.03	0.04; **0.23***	0.07[a]	0.08[b]
Anxiety (pregnancy 3rd trimester)	**0.20***; 0.05			
Depression (pregnancy 3rd trimester)	**0.18***; 0.16			
Anxiety (at 1 week post partum)		**0.39*; 0.32***	0.40*[a]	**0.53***[b]
Depression (at 1 week post-partum)		**0.43*; 0.44***	0.40*[a]	**0.56***[b]
ASD probable diagnosis			**0.37***[a]	
ASD severity				**0.73***[b]
Previous traumatic birth	0.03; 0.04	0.03; −0.09	0.02	0.04[b]
Previous perinatal loss	0.09; −0.16	**0.15*;** 0.08	0.14*[a]	0.06[b]

**p* < 0.050.
[a]*Correlations calculated regardless of the gender as it was an independent variable in the logistic regression of PTSD at 1 month.*
[b]*Correlations calculated regardless of the gender as it was an independent variable in the regression of PTSD (continuous scores).*
All values that were significant have a star and are in bold.

TABLE 4 | Logistic regression of ASD at 1 week for mothers according to type of birth.

ASD at 1 week	Odd ratio	*p*-value	95% confidence interval	
Anxiety in 3rd trimester	1.09	0.276	0.93	1.27
Depression in 3rd trimester	1.17	0.074	0.95	1.38
Mode of birth:				
Planned C-section	1.17	0.752	0.42	3.22
Unplanned operative birth	3.1	0.032	0.16	8.74

TABLE 5 | Logistic regression of ASD at 1 week for fathers according to type of birth.

ASD at 1 week	Odd ratio	*p*-value	95% confidence interval	
Age	0.9	0.089	0.8	1.01
Mode of birth:				
Planned C-section	0.81	0.728	0.25	2.61
Unplanned operative birth	1.26	0.675	0.43	3.72

significant (both p=ns). In the logistic regression [$\chi^2_{(5,N=108)} = 31.43$; $p < 0.00$], the whole model was significant. Anxiety and depression symptoms showed a significant influence on probable PTSD at 1 month post-partum but not on mode of birth (see **Table 7**). For fathers, this analysis could not be not performed due to small sample size (men who attended a PCS and had a probable PTSD = 2).

For PTSD symptoms, the mean severity score for mothers was 6.78 (SD = 6.94) and 3.54 (SD = 4.49) for fathers. This difference was significant ($z = 5.46$; $p < 0.0001$; $d = 0.517$) and in accordance with hypothesis 1. The three symptom cluster scores of PTSD were also higher for mothers than fathers, as predicted in hypothesis 1 (see **Table 8**).

TABLE 6 | Differences in ASD symptom severity according to gender (*T*-test).

	Mothers	Fathers	*z*	*p*	*d*
Arousal symptoms [mean (SD)]	(*n* = 306) 8.95 (3.90)	(*n* = 150) 7.88 (2.73)	2.40	0.0165	0.302
Avoidance symptoms [mean (SD)]	(*n* = 158) 3.94 (1.52)	(*n* = 91) 3.61 (1.10)	1.69	0.0451	0.236
Negative emotions symptoms [mean (SD)]	(*n* = 308) 2.81 (1.33)	(*n* = 151) 2.43 (0.92)	3.37	0.0008	0.307
Reexperiencing symptoms [mean (SD)]	5.62 (2.60)	4.92 (1.44)	2.27	0.0232	0.309

TABLE 7 | Logistic regression of PTSD at 1 month for mothers according to type of birth.

PTSD at 1 week	Odd ratio	*p*-value	95% confidence interval	
Anxiety at 1 week post-partum	1.22	0.005	1.06	1.4
Depression at 1 week post-partum	1.16	0.03	1.01	1.32
Previous perinatal loss	2.61	0.073	0.92	7.43
Mode of birth:	1.54	0.516	0.42	5.72
Planned C-section				
Unplanned operative birth	2.71	0.083	0.88	8.4

TABLE 8 | Differences in PTSD symptom severity according to gender (*T*-test).

	Mothers	Fathers	*z*	*p*	*d*
	($n = 286$)	($n = 141$)			
Arousal symptoms [mean (SD)]	3.33 (3.23)	1.85 (2.21)	4.64	0.0165	0.502
	($n = 287$)	($n = 139$)			
Avoidance symptoms [mean (SD)]	2.08 (2.90)	1.19 (2.16)	3.71	0.0002	0.332
	($n = 288$)	($n = 141$)			
Reexperiencing symptoms [mean (SD)]	1.38 (2.26)	0.54 (1.41)	4.99	<0.001	0.415

TABLE 9 | Proportions of mothers and fathers having PTSD regarding ASD status.

	No ASD: *n* (%) mothers; fathers	ASD: *n* (%) mothers; fathers
No PTSD (*N*; %)	51 (96.23%)[a]; 39 (100%)[b]	52 (59.77%)[a]; 35 (83.33%)[b]
PTSD (*N*; %)	2 (3.77%)[a]; 0[b]	35 (40.23%)[a]; 7 (16.67%)[b]

[a] $[\chi^2_{(1,N=140)} = 22.51; p < 0.0001]$.
[b] $[\chi^2_{(1,N=81)} = 7.11; p = 0.008]$.

TABLE 10 | Logistic regression of PTSD at 1 month.

PTSD at 1 month	Odd ratio	*p*-value	95% confidence interval	
ASD	8.64	0.006	1.85	40.42
Gender	0.49	0.192	0.17	1.42
Anxiety at 1 week	1.11	0.098	0.97	1.27
Depression at 1 week	1.19	0.008	1.05	1.37
Previous perinatal loss	2.14	0.107	0.85	5.39

TABLE 11 | Regression of PTSD at 1 month (continuous score).

PTSD severity at 1 month	coefficient	*p-value*	95% confidence interval	
ASD severity	0.55	<0.0001	0.43	0.67
Gender	−0.87	0.192	−2.19	0.44
Anxiety at 1 week	0.14	0.194	−0.07	0.36
Depression at 1 week	0.25	0.029	0.03	0.47
Previous perinatal loss	0.01	0.984	−1.34	1.37

TABLE 12 | Regression of PTSD (continuous score) at 1 month with interaction of ASD and gender.

PTSD at 1 month	Coefficient	*p*-value	95% confidence interval	
ASD severity	0.55	<0.0001	0.42	0.67
Gender: men	−1.58	0.533	−6.58	3.42
Gender and ASD combined	−0.36	0.772	−0.21	0.29
Anxiety at 1 week	0.14	0.207	−0.08	0.36
Depression at 1 week	0.25	0.029	0.03	0.47
Previous perinatal loss	0.02	0.977	−1.34	1.38

ASD as a Predictor of PTSD After Childbirth

ASD was a predictor of PTSD: 32.6% of parents with probable ASD had probable PTSD after 1 month, whereas 97% of parents without probable ASD did not develop probable PTSD at 1 month post-partum (see **Table 9**). When participants had probable ASD, their risk to develop probable PTSD was 8.6 times than those without probable ASD, even after including gender, anxiety/depression at 1 week, and previous perinatal loss in the regression. The regression model was significant $[\chi^2_{(5,N=182)} = 64.72; p < 0.0001]$ and explained 33.3% of the variance of probable PTSD diagnosis (see **Table 10**).

According to the regression model (**Table 11**), the ASD severity score was also a predictor of the PTSD severity score at 1 month post-partum. The model $[\chi^2_{(4,N=219]} = 72.83; p < 0.0001]$ explained 57% of the variance of PTSD symptoms severity score.

To determine if probable ASD was a stronger predictor of probable PTSD for mothers than fathers, a logistic regression was conducted, where probable ASD and gender were combined. However, this was not possible, as the number of fathers with probable PTSD was insufficient. Thus, a linear regression was conducted, including an interaction between ASD symptoms and gender. No differences in the predictive aspect of ASD symptoms according to gender were found (**Table 12**). The model $[\chi^2_{(5,N=219)} = 58.02; p < 0.0001]$ explained 58% of the variance of PTSD.

DISCUSSION

This prospective population-based cohort study firstly aimed to compare the prevalence of ASD and PTSD probable diagnosis and symptoms severity between mothers and fathers following childbirth, while considering other comorbid variables, such as anxiety, depression, obstetric variables, and previous perinatal loss. The second aim of this study was to determine if probable ASD was a predictor of probable PTSD after childbirth. We found that 63.9% of mothers and 51.7% of fathers presented symptoms of ASD at 1 week post-partum and 20.7% of mothers and 7.2% of fathers reported PTSD symptoms after 1 month, confirming hypothesized gender differences. Probable ASD was found to be a predictor of probable PTSD after childbirth, confirming hypothesis 2. Those findings are important because they underline the importance of early screening of ASD and its potential relation to future PTSD development.

It is worth noting that in the third trimester, probable PTSD rates were 20.3% for fathers and 24.3% for mothers. These rates correspond to high risk samples (10). In our study, this can perhaps be explained by a previous traumatic birth (13.7%) or a previous perinatal loss (21.8%) experienced by the participants, in line with the theoretical framework highlighting previous traumatic birth or problems associated with previous pregnancy as risk factors for PTSD (54).

Unlike prevalence rates of PTSD-CB, prevalence of general psychological distress in the third trimester (mothers: 20.2%; fathers: 10.9%) is more in line with community samples in the literature (8, 31). In our study, only depression symptoms showed as a significant confounder in the prediction of PTSD. However, this may be due to the relatively low level of anxiety in the sample in comparison to the high scores of ASD and PTSD symptoms.

The maternal prevalence rate of probable ASD diagnosis, regardless of the delivery mode, was higher than that in other studies (12), but was more similar to rates found in the NICU (35, 38, 48, 65). Thus, as indicated by the probable PTSD rates in the third trimester, our sample corresponds more to a high-risk sample.

The prevalence of probable PTSD diagnosis regardless of the delivery mode in our study of 20.7% for mothers at 1 month post-partum is in accordance with a systematic review reporting a rate of 18.5% for high-risk samples (11). The suggestion that we have a high-risk sample from the third trimester data is born out post-partum, for mothers at least. For fathers, given the scarcity of studies, our prevalence rate of probable PTSD of 7.2% is within the current estimates: 0–5% (27, 28, 31), with a maximum of 12% depending on sampling method (30).

As hypothesized, in our study, gender differences were found in ASD and PTSD (prevalence, symptoms and clusters) between mothers and fathers. Mothers had a significantly higher rate of probable ASD diagnosis and symptom severity than fathers. These gender differences in severity score add to the evidence of gender differences in NICU parents (38, 48). Gender differences in probable ASD diagnosis are less consistent. Our results correspond to a study in NICU parents (35), though contrasts others, where no differences were found (38, 48). Whether differences in evidence are due to methodological differences or other factors, such as reasons for NICU admission, are as yet unclear and should be further investigated.

Mothers also showed a higher probable PTSD diagnosis rate and symptom severity than fathers. Such gender differences in probable diagnosis rates have also been seen in other studies (37), though these differences were not always significant (33, 35). Gender differences in symptom severity scores are also in line with previous studies (27, 30) Gender differences in ASD and PTSD could possibly be explained by "living" (direct exposure) being more predictive of ASD than "witnessing" (indirect exposure) a traumatic event, or that fathers put their spouse's needs first, resulting in the tendency to underreport their symptoms (27). Symptom severity was higher for mothers following birth across all ASD and PTSD symptom clusters. In the NICU, studies also found a significant difference for re-experiencing symptoms and arousal (32, 33, 37). Mothers may report more arousal symptoms, as they include sleep disturbance, a common symptom in the post-partum period (16).

Contrary to previous studies (1, 54, 66), we found no evidence that OB (PCS or UOB) is a risk factor for either ASD or PTSD symptoms in mothers. There was no significant difference in probable ASD diagnosis rates for mothers or fathers regarding the delivery mode. However, in the logistic regression models, the risk to develop ASD was 3.1 times higher in mothers following UOB. Therefore, our hypothesis that there would be differences between probable parental PTSD and ASD by birth mode was not supported. Results may be explained by the fact that, according to Beck (67), "what is found traumatic lies in the eye of the beholder" (p.2). This underlines the importance of the subjective birth experience, as found in some studies (10, 54, 68, 69). According to Garthus-Niegel et al. (68), even if the objective birth experience can lead to PTSD symptoms, the subjective birth experience is much more important. The lack of difference across birth modes for fathers may also indicate that birth mode may not carry the same risk for ASD and PTSD diagnosis in fathers. Indeed, a previous study found that childbirth is a traumatic event for men, regardless of delivery mode (70). Therefore, future studies should further investigate risk factors for fathers, as mothers and fathers may not share the same.

Although many mothers and fathers with ASD symptoms at T2 did not go on to develop PTSD symptoms at T3, ASD was found to be a predictor of PTSD at 1 month post-partum across probable PTSD diagnosis and symptom severity scores. This finding is supported by several studies in different contexts, like the NICU or PICU (40, 42). However, other studies found that ASD was not specific enough to predict PTSD (43–45). We found that 97% of parents without probable ASD did not develop probable PTSD post-partum, whereas 32.6% of parents with probable ASD had probable PTSD. Similar rates were found in the PICU (42). Identifying those with ASD and intervening with a low-level intervention may go a long way to alleviate distressing symptoms in the immediate aftermath post-partum, but also prevent PTSD from developing in a third of parents. Our results suggest that probable ASD is a greater predictor in mothers, adding nuance to this suggestion. Indeed, 40.23% of mothers with probable ASD developed probable PTSD, compared to only 16% of fathers. Thus, interventions following ASD screening may be more effective in reducing the risk of full PTSD for mothers. The lower rates of fathers with probable ASD going on to have probable PTSD again, reiterates the idea that perhaps the risk factors in PTSD development for fathers are different from those for mothers; through identification of these factors, more targeted interventions may be possible for fathers.

Strengths and Limitations

A major strength of our prospective population-based study is that we were able to compare self-reported *parental* ASD and PTSD symptoms and probable diagnosis after childbirth. Furthermore, comorbid variables, such as mode of birth, previous perinatal loss, as well as anxiety and depression symptoms, were measured at all time points and included in all regressions assessing ASD as a predictor of PTSD. Additional strengths of our study were the large sample size including mothers and fathers and the relatively high response rates.

An important limitation of the study was the convenience sample (homogeneity): all participants were recruited in the same university hospital and had to speak French, thus limiting the generalizability of the findings. The measurement of anxiety/depression, ASD and PTSD with self-report questionnaires, rather than by clinical interviews, may have overestimated the prevalence of psychological distress, as well as probable ASD and PTSD (11, 71). In addition, it should be noted that the assessment of PTSD in our study was based on DSM-IV, as no validated self-report measure for PTSD according to DSM-5 was available at the beginning of the study. Finally, it is possible that "false positives" were identified when conducting routine assessment or screening in the post-partum context, as some factors commonly associated with having a newborn (e.g., increased vigilance) can overestimate rates of PTSD following childbirth (72).

Clinical Implications and Suggestions for Future Research

The high proportion of mothers and fathers experiencing ASD and PTSD symptoms as well as probable diagnosis confirms that childbirth can be a traumatic event for *both* parents. In addition, the perinatal period can be distressing for *both* parents, with approximately one fourth of the parents presenting with anxiety and depression symptoms. Therefore, it is important to also care for fathers. Healthcare professionals should strive to better include fathers in the antenatal and post-natal checkups (73).

The Odds ratio of probable ASD diagnosis was higher for mothers following UOB, compared to mothers following VB or PCS. This suggests that birth mode may be influencing the mother's experience of her birth, resulting in trauma symptoms in the immediate aftermath. However, this was not the case for probable PTSD diagnosis. While birth mode may not influence directly PTSD, it may show an influence through ASD. Good preparation of the mother, in particular, for what happens during an operative birth, may function as a prevention method for both ASD and subsequent PTSD development.

Early screening of ASD symptoms would appear to be a good prevention method to detect parents at risk of developing PTSD, particularly for mothers. It is currently recommended to assess anxiety/depression symptoms and psychological well-being of parents as soon as possible during the pregnancy and after birth (74, 75). This should also include ASD. Therefore, all healthcare professionals, including nurses and midwives on post-partum wards, should be trained to recognize ASD. They are best placed to observe and care for mothers during their hospital stay, as well as interact with fathers. This would allow the timely referral of parents to mental health specialists for those who are in need.

More research is required to fully understand the most important risk factors for fathers' development of PTSD-CB. Obstetric variables for fathers should be measured in future studies. Our evidence suggests that partners may have different risk factors, or risk factors may have a different relative importance, compared to mothers. Finally, future studies should assess PTSD with a self-report questionnaire based on DSM-5 criteria or make use of clinical diagnostic tools.

CONCLUSION

This study shows that probable ASD diagnosis after childbirth is highly prevalent in mothers and fathers. Probable PTSD diagnosis after 1 month was present for one fifth of mothers and 7% of fathers. Caution should be taken when interpreting those prevalence rates, as the sample in our study corresponds to a high-risk sample. Mothers presented higher scores of ASD and PTSD symptoms than fathers. Probable ASD diagnosis was found to be a predictor of probable PTSD diagnosis 1 month after childbirth. Early screening of ASD symptoms may help identify parents at risk of developing PTSD.

ETHICS STATEMENT

The studies involving human participants were reviewed and approved by the ethics committee of the Canton Vaud, Switzerland. The patients/participants provided their written informed consent to participate in this study.

AUTHOR CONTRIBUTIONS

AH conceived of the study and its design, and coordinated the data collection, participated in the data analysis, and critically reviewed the manuscript. SS participated in the coordination of the study and critically reviewed the manuscript. ES conducted part of the data collection and data analysis under supervision of SS and AH. All authors co-wrote parts of the manuscript. All authors read and approved the final manuscript.

ACKNOWLEDGMENTS

We would like to thank Mr. Berthoud of Superpapa and the entire Lausanne Perinatal Research Group, especially Cassie Pernet, Joanne Horisberger, Lara Schütz, Yasmina Lotfi Mahmoud, Lauranne Jan du Chêne, Vania Sandoz, Priska Udriot, Anna Favero, Leah Gilbert, and Céline Favrod for their precious help with recruitment and data collection. We thank Dr. Perluigi Ballabeni for his help with the statistical analysis and Professors Tolsa, Vial, and Baud for institutional support.

REFERENCES

1. Horsch A, Garthus-Niegel SJC. Posttraumatic stress disorder following childbirth. In: Pickles C, Herring J, editors. *Childbirth, Vulnerability and Law: Exploring Issues of Violence and Control.* London: Routledge (2019). pp. 49–66. Available online at: https://www.routledge.com/Childbirth-Vulnerability-and-Law-Exploring-Issues-of-Violence-and-Control/Herring-Pickles/p/book/9781138335493
2. American Psychiatric Association, American Psychiatric Association, editors. *Diagnostic and Statistical Manual of Mental Disorders: DSM-5.* 5th ed. Washington, DC: American Psychiatric Association (2013). p. 947. doi: 10.1176/appi.books.9780890425596
3. Bryant RA. The current evidence for acute stress disorder. *Curr Psychiatry Rep.* (2018) 20:111. doi: 10.1007/s11920-018-0976-x
4. Shaw RJ, Bernard RS, DeBlois T, Ikuta LM, Ginzburg K, Koopman C. The relationship between acute stress disorder and posttraumatic stress disorder in the neonatal intensive care unit. *Psychosomatics.* (2009) 50:131–7. doi: 10.1176/appi.psy.50.2.131
5. Grekin R, O'Hara MW. Prevalence and risk factors of postpartum posttraumatic stress disorder: a meta-analysis. *Clin Psychol Rev.* (2014) 34:389–401. doi: 10.1016/j.cpr.2014.05.003
6. Denis A, Parant O, Callahan S. Post-traumatic stress disorder related to birth: a prospective longitudinal study in a French population. *J Reprod Infant Psychol.* (2011) 29:125–35. doi: 10.1080/02646838.2010.513048
7. Parfitt Y, Ayers S. Transition to parenthood and mental health in first-time parents: maternal health and transition to parenthood. *Infant Ment Health J.* (2014) 35:263–73. doi: 10.1002/imhj.21443
8. Dennis C-L, Falah-Hassani K, Shiri R. Prevalence of antenatal and postnatal anxiety: systematic review and meta-analysis. *Br J Psychiatry.* (2017) 210:315–23. doi: 10.1192/bjp.bp.116.187179
9. Zerach G, Magal O. Exposure to stress during childbirth, dyadic adjustment, partner's resilience, and psychological distress among first-time fathers. *Psychol Men Masculinity.* (2017) 18:123–33. doi: 10.1037/men0000048
10. Cook N, Ayers S, Horsch A. Maternal posttraumatic stress disorder during the perinatal period and child outcomes: a systematic review. *J Affect Disord.* (2018) 225:18–31. doi: 10.1016/j.jad.2017.07.045
11. Yildiz PD, Ayers S, Phillips L. The prevalence of posttraumatic stress disorder in pregnancy and after birth: a systematic review and meta-analysis. *J Affect Disord.* (2017) 208:634–45. doi: 10.1016/j.jad.2016.10.009
12. Creedy DK, Shochet IM, Horsfall J. Childbirth and the development of acute trauma symptoms: incidence and contributing factors. *Birth.* (2000) 27:104–11. doi: 10.1046/j.1523-536x.2000.00104.x
13. Garthus-Niegel S, Horsch A, Handtke E, von Soest T, Ayers S, Weidner K, et al. The impact of postpartum posttraumatic stress and depression symptoms on couples' relationship satisfaction: a population-based prospective study. *Front Psychol.* (2018) 9:1728. doi: 10.3389/fpsyg.2018.01728
14. Horsch A, Stuijfzand S. Intergenerational transfer of perinatal trauma-related consequences. *J Reprod Infant Psychol.* (2019) 37:221–3. doi: 10.1080/02646838.2019.1629190
15. Fenech G, Thomson G. Tormented by ghosts from their past': a meta-synthesis to explore the psychosocial implications of a traumatic birth on maternal well-being. *Midwifery.* (2014) 30:185–93. doi: 10.1016/j.midw.2013.12.004
16. McKenzie-McHarg K, Ayers S, Ford E, Horsch A, Jomeen J, Sawyer A, et al. Post-traumatic stress disorder following childbirth: an update of current issues and recommendations for future research. *J Reprod Infant Psychol.* (2015) 33:219–37. doi: 10.1080/02646838.2015.1031646
17. Simpson M, Catling C. Understanding psychological traumatic birth experiences: a literature review. *Women Birth.* (2016) 29:203–7. doi: 10.1016/j.wombi.2015.10.009
18. Dekel S, Thiel F, Dishy G, Ashenfarb AL. Is childbirth-induced PTSD associated with low maternal attachment? *Arch Womens Ment Health.* (2018) 22:119–22. doi: 10.1007/s00737-018-0853-y
19. Williams C, Patricia Taylor E, Schwannauer M. A web-based survey of mother-infant bond, attachment experiences, and metacognition in posttraumatic stress following childbirth: postnatal stress, attachment, and metacognition. *Infant Ment Health J.* (2016) 37:259–73. doi: 10.1002/imhj.21564
20. Garthus-Niegel S, Horsch A, Ayers S, Junge-Hoffmeister J, Weidner K, Eberhard-Gran M. The influence of postpartum PTSD on breastfeeding: a longitudinal population-based study. *Birth.* (2017) 45:193–201. doi: 10.1111/birt.12328
21. Horsch A, Vial Y, Favrod C, Harari MM, Blackwell SE, Watson P, et al. Reducing intrusive traumatic memories after emergency caesarean section: a proof-of-principle randomized controlled study. *Behav Res Ther.* (2017) 94:36–47. doi: 10.1016/j.brat.2017.03.018
22. Garthus-Niegel S, Horsch A, Bickle Graz M, Martini J, von Soest T, Weidner K, et al. The prospective relationship between postpartum PTSD and child sleep: a 2-year follow-up study. *J Affect Disord.* (2018) 241:71–9. doi: 10.1016/j.jad.2018.07.067
23. Bauer A, Parsonage M, Knapp M, Iemmi V, Adelaja B. *The Costs of Perinatal Mental Health Problems.* Centre for Mental Health. p. 44.
24. Johnson MP. The implications of unfulfilled expectations and perceived pressure to attend the birth on men's stress levels following birth attendance: a longitudinal study. *J Psychosom Obstet Gynecol.* (2002) 23:173–82. doi: 10.3109/01674820209074670
25. Lindberg I, Engström Å. A qualitative study of new fathers' experiences of care in relation to complicated childbirth. *Sex Reprod Healthc.* (2013) 4:147–52. doi: 10.1016/j.srhc.2013.10.002
26. Ayers S, Wright DB, Wells N. Symptoms of post-traumatic stress disorder in couples after birth: association with the couple's relationship and parent–baby bond. *J Reprod Infant Psychol.* (2007) 25:40–50. doi: 10.1080/02646830601117175
27. Bradley R, Slade P, Leviston A. Low rates of PTSD in men attending childbirth: a preliminary study. *Br J Clin Psychol.* (2008) 47:295–302. doi: 10.1348/014466508X279495
28. Bradley R, Slade P. A review of mental health problems in fathers following the birth of a child. *J Reprod Infant Psychol.* (2011) 29:19–42. doi: 10.1080/02646838.2010.513047
29. Helle N, Barkmann C, Ehrhardt S, Bindt C. Postpartum posttraumatic and acute stress in mothers and fathers of infants with very low birth weight: cross-sectional results from a controlled multicenter cohort study. *J Affect Disord.* (2018) 235:467–73. doi: 10.1016/j.jad.2018.04.013
30. Parfitt YM, Ayers S. The effect of post-natal symptoms of post-traumatic stress and depression on the couple's relationship and parent–baby bond. *J Reprod Infant Psychol.* (2009) 27:127–42. doi: 10.1080/02646830802350831
31. Zerach G, Magal O. Anxiety sensitivity among first-time fathers moderates the relationship between exposure to stress during birth and posttraumatic stress symptoms. *J Nerv Ment Dis.* (2016) 204:381–7. doi: 10.1097/NMD.0000000000000482
32. Aftyka A, Rybojad B, Rosa W, Wróbel A, Karakuła-Juchnowicz H. Risk factors for the development of post-traumatic stress disorder and coping strategies in mothers and fathers following infant hospitalisation in the neonatal intensive care unit. *J Clin Nurs.* (2017) 26:4436–45. doi: 10.1111/jocn.13773
33. Aftyka A, Rybojad B, Rozalska-Walaszek I, Rzońca P, Humeniuk E. Post-traumatic stress disorder in parents of children hospitalized in the neonatal intensive care unit (NICU): medical and demographic risk factors. *Psychiatr Danub.* (2014) 26:0–352.
34. Koliouli F, Gaudron CZ, Raynaud J-P. Stress, coping, and post-traumatic stress disorder of French fathers of premature infants. *Newborn Infant Nurs Rev.* (2016) 16:110–4. doi: 10.1053/j.nainr.2016.08.003
35. Lefkowitz DS, Baxt C, Evans JR. Prevalence and correlates of posttraumatic stress and postpartum depression in parents of infants in the neonatal intensive care unit (NICU). *J Clin Psychol Med Settings.* (2010) 17:230–7. doi: 10.1007/s10880-010-9202-7
36. McCarthy MC, Ashley DM, Lee KJ, Anderson VA. Predictors of acute and posttraumatic stress symptoms in parents following their child's cancer diagnosis: parent traumatic stress and childhood cancer. *J Trauma Stress.* (2012) 25:558–66. doi: 10.1002/jts.21745
37. Yaman S, Altay N. Posttraumatic stress and experiences of parents with a newborn in the neonatal intensive care unit. *J Reprod Infant Psychol.* (2015) 33:140–52. doi: 10.1080/02646838.2014.990872
38. Barr P. Acute traumatic stress in neonatal intensive care unit parents: relation to existential emotion-based personality predispositions. *J Loss Trauma.* (2010) 15:106–22. doi: 10.1080/15325020903373128

39. Roque ATF, Lasiuk GC, Radünz V, Hegadoren K. Scoping review of the mental health of parents of infants in the NICU. *J Obstet Gynecol Neonatal Nurs.* (2017) 46:576–87. doi: 10.1016/j.jogn.2017.02.005
40. Shaw RJ, Bernard RS, Storfer-Isser A, Rhine W, Horwitz SM. Parental coping in the neonatal intensive care unit. *J Clin Psychol Med Settings.* (2013) 20:135–42. doi: 10.1007/s10880-012-9328-x
41. Patiño-Fernández AM, Pai ALH, Alderfer M, Hwang W-T, Reilly A, Kazak AE. Acute stress in parents of children newly diagnosed with cancer. *Pediatr Blood Cancer.* (2008) 50:289–92. doi: 10.1002/pbc.21262
42. Balluffi A, Kassam-Adams N, Kazak A, Tucker M, Dominguez T, Helfaer M. Traumatic stress in parents of children admitted to the pediatric intensive care unit. *Pediatr Crit Care Med.* (2004) 5:547–53. doi: 10.1097/01.PCC.0000137354.19807.44
43. Bryant RA. Acute stress disorder as a predictor of posttraumatic stress disorder: a systematic review. *J Clin Psychiatry.* (2011) 72:233–9. doi: 10.4088/JCP.09r05072blu
44. Bryant RA, Friedman MJ, Spiegel D, Ursano R, Strain J. A review of acute stress disorder in DSM-5. *Depress Anxiety.* (2011) 28:802–17. doi: 10.1002/da.20737
45. Kassam-Adams N, Fleisher CL, Winston FK. Acute stress disorder and posttraumatic stress disorder in parents of injured children. *J Trauma Stress.* (2009) 22:294–302. doi: 10.1002/jts.20424
46. Bryant RA, Harvey AG. Gender differences in the relationship between acute stress disorder and posttraumatic stress disorder following motor vehicle accidents. *Aust N Z J Psychiatry.* (2003) 37:226–9. doi: 10.1046/j.1440-1614.2003.01130.x
47. Olff M. Sex and gender differences in post-traumatic stress disorder: an update. *Eur J Psychotraumatology.* (2017) 8:1351204. doi: 10.1080/20008198.2017.1351204
48. Shaw RJ, Deblois T, Ikuta L, Ginzburg K, Fleisher B, Koopman C. Acute stress disorder among parents of infants in the neonatal intensive care nursery. *Psychosomatics.* (2006) 47:206–12. doi: 10.1176/appi.psy.47.3.206
49. Gamba Szijarto S, Forcada Guex M, Borghini A, Pierrehumbert B, Ansermet F, Müller Nix C. État de stress post-traumatique chez les mères et chez les pères d'enfants prématurés : similitudes et différences. *Neuropsychiatr Enfance Adolesc.* (2009) 57:385–91. doi: 10.1016/j.neurenf.2009.04.001
50. Ionio C, Colombo C, Brazzoduro V, Mascheroni E, Confalonieri E, Castoldi F, et al. Mothers and fathers in NICU: the impact of preterm birth on parental distress. *Eur J Psychol.* (2016) 12:604–21. doi: 10.5964/ejop.v12i4.1093
51. Darwin Z, Galdas P, Hinchliff S, Littlewood E, McMillan D, McGowan L, et al. Fathers' views and experiences of their own mental health during pregnancy and the first postnatal year: a qualitative interview study of men participating in the UK Born and Bred in Yorkshire (BaBY) cohort. *BMC Pregnancy Childbirth.* (2017) 17:45. doi: 10.1186/s12884-017-1229-4
52. Gürber S, Baumeler L, Grob A, Surbek D, Stadlmayr W. Antenatal depressive symptoms and subjective birth experience in association with postpartum depressive symptoms and acute stress reaction in mothers and fathers: a longitudinal path analysis. *Eur J Obstet Gynecol Reprod Biol.* (2017) 215:68–74. doi: 10.1016/j.ejogrb.2017.05.021
53. Iles J, Slade P, Spiby H. Posttraumatic stress symptoms and postpartum depression in couples after childbirth: the role of partner support and attachment. *J Anxiety Disord.* (2011) 25:520–30. doi: 10.1016/j.janxdis.2010.12.006
54. Ayers S, Bond R, Bertullies S, Wijma K. The aetiology of post-traumatic stress following childbirth: a meta-analysis and theoretical framework. *Psychol Med.* (2016) 46:1121–34. doi: 10.1017/S0033291715002706
55. Andersen LB, Melvaer LB, Videbech P, Lamont RF, Joergensen JS. Risk factors for developing post-traumatic stress disorder following childbirth: a systematic review. *Acta Obstet Gynecol Scand.* (2012) 91:1261–72. doi: 10.1111/j.1600-0412.2012.01476.x
56. King L, McKenzie-McHarg K, Horsch A. Testing a cognitive model to predict posttraumatic stress disorder following childbirth. *BMC Pregnancy Childbirth.* (2017) 17:32. doi: 10.1186/s12884-016-1194-3
57. Birmes P, Brunet A, Benoit M, Defer S, Hatton L, Sztulman H, et al. Validation of the peritraumatic dissociative experiences questionnaire self-report version in two samples of French-speaking individuals exposed to trauma. *Eur Psychiatry.* (2005) 20:145–51. doi: 10.1016/j.eurpsy.2004.06.033
58. Bryant RA, Harvey AG. *Acute Stress Disorder: A Handbook of Theory, Assessment, and Treatment.* Washington, DC: American Psychological Association (2000). doi: 10.1037/10346-000
59. Bryant RA, Moulds ML, Guthrie RM. Acute stress disorder scale: a self-report measure of acute stress disorder. *Psychol Assess.* (2000) 12:61–8. doi: 10.1037/1040-3590.12.1.61
60. Hearn M, Ceschi G, Brillon P, Fürst G, Van der Linden M. A French adaptation of the posttraumatic diagnostic scale. *Can J Behav Sci Can Sci Comport.* (2012) 44:16–28. doi: 10.1037/a0025591
61. Foa EB, Cashman L, Jaycox L, Perry K. The validation of a self-report measure of posttraumatic stress disorder: the posttraumatic diagnostic scale. *Psychol Assess.* (1997) 9:445–51. doi: 10.1037/1040-3590.9.4.445
62. Langevin V, François M, Boini S, Riou A. Hospital anxiety and depression scale (HADS)-article de revue-INRS. *Doc Pour Médecin Trav.* (2011) 481–5.
63. Zigmond AS, Snaith RP. The hospital anxiety and depression scale. *Acta Psychiatr Scand.* (1983) 67:361–70. doi: 10.1111/j.1600-0447.1983.tb09716.x
64. Largo R, Pfister D, Molinari L, Kundu S, Lipp A, Duc G. Significance of prenatal, perinatal and postnatal factors in the development of AGA-preterm children at 5–7 years. *Dev Med Child Neurol.* 31:440–56.
65. Vanderbilt D, Bushley T, Young R, Frank DA. Acute posttraumatic stress symptoms among urban mothers with newborns in the neonatal intensive care unit: a preliminary study. *J Dev Behav Pediatr.* (2009) 30:50–6. doi: 10.1097/DBP.0b013e318196b0de
66. Goutaudier N, Séjourné N, Bui É, Cazenave N, Chabrol H. L'accouchement prématuré: une naissance traumatique? Symptômes de stress posttraumatique et variables associées. *Gynécologie Obstétrique Fertil.* (2014) 42:749–54. doi: 10.1016/j.gyobfe.2014.05.004
67. Beck CT. Middle range theory of traumatic childbirth: the ever-widening ripple effect. *Glob Qual Nurs Res.* (2015) 2:2333393615575313. doi: 10.1177/2333393615575313
68. Garthus-Niegel S, von Soest T, Vollrath ME, Eberhard-Gran M. The impact of subjective birth experiences on post-traumatic stress symptoms: a longitudinal study. *Arch Womens Ment Health.* (2013) 16:1–10. doi: 10.1007/s00737-012-0301-3
69. Dekel S, Stuebe C, Dishy G. Childbirth Induced posttraumatic stress syndrome: a systematic review of prevalence and risk factors. *Front Psychol.* (2017) 8:560. doi: 10.3389/fpsyg.2017.00560
70. Inglis C, Sharman R, Reed R. Paternal mental health following perceived traumatic childbirth. *Midwifery.* (2016) 41:125–31. doi: 10.1016/j.midw.2016.08.008
71. Woolf C, Muscara F, Anderson VA, McCarthy MC. Early traumatic stress responses in parents following a serious illness in their child: a systematic review. *J Clin Psychol Med Settings.* (2016) 23:53–66. doi: 10.1007/s10880-015-9430-y
72. Horsch A, Ayers S. Childbirth and Stress. In: Fink G, editor. *Stress: Concepts, Cognition, Emotion, and Behavior.* San Diego: Elsevier (2016). p. 325–330. doi: 10.1016/B978-0-12-800951-2.00040-6
73. Elmir R, Schmied V. A meta-ethnographic synthesis of fathers' experiences of complicated births that are potentially traumatic. *Midwifery.* (2016) 32:66–74. doi: 10.1016/j.midw.2015.09.008
74. Austin M-P, Highet N, Expert Group. *Mental Health Care in the Perinatal Period: Australian Clinical Practice Guideline.* Melbourne, VIC: Centre of Perinatal Excellence (2017).
75. Hall MF. How to help women at risk for acute stress disorder after childbirth. *Nurs Womens Health.* (2014) 18:449–54. doi: 10.1111/1751-486X.12157

22

Posttraumatic Stress Disorder, Suicidal Ideation, and Suicidal Self-Directed Violence among U.S. Military Personnel and Veterans

Ryan Holliday[1,2], Lauren M. Borges[1,2], Kelly A. Stearns-Yoder[1,3], Adam S. Hoffberg[1], Lisa A. Brenner[1,2,3,4] and Lindsey L. Monteith[1,2]*

[1] Rocky Mountain Mental Illness Research, Education and Clinical Center for Veteran Suicide Prevention, Aurora, CO, United States, [2] Department of Psychiatry, University of Colorado Anschutz Medical Campus, Aurora, CO, United States, [3] Department of Physical Medicine and Rehabilitation, University of Colorado Anschutz Medical Campus, Aurora, CO, United States, [4] Department of Neurology, University of Colorado Anschutz Medical Campus, Aurora, CO, United States

Edited by:
Moshe Bensimon,
Bar-Ilan University, Israel

Reviewed by:
Leah Shelef,
Israeli Air Force, Israel
Michela Bonafede,
National Institute for Insurance Against Accidents at Work (INAIL), Italy
Eyal Fruchter,
Technion Israel Institute of Technology, Israel

***Correspondence:**
Ryan Holliday
ryan.holliday@va.gov

Rates of suicide and posttraumatic stress disorder remain high among United States military personnel and veterans. Building upon prior work, we conducted a systematic review of research published from 2010 to 2018 regarding: (1) the prevalence of suicidal ideation, suicide attempt, and suicide among United States military personnel and veterans diagnosed with posttraumatic stress disorder; (2) whether posttraumatic stress disorder was associated with suicidal ideation, suicide attempt, and suicide among United States military personnel and veterans. 2,106 titles and abstracts were screened, with 48 articles included. Overall risk of bias was generally high for studies on suicidal ideation or suicide attempt and low for studies on suicide. Across studies, rates of suicidal ideation, suicide attempt, and suicide widely varied based on study methodology and assessment approaches. Findings regarding the association between posttraumatic stress disorder diagnosis with suicidal ideation and suicide were generally mixed, and some studies reported that posttraumatic stress disorder was associated with lower risk for suicide. In contrast, most studies reported significant associations between posttraumatic stress disorder and suicide attempt. These findings suggest complex associations between posttraumatic stress disorder and suicidal ideation, suicide attempt, and suicide, which are likely influenced by other factors (e.g., psychiatric comorbidity). In addition, most samples were comprised of veterans, rather than military personnel. Further research is warranted to elucidate associations between posttraumatic stress disorder and suicidal ideation, suicide attempt, and suicide, including identification of moderators and mediators of this relationship. Addressing this among United States military personnel, by gender, and in relation to different trauma types is also necessary.

Keywords: posttraumatic stress disorder, suicidal ideation, suicide attempt, suicide, military personnel, veteran, systematic review

INTRODUCTION

Within the United States (U.S.), suicide remains a significant public health concern, with the Centers for Disease Control and Prevention (CDC) recently reporting it as the tenth overall leading cause of death (Heron, 2018). Risk for suicide is especially pronounced among U.S. military personnel and veterans, among whom adjusted suicide rates have, at times, outpaced suicide rates in the general U.S. non-veteran adult population (Reimann and Mazuchowski, 2018; Department of Veterans Affairs, 2019). As such, preventing suicide among military personnel and veterans remains a top clinical priority of the Departments of Defense and VA.

Efforts have been made to understand why U.S. military personnel and veterans are at increased risk for suicide, compared to civilians. Although suicide is understood to be etiologically complex, one potential conduit of increased risk is through traumatic experiences and their sequelae. Military personnel and veterans experience trauma with heightened propensity, both in terms of military- and non-military-related trauma, such as combat-related experiences, military sexual assault, childhood abuse, and intimate partner violence (Gates et al., 2012; Lehavot et al., 2018). Military personnel and veterans also experience high rates of posttraumatic stress disorder (PTSD) (Gates et al., 2012; Lehavot et al., 2018). As such, researchers have posited elevated rates of PTSD as a potential explanation for suicidal ideation (SI), suicide attempt (SA), and suicide among service members and veterans (Pompili et al., 2013). Indeed, prior systematic reviews and meta-analyses of the relationship between PTSD and suicide have reported significant associations between PTSD and suicide risk (Krysinska and Lester, 2010; Kanwar et al., 2013; Panagioti et al., 2015). However, to date, only one such review has focused specifically on military personnel and veterans (Pompili et al., 2013).

Pompili et al. (2013) conducted a systematic review of literature published from 1980 to 2010 regarding the association between PTSD with SI and suicidal self-directed violence (S-SDV; e.g., suicide attempt, suicide) among U.S. and Canadian military personnel and veterans. Based on their review of 18 studies, they concluded that PTSD was associated with SI, SA, and suicide. Pompili et al. further noted, however, that PTSD was associated with several mental health outcomes (e.g., psychiatric comorbidity), which may have partially accounted for the reported associations. As such, it remains difficult to ascertain to what extent PTSD independently explains heightened risk for SI, SA, and suicide among U.S. military personnel and veterans.

While the aforementioned systematic review was seminal in its focus on military personnel and veterans, the review focused on "war-related PTSD" (e.g., combat-related), limiting inference regarding PTSD from other prevalent military- or non-military related traumatic exposures (e.g., military sexual assault, childhood abuse). Another limitation of the prior review was the inclusion of studies focused on PTSD symptoms, limiting the ability to draw precise inferences regarding PTSD diagnosis, as those without a diagnosis of PTSD may have been included. In addition, since 2010, veterans from the recent conflicts in Afghanistan and Iraq have experienced high rates of deployment-related experiences, such as combat and sexual assault (Street et al., 2009; Vasterling et al., 2010; Barth et al., 2016). While some of these experiences are not necessarily unique to deployment (e.g., sexual assault can occur during training or while stateside), deployment can disrupt pre-deployment life and family functioning. For example, Paley et al. (2013) noted that deployment can introduce a number of challenges, including disruptions in family routine, extended separation from friends and family, and parenting challenges following return due to mental health sequelae. These disruptions appear particularly salient in driving PTSD symptomatology following military-related trauma (Polusny et al., 2014). This, in turn, may result in differing clinical presentations in more recent research with military personnel and veterans that could impact associations of PTSD with SI and S-SDV. As such, an updated review of the literature published since 2010 is critical.

Finally, a number of prior reviews discussed SI, SA, and suicide as categorically-similar constructs, rather than differentiating between these outcomes. This is problematic to discerning optimal clinical care to mitigate risk among service members and veterans with PTSD (Holliday et al., 2019). The VA and Department of Defense have mandated a specific classification system and nomenclature for suicide, the Centers for Disease Control and Prevention's (CDC) Suicidal Self-Directed Violence Classification System (Crosby et al., 2011), to distinguish these constructs. The CDC defines suicidal ideation as "thoughts of engaging in suicide-related behavior" (p. 90), suicide attempt as "a non-fatal self-directed potentially injurious behavior with any intent to die as a result of the behavior... which may or may not result in injury" (p. 21), and suicide as "death caused by self-directed injurious behavior with any intent to die as a result of the behavior" (p. 23). As these constructs have distinct underlying theoretical underpinnings, as well as divergent risk factors (Joiner, 2007; Nock et al., 2008; Klonsky and May, 2015; Klonsky et al., 2016; May and Klonsky, 2016), delineating the extent to which a diagnosis of PTSD is associated with SI, SA, and suicide remains crucial.

The current systematic review aimed to address these limitations and provide an enhanced update of research examining the association between PTSD diagnosis and SI, SA, and suicide among U.S. military personnel and veterans. To update prior work (c.f. Pompili et al., 2013), this review focused on literature published between 2010 and 2018. Specifically, we focused on two key questions (KQ):

KQ1. What is the prevalence of SI, SA, and suicide among U.S. military personnel and veterans with a diagnosis of PTSD?

KQ2. Is PTSD diagnosis associated with SI, SA, and suicide among U.S. military personnel and veterans?

METHODS

Methods and presentation of results map onto the Preferred Reporting Items for Systematic Reviews and Meta-Analyses (PRISMA) guidelines (Moher et al., 2009). This systematic review was registered in PROSPERO (CRD42018089267). We conducted a systematic search of literature published between

January 1, 2010 and April 25, 2018 in the following electronic databases: OVID MEDLINE, EMBASE, OVID PsycINFO, Web of Science, Cumulative Index to Nursing and Allied Health Literature (CINAHL), Published International Literature On Traumatic Stress (PILOTS), and Cochrane Library. The search strategy was developed using medical subject heading terms (MeSH) and relevant text and key words in OVID MEDLINE, then replicated in each database (see **Supplementary Table 1** for additional information). Google Scholar was also searched to identify gray literature studies that met inclusion criteria but had been published outside traditional academic distribution channels or were not yet indexed in electronic databases. Reference lists were also mined for relevant publications not already identified.

Eligibility criteria were defined in accordance with the Population, Intervention, Comparators, Outcomes, Timing/Setting (PI[E]COTS) framework (Moher et al., 2009; Matchar, 2012). In particular, inclusion criteria were as follows: Population(s): U.S. military personnel and/or veterans; Intervention/Exposure(s): (1) Assessment and diagnosis of PTSD and (2) assessment or documentation of SI, SA, or suicide; Comparator(s): A comparison group was not required for KQ1; however, for KQ2, a comparator of no PTSD diagnosis was required; Outcome(s): Prevalence of SI, SA, or suicide among those with PTSD (KQ1); reported on the association between PTSD and SI, SA, or suicide (KQ2); and Timing/Setting: No restrictions based on timing, setting, or study design. Additional criteria for inclusion were: (1) presentation of original study data in a peer-reviewed journal article; (2) adequate data to address KQ1 and/or KQ2 (i.e., reported rate and/or association between PTSD and SI, SA, or suicide within text); (3) the full-text article was in English; and (4) published between January 1, 2010 and April 25, 2018. Exclusion criteria were as follows: (1) duplicate datasets (i.e., re-analysis of a previously reported dataset) and (2) inadequate data (i.e., inability to calculate rates or associations based on content reported within the manuscript); (3) dissertations, conference proceedings, commentaries, editorials, letters, books, book chapters, duplicate datasets, and reviews.

Databases were searched sequentially on the same day. Complete citations were exported and de-duplicated using EndNote X8 reference management software (Thomson Reuters, New York City, NY, USA). References were then exported into Covidence review software. Review of studies for inclusion was based on previously-used systematic review frameworks, including those used by the study team (Hoffberg et al., 2020).

For the PRISMA screening stage, at least two reviewers (RH, LMB, KSY, LAB) independently screened each title and abstract for retrieval. When not in agreement, a third reviewer (LLM) evaluated the record for the final retrieval decision. All co-authors have experience conducting research on PTSD and SI and S-SDV among U.S. veterans and have previously published in this domain (e.g., Brenner et al., 2011a; Holliday et al., 2018b; Barnes et al., 2019; Monteith et al., 2019).

Covidence was also used to evaluate records selected for the PRISMA eligibility stage of the review. Each full-text record was assessed by at least two reviewers (RH, LMB, KSY, LAB). The decision process was stepwise and based on the PICOTS model. Each reviewer progressed through the PICOTS decision tree until either all inclusion criteria were met or the record was excluded for a particular reason. Any disagreements at this stage were similarly resolved by a third blind reviewer (LLM).

Data from full-text articles selected for inclusion were abstracted into tables by three authors (RH, LMB, and LLM). Conflicts were resolved by group consensus, with RH making the final determination for inclusion. The preliminary data abstraction template was tested before being finalized. The following information was extracted: source article, population/sample (e.g., composed of military personnel or veterans, proportion of males and females within the sample, index trauma), measurement of PTSD, measurement of SI/SA/suicide, prevalence of SI/SA/suicide among those diagnosed with PTSD (KQ1), association of PTSD to SI/SA/suicide (KQ2), and additional relevant results. As variability of study designs and outcome measurements precluded a meta-analytic approach, a descriptive synthesis approach was conducted (McKenzie and Brennan, 2019). For each study included, the sample was described based on composition (i.e., military personnel or veteran) and proportion of males/females; however, due to infrequent reporting across studies, index trauma could not consistently be assessed and was thus not reported.

Included articles were classified by study design using the Taxonomy of Study Design Tool (Hartling et al., 2010) in a custom Research Electronic Data Capture (REDCap) database (Harris et al., 2009). Study design was assessed independently (KSY, ASH), with conflicts resolved by a third author (RH). Each of these authors had prior experience conducting systematic reviews or meta-analyses (Bahraini et al., 2013; Hoffberg et al., 2018, 2020; Holliday et al., 2018a; Creech et al., 2019).

After reaching consensus on study design, risk of bias was assessed using the Effective Public Health Practice Project (EPHPP) quality assessment tool for quantitative studies (Thomas et al., 2004). Bias items included selection bias, study design, confounders, blinding, data collection, withdrawals/dropouts, and other sources (e.g., no disclosure of conflicts of interest). Each of these domains, if applicable, were rated as having a low, moderate, or high risk of bias based on standard guidelines (see Thomas et al., 2004 for additional information). An overall risk of bias rating was then generated using standard guidelines (Effective Public Health Practice Project, 1998a,b), such that studies rated as having no high risk of bias domain ratings were classified as low overall risk of bias, studies having up to one high risk of bias domain rating were classified as moderate overall risk of bias, and studies having two or more high risk of bias domain ratings were classified as high overall risk of bias. Risk of bias was evaluated independently by KSY and ASH, with discrepancies discussed among KSY, ASH, and RH until achieving consensus. Both KSY and ASH had prior experience evaluating risk of bias in prior systematic reviews (e.g., Hoffberg et al., 2018, 2020).

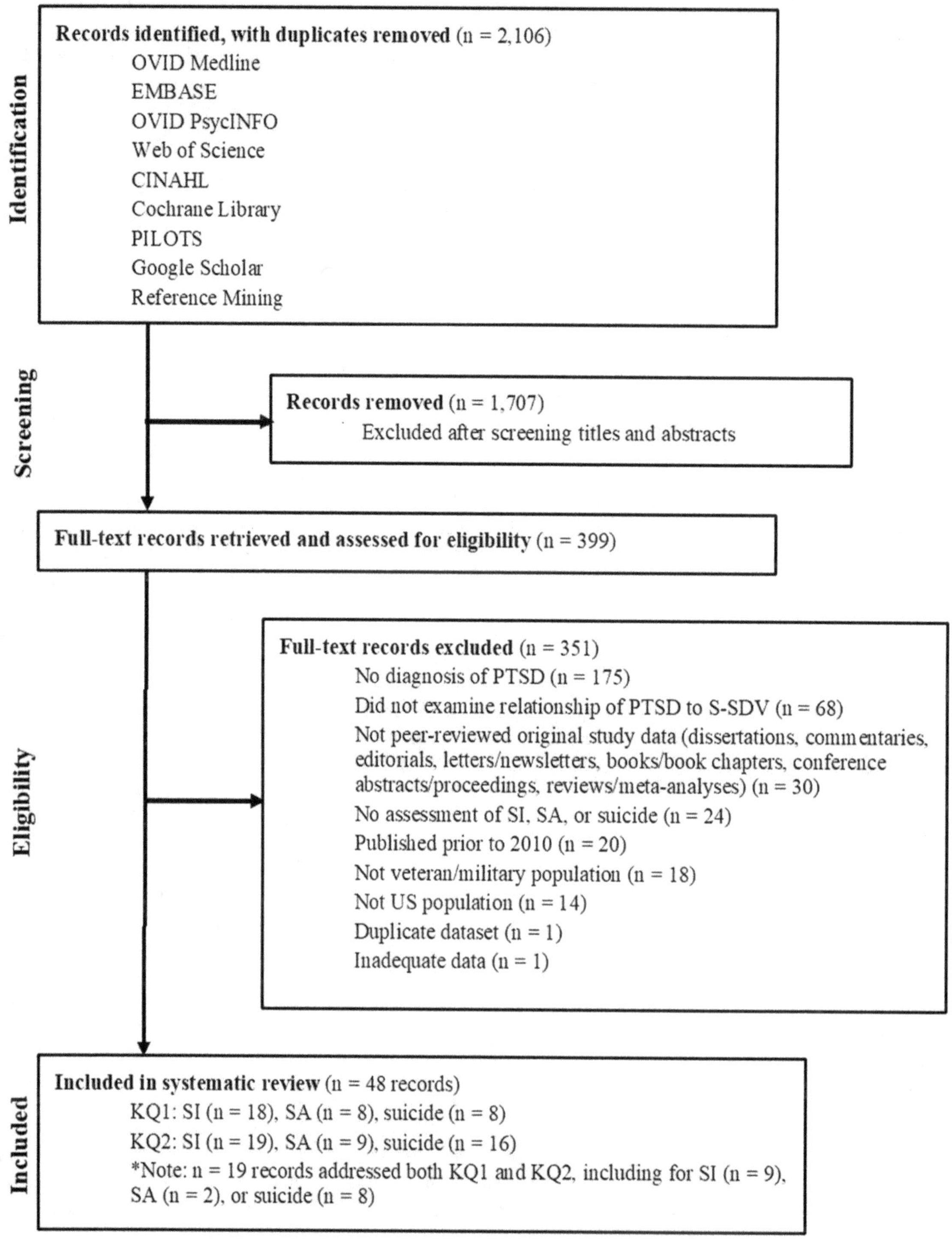

FIGURE 1 | PRISMA literature flow diagram.

RESULTS

Study Selection

As depicted in **Figure 1**, 2,106 titles and abstracts identified in electronic searches were screened after removing duplicates. Following screening, 399 full-text articles were assessed for eligibility. Based on our PICOTS criteria, 351 of these full-text articles were subsequently excluded, resulting in 48 articles included for KQ1 and/or KQ2. Risk of bias for these articles is reported in **Table 1**.

TABLE 1 | Risk of bias ratings for each study ($N = 48$).

Study	Study design	Source of bias						Overall bias
		Selection bias	Study design	Confounders	Blinding	Data collection	Withdrawals/ dropouts	
Alexander et al. (2014)	Case control	●	●	●	●	●	⊖	●
Bachynski et al. (2012)	Cross-sectional	○	●	○	●	○	⊖	●
Barnes et al. (2012)	Cross-sectional	●	●	○	●	●	⊖	●
Black et al. (2011)	Cross-sectional	○	●	○	●	○	⊖	●
Blakey et al. (2018)	Cross-sectional	●	●	○	●	○	⊖	●
Bohnert et al. (2013)	Retrospective cohort	○	●	○	●	○	○	○
Braden et al. (2015)	Cross-sectional	●	●	●	●	○	⊖	●
Brenner et al. (2011a)	Case control	●	●	○	●	○	○	○
Brenner et al. (2011b)	Retrospective cohort	○	●	○	●	○	○	○
Carroll et al. (2017)	Cross-sectional	●	●	●	●	●	⊖	●
Cohen et al. (2015)	Retrospective cohort	○	●	○	●	○	⊖	○
Conner et al. (2013)	Retrospective cohort	○	●	○	●	○	⊖	○
Conner et al. (2014)	Cross-sectional	○	●	○	●	○	⊖	●
Cornelius et al. (2012)	Cross-sectional	●	●	○	●	●	⊖	●
Corson et al. (2013)	Case control	●	●	○	●	●	⊖	○
Cox et al. (2016)	Before-after	●	●	●	●	●	●	●
Denneson et al. (2014)	Retrospective cohort	○	●	○	●	●	○	●
Dobscha et al. (2014)	Case control	○	●	○	●	○	○	○
Elbogen et al. (2018)	Cross-sectional	●	●	○	●	○	⊖	●
Finley et al. (2015)	Retrospective cohort	○	●	○	●	○	○	○
Ganocy et al. (2016)	Cross-sectional	●	●	●	●	○	⊖	●
Gradus et al. (2014)	Retrospective cohort	○	●	○	●	○	○	○
Green et al. (2010)	Cross-sectional	●	●	○	●	○	⊖	●
Hyman et al. (2012)	Cross-sectional	○	●	○	●	○	⊖	●
Ilgen et al. (2010a)	Case control	○	●	○	●	○	○	○
Ilgen et al. (2010b)	Retrospective cohort	○	●	○	●	○	○	○
Ilgen et al. (2012)	Retrospective cohort	○	●	○	●	○	○	○
Kachadourian et al. (2018)	Cross-sectional	●	●	○	●	○	⊖	●
Kessler et al. (2015)	Nested case control	○	●	○	●	○	○	○
Kimbrel et al. (2016)	Cross-sectional	●	●	○	●	○	⊖	●
Kimbrel et al. (2017)	Cross-sectional	●	●	○	●	○	⊖	●
Kimbrel et al. (2018a)	Cross-sectional	●	●	○	●	○	⊖	●
Kimbrel et al. (2018b)	Cross-sectional	●	●	○	●	○	⊖	●
Kittel et al. (2016)	Cross-sectional	●	●	○	●	○	⊖	●
Kopacz et al. (2016)	Cross-sectional	●	●	○	●	●	⊖	●
Legarreta et al. (2015)	Cross-sectional	●	●	○	●	○	⊖	●
Lemaire and Graham (2011)	Cross-sectional	○	●	○	●	●	⊖	●
Louzon et al. (2016)	Case control	○	●	○	●	○	○	○
Magruder et al. (2012)	Cross-sectional	●	●	○	●	○	⊖	●
Maguen et al. (2012)	Cross-sectional	●	●	○	●	●	⊖	●
Matthews et al. (2012)	Cross-sectional	●	●	○	●	○	⊖	●
Monteith et al. (2016)	Cross-sectional	●	●	○	●	●	⊖	●
Ribeiro et al. (2012)	Randomized controlled trial	●	●	●	●	○	●	●
(Shen et al., 2016)	Retrospective cohort	○	●	○	●	○	○	○

(Continued)

TABLE 1 | Continued

Study	Study design	Source of bias						Overall bias
		Selection bias	Study design	Confounders	Blinding	Data collection	Withdrawals/ dropouts	
Skopp et al. (2012)	Case control	○	●	○	●	○	○	○
Smith et al. (2015)	Cross-sectional	●	●	●	●	●	⊖	●
Suris et al. (2011)	Cross-sectional	●	●	●	●	○	⊖	●
Wisco et al. (2014)	Cross-sectional	●	●	○	●	●	⊖	●

Risk of bias: ○ = low; • = moderate; • = high; ⊖ = not applicable.

Synthesis of Literature

KQ1: Prevalence of SI Among Military Personnel and Veterans With PTSD

Eighteen studies reported on the prevalence of SI among U.S. military personnel or veterans diagnosed with PTSD. Rates of SI across studies ranged from 1.98 to 71.89% (**Table 2**). However, the overwhelming majority of included studies (n = 13) had a high overall risk of bias. Three had an overall moderate risk of bias and reported rates of SI ranging from 35.71 to 44.90% (Magruder et al., 2012; Denneson et al., 2014; Cox et al., 2016). Only two studies had a low overall risk of bias, reporting that 3.21–34.81% of veterans with PTSD had SI (Corson et al., 2013; Cohen et al., 2015). Of studies relying on interview or assessment measures, current/recent rates of SI ranged from 1.98 to 44.9%, whereas lifetime rates varied more broadly, from 17.39 to 71.89%. All of these studies focused on veterans; none focused exclusively on military personnel. Studies evaluating lifetime SI often comprised fairly small clinical samples, whereas studies reporting on more recent SI involved much larger samples, typically comprising treatment-seeking Operation Enduring Freedom/Operation Iraqi Freedom (OEF/OIF) veterans.

KQ1: Prevalence of SA Among Military Personnel and Veterans With PTSD

The eight studies on rates of SA among those diagnosed with PTSD reported rates ranging from 0.31 to 38.71% (**Table 3**). Only one included study was determined to have a low overall risk of bias (Gradus et al., 2014), and one had a moderate overall risk of bias (Kimbrel et al., 2016). Of note, all of the studies on the prevalence of SA among those with PTSD focused on veterans; none reported on rates of SA among military personnel with PTSD.

KQ1: Prevalence of Suicide Among Military Personnel and Veterans With PTSD

Eight studies were included that reported on the prevalence of suicide among military personnel and veterans diagnosed with PTSD (**Table 4**). Strength of evidence appeared strong for these studies, as the majority of included studies were determined to have a low overall risk of bias (n = 5; Ilgen et al., 2010b; Brenner et al., 2011b; Bohnert et al., 2013; Louzon et al., 2016; Shen et al., 2016). Four studies reported the percent of military personnel or veterans with PTSD who died by suicide, with a range of <0.01–0.30% (Brenner et al., 2011b; Bohnert et al., 2013; Conner et al., 2014; Louzon et al., 2016). An additional four studies reported rates per person-years, ranging from 55.1 to 159.9 per 100,000 (Ilgen et al., 2010b; Black et al., 2011; Bachynski et al., 2012; Louzon et al., 2016), with rates ranging based on timeframe (e.g., per-person year, per-person quarter).

KQ2: Association of PTSD With SI Among Military Personnel and Veterans

Nineteen studies reported on the association between PTSD and SI. The majority of included studies were determined to have a high overall risk of bias (n = 13), four had a moderate risk of bias (Magruder et al., 2012; Denneson et al., 2014; Monteith et al., 2016; Kimbrel et al., 2018a), and only two studies had a low overall risk of bias (Corson et al., 2013; Finley et al., 2015). Bivariate associations between PTSD and SI were generally significant (significant in ten studies, non-significant in three studies; **Table 2**). In contrast, results regarding the association between PTSD and SI at the multivariate level were mixed. Of the fourteen studies reporting multivariate results regarding the association between PTSD and SI, seven reported significant associations, and seven reported non-significant associations. All of the studies reporting significant bivariate or multivariate associations between PTSD and SI reported that these were positively, rather than inversely, associated.

KQ2: Association of PTSD With SA Among Military Personnel and Veterans

Nine studies examined the relationship between PTSD and SA. Only three had a low overall risk of bias (Brenner et al., 2011a; Gradus et al., 2014; Finley et al., 2015), all of which reported significant associations between PTSD and SA (**Table 3**). In fact, all but two studies reported significant positive associations at the bivariate and/or multivariate level. In addition, all but one study focused on veterans (versus military personnel).

KQ2: Association of PTSD With Suicide Among Military Personnel and Veterans

Sixteen studies examined the relationship between PTSD and suicide (**Table 4**), with the majority having a low overall risk of bias (n = 11; Ilgen et al., 2010a,b, 2012; Brenner et al., 2011b; Skopp et al., 2012; Bohnert et al., 2013; Conner et al., 2013; Dobscha et al., 2014; Kessler et al., 2015; Louzon et al., 2016; Shen et al., 2016). Among these 16 studies, findings were mixed. Nine studies, four of which used multivariate analyses, reported that those diagnosed with PTSD were at

TABLE 2 | SI among military personnel and veterans with PTSD ($n = 28$).

Study	Population/sample	Measurement of PTSD	Measurement of SI	Prevalence of SI among those with PTSD	Relationship of PTSD to SI	Notes
Barnes et al. (2012)	92 male OEF/OIF veterans with combat-related PTSD presenting for VA outpatient PTSD treatment.	Clinical interview (including CAPS for DSM-IV)	Interview question: "Have you had thoughts about death or about killing yourself?" (Yes/No; lifetime)	16 (17.39%) endorsed lifetime SI.*	Did not analyze relationship.	Exclusion criteria of TBI-related LOC > 30 min or PTA > 24 h.
Blakey et al. (2018)	667 OEF/OIF/OND veterans (81.0% male), active duty personnel, and National Guard and Reserve members who had served since September 11, 2001 and endorsed chronic pain.	SCID-IV	BSS and/or BDI-II item 9	Not reported.	PTSD was associated with SI on a bivariate level, $P = 0.17$, $p < 0.01$. After accounting for demographics, chronic pain intensity and interference, and comorbid MH conditions, PTSD remained a significant correlate (OR = 2.25, 95% CI: 1.18–4.24, $p = 0.01$).	Disagreement in SI scoring on BSS and BDI-II item 9 was present for 65 (51.18%) of SI data.*
Braden et al. (2015)	110 veterans (90.9% male) with a primary mood disorder diagnosis	SCID-IV	BSS	Not reported.	Accounting for demographics, PTSD was not associated with SI, $p > 0.05$; however, poorer physical health, prior psychiatric hospitalization, and past SA were associated in this sample.	Participants were excluded for a diagnosis of bipolar disorder, schizophrenia, dementia, organic brain damage, and intellectual disability.
Carroll et al. (2017)	217 male Iraq/Afghanistan-era veterans with combat-related PTSD entering a PTSD residential program.	"Intake procedures" (measure not reported)	Interview question: "Have you ever had serious thoughts of committing suicide?" (Yes/No; lifetime)	156 (71.89%) endorsed lifetime SI.	Did not analyze relationship.	Inclusion was based on presence of combat-related PTSD diagnosis. Participants were excluded based on presence of psychotic symptoms, unwillingness to stop using drugs/alcohol, and medical conditions impeding engagement in treatment.
Cohen et al. (2015)	186,460 OEF/OIF/OND veterans (90.6% male) with PTSD and an initial VHA visit from January 1, 2007 to September 30, 2011.	VA medical record	VA medical record	5,988 (3.21%) with PTSD had documented SI.*	Did not analyze relationship.	Veterans with a diagnosis of bipolar disorder or schizophrenia were excluded.
Cornelius et al. (2012)	101 veterans (89.1%) using VHA outpatient behavioral health services.	SCID-IV	BDI item 9	2 (1.98%) of those with PTSD endorsed SI.	PTSD was not associated with SI at a bivariate level, $\chi^2 = 0.08$, $p = 0.775$.	

(Continued)

TABLE 2 | Continued

Study	Population/sample	Measurement of PTSD	Measurement of SI	Prevalence of SI among those with PTSD	Relationship of PTSD to SI	Notes
Corson et al. (2013)	1,340 veterans (89.4% male) using VHA care with a positive depression screen (PHQ-2).	VA medical record	PHQ-9 item 9 and VA Pocket Card Risk Assessment	235 (34.81%) of those with PTSD endorsed SI.*	Bivariate associations between PTSD and SI were not significant, $p = 0.06$. After controlling for age, sex, marital status, branch, PHQ-2 scores, SUD, and when SI was assessed, PTSD was not predictive of SI (AOR = 1.18, 95% CI: 0.93–1.50, $p = 0.186$). Rather, the only significant MH diagnoses predictive of SI were depression and bipolar/schizophrenia.	
Cox et al. (2016)	289 veterans (89.0% male) receiving Prolonged Exposure Therapy from a VHA clinic.	CAPS for DSM-IV or PSS-I	BDI-II item 9	127 (43.94%) endorsed SI.	Did not analyze relationship.	Inclusion criterion of at least 2 timepoints of SI measurement.
Denneson et al. (2014)	465 OEF/OIF veterans (87.5% male) new to VA care who screened positive for depression.	VA medical record	PHQ-9 item 9 and/or VA Pocket Card Risk Assessment	80 (35.71%) with documented PTSD screened positive for SI.*	PTSD diagnosis was not associated with SI on a bivariate, $p = 0.07$, or multivariate level (AOR = 1.10; 95% CI: 0.72-1.69, $p = 0.67$). Multivariate results found depression to be a significant correlate adjusting for sex, age, race/ethnicity, rurality, marital status, SI assessment by MH clinician, and MH comorbidity.	
Elbogen et al. (2018)	2,543 Iraq/Afghanistan-era veterans, active duty personnel, and reserve forces (80.2% male).	SCID-IV	BSS	205 (28.55%) with PTSD endorsed SI.*	Accounting for demographics and resiliency, childhood abuse, pain, and depression, but not PTSD (OR = 1.34, 95% CI: 0.94–1.90, $p = 0.106$), were associated with SI.	Most participants were registered at a VA medical facility.
Finley et al. (2015)	211,652 veterans (86.4% male) receiving VA care during FY 2009-2011.	VA medical record	VA medical record	Not reported.	Accounting for demographics and MH comorbidity, PTSD was associated with SI (OR = 2.3, 95% CI: 2.0–2.6, $p < 0.01$), with risk increasing in the presence of MH comorbidity (e.g., depression, SUD).	
Ganocy et al. (2016)	418 Army National Guard personnel (88.0% male) participating in a longitudinal cohort study.	CAPS for DSM-IV (lifetime)	C-SSRS	Not reported.	Bivariate associations between lifetime PTSD and SI were significant, $r = 0.24$, $p < 0.01$.	The number of participants endorsing lifetime PTSD (28; 6.8%), as well as SI (32; 7.7%), were small.

(Continued)

TABLE 2 | Continued

Study	Population/sample	Measurement of PTSD	Measurement of SI	Prevalence of SI among those with PTSD	Relationship of PTSD to SI	Notes
Green et al. (2010)	497 deployed OEF/OIF veterans (83.1% male).	SCID-IV	BSS	41 (21.69%) with PTSD had past-week SI.	Those diagnosed with PTSD reported higher BSS scores at a bivariate level, $t = -4.98$, $p < 0.001$.	Veterans without lifetime trauma exposure were excluded.
Kachadourian et al. (2018)	93 veterans (93.5% male) with comorbid PTSD and alcohol dependence participating in an RCT.	SCID-IV	C-SSRS (lifetime)	60 (63.83%) with PTSD reported lifetime SI.	Did not analyze relationship.	Exclusion criteria of pregnancy, schizophrenia, schizophrenia-type disorders, bipolar disorder, active SI or homicidal ideation, use of medication likely to influence alcohol consumption, and Prazosin contraindication.
Kimbrel et al. (2017)	3,233 Iraq/Afghanistan-era veterans (79.7% male).	SCID-IV (lifetime)	BSS	Not reported.	Adjusting for sex, lifetime depression, lifetime alcohol use disorder, lifetime non-cannabis drug use disorder, lifetime cannabis use disorder, childhood sexual abuse, and combat exposure, lifetime PTSD diagnosis (OR = 2.08, 95% CI: 1.50–2.89, $p < 0.001$) as well as depression, childhood sexual abuse, combat exposure, and cannabis use disorder were associated with SI.	The majority of veterans were enrolled in VHA care.
Kimbrel et al. (2018a)	1,143 veterans (95.9% male) seeking PTSD treatment.	SCID-IV	BDI-II Item 9	Not reported.	PTSD was associated with presence of SI (OR = 2.13; 95% CI: 1.43–3.18, $p < 0.05$), accounting for gender, age, combat exposure, and NSSI.	
Kittel et al. (2016)	130 (85.3% male) Iraq and Afghanistan-era veterans enrolled in VHA care.	CAPS for DSM-IV	BSS	Not reported.	A bivariate, positive relationship between current PTSD diagnosis and past week SI severity was significant, $p = 0.002$.	Participants were excluded if endorsed SI, intent or plan warranting crisis intervention; none excluded based on this criterion.
Kopacz et al. (2016)	472 (94.1% male) veterans admitted for treatment at one of two VA PTSD Residential Rehabilitation Programs	Clinical interview and unreported assessment measures	Affirmative response to: "Have you ever had serious thoughts of committing suicide?" (lifetime)	336 (71.19%) reported a lifetime history of SI*	Not reported.	
Legarreta et al. (2015)	95 veterans (77.9% male) who reported at least one lifetime *DSM–5* Criterion A traumatic event.	Checklist created using SCID-IV, Trauma Symptom Index, HAM-D, Profile of Mood States, and methodical query	C-SSRS (lifetime)	47 (49.47%) with PTSD endorsed lifetime SI.*	PTSD was associated with lifetime SI at a bivariate level, $\chi^2 = 5.05$, $p = 0.03$.	Exclusion criteria of major sensorimotor handicaps, IQ < 80, and psychosis. Unvalidated measure of PTSD.

(Continued)

TABLE 2 | Continued

Study	Population/sample	Measurement of PTSD	Measurement of SI	Prevalence of SI among those with PTSD	Relationship of PTSD to SI	Notes
Lemaire and Graham (2011)	1,740 OEF/OIF veterans (84.1% male) participating in routine VA mental health screening.	VA medical record	Clinical interview	64 (12.88%) with PTSD reported SI.*	PTSD was associated with documented SI at the bivariate level (OR = 10.02, 95% CI: 4.02–24.97, $p < 0.001$). PTSD was not significant and thus not included in the final forward stepwise multivariate regression predicting SI. Rather, depressive disorders, social support, gender, and prior SA were noted correlates in this model.	
Magruder et al. (2012)	816 veterans (83.9% male) randomly selected from 4 Southeast VA hospitals.	CAPS for DSM-IV	MINI Suicidality module	44 (44.90%) with PTSD reported current SI.*	PTSD was positively associated with current SI at the bivariate level, $p < 0.01$. In multivariate analyses, PTSD was associated with SI in the presence of other comorbidities (depression, anxiety disorders; OR = 4.02, 95% CI: 1.95–8.29, $p < 0.05$).	Women oversampled.
Maguen et al. (2012)	259 male Vietnam veterans participating in a national survey.	SCID for DSM-III-R	Affirmative response: "Have you ever felt so low that you thought of committing suicide?" (lifetime)	Not reported.	After adjusting for demographic variables, killing experiences, depression, SUD, and PTSD (OR = 3.42, 95% CI = 1.09–10.73, $p < 0.05$) were associated with SI.	Weighted results to population of 1.3 million veterans.
Matthews et al. (2012)	26 male combat-exposed OEF/OIF veterans evaluated at an outpatient mood or psychiatric emergency clinic.	Semi-structured clinical interview	Comprehensive Suicide Risk Assessment (lifetime)	13 (54.16%) with PTSD endorsed lifetime SI.	Did not analyze relationship.	Exclusion criteria of alcohol/substance dependence in past 30 days; lifetime ADHD; psychotic, bipolar, chronic pain disorders; active medical problems; or claustrophobia.
Monteith et al. (2016)	354 (87.6% male) veterans accessing VHA care.	VA medical record	BSS	Not reported.	PTSD was associated with SI presence, $r = 0.12$, $p < 0.05$, and severity, $r = 0.23$, $p < 0.01$. When age, gender, combat exposure, depressive disorders, PTSD diagnosis, negative affect, past SA, military sexual trauma, and an interactive term of military sexual trauma x gender were included in a regression model, lifetime PTSD diagnosis was no longer associated with SI severity, $B = 0.08$, 95% CI: 0.06–2.06, $p = 0.80$.	
Ribeiro et al. (2012)	311 military personnel (82.0% male) referred for suicide-focused treatment.	DIS	MSSI	Not reported.	PTSD was associated with SI at the bivariate level, $r = 0.20$, $p < 0.01$. After accounting for baseline hopelessness, depression, anxiety, drug abuse, alcohol abuse, and insomnia symptoms, PTSD was not associated with SI, $p > 0.05$.	Results did not account for sociodemographic variables (e.g., gender).

(Continued)

TABLE 2 | Continued

Study	Population/sample	Measurement of PTSD	Measurement of SI	Prevalence of SI among those with PTSD	Relationship of PTSD to SI	Notes
Smith et al. (2015)	832 veterans (gender breakdown not reported) entering a VHA or non-profit PTSD residential program.	Prior primary diagnosis of PTSD (measure not reported)	Interview question: "Have you ever had serious thoughts of committing suicide?" (Yes/No; lifetime)	194 (71.06%) reported a lifetime history of SI.*	Did not analyze relationship.	Article reported a total sample of 832; however, suicide-related data were only reported for 273 veterans. Exclusion criteria of active psychosis, unwillingness to discontinue substance misuse, and medical conditions that would hinder/prevent engagement in treatment.
Suris et al. (2011)	128 veterans (11% male) currently diagnosed with military sexual assault-related PTSD participating in a PTSD RCT.	CAPS for DSM-IV	BDI-II Item 9	59 (46.09%) of sample endorsed SI.*	Did not analyze relationship.	Exclusion criterion of "active suicidality."
Wisco et al. (2014)	1,649 deployed OEF/OIF/OND veterans (49.9% male).	SCID for DSM-IV (lifetime)	MINI Suicidality module	375 (30.00%) of veterans with a lifetime diagnosis of PTSD reported current SI.*	Those with PTSD reported SI more frequently at a bivariate level, $V = 0.19$, $p < 0.001$. After accounting for age, gender, ethnicity, race, combat and postbattle experiences, postdeployment support, depressive symptoms, alcohol problems, and TBI, lifetime PTSD was associated with SI: $RR = 2.16$, 95% CI: 1.29-3.61, $p < 0.05$.	Participants deemed to be at "high suicide risk" were excluded. Oversampled veterans with probable PTSD. Results were significant for both males and females for gender-stratified.

Calculated using data reported in manuscript.

BDI-II, Beck Depression Inventory-II; BSS, Beck Scale for Suicide Ideation; C-SSRS, Columbia-Suicide Severity Rating Scale; CAPS, Clinician Administered PTSD Scale; DIS, Diagnostic Interview Schedule; DSM-IV, Diagnostic and Statistical Manual of Mental Disorders-IV; FY, fiscal year; HAM-D, Hamilton Rating Scale for Depression; IQ, intelligence quotient; LOC, loss of consciousness; MH, mental health; MINI, Mini International. Neuropsychiatric Interview; MSSI, Modified Scale for Suicidal Ideation; NSSI, non-suicidal self-injury; OR, odds ratio; PHQ-2: Patient Health Questionnaire-2; PHQ-9: Patient Health Questionnaire-9; PTA, posttraumatic amnesia; PSS-I, Posttraumatic Symptom Interview; PTSD, posttraumatic stress disorder; RCT, randomized clinical trial; RR, relative risk; SCID for DSM-III-R, Structured Clinical Interview for DSM-III-R; SCID-IV, Structured Clinical Interview for DSM-IV; SUD, substance use disorder; TBI, traumatic brain injury; VA, Department of Veterans Affairs; VHA, Veterans Health Administration.

TABLE 3 | SA among Military Personnel and Veterans with PTSD ($n = 15$).

Study	Population/sample	Measurement of PTSD	Measurement of SA	Prevalence of SA among those with PTSD	Relationship of PTSD to SA	Notes
Barnes et al. (2012)	92 male OEF/OIF veterans with combat-related PTSD presenting for VA outpatient PTSD treatment.	Clinical interview (including CAPS for DSM-IV)	Interview question: "Have you ever attempted suicide?" (Yes/No; lifetime)	5 (5.43%) reported a history of SA.*	Did not analyze relationship	Excluded if loss of consciousness exceeded 30 min or posttraumatic amnesia exceeded 24 h.
Brenner et al. (2011a)	241 veterans (83.0% male) using VHA care.	VA medical record	VA medical record	Not reported.	Bivariate associations between PTSD and SA were significant, $\chi^2 = 10.7$, $p = 0.001$. In a multivariate regression of PTSD and TBI, PTSD was a predictor of SA (OR = 2.85, 95% CI: 1.55–5.22, $p = 0.0007$).	Veterans with SA history were matched to controls with no SA history, based on gender and age.
Carroll et al. (2017)	217 male Iraq/Afghanistan-era veterans with combat-related PTSD entering a PTSD residential program.	"Intake procedures" (measure not reported)	Interview question: "Have you attempted suicide in your lifetime?" (Yes/No; lifetime)	84 (38.71%) endorsed lifetime SA.	Did not analyze relationship.	Inclusion was based on presence of combat-related PTSD diagnosis. Participants were excluded based on presence of psychotic symptoms, unwillingness to stop using drugs/alcohol, and medical conditions impeding engagement in treatment.
Finley et al. (2015)	211,652 veterans (86.4% male) receiving VA care during FY 2009-2011.	VA medical record	VA medical record	Not reported.	Accounting for demographics and MH comorbidity, PTSD was associated with SA (OR = 1.8, 95% CI: 1.2–2.8, $p < 0.01$), with risk increasing in the presence of MH comorbidity (e.g., depression, SUD).	
Gradus et al. (2014)	68,506 veterans (92.1% male) using VHA care.	VA medical record	VA medical record	49 (0.31%) with PTSD had a documented prior SA*	Adjusting for marital status, depression, alcohol/drug abuse/dependence, anxiety disorder diagnoses, and intentional self-harm, PTSD was associated with non-fatal intentional self-harm in both males (RR = 3.2, 95% CI = 2.3, 4.5) and females (RR = 16, 95% CI = 4.8, 56).	SA classified as "non-fatal intentional self-harm."
Kachadourian et al. (2018)	93 veterans (93.5% male) with comorbid PTSD and alcohol dependence participating in an RCT.	SCID-IV	C-SSRS (lifetime)	19 (21.59%) with PTSD reported lifetime SA.	Did not analyze relationship.	Exclusion criteria of pregnancy, schizophrenia, schizophrenia-type disorders, bipolar disorder, active SI or homicidal ideation, use of medication likely to influence alcohol consumption, and Prazosin contraindication.

(Continued)

TABLE 3 | Continued

Study	Population/sample	Measurement of PTSD	Measurement of SA	Prevalence of SA among those with PTSD	Relationship of PTSD to SA	Notes
Kimbrel et al. (2016)	292 veterans (67.5% male) deployed in support of Iraq and Afghanistan conflicts.	CAPS for DSM-IV (lifetime)	C-SSRS (lifetime)	19 (13.1%) with lifetime PTSD endorsed lifetime SA.*	Bivariate associations between PTSD and SA not significant, $\chi^2 = 2.379$, $p = 0.12$. PTSD was not significant in multivariate model that included gender, age, race, sexual orientation, psychiatric diagnoses, combat exposure, and non-suicidal self-injury: OR = 0.364, 95% CI: 0.11–1.22, $p > 0.05$.	Small sample reporting lifetime SA (30; 10.0%)
Kimbrel et al. (2017)	3233 Iraq/Afghanistan-era veterans (79.7% male).	SCID-IV (lifetime)	BSS (lifetime)	Not reported.	Adjusting for sex, lifetime depression, lifetime alcohol use disorder, lifetime non-cannabis drug use disorder, lifetime cannabis use disorder, childhood sexual abuse, and combat exposure, PTSD was associated with SA (OR = 2.60, 95% CI: 1.87–3.61, $p < 0.001$).	Most participants were enrolled in VHA care.
Kimbrel et al. (2018b)	292 Iraq/Afghanistan-era veterans (67.5% male).	CAPS for DSM-IV (lifetime)	C-SSRS (lifetime)	Not reported.	After accounting for sociodemographics, combat exposure, traumatic life events, TBI, depression, alcohol use disorder, and non-cannabis drug use disorder, and cannabis use disorder, PTSD was not associated with SA (OR =0.52, 95% CI: 0.18–1.50, $p > 0.05$). Rather, sex, combat exposure, depression, and cannabis use disorder were positively associated with SA.	
Kopacz et al. (2016)	472 (94.1% male) veterans admitted for treatment at one of two VA PTSD Residential Rehabilitation Programs.	Clinical interview and unreported assessment measures	Affirmative response to: "Have you attempted suicide in your lifetime?" (lifetime)	171 (36.23%) reported lifetime SA.*	Not reported.	
Legarreta et al. (2015)	95 veterans (77.9% male) who reported at least one lifetime *DSM–5* Criterion A traumatic event.	Checklist created from SCID-IV, Trauma Symptom Index, HAM-D, Profile of Mood States, and methodical query	C-SSRS (lifetime)	24 (36.92%) with PTSD reported lifetime SA.*	Not reported	Exclusion criteria of major sensorimotor handicaps, IQ < 80, and psychosis. Unvalidated measure of PTSD.
Maguen et al. (2012)	259 male Vietnam veterans in a national survey.	SCID for DSM-III-R	Affirmative response to: "Have you ever attempted suicide?" (lifetime)	Not reported	PTSD was associated with SA in multivariate models that also included demographic variables, depression SUD, combat experiences, and killing experiences (OR = 5.52, 95% CI = 1.21–25.29, $p < 0.05$).	Weighted results.
Monteith et al. (2016)	354 (87.6% male) veterans accessing VHA care.	VA medical record	BSS (lifetime)	Not reported.	There was a significant bivariate relationship between PTSD and lifetime SA, $r = 0.16$, $p < 0.01$.	

(Continued)

TABLE 3 | Continued

Study	Population/sample	Measurement of PTSD	Measurement of SA	Prevalence of SA among those with PTSD	Relationship of PTSD to SA	Notes
Ribeiro et al. (2012)	311 military personnel (82.0% male) referred for suicide-focused treatment.	DIS	Clinical interview assessing whether a SA occurred since baseline during one-month follow-up	Not reported.	Accounting for baseline hopelessness, depression, anxiety, drug abuse, alcohol abuse, and insomnia symptoms, PTSD significantly predicted SA, Exp(B) = 6.71; Wald coefficient = 5.83, $p < 0.05$.	Results did not account for sociodemographic variables. Sample endorsing SA was small ($n = 10$).
Smith et al. (2015)	832 veterans (gender breakdown not reported) entering a VHA or non-profit PTSD residential program.	Prior primary diagnosis of PTSD (measure not reported)	Interview question: "Have you attempted suicide in your lifetime?" (Yes/No; lifetime)	85 (31.14%) reported a lifetime history of SA.*	Did not analyze relationship.	Article reported a total sample of 832; however, suicide-related data were only reported for 273 veterans. Exclusion criteria of active psychosis, unwillingness to discontinue substance misuse, and medical conditions that would hinder/prevent engagement in treatment.

*Calculated using data reported in manuscript.

BSS, Beck Scale for Suicide Ideation; C-SSRS, Columbia-Suicide Severity Rating Scale; CAPS, Clinician Administered PTSD Scale; DIS, Diagnostic Interview Schedule; DSM-IV, Diagnostic and Statistical Manual of Mental Disorders-IV; FY, fiscal year; HAM-D, Hamilton Rating Scale for Depression; IQ, intelligence quotient; MH, mental health; PHQ-2: Patient Health Questionnaire-2; PHQ-9: Patient Health Questionnaire-9; PTA, posttraumatic amnesia; PSS-I, Posttraumatic Symptom Interview; PTSD, posttraumatic stress disorder; RCT, randomized clinical trial; RR, relative risk; SCID for DSM-III-R, Structured Clinical Interview for DSM-III-R; SCID-IV, Structured Clinical Interview for DSM-IV; SUD, substance use disorder; TBI, traumatic brain injury; VA, Department of Veterans Affairs; VHA, Veterans Health Administration.

greater risk for suicide. Interestingly, in seven studies, five of which used multivariate analyses, PTSD was not a significant predictor of increased risk for suicide (Skopp et al., 2012; Alexander et al., 2014; Dobscha et al., 2014; Louzon et al., 2016), with three of these studies reporting that suicide risk was significantly lower among those diagnosed with PTSD (Conner et al., 2014; Kessler et al., 2015; Shen et al., 2016). When restricting to only studies with low overall risk of bias, results were still mixed, with six reporting significant positive associations (Ilgen et al., 2010a,b, 2012; Brenner et al., 2011b; Bohnert et al., 2013; Conner et al., 2013), three reporting non-significant associations (Skopp et al., 2012; Dobscha et al., 2014; Louzon et al., 2016), and two reporting significant inverse associations (Kessler et al., 2015; Shen et al., 2016).

DISCUSSION

Given the continued rise in rates of suicide among U.S. military personnel and veterans (Reimann and Mazuchowski, 2018; Department of Veterans Affairs, 2019), understanding the extent to which common mental health diagnoses, such as PTSD, are associated with SI, SA, and suicide is important. Building upon the systematic review by Pompili et al. (2013), the current systematic review provides an update of literature spanning 2010–2018, focused on U.S. service members and veterans. Importantly, this review is inclusive of cohorts spanning multiple service eras, including those who served in the recent conflicts based in Afghanistan and Iraq, a population with notably high rates of suicide (Department of Veterans Affairs, 2019).

KQ1

This systematic review is among the first to examine the prevalence of SI, SA, and suicide among U.S. military personnel and veterans with PTSD. Attempts to determine rates of SI, SA, and suicide across studies were largely impacted by differences in study methodology. Studies varied in their methods of assessing PTSD and suicide-related constructs (e.g., use of electronic medical records vs. validated semi-structured interviews), as well as in the temporality of these variables (e.g., lifetime vs. past month). This resulted in highly variable rates, especially among studies examining SI.

The majority of included studies examining KQ1 for SI and SA were also rated as having high bias in study methodology. This is likely driven, in part, by the fact that many of these studies were not designed to examine the prevalence of SI or SA. Rather, a number of studies examined PTSD, SI, or SA as secondary outcomes or covariates. In contrast, studies on suicide tended to have a low overall risk of bias, although suicide rates were still quite variable. Stronger methodology and consistent reporting regarding assessment and timeframe of PTSD, SI, and SA is needed for future research to ensure accurate depiction of reported rates.

KQ2

Research examining if PTSD is associated with SI and S-SDV was also mixed, suggesting a complex relationship. Only PTSD

TABLE 4 | Suicide among Military Personnel and Veterans with PTSD ($n = 16$).

Study	Population/sample	Measurement of PTSD	Measurement of Suicide	Prevalence of Suicide among those with PTSD	Relationship of PTSD to suicide	Notes
Alexander et al. (2014)	150 military service members (94.0% male).	DoDSER	DoDSER	Not reported.	PTSD was not associated with suicide at a bivariate level (OR = 3.34, 95% CI: 0.46–146.53, $p = 0.229$).	The control condition was relatively small ($n = 27$) due to unsuccessful oversampling.
Bachynski et al. (2012)	255 Army personnel (94.5% male) who died of suicide in 2007–2008.	Army Behavioral Health Integrated Data Environment	Army Behavioral Health Integrated Data Environment	Among those with PTSD, the suicide mortality rate per 100,000 person-years was 159.5.	Among those with PTSD, the RR was 5.6 (95% CI: 3.6–8.7, $p < 0.05$).	Data were consolidated from the Defense Casualty Information Processing System, the DoD Manpower Data Center, and the Defense Medical Surveillance System. Suicide decedents were compared against the Army as a whole using the Defense Medical Epidemiology Database. The sample of females who died by suicide was small (14; 5.5%).
Black et al. (2011)	874 Army soldiers (94.6% male) who died by suicide from 2001 to 2009.	DMSS	ABHIDE	Among those with PTSD, the mortality rate per 100,000 was 159.9.	The RR for suicide among those with PTSD was 12.61 (95% CI: 9.68 = 16.43, $p < 0.05$).	Those who died by suicide were compared to Army personnel over the same time period. Army-wide comparison data were obtained from DMSS and the Armed Forced Medical Examiner System of the Armed Forces Institute of Pathology. The sample of females who died by suicide was small (47; 5.4%).
Bohnert et al. (2013)	3,291,891 veterans (90.0% male) who used VHA care in FY 1999.	VA National Patient Care Database	NDI	226 (.11%) of those with PTSD died by suicide determined to be an "intentional overdose." *	Unadjusted analyses found PTSD was associated with a relative risk of 4.46 (95% CI: 3.85–5.18, $p < 0.05$) as it relates to suicides determined to be an "intentional overdose."	Veterans were followed through FY 2006. Study classified suicide by overdose as "intentional", "indeterminate intent", and "unintentional." Only "intentional was reported based on purpose of paper.
Brenner et al. (2011b)	7,850,472 veterans (89.8% male) using VHA care from FY 2001 to 2006.	VA medical record	NDI	849 (.30%) of those with PTSD died by suicide between FY 2001-2006.*	PTSD diagnosis was associated with higher rates of suicide ($p < 0.0001$).	
Conner et al. (2013)	2,962,810 male veterans who used VHA care in FY 1999 and were alive at start of FY 2000.	VA medical record	NDI	Not reported.	After adjusting for age, PTSD diagnosis was associated with increased risk for suicide (HR=1.61; 95% CI:1.34–1.93, $p < 0.05$). Risk was elevated in the presence of psychiatric comorbidity (HR = 2.30; 95% CI:2.39–2.82, $p < 0.05$).	

(Continued)

TABLE 4 | Continued

Study	Population/sample	Measurement of PTSD	Measurement of Suicide	Prevalence of Suicide among those with PTSD	Relationship of PTSD to suicide	Notes
Conner et al. (2014)	5,913,648 veterans (90.5% male) using VHA care in FY 2007–2008.	VA National Patient Care Database	NDI	423 (.08%) of those with PTSD died by suicide.	In an unadjusted model, PTSD was significantly associated with suicide (OR = 1.34, 95% CI: 1.21–1.48, $p < 0.001$). After adjusting for age, sex, marital status, urban-rural residence, region of country, service era, deployments, new to VHA, depression, alcohol use disorder, drug use disorder, anxiety disorder, bipolar disorder, and schizophrenia, PTSD was associated with decreased risk for suicide (OR = 0.774, 95% CI: 0.69–0.86, $p < 0.001$).	
Dobscha et al. (2014)	783 male veterans using VHA care.	VA medical record	State death certificate data	Not reported.	Bivariate associations between PTSD and suicide were not significant, $p = 0.70$.	In this case-control study, all veterans had contact with a VA primary care clinician. Data from all veterans who died in 2009 in an 11-state catchment area were used. Suicide decedents had care from their clinician 6 months prior to death. Controls were matched to cases 2:1 based on same clinician, sex, and age. Females were excluded from analyses due to males comprising 97% of the sample.
Hyman et al. (2012)	2,064,183, in 2005, and 1,981,810, in 2007, active duty military personnel (ranged from 80.3 to 93.9% male).	Military medical record	Reported as "DoD standardized suicide data"	Not reported.	Bivariate OR between PTSD and suicide exceeded 1 for Army (2005: 1.86; 2007: 4.51), and Air Force (2005: 7.40; 2007: 10.57).	The current study was a case-controlled analysis. The relationship between PTSD and suicide was not analyzed for Navy and Marines due to inadequate sampling. Results did not report 95% CI or p-values.
Ilgen et al. (2010a)	5,082 veterans (96.9% male) with SUDs using VHA care in FY 2002–2006.	VA medical record	NDI	Not reported.	Accounting for age, gender, race, and region, PTSD diagnosis was associated with increased risk of violent suicide (OR = 1.33; 95% CI: 1.10–1.62, $p < 0.001$) and nonviolent suicide (OR = 2.23; 95% CI: 1.70–2.92, $p < 0.001$).	Study examined violent (i.e., firearm, drowning, jumping, use of sharp object, or potentially violent measure) and non-violent (i.e., poisoning) suicide.
Ilgen et al. (2010b)	3,291,891 veterans (96.6% male) who used VHA care in FY 1999 and alive in FY 2000.	VA National Patient Care Database	NDI	Those with PTSD had a suicides rate of 68.6 per 100,000 person-years.	The unadjusted association between PTSD and suicide was significant (HR = 1.93, 95% CI: 1.79–2.08, $p > 0.05$). PTSD remained a significant predictor adjusted for age for both males (HR = 1.84, 95% CI: 1.70–1.98, $p < 0.05$) and females (HR = 3.50, 95% CI: 2.51–4.86, $p < 0.05$).	Veterans were followed up until death or at the end of FY 2006.

(Continued)

TABLE 4 | Continued

Study	Population/sample	Measurement of PTSD	Measurement of Suicide	Prevalence of Suicide among those with PTSD	Relationship of PTSD to suicide	Notes
Ilgen et al. (2012)	5,772,282 veterans (90.5% male) receiving VHA care in FY 2007–2008 and still alive at the start of FY 2008.	VA National Patient Care Database	NDI	Not reported.	Accounting for demographics and adjusting at the facility level, proportional hazards regression models found a significant association between PTSD and suicide (HR = 0.36, SE = 0.08, $p <$ 0.001).	
Kessler et al. (2015)	53,769 military personnel (gender breakdown not reported) with a psychiatric hospitalization.	HADS	Suicide in 12 months after discharge from inpatient hospitalization	Not reported.	PTSD diagnosed during hospitalization was associated with lower odds of suicide in the subsequent 12 months (OR = 0.4; 95% CI: 0.2–0.7, $p < 0.05$).	Hospitalizations occurred from 2004 to 2009.
Louzon et al. (2016)	391,492 veterans (92.7% male) using VHA care who received a unique PHQ-9 assessment in FY 2010.	VA medical record	NDI	43 (<0.01%) of those with PTSD died by suicide in FY 2010.* Suicide mortality per 100,000 person-years was calculated as 55.1 based on lifetime PTS diagnosis.	PTSD was not associated with suicide within this sample, $p = 0.746$. Rather, diagnoses of serious mental illness, anxiety, SUD, depression, and "other" diagnoses as well as age, gender, depression severity and SI as measured by the Patient Health Questionnaire-9, and encounter type during Patient Health Questionnaire-9 (i.e., primary care-mental health integration, standard primary care, inpatient mental health, and non-primary care-mental health integration outpatient mental health) were significant correlates of suicide.	
Shen et al. (2016)	3,795,823 military personnel (gender breakdown not reported).	TRICARE medical records	NDI	Suicide rate of those diagnosed with PTSD during the current quarter was 10.26 suicides per 100,000 person-quarter years in comparison to 15.90 and 10.35 per 100,000 person-quarter years for those diagnosed in the previous three quarters or four or more quarters ago respectively. The rate for those without PTSD was 3.94 per 100,000 person-quarter years.	Accounting for sex, race, age, marital status, dependent quantity, rank, Armed Forces Qualifying Test percentile, and military occupational specialty, all mental health diagnoses except PTSD were associated with increased risk for suicide. Specifically, those with PTSD had a lower risk for suicide (hazard ratio = 0.70, 95% CI: 0.57–0.86, $p = 0.001$).	Data were compiled for all U.S. military personnel between 2001 and 2011.

(Continued)

TABLE 4 | Continued

Study	Population/sample	Measurement of PTSD	Measurement of Suicide	Prevalence of Suicide among those with PTSD	Relationship of PTSD to suicide	Notes
Skopp et al. (2012)	8,782 active duty military personnel (93.6% male).	Military medical record	DoD Medical Mortality Registry	Not reported.	In multivariate analyses, mood disorders, partner relationship problems, and family circumstance problems, but not PTSD (OR: 1.1, 95% CI: 0.75–1.75, $p > 0.05$) were associated with suicide.	This case-control study examined a surveillance period from 2001 to 2009. Personnel were randomly selected and matched 4:1 by service, gender, race, age, entry into service, and years of service.

Calculated using data reported in manuscript.

ABHIDE, Army Behavioral Health Integrated Data Environment; CY, calendar year; DMSS, Defense Medical Surveillance System database; DoD, Department of Defense; DoDSER, DoD Suicide Event Report; FY, fiscal year; HADS, Historical Administrative Data System; NDI, National Death Index; PHQ-9: OR, odds ratio; Patient Health Questionnaire-9; PTSD, posttraumatic stress disorder; RR, relative risk; SUD, substance use disorder; VA, Department of Veterans Affairs; VHA, Veterans Health Administration.

and SA appeared to have a significant association that was largely maintained in the presence of covariates. In contrast, for studies reporting on the association between PTSD and SI or suicide, multivariate findings diverged, with some studies reporting non-significant associations. Further, in some studies, PTSD was even associated with decreased risk for suicide, further complicating conceptualization of this relationship.

Mixed findings regarding the association between PTSD with SI or suicide were maintained even when restricting studies to those with low overall risk of bias. This suggests that while study methodology and rigor are pertinent to synthesizing the literature base, factors outside of study quality may produce varied findings regarding the relationship between PTSD with both SI and suicide.

Several potential explanations can be posited as to why the relationship between PTSD and SI or suicide may be less robust. First and foremost, inclusion of other important correlates of SI and suicide may be more explanatory of risk than PTSD. Several included studies found other variables to be significant correlates of SI, SA, and suicide, including psychiatric comorbidities, psychosocial functioning (e.g., socioeconomic status, social support), and sociodemographic factors. In particular, across several studies, depression was a robust predictor of SI and S-SDV and thus may be more explanatory of suicide risk among U.S. military personnel and veterans with PTSD.

It is also important to note that a number of the studies which reported non-significant relationships between PTSD and SI or S-SDV relied on electronic medical records. There is sizable variability in the diagnostic validity of data obtained from medical records compared to diagnostic interviews (Holowka et al., 2014), suggesting that this may be an important factor to consider when interpreting these findings. The recency (e.g., past-month vs. lifetime) of PTSD, SI, and SA also can be difficult to ascertain from electronic medical records, which may further impact findings.

While our systematic review focused on the presence or absence of a PTSD diagnosis, a dichotomous focus on the presence or absence of a PTSD diagnosis likely does not provide sufficiently nuanced information regarding factors inherent to, or associated with, PTSD that may be driving risk within this population. The clinical presentation of PTSD can vary largely between patients based on heterogenous symptom profiles. In addition, specific symptoms of PTSD, such as guilt, social isolation, and trauma-related beliefs, have been posited as risk factors for suicide among military personnel and veterans (Bryan et al., 2013, 2017; DeBeer et al., 2014; Legarreta et al., 2015; McLean et al., 2017; Holliday et al., 2018a; Borges et al., 2020), but were not the focus of the current review. More research is needed to understand if specific components of PTSD are more strongly related to SI and suicide among military personnel and veterans.

Despite these potential explanations, none provide insight as to why the overwhelming majority of studies on SA found that PTSD was associated with SA, while many studies on SI and suicide did not. Research noting inherent differences in what motivates progression from SI to S-SDV (Nock et al., 2008) may explain some of these differences in findings regarding SI and

SA, but would not necessarily explain inconsistencies between findings on SA vs. suicide. One alternate explanation is that, for KQ2, the number of SA studies, particularly low risk of bias studies, were far fewer; as such, inclusion of additional studies may regress toward a more confident understanding of the relationship between PTSD diagnosis and SA. Overall risk of bias for studies on SA were largely rated as moderate to high, leading to potentially spurious findings in comparison to the majority of studies on suicide, which were generally rated as low. This further reinforces the need for additional investigation of the relationship between PTSD and SA, using consistent, sound methodology.

Additional factors underlying S-SDV may also explain variance. For instance, differing means of attempting suicide (e.g., firearms vs. overdose) vary in lethality, as the overwhelming majority of individuals who use a firearm to attempt suicide die (Spicer and Miller, 2000). It is possible that those who survive a SA using a less lethal means differ in their precipitants and drivers of suicide risk in comparison to those who use more lethal means (e.g., firearms). Given that military personnel and veterans have high rates of access to highly lethal means (e.g., firearms; Cleveland et al., 2017) as well as the potential interrelationship between trauma and firearm access (Monteith et al., 2020; Sadler et al., 2020; Simonetti et al., 2020; Stanley et al., 2020), longitudinal research must be prioritized to further understand if PTSD is associated with using different types of lethal means to enact S-SDV.

Limitations and Future Research

While this systematic review provides important insight into research published since 2010, several factors limit comprehensive inferences regarding this body of literature. A number of studies did not report rates of SI, SA, or suicide specific to those diagnosed with PTSD, precluding inclusion for KQ1. Included study samples were also overwhelmingly male and veteran, which generally reflects the compositions of the U.S. military and veteran populations. Nonetheless, as most studies reviewed did not adequately sample women or report rates or associations separately based on gender, future studies should consider oversampling women to facilitate exploring whether associations between PTSD with SI, SA, and suicide differ by gender.

Moreover, while our review expanded beyond war-related trauma (Pompili et al., 2013) to also include non-combat-related trauma (e.g., military sexual assault), only a limited number of studies specifically assessed and reported on trauma type or focused on non-combat-related PTSD. Because of this, it was not possible to differentiate rates and associations based on types of trauma. Therefore, given research suggesting that risk (e.g., for SI) may differ based on trauma type (Blais and Monteith, 2019), researchers should assess and report type of index trauma among their samples, especially in research pertaining to SI, SA, and suicide.

The current systematic review also focused on PTSD diagnosis, excluding studies relying on self-report symptom inventories (e.g., PTSD Checklist). While these inventories are psychometrically valid and can determine probable diagnoses, they should not be used to infer a formal diagnosis. As this was a departure from prior systematic reviews (e.g., Pompili et al., 2013), it may contribute to differences in findings. A number of studies also used single-item self-report measures of SI and SA. While these items were face valid, their psychometric properties relative to a clinical interview or formal assessment measure is debatable. Further inquiry is needed to understand how method of assessing SI and SA may impact findings.

Included studies were also predominantly cross-sectional. While still informative, such studies were rated as having higher risk of bias as this type of design precludes understanding the temporal relationship between PTSD with SI and SA (i.e., if PTSD precedes subsequent SI and SA). Longitudinal research was limited in this body of literature, and in particular, prospective cohort studies are warranted to further elucidate drivers of suicide risk.

Finally, studies largely differed in the factors that they accounted for in multivariate analyses. Because analytic approaches differed across studies, it is difficult to infer if associations between PTSD with SI, SA, and suicide would have differed based on inclusion of additional variables. As such, researchers should ensure multivariate analyses with PTSD also include correlates of SI, SA, and suicide identified in this review (e.g., depression) to better understand the magnitude and direction of the association with PTSD. Consistent inclusion of these factors would also facilitate future research focused on understanding potential moderators and mediators of the association between PTSD and SI, SA, and suicide (e.g., meta-regression).

CONCLUSIONS

When interpreting findings within the context of these limitations, this systematic review provides insight into the prevalence of SI, SA, and suicide among U.S. military personnel and veterans. Results provide continued, yet tentative, support that PTSD diagnosis is likely associated with SI, SA, and suicide at a bivariate level. Because of this, clinicians should continue to assess for PTSD, as well as associated psychiatric comorbidities (e.g., depression), in the context of suicide risk assessment when working with trauma-exposed U.S. military personnel and veterans. Similarly, clinicians should continue to screen for SI and prior SA when working with military personnel and veterans diagnosed with PTSD.

For many service members and veterans, PTSD may not be the sole driver of suicide risk, as SI, SA, and suicide are likely the result of an accumulation of numerous comorbid risk factors (e.g., depression) and other trauma-related sequelae (e.g., low social support; Lemaire and Graham, 2011). It is important to note that PTSD likely also increases risk for psychiatric comorbidity and decreased psychosocial functioning (Pietrzak et al., 2010; Hefner and Rosenheck, 2019). Therefore, PTSD may increase risk through indirect pathways (e.g., PTSD increases risk for depression, which, in turn, increases risk for suicide; e.g., McKinney et al., 2017).

Given the lack of consistency in multivariate results, further synthesis of the literature remains warranted. Analytic approaches that account for methodological differences between studies (e.g., diagnostic interview vs. electronic medical record) and also synthesize the role of potential covariates and other notable risk factors (e.g., depression) across studies is an integral next step. Additional understanding of specific aspects of PTSD (e.g., guilt, social isolation, trauma-related beliefs) that potentially moderate or mediate the relationship between PTSD diagnosis with SI, SA, and suicide would also further elucidate factors potentially impacting risk among U.S. military personnel and veterans. Identification of specific drivers of risk would be particularly important to inform clinical assessment and evidence-based treatment to prevent SI and S-SDV among U.S. military personnel and veterans with PTSD.

AUTHOR CONTRIBUTIONS

All authors contributed to potential study inclusion, review, and writing of the finalized manuscript.

FUNDING

This work was supported in part by the Department of Veterans Affairs (VA); the Rocky Mountain Mental Illness Research, Education and Clinical Center for Veteran Suicide Prevention; and the VA Office of Academic Affiliations, Advanced Fellowship Program in Mental Illness Research and Treatment. The views expressed are those of the authors and do not necessarily represent the views or policy of the VA or the United States Government.

REFERENCES

Alexander, C. L., Reger, M. A., Smolenski, D. J., and Fullerton, N. R. (2014). Comparing U.S. Army suicide cases to a control sample: initial data and methodological lessons. *Military Med.* 179, 1062–1066. doi: 10.7205/MILMED-D-13-00574

Bachynski, K. E., Canham-Chervak, M., Black, S. A., Dada, E. O., Millikan, A. M., and Jone, B. H. (2012). Mental health risk factors for suicides in the US Army, 2007-8. *Injury Prevention* 18, 405–412. doi: 10.1136/injuryprev-2011-040112

Bahraini, N. H., Simpson, G. K., Brenner, L. A., Hoffberg, A. S., and Schneider, A. L. (2013). Suicidal ideation and behaviours after traumatic brain injury: a systematic review. *Brain Impairment* 14, 92–112. doi: 10.1017/BrImp.2013.11

Barnes, S. M., Monteith, L. L., Forster, J. E., Nazem, S., Borges, L. M., Stearns-Yoder, K. A., et al. (2019). Developing predictive models to enhance clinician prediction of suicide attempts among veterans with and without PTSD. *Suicide Life-Threatening Behav.* 49, 1094–1104. doi: 10.1111/sltb.12511

Barnes, S. M., Walter, K. H., and Chard, K. M. (2012). Does a history of mild traumatic brain injury increase suicide risk in veterans with PTSD? *Rehabil. Psychol.* 57, 18–26. doi: 10.1037/a0027007

Barth, S. K., Kimerling, R. E., Pavao, J., McCutcheon, S. J., Batten, S. V., Dursa, E., et al. (2016). Military sexual trauma among recent veterans: Correlates of sexual assault and sexual harassment. *Am. J. Prev. Med.* 50, 77–86. doi: 10.1016/j.amepre.2015.06.012

Black, S. A., Gallaway, M. S., Bell, M. R., and Ritchie, E. C. (2011). Prevalence and risk factors associated with suicides of Army soldiers 2001-2009. *Military Psychol.* 23, 433–451. doi: 10.1080/08995605.2011.590409

Blais, R. K., and Monteith, L. L. (2019). Suicide ideation in female survivors of military sexual trauma: the trauma source matters. *Suicide Life Threat. Behav.* 49, 643–652. doi: 10.1111/sltb.12464

Blakey, S. M., Wagner, H. R., Naylor, J., Brancu, M., Lane, I., Sallee, M., et al. (2018). Chronic Pain, TBI, and PTSD in military veterans: a link to suicidal ideation and violent impulses? *J. Pain* 19, 797–806. doi: 10.1016/j.jpain.2018.02.012

Bohnert, A. S. B., McCarthy, J. F., Ignacio, R. V., Ilgen, M. A., Eisenberg, A., and Blow, F. C. (2013). Misclassification of suicide deaths: examining the psychiatric history of overdose decedents. *Injury Prevention* 19, 326–330. doi: 10.1136/injuryprev-2012-040631

Borges, L. M., Bahraini, N. H., Dorsey Holliman, B., Gissen, M. R., Lawson, W. C., and Barnes, S. M. (2020). Veterans' perspectives on discussing moral injury in the context of evidence-based psychotherapies for PTSD and other VA treatment. *J. Clin. Psychol.* 76, 377–391. doi: 10.1002/jclp.22887

Braden, A., Overholser, J., Fisher, L., and Ridley, J. (2015). Life meaning is associated with suicidal ideation among depressed veterans. *Death Stud.* 39, 24–29. doi: 10.1080/07481187.2013.871604

Brenner, L. A., Betthauser, L. M., Homaifar, B. Y., Villarreal, E., Harwood, J. E., Staves, P. J., et al. (2011a). Posttraumatic stress disorder, traumatic brain injury, and suicide attempt history among veterans receiving mental health services. *Suicide Life Threat. Behav.* 41, 416–423.

Brenner, L. A., Ignacio, R. V., and Blow, F. C. (2011b). Suicide and traumatic brain injury among individuals seeking veterans health administration services. *J. Head Trauma Rehabilit.* 26, 257–264. doi: 10.1097/HTR.0b013e31821fdb6e

Bryan, C. J., Grove, J. L., and Kimbrel, N. A. (2017). Theory-driven models of self-directed violence among individuals with PTSD. *Curr. Opinion Psychol.* 14, 12–17. doi: 10.1016/j.copsyc.2016.09.007

Bryan, C. J., Ray-Sannerud, B., Morrow, C. E., and Etienne, N. (2013). Guilt is more strongly associated with suicidal ideation among military personnel with direct combat exposure. *J. Affect. Disord.* 148, 37–41. doi: 10.1016/j.jad.2012.11.044

Carroll, T. D., Currier, J. M., McCormick, W. H., and Drescher, K. D. (2017). Adverse childhood experiences and risk for suicidal behavior in male Iraq and Afghanistan veterans seeking PTSD treatment. *Psychol. Trauma* 9, 583–586. doi: 10.1037/tra0000250

Cleveland, E. C., Azrael, D., Simonetti, J. A., and Miller, M. (2017). Firearm ownership among American veterans: Findings from the 2015 National Firearm Survey. *Injury Epidemiology* 4:33. doi: 10.1186/s40621-017-0130-y

Cohen, B. E., Shi, Y., Neylan, T. C., Maguen, S., and Seal, K. H. (2015). Antipsychotic prescriptions in Iraq and Afghanistan veterans with posttraumatic stress disorder in Department of Veterans Affairs healthcare, 2007-2012. *J. Clin. Psychiatry* 76, 406–412. doi: 10.4088/JCP.13m08857

Conner, K. R., Bohnert, A. S., McCarthy, J. F., Valenstein, M., Bossarte, R., Ignacio, R., et al. (2013). Mental disorder comorbidity and suicide among 2.96 million men receiving care in the Veterans Health Administration health system. *J. Abnorm. Psychol.* 122, 256–263. doi: 10.1037/a0030163

Conner, K. R., Bossarte, R. M., He, H., Arora, J., Lu, N., Tu, X. M., et al. (2014). Posttraumatic stress disorder and suicide in 5.9 million individuals receiving care in the Veterans Health Administration health system. *J. Affect. Disord.* 166, 1–5. doi: 10.1016/j.jad.2014.04.067

Cornelius, J. R., Haas, G. L., Appelt, C. J., Walker, J. D., Fox, L. J., Kasckow, J. W., et al. (2012). Suicidal Ideation Associated with PCL Checklist-Ascertained PTSD among veterans treated for substance abuse. *Intern. J. Med. Biol. Front.* 18, 783–794.

Corson, K., Denneson, L. M., Bair, M. J., Helmer, D. A., Goulet, J. L., and Dobscha, S. K. (2013). Prevalence and correlates of suicidal ideation among Operation Enduring Freedom and Operation Iraqi Freedom veterans. *J. Affect. Disord.* 149, 291–298. doi: 10.1016/j.jad.2013.01.043

Cox, K. S., Mouilso, E. R., Venners, M. R., Defever, M. E., Duvivier, L., Rauch, S. A. M., et al. (2016). Reducing suicidal ideation through evidence-based treatment for posttraumatic stress disorder. *J. Psychiatr. Res.* 80, 59–63. doi: 10.1016/j.jpsychires.2016.05.011

Creech, S. K., Pulverman, C. S., Crawford, J. N., Holliday, R., Monteith, L. L., Lehavot, K., et al. (2019). Clinical complexity in women veterans: A systematic review of the recent evidence on mental health and physical health comorbidities. *Behav. Med.* doi: 10.1080/08964289.2019.1644283. [Epub ahead of print].

Crosby, A. E., Ortega, L., and Melanson, C. (2011). *Self-Directed Violence Surveillance: Uniform Definitions and Recommended Data Elements, version 1.0* Atlanta, GA: Centers for Disease Control and Prevention, National Center for Injury Prevention and Control.

DeBeer, B. B., Kimbrel, N. A., Meyer, E. C., Gulliver, S. B., and Morissette, S. B. (2014). Combined PTSD and depressive symptoms interact with post-deployment social support to predict suicidal ideation in Operation Enduring Freedom and Operation Iraqi Freedom veterans *Psychiatry Res.* 216, 357–362. doi: 10.1016/j.psychres.2014.02.010

Denneson, L. M., Corson, K., Helmer, D. A., Bair, M. J., and Dobscha, S. K. (2014). Mental health utilization of new-to-care Iraq and Afghanistan Veterans following suicidal ideation assessment. *Psychiatry Res.* 217, 147–153. doi: 10.1016/j.psychres.2014.03.017

Department of Veterans Affairs (2019). *2019 National Veteran Suicide Prevention Annual Report.* Retrieved from https://www.mentalhealth.va.gov/docs/data-sheets/2019/2019_National_Veteran_Suicide_Prevention_Annual_Report_508.pdf.

Dobscha, S. K., Denneson, L. M., Kovas, A. E., Teo, A., Forsberg, C. W., Kaplan, M. S., et al. (2014). Correlates of suicide among veterans treated in primary care: case-control study of a nationally representative sample. *J. Gen. Intern. Med.* 29, S853–S860. doi: 10.1007/s11606-014-3028-1

Elbogen, E. B., Wagner, H. R., Kimbrel, N. A., Brancu, M., Naylor, J., Graziano, R., et al. (2018). Risk factors for concurrent suicidal ideation and violent impulses in military veterans. *Psychol. Assess* 30, 425–435. doi: 10.1037/pas0000490

Finley, E. P., Bollinger, M., Noël, P. H., Amuan, M. E., Copeland, L. A., Pugh, J. A., et al. (2015). A national cohort study of the association between the polytrauma clinical triad and suicide-related behavior among US Veterans who served in Iraq and Afghanistan. *Am. J. Public Health* 105, 380–387. doi: 10.2105/AJPH.2014.301957

Ganocy, S. J., Goto, T., Chan, P. K., Cohen, G. H., Sampson, L., Galea, S., et al. (2016). Association of spirituality with mental health conditions in Ohio National Guard soldiers. *J. Nervous Mental Disease* 204, 524–529. doi: 10.1097/NMD.0000000000000519

Gates, M. A., Holowka, D. W., Vasterling, J. J., Keane, T. M., Marx, B. P., and Rosen, R. C. (2012). Posttraumatic stress disorder in veterans and military personnel: Epidemiology, screening, and case recognition. *Psychol. Serv.* 9, 361–382. doi: 10.1037/a0027649

Gradus, J. L., Leatherman, S., Raju, S., Ferguson, R., and Miller, M. (2014). Posttraumatic stress disorder, depression, and non-fatal intentional self-harm in Massachusetts veterans. *Injury Epidemiol.* 1:20. doi: 10.1186/s40621-014-0020-5

Green, K. T., Calhoun, P. S., Dennis, M. F., Beckham, J. C., Miller-Mumford, M., Fernandez, A., et al. (2010). Exploration of the resilience construct in posttraumatic stress disorder severity and functional correlates in military combat veterans who have served since September 11, 2001. *J. Clin. Psychiatry* 71, 823–830. doi: 10.4088/JCP.09m05780blu

Harris, P. A., Taylor, R., Thielke, R., Payne, J., Gonzalez, N., and Conde, J. G. (2009). Research electronic data capture (REDCap)–a metadata-driven methodology and workflow process for providing translational research informatics support. *J. Biomed. Inform.* 42, 377–381. doi: 10.1016/j.jbi.2008.08.010

Hartling, L., Bond, K., Harvey, K., Santaguida, P. L., Viswanathan, M., and Dryden, D. M. (2010). *Developing and Testing a Tool for the Classification of Study Designs in Systematic Reviews of Interventions and Exposures.* Rockville, MD: Agency for Healthcare Research and Quality.

Hefner, K., and Rosenheck, R. (2019). Multimorbidity among Veterans diagnosed with PTSD in the Veterans Health Administration nationally. *Psychiatric Quarterly* 90, 275–291. doi: 10.1007/s11126-019-09632-5

Heron, M. (2018). *Deaths: Leading causes for 2016.* Hyattsville, MD: National Center for Health Statistics. Available online at: https://www.cdc.gov/nchs/data/nvsr/nvsr67/nvsr67_06.pdf

Hoffberg, A. S., Spitzer, E., Mackelprang, J. L., Farro, S. A., and Brenner, L. A. (2018). Suicidal self-directed violence among homeless US veterans: a systematic review. *Suicide Life-Threat. Behav.* 48, 481–498. doi: 10.1111/sltb.12369

Hoffberg, A. S., Stearns-Yoder, K. A., and Brenner, L. A. (2020). The effectiveness of crisis line services: A systematic review. *Front. Public Health* 7:399. doi: 10.3389/fpubh.2019.00399

Holliday, R., Holder, N., Olson-Madden, J. H., and Monteith, L. L. (2019). Treating posttraumatic stress disorder in the presence of acute risk in veterans and active duty service members: a call for research. *J. Nervous Mental Disease* 207, 611–614. doi: 10.1097/NMD. 0000000000001022

Holliday, R., Holder, N., and Surís, A. (2018a). A single-arm meta-analysis of Cognitive Processing Therapy in addressing trauma-related negative beliefs. *J. Aggression Maltreat. Trauma* 10, 1145–1153. doi: 10.1080/10926771.2018.1429511

Holliday, R., Monteith, L. L., and Wortzel, H. S. (2018b). Understanding, assessing, and conceptualizing suicide risk among veterans with posttraumatic stress disorder. *Federal Practitioner* 35, 24–27.

Holowka, D. W., Marx, B. P., Gates, M. A., Litman, H. J., Ranganathan, G., Rosen, R. C., et al. (2014). PTSD diagnostic validity in Veterans Affairs electronic records of Iraq and Afghanistan veterans. *J. Consult. Clin. Psychol.* 82, 569–579. doi: 10.1037/a0036347

Hyman, J., Ireland, R., Frost, L., and Cottrell, L. (2012). Suicide incidence and risk factors in an active duty US military population. *Am. J. Public Health* 102, S138–146. doi: 10.2105/AJPH.2011.300484

Ilgen, M. A., Bohnert, A. S. B., Ignacio, R. V., McCarthy, J. F., Valenstein, M. M., Kim, H. M., et al. (2010a). Psychiatric diagnoses and risk of suicide in veterans. *Arch. Gen. Psychiatry* 67, 1152–1158. doi: 10.1001/archgenpsychiatry.2010.129

Ilgen, M. A., Conner, K. R., Valenstein, M., Austin, K., and Blow, F. C. (2010b). Violent and nonviolent suicide in veterans with substance-use disorders. *J. Stud. Alcohol Drugs* 71, 473–479. doi: 10.15288/jsad.2010.71.473

Ilgen, M. A., McCarthy, J. F., Ignacio, R. V., Bohnert, A. S. B., Valenstein, M., Blow, F. C., et al. (2012). Psychopathology, Iraq and Afghanistan service, and suicide among Veterans Health Administration patients. *J. Consult. Clin. Psychol.* 80, 323–330. doi: 10.1037/a0028266

Joiner, T. (2007). *Why people die by suicide.* Cambridge, MA: Harvard University Press.

Kachadourian, L. K., Gandelman, E., Ralevski, E., and Petrakis, I. L. (2018). Suicidal ideation in military veterans with alcohol dependence and PTSD: the role of hostility. *Am. J. Addictions* 27, 124–130. doi: 10.1111/ajad.12688

Kanwar, A., Malik, S., Prokop, L. J., Sim, L. A., Feldstein, D., Wang, Z., et al. (2013). The association between anxiety disorders and suicidal behaviors: a systematic review and meta-analysis. *Depress. Anxiety* 30, 917–929. doi: 10.1002/da.22074

Kessler, R. C., Warner, C. H., Ivany, C., Petukhova, M. V., Rose, S., Bromet, E. J., et al. (2015). Predicting suicides after psychiatric hospitalization in US army soldiers: the Army Study to Assess Risk and Resilience in Servicemembers (Army STARRS). *JAMA Psychiatry* 72, 49–57. doi: 10.1001/jamapsychiatry.2014.1754

Kimbrel, N. A., DeBeer, B. B., Meyer, E. C., Gulliver, S. B., and Morissette, S. B. (2016). Nonsuicidal self-injury and suicide attempts in Iraq/Afghanistan war veterans. *Psychiatry Res.* 243, 232–237. doi: 10.1016/j.psychres.2016.06.039

Kimbrel, N. A., Dedert, E. A., Van Voorhees, E. E., Elbogen, E. B., Naylor, J. C., Ryan Wagner, H., et al. (2017). Cannabis use disorder and suicide attempts in Iraq/Afghanistan-era veterans. *J. Psychiatr. Res.* 89, 1–5. doi: 10.1016/j.jpsychires.2017.01.002

Kimbrel, N. A., Meyer, E. C., DeBeer, B. B., Gulliver, S. B., and Morissette, S. B. (2018b). The impact of cannabis use disorder on suicidal and nonsuicidal self-injury in Iraq/Afghanistan-Era veterans with and without mental health disorders. *Suicide Life Threat. Behav.* 48, 140–148. doi: 10.1111/sltb.12345

Kimbrel, N. A., Thomas, S. P., Hicks, T. A., Hertzberg, M. A., Clancy, C. P., Elbogen, E. B., et al. (2018a). Wall/object punching: An important but under-recognized form of nonsuicidal self-injury. *Suicide Life Threat. Behav.* 48, 501–511. doi: 10.1111/sltb.12371

Kittel, J. A., DeBeer, B. B., Kimbrel, N. A., Matthieu, M. M., Meyer, E. C., Gulliver, S. B., et al. (2016). Does body mass index moderate the association between posttraumatic stress disorder symptoms and suicidal ideation in Iraq/Afghanistan veterans? *Psychiatry Res.* 244, 123–129.

doi: 10.1016/j.psychres.2016.07.039

Klonsky, E. D., and May, A. M. (2015). The Three-Step Theory (3ST): A new theory of suicide rooted in the "ideation-to-action" framework. *Int. J. Cogn. Ther.* 8, 114–129. doi: 10.1521/icjt.2015.8.2.114

Klonsky, E. D., May, A. M., and Saffer, B. Y. (2016). Suicide, suicide attempts, and suicidal ideation. *Annu. Rev. Clin. Psychol.* 12, 307–330. doi: 10.1116/ annurev-clinpsy-021815-093204

Kopacz, M. S., Currier, J. M., Drescher, K. D., and Pigeon, W. R. (2016). Suicidal behavior and spiritual functioning in a sample of veterans diagnosed with PTSD. *J. Inj. Violence Res.* 8, 6–14. doi: 10.5249/jivr.v8i1.728

Krysinska, K., and Lester, D. (2010). Post-traumatic stress disorder and suicide risk: A systematic review. *Archives Suicide Res.* 14, 1–23. doi: 10.1080/13811110903478997

Legarreta, M., Graham, J., North, L., Bueler, C. E., McGlade, E., and Yurgelun-Todd, D. (2015). DSM-5 posttraumatic stress disorder symptoms associated with suicide behaviors in veterans. *Psychol. Trauma* 7, 277–285. doi: 10.1037/tra0000026

Lehavot, K., Katon, J. G., Chen, J. A., Fortney, J. C., and Simpson, T. L. (2018). Post-traumatic stress disorder by gender and veteran status. *Am. J. Preventative Med.* 54, e1–e9. doi: 10.1016/j.amepre.2017.09.008

Lemaire, C. M., and Graham, D. P. (2011). Factors associated with suicidal ideation in OEF/OIF veterans. *J. Affect. Disord.* 130, 231–238. doi: 10.1016/j.jad.2010.10.021

Louzon, S. A., Bossarte, R., McCarthy, J. F., and Katz, I. R. (2016). Does suicidal ideation as measured by the PHQ-9 predict suicide among VA patients? *Psychiatric Services* 67, 517–522. doi: 10.1176/appi.ps.201500149

Magruder, K. M., Yeager, D., and Brawman-Mintzer, O. (2012). The Role of pain, functioning, and mental health in suicidality among Veterans Affairs primary care patients. *Am. J. Public Health* 102, S118–S124. doi: 10.2105/ajph.2011.300451

Maguen, S., Metzler, T. J., Bosch, J., Marmar, C. R., Knight, S. J., and Neylan, T. C. (2012). Killing in combat may be independently associated with suicidal ideation. *Depress. Anxiety* 29, 918–923. doi: 10.1002/da.21954

Matchar, D. B. (2012). Chapter 1: introduction to the methods guide for medical test reviews. *J. Gen. Intern. Med.* 27(Suppl 1), 4–10. doi: 10.1007/s11606-011-1798-2

Matthews, S., Spadoni, A., Knox, K., Strigo, I., and Simmons, A. (2012). Combat-exposed war veterans at risk for suicide show hyperactivation of prefrontal cortex and anterior cingulate during error processing. *Psychosom. Med.* 74, 471–475. doi: 10.1097/PSY.0b013e31824f888f

May, A. M., and Klonsky, E. D. (2016). What distinguishes suicide attempters from suicide ideators? A meta-analysis of potential factors. *Clin. Psychol.* 23, 5–20. doi: 10.1111/cpsp.12136

McKenzie, J. E., and Brennan, S. E. (2019). "Chapter 12: Synthesizing and presenting findings using other methods," in *Cochrane Handbook for Systematic Reviews of Interventions Version 6.0,* eds J. P. T. Higgins, J. Thomas, J. Chandler, M. Cumpston, T. Li, M. J. Page, and V. A. Welch. Available online at: www.training.cochrane.org/handbook

McKinney, J. M., Hirsch, J. K., and Britton, P. C. (2017). PTSD symptoms and suicide risk in Veterans: serial indirect effects via depression and anger. *J. Affect. Disord.* 214, 100–107. doi: 10.1016/j.jad.2017.03.008

McLean, C. P., Zang, Y., Zandberg, L., Bryan, C. J., Gay, N., Yarvis, J. S., et al. (2017). Predictors of suicidal ideation among active duty military personnel with posttraumatic stress disorder. *J. Affect. Disord.* 208, 392–398. doi: 10.1016/j.jad.2016.08.061

Moher, D., Liberati, A., Tetzlaff, J., Altman, D. G., and the, P. R. I. S. M. A., Group (2009). Preferred reporting items for systematic reviews and meta-analyses: the PRISMA statement. *PLoS Med.* 6:e1000097. doi: 10.1371/journal.pmed.1000097

Monteith, L. L., Bahraini, N. H., Matarazzo, B. B., Gerber, H. R., Soberay, K. A., and Forster, J. E. (2016). The influence of gender on suicidal ideation following military sexual trauma among Veterans in the Veterans Health Administration. *Psychiatry Res.* 244, 257–265. doi: 10.1016/j.psychres.2016.07.036

Monteith, L. L., Holliday, R., Dorsey Holliman, B., Brenner, L. A., and Simonetti, J. A. (2020). Understanding female veterans' experiences and perspectives of firearms. *J. Clin. Psychol.* doi: 10.1002/jclp.22952. [Epub ahead of print].

Monteith, L. L., Holliday, R., Schneider, A. L., Forster, J. E., and Bahraini, N. H. (2019). Identifying factors associated with suicidal ideation and suicide attempts following military sexual trauma. *J. Affect. Disord.* 252, 300–309. doi: 10.1016/j.jad.2019.04.038

Nock, M. K., Borges, G., Bromet, E. J., Cha, C. B., Kessler, R. C., and Lee, S. (2008). Suicide and suicidal behavior. *Epidemiol. Rev.* 30, 133–154. doi: 10.1093/epirev/mxn002

Paley, B., Lester, P., and Mogil, C. (2013). Family systems and ecological perspectives on the impact of deployment on military families. *Clin. Child Fam. Psychol. Rev.* 16, 245–265. doi: 10.1007/s10567-013-0138-y

Panagioti, M., Gooding, P. A., Triantafyllou, K., and Tarrier, N. (2015). Suicidality and posttraumatic stress disorder (PTSD) in adolescents: a systematic review and meta-analysis. *Soc. Psychiatry Psychiatr. Epidemiol.* 50, 525–537. doi: 10.1007/s00127-014-0978-x

Pietrzak, R. H., Goldstein, M. B., Malley, J. C., Rivers, A. J., and Southwick, S. M. (2010). Structure of posttraumatic stress disorder symptoms and psychosocial functioning in veterans of Operations Enduring Freedom and Iraqi Freedom. *Psychiatry Res.* 178, 323–329. doi: 10.1016/j.psychres.2010.04.039

Polusny, M. A., Kumpula, M. J., Meis, L. A., Erbes, C. R., Arbisi, P. A., Murdoch, M., et al. (2014). Gender differences in the effects of deployment-related stressors and pre-deployment risk factors on the development of PTSD symptoms in National Guard Soldiers deployed to Iraq and Afghanistan. *J. Psychiatr. Res.* 49, 1–9. doi: 10.1016/j.jpsychires.2013.09.016

Pompili, M., Sher, L., Serafini, G., Forte, A., Innamorati, M., Dominici, G., et al. (2013). Posttraumatic stress disorder and suicide risk among veterans: A literature review. *J. Nervous Mental Disorders* 201, 802–812. doi: 10.1097/NMD.0b013e3182a21458

Reimann, C. A., and Mazuchowski, E. L. (2018). Suicide rates among active duty service members compared with civilian counterparts, 2005-2014. *Mil. Med.* 183, 396–402. doi: 10.1093/milmed/usx209

Ribeiro, J. D., Pease, J. L., Gutierrez, P. M., Silva, C., Bernert, R. A., Rudd, M. D., et al. (2012). Sleep problems outperform depression and hopelessness as cross-sectional and longitudinal predictors of suicidal ideation and behavior in young adults in the military. *J. Affect. Disord.* 136, 743–750. doi: 10.1016/j.jad.2011.09.049

Sadler, A. G., Mengeling, M. A., Cook, B. L., and Torner, J. C. (2020). Factors associated with U.S. military women keeping guns or weapons nearby for personal security following deployment. *J. Women's Health.* doi: 10.1089/jwh.2019.8029. [Epub ahead of print].

Shen, Y. C., Cunha, J. M., and Williams, T. V. (2016). Time-varying associations of suicide with deployments, mental health conditions, and stressful life events among current and former US military personnel: A retrospective multivariate analysis. *Lancet Psychiatry* 3, 1039–1048. doi: 10.1016/S2215-0366(16)30304-2

Simonetti, J. A., Dorsey Holliman, B., Holliday, R., Brenner, L. A., and Monteith, L. L. (2020). Correction: firearm-related experiences and perceptions among United States male veterans: a qualitative interview study. *PLoS ONE* 15:e0231493. doi: 10.1371/journal.pone.0231493

Skopp, N. A., Trofimovich, L., Grimes, J., Oetjen-Gerdes, L., and Gahm, G. A. (2012). Relations between suicide and traumatic brain injury, psychiatric diagnoses, and relationship problems, active component, U.S. Armed Forces, 2001-2009. *MSMR* 19, 7–11.

Smith, P. N., Currier, J., and Drescher, K. (2015). Firearm ownersh veterans entering residential PTSD treatment: Associations with suicide ideation, attempts, and combat exposure. *Psychiatry Res.* 229, 220–224. doi: 10.1016/j.psychres.2015.07.031

Spicer, R. S., and Miller, T. R. (2000). Suicide acts in 8 states: incidence and case fatality rates by demographics and method. *Am. J. Public Health* 90, 1885–1891. doi: 10.2105/ajph.90.12.1885

Stanley, I. H., Hom, M. A., Marx, B. P., and Reger, M. A. (2020). Post-traumatic stress disorder and firearm ownership, access, and storage practices: a systematic review. *Clin. Psychol.* doi: 10.1111/cpsp.12358. [Epub ahead of print].

Street, A. E., Vogt, D., and Dutra, L. (2009). A new generation of women veterans: stressors faced by women deployed to Iraq and Afghanistan. *Clin. Psychol. Rev* 29, 685–694. doi: 10.1016/j.cpr.2009.08.007

Suris, A., Link-Malcolm, J., and North, C. S. (2011). Predictors of suicidal ideation in veterans with PTSD related to military sexual trauma. *J. Trauma. Stress* 605–608. doi: 10.1002/jts.20674

Thomas, B. H., Ciliska, D., Dobbins, M., and Micucci, S. (2004). A process for systematically reviewing the literature: Providing the research evidence for public health nursing interventions. *Worldviews on Evidence-Based Nursing* 1, 176–184. doi: 10.1111/j.1524-475X.2004.04006.x

Vasterling, J. J., Proctor, S. P., Friedman, M. J., Hoge, C. W., Heeren, T., King, L. A., et al. (2010). PTSD symptom increases in Iraq-deployed soldiers: comparison with nondeployed soldiers and associations with baseline symptoms, deployment experiences, and postdeployment stress. *J. Trauma. Stress* 23, 41–51. doi: 10.1002/jts.20487

Wisco, B. E., Marx, B. P., Holowka, D. W., Vasterling, J. J., Han, S. C., Chen, M. S., et al. (2014). Traumatic brain injury, PTSD, and current suicidal ideation among Iraq and Afghanistan U.S. veterans. *J. Traumatic Stress* 27, 244–248. doi: 10.1002/jts.21900

Permissions

All chapters in this book were first published in TPPSD, by Frontiers; hereby published with permission under the Creative Commons Attribution License or equivalent. Every chapter published in this book has been scrutinized by our experts. Their significance has been extensively debated. The topics covered herein carry significant findings which will fuel the growth of the discipline. They may even be implemented as practical applications or may be referred to as a beginning point for another development.

The contributors of this book come from diverse backgrounds, making this book a truly international effort. This book will bring forth new frontiers with its revolutionizing research information and detailed analysis of the nascent developments around the world.

We would like to thank all the contributing authors for lending their expertise to make the book truly unique.

They have played a crucial role in the development of this book. Without their invaluable contributions this book wouldn't have been possible. They have made vital efforts to compile up to date information on the varied aspects of this subject to make this book a valuable addition to the collection of many professionals and students.

This book was conceptualized with the vision of imparting up-to-date information and advanced data in this field. To ensure the same, a matchless editorial board was set up. Every individual on the board went through rigorous rounds of assessment to prove their worth. After which they invested a large part of their time researching and compiling the most relevant data for our readers.

The editorial board has been involved in producing this book since its inception. They have spent rigorous hours researching and exploring the diverse topics which have resulted in the successful publishing of this book. They have passed on their knowledge of decades through this book. To expedite this challenging task, the publisher supported the team at every step. A small team of assistant editors was also appointed to further simplify the editing procedure and attain best results for the readers.

Apart from the editorial board, the designing team has also invested a significant amount of their time in understanding the subject and creating the most relevant covers. They scrutinized every image to scout for the most suitable representation of the subject and create an appropriate cover for the book.

The publishing team has been an ardent support to the editorial, designing and production team. Their endless efforts to recruit the best for this project, has resulted in the accomplishment of this book. They are a veteran in the field of academics and their pool of knowledge is as vast as their experience in printing. Their expertise and guidance has proved useful at every step. Their uncompromising quality standards have made this book an exceptional effort. Their encouragement from time to time has been an inspiration for everyone.

The publisher and the editorial board hope that this book will prove to be a valuable piece of knowledge for researchers, students, practitioners and scholars across the globe.

List of Contributors

Cherise Rosen and Jennifer K. Melbourne
Department of Psychiatry, University of Illinois at Chicago, Chicago, IL, USA

Nev Jones
Felton Institute, San Francisco, CA, USA

Eleanor Longden
Greater Manchester West Mental Health NHS Foundation Trust, Psychosis Research Unit, Manchester, UK

Kayla A. Chase
Department of Psychiatry, University of California San Diego, La Jolla, CA, USA

Mona Shattell
Department of Community, Systems and Mental Health Nursing, Rush University, Chicago, IL, USA

Sarah K. Keedy
Department of Psychiatry, University of Chicago, Chicago, IL, USA

Rajiv P. Sharma
Department of Psychiatry, University of Illinois at Chicago, Chicago, IL, USA
Department of Psychiatry, Jesse Brown Veterans Affairs Medical Center, Chicago, IL, USA

Chelsea Church
School of Psychology, University of Glasgow, Glasgow, United Kingdom

Ole A. Andreassen, Ingrid Melle and Monica Aas
Division of Mental Health and Addiction, NORMENT K.G. Jebsen Centre for Psychosis Research, Oslo University Hospital and Institute of Clinical Medicine, University of Oslo, Oslo, Norway

Steinar Lorentzen
Institute of Clinical Medicine, University of Oslo, Oslo, Norway

Lucy H. Stevens
Tees Esk and Wear Valley NHS Mental Health Foundation Trust, Cleveland, UK

Helen M. Spencer and Douglas Turkington
Northumberland, Tyne and Wear NHS Mental Health Foundation Trust, Newcastle upon Tyne, UK

Yael Mazor, Marc Gelkopf and David Roe
Faculty of Social Welfare and Health Sciences, Department of Community Mental Health, University of Haifa, Haifa, Israel

Kim T. Mueser
Department of Occupational Therapy, Psychology and Psychiatry, Boston University Center for Psychiatric Rehabilitation, Boston, MA, USA

Rachel M. Brand and Neil Thomas
Centre for Mental Health, Swinburne University, Hawthorn, VIC, Australia
The Voices Clinic, Monash Alfred Psychiatry Research Centre, Alfred Hospital and Monash University Central Clinical School, Melbourne, VIC, Australia

Susan L. Rossell
Centre for Mental Health, Swinburne University, Hawthorn, VIC, Australia
The Voices Clinic, Monash Alfred Psychiatry Research Centre, Alfred Hospital and Monash University Central Clinical School, Melbourne, VIC, Australia
Psychiatry, St. Vincent's Hospital, Fitzroy, VIC, Australia

Sarah Bendall
Orygen: The National Centre of Excellence in Youth Mental Health, Parkville, VIC, Australia
The Centre for Youth Mental Health, The University of Melbourne, Parkville, VIC, Australia

Casey A. Cragin and Martha B. Straus
Department of Clinical Psychology, Antioch University New England, Keene, NH, USA

Dawn Blacker
CAARE Diagnostic and Treatment Center, Department of Pediatrics, University of California, Davis, Sacramento, USA

Laura M. Tully and Tara A. Niendam
UC Davis Imaging Research Center, Department of Psychiatry and Behavioral Sciences, University of California, Davis, Sacramento, USA

Michelle J. Bovin and Erika J. Wolf
VA National Center for PTSD, Boston, MA, USA
Boston University School of Medicine, Boston, MA, USA

Patricia A. Resick
Duke University Medical Center, Durham, NC, USA

Nadine Keen, Elaine C. M. Hunter and Emmanuelle Peters
South London and Maudsley NHS Foundation Trust, Psychological Interventions Clinic for outpatients with Psychosis (PICuP), London, United Kingdom
Department of Psychology, Institute of Psychiatry, Psychology and Neuroscience, King's College London, United Kingdom

Jason C. Lee and Joe Z. Tsien
Department of Neurology, Brain and Behavior Discovery Institute, Medical College of Georgia, Augusta University, Augusta, GA, USA

Lei Philip Wang
Department of Neurology, Brain and Behavior Discovery Institute, Medical College of Georgia, Augusta University, Augusta, GA, USA
Department of Psychiatry, Medical College of Georgia, Augusta University, Augusta, GA, USA

Kee-Hong Choi, Eunju Jaekal and Ga-Young Lee
Department of Psychology, Korea University, Seoul, Republic of Korea

Chao Wang, David Darmon and Kylee Bashirelahi
Traumatic Injury Research Program, Department of Military and Emergency Medicine, Uniformed Services University of the Health Sciences, Bethesda, MD, USA
The Henry M. Jackson Foundation for the Advancement of Military Medicine, Inc., Bethesda, MD, USA

Michelle E. Costanzo
The Henry M. Jackson Foundation for the Advancement of Military Medicine, Inc., Bethesda, MD, USA
Department of Medicine and Center for Neuroscience and Regenerative Medicine, Uniformed Services University of the Health Sciences, Bethesda, MD, USA

Paul E. Rapp and David O. Keyser
Traumatic Injury Research Program, Department of Military and Emergency Medicine, Uniformed Services University of the Health Sciences, Bethesda, MD, USA

Dominic E. Nathan
Traumatic Injury Research Program, Department of Military and Emergency Medicine, Uniformed Services University of the Health Sciences, Bethesda, MD, USA
The Henry M. Jackson Foundation for the Advancement of Military Medicine, Inc., Bethesda, MD, USA
Graduate School of Nursing, Uniformed Services University of the Health Sciences, Bethesda, MD, USA

Christopher J. Cellucci
Aquinas LLC, Berwyn, PA, USA

Michael J. Roy
Department of Medicine and Center for Neuroscience and Regenerative Medicine, Uniformed Services University of the Health Sciences, Bethesda, MD, USA

Amy Hardy
Institute of Psychiatry, Psychology & Neuroscience, King's College London, London, UK
Psychosis Clinical Academic Group, South London and Maudsley NHS Foundation Trust, London, UK

Sarah Swan
South London and Maudsley NHS Foundation Trust, London, UK

Nadine Keen, Nicola Reynolds and Juliana Onwumere
South London and Maudsley NHS Foundation Trust, London, UK
Department of Psychology, Institute of Psychiatry, Psychology and Neuroscience, King's College London, London, UK

Berta Britz
Berta Britz Consulting, Havertown, PA, USA

Hawkar Ibrahim
Department of Psychology, Clinical Psychology and Psychotherapy, Bielefeld University, Bielefeld, Germany
Department of Clinical Psychology, Koya University, Koya, Iraq

Chiya Q. Hassan
Department of Clinical Psychology, Koya University, Koya, Iraq

Anouk L. Grubaugh, Kimberly Veronee and Wilson Brown
Ralph H. Johnson Veterans Affairs Medical Center, Charleston, SC, United States
Department of Psychiatry and Behavioral Sciences, Medical University of South Carolina, Charleston, SC, United States

Charles Ellis
Department of Communication Sciences and Disorders, East Carolina University, Greenville, NC, United States

Rebecca G. Knapp
Department of Public Health Sciences, Medical University of South Carolina, Charleston, SC, United States

Katherine Berry, Filippo Varese and Sandra Bucci
Division of Psychology and Mental Health, School of Health Sciences, Manchester Academic Health Science Centre, The University of Manchester, Manchester, United Kingdom

Weili Lu and and Neisrein Mahmoud
Department of Psychiatric Rehabilitation and Counseling Professions, Rutgers University, Scotch Plains, NJ, United States

Kim T. Mueser
Center for Psychiatric Rehabilitation, Sargent College of Health and Rehabilitation Sciences, Boston University, Boston, MA, United States

Stanley D. Rosenberg
Department of Psychiatry, Dartmouth Medical School, Hanover, NH, United States
Dartmouth Trauma Intervention Research Center, Lebanon, NH, United States

Philip T. Yanos
Department of Psychology, John Jay College of Criminal Justice, CUNY, New York, NY, United States

Danessa Mayo and Tara A. Niendam
Imaging Research Center, Department of Psychiatry and Behavioral Sciences, University of California Davis, Sacramento, CA, USA

Sarah Corey, Leah H. Kelly, Seghel Yohannes, Alyssa L. Youngquist, Barbara K. Stuart and Rachel L. Loewy
Department of Psychiatry, University of California San Francisco, San Francisco, CA, USA

Craig Steel
School of Psychology and Clinical Language Sciences, University of Reading, Reading, UK

Elisabeth Schobinger and Suzannah Stuijfzand
Institute of higher Education and Research in Healthcare in French, University of Lausanne, Lausanne, Switzerland

Antje Horsch
Institute of higher Education and Research in Healthcare in French, University of Lausanne, Lausanne, Switzerland
Department Woman-Mother-Child, Lausanne University Hospital, Lausanne, Switzerland

Ryan Holliday, Lauren M. Borges and Lindsey L. Monteith
Rocky Mountain Mental Illness Research, Education and Clinical Center for Veteran Suicide Prevention, Aurora, CO, United States
Department of Psychiatry, University of Colorado Anschutz Medical Campus, Aurora, CO, United States

Kelly A. Stearns-Yoder
Rocky Mountain Mental Illness Research, Education and Clinical Center for Veteran Suicide Prevention, Aurora, CO, United States
Department of Physical Medicine and Rehabilitation, University of Colorado Anschutz Medical Campus, Aurora, CO, United States

Adam S. Hoffberg
Rocky Mountain Mental Illness Research, Education and Clinical Center for Veteran Suicide Prevention, Aurora, CO, United States

Lisa A. Brenner
Rocky Mountain Mental Illness Research, Education and Clinical Center for Veteran Suicide Prevention, Aurora, CO, United States
Department of Psychiatry, University of Colorado Anschutz Medical Campus, Aurora, CO, United States
Department of Physical Medicine and Rehabilitation, University of Colorado Anschutz Medical Campus, Aurora, CO, United States
Department of Neurology, University of Colorado Anschutz Medical Campus, Aurora, CO, United States

Index

www.ingramcontent.com/pod-product-compliance
Lightning Source LLC
LaVergne TN
LVHW080950210926
848485LV00004B/813